Current Readings on Money, Banking, and Financial Markets

1990 Edition

Current Readings on Money, Banking, and Financial Markets

1990 Edition

Edited by
James A. Wilcox
School of Business Administration
University of California at Berkeley

Frederic S. Mishkin
Consulting Editor
Columbia University

SCOTT, FORESMAN/LITTLE, BROWN HIGHER EDUCATION
A Division of Scott, Foresman and Company
Glenview, Illinois   London, England

ISBN 0-673-39923-0

Preface

Keeping abreast of developments in money, banking, and financial markets is challenging and exciting. In the past few years these developments have been rapid and important. A vast array of new financial instruments has appeared; deregulation of financial institutions has dramatically increased managerial latitude and blurred the traditional distinctions between institutions; record-breaking numbers of banks and thrift institutions have failed, dragging the thrifts' deposit insurance fund into insolvency with them; the thrust of monetary policy and even its underpinnings have shifted in the last decade; and financial markets have become increasingly internationalized. The readings in this book explore the driving forces behind these recent developments, document their extent, explain why these developments have altered the basic operation of many institutions and markets, and discuss the likely further evolution of financial instruments and institutions.

The readings in this collection cover material essential for courses both on money and banking and on financial markets and institutions. Three features in particular make this collection a genuine complement to whatever textbook is being used in such courses: its currency, its coverage, and its conciseness. Students and instructors alike will value the book's currency: virtually all of the readings were published over the past two years. This means that the most recent data, regulations, issues, policies, and opinions are contained here. No textbook can match that. Our annual updating of the readings ensures that the demand for this type of currency will always be met.

The topics and orientation of the articles make each of the selections accessible to students in undergraduate economics departments and business schools as well as in MBA programs. Most of the articles presume little or no familiarity with the jargon of the field, but instead strive to teach some of it. Used in conjunction with a textbook, this reader provides students with the necessary exposure to modern principles, the current institutional environment, and up-to-date facts. The readings also cover institutions, markets, instruments, and operations in more detail than textbooks normally do. Further, the range of topics included is broader than that in many readers.

Nonetheless, this collection is concise. Succinct treatments of each topic have been chosen, making the reader about half as long as such anthologies typically are and allowing the entire range of topics to be handled in a single course, if so desired. This conciseness also makes the reader less expensive than the competition. For students, the purchase price will be less than the cost of a photocopied collection of readings. For the instructor, the hassle of collecting the articles and the uncertainty of copyright regulations are eliminated.

The collection also affords flexibility. The six sections roughly parallel the most widely used textbooks in money and banking, financial institutions, and financial market courses. Readings within sections, or even entire sections, can be reordered or omitted if necessary to follow more closely the order of treatment in the textbook or the interest of the instructor.

Half of the book's material is contained in the first two sections. Together these sections cover the instruments, institutions, regulations, and operation of financial markets. The continuing, dramatic changes in these areas dictate that a large share of the book be devoted to them. Section One, Financial Markets and Interest Rates, begins with a review of developments in the financial system over the past decade. That is followed by an explanation of how the U.S. government bond market operates. The principles of diversification and of risk-return trade-offs are developed next. The term structure of interest rates is then investigated. Finally, attention turns to the recognition, measurement, and avoidance of interest rate risk in financial institutions.

Section Two, Financial Institutions, covers the evolution and recent deregulation of the financial institutions industry. The readings present the facts and arguments about the effects of deposit insurance and the problems the deposit insurance funds now face, interstate banking, and individual and aggregate bank and thrift failures. The difficulty and necessity of applying the portfolio approach to international lending are discussed. This section also addresses the reform and restructuring of the financial services industry.

Section Three, The Money Supply, shows the inroads new accounts have made at depository institutions and how, in practice, their existence makes the Federal Reserve's job more difficult. It also shows how common cash transactions are. The last article in this section addresses the role of deposit insurance in preventing bank runs.

Sections Four and Five address the short-run and long-run aspects of monetary policy. Section Four, Central Banking and Monetary Policy, illustrates how the Federal Reserve actually operates. The first two selections try to discern the approach the Federal Reserve will pursue under chair Alan Greenspan and detail the Fed's actions leading up to and in the wake of the October 19, 1987 stock market crash. The next two readings here describe, with numerous examples, how and why open market operations are conducted daily and the purposes and operation of the Fed's discount window.

Section Five, Monetary Theory, has a decidedly long-run focus. Milton Friedman argues that only institutional redesign will lead to improved performance by the Fed. The remaining readings demonstrate how and why the Fed can build and use its reputation to help achieve its macroeconomic goals.

The final section, International Finance, provides the international analogue to earlier sections. The workings of the foreign exchange market are described. The arguments for and against international policy coordination and a return to less-freely-floating exchange rates are then evaluated. The current short-run pressures and long-run implications of the international debt crisis are probed. Lastly, the implications of the proposed financial and economic deregulation of Europe in 1992 are explored.

In putting together this book, I have had the benefit of working with talented people. Special thinks go to the following for their comments and suggestions: Nathan Balke, Southern Methodist University; Ron Balvers, University of Notre Dame; Allin Cothrell, Elon (N.C.) College; Scott Hein, Texas Tech; John McArthur, Claremont College; Jeffrey Miller, University of Delaware; Peter Mlynaryk, CSU-Fullerton; and James L. Pierce, University of California at Berkeley. Thanks also to Bruce Kaplan at SF/LB for his help; to Stephanie Lee for her all-round assistance; and to Rick Mishkin for his good sense and ever-ebullient encouragement.

James A. Wilcox

Acknowledgments

Article 1: "Developments in the U.S. Financial System since the Mid-1970s," Thomas D. Simpson, *Federal Reserve Bulletin,* January 1988, Vol. 74, No. 1, pp. 1–13.

Article 2: "Treasury Bills," Timothy Q. Cook, Federal Reserve Bank of Richmond, *Instruments of the Money Market,* 1986, pp. 81–93.

Article 3: "Modern Financial Theory," Richard R. Simonds, *MSU Business Topics,* Winter 1978, pp. 54–63. Reprinted by permission of the College of Business, Michigan State University.

Article 4: "The Yield Curve and Inflation Expectations," C. Alan Garner, Federal Reserve Bank of Kansas City *Economic Review,* September/October 1987, pp. 3–15.

Article 5: "Measuring Interest Rate Risk: What Do We Really Know?" James E. McNulty. Reprinted from the *Journal of Retail Banking,* Spring/Summer 1986, Vol. VIII, Nos. 1 and 2, pp. 49–58. Copyright 1986 Lafferty Publications, 3945 Holcomb Bridge Rd., Suite 301, Norcross, GA 30092. By permission.

Article 6: "Hedging Interest Rate Risk with Financial Futures: Some Basic Principles," Michael T. Belongia and G. J. Santoni, Federal Reserve Bank of St. Louis *Review,* October 1984, pp. 15–25.

Article 7: "Interest Rate Swaps: Risk and Regulation," J. Gregg Whittaker, Federal Reserve Bank of Kansas City *Economic Review,* March 1987, pp. 3–13.

Article 8: "Deposit Insurance and Bank Failures," George J. Benston, Federal Reserve Bank of Atlanta *Economic Review,* March 1983, pp. 4–17.

Article 9: "FDIC Policies for Dealing with Failed and Troubled Institutions," Daria B. Caliguire and James B. Thomson, Federal Reserve Bank of Cleveland *Economic Commentary,* October 1, 1987, pp. 1–6.

Article 10: "The Thrift Industry: Reconstruction in Progress," Thomas M. Buynak, Federal Reserve Bank of Cleveland *Economic Commentary,* June 1, 1986, pp. 1–4.

Article 11: "Dangers of Capital Forbearance: The Case of the FSLIC and 'Zombie' S&Ls," Edward J. Kane, *Contemporary Policy Issues,* January 1987, pp. 77–83. Reprinted by permission of the author and Western Economic Association International.

Article 12: "Texas S&L Disasters Are Blamed, in Part, On Freewheeling Style," Leonard M. Apcar, *The Wall Street Journal,* July 13, 1987. Reprinted by permission of *The Wall Street Journal,* Dow Jones & Company, Inc. 1987. All rights reserved.

Article 13: "A Comparison of Risk-Based Capital and Risk-Based Deposit Insurance," Robert B. Avery and Terrence M. Belton, Federal Reserve Bank of Cleveland *Economic Review,* 1987 Quarter 4, pp. 20–30.

Article 14: "Interstate Bank Mergers and Competition in Banking," Paul Calem, Federal Reserve Bank of Philadelphia *Business Review,* January/February 1987, pp. 3–14.

Article 15: "Country Risk, Portfolio Decisions and Regulation in International Bank Lending," Ingo Walter, *Journal of Banking and Finance,* March 1981, Vol. 5:1, pp. 77–92. Reprinted by permission of North-Holland Information & Business Division, a branch of Elsevier Science Publishers B.V.

Article 16: "Bank Risk from Nonbank Activities," Elijah Brewer, III, Diana Fortier, and Christine Pavel, Federal Reserve Bank of Chicago *Economic Perspectives,* July/August, 1988, Vol. XII, Issue 4, pp. 14–26.

Article 17: "Banking Reform: An Overview of the Restructuring Debate," Mitchell Berlin, Federal Reserve Bank of Philadelphia *Business Review,* July/August 1988, pp. 3–14.

Article 18: "Uniting Investment and Commercial Banking," Michael C. Keeley and Randall J. Pozdena, Federal Reserve Bank of San Francisco *Weekly Letter,* June 19, 1987, pp. 1–3.

Article 19: "The Securitization of Housing Finance," Gordon H. Sellon, Jr. and Deana VanNahmen, Federal Reserve Bank of Kansas City *Economic Review,* July-August 1988, pp. 3–20.

Article 20: "Has Deregulation Ruined M1 as a Policy Guide?" Howard L. Roth, Federal Reserve Bank of Kansas City *Economic Review,* June 1987, pp. 24–37.

Article 21: "M1A—M.I.A.?" William T. Gavin and Michael R. Pakko, Federal Reserve Bank of Cleveland *Economic Commentary,* July 1, 1987, pp. 1–4.

Article 22: "A Cashless Society?" Michael C. Keeley, Federal Reserve Bank of San Francisco *Weekly Letter,* April 15, 1988, pp. 1–3.

Article 23: "Bank Runs, Deposit Insurance, and Bank Regulation, Part I," Charles T. Carlstrom, Federal Reserve Bank of Cleveland *Economic Commentary,* February 1, 1988, pp. 1–4.

Article 24: "The Impact of a New Federal Reserve Chairman," Edward J. Kane, *Contemporary Policy Issues,* Vol. VI, January 1988, pp. 88–97. Reprinted by permission of the author and the Western Economic Association International.

Article 25: "Happy Anniversary, Alan Greenspan," Lyle E. Gramley, *Mortgage Banking,* July 1988, Vol. 48, No. 10, pp. 38–42. Reprinted by permission of the Mortgage Bankers Association.

Article 26: "Federal Reserve Open Market Techniques," Howard L. Roth, Federal Reserve Bank of Kansas City *Economic Review,* March 1986, pp. 3–15.

Article 27: "The Discount Window," David L. Mengle, Federal Reserve Bank of Richmond *Economic Review,* May/June 1986, pp. 2–10.

Article 28: "Looking Forward," John P. Judd, Federal Reserve Bank of San Francisco *Weekly Letter,* July 8, 1988, pp. 1–3.

Article 29: "Why Does Velocity Matter?" Daniel L. Thornton, Federal Reserve Bank of St. Louis *Review,* December 1983, pp. 5–13.

Article 30: "The Case for Overhauling the Federal Reserve," Milton Friedman, *Challenge,* July/August 1985, pp. 4–12. Reprinted by permission of Hoover Press.

Article 31: "Time Inconsistency: A Potential Problem for Policymakers," Herb Taylor, Federal Reserve Bank of Philadelphia *Business Review,* March/April 1985, pp. 3–12.

Article 32: "Maintaining Central Bank Credibility," Anne Sibert and Stuart E. Weiner, Federal Reserve Bank of Kansas City *Economic Review,* September-October 1988, pp. 3–15.

Article 33: "Rules Versus Discretion: Making a Monetary Rule Operational," John B. Carlson, Federal Reserve Bank of Cleveland *Economic Review,* 1988 quarter 3, Vol. 24, No. 3, pp. 2–13.

Article 34: "A Guide to Foreign Exchange Markets," K. Alec Chrystal, Federal Reserve Bank of St. Louis *Review,* March 1984, pp. 5–18. Table 1 (left): Reprinted by permission of *The Wall Street Journal,* Dow Jones & Company, Inc. 1983. Table 1 (right): Reprinted by permission from the *Financial Times,* 8 September 1983. Table 3: Reprinted by permission of *The Wall Street Journal,* Dow Jones & Company, Inc. 1984. All rights reserved.

Article 35: "Distinguished Lecture on Economics in Government: Thinking About International Economic Coordination," Martin S. Feldstein, The Journal of Economic Perspectives, Vol. 2, No. 2, Spring 1988, pp. 3–13. Reprinted by permission of the author and the American Economic Association.

Article 36: "Louvre's Lesson—The World Needs a New Monetary System," C. Fred Bergsten, *The International Economy,* January/February 1988, Vol. 1, No. 2, pp. 70–75. Reprinted by permission.

Article 37: "Understanding International Debt Crisis," James R. Barth, Michael D. Bradley, and Paul C. Panayotacos, 19:1 *Case Western Reserve Journal of International Law,* Winter 1987, pp. 31–52. Reprinted by permission.

Article 38: "Financial Markets in Europe: Toward 1992," Morgan Guaranty Trust Company *World Financial Markets,* Issue 5, September 9, 1988, pp. 1–15. Reprinted by permission.

The views expressed in the articles from Federal Reserve Bank publications are those of the authors and not necessarily those of the Federal Reserve Bank or the Federal Reserve System.

Contents

SECTION ONE

Financial Markets and
Interest Rates

The readings in this section begin with an overview of the developments in financial markets of the past decade. An introduction to the workings of the market for Treasury bills follows. The next selection provides a framework for understanding how and why expected rates of return on financial assets, relative to those on Treasury bills for example, are related to risk. The relation between short and long term interest rates is then explored. The last three readings in this section address issues of interest rate risk. Because the yields on their assets adjust less often than those on their liabilities, financial institutions face this risk. These readings demonstrate how such risk can be measured and how it can be reduced by using financial futures and by using swaps.

"Developments in the U.S. Financial System Since the Mid-1970s" by Thomas D. Simpson begins by showing that all sectors of the economy have become much more debt-intensive and interest rates have become much more volatile. Coupled with worldwide economic slack and especially severe downturns in the energy and agriculture sectors, financial markets became more concerned with credit and interest rate risk. New strategies and financial instruments arose to ameliorate these risks for financial institutions and their customers. Examples include the emergence of widespread hedging with financial futures, increased reliance on variable-interest-rate loans and deposits, and the selling of mortgages and other loans these institutions originate. At the same time, some financial institutions, perhaps even inadvertently, chose riskier strategies and instruments.

"Treasury Bills" by Timothy Q. Cook provides a detailed description of the Treasury bill market. The mechanics of the auction the Fed conducts on behalf of the Treasury to sell new issues of bills is first explained. Then Cook discusses the fundamental default, liquidity, and other investment features of Treasury bills. Next the correct method of calculating yields on Treasury bills is presented. The article concludes with descriptions of who holds these bills and how the enormously active secondary market in Treasury bills functions.

"Modern Financial Theory" by Richard R. Simonds introduces the concepts that underlie the diversification of portfolios, the relation between expected risk and returns, and the notion of financial market efficiency. He begins by demonstrating simply why portfolio risk can be reduced through diversification and shows the optimal amount of diversification. The implications of these results are then used to demonstrate why the return on an asset rises, not with its own riskiness, but with the amount of extra risk that an asset imparts to the entire portfolio. Next, Simonds defines various concepts of efficiency and briefly notes some of the evidence for their relevance. The article concludes by outlining applications of each of the results developed in the article.

"The Yield Curve and Inflation Expectations" by C. Alan Garner begins with a definition of what the yield curve is and expounds the expectations theory of its shape and movement. That is followed by a numerical example of how an increase in the expected rate of inflation can affect the yield curve. Garner notes that other factors also influence the yield curve: The effects of government budget deficits, lower household savings rates, monetary policy, supply shocks, liquidity premia, and relative asset supplies are each examined. These factors are shown to preclude using yield curve shifts as a flawless barometer of shifts in expected inflation. The article reminds us that during 1987, for example, survey measures indicated long-term expected inflation was falling as long-term interest rates were rising.

Before interest rate risk can be managed, it should be quantified. In "Measuring Interest Rate Risk: What Do We Really Know?," James E. McNulty illustrates how to measure risk with each of the two major techniques that sophisticated managers currently use: gap analysis and duration analysis. He then assesses the relative virtues and vices of each method, arguing that since the strengths of one tend to be the weaknesses of the other, both should be used. In effect, the manager chooses a blend or portfolio of methods to use to achieve efficiency.

The article by Michael T. Belongia and G.J. Santoni, "Hedging Interest Rate Risk with Financial Futures: Some Basic Principles," works through examples to show how maturity mismatches between assets and liabilities expose a financial institution to interest rate risk. The authors then discuss the principles of hedging and demonstrate how Treasury bill futures contracts can be used to insulate a firm from such risk. They also emphasize two distinctions that are often forgotten in practice. The first is between the commonly used tactic that hedges cash flows and the tactic that hedges the net worth of the firm. The second distinction is between futures positions that reduce and those that increase interest rate risk.

Though financial futures can often be helpful in reducing interest rate risk, in practice they do not suffice. One problem is that contracts that specify delivery a year or more in the future are expensive and sometimes nonexistent. Another difficulty encountered is that the specific interest rate whose risk the institution is trying to hedge will not move perfectly with the Treasury bill rate. These are some of the shortcomings that led to the explosive growth of the interest rate swap market. The article by J. Gregg Whittaker, "Interest Rate Swaps: Risk and Regulation," defines what a swap is and describes why such agreements can be advantageous to both parties. The article then explores the risks involved in swap agreements and how banks manage those risks. Reasons for bank regulators' concern about these risks and proposals for monitoring and pricing them are also presented.

Article One

Developments in the U.S. Financial System since the Mid-1970s

Thomas D. Simpson, Associate Director, Division of Research and Statistics, prepared this article. *An earlier version of this article was presented at a conference on The New Financial System in Madrid, Spain, on October 8 and 9, 1987. The conference was organized by the Fundación fondo para la Investigación Económica y Social and the Fondation Internationale des Sciences Humaines.*

Since the mid-1970s, the United States has seen some of the most profound financial change in its history. New kinds of investment and credit arrangements have proliferated at a bewildering pace, accompanied by derivative instruments such as financial futures, options, and swaps. Underlying many of these developments has been an economy buffeted by inflation and disinflation and by large fiscal and external deficits. At the same time, competition in the financial marketplace has become more intense, the U.S. financial system has become more integrated with those abroad, and some parts of the financial system have been deregulated.

A perspective on this change can be gained by examining the expansion of debt owed by domestic nonfinancial sectors, shown in table 1. Between 1976 and mid-1987, aggregate debt (line 6) more than tripled, while the gross national product, a very rough index of the capacity to service this debt, rose much less. As a consequence, the ratio of debt to GNP, which had been relatively stable for most of the postwar period before the early 1980s, has climbed markedly in recent years. Pacing the expansion in total debt has been the indebtedness of the U.S. government (line 1), which grew nearly $1½ trillion over the 10½-year period, with the bulk of the expansion occurring during the 1980s. The share of outstanding federal debt held by commercial banks (line 1a) fell from about a fifth to only a little more

1. Debt owed by domestic nonfinancial sectors
Billions of dollars

Sector	Amount outstanding	
	1976:4	1987:2
1. U.S. government (Treasury)	515.8	1,873.9
a. Held by commercial banks.....	105.7	194.4
b. Held by others	409.1	1,679.5
2. State and local governments	233.5	535.1
a. Held by commercial banks.....	99.8	127.0e
b. Held by others	145.6	408.1
3. Nonfinancial corporations	586.2	1,767.8
a. Banks	171.3	526.5
b. Commercial paper..............	11.0	67.9
c. Corporate bonds	277.2	714.6
d. Other[1]	127.2	458.8
MEMO		
Equity (market value)	787.6	2,834.7
4. Farms and unincorporated		
businesses......................	322.5	1,094.4
a. Bank loans	32.8	67.0
b. Mortgages and other	289.7	982.4
5. Households	851.7	2,704.6
a. Consumer debt	243.9	719.3
Owed to commercial banks	118.0	317.6
Owed to others.................	125.9	401.7
b. Home mortgages	529.4	1,724.2
c. Other debt....................	78.4	261.1
6. Total domestic nonfinancial debt ...	2,509.7	7,930.8
MEMO		
GNP...............................	1,843.7	4,457.1
Debt as a percentage of GNP........	136.1	177.9

1. Includes mortgages and industrial development bonds.
e Estimated.

than a tenth—implying a massive absorption by the nonbank public, including foreign purchasers. The rise in state and local debt over this period (line 2) was less dramatic, again with most of it accumulated by nonbank holders.

The private sectors—households and nonfinancial businesses—also have been heavy borrowers, especially in recent years. Businesses (line 3) have tapped commercial banks and the bond market in volume; also of note is the sharp rise in commercial paper, a nonbank source of short-term funds used by a growing number of firms.

Growth of household indebtedness (line 5), including mortgages and consumer credit, also has been substantial. A surge in revolving consumer credit—mostly at commercial banks—associated with a proliferation and growing use of credit cards captured much attention around the mid-1980s. The trillion-dollar-plus advance in home mortgages (line 5b) has provided the raw material for a growing array of mortgage securities; in addition, a portion of the buildup of mortgage debt has reflected borrowing against accumulated home equity, a type of credit that has become popular of late while other forms of household debt have been losing their tax deductibility.

Because this period of rapid debt expansion also has been one of unrealized expectations and severe hardship for many, certain parts of the financial system, especially in the commercial bank and thrift (or savings) sectors have experienced severe strains. These strains have been evident in the earnings performance of the bank and thrift industries, including massive losses by many thrift institutions and impairment of the industry's insurance fund. The financial system has been responding to financial losses by developing new ways of shifting risk. A better understanding of trends in the U.S. financial system over the past ten years can be gained by reviewing the overall economic and financial background.

ECONOMIC AND FINANCIAL BACKGROUND

A major feature of the economic setting over the past decade or so has been the inflation–disinflation process. As chart 1 shows, inflation—as

measured by the consumer price index—picked up in the late 1970s from already advanced levels; reached a peak of about 13 percent in 1979 and 1980; and then fell off sharply. This inflationary experience profoundly affected the public's expectations of inflation, which were a primary factor in boosting interest rates in this period and in influencing wage negotiations in the labor markets. Many consumers borrowed large sums, which they expected to repay in greatly inflated dollars: real estate investments, which had been performing well in the inflationary setting, were especially favored. In the event, after 1981, earnings and prices, including real estate prices, grew much less rapidly than expected, placing debt-servicing strains on many borrowers.

Fiscal deficits widened sharply in the early 1980s, reaching the $200 billion area (5 percent of GNP) in the expansion years 1985 and 1986 (chart 2). The resulting pressures on financial markets are widely thought to have contributed to the dollar's strength over much of the first half of the 1980s, and to a worsening current account position (chart 2). The growing availability of savings from abroad likely acted to limit upward

2. Current account deficit, federal deficit, and exchange value of the U.S. dollar

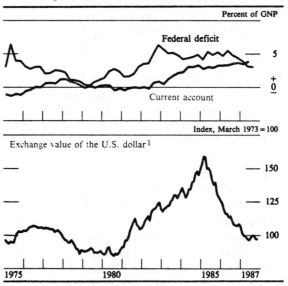

Percent of GNP

Federal deficit

Current account

Index, March 1973 = 100

Exchange value of the U.S. dollar [1]

1. Consumer price index

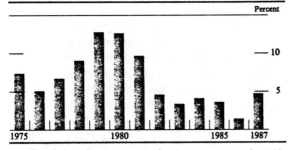

Percent

1. Growth from fourth quarter to fourth quarter, except for 1987, when data shown are through the third quarter.

1. Index of weighted average exchange value of the U.S. dollar against currencies of other Group of Ten countries plus Switzerland. Weights are global trade from 1972 through 1976 for each of the G-10.

movements in domestic interest rates. Foreign sources of funds thus reduced the extent to which interest-sensitive sectors of the economy, such as housing and investment, were constrained by resource transfers necessitated by large fiscal deficits. Conversely, export industries and those competing with imports bore more of the burden of the adjustment, and weaker earnings in these industries added to debt-servicing strains.

The agricultural sector was particularly hard hit. Prices paid to U.S. farmers over the first half of the 1980s were depressed by the strong dollar and enlarged supplies of non-U.S. producers. Weak output prices contributed to the sharp decline in farm income. Weaker income, together with historically high interest rates over much of this period, placed heavy debt-servicing strains on farm borrowers and stress on many of their creditors. A plunge in the value of farmland used as collateral exacerbated the situation.

Energy producers, especially around the mid-1980s, also were adversely affected by external developments, in particular the decline in oil prices. Although lower energy prices enabled the incomes of many borrowers to stretch further, energy producers experienced a sharp drop in their earnings and in their ability to service their debts. Owing to the geographic concentration of the energy industry, this development contributed to a generalized weakness in the so-called oil patch, most notably Texas.

Bank loans to several heavily indebted developing countries also have soured. These countries have had difficulties servicing their external debt because of weak markets for their exports, high interest costs on these loans over much of this period, and their macroeconomic and structural policies. While much progress has been made by these countries as a group, interest payments on some loans have been disrupted, and banks in the United States and elsewhere have made large provisions for losses on developing-country debt.

Meanwhile, debt growth in the household and business sectors has greatly outpaced income in recent years (chart 3), adding to concerns about credit quality. The degree to which the surge in household debt has strained the household sector is somewhat uncertain because, in the aggregate,

3. Debt ratios

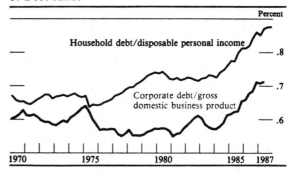

it has for most of this period been accompanied by a massive buildup of financial assets. Those household units that have accumulated large amounts of assets along with debt have built a cushion in the event that debt-servicing strains become excessive. The large buildup of debt in the corporate sector has been associated with a wave of mergers, acquisitions, and corporate restructurings, in which equity has been retired with the proceeds of debt issuance. Corporations that have increased their leverage in this way are viewed as more vulnerable to an earnings disruption, although many analysts believe that such higher levels of corporate leveraging impose more discipline on management to maximize earnings from the corporation's assets and thereby to enlarge the cash flow available for debt service.

In reflection of the various debt strains, delinquency rates on bank loans have been very high in recent years (table 2). In particular, farm loan delinquencies have been on the order of 10 percent or higher. Delinquencies on commercial and industrial loans, real estate loans, and consumer loans, while distinctly lower than on farm loans, have been at historically high levels. Loan charge-offs, which generally follow delinquencies, have risen considerably in recent years, with increases evident in all major categories.

Downgradings of corporate debt in relation to upgradings (chart 4) are another indicator of credit quality in the business sector. Over the 1980s, the number of downgradings has been very high. Indeed, in the economic expansion since the 1981–82 recession, an unusually high number of bonds have been downgraded in that the number of downgradings typically falls as an

2. Delinquency rates at large insured commercial banks, by type of loan[1]

Delinquent loans as a percent of average amount outstanding, annual rate

Type of loan	1983[2]	1984[2]	1985[2]	1986				1987[3]	
				Q1	Q2	Q3	Q4	Q1	Q2
Real estate loans	6.61	5.79	5.25	5.46	5.30	5.02	5.19	5.44	5.08
Commercial and industrial loans ..	7.39	6.18	5.59	5.55	5.72	5.79	5.52	6.45	6.33
Consumer loans	2.65	2.59	3.01	3.38	3.20	3.17	3.33	3.44	3.29
Farm loans	10.85	11.14	9.39	12.60	12.52	10.58	10.36	13.87	12.66
Other loans in domestic offices[4].	3.78	2.64	2.47	2.22	2.10	2.04	2.03	7.14	6.77
Loans in foreign offices...........	4.95	5.76	5.50	4.62	4.55	4.39	4.52	n.a.	n.a.
Total................	5.74	5.11	4.73	4.59	4.55	4.44	4.46	5.82	5.57
MEMO Total for all banks....	5.54	5.01	4.78	4.84	4.79	4.62	4.61	5.72	5.45

1. Delinquent loans include nonaccrual loans, as well as those past due 30 days or more and still accruing. These data are for banks with at least $300 million in assets, except the last row, which is calculated for all insured U.S.-chartered commercial banks.
2. Figures for 1983, 1984, and 1985 are averages of quarterly data.
3. Series break: Beginning in March 1987, banks report delinquent loans in domestic offices and foreign offices on a consolidated basis.

Thus, loans previously reported for foreign offices are now included in loans by type. Also, in contrast to earlier data, which are averages of quarter ends, first-quarter data for 1987 are calculated on an end-of-quarter basis.
4. Beginning in 1987, includes other loans booked in foreign offices.
n.a. Not available.

expansion matures. In part, downgradings in recent years have reflected the sharp rise in corporate leveraging.

Overall, the period since the mid-1970s has been one of greater interest rate risk. Interest rate volatility increased greatly at the end of the 1970s—at a time of higher interest rates (chart 5)—an event widely associated with the Federal Reserve's shift to a reserves-based operating procedure in October 1979. The objective of the operating procedure was to obtain tighter control over the money stock in order to curb inflationary pressures more effectively. A by-product of this change was more scope for movements in

short-term interest rates. As shown in table 3, both short-term and long-term rates became much more volatile beginning in late 1979 and continuing through the early 1980s. Volatility diminished subsequently, but it remains above that of the 1970s. These events heightened the sensitivity of financial market participants to interest rate risk, leading to many behavioral adaptations and new financial products—including financial futures and options. In particular, savings institutions that traditionally had raised short-term funds to hold long-term assets sought various ways to control and limit exposure to interest rate risk; some did so through changes in portfo-

4. Changes in Moody's corporate bond ratings

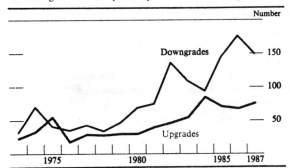

Data for 1987 plotted through the second quarter.
SOURCE. Moody's Investors Service.

5. Treasury rates[1]

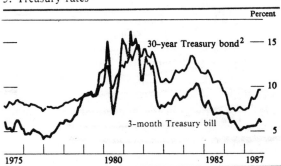

1. Monthly data.
2. Before February 1977, data shown are for 20-year Treasury bonds.

3. Interest rate volatility measured as the standard deviation of daily changes

Basis points

Period	Treasury bills (3-month)	Certificates of deposit (3-month)	Treasury bonds (30-year)
1975–79[1]	7.1	6.0	2.7
1979–82[2]	28.9	32.4	14.4
1982–87[3]	8.1	8.9	8.0

1. September 1975 through August 1979 for 3-month bills and CDs. For the 30-year bond, the period is September 1977 through August 1979.
2. October 1979 through September 1982.
3. October 1982 through September 1987.

lio management, including the use of interest rate futures and other hedging instruments.

Other developments have had a significant impact on the financial system since the mid-1970s. The deregulation of deposit rates began in mid-1978, when a new retail deposit instrument, the six-month money market certificate, was introduced with a regulatory rate ceiling that adjusted with rates in the open market. In early 1980, the Congress enacted the Depository Institutions Deregulation and Monetary Control Act, landmark legislation that mandated the removal of all interest rate ceilings in an orderly fashion by April 1986. In practice, rate ceilings were taken off in stages, with the final measures occurring in early 1986. At present, banks are prohibited from paying interest only on demand deposits.

Asset quality problems of U.S. banks have taken their toll on bank earnings, especially for some institutions (chart 6). Earnings as a percentage of assets weakened over much of the 1980s, with the erosion being highly pronounced at the poorer-performing institutions (the lowest

5 percent in earnings). In the thrift industry (chart 7), earnings were depressed in the early 1980s by the adverse movement in interest margins accompanying the sharp rise in rate levels. Subsequently, the top half of the industry has recovered, while the poorer earners have slipped dramatically. The bottom segment of the industry has created extraordinary difficulties for the Federal Savings and Loan Insurance Corporation, which has recently required legislative action to provide more financial resources to deal with insolvent institutions.

The earnings problems faced by U.S. banking and thrift organizations added to their costs of raising funds in the wholesale markets. Moreover, regulatory policy has shifted toward increased capital requirements for banks and thrift institutions. As capital requirements have become more binding, banks and thrift institutions have sought new ways of conducting business without adding to their assets that are subject to such requirements and have turned to so-called off-balance-sheet activities and loan sales.

The increasing sophistication of borrowers and lenders in the financial marketplace is another important factor contributing to change in the financial system. Against the backdrop of the computer revolution and vast improvements in telecommunications, investors have become more aware of alternatives and more sensitized to differentials in yields and risk, while borrowers have become more aware of alternative borrowing opportunities. Closely related to the growing awareness of investment and borrowing alternatives has been a rising level of competition

6. Dispersion of commercial bank earnings

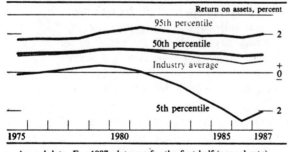

Annual data. For 1987, data are for the first half (annual rate).

7. Dispersion of thrift institution earnings

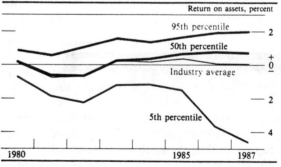

Annual data for FSLIC-insured institutions. For 1987, data are for the first quarter (annual rate).

in the financial marketplace. In the banking sector, foreign banks have gained a presence in U.S. credit markets by establishing a large number of banking offices, mainly in major money centers, and have aggressively pursued U.S. customers by emphasizing credit services and offering attractive terms. The number of branches and agencies of foreign banks has more than tripled over the past decade, while their share of the loan market—especially business loans—has climbed.

Access by businesses to the open markets has improved over this period, most visibly in the commercial paper market, which has expanded several-fold from only about $10 billion outstanding in the mid-1970s. Many borrowers have entered this market, aided by bank credit lines supporting their paper issuance or by bank standby letters of credit. Also, a growing number of firms has been able to tap the bond market for long-term credit as the high-yield or "junk bond" market mushroomed in the mid-1980s.

RESPONSES OF THE
U.S. FINANCIAL SYSTEM

Against the background of heightened interest rate and credit risk and growing competition, financial institutions and markets have responded in many ways, only some of which can be highlighted in this article. Among the more important have been the increasing reliance on futures markets as a means of shifting risk, generally more prompt adjustment of deposit and loan rates to changes in open market rates, off-balance-sheet activities and asset sales by depositories, and securitization of credit.

Financial Futures

Activity in financial futures and options has soared since the introduction of these instruments in the 1970s. The number of contracts and types of users of these so-called derivative instruments have expanded greatly, contributing to the sharp rise in trading volume. A great deal of attention has focused on the markets for financial futures and options in the wake of the stock market crash in October 1987. Public scrutiny

has centered on the possible contribution of these instruments to market volatility—including the collapse on October 19—while users of these instruments have been reassessing the degree to which they satisfy hedging needs, especially in the event of extreme market turbulence.

Interest rate futures were introduced in 1976 and have figured prominently in efforts to shift interest rate risk in the more volatile rate environment of the late 1970s and early 1980s. Interest rate futures are one means available to commercial banks and savings institutions to limit their exposure to interest rate risk associated with maturity mismatches, traditionally a more serious problem for thrift institutions, which have depended on short-term deposits to fund long-term mortgages. Interest rate futures also have been used by underwriters of credit market instruments to limit their exposure to interest rate risk while they are originating and distributing new issues. Perhaps the major users of interest rate futures, however, have been securities dealers with large trading-account positions.

While many types of interest rate futures are available, those on Treasury bills, Eurodollar deposits, and Treasury bonds have come to dominate the market. Because the correlation between prices for these instruments and those on other securities is less than perfect, market participants using such futures contracts to cover positions in other securities are left with some risk, so-called basis risk. On occasion, hedgers using contracts in these instruments, especially futures on Treasury bonds, to cover positions in other securities, such as mortgage securities, have incurred appreciable losses owing to differential movements in prices.

Futures and options on stock indexes were introduced around the time of the advance in prices of equities in 1982. These instruments enable market participants to shift the risk associated with generalized market price developments. To many investors, the availability of futures and options has been viewed as a means of protecting the value of a portfolio of securities, so-called portfolio insurance, by selling a futures contract or acquiring a put option on a stock price index matching the securities actually held by the investor. Thus, losses arising from a market decline can be limited. Others have come to view the futures and options markets as a low-cost means of participating in general advances or declines in markets; transactions costs associated with positions in options and futures typically have been lower than those for cash positions. As a consequence, price movements frequently occur in futures and options contracts before they appear in the cash market; indeed, many sophisticated arbitrage strategies have been developed to profit from this disparity. Particularly controversial have been computer-driven "program trading" strategies involving the purchase or sale of a diversified basket of stocks. Some believe that program trading, including arbitrage strategies, has contributed to stock market volatility in recent years, especially to the collapse in mid-October 1987. Studies have been undertaken to examine the causes of that collapse, with particular emphasis on the role of portfolio insurance and arbitrage strategies. In addition, difficulties in getting prompt execution of orders in the cash market and the apparent tendency for index futures to trade below comparable prices in the cash market at that time have led to a reexamination of the use of index futures and options for hedging or arbitrage by many in the market.

In principle, financial futures and options have enabled market participants to shift interest rate and market risk toward economic units that may be better positioned and more willing to absorb it. As previously noted, the availability of financial futures and options probably has encouraged more underwriting and trading, tending to enhance liquidity and affording borrowers greater access to the markets. On the other hand, hedgers using these instruments still are left with the risk that the price of the hedging instrument and the underlying position being hedged can diverge, especially under turbulent market conditions. In addition, futures and options contracts enable those who are ill-equipped to handle the risk to engage more easily in speculation, with adverse consequences for other participants as well as for the functioning of the financial markets.

Pricing of Loans and Deposits

At commercial banks, the process of deregula-

tion of retail deposit rates, together with competitive forces, has led to prompter adjustment of deposit rates to movements in open market rates. The resulting pressures on costs also have contributed to the faster adjustment of loan rates to open market rates. This development has been especially significant for small and medium-sized banks. Larger banks traditionally have relied more on wholesale funds and have long been under more pressure to keep loan rates in alignment with those in the open market: their wholesale borrowing costs, primarily the rates on CDs and federal funds, tend to move closely with other open market rates, and their customers tend to have better access to competing sources of credit. Before the late 1970s, when the deregulation process began, deposit and loan rates at small and medium-sized banks moved very little, even when open market rates swung quite sharply. Since deregulation began, such rates at small- and medium-sized banks have become more responsive to market developments.

The pricing of business loans also became more directly tied to open market rates over this period, especially at larger banks. Contributing to the shift from the prime rate, an administered rate, to an open market reference rate were foreign banks that were seeking a market share in the United States through their branches and agencies. Today, business loan customers commonly have loan commitments with both prime and open market base-rate options. In practice, customers of the money center banks elect loans with a money market reference rate more often than they choose prime rate loans, as table 4 shows. In May 1987, only a fifth of business loans extended by the very large money center banks

4. Pricing of business loan extensions at U.S. banks, May 1987

Percent of loan extensions

Reference rate	Nine money center banks	Other large banks[1]	Other banks
Prime rate	21.1	29.0	54.0
Federal funds rate...	37.7	25.8	16.7
Other domestic money market rate	25.5	20.7	12.0
Foreign rate	4.3	9.4	6.2
Other	11.4	15.1	11.0

1. Banks with assets of about $5 billion or more.

were linked to the prime rate, while nearly two-fifths were linked to the federal funds rate and another one-fourth were tied to other domestic money market rates, such as the CD or Treasury bill rate. Loans linked to interest rates outside the United States (including the LIBOR) and priced in other ways represented only a small fraction of the total. At other large banks, the prime-based share is a little larger, and the open-market-based share, smaller but still well above that of a decade earlier. Most business loans made by the smaller banks continue to be tied to the prime, although market-based lending by these institutions has become significant.

Meanwhile, some larger banks have sought to use deregulated retail deposits as a means of reducing their dependence on wholesale funds. Retail deposits generally have been viewed as a more stable source of funds than are wholesale or managed liabilities, especially at a time when the availability of funds in the wholesale market appears to be sensitive to shifts in sentiment about the strength of banking organizations. Moreover, some institutions evidently have viewed the substitution of core deposits for wholesale funds as a means of lowering interest costs over the long run; at times, banks have used their freedom to set retail deposit rates to bid aggressively for such balances, apparently expecting to reduce their rates after an introductory period or roll them over at lower rates. For example, the share of assets funded by retail core deposits rose appreciably from a very low level at large money center banks in late 1982, after a major deregulatory measure that introduced the money market deposit account, and it has subsequently edged higher.

Viewed somewhat differently, the concern about the quality of large bank loan portfolios, heightened since 1982 by events involving developing-country debt, has added to the premium over open market rates that banks, some highly vulnerable banks in particular, have had to pay on wholesale deposits, while also adding to the attractiveness of federally insured retail deposits. The added premium that many banks now pay has put upward pressure on bank costs, and therefore more high-grade corporate borrowers have gone directly to the open market for credit. In essence, the attractiveness of credit offered by

banking organizations has fallen for many premium customers, as open market credit has become relatively less costly to them.

Capital Requirements, Standby Letters of Credit, and Loan Sales

In the midst of the profound changes taking place in the financial system, the capital requirements on the large banks have been stiffened, in recognition of the increased risk exposure of these banks and a desire to limit exposure of the federal deposit insurance fund. Capital requirements for the large banks were tightened both formally, by specifying a minimum primary capital ratio, and informally, through the examination and applications process. Because off-balance-sheet activities were initially excluded from formal capital requirements, banks had an incentive to expand such activities in lieu of placing loans on their books. In particular, standby letters of credit soared from about $40 billion in 1980 to almost $170 billion in 1985 (chart 8) . Through a standby letter of credit (SLC), a bank could support the commercial paper, notes, or bonds of a customer without maintaining the level of capital that would be required if the customer's obligation had been booked as a loan. The market regards the customer's obligation backed by the SLC much as it regards the bank's obligation, thereby securing the customer access to markets on terms comparable with those for the bank. This development has encouraged the separation of the credit support function of commercial banks from the funding function. Since 1985, however, the volume of SLCs has leveled off as regulators have increasingly taken SLCs

8. Standby letters of credit at all
   insured commercial banks

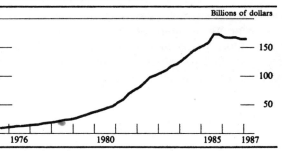

Quarterly data.

into account informally in the examination and applications review processes, as the credit ratings of some banks deteriorated relative to their top customers, and as support grew for a proposed risk-based capital standard that would include such off-balance-sheet activities in the formal computation of capital requirements. That proposal took on an international dimension when authorities of the United States and the United Kingdom proposed common treatment of capital standards and, subsequently, when other nations became involved.

Larger banks also have increasingly originated loans with a view to selling them or offering participations. In this way, they can collect origination and servicing fees by advancing credit to an established customer yet need not hold capital against it, provided the buyer of the loan does not have recourse to the bank in the event of default (through a standby letter of credit or other guarantee). To date, banks—including foreign banks—presumably with less binding capital requirements have bought a good portion of such loans sold by large banks. This development further unbundles the traditional banking relationship by separating the lending function, in this case into origination and funding components. Although most of these asset sales have taken the form of business loans, a few banks, with the aid of investment bankers, have structured sales of automobile loans and other receivables, most notably credit card receivables, in the form of pass-through participations in a pool of such claims or bonds backed by receivables.

④ *Adaptations by Savings Institutions*

Savings institutions better appreciated the extent of their vulnerability to interest rate risk in the early 1980s after the rise in the level of interest rates across the maturity spectrum. This increase in interest rates quickly added to the cost of funds at thrift institutions, predominantly for shorter-term deposits, while returns on holdings of fixed-rate mortgages did not register a compensating increase. Indeed, under these circumstances mortgage borrowers with relatively low fixed rates became less inclined to prepay, leading to an even more sluggish upward adjustment

of asset returns to the new higher level of market rates. As a consequence, savings institutions incurred record losses in the early 1980s and failures soared.

Many of the surviving institutions have devoted greater effort to managing interest rate risk. These institutions and their supervisors now follow more closely their exposure to interest rate risk by monitoring gaps between the maturities of assets and liabilities. Several methods have been used to shorten the repricing interval on assets and to lengthen the repricing interval on liabilities. One is the adjustable-rate mortgage (ARM). Such mortgages typically have the same maturity as the standard fixed-rate mortgage but carry interest rates that adjust at regular intervals to a benchmark rate. Commonly used benchmark rates are the yield on one-year Treasury securities and a published measure of the cost of funds to savings institutions. The share of conventional mortgages with adjustable-rate features was one-half or more of the total originated from mid-1983 to late 1985, a time when initial rates on these mortgages were low compared with those on fixed-rate mortgages. Borrowers nonetheless continue to show a preference for fixed-rate mortgages. Strong borrower interest in ARMs has been evident only when rather large rate differentials between ARMs and fixed-rate mortgages have prevailed, with such differentials enlarged at times by concessionary terms granted by the lender in the first year of the mortgage. Moreover, data on refinancings in 1986 and early 1987 indicate that many ARM borrowers are quick to refinance with fixed-rate mortgage credit when such rates fall markedly.

Another method used by savings institutions to shorten the effective maturity of their assets is the collateralized mortgage obligation (CMO). The CMO is a multiclass pay-through bond secured by mortgages or mortgage securities. Repayments (including prepayments) are applied to different classes of bondholders at different rates. The CMO enables the cash flow from a pool of mortgages, which is inherently uncertain because of the prepayment option to be structured into various broad maturity classes. Savings institutions have found the short maturity classes of CMOs an attractive form in which to hold mortgage assets because such CMOs have effective maturities more in line with maturities on deposit liabilities and because they have yields that exceed those on highly liquid money market instruments. Recently, CMOs have been offered with an adjustable-rate feature, further enhancing the appeal to many thrift institutions. As noted below, CMO issuance has soared in recent years, with savings institutions thought to be important holders of the short maturity classes. In some cases, thrift institutions retain the shorter maturity classes of CMOs that they themselves issue while in others they acquire these classes from other issuers.

Savings institutions also have attempted to lengthen effective maturities of liabilities. A technique used by many savings institutions is the interest rate swap, in which the thrift in effect trades an adjustable-rate obligation—that is, a regularly repriced obligation—for a fixed-rate obligation. The overall swap market has grown dramatically from virtually nothing in the early 1980s to several hundred billion dollars recently, with savings institutions holding a significant share of the fixed-rate component.

Savings institutions also compete aggressively for longer-term retail deposits. In relation to commercial banks they typically offer a larger premium for time deposit balances than for more liquid accounts and generally have been more successful than commercial banks in attracting time deposits, despite adverse publicity about the financial condition of the thrift industry.

Another device recently developed by savings institutions to reduce risk is the mortgage strip, in which the interest flow from a pool of mortgages and the principal are divided and sold as separate interest-only and principal-only securities. For the interest-only security, the average length of the interest flow depends on the level of interest rates. As interest rates fall and principal prepayments pick up, cash flow on the interest-only security declines. Conversely, if interest rates rise and prepayment activity slows, cash flow on the interest-only security improves. As a consequence, the interest-only security is thought to be a hedge against a rise in market rates for an institution with a maturity mismatch in the form of more long-term assets than liabilities. Some thrift institutions reportedly have acquired interest-only portions of mortgage pools as a hedge.

Meanwhile, the savings industry has responded to maturity imbalances, higher capital requirements, and borrower preferences for fixed-rate mortgages by originating fixed-rate mortgages for sale. In this way, thrift institutions can meet customer demands for mortgages and earn an origination and servicing fee while not aggravating maturity mismatches or adding to capital requirements. Fixed-rate mortgages are sold to other depository institutions but most often to the Federal National Mortgage Association (FNMA) or the Federal Home Loan Mortgage Corporation (FHLMC), two federally related agencies that play a central role in the secondary mortgage market. These institutions pool such mortgages and issue pass-throughs, by which holders receive an undivided interest in the pool. Savings institutions also swap mortgages for mortgage pass-through securities that contain the mortgages sold. Pass-through securities are more liquid than the underlying mortgages and can be used as collateral for certain kinds of borrowing. Another federal institution, the Government National Mortgage Association (GNMA), guarantees payments on pass-through securities issued against pools of federally insured mortgage loans.

Securitization

The securitization of loans, another major recent development in financial markets, has been most evident for mortgages. The most prominent instrument is the mortgage pass-through security. As chart 9 illustrates, mortgage pass-throughs have grown from miniscule proportions of all residential mortgage debt in the early 1970s to about one-third, or $600 billion, in mid-1987. The strong growth in mortgages in 1985 and 1986 and borrower preference for fixed-rate mortgages helped to boost pass-through volume substantially. Federally related mortgage pass-throughs—those guaranteed or issued by GNMA, FNMA, and FHLMC—account for all but a small portion of mortgage pass-throughs. The standardization requirements for underlying mortgages, the liquidity generated by the size of

securitization of loans is most prominent for MORTGAGES via PASS-THROUGH SECURITY.

9. Home mortgage debt outstanding

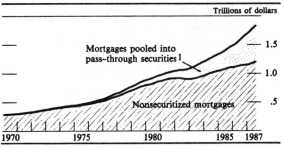

1. Pools include GNMA, FHLMC, and FNMA pass-throughs only.

the market, and the federal support of the pools have led to their dominance in the market. Nevertheless, even though such securities are not viewed as entailing much, if any, credit risk to investors, they do embody a significant amount of prepayment risk. As already noted, mortgage prepayments tend to rise as mortgage rates fall—reflecting refinancing of existing mortgages and more turnover of homes—and to decline as mortgage rates increase; this relationship is a relatively loose one, however, and thus the slippages add to prepayment uncertainty and risk. Consequently, mortgage pass-through yields contain a premium over federal government securities, with comparable expected maturities, that reflects such prepayment uncertainty. This premium tends to vary directly with interest rate volatility.

Mortgage pass-through securities have become the raw material for various derivative products. These include the CMOs and interest-only and principal-only obligations issued by private entities. Such instruments represent an alternative for dealing with prepayments and prepayment uncertainty. In view of the complexity of administering mortgage securities—such as assembling and maintaining records on the underlying mortgages, principal and interest payments, and prepayments—the introduction of these instruments and development of these markets have been highly dependent on advances in computer and information technology.

The concept of the pass-through subsequently has been extended to other kinds of loans, mainly automobile loans and credit card receivables. The latter represent unsecured loans while the former, like mortgages, are collateralized by the automobiles being financed; letters of credit have

been used to enhance both types of pass-throughs. Banks selling off such loans are able to relieve some pressure on capital positions while collecting origination and servicing fees. For such consumer receivables, prepayment uncertainty is minimal, in part because the incentive to prepay when interest rates change is relatively small. At present, the amount of securitized automobile and credit card receivables is rather small, on the order of $15 billion, mostly in the form of automobile securities. While banks have been the only issuers of credit card pass-through securities, automobile finance subsidiaries are thought to have a larger share in the securitization of automobile paper.

The term "securitization" has been applied to much more than pools of mortgages and consumer loans and their derivative instruments. Some have viewed as securitization the sale of business loans and the growing reliance on the commercial paper market by firms that had been heavily dependent on commercial banks; such loans and paper may be enhanced by bank standby letters of credit or loan commitments. In addition, the growing ability of many lower-rated firms to tap the bond market as an alternative to long-term bank financing has been regarded as securitization. Clearly, the wider availability of information on such credits and in the case of low-rated bonds, the recognition of the benefits of diversification (including through mutual funds), have reinforced the securitization trend. Issuance of high-yield (or below-investment-grade) bonds roughly doubled from mid-1985 to mid-1987, at a time when investors also absorbed a larger volume of bonds offered by investment-grade issuers (see chart 10). The market for

10. Gross issuance of nonfinancial corporate bonds

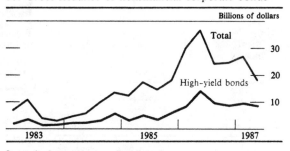

Quarterly data, not seasonally adjusted.

low-grade bonds, however, received a setback following the mid-October stock market crash—as investors evidently reassessed the prospects for debt service in the event of an economic slowdown or a less favorable climate for asset sales—and the volume of offerings has fallen markedly. Whether the market can regain its earlier momentum remains an open question.

As securitized assets work their way into investor portfolios and compete with traditional securities, the linkage between interest rates on loans that can be securitized and those on open market instruments becomes tighter. Not only does investor behavior directed toward maximizing yield—adjusted for credit, interest rate, and prepayment risk—act to bring rates on loans that can be securitized into line, but the originators of loans and the underwriters of securitized assets must keep a close eye on yields on competing assets in investor portfolios when they make loans or acquire them for securitization. Table 5 illustrates the tightening linkages between the commitment rate on fixed-rate home loans and the 10-year Treasury bond yield, a maturity that is roughly comparable with the expected life of 30-year mortgages. The change in the mortgage rate measured in basis points in the week following a change in the Treasury yield (standardized to be a 10-basis-point change) has quadrupled from the 1975–79 period to the 1986–87 period. In the late 1970s, the short-run responsiveness of mortgage rates was minimal: a change of only 2 basis points on average per each change of 10 basis points in Treasury yields. Responsiveness picked up a little over the first half of the 1980s, and in the past couple of years, with the surge in the volume of mortgage pass-throughs, the change in the mortgage rate climbed to more than 8 basis points on average per change of 10 basis

5. Change in mortgage rate in week after change in 10-year Treasury yield[1]

Basis points

1975–79	2.0
1980–82	3.2
1983–85	4.0
1986–87	8.2

1. The mortgage rate is the commitment rate on fixed-rate home loans. Both rates are weekly averages; 1987 observations are through mid-November.

points in the Treasury rate. In the spring of 1987, at a time when bond prices plunged in close association with a plunge in the dollar, stories abounded of mortgage lenders adjusting their rates daily, or even more frequently, in conjunction with developments in foreign exchange markets and domestic credit markets.

CONCLUSION

The financial system in the United States has been affected greatly over the past decade or so by drastic alterations in the economic setting. Interest rates have swung widely over this period, in large part reflecting changing inflation experience and expectations; in addition, interest rates have come to be viewed as inherently more volatile than was thought in the mid-1970s. While the U.S. economy has been expanding steadily since late 1982 and overall slack in resource utilization has diminished, debt-servicing strains on many borrowers have been substantial. These strains have reflected not only a much-diminished rate of inflation, including that on real estate acquired as an inflation hedge, but also a depressed agricultural sector, weakness in the energy sector, and other imbalances associated with large fiscal deficits and a massive erosion in the U.S. net export position. Bank lenders also have been affected by the debt problems of some developing countries.

The confluence of these events—resulting to an important degree from disinflation, global economic slack, and a strong dollar—clearly was not envisioned by financial institutions and markets. Nevertheless, it has had a pronounced effect on attitudes and behavior. Participants in financial markets generally have become more aware and sensitive to interest rate and credit risk. Against this background, a growing array of financial products have been developed to enable financial institutions and others to adjust and shift risk exposure to better suit their preferences and absorption capacities. The degree to which risk can be limited through derivative products, however, has been called into question by events surrounding the stock market crash in October 1987.

Commercial banks and savings institutions have experienced large loan losses, owing to the concentration of debt-servicing strains on their customers. Measures taken by these institutions in recent years to limit risk exposure are expected to reduce their vulnerability to economic shocks in the future. The growing use of hedging instruments is one such development. However, many of these instruments, especially those involving mortgages and their uncertain prepayments, contain elements of risk that are not fully known and may not be fully understood by all users.

The securitization of loans is another method developed by depository institutions to manage risk. Commercial banks and savings institutions have been able to continue to originate and service credit by selling loans, while avoiding losses associated with changes in credit or interest rate risk, provided that these loans are not sold with recourse to the originator. When recourse is provided, however, the capital positions of these institutions and their federal deposit insurance funds are exposed. Also of some concern are the consequences for bank and thrift portfolios of selling loans if they represent higher-quality credits. In these circumstances, the average quality of loans remaining in the loan portfolios could decline.

Federal exposure continues to be important in the market for mortgage pass-through securities, the largest area of securitization thus far. Indeed, in this period of heightened concern about credit quality and financial stability, investors seem to have sought the protection of a direct or indirect federal credit enhancement. Nevertheless, many investors are adding riskier securities to their portfolios, such as below-investment-grade bonds. The associated risks of borrower default are thus passed directly to investor portfolios rather than to the capital positions of banks and thrift institutions.

These developments, by affecting the incidence of economic losses and the exposure of the financial system, may influence spending behavior and the way the economy functions. Spending behavior may change if economic losses are absorbed directly into the public's portfolios rather than being absorbed by the capital positions of banks and thrift institutions. More important, the securitization process has hastened the effect of interest rate and credit market developments on loan markets. Moreover, in this era of tighter integration of U.S. financial markets with those abroad, international influences on domestic credit markets, including loan markets, are growing. □

Article Two

TREASURY BILLS

Timothy Q. Cook

Treasury bills are short-term obligations of the United States Government. Bills are generally considered to be totally free of default risk and are the most marketable of all money market instruments. They are held by a wide range of investors including individuals, financial institutions, corporations and foreigners. Treasury bills are also an important tool in federal debt management and in the execution of monetary policy. Persistent federal deficits have resulted in rapid growth in Treasury bills in recent years. At the end of 1985 the outstanding volume was $400 billion, the largest for any money market instrument.

TREASURY BILL AUCTIONS

The Treasury sells bills at regularly scheduled auctions to refinance maturing issues and, if necessary, to help finance current federal deficits. The Treasury also sells bills on an irregular basis to smooth out the uneven flow of revenues from corporate and individual tax receipts.

Regularly Scheduled Issues   Treasury bills were first authorized by Congress in 1929. After experimenting with a number of bill maturities the Treasury in 1937 settled on the exclusive issue of three-month bills. In December 1958 these were supplemented with six-month bills in the regular weekly auctions. In 1959 the Treasury began to auction one-year bills on a quarterly basis. The quarterly auction of one-year bills was replaced by an auction occurring every four weeks in August 1963. The Treasury added a nine-month maturity to the monthly auction in September 1966 but the sale of this maturity was discontinued in late 1972. Since then, the only regular bill offerings have been the offerings of three- and six-month bills every week and the offerings of one-year bills every four weeks. The Treasury has increased the size of its weekly and monthly bill auctions as new money has been needed to meet enlarged federal borrowing requirements. In 1985 monthly sales of one-year bills averaged $8.6 billion, while the weekly auctions of three- and six-month bills both ranged from $6.5 to $7.5 billion.

Irregularly Scheduled Issues Prior to the mid-1970s the Treasury sold bills on an irregular basis through the use of tax anticipation bills.[1] Introduced in October 1951, tax anticipation bills were designed specifically to help smooth out the Treasury's uneven flow of tax receipts while providing corporations with an investment vehicle for funds accumulated for tax payments. These bills were accepted at par on the tax date in payment for taxes due—hence the name, tax anticipation bills. They actually matured a week later, usually on the 22nd of the month. Tax anticipation bills did not have to be used for tax payments, and some investors chose to hold them to maturity.

No tax anticipation bills have been issued since 1974. In their place the Treasury has raised money on an irregular basis through the sale of "cash management" bills, which are typically "reopenings" or sales of bills that mature on the same date as an outstanding issue of bills. Cash management bills are designed to bridge low points in the Treasury's cash balances. Like tax anticipation bills, many cash management bills help finance the Treasury's requirements until tax payments are received. For this reason they frequently have maturities that fall after one of the five major federal tax dates. Thirty-eight issues of cash management bills were sold in the period from 1981 through 1985. The maturities of these issues ranged from 3 to 168 days and averaged 56 days.

Auctioning New Bills The Treasury sells bills at a discount through competitive auctions; the return to the investor is the difference between the purchase price of the bill and its face or par value. Treasury bills are currently sold in minimum amounts of $10,000 and multiples of $5,000 above the minimum. Treasury bills are issued only in book-entry form. Under this arrangement ownership is recorded in a book-entry account established at the Treasury and investors receive only a receipt as evidence of purchase.

Weekly offerings of three- and six-month bills are typically announced on Tuesday and the amount of the offering is set at that time. The auction is usually conducted on the following Monday, with delivery and payment on the following Thursday. Bids, or tenders, in the weekly auctions must be presented at Federal Reserve Banks or their branches, which act as agents for the Treasury, by 1:00 p.m. New York time on the day of the auction.[2]

Bids may be made on a competitive or noncompetitive basis. In making a competitive bid the investor states the quantity of bills desired and the price he is willing to pay. A subscriber may enter more than one bid indicating the various quantities he is willing to take at different prices. Competitive bids, which are

---

[1] Tax anticipation bills are described in more detail in Nelson [1977].

[2] For a detailed description of the mechanics of purchasing Treasury bills see Tucker [1987].

usually made by large investors who are in close contact with the market, comprise the largest portion of subscriptions on a dollar basis. In making a noncompetitive bid the investor indicates the quantity of bills desired and agrees to pay the weighted-average price of accepted competitive bids. Individuals and other small investors usually enter noncompetitive bids, which are limited to $1,000,000 for each new offering of three- and six-month bills. In recent years the dollar amount of noncompetitive awards as a percent of total awards has generally ranged from 10 to 25 percent of the total auction amount. As shown in Chart 1, the percent awarded to noncompetitive bids typically rises in periods of high interest rates.

After subscription books at the various Federal Reserve Banks and branches are closed at 1:00 p.m., the bids are tabulated and submitted to the Treasury for allocation. The Treasury first allocates whatever part of the total offering is needed to fill all the noncompetitive bids. The remainder is then allocated to those competitive bidders submitting the highest offers, ranging downward from the highest bid until the total amount offered is allocated. The "stop-out price" is the lowest price, or highest yield, at which bills are awarded. Usually only a portion of

Chart 1
NONCOMPETITIVE BIDS AT WEEKLY AUCTION
COMPARED TO LEVEL OF RATES

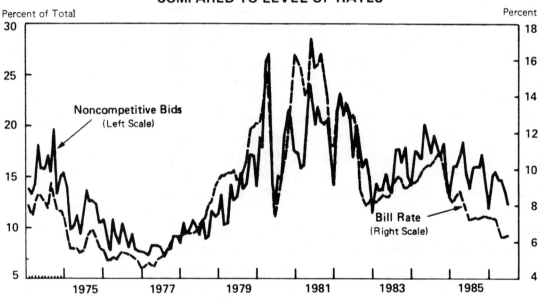

Note: Monthly data are averages of weekly figures.

Source: *Treasury Bulletin; Federal Reserve Bulletin.*

the total bids made at this price is accepted. The average issuing price is then computed as a weighted-average of the competitive bids accepted.

In the weekly auction of July 14, 1986, for example, accepted bids for the three-month bills ranged from a high of $98.547 per $100 of face amount (equivalent to an annual discount rate of 5.75 percent) to a stop-out price of $98.536 (5.79 percent). A total of $7,412 million of bids was accepted, $1,067 million of which was for noncompetitive tenders accepted at the average issuing price of $98.539 (5.78 percent). The relatively small proportion (14 percent) of bills purchased on a noncompetitive basis was typical given the low level of interest rates prevailing at the time of the auction.

In addition to the regular weekly auction, one-year bills are auctioned every fourth Thursday for issue the following Thursday and special auctions are held for cash management bills. The procedure for these auctions is similar to the weekly auctions.

INVESTMENT CHARACTERISTICS

Four investment characteristics of Treasury bills distinguish them from other money market instruments and consequently influence investor decisions to purchase bills. These include (1) lack of default risk, (2) liquidity, (3) favorable tax status, and (4) a low minimum denomination.

Default Risk   Treasury bills are generally considered to be free of default risk because they are obligations of the federal government. In contrast, even the highest grade of other money market instruments, such as commercial paper or CDs, is perceived to have some degree of default risk. Concern over default risk typically increases in times of weak economic conditions. In such periods the risk-free feature of bills becomes more valuable to some investors.

Because Treasury bills are free of default risk, various regulations permit them to be used for purposes that often cannot be served by other money market instruments. For example, banks use bills to make repurchase agreements free of reserve requirements with businesses and state and local governments, and banks use bills to satisfy pledging requirements on state and local and federal deposits. Treasury bills are widely accepted as collateral for selling short various financial securities and can be used instead of cash to satisfy initial margin requirements against futures market positions. And Treasury bills are always a permissible investment for state and local governments, while many other types of money market instruments frequently are not.

Liquidity   A second characteristic of bills is their high degree of liquidity. Liquidity refers mainly to the ability of investors to convert an asset into cash quickly at a low transactions cost. Investors in Treasury bills have this ability because bills are a homogeneous instrument and the bill market is highly organized and efficient. A measure of the liquidity of a financial asset is the spread between the price at which securities dealers buy it (the bid price) and the price at which they sell it (the asked price). In recent years the "bid-asked" spread on actively traded bills has been only two to four basis points, which is lower than for any other money market instrument.

Taxes   Unlike other money market instruments, the income earned on Treasury bills is exempt from all state and local income taxes. Given a state income tax rate (t), the relationship between, say, the CD rate (RCD) and the bill rate (RTB) that leaves an investor indifferent between the two, other considerations aside, is

$$RCD(1 - t) = RTB.$$

From this formula it can be seen that the advantage of the tax-exempt feature for a particular investor depends on (1) the investor's state and local tax rate and (2) the current level of interest rates. For a given before-tax yield differential between bill rates and CD rates, the higher the state and local income tax rate and the higher the level of interest rates, the more attractive bills become. The interest rate differential at which an investor subject to a marginal state income tax rate of 6 percent is indifferent between bills and CDs rises from 32 basis points when the Treasury bill rate is 5 percent to 64 basis points when the Treasury bill rate is 10 percent.

This characteristic of bills is relevant only for some investors. Other investors, such as state and local governments, are not subject to state income taxes. Still other investors, such as commercial banks in most states, pay a "franchise" or "excise" tax that in fact requires them to pay state taxes on interest income from Treasury bills.[3]

Minimum Denomination   A fourth investment characteristic of Treasury bills is their relatively low minimum denomination. Prior to 1970, the minimum denomination of bills was $1,000. In early 1970 the minimum denomination was raised from $1,000 to $10,000. The stated purposes of this change were to discourage noncompetitive bids by small investors, reduce the costs of processing many small subscriptions yielding only a small volume of funds, and discourage the exodus of funds from financial intermediaries and the mortgage market. Despite the increase in the minimum denomination of bills, investors continued to shift substantial amounts of funds out of deposit institutions into the bill market in

---

[3] Details on the taxation of Treasury bill interest income for different investors are provided in Cook and Lawler [1983].

periods of high interest rates such as 1973 and 1974. This activity was generally referred to as "disintermediation."

Even at $10,000 the minimum denomination of Treasury bills is far below the minimum denomination required to purchase other short-term securities, with the exception of some federally sponsored agency and municipal securities. Typically, it takes at least $100,000 to purchase money market instruments such as CDs or commercial paper.

INVESTORS

Because of their unique investment characteristics Treasury bills are held by a wide variety of investors. Comprehensive data on Treasury bill holdings are not available. Available information suggests that individuals, money market mutual funds, commercial banks, the Federal Reserve and foreigners are among the largest investors in bills.

Individuals   Because Treasury bills have a relatively low minimum denomination and can be purchased at Federal Reserve Banks and branches without any service charge, the direct investment by individuals in bills has been greater than in any other money market instrument. (Since the late 1970s individuals have been heavy indirect investors in all money market instruments through their investment in money market funds.) The percentage of bills awarded to noncompetitive bidders at the weekly Treasury bill auctions is a widely used barometer of individual investment activity in the bill market. Chart 1 shows that this percentage moves closely with the level of interest rates. In recent years the major reason for this relationship appears to be that individuals as a group benefit most from the exemption of Treasury bill interest income from state and local income taxes. For a given spread between Treasury bill and other money market rates this exemption makes bills more attractive—relative to other short-term investments— the higher the level of interest rates. Hence, investment in bills by individuals rises with the level of interest rates.

Money Market Funds   Money market funds held $20.4 billion of Treasury bills at year-end 1985, representing 9.8% of their total assets. Several money market funds buy only Treasury bills in order to appeal to the most risk-averse investors. The relatively small investment by money market funds in bills partly reflects the fact that the tax-exemption on bill interest income generally cannot be passed through to the money fund shareholder.

Commercial Banks   At the end of 1985 commercial banks held about $140 billion of U.S. Treasury securities. A very rough estimate is that about $40 billion of this was Treasury bills. Banks' holding of bills tends to vary inversely with the demand for business loans. When loan demand is slack, banks increase their holdings of Treasury securities. Conversely, when loan demand is increasing, banks reduce their holdings of Treasury securities in order to expand loans. Of course, banks finance increases in business loans not only through the sale of securities but also through the issuance of liabilities such as CDs. Further, as noted above, banks also use Treasury bills to satisfy various collateral requirements and to make repurchase agreements with businesses and state and local governments.

Federal Reserve System   The Federal Reserve System's holdings of Treasury bills at year-end 1985 was $85.4 billion, which represented about half its total holdings of Treasury securities. Treasury bills perform an important role in the implementation of monetary policy. The Federal Reserve System pursues its monetary policy objectives by altering the level of reserves available to depository institutions in order to influence short-term interest rates and the money supply. (See the Federal funds chapter for a discussion of Federal Reserve operating procedures.) The Federal Reserve changes the level of reserves primarily through the purchase and sale of Treasury bills, either outright in the bill market or on a temporary basis in the market for repurchase agreements (RPs). RPs are the purchase or sale of bills under an agreement to reverse the transaction one or more days later. RPs have a temporary effect on the supply of bank reserves and are typically used to offset temporary fluctuations in reserves arising from other sources, such as changes in Treasury deposits at the Federal Reserve Banks. On a day-to-day basis most Federal Reserve operations are RPs. The increase in the Fed's outright holdings of bills over long periods of time reflects permanent increases in the level of reserves and money.

Foreign and Other Investors   Data on total foreign holdings of Treasury bills are not available, but foreign official institutions held $53 billion of bills (including some nonmarketable certificates of indebtedness) at the end of 1985. Other investors in Treasury bills are nonbank financial institutions, nonfinancial corporations, and state and local governments. The share of bills held by state and local governments has fallen in recent years, reflecting the increased investment flexibility available to many of these governments.

YIELDS

Treasury bill yields are generally quoted on a discount basis using a 360-day year. Under this procedure the stated rate of return on a bill of a given maturity is calculated by dividing the discount by par and expressing this percentage at an annual rate, using a 360-day year. For example, in the weekly auction of July 14, 1986, discussed above, an average price of $98.539 per $100 of face amount for a three-month (91-day) bill produced an annual rate of return on a discount basis of

$$\frac{100 - 98.539}{100} \times \frac{360}{91} = 5.78\%.$$

To calculate the true investment yield of a Treasury bill for comparison with other yields, the discount must be divided by the price and a 365-day year used. In the above example the true yield is

$$\frac{100 - 98.539}{98.539} \times \frac{365}{91} = 5.95\%.$$

As this example illustrates, the yield calculated on a discount basis understates the true yield of a Treasury bill.[4] The difference between the true yield of a bill and the discount yield is greater the longer the maturity of the bill and the higher the level of interest rates. For example, at an interest rate level of 12 percent the difference between the true yield and the yield calculated on a discount basis is 55 basis points at the three-month maturity and 95 basis points at the six-month maturity.

Yield Spreads Most money market rates move together closely over time. Perhaps more than any other money market rate, however, the rate on Treasury bills has at times diverged substantially from other short-term rates. Chart 2 shows that the differential between the three-month prime CD rate and the three-month Treasury bill rate varies greatly over time. In attempting to understand the highly variable spread between bill rates and other money market rates, it is useful to focus on three factors: default risk, taxes, and disintermediation.

The most common explanation of the spread between Treasury bill and other money market rates focuses on default risk. According to this explanation, the spreads between other short-term rates and bill rates vary over time due to a cyclical risk premium pushing up the yields on private sector money market instruments relative to the yields on Treasury bills in periods of weak economic activity. Throughout the money market, spreads between yields of securities that differ in their degree of default risk typically rise in recessions and this effect has

---

[4] For a three- or six-month Treasury bill the formula to convert a discount yield (rd) to a true investment yield (r) is:

$$r = \frac{365 \times rd}{360 - (rd \times t)},$$

where t is days to maturity and the interest rates are expressed in decimal form.

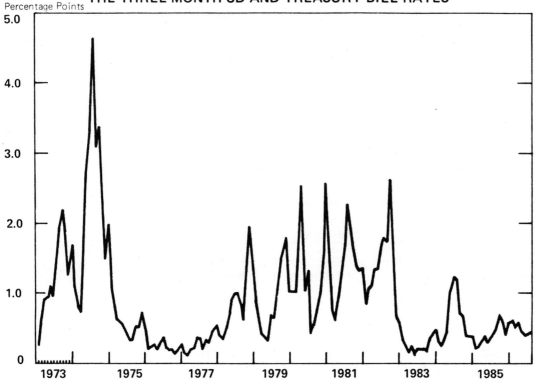

Chart 2
THE SPREAD BETWEEN
THE THREE-MONTH CD AND TREASURY BILL RATES

Percentage Points

Source: *Federal Reserve Bulletin.*

clearly been evident in the spread between Treasury bill and other money market rates. (See, for example, the spread between the prime and medium-grade commercial paper rates shown in the commercial paper chapter of this book.) Default risk can also cause the spread to rise in periods of concern over the fragility of the financial system. One major such episode occurred in August 1982 when the failure of a securities dealer along with heightened concern over the ability of some foreign countries to pay off loans to U.S. commercial banks increased investor worries over the soundness of the nation's financial system and resulted in a sharp increase of almost a full percentage point in the spread between CD and bill rates.

Another possible factor influencing the spread between the bill rate and other short-term rates is the exemption of Treasury bills from state and local income tax.

As noted above, the higher the level of interest rates the wider the spread between bill rates and other short-term rates that is necessary to leave an investor with a given state income tax rate indifferent between bills and other money market instruments. Consequently, as interest rates rise, this tax feature of bills induces some investors to increase their purchases of bills, thereby putting upward pressure on the spread between bill rates and other rates. Evidence in favor of this effect is that the spread typically rises in high interest rates periods and falls in low interest rate periods.

This is not to say that the tax-exempt feature of bills must cause the spread to rise with the level of interest rates. As noted above, many investors in the bill market are not subject to state and local income taxes. If, however, investors subject to state income tax rate (t) dominated the bill market, then the observed relationship between the CD rate (RCD) and the bill rate (RTB)—taking default risk into account—would be:

$$RCD(1 - t) = RTB + Default\ Risk\ Premium.$$

One study [Cook and Lawler, 1983] using data from 1979 through mid-1983, when the spread between the CD and Treasury bill rates was particularly volatile, found that the simple model represented by the equation above did a good job of explaining the spread in that period. This study estimated that the average value of (t) over that period was in the neighborhood of 8 percent, which is well within the range of state individual income tax rates on interest income.

A third factor that prior to the late 1970s may have affected the spread in periods of high interest rates such as 1969, 1973 and 1974 is disintermediation. In these periods the large differential between market interest rates and Regulation Q ceiling rates at the depository institutions induced many individuals to move their funds out of these institutions and into the bill market. The large purchases of Treasury bills by individuals in these periods may have driven bill rates down relative to the rates on other money market instruments.[5] Ceilings on savings type deposits at depository institutions were partially eliminated in 1978 with the introduction of $10,000 money market certificates and then totally eliminated in late 1982 with the introduction of money market deposit accounts (MMDAs).

Yield Curves   Money market yield curves show the relationship between maturity and yield on money market instruments. An interesting aspect of the Treasury bill yield curve is that it generally has shown greater upward slope than the yield

---

[5] This explanation is given in more detail in Cook [1981].

curves of private money market instruments such as CDs. Thus, the spread between the one-month CD and Treasury bill yields has usually exceeded the spread between the three-month CD and Treasury bill yields. Similarly, the three-month spread has usually exceeded the spread between the six-month CD and Treasury bill yields. The reasons underlying the differential behavior of the Treasury bill and CD yield curves are not entirely clear. According to one study [Rowe, Lawler and Cook, 1986] a key factor is the dominant role of the Treasury in the bill market.

SECONDARY MARKET[6]

The market for Treasury bills is the largest and most efficient for any money market instrument. At the heart of this market is a group of securities dealers known as primary dealers, who purchase a large portion of the Treasury bills sold at auction and make an active secondary market for these securities. Dealers earn the designation of primary dealer from the Federal Reserve after a period of observation of their customer base, business volume, participation in Treasury auctions, ability and commitment to make markets, and the financial strength of the firm. With this designation comes a number of advantages including market recognition and the possibility of daily contact with the Federal Reserve's trading desk since the Fed selects its trading partners for the conduct of monetary policy from the list of primary dealers. In mid-1986 there were 37 primary dealers. Of these, 14 were operated as departments of commercial banks and 23 were nonbank dealers. In addition to the primary dealers, there are a large number of bank and nonbank "secondary" dealers in Government securities. The number of these dealers is unknown, but estimates range from 300 to 500.

The primary dealers make markets by buying and selling securities for their own account. The marketplace is decentralized with most trading transacted over the telephone. As shown in the table, daily average trading in Treasury securities by the primary dealers in 1985 was $75.3 billion, $32.9 billion of which was in Treasury bills. About half of the trading in Treasury securities was with the dealers' customers, including depository institutions, insurance companies, pension funds, nonfinancial corporations, and state and local governments. Dealers also trade actively with each other, mostly through brokers who match buyers and sellers for a commission. Brokers display bid and asked prices via closed circuit television screens located in the trading rooms of the primary dealers, thereby providing them with rapid access to this information, yet maintaining anonymity in their trades.

---

[6] The chapter on repurchase agreements contains more detail on the secondary market for Treasury securities. Also, see McCurdy [1977-78] and General Accounting Office [1985].

TRANSACTIONS IN UNITED STATES GOVERNMENT SECURITIES BY DEALERS REPORTING TO THE FEDERAL RESERVE BANK OF NEW YORK

Year	By Maturity (in billions of dollars, daily averages)			By Trading Participant (as a percentage of total)		
	Due within one year	Due in one year or more	Total	Dealers	Brokers	All others
1981	14.8	10.0	24.7	6.6	47.5	45.9
1982	18.4	13.9	32.3	5.5	49.0	45.5
1983	22.4	19.7	42.1	5.4	49.9	44.7
1984	26.0	26.7	52.8	5.5	48.5	46.0
1985	32.9	42.4	75.3	4.4	48.1	47.5

Source: *Federal Reserve Bulletin.*

As noted above, an indication of the efficiency of the bill market is the narrow bid-asked spread on bills. The bid-asked spread varies over time, largely depending on the volatility of interest rates. The more volatile are interest rates, the greater the spread required by dealers in compensation for the risk of taking a position. Hence, bid-asked spreads tend to rise in periods of increased interest rate volatility. Prior to October 1979 the bid-asked spread on the most actively traded three-month bills was generally only two basis points—i.e., $50 per $1 million. On October 6, 1979 the Federal Reserve announced a change in operating procedures that resulted in much greater volatility in short-term interest rates. (See the chapter on Federal funds for a discussion of these procedures.) Subsequently, the bid-asked spread on Treasury bills rose to as high as eight to ten basis points. In 1982 the Fed reverted to a procedure similar to its pre-October 1979 procedure and since then the bid-asked spread has been in a range of two to four basis points.

References

Cook, Timothy Q. "Determinants of the Spread Between Treasury Bill and Private Sector Money Market Rates." *Journal of Economics and Business* 33 (Spring 1981), pp. 177-87.

——— and Thomas A. Lawler. "The Behavior of the Spread Between Treasury Bill Rates and Private Money Market Rates Since 1978." Federal Reserve Bank of Richmond, *Economic Review* 69 (November/December 1983), pp. 3-15.

General Accounting Office. *Survey of the Federal Reserve System's Supervision of the Treasury Securities Market.* Report prepared for the Subcommittee on Domestic Monetary Policy of the House Committee on Banking Finance and Urban Affairs. 99th Cong., 1st sess., May 1985.

McCurdy, Christopher J. "The Dealer Market for United States Government Securities." Federal Reserve Bank of New York, *Quarterly Review* 2 (Winter 1977-78), pp. 35-47.

Monhollon, Jimmie R. "Treasury Bills." In *Instruments of the Money Market*, 4th ed. Edited by Timothy Q. Cook. Richmond: Federal Reserve Bank of Richmond, 1977.

Nelson, Jane F. "Tax Anticipation Bills." In *Instruments of the Money Market*, 4th ed. Edited by Timothy Q. Cook. Richmond: Federal Reserve Bank of Richmond, 1977.

Rowe, Timothy D., Thomas A. Lawler, and Timothy Q. Cook. "Treasury Bill Versus Private Money Market Yield Curves." Federal Reserve Bank of Richmond, *Economic Review* 72 (July/August 1986), pp. 3-12.

Tucker, James F. "Buying Treasury Securities at Federal Reserve Banks." Federal Reserve Bank of Richmond, 1987.

Article Three

Richard R. Simonds

Modern Financial Theory

Developments in the past twenty-five years have application to public utility regulation, to investor portfolio selection, and to corporate capital budgeting.

The most significant academic developments in finance in the past twenty-five years have been portfolio theory, capital market theory, and efficient market theory. Portfolio theory is concerned with how a risk-averse investor should go about selecting an optimal portfolio of investment assets. Capital market theory extends portfolio theory and attempts to describe the way in which the equilibrium market price or expected return of an individual investment asset is related to the asset's risk of return. Efficient market theory deals with the relationship between information and security prices and the resulting implications for investors.

This article attempts to present the major theoretical concepts in these areas in as nontechnical a manner as possible. Several statistical terms are used along the way but only after the meaning of each is sufficiently developed. Second, empirical support for these theories is briefly summarized. Third, three applications of these theories are illustrated. Although the applications presented are by no means exhaustive, they indicate the scope of the impact of recent academic developments on financial analysis.

Portfolio theory

The one-period return on an individual invest-ment asset during a specified time is equal to the change in the market value of the asset plus any cash distributions received divided by the initial market value.[1] The return for the ith asset, $\tilde{R}_i$, is given by

$$\tilde{R}_i = \frac{\tilde{V}_{i1} - V_{i0} + \tilde{D}_{i1}}{V_{i0}}, \qquad (1)$$

where

$\tilde{V}_{i1} = i^{th}$ asset market value at the end of the period;

$V_{i0} = i^{th}$ asset market value at the beginning of the period; and

$\tilde{D}_{i1} = i^{th}$ asset cash distribution during the period.[2]

The return on a portfolio, $\tilde{R}_p$, is a weighted average of the returns on the individual assets in the portfolio. That is, for n assets,

$$\tilde{R}_p = A_1\tilde{R}_1 + A_2\tilde{R}_2 + \ldots + A_n\tilde{R}_n, \qquad (2)$$

where A_i equals the proportion of the initial investment committed to the ith asset, and the sum of the A_i's is one.

Expected return. Each return, $\tilde{R}_i$, is uncertain at the beginning of the period. A useful way to deal with this uncertainty is to assign subjective probabilities to possible return outcomes. Having done

Richard R. Simonds is a member of the faculty of the Graduate School of Business Administration at Michigan State University.

so, the expected return may be computed. The expected return is the weighted average of all possible returns where the weights are equal to the probabilities or relative chances of each level of return occurring. The probability of R_{ij}, where R_{ij} represents the jth level of return for the ith asset, is designated P_{ij}, and the sum of the probabilities, P_{i1}, P_{i2}, . . . , P_{im}, for m possible return levels must equal one. The expected value of $\tilde{R}_i$, $E(\tilde{R}_i)$, given the m possible outcomes shown in Exhibit 1, is

$$E(\tilde{R}_i) = \sum_{j=1}^{m} R_{ij}P_{ij}$$

$$= .1(.05) + .2(.06) + .4(.07)$$
$$+ .2(.08) + .1(.09)$$
$$= .07 \text{ or } 7\%. \tag{3}$$

EXHIBIT 1

SYMMETRIC PROBABILITY DISTRIBUTION OF RETURN
FOR THE ith ASSET IN PORTFOLIO p

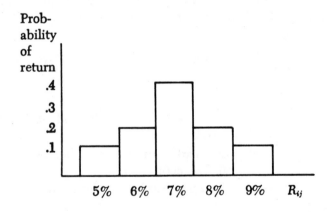

In accordance with expression (2), the expected value of the portfolio return, $E(\tilde{R}_p)$, is equal to a weighted average of the n individual assets' expected returns,

$$E(\tilde{R}_p) = A_1(\tilde{R}_1) + A_2E(\tilde{R}_2) + \cdots$$
$$+ A_nE(\tilde{R}_n),$$
$$= \sum_{i=1}^{n} A_iE(\tilde{R}_i). \tag{4}$$

Therefore, the contribution of each asset to the expected portfolio return is its own expected return.

Risk of return. The risk of the portfolio return might be stated in terms of a dispersion measure which takes into account both the likelihood of $\tilde{R}_p$ being less than $E(\tilde{R}_p)$ and the size of the downside deviations. However, if the distribution for $\tilde{R}_p$ is symmetric, a measure of dispersion based on both the upside and downside deviations from the expected return level may be used even though it is only the downside deviations which leave the investor less well off than if the outcome had been the expected value. Since security returns and hence portfolio returns appear to be approximately symmetric, it is this two-sided measure of dispersion that is generally used.[3] The variance of return is just such a two-sided measure and is defined as the weighted average of squared deviations from the expected return. The variance of the portfolio single-period return, designated $\sigma^2(\tilde{R}_p)$, is given by

$$\sigma^2(\tilde{R}_p) = \sum_{j=1}^{m} [R_{pj} - E(\tilde{R}_p)]^2 P_{pj}. \tag{5}$$

Correspondingly, for a single asset the variance is

$$\sigma^2(\tilde{R}_i) = \sum_{j=1}^{m} [R_{ij} - E(\tilde{R}_i)]^2 P_{ij}, \tag{6}$$

and for the security depicted in Exhibit 1

$$\sigma^2(\tilde{R}_i) = (-.02)^2 (.1) + (-.01)^2 (.2)$$
$$+ (0)^2 (.4) + (.01)^2 (.2) + (.02)^2 (.1)$$
$$= .00012.$$

The variance of the return on an n-asset portfolio with asset weights A_i, $i = 1, \ldots, n$, is also expressible as

$$\sigma^2(\tilde{R}_p) = \sum_{i=1}^{n} A_i \text{ covariance } (\tilde{R}_i, \tilde{R}_p), \tag{7}$$

where the covariance $(\tilde{R}_i, \tilde{R}_p)$ measures the magnitude of the comovement of the returns on the ith asset and the returns on the portfolio, p, of which asset i is a member.[4] The covariance $(\tilde{R}_i, \tilde{R}_p)$ is expressible as

covariance $(\tilde{R}_i, \tilde{R}_p) = $ (correlation between $\tilde{R}_i$ and $\tilde{R}_p$)
$$\times \sqrt{\sigma^2(\tilde{R}_i) \sigma^2(\tilde{R}_p)}. \tag{8}$$

Expression (7) is significant because it indicates that the contribution of the ith asset to the risk of portfolio p is the covariance $(\tilde{R}_i, \tilde{R}_p)$, and the relative risk of security i in portfolio p is

$$\frac{\text{covariance } (\tilde{R}_i, \tilde{R}_p)}{\sigma^2(\tilde{R}_p)} = \beta_{ip}. \quad (9)$$

Alternatively, if one considers a portfolio of n assets in which $A_i = 1/n$, $i = 1, \ldots, n$, then $\sigma^2(\tilde{R}_p)$ may be expressed as

$$\sigma^2(\tilde{R}_p) = \frac{\text{average security return variance}}{n}$$

$$+ \left(\frac{n-1}{n}\right)$$

$$\times \left(\begin{array}{c}\text{average covariance between}\\ \text{returns for pairs of securities}\\ \text{comprising portfolio } p\end{array}\right). (10)$$

Two of the most important results of portfolio theory are presented in expressions (7) and (10). Expression (7) shows that the risk contribution of asset i to portfolio p is measured by the covariance $(\tilde{R}_i, \tilde{R}_p)$ and *not* the variance of its own return, $\sigma^2(\tilde{R}_i)$. Expression (10) shows that as a portfolio is expanded to include large numbers of assets, the portfolio variance may not be reduced beyond the average covariance of returns for pairs of securities comprising the portfolio.[6] Consequently, simple diversification in risky assets can be only partially effective in reducing risk.

EXHIBIT 2

TWO-PARAMETER PORTFOLIO MODEL
WITH TWO ASSETS

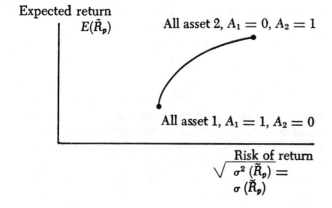

Two-Parameter Model. Employing expressions (4) and (7), one may calculate $E(\tilde{R}_p)$ and $\sigma^2(\tilde{R}_p)$ for an n-asset portfolio with given weights, A_i. Specifically, if $n = 2$, the possible combinations of expected return and risk for different levels of A_1 and A_2, with the restriction that $A_1 + A_2 = 1$, are indicated by the curved line in Exhibit 2.

Note that it is customary to represent the risk of the portfolio as the standard deviation of the return, which is the square-root of the return variance. The less the returns for assets 1 and 2 are positively correlated, the greater is the curvature of the line representing the locations attainable by combining the two assets.

Next assume that the investor has assigned subjective probability distributions to the returns for all risky investment assets. The set of possible portfolio risk-return pairs resulting from different combinations of these assets would appear as the shaded area shown in Exhibit 3. (Momentarily disregard the straight line shown.) Only the darkened border

EXHIBIT 3

TWO-PARAMETER PORTFOLIO
MODEL WITH n ASSETS

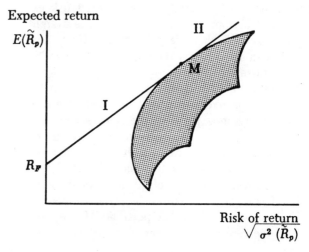

of this set will be of interest to an investor, however. This so-called efficient set offers the highest expected return for a given risk level.[7] Which point on the efficient set of risky assets is best depends on the investor's willingness to accept additional risk in order to increase the level of expected portfolio returns.

Capital market theory

Equilibrium Models. Capital market theory seeks to explain the relationship between the expected equilibrium returns on investment assets and their risk of return. Although several slightly different capital market equilibrium models are derivable from two-parameter portfolio theory, depending on the assumptions imposed, only the best-known model, the Sharpe-Lintner Capital Asset Pricing Model, is discussed here.[8]

If a risk-free asset is available with a return R_F, where R_F is a certain rate at which investors may borrow or lend, the new efficient set becomes the straight line emanating from R_F tangent to the original efficient set of risky assets at point M. Anywhere along the straight line is attainable given the proper allocation of funds to the portfolio M and the risk-free asset. If the investor desires to be in region I, funds are invested in the riskless asset, whereas in region II funds are borrowed at the riskless rate and invested in the portfolio M. The combination of riskless asset and portfolio M selected depends on the investor's level of desired risk exposure. Furthermore, all locations along the straight line offer returns that are perfectly positively correlated with the returns on portfolio M since R_F is a certain rate of return.

If investors' expectations regarding uncertain future returns for investment assets are homogeneous, that is, all investors perceive the same set of risk-return pairs, all investors will choose to hold the portfolio M in combination with the riskless asset.[9] Consequently, M is the market portfolio itself, which is the portfolio of all investment assets.

By referring back to expression (7) and replacing portfolio p with the market portfolio M the variance of the return on the market portfolio is seen to be

$$\sigma^2(\tilde{R}_m) = \sum_{i=1}^{n} A_i \text{ covariance } (\tilde{R}_i, \tilde{R}_m). \quad (11)$$

The relative risk of the ith asset in the market portfolio, which is referred to as the ith asset's beta co-

efficient, is, from expression (9), seen to be equal to

$$\beta_{im} = \frac{\text{covariance } (\tilde{R}_i, \tilde{R}_m)}{\sigma^2(\tilde{R}_m)}. \quad (12)$$

Next consider a fractional investment of A_1 in the market portfolio and $(1 - A_1)$ in the riskless asset; then the portfolio return, $\tilde{R}_p$, is

$$\tilde{R}_p = A_1 \tilde{R}_m + (1 - A_1)\tilde{R}_F, \quad (13)$$

and the expected portfolio return is

$$E(\tilde{R}_p) = A_1 E(\tilde{R}_m) + (1 - A_1)R_F. \quad (14)$$

Beta for the portfolio is

$$\beta_{pm} = \frac{\text{covariance } (\tilde{R}_p, \tilde{R}_m)}{\sigma^2(\tilde{R}_m)}, \quad (15)$$

which, using equation (13), may be expressed as

$$\beta_{pm} = \frac{\text{covariance } (A_1 \tilde{R}_m + (1 - A_1)R_F, \tilde{R}_m)}{\sigma^2(\tilde{R}_m)}$$

or

$$= \frac{A_1 \text{ covariance } (\tilde{R}_m, \tilde{R}_m) + (1 - A_1) \text{ covariance } (R_F, \tilde{R}_m)}{\sigma^2(\tilde{R}_m)}. \quad (16)$$

Since R_F is a certain rate of return, then expression (16) for β_{pm} reduces to

$$\beta_{pm} = \frac{A_1 \sigma^2(\tilde{R}_m) + (1 - A_1)(0)}{\sigma^2(\tilde{R}_m)} = A_1. \quad (17)$$

Using this result for β_{pm} in expression (14) we arrive at

$$E(\tilde{R}_p) = \beta_{pm} E(\tilde{R}_m) + (1 - \beta_{pm})R_F. \quad (18)$$

Equation (18) is the Capital Asset Pricing Model (CAPM) developed simultaneously by William F. Sharpe and John Lintner. Although it was developed here for portfolios on the efficient set, it can be shown to hold for *each* risky asset in the market portfolio.[10] For each risky asset the relationship between expected return and risk is

$$E(\tilde{R}_i) = R_F(1 - \beta_{im}) + \beta_{im}E(\tilde{R}_m),$$

or

$$E(\tilde{R}_i) = R_F + [E(\tilde{R}_m) - R_F]\beta_{im}. \quad (19)$$

Note that it is the relative risk contribution, β_{im}, of the security to the market portfolio risk that establishes the expected return on the asset and not the total variability of asset return, $\sigma^2(\tilde{R}_i)$. This perspective of risk has dramatic consequences, as will be seen when applications of the CAPM are discussed below.

Beta Coefficients. It is common practice to use

past realized data for security and market returns to estimate beta coefficients for individual securities or portfolios.[11] Employing the market-model regression equation

$$\tilde{R}_i = a_i + b_i\tilde{R}_m + \tilde{e}_i, \qquad (20)$$

estimates are obtained for b_i using standard statistical techniques. Exhibit 4 shows a regression line fitted to monthly observations on $\tilde{R}_i$ and $\tilde{R}_m$.

EXHIBIT 4

MARKET-MODEL REGRESSION EQUATION

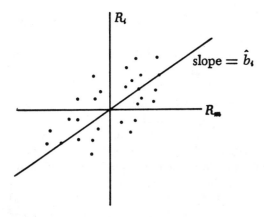

When the error term $\tilde{e}_i$ is assumed independent of $\tilde{R}_m$, the b_i term is equal to covariance $(\tilde{R}_i\tilde{R}_m)/\sigma^2(\tilde{R}_m)$, which is β_{im}. Therefore the estimates of b_i, denoted $\hat{b}_i$, are used as estimates of β_{im}.[12] Equation (20) also provides another description of beta. Beta reflects the sensitivity of the ith asset's returns to the returns on the market as a whole. Beta coefficients over one are deemed more risky than the market, and beta coefficients under one less risky than the market, since the market portfolio itself must have a beta coefficient of one.

If one were to consider equation (20) written separately for many individual securities it becomes clear that the return on a portfolio of n equally weighted securities may be expressed as

$$\tilde{R}_p = \frac{1}{n}\sum_{i=1}^{n} a_i + \frac{1}{n}\sum_{i=1}^{n} b_i(\tilde{R}_m) + \frac{1}{n}\sum_{i=1}^{n} \tilde{e}_i. \quad (21)$$

Alternatively, equation (21) may be expressed as

$$\tilde{R}_p = \bar{a}_i + \bar{b}_i(\tilde{R}_m) + \frac{1}{n}\sum_{i=1}^{n} \tilde{e}_i, \qquad (22)$$

or using notation to reflect that R_p is the return on a portfolio,

$$\tilde{R}_p = a_p + b_p(\tilde{R}_m) + \tilde{e}_p, \qquad (23)$$

where $\bar{a}_i = a_p$ and $\bar{b}_i = b_p$ are averages for the n securities. If the $\tilde{e}_i$ terms are independent of each other, then

$$\sigma^2(\tilde{R}_p) = (b_p)^2\sigma^2(\tilde{R}_m)$$
$$+ \frac{1}{n}(\text{average variance of the } \tilde{e}_i\text{'s}). \qquad (24)$$

Consequently, as n gets very large the risk of the portfolio can be reduced to that resulting from the comovement of the portfolio returns with the market returns. Variations independent of general market returns can be diversified away, but risk cannot be completely eliminated through diversification. This is the same conclusion we arrive at in expression (10). The standard deviation of the $\tilde{e}_p$ term has come to be called the unsystematic risk and the standard deviation of the $b_p\tilde{R}_m$ term the systematic risk. Diversification can effectively eliminate the unsystematic risk but has no such effect on the systematic risk.

Empirical Evidence. The Sharpe-Lintner CAPM was developed based on the normative idea that risk-averse investors should make portfolio choices based on the expected level and standard deviation of portfolio returns, assumed homogeneous expectations, and on the assumed presence of a risk-free rate for borrowing and lending.[13] Therefore, the model is referred to as a two-parameter market equilibrium model. Since expression (19) is stated in terms of expected returns which are unobservable, it may not be tested directly. Various researchers have, however, conducted indirect tests by using data on realized returns for New York Stock Exchange securities. Most notable of these tests are the studies by Eugene Fama and James MacBeth and by Fischer Black, Michael Jensen, and Myron Scholes.[14] Their empirical evidence suggests that the relationship between expected security returns and betas, β_{im}'s, is linear and that beta is the only required factor to explain the differences in levels of expected returns among securities. These findings are consistent with the Sharpe-Lintner CAPM.[15]

Furthermore, these findings support the proposition that securities are priced consistent with a two-parameter portfolio model used to describe how investors should select investment portfolios.

Efficient capital market theory

In an efficient capital market, individual security prices fully reflect all available information. Prices adjust completely and instantaneously to new information. Current security prices represent "correct" or unbiased assessments of all information available at the moment.

Academic researchers have attempted to test the extent to which security markets appear to behave as efficient markets.[16] Three classes of testable propositions derivable from the efficient market theory have been examined.[17] First, do current security prices fully reflect all information available in the sequences of past security prices and return data? This proposition is often referred to as the random walk hypothesis, which implies that successive security returns are not statistically associated. To examine this proposition, researchers have tested complicated buying and selling rules based on securities' past price performances. Such rules have not generated returns sufficiently greater than those available through buy-and-hold strategies to warrant investors behaving in a manner not consistent with the notion that this first efficient market proposition is correct.

"Portfolio theory and capital market theory may be used to estimate both the risk of the equity and the level of expected equity return."

A second testable proposition is that security prices adjust fully and instantaneously to *new* publicly available information. The empirical research regarding this proposition is preponderantly supportive. Studies conducted concerning earnings announcements, announced changes in accounting practices, mergers, stock splits, newly filed SEC documents, and so forth, have all supported this second proposition. It should be kept in mind, however, that even though the evidence reported would not lead one to reject this second proposition, any real market is surely not completely consistent with it either. The important point is that the evidence suggests that individual investors are best off conducting their affairs as if the proposition were correct. Finally, if this second proposition concerning publicly available information is correct, it is only because individual investors are trying to identify securities whose current prices do not reflect their intrinsic values and are making investment decisions based on these assessments. This activity is the driving force behind market efficiency. By so behaving, investors are causing the market to behave in accordance with this second proposition.

A third testable proposition is that no sector can, through superior analysis of publicly available information or through access to nonpublicly available information, realize superior investment performance. Research by Michael Jensen in which he examined mutual fund performance strongly suggests that once returns are adjusted for risk these managers have been unable to outperform other investors.[18] On the other hand, evidence from other studies of stock trading by insiders (managers and directors) and New York Stock Exchange specialists suggests that these individuals are privy to information not reflected in current stock prices which may be used to achieve superior returns.[19] This last bit of evidence against the idea of complete market efficiency does not appear to affect the general conclusion that if investors only have access to publicly available information they are wise to act as if the market were efficient.

Applications

Almost every facet of financial analysis has been affected by the theories described above. This pervasiveness is illustrated here by examining the impact of modern financial theory on public utility regulation, investor portfolio selection, and corporate capital budgeting. Although this examination must necessarily be brief, an effort has been made to point out several practical problems encountered when trying to apply these theories. This effort is important lest the reader get the false impression that modern financial theory has reduced many areas of financial analysis to mechanical formula manipulation.

Public Utility Regulation. Public utility rate of return regulation is based on the legal principle that "the return to the equity owner should be commensurate with returns on investments in other enterprises having corresponding risk."[20] One concept of commensurate return is the market rate of return which investors expect when they purchase other equity shares of comparable risk. If estimates of the risk and associated expected rate of return alluded to in the legal principle above can be obtained for a utility's stock, these estimates may be used along with debt costs to determine a "fair" company rate of return on assets. This company rate of return may be applied to a rate base such as the book value of capital investment to determine utility service rates.

Portfolio theory and capital market theory may be used to estimate both the risk of the equity and the level of expected equity return. As seen in expression (12), for a well-diversified investor the relevant risk measure of a security is its beta coefficient. Expression (19) specifies the level of expected return for a security with known beta, and it also shows all securities with the same beta have the same expected return. Modern financial theory offers a conceptually sound approach to the implementation of the legal principle of "fair" return in regulatory cases and in fact has been used for this purpose.

Testimony has been offered in regulatory cases such as those involving Communications Satellite Corporation, in which experts were requested to prepare an analysis of Comsat's risk in a portfolio context and to estimate Comsat's expected return on equity capital.[21] Two major problems arise in such an analysis. First, a firm's true equity beta coefficient can only be estimated (see expression [20] for the standard statistical approach), and therefore a firm's inherent risk level may not be known exactly. Furthermore, since the "real" or inherent beta coefficient is determined by a firm's operating and financial characteristics, only if these remain constant over time will the theoretical beta remain constant. Consequently, errors may arise

from two sources in predicting the future riskiness of a utility's equity shares.

Second, a major problem arises in using expression (19) to estimate the expected return on the utility's equity since values for the expected market return, $E(\tilde{R}_m)$, and risk-free rate, R_F, must be specified. These can only be specified subjectively, which, of course, means that $E(\tilde{R}_j)$, the expected equity return, is a subjective estimate. One meaningful way to proceed, however, is not to generate one estimate but to explore the range of estimates that result when different combinations of $E(\tilde{R}_m)$ and R_F are inserted. Given the limitations cited here it would not appear sensible to consider the CAPM alone a sufficient basis for regulatory decisions but rather one approach to determining the utility's required equity return which should be considered in regulatory proceedings.

Index Funds. An index fund is an investment fund constructed so that its rate of return behavior is approximately the same as that of a major index, such as the Standard & Poor's 500. Therefore, except for transaction costs and compositional differences, these funds offer the same return as the indices they attempt to imitate. The motivation for such funds arises from efficient market theory and portfolio theory.[22]

"It follows that product diversification by a firm for the sole purpose of reducing the variability of the firm's return is not beneficial to investors since they can achieve the same or better diversification within their own investment portfolios."

First, in an efficient market, investors are not able to use publicly available information to identify undervalued or overvalued securities; therefore, market prices reflect intrinsic values. Second, we have shown that the efficient set of portfolios (greatest expected return for a given risk level) is the locus of points on the straight line extending from the risk-free rate through and beyond the market portfolio. All investors should be somewhere on the straight line of efficient portfolios. By combining an investment in the market portfolio with an investment in the risk-free asset one may obtain efficient portfolios less risky than the market portfolio. An efficient portfolio riskier than the market portfolio is achieved by borrowing at the risk-free rate and investing in the market portfolio.

If the Standard & Poor's 500 index is a good surrogate for the market portfolio, investors may approximate the market portfolio by holding the index fund. If less risk is desired part of the investor's wealth can be diverted to short-term Treasury Bills, which serve as a substitute for a risk-free asset. Positions riskier than the market may also be achievable by buying on margin.[23] However, since actual margin loan rates are greater than the risk-free rate, the leveraging process is not as effective as that shown for region II in Exhibit 3. The slope of the efficient set is diminished for points past the market portfolio M.

Capital Budgeting. The two-parameter portfolio model has been applied in the capital budgeting area to develop a new market portfolio concept of project risk. This perspective suggests that the management of a publicly held firm should not be concerned with the impact a project has on the firm's total variability of return but rather with the project's relative risk. The relative risk is the incremental effect of the project on the variability of returns on a portfolio of investment assets held by a well-diversified investor holding the firm's stock. This is the same concept of risk we developed earlier for investment assets held in a portfolio and was represented by the asset's beta coefficient. It follows that product diversification by a firm for the sole purpose of reducing the variability of the firm's return is not beneficial to investors since they can achieve the same or better diversification within their own investment portfolio. The market portfolio concept of project risk shifts the emphasis away from measuring risk in the narrow context of the firm to measuring it in the context of the entire market of investment assets.

Associated with a project's relative risk measure is a required rate of return on the investment project. This rate of return is estimable using expression (19) for the Sharpe-Lintner CAPM. If the pre-

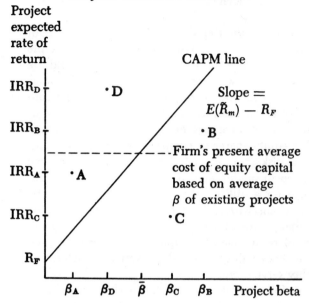

EXHIBIT 5

PROJECT SELECTION CRITERION

dicted internal rate of return (IRR) on the equity financed portion of a capital investment project does not exceed the project's required rate of return, the project is not acceptable. This required return is represented by the straight line of slope $E(\tilde{R}_m) - R_F$ in Exhibit 5 for a firm with a fixed capital structure.[24]

The project's expected rate of return is interpreted to be the expected return on the equity financed portion of the project. Or, stated differently, we now wish to consider the return of the project based on the generated cash flows adjusted for debt charges and the amount of the investment in the project reduced by the portion financed through debt. The project beta is considered to be the covariance between the return on the equity financed portion and the market return. Projects are positioned in Exhibit 5 by their estimated internal rates of return on the equity financed portion and their estimated betas. If a project lies above the CAPM line of slope $E(\tilde{R}_m) - R_F$ it is acceptable; otherwise it is not. Consequently, projects A and D are acceptable while C and B are not. Note that project A is acceptable even though its expected equity return is below the firm's average cost of equity capital. Apparently project A is sufficiently less risky than the firm's average project to warrant its acceptance.

Estimating betas for capital investment projects is especially difficult, much more so than for publicly traded securities. Several approaches are available, however. First, it may be possible to identify an existing firm, whose stock is publicly traded, which is involved in activities that approximate the project the firm is considering.[25] If such is the case, statistically estimated betas using historical stock return data for this firm may provide an adequate estimate of the project's beta.

Second, if the project is similar to one with which the firm has had prior experience, it may be possible to construct historical rates of return on the equity financed portion for different time periods and combine these with the corresponding market returns (actually a surrogate such as the Standard & Poor's 500) to estimate a beta coefficient using expression (20).[26] Third, the firm might resort to constructing a simulation model of the project under consideration to help in estimating its beta.

Summary

Modern financial theory and empirical evidence suggest that investors are well advised to make investment decisions assuming that security prices fully and instantaneously reflect all publicly available information. Furthermore, investors should hold efficient portfolios. Efficient portfolios offer the highest possible level of expected return for a given level of risk and represent combinations of a risk-free asset and the market portfolio.

When investors hold efficient portfolios, the risk of an individual asset is measured in terms of how much it contributes to the efficient portfolio's risk of return. This contribution is not adequately represented by the individual asset's total variability of return since a portion of this variation may be diversified away. The proper measure of the asset's risk contribution is its beta coefficient, which is based on the covariation between the asset's returns and returns on the market portfolio. The higher this covariation, the more the asset contributes to the risk of an efficient portfolio.

The Sharpe-Lintner capital asset pricing model (CAPM) expresses the equilibrium relationship between the expected return on an individual investment asset and its risk stated as a beta coefficient. The CAPM has been used extensively to analyze theoretical and practical problems in finance. Applications of the model in public utility regulation and corporate capital budgeting were illustrated here. A particularly striking conclusion is that the risk of a capital investment project and its associated required level of return should not be judged on the basis of the project's total variability returns. The proper basis of evaluation is to examine how the project's returns are estimated to covary with the returns on the market portfolio.

---

1. Although the theory is properly presented in terms of all investment assets, most applications have focused on financial assets.
2. The tilde, $\sim$, on $\tilde{R}_i$, $\tilde{V}_{i1}$, and $\tilde{D}_{i1}$ indicates that these quantities are uncertain at the beginning of the period and hence are random variables.
3. In fact, return distributions on individual securities and portfolios are approximately normal, with monthly returns better described by the normal distribution than daily returns. See Eugene Fama, *Foundations of Finance* (New York: Basic Books, 1976), chapter 1.
4. $$\sigma^2(\tilde{R}_p) = \sum_{i=1}^{n} \sum_{k=1}^{n} A_i A_k \text{ covariance } (\tilde{R}_i, \tilde{R}_k),$$

therefore,

$$\sigma^2(\tilde{R}_p) = \sum_{i=1}^{n} A_i [\sum_{k=1}^{n} \text{ covariance } (\tilde{R}_i, A_k \tilde{R}_k)],$$

and since

$$\tilde{R}_p = \sum_{k=1}^{n} A_k \tilde{R}_k, \text{ and } \sum_{i=1}^{n} A_i = 1,$$

$$\sigma^2(\tilde{R}_p) = \sum_{i=1}^{n} A_i \text{ covariance } (\tilde{R}_i, \tilde{R}_p).$$

5. See Fama, *Foundations of Finance*, p. 252. It should be emphasized that the notion that the effects of single-period risk of return tend to cancel out in the longer run is incorrect. The relationship between the future value of a security and the sequence of its n single-period returns is

Future Value $= [(1 + \tilde{R}_1)(1 + \tilde{R}_2)(1 + \tilde{R}_3) \ldots$
$(1 + \tilde{R}_n)]$ (Current Value),

where the subscript refers to the time period. For commonly encountered levels of security returns,

Future Value $\simeq [1 + \tilde{R}_1 + \tilde{R}_2 + \tilde{R}_3 + \ldots$
$+ \tilde{R}_n]$ (Current Value).

If the returns, $\tilde{R}_i$, are independent and of constant variance, σ^2, then the variance of the future security value after n periods is equal to $\sigma^2 \times$ (current value) $\times$ (n), or n times the variance of the security value one period hence. Single-period risk effects do not cancel out in the longer run.
6. Almost all security returns appear to be positively cor-

related with one another, implying positive covariances between asset returns. The average covariance of returns discussed here can therefore be presumed to be positive. See Fama, *Foundations of Finance*, pp. 251–54.

7. The use of the word *efficient* here is not to be confused with its usage in describing capital markets.

8. See Michael Jensen, "Capital Markets: Theory and Evidence," *Bell Journal of Economics and Management Science* 3 (Autumn 1972):357–98, for an excellent presentation of other models.

9. This result is frequently referred to as the separation theorem.

10. The best presentation of the complete derivation of the Sharpe-Lintner CAPM is found in Fama, *Foundations of Finance*, chapter 8.

11. A surrogate for the market return, such as the return on the Standard & Poor's 500 index, is usually employed in this process.

12. An alternative market model specification is stated in terms of excess returns, namely,

$$\tilde{R}_i - R_f = a_i + b_i(\tilde{R}_m - R_f) + \tilde{e}_i.$$

This form is also used by some investigators to obtain estimates of β_{im}.

13. It is also assumed that investors do not incur transaction costs and are indifferent to capital gains or dividends.

14. Eugene Fama and James MacBeth, "Risk, Return and Equilibrium: Empirical Tests," *Journal of Political Economy* 71 (May-June 1971): 607–36, and Fischer Black, Michael Jensen, and Myron Scholes, "The Capital Asset Pricing Model: Some Empirical Tests," in Michael Jensen, ed., *Studies in the Theory of Capital Markets* (New York: Praeger, 1972), pp. 79–121.

15. It must be stated that although these findings are consistent with the Sharpe-Lintner CAPM other evidence suggests that a slightly different version of a two-parameter capital market equilibrium model which does not presume the presence of a risk-free asset is superior. Black has presented such a model in which the expected return on a riskless portfolio ($\beta_{pm} = 0$) replaces the risk-free rate in equation (19). The linearity of the relationship between $E(R_i)$ and β_{im} and the singular importance of β_{im} is not altered in any way, however. See Fama, *Foundations of Finance*,

chapter 8, for an excellent discussion of the differences between the various two-parameter capital market equilibrium models which have been developed.

16. Most of this testing has been conducted using securities traded on the New York Stock Exchange. Caution should be exercised in generalizing these test results to all security markets.

17. Most of the studies of market efficiency are also implicitly testing a market equilibrium model. See Fama, *Foundations of Finance*, chapter 5, for a discussion of this point.

18. Michael Jensen, "The Performance of Mutual Funds in the Period 1945–1964," *Journal of Finance* 23 (May 1968: 389–416.

19. Jeffrey Jaffe, "Special Information and Insider Trading," *Journal of Business* 47 (July 1974): 410–28.

20. Supreme Court Decision in *Federal Power Commission et al. v. Hope Natural Gas Company*, 320 U.S. 591 (1949) at 603.

21. Federal Communications Commission, Communications Satellite Corporation. Prepared Testimony, S. J. Meyers. F.C.C. Docket 16070; 1972.

22. The appeal of index funds stems from efficient market and efficient portfolio considerations. However, if a majority of investors were to invest in a few index funds the market would no longer be efficient. This would destroy the underlying basis for index funds.

23. Most institutions are legally precluded from buying on margin, however.

24. Questions concerning the optimal capital structure are not considered here. See Mark Rubinstein, "Mean-Variance Synthesis," *Journal of Finance* 28 (March 1973): 167–81, and Robert Hamada, "The Effect of the Firm's Capital Structure on the Systematic Risk of Common Stocks," *Journal of Finance* 27 (May 1972): 435–52, for applications of the CAPM model to questions relating to capital structure.

25. One should in this process adjust the beta coefficient for differences in capital structure that may exist. See Rubinstein, "Mean-Variance Synthesis."

26. See James Van Horne, *Financial Management and Policy*, 4th ed. (Englewood Cliffs: Prentice-Hall, 1977), pp. 175–78.

Article Four

The Yield Curve
And Inflation Expectations

By C. Alan Garner

Long-term interest rates rose sharply relative to short-term rates in the first half of 1987. The resulting difference between yields on long-term bonds and short-term bills was the largest since 1984. This dramatic rise in long-term rates relative to short-term rates steepened the yield curve, which shows how security yields vary as the term to maturity lengthens. Did this steepening of the yield curve carry a message for business forecasters and decisionmakers?

Many economic and financial analysts viewed the steepening of the yield curve as a sign of rising inflation expectations. The curve steepened amid general concern about the inflation outlook. Oil prices had firmed after declining sharply in 1986, industrial commodity prices were increasing rapidly, and the depreciation of the dollar against other major currencies was raising import prices. Other analysts were skeptical, however, feeling that an increase in long-term inflation

expectations was unwarranted and that the steepening of the yield curve was reflecting other factors.

This article examines whether the shape of the yield curve can give useful information about inflation expectations. The first section explains how increasing inflation expectations could steepen the yield curve. But the second section shows that other factors could steepen the curve without increasing expected inflation. The third section examines recent evidence on inflation expectations and the shape of the yield curve. The yield curve is found to be a useful—but not infallible—indicator of inflation expectations.

Inflation expectations and the steepening yield curve

The view that the yield curve is an indicator of inflation expectations has a basis in economic theory. Inflation expectations influence the shape of the yield curve by affecting expected short-term interest rates. When investors revise their expectations about long-term future inflation rates upward, theory predicts the yield curve will

C. Alan Garner is a senior economist at the Federal Reserve Bank of Kansas City. Thomas J. Merfeld, an assistant economist at the bank, assisted in the preparation of the article.

CHART 1
Yield curve shapes

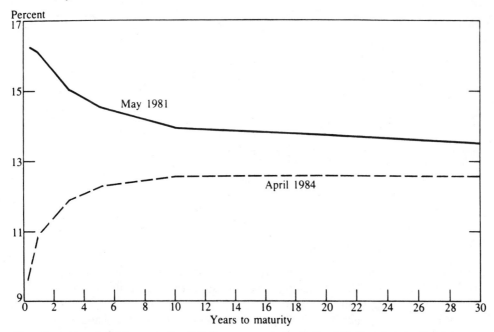

Note: Curves are plotted by connecting U.S. Treasury constant-maturity yields for selected maturities.

steepen. This section shows how a worsening of the long-term inflation outlook affects the shape of the yield curve.

The Treasury yield curve

The yield curve shows how security yields vary as the term to maturity of the securities increases. For yield comparisons to be meaningful, the securities must have similar default risk and tax considerations. Economists typically focus on the yield curve for U.S. Treasury securities because Treasury bills, notes, and bonds are free of default risk. Moreover, yield data are readily available since Treasury securities are traded in active secondary markets.[1]

The shape of the Treasury yield curve has varied substantially over time. Chart 1 illustrates some commonly observed shapes. Long-term interest rates have been greater than short-term rates, on average, over long periods of U.S. history. And short-term interest rates typically have fluctuated over a wider range than long-term rates. This fluctuation has produced both upward-sloping yield curves, as in May 1981, and downward-sloping yield curves, as in April 1984. The yield curve has often sloped upward near business cycle troughs and downward in boom periods.

---

[1] The Treasury yields in this article are constant-maturity yields estimated by the U.S. Treasury. Daily yield curves are constructed from quotations reported by five leading government securities dealers. The yield curve is fitted by eye and based only on the most actively traded issues. Constant-maturity yields are read from the curve at specified maturities. This method permits estimation of the yield for a ten-year maturity, for example, even if no outstanding security has exactly ten years remaining to maturity.

The expectations theory

The expectations theory provides an explanation for the shape of the yield curve. This theory asserts that financial markets determine security yields so that the return from holding a multiyear security until maturity equals the expected average return from holding a series of one-year securities over the same period.

A numerical example helps illustrate the expectations theory. Suppose investors have only two options for investing over a three-year period. One option is to purchase a security maturing in one year, to reinvest the proceeds from this security at the end of the year in another one-year security, and to follow the same procedure at the end of the second year. The other option is to purchase a security maturing in three years and hold it to maturity. Suppose that a one-year security currently yields 4 percent and that one-year securities are expected to yield 5 percent and 6 percent in the following two years. A three-year security currently must provide a 5 percent annual return to match the expected average return from holding three successive one-year securities.[2] Investors will adjust their portfolios until the expected return over the three-year horizon is equalized. Investors will buy the three-year security only if it yields more than the currently available one-year security because they expect the proceeds from the one-year security to be reinvested later at higher short-term rates. That is, the yield curve will slope upward to reflect investors' expectations of future interest rates.

The expectations theory implies that the shape of the yield curve depends on the expected pattern of short-term interest rates. As the numerical example shows, long-term interest rates exceed current short-term rates if short-term rates are expected to rise. The yield curve thus slopes upward. In contrast, long-term interest rates are less than current short-term rates if short-term interest rates are expected to fall. In this case, the yield curve slopes downward.

The Fisher effect

How does expected inflation affect the shape of the yield curve? The link between market interest rates and expected inflation is called the Fisher effect.[3] The Fisher effect implies that an increase in expected inflation could steepen the yield curve by raising the expected level of future short-term interest rates.

A market interest rate can be divided conceptually into a required real rate of return and the expected inflation rate over the relevant period. Market interest rates are nominal rates, measured in current dollars. But investors are concerned about their real, or inflation-adjusted, returns. As a result, investors demand nominal returns that are high enough to protect them against expected inflation and still yield a real return that makes lending attractive.[4] If the expected inflation rate

---

[2] This article uses arithmetic averages of interest rates to simplify the exposition. Geometric averages are appropriate, but the arithmetic averages provide close approximations in these examples. For further discussion of the expectations theory, see George G. Kaufman, *Money, the Financial System, and the Economy*, Third Edition, Houghton Mifflin, Boston, 1981.

[3] The Fisher effect is named for Irving Fisher, a famous American economist. Fisher's work is summarized in George G. Kaufman, *Money, the Financial System, and the Economy*. This discussion of the Fisher effect neglects the role of income taxes. Income taxes are incorporated into the Fisher effect in Michael R. Darby, "The Financial and Tax Effects of Monetary Policy on Interest Rates," *Economic Inquiry*, June 1975, pp. 266-276.

[4] Required real interest rates are determined by the interaction of such macroeconomic factors as saving rates, investment opportunities, and government policies. Economists represent these factors with general equilibrium models of the economy. For example, see Joe Peek and James A. Wilcox, "The Postwar Stability of the Fisher Effect," *Journal of Finance*, September 1983, pp. 1111-1124.

TABLE 1
Inflation expectations and the yield spread

	One-Year Rates			Three-Year Rate	Yield Spread
Example 1	First Year	Second Year	Third Year		
Required real rate	2	2	2	2	—
Expected inflation	2	3	4	3	—
Nominal rate	4	5	6	5	1
Example 2					
Required real rate	2	2	2	2	—
Expected inflation	2	4	6	4	—
Nominal rate	4	6	8	6	2

Note: Numbers are annual percentage rates. Three-year rates are averages of the one-year rates. The yield spread is the difference between the three-year nominal rate and the first year one-year nominal rate.

rises, the market interest rate must rise to preserve this required real return.

The Fisher effect is illustrated by the first example in Table 1. The required real rate of return is assumed to be 2 percent in all three periods. In the first year, the inflation rate is also expected to be 2 percent, implying that the nominal interest rate on a one-year security must be 4 percent to give investors the required real return. The expected inflation rate in the second year is 3 percent. The nominal interest rate on a one-year security over the second year must rise to 5 percent if the real return is to remain at the required 2 percent. Similarly, if the expected inflation rate is 4 percent in the third year, a one-year security must yield 6 percent to give investors a real return of 2 percent. Since the average of these one-year nominal rates is 5 percent, a three-year security must provide the same

5 percent return according to the expectations theory. This nominal return is the sum of the required real return of 2 percent and the expected average inflation rate of 3 percent over the three-year period.

The second example in Table 1 shows how a worsening of inflation expectations steepens the yield curve. Suppose investors raise their estimates of future inflation to 4 percent for the second year and 6 percent for the third year, perhaps because of policy changes or economic disturbances. The Fisher effect implies that short-term nominal interest rates also must increase—to 6 percent the second year and 8 percent the third year—to maintain the required 2 percent real rate of return. As a result, the yield on a three-year security must rise to 6 percent, the average expected return from holding three successive one-year securities.

CHART 2
The steepening yield curve

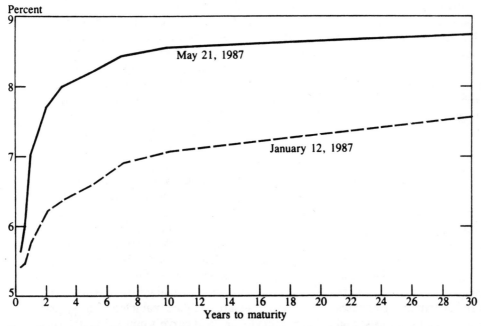

Note: Curves are plotted by connecting U.S. Treasury constant-maturity yields for selected maturities.

The steepening of the yield curve in response to higher expected inflation can be seen in the widening spread between the nominal yields on one-year and three-year securities. The yield spread in Table 1 is the nominal interest rate on the three-year security minus the nominal rate on the first one-year security. The yield spread in the first example is one percentage point. The spread increases to two percentage points in the second example because of the higher nominal rate on three-year securities. Thus, an increase in expected future inflation rates can steepen the yield curve, reflecting a larger spread between the yields on long-term and short-term securities.

Recent steepening of the yield curve

Such an increase in expected inflation rates could presumably have contributed to the sharp steepening of the yield curve for U.S. Treasury securities in the first half of 1987. Chart 2 shows yields on Treasury securities for two dates during this period. Yields on 30-year Treasury bonds rose from 7.4 percent in January to 8.8 percent in May. Three-month Treasury bill rates, in contrast, increased comparatively little, ranging from 5.4 percent to 5.7 percent over the period. The yield curve thus steepened dramatically as long-term rates rose relative to short-term rates.

Analysts disagreed about why the yield curve had steepened so sharply.[5] Some felt the steepen-

[5] See Bear Stearns and Company, *Analysts' Viewpoint*, May 5, 1987; William N. Griggs and Leonard J. Santow, *Griggs and Santow Report*, May 18, 1987; and Henry Kaufman, *Comments on Credit*, Salomon Brothers, May 15, 1987. The view that the bond market overreacted to the inflation threat is found in Maury N. Harris, *Update*, PaineWebber Inc., May 22, 1987.

ing reflected a sudden worsening of inflation expectations. These analysts noted that oil prices had firmed, that commodity prices had increased rapidly in both the spot and futures markets, and that the large depreciation of the dollar threatened to raise the U.S. inflation rate. Other analysts believed that the inflation outlook had not worsened substantially. These analysts felt the United States would not experience sharply higher inflation because of sluggish growth in domestic spending, low utilization rates for industrial capacity, and modest wage inflation.

Other factors affecting the yield curve

Those analysts who believed that the long-term inflation outlook had not worsened substantially attributed the steepening of the yield curve to factors other than rising long-term inflation expectations. For example, depreciation of the dollar may have increased the perceived risk of future exchange rate changes and discouraged purchases of long-term Treasury securities by Japanese and other foreign investors, forcing the yields on these securities higher. Such an explanation is not without foundation; a variety of macroeconomic and financial factors can cause the yield curve to steepen without changing long-term inflation expectations.

Macroeconomic factors

In addition to affecting expectations about long-term inflation rates, macroeconomic disturbances and policy changes can alter expectations about real interest rates and short-term inflation rates. Changes in investors' required real returns for future years can affect the shape of the yield curve even when inflation expectations are constant. And supply shocks, such as falling oil prices, can affect short-term inflation expectations without affecting the long-term inflation outlook appreciably. Thus, a steepening of the yield curve does

not necessarily imply higher long-term inflation expectations. Three possible economic scenarios help illustrate these points.

Saving and budget deficits. The yield curve can steepen even with unchanged inflation expectations if investors raise their required real interest rates for future years. The required real rate, which can be viewed as the price of credit, depends on the supply of and demand for funds. Funds are provided through private saving, growth of the domestic money supply, and capital inflows from abroad. Funds are demanded for private investment and government budget deficits. Lower private saving, declines in the real money supply, and reduced capital inflows decrease the supply of funds and raise the required real rate. A larger government deficit and stronger private investment raise the required real rate by increasing the demand for funds.

Many economists believe that a low saving rate and large government budget deficits have put upward pressure on future real interest rates, contributing to the yield curve's upward slope. This upward-sloping yield curve would steepen further if a growing government deficit or further declines in private saving caused investors to raise their required real rates for future years even higher.

Table 2 illustrates how an increase in the future real returns required by investors could steepen the yield curve. The first example has a constant required real rate of 2 percent and is identical to the first example in Table 1. The yield spread between one-year and three-year securities is one percentage point. In the second example, required real rates rise from 2 percent for the first year to 3 percent for the second year and 4 percent for the third year. Expected inflation is the same in both examples. Short-term nominal rates increase more in the second example because of the higher real rates in the second and third years. The average expected return from three successive investments in one-year securities is 6 per-

TABLE 2
Real interest rates and the yield spread

| | One-Year Rates | | | | |
Example 1	First Year	Second Year	Third Year	Three-Year Rate	Yield Spread
Required real rate	2	2	2	2	—
Expected inflation	2	3	4	3	—
Nominal rate	4	5	6	5	1
Example 2					
Required real rate	2	3	4	3	—
Expected inflation	2	3	4	3	—
Nominal rate	4	6	8	6	2

Note: Numbers are annual percentage rates. Three-year rates are averages of the one-year rates. The yield spread is the difference between the three-year nominal rate and the first year one-year nominal rate.

cent. According to the expectations theory, the three-year security must also yield 6 percent. As a result, the yield spread between one-year and three-year securities widens to two percentage points with no change in expected inflation.

Monetary policy. The yield curve also can steepen because of monetary policy changes. An easing of monetary policy when the economy is already producing near its capacity is one example. Such a policy would initially expand the real money supply, lowering required short-term real interest rates. With long-term real interest rates unchanged, the yield curve would steepen. Lower interest rates, in turn, would stimulate domestic spending, putting upward pressure on prices. Expected inflation would likely rise. As discussed previously, an increase in inflation expectations would cause long-term nominal interest rates to rise. Thus, both the initial decline in short-term

required real rates and the later rise in long-term nominal rates would steepen the yield curve.

Supply shocks. Supply shocks, such as changes in the price of oil or the exchange rate, can affect the shape of the yield curve by changing short-term inflation expectations much more than long-term inflation expectations. Changes in the price of oil, for example, have only a temporary effect on inflation and should not appreciably alter long-term inflation expectations. Over long time horizons, inflation depends primarily on such fundamental macroeconomic factors as the growth rates of the money supply and labor productivity. A change in the exchange rate also has temporary effects on inflation and should primarily affect short-term inflation expectations. Supply shocks can thus alter the shape of the yield curve by changing short-term inflation expectations much more than long-term inflation expectations, thus changing the relationship between yields on short-term and long-term securities.

One supply shock that might have affected the yield curve was the sharp drop in crude oil prices in late 1985 and early 1986. Falling oil prices reduced the U.S. inflation rate substantially in 1986. Short-term inflation expectations also declined, causing short-term nominal interest rates to fall because of the Fisher effect. According to the expectations theory, long-term interest rates decline less than short-term rates under such circumstances. As a result, the yield curve temporarily steepened.

Financial factors

The shape of the yield curve also depends on financial factors that are unrelated to inflation expectations. Two such factors are liquidity premiums and relative asset supplies.

Liquidity premiums. Long-term interest rates incorporate an additional component, the liquidity premium, that is not explained by the expectations theory. A liquidity premium reflects the greater risk of long-term securities. Because liquidity premiums fluctuate over time, changes in the shape of the yield curve cannot be explained solely by changes in expected short-term interest rates.[6]

The size of the liquidity premium reflects investors' perceptions of interest rate risk.[7] A sud-den increase in interest rates could quickly reduce the market value of investors' long-term securities portfolios. As a result, investors demand a positive term premium before they will give up the relative safety of short-term financial assets and invest in riskier long-term securities.

Liquidity premiums can fluctuate without accompanying changes in inflation expectations. The size of the premium reflects many factors affecting the degree of uncertainty about future interest rates. Uncertainty about future inflation rates is one such factor. Another is exchange rate uncertainty since foreign investors generally care about the value of their securities portfolios in terms of their own currencies. Other factors include changes in Federal Reserve operating procedures and deposit deregulation at commercial banks and thrift institutions. Changes in these factors might alter investors' perceptions of interest rate risk, causing liquidity premiums to vary without a change in expected inflation.

Relative asset supplies. Relative supplies of short-term and long-term securities also may affect the yield curve. Asset supplies do not affect the shape of the yield curve in the expectations theory. This theory assumes that many borrowers and lenders can easily shift from one maturity to another to obtain the most favorable yield. As a result, changing relative supplies of short-term and long-term securities would not affect the slope of the yield curve. A greater supply of long-term securities, for example, would not steepen the yield curve because investors can easily be attracted away from other maturities.

[6] Studies finding evidence of changing term premiums include David S. Jones and V. Vance Roley, "Rational Expectations and the Expectations Model of the Term Structure," *Journal of Monetary Economics*, September 1983, pp. 453-465; Edward J. Kane, "Nested Tests of Alternative Term-Structure Theories," *Review of Economics and Statistics*, February 1983, pp. 115-123; and N. Gregory Mankiw, "The Term Structure of Interest Rates Revisited," *Brookings Papers on Economic Activity*, 1986:1, pp. 61-96.

[7] Although theories of asset pricing imply that term premiums should reflect risk, the empirical evidence is mixed. Mankiw,

for example, finds little evidence that risk explains observed interest rate fluctuations. Engle, Lilien, and Robins conclude, however, that term premiums reflect the risk of unexpected interest rate changes. See Robert F. Engle, David M. Lilien, and Russell P. Robins, "Estimating Time Varying Risk Premia in the Term Structure: The ARCH-M Model," *Econometrica*, March 1987, pp. 391-407; and N. Gregory Mankiw, "The Term Structure of Interest Rates Revisited."

Some economists believe, however, that an increase in the supply of long-term securities raises long-term interest rates relative to short-term rates. This view is often called the market segmentation theory since the theory assumes securities markets are divided into distinct maturity segments with little movement by investors from one segment to another.[8] An increase in the supply of long-term securities would depress the price of these securities because investors cannot shift easily from one maturity to another. The yields of long-term securities would rise because security prices and yields move inversely. A changing maturity structure for government debt could thus steepen the Treasury yield curve even when inflation expectations are stable.

In sum, the spread between long-term and short-term interest rates is an imperfect indicator of long-run inflation expectations. Various macroeconomic factors can steepen the yield curve by altering required real interest rates and short-term inflation expectations as well as long-term inflation expectations. Financial factors can alter the shape of the yield curve through changing liquidity premiums and changing relative asset supplies. The yield curve reflects many forces, long-term inflation expectations being just one.

The yield curve and inflation expectations in the 1980s

Because of the factors described in the previous section, the yield curve is not a perfectly reliable indicator of inflation expectations. In practice, however, the yield curve might still be a good indicator of inflation expectations. Have changes in the shape of the yield curve been closely associated with changing inflation expectations in the 1980s?

Comparison with survey data

One way to see whether changes in the steepness of the yield curve have been a good indicator of changes in expected inflation is to compare the yield spread on securities with corresponding data on inflation expectations. No one measure of inflation expectations is generally accepted as being correct, and measures of long-term inflation expectations are especially scarce. However, surveys of inflation expectations have been used widely in economic research. Alternative measures of inflation expectations often are produced by statistical procedures involving arbitrary assumptions about the economic structure and the information available to forecasters. As a result, survey measures of expected inflation are probably as valid as any other measure currently available.

The yield spread and a corresponding expected inflation spread are presented in Chart 3 for the 1980s. The yield spread is the difference between the yields on ten-year Treasury securities and on one-year Treasury securities. The expected inflation spread is the difference between the expected inflation rate over a ten-year horizon and the expected inflation rate over a one-year horizon. The expected inflation spread is measured by the difference between ten-year inflation expectations from the Decision-Makers Poll and the actual inflation rate one year ahead.[9] The

[8] The market segmentation view is stated in J.M. Culbertson, "The Term Structure of Interest Rates," *Quarterly Journal of Economics,* November 1957, pp. 485-517. Empirical evidence supporting asset supply effects is found in Benjamin M. Friedman, "Financial Flow Variables and the Short-Run Determination of Long-Term Interest Rates," *Journal of Political Economy,* August 1977, pp. 661-689; and V. Vance Roley, "The Determinants of the Treasury Security Yield Curve," *Journal of Finance,* December 1981, pp. 1103-1126.

[9] Richard B. Hoey and Helen Hotchkiss, *Decision-Makers Poll,* Drexel Burnham Lambert Inc., June 4, 1987. This poll is the only available survey measure of long-term inflation expecta-

ten-year inflation forecast is compared with the actual one year ahead inflation rate because one-year survey expectations were not available over most of the 1980s. The one year ahead inflation rate is probably a good substitute for short-term inflation expectations because economic conditions and policies often change gradually. Therefore, forecasters have fairly accurate short-term expectations.[10] According to the expectations theory, the yield spread should increase when the difference between ten-year and one-year inflation expectations widens.

The yield spread and the expected inflation spread have had a positive association over the 1980s. Chart 3 shows that an increase in the expected inflation spread was often accompanied

by an increase in the yield spread, as in late 1981. However, the two variables moved in opposite directions in late 1984 and at other times. A positive relationship is confirmed by computing the correlation coefficient between the expected inflation spread and the yield spread. A correlation coefficient measures the degree of association between two variables. The correlation coefficient between the expected inflation spread and the yield spread is positive over the 1980s.[11] However, the correlation coefficient is smaller than one in value, which implies that the expected inflation spread and the yield spread did not always vary together. Therefore, the correlation coefficient is consistent with the view that the shape of the yield curve reflects expected inflation but is also affected by other factors.

Some of these other factors in the 1980s were changing required real interest rates and changing liquidity premiums. Real interest rates were affected by large fluctuations in real economic growth, a mushrooming federal deficit, and changes in Federal Reserve operating procedures.[12] Moreover, interest rates were excep-

tions. The survey probably provides a reasonably good measure of the inflation rate expected by Treasury market participants because the survey includes many financial officers and portfolio managers who regularly make financial decisions. However, the accuracy of the long-term inflation expectations cannot be determined at this point because the survey has not been conducted long enough to permit a comparison of actual and expected values. The survey has been conducted intermittently since September 1978.

Box-Jenkins forecasts of the CPI also were computed for comparison with the Decision-Makers survey. Box-Jenkins statistical models, which predict inflation solely by extrapolating past changes in prices, neglect such other potentially useful information as money growth rates and real economic growth. The Box-Jenkins model was reestimated before each Decision-Makers survey date so that the statistical model used only information that was available to survey respondents at the time. The ten-year Box-Jenkins forecast and the ten-year survey measure of expected inflation have a correlation coefficient of 0.83. This correlation coefficient is statistically different from zero at the 1 percent significance level.

[10] Using the actual one year ahead inflation rate as a substitute for the short-term inflation expectation can also be justified by the rational expectations hypothesis, which implies that the one-year inflation expectation differs from the actual one year ahead inflation rate by a random error with zero mean. This representation of expected inflation is employed in several empirical studies, including Benjamin M. Friedman and V. Vance Roley, "Investors' Portfolio Behavior Under Alternative Models of Long-Term Interest Rate Expectations: Unitary, Rational, or Autoregressive," *Econometrica*, November 1979, pp. 1475-1497.

[11] The Pearson correlation coefficient between the expected inflation spread and the yield spread is 0.52 over the period from October 1980 to June 1986. This correlation coefficient is statistically different from zero at the 1 percent significance level.

The results are qualitatively similar when Box-Jenkins inflation forecasts are employed. If one-year Box-Jenkins forecasts are substituted for the actual one year ahead inflation rate in computing the expected inflation spread, the correlation coefficient between the yield spread and the expected inflation spread is 0.47 over the period from October 1980 to May 1987. This correlation coefficient is statistically significant at the 1 percent significance level. If the expected inflation spread equals the ten-year Box-Jenkins inflation forecast minus the one-year Box-Jenkins forecast, the correlation coefficient is 0.67 and is also significant at the 1 percent level.

[12] Another important influence on the yield curve in the 1980s may have been the large reductions in personal and corporate tax rates. The Treasury yield curve is plotted with pre-tax nominal interest rates, but investors care about their after-tax real returns. If investors expect their tax rates to fall in the years ahead, lower long-term nominal interest rates will provide the same after-tax

CHART 3

The yield spread and the expected inflation spread

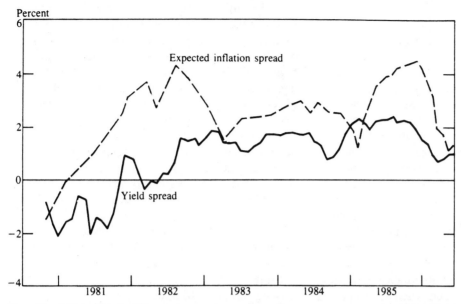

Note: The yield spread is the difference between the ten-year and one-year constant-maturity yields on U.S. Treasury securities. The expected inflation spread is the ten-year inflation expectation from the Decision-Makers Poll minus the actual one year ahead inflation rate.

tionally volatile in the 1980-82 period. High interest rate volatility and other economic uncertainties may have caused increasing risk premiums for long-term securities in this period.

Evidence from the Decision-Makers Poll shows that the steepening of the Treasury yield curve in the first half of this year did not signal an increase in long-term inflation expectations. The dramatic steepening of the Treasury yield curve in April and May was accompanied by slightly lower long-term inflation expectations; the ten-year inflation expectation in the Decision-Makers Poll actually declined from 5.5 percent in March to 5.3 percent in May. Short-term inflation expec-

tations did increase, however, with the 12-month inflation forecast from the Decision-Makers Poll rising from 4.0 percent in March to 4.7 percent in May.[13] The decrease in ten-year inflation expectations in tandem with the increase in 12-month inflation expectations should have flattened the yield curve under the expectations theory, contrary to what actually occurred. Comparisons between the yield spread and survey data show,

[13] Both 12-month and ten-year inflation expectations declined slightly from May to June. The 12-month inflation expectation declined to 4.57 percent in the June Decision-Makers Poll, and the ten-year inflation expectation declined to 5.25 percent. A widely quoted survey of business economists shows that forecasts of consumer price inflation in 1987 worsened from 4.1 percent in the March survey to 4.7 percent in the August survey. See Robert J. Eggert, *Blue Chip Economic Indicators*, March 10 and August 10, 1987.

average real return. Expected tax rate changes could thus affect the steepness of the yield curve. This effect has received little attention in tests of the expectations theory and deserves further study.

therefore, that a steepening or flattening of the yield curve is not always due to changing inflation expectations.

Other indicators of inflation expectations

Despite the imperfect correlation between the yield spread and the expected inflation spread, the yield curve may still play a useful role as an indicator of inflation expectations if it is used in combination with other expectations indicators and fundamental economic analysis. Business forecasters and decisionmakers usually can have more confidence in the signals provided by a steepening or flattening yield curve if other indicators of inflation expectations give a similar message. Several market prices besides security yields may be useful in judging inflation expectations. The exchange rate of the dollar with other major currencies is one possible indicator since the dollar is likely to depreciate when market participants expect the U.S. inflation rate to rise relative to foreign inflation rates. Sensitive commodity prices also may rise when the general inflation rate is expected to worsen. Businesses may increase their stocks of storable commodities when higher inflation and stronger economic activity are expected. However, greater demand for commodities could push commodity prices higher before inflation is observed in more sluggish wages and prices. Rapid gains in the prices of gold and other precious metals are often viewed as a sign of increasing inflation expectations since these metals have served traditionally as inflation hedges.[14]

---

[14] For more information about the relationship between auction-market prices and inflation expectations, see Brian R. Horrigan, "Monetary Indicators, Commodity Prices, and Inflation," Federal Reserve Bank of Philadelphia, Working Paper No. 86-7, April 1986; and Carl E. Walsh, "Interest Rates and Exchange Rates," *Weekly Letter*, Federal Reserve Bank of San Francisco, June 5, 1987.

Analysts, therefore, should monitor several market prices and yields that typically indicate changing inflation expectations. Focusing exclusively on the yield curve or any other expectations indicator could be misleading since many prices of financial instruments and commodities are highly volatile. This volatility reflects factors that are specific to the particular market as well as general economic news and policies. However, market-specific disturbances are unlikely to affect an entire set of indicators. The yield spread should be used, therefore, along with other information variables that quickly reflect market reactions to economic disturbances and policy changes.

Security yields and other expectations indicators should supplement rather than replace fundamental economic analysis, however. Analyzing fundamental determinants helps forecasters confirm or revise their previous views about the economic situation and gives better estimates of the factors driving inflation. Market prices and yields are useful primarily because they reflect new information about fundamental economic trends and policies. However, these indicators are affected by market-specific disturbances as well as a variety of macroeconomic influences. Also, at times, market expectations may simply be wrong. During the first half of 1987, for example, market prices and yields correctly reflected an increase in short-term inflation expectations, but a steepening yield curve erroneously indicated a rise in long-term inflation expectations.

Conclusion

The steepening of the Treasury yield curve during the first half of 1987 has been viewed as an indicator of rising inflation expectations. According to the expectations theory, expectations of higher inflation in the years ahead could steepen the yield curve since higher expected inflation should raise expected short-term nominal interest rates. However, a steepening of the yield curve also could reflect an increase in future required real interest rates or bigger liquidity premiums on long-term securities. Real interest rates have been affected in the 1980s by such macroeconomic factors as wide swings in economic activity and a series of large federal budget deficits. Liquidity premiums have probably been influenced by interest rate volatility and uncertainty about the future foreign exchange value of the dollar.

To the extent that survey data give a reliable measure of long-term inflation expectations, evidence from the 1980s shows that the yield spread and inflation expectations have not always varied together. The steepening of the Treasury yield curve in the first half of 1987 is a case in point. The ten-year inflation expectation from the Decision-Makers Poll actually decreased at the same time that long-term interest rates were rising. Although the cause of the sharp increase in long-term interest rates remains puzzling, an alternative explanation may be that Japanese and other foreign investors required higher long-term interest rates to compensate for a perceived rise in exchange rate risk. Twelve-month inflation expectations from the same survey did increase, however, which was consistent with rising commodity prices and such fundamental determinants as the falling dollar and firming oil prices. Business forecasters and decisionmakers, therefore, should examine a variety of expectations indicators and fundamental economic determinants rather than giving excessive weight to the shape of the yield curve.

Article Five

Both gap analysis and duration analysis have their limitations in measuring rate risk; however, each provides information that the other does not.

Measuring Interest Rate Risk: What Do We Really Know?

JAMES E. MCNULTY

With bankers exhorted from all sides to reduce interest rate risk, increasing attention is directed to how that risk can best be measured. Without the ability to measure interest rate risk, proper management is impossible.

Gap analysis, the method most commonly used for measuring interest rate risk, has come under significant criticism in the past few years from advocates of an alternative approach, duration analysis. George Kaufman, for example, states that "duration analysis has substantial advantages over alternative techniques for measuring interest rate risk," such as asset-liability gap analysis.[1] Both Kaufman and Alden Toevs argue that the standard asset-liability gap analysis (henceforth referred to as gap analysis) provides an arbitrary set of numbers that fails to measure accurately a financial institution's interest rate risk. This, says Toevs, may provide false signals that net interest income is protected from rate changes. Additional shortcomings, according to Toevs, include the "inability to generate a simple and reliable index of interest rate risk exposure" and "unnecessary restrictions imposed on the bank's choice of assets and liabilities," which may fail to meet the needs of bank customers for certain maturities of deposits and loans.[2]

The purpose of this article is to evaluate gap analysis in light of four major criticisms that have been advanced in the literature. Part of the process will be to compare the two approaches to interest rate risk measurement—gap analysis and duration analysis. How well do these two approaches measure interest rate risk? What are the primary strengths and weaknesses of each? What are the assumptions and how valid are they? What is the relationship between the two approaches? Are they really in conflict with one another, or are they complementary?

Gap Analysis

Most readers are familiar with gap analysis, so only a brief summary is presented here.[3] Table 1 illustrates the technique: A hypothetical financial institution's balance sheet has been segmented by maturity. The individual assets and liabilities of this institution are placed in separate columns or

James E. McNulty is vice president-economist at the Federal Home Loan Bank of Atlanta and adjunct professor of finance at Emory University, Atlanta.

Table 1. Gap Analysis — An Example
(in $ Millions)

| | Maturity or Time to Re-pricing | | | |
	1 Year	2 Years	3 Years	Total
Assets	$ 50	$ 50	$200	$300
Liabilities and Net Worth	100	100	100	300
Gap	− 50	− 50	100	0
Cumulative Gap	− 50	−100	0	0

Assumptions

1. Interest rates increase by 500 basis points at all maturity levels at the beginning of year one.

2. All assets and liabilities are re-priced at the beginning of the year in which they mature.

3. Changes in spreads, rate volatility, prepayments, and all other factors affecting income are ignored.

4. The fact that no explicit interest is paid on net worth is ignored to simplify the arithmetic. Thus, net worth is treated the same as a liability item.

Effect of a 500-Basis-Point Increase in Rates

Effect in Year One
  Income Change:
    Assets x Rate Change
    50 x .05   =   + 2.50
  Expense Change:
    Liabilities x Rate Change
    100 x .05   =   + 5.00

  Net Income: −2.50
  Net Income Calculated from Cumulative Gap Formula:
    CUMGAP x CHRATES
    −50 x .05   =   −2.50

Effect in Year Two
  Income Change:
    Assets* x Rate Change
    100 x .05   =   + 5.00
  Expense Change:
    Liabilities* x Rate Change
    200 x .05   =   + 10.00

  Net Income: −5.00
  Net Income Calculated from Cumulative Gap Formula:
    CUMGAP x CHRATES
    −100 x .05   =   −5.00

Effect in Year Three
  No change — Net income returns to the level of the base year since all assets and liabilities have been repriced.

* Includes all assets or liabilities that are re-priced either in or before the given year.

"maturity buckets" designating when they mature or when they can be re-priced. This institution has $300 million in total assets, of which $200 million will mature at the beginning of year three. For ease of exposition, assume that the longest maturity of any asset or liability is three years. Gap analysis can be extended to as many maturity buckets as the user wants. The choice depends entirely on the personal preferences of the user and the balance sheet of the financial institution.

One measure of interest rate risk used in this approach is the gap—the difference between assets and liabilities in a certain maturity category. If liabilities exceed assets, as they do in the one- and two-year maturity categories, the gap is negative. The cumulative gap can be derived by simply summing up the individual gaps. For the first maturity bucket, the individual and cumulative gaps are the same, −$50 million. For the second maturity bucket, the cumulative gap is −$100 million, reflecting a −$50 million gap in each of the first two buckets.

The cumulative gap is a direct measure of interest rate sensitivity. This can be seen from the following formula:

$$CHINCOME(t) = CUMGAP(t) \times CHRATES$$

Where:

CHINCOME(t) = the change in a financial institution's net income in period t which results from a given change in interest rates. (The change is measured from some base year, rather than as a year-to-year change.)

CUMGAP(t) = the cumulative gap at the end of that period of time.

CHRATES = a permanent once and for all change in all interest rates at all maturity levels.

The use of this formula can be seen in the examples in Table 1, which examine the effect of a 500-basis-point increase in interest rates on net income. The institution has $100 million in liabilities, which will re-price at the higher interest rates at the beginning of year one. This will raise interest expense by $5 million, which will be partially offset by the increased income from the $50 million in assets, which will re-price at the same time. The difference, which is the cumulative gap of $50 million, indicates the excess amount of liabilities.

The decline in net income of $2.5 million can be calculated two ways, as shown on the table. The second method, which is a direct application of the previously stated formula, highlights the significance of the cumulative gap. The reader can follow the arithmetic for years two and three in the same fashion.

As shown, the cumulative gap tells you how many more liabilities (assets) re-price than assets (liabilities) at the end of a certain period of time. If interest rates go up, institutions with negative cumulative gaps will be hurt. If rates go down, these institutions will experience a gain in net income.

In the example, if rates go down by 300 basis points, net income will go up by $1.5 million, which equals the cumulative gap (−$50 million) times the change in rates (−0.03). The cumulative gap, therefore, shows how much of a "bet" an institution is making on interest rates. The institution in the example has a negative cumulative gap in the shorter maturities and will lose its bet if rates go up and gain if rates come down. An institution that has a positive gap will lose if rates go down and gain if rates rise. Again, these relationships follow directly from the formula.

Most of the proposed strategies for reducing interest rate risk can be looked at in gap analysis terms. Sales of longer term fixed-rate loans, with the proceeds reinvested in shorter term assets, reduce the short-term gaps by adding assets to these maturity buckets. Shifting new lending from fixed-rate to adjustable-rate consumer or mortgage loans does the same thing. For institutions with too many long-term assets, other strategies work by moving liabilities from the near-term maturity buckets to those with longer maturities. These include interest rate swaps, financial futures (which can also be used on the asset side), and extension of the maturity of deposit liabilities.

Limitations of Gap

Criticism One. The first criticism leveled at the gap approach is that the individual gap numbers are arbitrary, since they depend on the size of the maturity buckets chosen by the person doing the analysis. For example, if the two- and three-year buckets in Table 1 were combined, the analysis would show a gap of +$50 million rather than a −$50 million and +$100 million.

It is also argued that if the buckets are too large there can be significant interest rate risk even within a single maturity bucket.[4] Suppose that the one-year gap is zero, but all the liabilities mature at the

---

In gap analysis, the crucial measure of interest rate risk is the cumulative gap, not the individual gaps.

---

beginning of the period and all the assets mature at the end. If rates were to increase, the institution could suffer a significant loss of income during the year, even though its gap analysis suggested it had no interest rate risk.

This criticism does not invalidate gap analysis; it simply indicates that the size of the maturity buckets has to be determined by someone who has a thorough knowledge of the nature of the interest rate risk facing the institution. For the traditional savings and loan association with large amounts of 20-30 year assets and 0-6 month liabilities, a limited number of maturity buckets may be appropriate because the main source of the interest rate risk is obvious. For a retail bank, a more comprehensive analysis using a larger number of maturity categories would be necessary. The fact that the user has to choose the proper level of disaggregation does not establish that the technique itself is faulty.[5]

A more important "defense" of gap analysis from the criticism of arbitrariness follows from the formula discussed above, which establishes that the crucial measure of interest rate risk is the cumulative gap, not the individual gaps. The cumulative gap at a given point in time is completely independent of the size of the individual maturity buckets because the cumulative gap measures the excess amount of liabilities (assets) that will have re-priced by the end of a given period of time in the future. For example, in Table 1 the gap of −$50 means that $50 million more liabilities will re-price during the second year. The cumulative gap of −$100 means that $100 million more liabilities will have re-priced *by the end* of year two. Since the cumulative gap is measured by summing up the individual gaps, it must be independent of the period of time used to construct the individual gaps. Any item that is omitted from one maturity bucket will be picked up in another.

Criticism Two. A second criticism leveled at gap analysis is that the standards required to "immunize" or to protect the institution from interest rate changes are impossible to achieve. Toevs implicitly argues that complete immunization would require calculating the gaps using daily maturity buckets and setting all the daily gaps equal to zero, which is simply not practical. The institution is thus left without a realistic goal to strive for in managing its interest rate risk.[6]

In actual practice, however, it is relatively easy to develop tolerance levels for key financial ratios such as the cumulative gap to total assets at various maturity levels. For example, one approach might be to let the ratios deviate within a range of, say, +3% to −3%, or +5% to −5%, and take action to reduce the gap only when it falls outside that range. This would not provide complete protection against interest rate changes, but the amount of protection it would provide is easily measurable using the standard gap formula above. For instance, a $100-million institution with a −$5 million (−5%) cumulative gap at one year would be exposed to a potential decline in net interest income of $100,000, if interest rates rose by 200 basis points ($5 million × .02 = $100,000). This can be compared with the institution's capital position to determine if this level of risk is acceptable.

The idea that the gaps need to be calculated at one day maturities and set equal to zero assumes that complete avoidance of all interest rate risk is a realistic goal. Interestingly, few gap analysis practitioners advocate anything like zero gap strategy. Assuming some interest rate risk is probably unavoidable in conducting the business of a financial institution, but the amount of risk inherent in the balance sheet should be carefully measured so that the level of risk that the institution does take on becomes a management decision.[7]

Criticism Three. The critics' third point is that gap analysis "unnecessarily constrains the bank's choice of assets and liabilities, which reduces the bank's ability to accommodate customer demands for bank services."[8] For instance, if a bank has six month deposits, it has to have an equal amount of six month loans. If the bank's customers want something other than six month loans, the bank will be left watching as its customers go somewhere else. Several points need to be made in response to this.

First of all, it assumes that financial institutions must follow a pure zero-gap strategy. As indicated above, this is clearly not the case. Second, numerous tools and techniques are available for altering the maturities of assets and liabilities to reduce interest rate risk and still accommodate customer demands. With the development of the interest rate swap market, for example, financial institutions have a way of changing the maturity of their liabilities so that this situation need not arise.[9]

Such maturity transformations can reduce potential profits, however. With an upward sloping yield curve, extending the maturity of a liability by using, for example, interest rate swaps will increase the cost of the liability. This highlights another aspect of the third objection to gap analysis—the impact on profitability. As Stanley Diller expresses it, "The traditional gap approach allows one side of a balance sheet to dictate what will be on the other, at the expense of profits."[10] Diller argues that because of the movement toward matched maturities, spreads between yields on assets and liability costs at the same maturity are being compressed so that institutions that match maturities dollar-for-dollar may earn an unsatisfactory rate of return.

This is simply a reflection of one of the basic principles of finance—the risk-return trade off. The expected rate of return on any project or set of projects depends upon the risk of the project. To earn a higher expected return, you need to take more risk. If you don't take any risk, you only earn the risk-free rate of return, which can be approximated by the three-month U.S. Treasury bill rate, for example.

Table 2 illustrates a common risk-return dilemma facing institutions mixing fixed-rate loans. The purpose of the example is to illustrate that gap analysis provides certain important information about the timing of the impact of various asset and liability management strategies on profitability that duration analysis does not provide. The institution has the opportunity to make fixed-rate loans with an expected life of 12 years at a rate of 12.5 percent. The institution can finance these asset acquisitions with one-year deposits yielding 8 percent and earn a 450-basis-point spread the first year. This spread comes only with enormous risk, however.

The second alternative is to finance the asset acquisition with 10-year liabilities at a cost of 11 percent. While this eliminates much of the interest rate risk, it leaves the institution with a spread of only 150 basis points. For most institutions, this would not be enough to even pay operating costs, let alone produce a profit.

The third alternative would be to finance the acquisition of the 12-year asset with five-year liabilities at a cost of 10 percent. This produces a 250-basis-point spread, but it entails some interest rate risk. The amount of risk involved can be measured by the cumulative gap. For years one through five, profits are completely protected, as reflected in the cumulative gap of zero. The institution's profitability is at risk in year six after the liability matures. If rates remain stable or decline, the institution can extend the maturity of the liability and preserve or increase the spread. If rates rise substantially, the spread will erode, and the institution could suffer a loss on the transaction.

Rightly or wrongly, many institutions today are apparently choosing this third alternative. For example, conversations with interest rate swap dealers indicate a significant interest in five-year swaps by savings institutions as a result of recent rate declines. The same thing has happened to the demand for intermediate-term Federal Home Loan Bank advances.

It should be emphasized that gap analysis provides important information about the interest rate risk inherent in this transaction that duration analysis does not provide. Duration analysis would show that if the institution pursued strategies one or three and interest rates rose, the market value of the institution would decline. It also would show that the decline would be less for strategy three than for strategy two because of the longer liability maturity in strategy three. But duration analysis says nothing about *when* the institution's net interest margin is at risk.

In evaluating the third criticism of gap analysis, it should be clear that gap analysis does not impose artificial constraints on the balance sheet, and it does not require pure matched maturities. In fact, the example shows that it can be a useful tool for analyzing the relative risk of different strategies, each of which involves some degree of maturity mismatch. A case study presented later in this article illustrates one approach to asset and liability management that, through a blending of gap and

Table 2. Gap Analysis for Alternative Strategies
(in $ Millions)

	Maturity or Time to Re-pricing			
	Under 1 Year	1-4 Years	5-9 Years	10 Years + Over
Strategy 1:				
Assets	—	—	—	$100 (12.5%)
Liabilities and Net Worth	$100 (8.0%)	—	—	—
Gap	−100	0	0	100
Cumulative Gap	−100	−100	−100	0
Strategy 2:				
Assets	—	—	—	100 (12.5%)
Liabilities and Net Worth	—	—	—	100 (11.0%)
Gap	0	0	0	0
Cumulative Gap	0	0	0	0
Strategy 3:				
Assets	—	—	—	100 (12.5%)
Liabilities and Net Worth	—	—	100 (10.0)	0
Gap	0	0	−100	100
Cumulative Gap	0	0	−100	0

duration analysis, produces a relatively low level of interest rate risk without pure dollar matching of maturities for each transaction.

Criticism Four. A fourth major criticism of gap analysis is the "inability of the model to generate a simple and reliable index of interest rate risk exposure."[11] Rather than providing a single number that tells management exactly what its risk is, gap analysis produces too many numbers—so many that interpretation becomes muddled, say the critics. Toevs has commented that different people can often look at the same gap report and come to completely different conclusions as to what the risk is and what strategies should be followed to reduce it.

But if interest rate risk management is important —and no one argues that it is not—then a single number may obliterate or distort the effect of a large number of contingencies, options, and other technical and special factors that affect that risk. As

Table 3. Calculating the Macaulay Duration for a
6-year, $100 Par Value Bond
(Paying a 12% Annual Coupon Rate, Priced to Yield 10%)

(1) Cash Flow Period (years)	(2) Cash Flow	(3) Present Value of Cash Flow (discounted at 10%)	(4) Weights (col. 3 ÷108.71)	(5) Weighted Cash Flow Periods (col. 4 x col. 1)
1	$ 12	$ 10.91	.1004	.10
2	12	9.92	.0913	.18
3	12	9.02	.0830	.25
4	12	8.20	.0754	.30
5	12	7.45	.0685	.34
6	112	63.22	.5815	3.49
Column Sum		$108.71	1.0000	4.67

(Totals of individual figures given may differ from sums because of rounding off.)

Source: Adapted from Robert A. Ott, "Duration Analysis and Minimizing Interest Rate Risk,"*Review,* Federal Home Loan Bank of Atlanta (December 1984), p. 2, as corrected.

seen in the previous example, the timing of interest rate exposure is one factor that financial managers will want to be aware of. Another example is the prepayment option provided to the mortgage borrower. This is one-sided since it will be exercised much more frequently if interest rates go down.

Interest rate risk, then, is a multi-dimensional concept; there are so many factors affecting it that to rely on a single number by itself would, no doubt, hide many of them. The economist attempting to forecast the behavior of the economy uses many indicators—gross national product (real and nominal), the money supply, employment and unemployment, retail sales, industrial production, to name only a few. The manager of a financial institution also needs numerous bits of information. For example, what is the cumulative gap at one year, three years, five years? How are the gaps affected by various prepayment assumptions? What is the effect of different assumptions about passbook savings? The manager will also want to know the duration of his assets and liabilities to put this information into perspective and to see the overall degree of risk in the balance sheet.

Duration Analysis: Assumptions

Duration analysis begins with a completely different premise than gap analysis. Gap analysis is concerned only with the net interest margin and its effect on net income, as measured by conventional accounting practices. Duration analysis ignores accounting considerations and concentrates on the market value of the net worth of the firm. As Toevs expresses it, "the current market value of net worth represents the present value of this and all future years' net interest income. If net worth declines, then some or all yearly net interest incomes must decline. That is, market value of net worth is a leading indicator of the stream of net interest incomes."[12]

Duration had its origins in the area of bond portfolio management. In fact, duration is a measure of the average life of a stream of payments, such as those that might be produced by a bond. To the bond analyst, duration is often a better measure of the average life of a financial contract than maturity. Maturity only tells you when the final payment is due; it says nothing about the size or timing of either the interest payments or any early repayment of principal. The standard Macaulay duration measure can be calculated as follows:

$$D = \frac{\displaystyle\sum_{t=1}^{n} \frac{P_t}{(1+r)^t} \times (t)}{\displaystyle\sum_{t=1}^{n} \frac{P_t}{(1+r)^t}}$$

Where
D = the Macaulay duration measure
P_t = payment of interest or principal at time t
t = the amount of time before the cash flow (P) is received
n = the final maturity of the financial contract
r = current market interest rates for the security under consideration

Table 3 gives an example of how the Macaulay duration is calculated. Notice that each payment has a weight, the weights sum to 1.00, and each weight is the ratio of the present value of that cash flow to the total present value of all the cash flows ($108.71). Each cash flow is thus weighted by its importance in determining the total present value of the financial contract. Since present value is equal to the price of the bond (because no one would pay more or sell for less than the bond is worth), the weights reflect the importance of each cash flow in determining the price of the financial instrument. Duration, which in this case is 4.67 years, is simply a weighted average measure of maturity.

Duration is also a direct measure of the sensitivity of market value to changes in interest rates. The measurement, however, is only approximate, as the following formula indicates:

$$\Delta P \cong -d \times \Delta i$$

Where:
ΔP = the percent change in price for the asset or liability
d = the duration of that asset or liability
Δi = the change in market yield for the financial instrument under consideration

For instance, if rates increase by 10 basis points and the duration of a bond is 3 years, the percentage change in price will be about -0.3 percent (i.e., $-3 \times .001 = -.003$). For small changes in interest rates, the approximation produced by this formula is reasonably accurate. For large changes, however, this is not the case.

Duration is measured in units of time, since it is a measure of average maturity, but duration is almost always smaller than maturity. The exception would be a zero coupon bond or a discount security such as a Treasury bill. For these instruments, duration and maturity are equal.

Advocates of the duration approach to interest rate risk management, such as Kaufman and Toevs, suggest that the durations of the institution's assets and liabilities be calculated separately. If the duration of assets exceeds the duration of liabilities, as it would, for example, at most savings institutions, the market value of the assets will decline more than the market value of the liabilities when interest rates rise. This means, of course, that the institution sees its profits erode when interest rates rise and experiences a gain when rates fall. Interest rate sensitivity is therefore eliminated when the duration of the assets equals the duration of the liabilities. Duration matching thus replaces asset and liability maturity matching as the key element in this approach to interest rate risk management.

Its advocates contend that duration overcomes the four primary limitations of gap analysis. First,

duration is unique—it is not an arbitrary number that depends upon the size of a maturity bucket. Second, it provides a clear and practical goal that will "immunize" the institution from interest rate changes. While setting all daily gaps equal to zero is clearly impossible, approximate duration matching is feasible.

Third, duration allows the institution to offer different maturities for deposits and loans, thus meeting customer needs without taking on undue interest rate risk. This is possible because one of the

---

Duration analysis is a direct measure of the sensitivity of market value to changes in interest rates.

---

mathematical properties of duration is that durations can be averaged. If a customer wants loans that have a duration of three years, these can be funded with equal amounts of one- and five-year (duration) liabilities or two- and four-year liabilities, or any other combination with an average duration of three years. This is extremely important because it allows the financial institution to continue to perform one of the classic functions of financial intermediaries—to "intermediate" between various maturities to meet the needs of both depositors and borrowers. These needs, of course, will not always be for the same maturity. Customers may want short-term deposits, for example, while borrowers may prefer longer term loans.

Since duration provides a single number—the difference between the duration of assets and liabilities—as a convenient summary measure of interest rate risk, it also overcomes the fourth alleged limitation of gap analysis—the lack of any such summary statistic. Nonetheless, it needs to be emphasized that duration also has limitations.[13]

Limitations of Duration Analysis

The limitations of duration follow from the assumptions. Immunization against interest rate changes using the standard Macaulay duration measure requires that the interest rate change be a proportionate, once and for all, change in all interest rates at all maturity levels. In other words, the yield curve moves upward by a constant percentage amount, say 10 percent. If short-term rates were 8

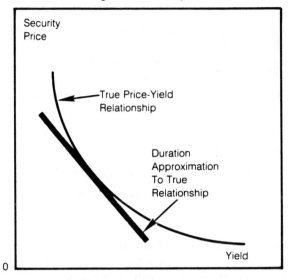

Figure 1. Convexity

Security Price

True Price-Yield Relationship

Duration Approximation To True Relationship

Yield

0

percent, they increase to 8.8 percent. If long-term rates were 10 percent, they increase to 11 percent. If the interest rate change is of any other type, the financial institution will not be immunized against that particular rate change. In the course of an interest rate cycle, however, short-term rates usually go up more than long-term rates.

It is possible to construct different duration measures for different rate change environments. In effect, one needs to know in advance what type of rate change to expect in order to know what duration measure to use. However, the whole idea of interest rate risk mangement is to protect institutions against *unforeseen* rate changes. The savings and loan crisis of 1981-82 occurred because no one thought short-term rates could go as high as they did.

Another limitation of duration analysis stems from the fact that, as noted above, duration is only an approximation. Figure 1 shows a typical price-yield relationship for a U.S. Treasury security. When yields go up, of course, bond prices go down, which accounts for the fact that the curve is downward sloping. However, the relationship is not linear; it is convex and duration provides only a linear approximation to the true relationship. If the asset and liability do not have the same convexity, duration will not match the market value changes on both sides of the balance sheet. If the asset is a mortgage and the liability is a time deposit or interest rate

swap, the "convexities" will not be the same. The reason is that the mortgage amortizes, and it is also likely to be repaid if rates come down, while the liability does not have this feature.[14]

Related to this is the phenomenon of "duration drift." Even if asset and liability durations are matched initially, they will not necessarily remain this way over time. Robert Ott presents a situation in which a package of mortgage loans is financed with a combination of five- and 10-year loans from the Federal Home Loan Bank. Initially the duration of the assets equals that of the liabilities at 5.3 years. After four years, the duration of the assets declines slowly to only five years, but the duration of the liabilities drops to about three years. After eight years, the duration mismatch is even greater. This situation occurs because, while initial durations were matched, initial maturities were not.

A Case Study: Blending Gap and Duration Analysis

The Federal Home Loan Bank of Atlanta uses both gap and duration analysis to measure its interest rate risk, with the primary focus on gap analysis. The following example shows how the two can complement one another. When the Bank participates in an issue of FHLB System debt, it may use a portion of the proceeds to purchase U.S. Treasury securities of comparable maturity. This hedge protects the Bank in the event interest rates fall and loans have to be made at lower rates. For the five-year maturity, the gap report would be affected by this transaction as follows:

Assets	
U.S. Treasury Securities	+50
Liabilities	
FHLB Consolidated Obligations	+50
Gap	No Change

When five-year loans are made, the hedge securities are sold so there is again no change in the gap. The loans would simply replace the hedge securities in the asset account above.

The Bank is required to stand ready to make loans in a full range of maturities out to 10 years. As a practical matter, however, it is impossible to hold hedge securities in all maturity ranges at all times. What is done is to use hedge securities of one maturity to fund loan demand at another maturity on a weighted basis. The weights are derived from duration analysis.

Suppose a hypothetical reduction in interest rates of 10 basis points would raise the price of $1 million of three-year securities by $2,000. An identical change in rates would, of course, have a larger effect on the price of five-year securities; let's say this effect is $3,000. Then it would require the sale of only $0.67 million of five-year securities to hedge a $1 million three-year advance. This hedge would, in effect, protect the market value of the Bank's net worth.

This type of duration-weighted hedge transaction is also used to improve the Bank's gap. For example, in one situation the Bank faced a demand for $75 million of three-year advances. At that time, the Bank had a negative gap (excess of liabilities over assets) at the three-year maturity, so the additional three-year assets were welcome. At the same time, the gap in the five-year area was positive. By selling approximately $50 million of five-year hedge (Treasury) securities to fund this advance and reducing its overnight assets (federal funds sold) by $25 million, the Bank was able to reduce both the three-year and five-year gaps.

Another important aspect of this process is the calculation of overall duration measures for the Bank's balance sheet. By providing a summary risk measure, the duration calculation can tell the Bank which gaps need to be closed. This provides important information when decisions about the maturity of new debt issues are made. Given the importance of interest rate risk management, the two methods—gap and duration—are then compared so as to be sure they both point in the same direction. At the end of June 1985, for example, the durations of assets and liabilities were approximately 12.6 and 13.1 months, respectively. At the same time, the cumulative gap at most maturity levels out to five years was positive, but less than 4 percent of assets. Both the gap and duration measures suggest a very modest, almost negligible, risk exposure to falling interest rates.

Conclusion: Are Gap and Duration in Conflict?

The reader who has followed the discussion to this point may see himself in a dilemma. Interest rate risk management may be crucial to bank performance, and the regulators are now attempting to measure each institution's risk with double digit precision. Nonetheless, both the two principal tools for measuring this risk have significant limitations. What is one to do?

The advocates of duration analysis have provided a useful service in highlighting the limitations of gap analysis. However, duration is also based on a number of restrictive assumptions so that exclusive reliance on it could lead to significant problems if

---

Gap analysis and duration analysis can be used as complementary approaches to interest rate risk management.

---

these assumptions are invalid. In the opinion of the author, the limitations of gap are not as severe as its critics contend, and gap analysis can continue to be a primary tool of interest rate risk management.

Duration asks a completely different question than gap. By ignoring accounting considerations and the timing of the effect of interest rate changes, it calls the analyst's attention to the effect of interest rate changes on market value. Since the focus of the two approaches is completely different, the limitations should tend to offset one another.

Consider the following example of the interrelationship between gap and duration. A retail bank has a positive gap (excess assets) of $100 million at four years and a negative gap (excess liabilities) of $100 million at seven years. It can add four-year liabilities to correct the first situation; it can add seven-year assets to correct the second. Assume the overall duration on the asset side exceeds the duration on the liability side by a significant amount. Adding four-year liabilities will help correct the duration imbalance while adding seven-year assets will worsen it. (The sources or uses of the funds are ignored for simplicity). While the gaps are equal in dollar amount, closing one will reduce the overall level of interest rate risk, while closing the other would increase it and thus be counterproductive. Duration, then, can tell the financial manager which gaps need to be closed.

At the very least, each approach provides information that the other does not. As indicated in this example and in the case study, it is possible to use the two as complementary rather than competing approaches to interest rate risk management.

Notes

1. George Kaufman, "Measuring and Managing Interest Rate Risk: A Primer," *Economic Perspectives*, Federal Reserve Bank of Chicago (January-February 1984), 16-29.

2. Alden Toevs, "Gap Management: Managing Interest Rate Risk in Banks and Thrifts," *Economic Review*, Federal Reserve Bank of San Francisco (Spring 1983).

3. A more detailed summary of gap analysis is contained in Steven J. Goldstein and Eric I. Hemel, "Gap Analysis: Using Section H of the Quarterly Report," Office of Policy and Economic Research, Federal Home Loan Bank Board, July 1984; and Joseph Sinkey, *Commercial Bank Financial Management* (New York: Macmillan, 1983), 493-509. An extensive bibliography can be found in Sinkey, 512-15.

4. Toevs, "Gap Management," 22-23.

5. An analogy might be useful to reinforce this point. For over 40 years, economists have been using multiple regression analysis to estimate the relationship between the demand for individual commodities and their price. In their analysis, a choice has to be made as to the level of detail at which the analysis should be conducted (e.g., meat in general, or beef, pork and veal separately). The choice clearly depends on what the analysis is to be used for. The fact that a choice has to be made does not establish that multiple regression is a faulty technique.

6. Toevs, "Gap Management," 23-34.

7. See, for example, Goldstein and Hemel, "Gap Analysis," 16-17.

8. Toevs, "Gap Management," 20.

9. An interest rate swap is an "interest-exchange agreement." One party, say a savings institution, has a short-term liability on which it makes variable-rate payments. Another party has a fixed-rate, longer term liability. The two institutions enter into an agreement whereby the party with short-term liability agrees to pay the interest expense that would be paid by the party with the long-term obligation, and the other institution does the reverse. In actual practice, no exchange of principal occurs and the short-term payments are tied to an index.

10. Stanley Diller, "Parametric Analysis of Fixed Income Securities: Options, Passthroughs, Convexity, Asset Liability Management" (New York: Goldman Sachs, Financial Strategies Group, June 1984).

11. Toevs, "Gap Management," 31.

12. Alden Toevs and Jeffrey Wernick, "Hedging Interest Rate Risk Inclusive of Prepayment and Credit Risks," in *Identification and Control of Risk in the Thrift Industry*, Proceedings of the Ninth Annual Conference, Federal Home Loan Bank of San Francisco (December 1983), 99. For a more detailed description of the principles of duration and a discussion of the calculation of duration statistics see Kaufman, "Managing Interest Rate Risk," 16-29; Robert A. Ott, "Duration Analysis and Minimizing Interest Rate Risk," *Review*, Federal Home Loan Bank of Atlanta (December 1984) 1-5; or Alan Winger, "Duration in the Analysis of Interest Rate Risk," *Quarterly Review*, Federal Home Loan Bank of Cincinnati (First Quarter 1984).

13. This is discussed more extensively in Ott, "Duration Analysis," 1-5.

14. Methods of dealing with this problem, such as by using strips of FHLB advances or certificates of deposit with different maturities are discussed in Diller, "Parametric Analysis" and Toevs and Wernick, "Hedging Interest Rate Risk." As the number of different liability maturities is increased, the problems created by convexity are reduced, because cash flows are more closely matched. But this is precisely what gap analysis would suggest.

Article Six

Hedging Interest Rate Risk with Financial Futures: Some Basic Principles

Michael T. Belongia and G. J. Santoni

FOR much of the postwar period, stable rates of inflation — accompanied by stable levels of interest rates — created a comforting economic environment for managers of depository institutions. Beginning in the mid-1970s, however, more variable interest rates, brought about in part by more variable inflation, caused a substantial change in the economic conditions facing depository institutions. Offering long-term credit at fixed rates became riskier as larger and more frequent unexpected changes in interest rates introduced more variation into the market value of these assets.[1]

This article describes how variation in interest rates affects the market value of depository institutions. The discussion then demonstrates how financial futures contracts might be used to hedge some of the interest rate risk of a portfolio composed of interest-sensitive deposit accounts and loans of unmatched maturities. Although some regulatory authorities have denied or strictly regulated the use of futures contracts by de-

pository institutions in the belief that futures trading is risky and unduly speculative, we argue that the judicious use of futures can reduce the firm's exposure to interest rate fluctuations.[2]

DURATION GAP AND INTEREST RATE RISK

In the mid-1970s, when large fluctuations in interest rates began to occur, it became increasingly evident that depository institutions needed some measure of the relative risks associated with various portfolio holdings. One approach to the measurement of interest rate risk is called Duration Gap analysis. "Duration" refers to the "average" life of some group of assets or liabilities. "Gap" refers to the difference between the durations of an institution's assets and its liabilities.[3]

Michael T. Belongia is an economist and G. J. Santoni is a senior economist at the Federal Reserve Bank of St. Louis. John G. Schulte provided research assistance.

[1]For a general description of events that have introduced or increased interest rate risk, see Carrington and Hertzberg (1984) and Koch, et al. (1982).

[2]Legal restrictions and guidelines on the use of financial futures by different types of financial institutions are summarized in Lower (1982). A comparison of statutes on the use of futures by insurance companies is made in Gottlieb (1984).

[3]For more detailed discussions of duration analysis and its application to financial institution portfolios, see Kaufman (1984); Bierwag, Kaufman and Toevs (1983); Toevs (1983); Santoni (1984); Samuelson (1944); and Hicks (1939), pp. 184–88.

Table 1

Expected Streams of Receipts and Payments

	Day				
	0	90	180	270	360
Panel A: No Change in Interest Rates					
Asset (loan)					
Receipts					$1,000.00
Payments	$909.09				
Liabilities (borrowings)					
Receipts	909.09	$926.75	$944.76	$963.11	
Payments		926.75	944.76	963.11	981.82
Net Receipts	-0-	-0-	-0-	-0-	$ 18.18

Present Value $18.18/1.10 = $16.53

	0	90	180	270	360
Panel B: Interest Rates Rise by 200 Basis Points					
Asset (loan)					
Receipts					$1,000.00
Payments	$909.09				
Liabilities (borrowings)					
Receipts	909.09	$926.75	$949.10	$971.98	
Payments		926.75	949.10	971.98	995.42
Net Receipts	-0-	-0-	-0-	-0-	$ 4.58

Present Value = $4.58/1.12 = $4.09

	0	90	180	270	360
Panel C: Interest Rates Fall by 200 Basis Points					
Asset (loan)					
Receipts					$1,000.00
Payments	$909.09				
Liabilities (borrowings)					
Receipts	909.09	$926.75	$940.35	$954.15	
Payments		926.75	940.35	954.15	968.15
Net Receipts	-0-	-0-	-0-	-0-	$ 31.85

Present Value = $31.85/1.08 = $29.49

An Example

The risk introduced into a portfolio of assets and liabilities of different duration is illustrated in tables 1 and 2. In this example, for expositional simplicity, the firm's planned life is assumed to be only one year. It has extended a loan with a face value of $1,000 to be repaid in a single payment at the end of the year at an interest rate of 10 percent. The present value of the loan, and, thus, the amount paid out by the firm to the borrower, is $909.09. To finance this loan, the firm borrows $909.09 for 90 days at 8 percent interest. The two percentage-point spread is the return earned by the firm for employing its specialized capital in intermediating between borrowers and lenders.

The amount that the firm will owe in three months time is $926.75 (= $909.09(1.08)$^{.25}$), which it plans to pay by borrowing this amount for another 90 days. Because the firm's proceeds from the new loan and its payment of the old loan cancel, its net receipts at this time are zero. The firm anticipates being able to roll the loan over every 90 days at the same interest rate. Consequently, at the end of 180 days, the firm expects to owe $944.76 (= $926.75(1.08)$^{.25}$), which it plans to pay with new borrowings. At the end of the year, the firm

Table 2

Interest Rate Changes and the Present Value of a Portfolio of Assets and Liabilities of Different Durations

Panel A: Initial Conditions

Present Values

Asset:	Liability:
$\dfrac{\$1,000.00}{1.10} = \$909.09$	$\dfrac{\$981.82}{1.10} = \$892.56$
	Equity:
	$\$909.09 - \$892.56 = \$16.53$

Panel B: All Interest Rates Rise by 200 Basis Points

Present Values

Asset:	Liability:
$\dfrac{\$1,000.00}{1.12} = \$892.86$	$\dfrac{\$995.42}{1.12} = \$888.77$
	Equity:
	$\$892.86 - \$888.77 = \$4.09$
	Percentage change in equity = -75.26

anticipates having to pay $981.82 (= $909.09 × 1.08). This amount will be paid out of the $1,000 proceeds from its matured asset. The firm's expected net receipt at year-end is $18.18, as shown in panel A of table 1.

Panel A of table 2 is a balance sheet summary of the present value of this investment plan. The present value of the expected net receipt at year-end is $16.53 and is equal to the difference between the present value of the asset, $909.09 (= $1,000/1.10), and the present value of the expected liability, $892.56 (= $981.82/1.10). Both future values are discounted at 10 percent, the firm's opportunity cost.

The Effects of Changing Interest Rates on Equity

This package of assets and liabilities is subject to considerable interest rate risk because the 10 percent interest rate on the firm's loan is fixed for one year while its borrowings must be refunded every 90 days. In this example, the gap between the durations of the

asset and liability is 270 days (= 360 − 90).[4] As a practical matter, the asset's longer duration implies that a given change in interest rates will change the present value of the asset more than it will affect the present value of the liability. This difference, of course, will change the value of the firm's equity.

Panel B of table 1 shows the effect of an unexpected 200 basis-point rise in interest rates. The increase raises the firm's anticipated refunding costs. As a result, the amount the firm expects to pay at year-end increases to $995.42. Net receipts fall to $4.58 and the present value of the investment plan falls to $4.09.

Panel B of table 2 presents a balance sheet summary of the effect of the change on the present values of the asset, liability and owner equity. The increase in interest rates reduces the present values of both the asset and liability, but the asset value falls by relatively more because its life is fixed for one year, while the liability must be rolled over in 90 days at a higher interest rate. The increase in interest rates causes owner equity to fall by $12.44, or about 75 percent. In contrast, had the interest rate declined by 200 basis points, the net present value of the firm's equity would have risen to $29.49 (see panel C of table 1), an increase of about 78 percent.

This extreme volatility in the firm's equity is due to the mismatch of the durations of the asset and liability that make up the firm's portfolio. Table 3 illustrates this point. The only difference between this and earlier examples is that, in table 3, the duration of the liability has been lengthened to match the duration of the asset. While a 200 basis-point increase in the interest rate still causes the present value of the portfolio to fall, the change, − $0.30 or − 1.8 percent, is much less than before. Clearly, matching the durations of the asset and liability exposes the value of the portfolio to much lower interest rate risk.

COPING WITH THE GAP

Depository institutions, particularly savings and loan associations, maintain portfolios of assets and liabilities that are similar to the one shown in the initial example.[5] That is, the duration of their assets

---

[4]The durations of single-payment financial instruments are equal to the maturities of the instruments. In other cases, calculation of duration is not as straightforward. See footnote 3.

[5]Savings and loan associations are required to maintain a significant share of their portfolios in long-term home mortgages in order to obtain federal insurance of deposits. See Federal Home Loan Bank Act of 1932, sec. 4(a).

Table 3

Interest Rate Changes and the Present Value of a Portfolio of Assets and Liabilities of the Same Duration

Panel A: Initial Conditions

Present Values

Asset:		Liability:	
$\dfrac{\$1{,}000.00}{1.10} = \$909.09$		$\dfrac{\$981.82}{1.10} =$	$\$892.56$
		Equity:	
		$\$909.09 - \$892.56 = \$16.53$	

Panel B: All Interest Rates Rise by 200 Basis Points

Present Values

Asset:		Liability:	
$\dfrac{\$1{,}000.00}{1.12} = \$892.86$		$\dfrac{\$981.82}{1.12} =$	$\$876.63$
		Equity:	
		$\$892.86 - \$876.63 = \$16.23$	
		Percentage change in equity = -1.8	

typically is longer than the duration of their liabilities. As a result, the market values of these institutions have been particularly sensitive to interest rate fluctuations. This, along with the recent experience of highly variable interest rates, has led these institutions to seek out methods to reduce their exposure to interest rate risk. Among other things, these firms have made greater use of floating rate loans and interest rate swap agreements. Recent regulatory changes have allowed them to allocate more of their loan portfolios to short-term consumer loans. In addition, a number of institutions are using financial futures to reduce their exposure to interest rate risk.[6]

---

[6]See Booth, Smith and Stolz (1984). While a number of financial firms are employing the futures market, it seems that accounting requirements have discouraged the use of futures to hedge interest rate risk. Until recently, regulators and accountants feared that losses from futures transactions could be hidden in financial reports. Therefore, they would not permit a hedge to count as one transaction with spot gains or losses offsetting futures markets losses or gains. Instead, they required futures losses to be marked to the market while spot gains could be deferred. This asymmetric treatment of gains and losses on the two sides of a hedge distorted earnings estimates and, therefore, discouraged the use of futures.

Futures Markets and Risk

It may seem odd that the futures market, which is generally thought of as being very risky, can be used to reduce risk. Futures trading is risky for people who bet on the future price movements of particular commodities or financial instruments by taking long or short positions in futures contracts. Such speculative bets on future price movements, however, are not unique to futures market trading. The nature of most types of businesses requires a speculative bet about the future course of a particular price.

Growing crops, for example, gives farmers long positions in physical commodities during the growing season. These long positions expose the farmer to the risk of price declines — declines that can reduce the profits from efficient farming (the activity that the farmer specializes in). Judicious use of the futures market allows the farmer to offset his long position in the commodity by selling futures contracts. Since the sale reduces his net holdings of the commodity, the farmer's exposure to the risk of future price declines is reduced. Similarly, futures trading presents depository institutions with the opportunity to reduce their exposure to the risk of interest rate changes.

Futures Contracts

A futures contract is an agreement between a seller and a buyer to trade some well-defined item (wheat, corn, Treasury bills) at some specified future date at a price agreed upon *now* but paid in the future at the time of delivery. The futures price is a prediction about what the price of the item will be at the time of delivery.

In the case of commodities, the price of the good today (the spot price), on average, will be equal to the futures price minus the cost of storage, insurance and foregone interest associated with holding the good over the interval of the contract. A similar relationship exists between the spot and futures prices of financial instruments. However, since the storage and insurance cost of holding these instruments is very low, the spread between the spot and futures prices is largely determined by the interest cost.

See Morris (1984) for more detail on changes in accounting standards. Asay, et al. (1981) provide examples of how former accounting standards discouraged the use of futures by banks and thrift institutions.

The Relationship Between Spot and Futures Markets for Treasury Bills: An Illustration

In January 1976, the International Monetary Market (IMM), now part of the Chicago Mercantile Exchange (CME), began trading futures contracts in 13-week Treasury bills.[7] The basic contract is for $1 million with contracts maturing once each quarter in the third week of March, June, September and December. Since there are eight contracts outstanding, the most distant delivery date varies between 21 and 24 months into the future.

Panel A of table 4 presents quotations for Treasury bill futures for the trading day of August 7, 1984. Panel B of table 4 lists spot quotations for Treasury bills for the same trading day.[8]

Panel A of table 4 is interpreted as follows: September Treasury bill futures were trading at a discount of 10.49 percent on August 7, 1984. Any person trading this contract obtained the right to buy (sell) a Treasury bill the third week in September with a remaining maturity of 13 weeks at a discount rate of 10.49 percent. A similar statement holds for the other contracts listed in panel A.

Panel B lists spot market quotations. For example, Treasury bills due to mature August 9, 1984, traded at a discount of 9.91 percent (bid) to 9.79 percent (ask), while those maturing September 20, 1984, traded at a discount of 9.95 (bid) to 9.91 (ask), etc.

We noted earlier that the spot and futures markets must be closely related, and the data in panels A and B can be used to illustrate this point. For example, on August 7, 1984, an investor could purchase a Treasury bill due to mature December 20, 1984 (i.e., 134 days later). If he purchases the bill on the spot market, he obtains the asked discount of 10.39 percent. At this discount rate, the price he pays for the bill is $96.41 per $100 of face value.[9]

Table 4
Market Quotations for U.S. Treasury Bills: August 7, 1984[1]

Panel A: Treasury Bill Futures (IMM)

	Contract	Discount settle
1984	September	10.49
	December	10.85
1985	March	11.13
	June	11.35
	September	11.52
	December	11.66
1986	March	11.79
	June	11.90

Panel B: Treasury Bill Spot

	Discount	
Maturity Date	Bid	Ask
August 9, 1984	9.91	9.79
September 20, 1984	9.95	9.91
December 20, 1984	10.45	10.39
March 21, 1985	10.63	10.56
June 13, 1985	10.72	10.66
July 11, 1985	10.73	10.69

[1]*Wall Street Journal*, August 8, 1984, pp. 38–9.

Alternatively, the investor could purchase a futures contract that gives him the right to buy a Treasury bill in September that will mature the third week in December. This alternative gives him a discount rate of 10.49 percent. Buying the Treasury bill in September at this discount would require a payment of $97.54.[10] This payment will be made 43 days into the future, roughly, September 20, and the present value of the payment on August 7 is $96.44.[11] Notice that this is very near the amount that the investor would pay ($96.41) if he were to purchase a Treasury bill on the spot market that matured during the third week of December.

Of course, other alternatives are open to the investor as well. He could, for example, buy a Treasury bill that matured the third week in March on the spot market.

---

[7]Futures contracts in other types of financial instruments, such as GNMA passthrough certificate contracts, 90-day CDs, Treasury bonds and Treasury notes, also are available at the Chicago Board of Trade.

[8]The information in table 3 is taken from pages 38 and 39 of the August 8, 1984, *Wall Street Journal*. The actual tables in the *Wall Street Journal* contain more information than is presented here. For our purposes, however, the additional information is extraneous.

[9]$96.41 = $100/(1.1039)^{37}. The discount factor is raised to the power of 134/360 = .37. This calculation is slightly different from the discount calculation used in determining actual trading prices, but

numerical differences between the two formulas are small. See Stigum (1981) for the market's discount formula.

[10]$97.54 = $100/(1.1049)^{25}.

[11]$96.44 = $97.54/(1.0991)^{12}. The interest rate used in the calculation is the rate on August 7 for a security maturing on September 20 (43 days in the future).

The present cost of doing this should be near the present cost of buying a futures contract that allows him to purchase a Treasury bill in December maturing the third week in March. Table 5 uses the data in table 4 to compare the present costs of this and other alternatives. In each case, the present costs of employing the spot vs. the futures market are very close.[12] Because a close relationship between these markets exists, the Treasury bill futures market can be used effectively to hedge interest rate risk.[13]

HEDGING THE GAP

The Streams of Receipts and Payments

The example in table 1 can be used to illustrate how futures contracts can be applied to hedge the interest rate risk caused by the mismatch in the lives (durations) of the firm's assets and liabilities. Considerable confusion appears to exist as to what the firm's hedging objective should be and how hedges should be constructed. One possible hedging strategy is to protect the equity of the firm (in the present value sense) from interest rate fluctuations. Another often-cited strategy is to minimize discrepancies between cash flows over time. It seems clear, however, that firm owners will choose a hedge that protects their net wealth (present value of the firm's equity). This focus on net wealth is crucial because, as the examples show, reducing cash flow mismatches to zero does not minimize the exposure of the firm's equity to interest rate changes.

Hedging Net Wealth: An Example

Suppose it is September 15, 1984, and the firm initiates the transactions summarized earlier in panel A of table 1. In addition, to hedge each of its three refunding requirements, the firm sells December, March and June futures contracts at 10 percent discounts.[14] The price of each contract is $1,000/(1.10)^{.25} =$

---

[12]Small differences are due to the existence of transaction costs. If the differences were large, profitable arbitrage opportunities would exist. These, of course, would vanish quickly as traders took advantage of the situation.

[13]There is, of course, the problem that the spot instrument being hedged may not be identical to the futures market instrument. If so, the price of one may diverge from the other because of a change in a factor that affects the price of one but not the other. This is called "basis risk" and is ignored in the following examples.

[14]A flat yield curve is assumed for ease of exposition. The examples become more complicated if the yield curve slopes up or down and/or the spread between borrowing and lending rates changes.

Table 5

The Relationship Between Treasury Bill Spot and Futures Prices: August 7, 1984, Per $100 of Face Value

Case 1: Purchase of a Treasury bill that matures the third week in December 1984

	Present Cost
Spot Market Purchase	$96.41
September Futures Purchase	96.44
Difference	.03

Case 2: Purchase of a Treasury bill that matures the third week in March 1985

	Present Cost
Spot Market Purchase	$93.92
December Futures Purchase	93.94
Difference	.02

Case 3: Purchase of a Treasury bill that matures the third week in June 1985

	Present Cost
Spot Market Purchase	$91.45
March Futures Purchase	91.47
Difference	.02

$976.45. These contracts obligate the firm to deliver a 13-week Treasury bill with a face value of $1,000 during the third week of December, March and June in exchange for $976.45.

Panel A of table 6 presents the firm's expected streams of receipts and payments given the structure of interest rates on September 15. It is identical to panel A of table 1 except that the streams of receipts and payments generated by the futures contract are included. The futures contract generates a certain stream of receipts equal to $976.45 in December, March and June in exchange for delivery of the 90-day Treasury bills. The firm must acquire these bills in order to make delivery and, on September 15, the expected cost of acquiring each of the Treasury bills is $976.45. If interest rates remain unchanged, expected and actual costs will be the same so that the actual receipts and payments generated by the futures contract net out in each period. The net flow of receipts is zero until year-end when the firm receives $18.18. The present value of this amount is $16.53.

In panel B, interest rates are assumed to rise unexpectedly by 200 basis points immediately following

Table 6

Expected Streams of Receipts and Payments

			Day		
	0	90	180	270	360
Panel A: No Change in Interest Rates					
Asset (loan)					
Receipts					$1,000.00
Payments	$909.09				
Asset (futures)					
Receipts		$976.45	$976.45	$976.45	
Liabilities (borrowings)					
Receipts	909.09	926.75	944.76	963.11	
Payments		926.75	944.76	963.11	981.82
Liabilities (futures)					
Payments		976.45	976.45	976.45	
Net Receipts	-0-	-0-	-0-	-0-	$ 18.18

Present Value = $18.18/1.10 = $16.53

Panel B: Interest Rates Rise by 200 Basis Points					
Asset (loan)					
Receipts					$1,000.00
Payments	$909.09				
Asset (futures)					
Receipts		$976.45	$976.45	$976.45	
Liabilities (borrowings)					
Receipts	909.09	926.75	949.10	971.98	
Payments		926.75	949.10	971.98	995.42
Liabilities (futures)					
Payments		972.07	972.07	972.07	
Net Receipts	-0-	$ 4.38	$ 4.38	$ 4.38	$ 4.58

Present Value = $4.38/(1.12)$^{.25}$ + $4.38/(1.12)$^{.50}$ + $4.38/(1.12)$^{.75}$ + $4.58/(1.12) = $16.50

Panel C: Interest Rates Fall by 200 Basis Points					
Asset (loan)					
Receipts					$1,000.00
Payments	$909.09				
Asset (futures)					
Receipts		$976.45	$976.45	$976.45	
Liabilities (borrowings)					
Receipts	909.09	926.75	940.35	954.15	
Payments		926.75	940.35	954.15	968.15
Liabilities (futures)					
Payments		980.94	980.94	980.94	
Net Receipts	-0-	$ -4.49	$ -4.49	$ -4.49	$ 31.85

Present Value = $-\$4.49/(1.08)$^{.25}$ - $4.49/(1.08)$^{.50}$ - $4.49/(1.08)$^{.75}$ + $31.85/(1.08) = $16.52

the firm's September 15 transactions. As in panel B of table 1, the increase in interest rates raises the firm's refunding cost and reduces the net year-end receipt to $4.58. In addition, however, the increase in interest rates reduces the expected cost of acquiring the Treasury bill to $972.07. Since the firm will receive $976.45 upon delivery of the Treasury bills, the futures contract will generate a net flow of receipts equal to $4.38 in December, March and June. The present value of this flow added to the present value of the net receipt at year-end ($4.58) is $16.50, which is nearly identical to the present value for the case in which interest rates remained unchanged (the small difference is due to rounding errors).

Panel C illustrates the outcome for a 200 basis-point decline in interest rates. In this case, the futures contract generates negative net receipts for the firm in December, March and June. The present value of this negative flow added to the present value of the higher positive net receipt at year-end sum to $16.52. As the examples show, this hedge protects the net wealth of the firm regardless of the direction of the change in interest rates.

While this hedge protects net wealth from changes in interest rates, it does so by allowing net cash receipts to vary. Net cash receipts, both in amount and timing, are considerably different in panels A, B and C. In panel A, net receipts are $18.18 at year-end while in panel B net receipts are spread out over the year and total only $17.72. In panel C, the firm has negative net receipts during the year and a large positive net receipt at year-end for a total of $18.38. However, the present value of the firm is the same in all three cases.

The Balance Sheet

Panel A of table 7 presents the firm's balance sheet position in terms of present values. The futures contracts are entered as both assets and liabilities, leaving equity the same as that shown in panel A of table 2.[15] The futures asset is the present value of the future receipt of a *fixed* amount. The futures liability, on the other hand, is the present value of the *expected* cost of covering the futures contract given the structure of interest rates on September 15. Panels B and C illus-

trate the effect on the present values of the firm's assets, liabilities and equity if, immediately following the above transactions, interest rates rise unexpectedly (panel B) or fall unexpectedly (panel C) by 200 basis points.

An unexpected increase in interest rates causes the present value of the loan to fall relative to the present value of the liability. By itself, this would cause a reduction in the firm's equity. At the same time, however, the increase in interest rates generates a positive expected net cash flow from the futures contracts, which, of course, has a positive net present value. Other things the same, this causes equity to rise. The net effect of both changes is that equity remains unchanged. The reverse occurs if interest rates decline by 200 basis points.

This hedge has eliminated the firm's exposure to interest rate risk. In contrast, recall that a 200 basis-point change in the interest rate causes the equity of the unhedged firm in table 2 to change by about 75 percent.

Hedging as a "Profit Center"

The purpose of hedging is to reduce the variance of a firm owner's wealth. In a textbook example of a perfect hedge, the gain or loss from a short position in the futures market will offset exactly the compensating loss or gain on the spot assets and liabilities held by the firm. A hedge is constructed because — in the presence of an uncertain future — wealth is greater if the institution foregoes a profit stream that is higher on average (if it goes unhedged) in exchange for a profit stream that is lower on average (by the cost of the hedging operations) but more certain.

Some portfolio managers, however, lose sight of this fact and assume speculative positions in the futures market with the objective of earning profits from the position if interest rates change in their favor. While speculative positions in futures (or spot instruments) can increase earnings, they can have the opposite effect as well.

One potentially significant danger in the use of futures contracts to hedge interest rate risk is that the firm may misunderstand the nature of the hedging function. Trading futures for hedging is *not* intended to generate profits from the trading itself. Rather, its purpose is to establish futures positions so that the owner's wealth is held constant; this will occur if the increase (decrease) in the value of the firm's spot holdings of assets and liabilities is offset exactly by the loss (gain) in the futures market.

---

[15]Strictly speaking, futures contracts entered into by member banks of the Federal Reserve System are treated as balance sheet memoranda items. These are reported on Schedule L, Commitments and Contingencies, of the Call Report. Hence, for accounting purposes, futures contracts do not affect the assets and liabilities of the firm until the contracts are exercised.

Table 7

Interest Rate Changes and the Present Value of a Hedged Firm

Panel A: Initial Conditions (9/15/84)

Present Values

Assets:		Liabilities:	
Loan: $1,000.00/1.10 =	$ 909.09	90-day CD: $981.82/1.10 =	$ 892.56
Contracted Future Receipts		Expected Cost of Covering the Futures Contract:	
December Future: $976.45/(1.10)^{25} =	953.46	December Future: $976.45/(1.10)^{25} =	953.46
March Future: $976.45/(1.10)^{50} =	931.01	March Future: $976.45/(1.10)^{50} =	931.01
June Future: $976.45/(1.10)^{75} =	909.09	June Future: $976.45/(1.10)^{75} =	909.09
	3,702.65		3,686.12
		Equity:	16.53
			3,702.65

Panel B: All Interest Rates Rise by 200 Basis Points

Note: The expected cost of covering each contract falls to $1,000/(1.12)^{25} = $972.07 while the contracted future receipt remains unchanged.

Present Values

Assets:		Liabilities:	
Loan: $1,000.00/1.12 =	$ 892.86	90-day CD: $995.42/1.12 =	$ 888.77
Contracted Future Receipts:		Expected Cost of Covering Futures Contract:	
December Future: $976.45/(1.12)^{25} =	949.17	December Future: $972.07/(1.12)^{25} =	944.92
March Future: $976.45/(1.12)^{50} =	922.66	March Future: $972.07/(1.12)^{50} =	918.52
June Future: $976.45/(1.12)^{75} =	896.88	June Future: $972.07/(1.12)^{75} =	892.86
	3,661.57		3,645.07
		Equity:	16.50
			3,661.57

Panel C: All Interest Rates Fall by 200 Basis Points

Note: The expected cost of covering each contract rises to $1,000/(1.08)^{25} = $980.94

Present Values

Assets:		Liabilities:	
Loan: $1,000.00/1.08 =	$ 925.93	90-day CD: $968.15/1.08 =	$ 896.44
Contracted Future Receipts:		Expected Cost of Covering Futures Contract:	
December Future: $976.45/(1.08)^{25} =	957.84	December Future: $980.94/(1.08)^{25} =	962.25
March Future: $976.45/(1.08)^{50} =	939.59	March Future: $980.94/(1.08)^{50} =	943.91
June Future: $976.45/(1.08)^{75} =	921.68	June Future: $980.94/(1.08)^{75} =	925.92
	3,745.04		3,728.52
		Equity:	16.52
			3,745.04

Real World Complications in Hedging

The examples in tables 6 and 7 simplify real world problems to illustrate the basic concepts of interest rate risk and hedging. In practice, a number of complicating factors will make the construction of a hedge considerably more difficult.

The first difficulty to note is that the calculation of present values for a large portfolio composed of many different assets and liabilities will require a great deal of information. Moreover, resources will be needed to estimate interest elasticities (or durations). And, unlike our examples, which are based on single-payment loans and deposits of known durations, firms face the additional problem of loans that are subject to early payment and deposits that are subject to early withdrawal.

Even with a good estimate of its exposure to interest rate risk, firms will face practical problems in implementing a hedge. Typically, liquidity is very thin in futures contracts dated for delivery more than nine months in the future. Firms also are not likely to find futures contracts for the exact dollar amount they wish to hedge or for the specific spot asset or liability being hedged. For example, money market certificates (MMCs) might be hedged with Treasury bill futures. It is possible, however, that interest rates on MMCs and Treasury bill futures will not move by identical amounts or in the same direction, an event that will reduce the effectiveness of a hedge. When the futures contract does not correspond exactly to the spot commodity, as in this case, the firm is exposed to "basis" risk.

Firms also face the possibility of changes in the slope of the yield curve; that is, unlike our examples, short- and long-term rates could change by differing amounts. If, for example, long rates increased 200 basis points but short rates increased only 100 basis points, the change in the difference between the present values of spot assets and spot liabilities would not be completely offset by a change in the difference between the present values of the futures asset and liability. True hedges, however, are implemented under the expectation of no change in the yield curve's slope. It is easy to see, therefore, that hedging does not eliminate this source of risk.

SUMMARY

Higher and more variable interest rates have increased the risk faced by financial institutions associated with attracting deposit funds and extending credit. This article presented some simple examples of techniques that can isolate and quantify sources of a financial institution's exposure to interest rate risk. The discussion also described how financial futures can be used to reduce this risk. A simple hedging example indicated that relatively conservative use of futures markets can have a potentially large impact on reducing risk exposure. The use of futures trading is a threat to the long-run performance of a financial firm only if applied in a manner inconsistent with hedging.

REFERENCES

Asay, Michael R., Gişela A. Gonzalez, and Benjamin Wolkowitz. "Financial Futures, Bank Portfolio Risk, and Accounting," *Journal of Futures Markets* (Winter 1981), pp. 607–18.

Bierwag, G. O., George G. Kaufman and Alden Toevs. "Bond Portfolio Immunization and Stochastic Process Risk," *Journal of Bank Research* (Winter 1983), pp. 282–91.

Booth, James R., Richard L. Smith, and Richard W. Stolz. "Use of Interest Rate Futures by Financial Institutions," *Journal of Bank Research* (Spring 1984), pp. 15–20.

Carrington, Tim, and Daniel Hertzberg. "Financial Institutions Are Showing the Strain of a Decade of Turmoil," *Wall Street Journal* (September 5, 1984).

Federal Home Loan Bank Act of 1932. Public No. 304, 72 Cong., HR 12280.

Gay, G. D., and R. W. Kolb. "The Management of Interest Rate Risk," *Journal of Portfolio Management* (Winter 1983), pp. 65–70.

Gottlieb, Paul M. "New York and Connecticut Permit Insurers to Use Futures and Options: A Comparison," Chicago Mercantile Exchange *Market Perspectives* (May/June 1984), pp. 1–6.

Hicks, J. R. *Value and Capital* (Oxford: Clarendon Press, 1939).

Kaufman, George G. "Measuring and Managing Interest Rate Risk: A Primer," Federal Reserve Bank of Chicago *Economic Perspectives* (January-February 1984), pp. 16–29.

Koch, Donald L., Delores W. Steinhauser and Pamela Whigham. "Financial Futures as a Risk Management Tool for Banks and S&Ls," Federal Reserve Bank of Atlanta *Economic Review* (September 1982), pp. 4–14.

Kolb, R. W. *Interest Rate Futures: A Comprehensive Introduction* (Robert F. Dame, Inc., 1982).

Kolb, Robert W., Stephen G. Timme and Gerald D. Gay. "Macro Versus Micro Futures Hedges at Commercial Banks," *Journal of Futures Markets* (Spring 1984), pp. 47–54.

Lower, Robert C. *Futures Trading and Financial Institutions: The Regulatory Environment* (Chicago Mercantile Exchange, 1982).

Morris, John. "FASB Issues Rules for Futures Accounting," *American Banker* (August 24, 1984).

Olson, Ronald L. and Donald G. Simonson. "Gap Management and Market Rate Sensitivity in Banks," *Journal of Bank Research* (Spring 1982), pp. 53–58.

Samuelson, P. A. "The Effect of Interest Rate Increases on the Banking System," *American Economic Review* (March 1944), pp. 16–27.

Santoni, G. J. "Interest Rate Risk and the Stock Prices of Financial Institutions," this *Review* (August/September 1984).

Simonson, Donald G., and George H. Hempel. "Improving Gap Management for Controlling Interest Rate Risk," *Journal of Bank Research* (Summer 1982), pp. 109–15.

Stigum, Marcia. *Money Market Calculations: Yields, Break-Evens and Arbitrage* (Dow Jones-Irwin, 1981).

Toevs, Alden. "Gap Management: Managing Interest Rate Risk in Banks and Thrifts," *Federal Reserve Bank of San Francisco Economic Review* (Spring 1983), pp. 20–35.

Wardrep, Bruce N. and James F. Buch. "The Efficacy of Hedging with Financial Futures: A Historical Perspective," *Journal of Futures Markets* (Fall 1982), pp. 243–54.

GLOSSARY

Basis	The price or yield difference between a futures contract and the cash instrument being hedged
Basis point	1/100 of 1 percent
Delivery month	A specified month within which delivery may be made under the terms of the futures contract
Discount yield	The ratio of the annualized discount to the par value
Evening up	Buying or selling to offset or liquidate an existing market position
Futures contract	A standardized contract, traded on an organized exchange, to buy or sell a fixed quantity of a defined commodity at a price agreed to now but delivered in the future
Gap analysis	A technique to measure interest rate sensitivity
Hedge	An attempt to reduce risk by taking a futures position opposite to an existing cash position
Interest rate swap	The exchange of two financial assets (liabilities) which have the same present value but which generate different streams of receipts (payments)
Long hedge	A hedge in which the futures contract is bought (long position)
Macro-hedge	A hedge designed to reduce the net portfolio risk of an organization
Micro-hedge	A hedge designed to reduce the risk of holding a particular asset or liability
Open interest	The number of open futures contracts, that is, unliquidated purchases *or* sales of futures contracts
Short hedge	A hedge that involves selling a futures contract (short position)
Spot price	The current market price of the actual physical commodity

Article Seven

Interest Rate Swaps: Risk and Regulation

By J. Gregg Whittaker

The rapid growth of "off-balance sheet" activities by banks in recent years has given rise to a number of concerns. These activities create commitments for banks that are not reflected on their balance sheets as either assets or liabilities. As a result, it is often difficult for investors, regulators, and even bank managers to determine the risk exposure of banks engaging in such activities. One of the most rapidly growing of these activities is the interest rate swap.

While enhancing financial market efficiency in many respects, interest rate swaps give rise to new risks for banks. Bank regulators are concerned that the role played by banks in the swap market may lead banks to incur too much risk or risk for which they are not adequately compensated. Current regulatory capital requirements for banks apply only to risks arising from a bank's assets. And since swaps are not considered an asset and

J. Gregg Whittaker is an assistant economist at the Federal Reserve Bank of Kansas City. Bryon Higgins, a vice president and economist at the bank, supervised the preparation of the article.

do not affect the balance sheet, they can lead to increased risk exposure without requiring the bank to hold additional amounts of capital. Therefore, the potential may exist for excessive risk-taking and underpricing of this highly leveraged instrument. Bank regulators have recently proposed revising capital guidelines to help control these risks.

The first section of the article explains how interest rate swaps work and documents the recent growth of the swap market. The second section explores the risks of swaps and risk management techniques. The third section discusses proposed regulatory changes and other possible improvements for limiting the risks for banks involved in interest rate swaps.

What are interest rate swaps?

An interest rate swap is a financial transaction in which fixed interest is exchanged for floating interest of the same currency. Swaps were originally liability based exchanges of interest payment streams on debt obligations. More recently, however, asset based swaps have been arranged as well, exchanges of interest income streams on assets. Swaps are among the most versatile of all financial instruments. They can be used to obtain cheaper funds or to manage interest rate risks. All swaps are based on one central principle: one participant exchanging an advantage in one credit market for an advantage available to another participant in a different credit market. The advantage can be reduced costs or greater availability of funds. Swaps enable borrowers to tap markets where they can obtain the best relative terms and then swap obligations to obtain the desired interest rate structure.

Reasons for swaps

Some interest rate swaps are arranged to reduce borrowing costs through financial arbitrage. There are opportunities for financial arbitrage when borrowing costs for the same borrowers differ across various credit markets. For instance, bond market investors are very concerned about credit quality because they are lending for long periods at a fixed interest rate. Because there is no opportunity to adjust the lending rate to reflect changes in the financial condition of the bond issuer, the yield on fixed-rate bonds typically includes a large risk premium for bonds issued by firms that are perceived as having a relatively high risk of default. The risk premium for such firms is much smaller in floating-rate banking markets where lenders can adjust the lending rate in line with the financial condition of the borrower. Therefore, while a firm with a lower credit rating has a comparative advantage in raising short-term floating-rate debt, a firm with a high credit rating has a comparative advantage in raising long-term fixed-rate debt. As a result, a bond issue in conjunction with an interest rate swap can lower the cost of floating-rate funds for a highly creditworthy company. The lower rated firm that must pay a relatively large premium for borrowing in the bond market can use a swap to

lower its costs by borrowing short-term floating-rate funds and swapping for the fixed-rate payments of the more creditworthy firm.[1]

Interest rate swaps can also be used to reduce interest rate risk. For example, savings and loan institutions (S&L's) have traditionally funded fixed-rate mortgage loans with short-term deposits. The danger of this kind of maturity mismatch was demonstrated in the late 1970s and early 1980s by the heavy losses S&L's sustained as a result of the rise in interest rates. An S&L can now swap its floating-rate interest payments on short-term deposits for fixed interest payments, or it could swap its fixed-rate interest income on mortgage loans for floating-rate interest income. By doing so, it better matches the income stream on its assets to the payment stream on its liabilities, thereby reducing the risk of a capital loss due to an unexpected increase in interest rates.

Participants in swap markets

There are two classes of participants in the swap market: end-users and intermediaries. End-users are those who want to swap their interest payment stream for a different type of payment stream. Intermediaries help arrange the swaps, collect and disburse the payments that are swapped, and assume the risk of default by end-users.

A variety of end-users participate in the swap market. International lending agencies were among the first to engage in swaps. Sovereign governments and their agencies also were early participants. Most recently, nonfinancial corpora-

---

[1] The lower rated firm does, however, incur rollover risk—the risk that its financial condition will deteriorate to the point that short-term financing is either unavailable or available only at higher rates. Even if the firm could continue to borrow, the floating-rate interest it receives in the swap could be insufficient to cover the higher costs of its floating-rate debt.

tions and many financial institutions have begun participating in the swap market as well.

The role of large commercial banks and securities firms as intermediaries has increased in recent years. When the swap market began in the early 1980s, intermediaries served merely as brokers. In arranging swaps between end-users, intermediaries had the obvious disadvantage of having to find end-users with equal but opposite needs. Recognizing the limitation of arranging swaps that required a "double coincidence of wants," intermediaries began playing a larger role.

Intermediaries now maintain inventories of standardized swaps and some even quote prices at which they will buy and sell swaps from qualified end-users. Instead of just arranging swaps between end-users, intermediaries themselves now enter into swaps with end-users even before finding offsetting swaps with other end-users. What may appear to be a single swap between two end-users is actually two swaps in which the intermediary itself has a contractual obligation to each of the end-users. Intermediaries have thus come to play the role of dealers, increasing the liquidity of the swap market and making it more convenient for end-users to arrange swaps.

Intermediaries earn fees for arranging and servicing swaps. The fees depend on the complexity of the swap agreement and, therefore, on the amount of services the intermediary provides. Fees on a standard interest rate swap usually range from 7 to 12 basis points a year but can be higher for more complex swaps, especially those tailored specifically to the needs of the customer. Since swaps are frequently arranged in conjunction with the initial borrowing of funds, the intermediary may cut fees on the swap to get other business from the customer. For example, a bank may charge a lower fee on a swap in exchange for the lead underwriter position in an accompanying Eurobond issue.[2]

How swaps work

An intermediary can arrange a swap that allows the end-users to reduce their borrowing costs or better match their interest payments with their expected income streams. The interest payments to be swapped are based on a "notional" amount of principal—notional in that the principal is not actually exchanged but merely serves as the basis for calculating the amount each end-user pays. Only the interest payments are swapped.

An example shows how both end-users can benefit from an interest rate swap. Suppose company XYZ, a nonfinancial firm with a low credit rating, seeks fixed-rate dollar funds for a long-term investment project, while Eurobank, a bank that has a high credit rating, seeks floating-rate dollar funds to finance its short-term loan portfolio. Since Eurobank has a higher credit rating than XYZ, it can borrow funds of any type at lower rates than those available to XYZ. Assume company XYZ can borrow floating-rate funds at 1 percent over LIBOR (the London Interbank Offering Rate) while Eurobank can borrow at 0.5 percent over LIBOR. Further assume that Eurobank can borrow at 12 percent in the bond market while XYZ can borrow at a 14 percent fixed rate. While Eurobank has an advantage in both credit markets, it has a greater advantage in one market than in the other. Compared with Eurobank, XYZ must pay a two percentage point premium for fixed-rate funds but only a 0.5 percentage point premium for floating-rate funds. This difference creates a borrowing wedge that can be exploited through an interest rate swap.

Chart 1 shows the mechanics of an interest rate swap. Eurobank issues seven-year fixed-rate Eurobonds at 12 percent, and XYZ takes out a

---

[2] A Eurobond is a bond issued outside the confines of any national capital market and may or may not be denominated in the currency of the issuer.

CHART 1
Interest rate swap

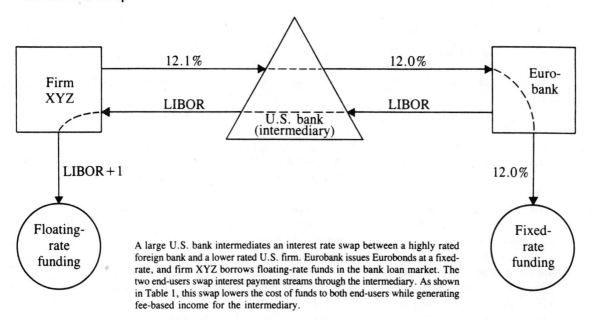

A large U.S. bank intermediates an interest rate swap between a highly rated foreign bank and a lower rated U.S. firm. Eurobank issues Eurobonds at a fixed-rate, and firm XYZ borrows floating-rate funds in the bank loan market. The two end-users swap interest payment streams through the intermediary. As shown in Table 1, this swap lowers the cost of funds to both end-users while generating fee-based income for the intermediary.

floating-rate bank loan on which it pays LIBOR plus 1 percent. Eurobank and XYZ then swap interest payments through the intermediary. XYZ pays Eurobank's fixed-rate obligation of 12 percent, plus an intermediation fee of 0.1 percent to the large U.S. bank. Eurobank pays the LIBOR part of XYZ's floating-rate interest payment, leaving XYZ to pay the remaining 1 percent. Thus, Eurobank has a floating-rate obligation to pay the LIBOR rate, while XYZ has a total or "all-in" fixed-rate obligation of 13.1 percent (12 percent + 0.1 percent + 1 percent).

As a result of the swap, both Eurobank and XYZ are able to obtain the interest rate structures they desire and to reduce their borrowing costs. Eurobank is financing its floating-rate loan portfolio with floating-rate funds, while XYZ has locked in the borrowing cost to finance its long-term investment project by swapping for fixed-rate funds. And, as shown in Table 1, both have

done so at reduced costs. The swap enables Eurobank to reduce its cost of floating-rate debt by 50 basis points from LIBOR + 0.5 percent to LIBOR. XYZ's cost of fixed-rate debt has fallen from 14.0 percent without the swap to 13.1 percent with the swap, a savings of 90 basis points.

The intermediary earns an intermediation fee based on the spread between the fixed rate paid and the fixed rate received. Swap prices are quoted as a spread over a fixed-rate index versus a floating-rate index, such as the seven-year Treasury bond rate plus 60 basis points versus the six-month LIBOR rate. The bank gives a bid price to the floating-rate payer and an offer price to the fixed-rate payer. The bid is the fixed rate that the bank pays in a swap and the offer is the fixed rate it receives. In Chart 1, the bid is 12 percent and the offer is 12.1 percent. The intermediary's profit is the offer minus the bid, or ten

TABLE 1
Analysis of swap payments

XYZ's cost		Intermediary's fees		Eurobank's costs	
Payment on debt:		Receipt from XYZ:	12.1%	Payment on debt:	12.0%
LIBOR + 1.0%					
+ Payment to intermediary:	12.1%	− Payment to XYZ: LIBOR		+ Payment to intermediary:	LIBOR
− Receipt from intermediary:	LIBOR	+ Receipt from Eurobank: LIBOR		− Receipt from intermediary:	12.0%
= All-in-cost:	13.1%	− Payment to Eurobank: 12.0%		= All-in-costs:	LIBOR
		= Total Fees: 0.1%			

XYZ's saving				Eurobank's saving	
Best fixed-rate alternative:	14.0%			Best floating-rate alternative: LIBOR + 0.5%	
− Cost with swap:	13.1%			− Cost with swap:	LIBOR
= Total saving:	0.9%			= Total saving:	0.5%

basis points in this example. Thus, the intermediary earns a profit by arranging a swap while both of the end-users obtain funds at a lower cost.

Growth of swaps

The swap market has grown rapidly in recent years. Virtually nonexistent as late as 1981, the interest rate swap market worldwide grew to about $170 billion of notional principal outstanding by the end of 1985 and to between $350 and $400 billion by the end of 1986.[3] Thus, interest rate swaps have become an important part of the global capital market.

This rapid growth has been due to several factors. A major cause of the dramatic growth has been the increased demand for protection against interest rate risk. Heightened interest rate volatility has caused bank customers to try new techniques for matching the interest rate exposures of their assets and their liabilities. Increased com-

---

[3] Data for 1985 were taken from the International Swap Dealers Association (ISDA) 1985 annual survey. Preliminary data for 1986 were kindly provided by Kenneth McCormick, cochairman of the ISDA. Since the 1986 annual survey has not been completed, the 1986 data are based on quarterly statistical data gathered throughout the year by the ISDA.

petition also has stimulated innovation. Worldwide deregulation in the banking industry has increased the competition banks face on all sides, at home and abroad. Competition has been further stimulated by technological advances in telecommunications and computer systems that have increased international financial mobility. As a result, banks have tried to find new ways of generating income, while borrowers have sought lower borrowing costs and protection from interest rate risk.

Risks and risk management

The role of banks as intermediaries in swap transactions has exposed them to new and varied risks. The risks arise because, under certain circumstances, swaps can cause banks to suffer capital losses. There is also concern that banks may be underpricing their services and are not being adequately compensated for the risks they bear. However, banks have developed methods for limiting the risks involved in intermediating swaps.

Intermediation of a swap requires that the bank enter into a financial contract with each of the end-users. In the example above, the U.S. bank that arranges the swap between company XYZ and Eurobank has a contractual obligation to each. Instead of the two end-users agreeing to exchange interest payments with one another directly, they each enter into separate contracts with the U.S. bank acting as the intermediary. Firm XYZ agrees to pay the U.S. bank a fixed-rate stream of payments in exchange for the floating-rate stream from the bank, and Eurobank agrees to pay the U.S. bank a floating-rate stream of payments in exchange for the fixed-rate stream from the U.S. bank. Neither end-user has any obligation to the other. They may not even know the other's identity. The intermediary, in effect, enters into two separate contracts that are offsetting except for the fee earned for serving as the intermediary.

Their role as intermediaries between end-users in interest rate swaps exposes banks to two types of risk, price risk and credit risk.

Price risk

Price risk occurs from banks "warehousing" swaps—from arranging a swap contract with one end-user without having arranged an offsetting swap with another end-user. Until an offsetting swap is arranged, the bank has an open swap position and is vulnerable to an adverse change in swap prices.

The most common reason for a change in swap prices is a change in interest rates—a change that could cause the bank to suffer a loss on its swap. For example, if the bank has an open swap in which it pays XYZ a variable interest rate in exchange for a fixed interest rate, an increase in market interest rates would lead to an increase in the payments the bank makes but no change in the payments it receives. In this case, the bank incurs a capital loss just as it would if it were funding long-term fixed-rate loans with floating-rate deposits. Banks warehouse only a small amount of swaps relative to the total amount of swaps outstanding, however. As a result, only a small portion of a bank's total swap portfolio is subject to price risk.

Banks hedge to limit the price risk of an open swap. The predominant means of hedging is to offset an open swap position through the purchase or sale of Treasury securities. A bank that is a fixed-rate payer in an open interest rate swap can limit the interest rate risk of that position by buying a Treasury security whose price will change by the same amount as the price of the swap, but in the opposite direction. With this hedge, an unexpected change in interest rates will not affect the market value of the banks' overall portfolio because the resulting change in the price of the swap will be offset by a corresponding change in the price of the Treasury security. Because buying Treasury securities outright requires the bank to commit capital, however, banks often use the futures market rather than the cash market to hedge their open swap positions with maturities short enough to be offset with a futures contract.[4]

Although hedging through use of Treasury securities is widespread, it is difficult to entirely offset the risk of an open swap position in this way. It is difficult to design a position in Treasury securities—cash or futures—that exactly offsets the interest rate risk of a swap. In practice, banks can offset only a portion of the price risk of a swap through hedging in the Treasury securities market. For this reason, banks are usually reluctant to have substantial open swap positions on their books for long periods.

Credit risk

Credit risk is the main concern of regulators and banks. Banks' credit risk exists on all swaps in which the bank is the intermediary between two end-users. Suppose a bank enters into two perfectly matched, offsetting swaps with XYZ and Eurobank. If interest rates change, the value of one swap will fall while the value of the other rises by an equal amount, providing the bank with a hedge against price risk. But if one of the end-users defaults, the bank loses the hedging value of the offsetting swap and may suffer a capital loss.

Consider again the previous example where the bank pays fixed-rate interest to Eurobank in exchange for floating-rate interest, while the bank pays floating-rate interest to XYZ in exchange for fixed-rate interest. If interest rates fall and XYZ subsequently defaults, the bank is left with an obligation to continue making the agreed upon fixed-rate payments to Eurobank, but is now

receiving less in floating-rate payments. On the other hand, suppose that Eurobank, the floating-rate payer, defaults after interest rates have risen. The bank is now left with an obligation to pay XYZ the higher floating rate, but continues to receive the same fixed rate. In both cases, the bank serving as intermediary would incur a capital loss. Changes in interest rates, therefore, can cause losses on banks' swap activities even if the bank immediately offsets one swap with another. Because losses can be incurred in this case only if one of the end-users defaults, this type of risk is called credit risk.

Two of the most critical aspects of managing credit risk in the swap market are the banks' pricing procedures and the degree of portfolio diversification. Banks must make sure that the price of the service they provide adequately reflects the risk inherent in the arrangement. Just as investors demand a higher yield on bonds issued by a firm with a Baa credit rating than on commercial paper issued by a firm with a Aaa credit rating, banks must charge more for long-term swaps with end-users that have a low credit rating than for short-term swaps with end-users that have a high credit rating. In both cases, the risk of entering into a financial contract varies directly with the length of the contract and the creditworthiness of the other party to the contract. An individual risky swap need not endanger the financial position of the bank as long as the bank is adequately compensated for the risk and has diversified its swap portfolio so that default by any one customer or group of customers does not substantially impair the bank's earnings or capital position.

The credit risk of interest rate swaps can also be limited by the enforcement of strict credit standards. Perhaps the most important means of limiting risk is to enter into swaps only with creditworthy customers. Typically, the credit department of a bank must agree to the swap before the contract is made. Moreover, banks ordinarily monitor the customer's financial position through-

---

[4] See *Recent Innovations in International Banking*, Bank for International Settlements, April 1986, p. 48.

out the life of the swap. Banks may require less creditworthy customers to post collateral or use other credit enhancements that further reduce the risk to the bank in case of a default. The amount of protection collateralization provides is uncertain, however, because the legal status of collateral posted against swaps has not been tested in court. And as the swap market continues to grow, regulators are concerned that credit standards may deteriorate as banks try to accommodate more and often less creditworthy customers.

Regulation of swaps

Regulators are concerned about the risks involved in swap intermediation. However, prohibiting bank participation in the swap market could reduce financial market efficiency. To strike a balance, regulators are studying ways to impose capital requirements on banks' swap activities.

Reasons for concern

Even though banks have developed methods of limiting the risks of swaps, concerns have been expressed about the effect swaps have on the safety of banks and the soundness of the financial system. Some of these concerns result from the rapid growth of swaps. The $400 billion increase in interest rate swaps over the past six years raises questions about whether end-users, financial regulators, and the banks themselves fully understand the risks inherent in swaps. The questions are even more troublesome because nearly all the growth has occurred during a period of declining interest rates. The risk characteristics of interest rate swaps may change when interest rates increase. Moreover, a recession could cause financial stresses that could lead to defaults on swaps with a cumulative effect on the financial position of intermediaries. Although such issues cannot be resolved now, planning for such adverse circumstances seems wise.

Another concern is that banks, possibly unfamiliar with the full range of risks that could be encountered, may be too aggressive in pricing interest rate swaps. Only if the financial institutions offering new financial instruments fully understand the risks inherent in those instruments can the pricing fully reflect the risks. However, given the disagreements among the banks themselves regarding the appropriate means of measuring risk and pricing swaps, regulators are concerned that banks may be underpricing their services. The interest rate swap market has become so competitive in recent years that the margins for banks acting as intermediaries have been substantially reduced. There is a fear that to gain market share in interest rate swaps, intermediaries may be underpricing the services they provide—that the return for intermediating interest rate swaps may not be commensurate with the risks.

This concern is exacerbated by existing strains on the banking system caused by losses from loans to less developed countries, energy firms, and the agricultural and real estate sectors. Losses incurred in traditional banking business may make some banks overzealous in trying to earn fees from off-balance sheet activities. The temptation to do so is more acute because the deposit insurance system, which bases insurance fees on total assets rather than on the risk of the activities, can encourage excessive risk-taking by banks.[5] Although there is no evidence that banks engaging in swaps have suffered substantial losses as a result of these activities, there is a danger that new entrants into the swap market or existing participants in adverse financial circumstances might be too aggressive in seeking out new swap business to compensate for losses in traditional lending activities.

---

[5] For a detailed discussion of the moral hazard problem, see William R. Keeton, "Deposit Insurance and the Deregulation of Deposit Rates," *Economic Review*, Federal Reserve Bank of Kansas City, April 1984.

A further concern arises from the nature of swaps themselves. Interest rate swaps can change the risk exposure of end-users or intermediaries. This capability can be used to reduce interest rate risk by hedging existing assets or liabilities. But the same capability also could be used to speculate on future movements in interest rates. A bank that had a "view" on the direction of interest rate movements could use the highly leveraged method of entering into unmatched interest rate swaps to bet the money of shareholders, uninsured depositors, and the deposit insurance system in the hope of earning large profits. But the counterpart of the chance for making large profits is the risk of incurring large losses. For example, a bank that believes that interest rates will rise could easily take an open position in which it is the fixed-rate payer on a substantial amount of swaps. If interest rates were to subsequently fall, however, the bank would suffer a significant capital loss.

Financial market safety and efficiency

One possible response to such concerns about the effect of interest rate swaps on the safety and soundness of the banking system could be for regulators to prohibit bank participation in the swap market altogether. However, such an outright prohibition would place banks at a disadvantage relative to securities firms in competing for the business of corporate customers with increasingly complex needs to raise funds in capital markets. Large bank holding companies are engaging increasingly in a wide range of capital market activities, both in the domestic credit markets and in foreign markets. Inability to offer interest rate swaps in conjunction with borrowing in Eurodollar markets, for example, could erode banks' earnings from capital market services for their customers. Moreover, inability to provide a full range of services could impair long-standing customer relationships between banks and corporate customers.

Prohibiting banks from participating in interest rate swaps could also reduce the safety of financial markets. Interest rate swaps can contribute to the safety of financial markets by providing a means of hedging interest rate risk. Financial futures contracts do not ordinarily extend beyond two years. Therefore, interest rate swaps provide the most efficient method for both financial and nonfinancial businesses to guard against the adverse effects of interest rate volatility.

Swaps can also enhance the efficiency of financial markets by allowing banks to "unbundle" risks that have traditionally been inseparable, allowing risks to be redistributed to those best able to bear them. For instance, end-users can use swaps to manage the interest rate risk of their portfolios and transfer the credit risk of the swap itself to the intermediary, who may be in a better position to manage the credit risk.[6] More generally, swaps can be used to improve the efficiency of financial markets by reducing borrowing costs. Borrowers can use swaps to improve the terms of loans and increase the availability of funds by tapping a wider range of credit markets.[7]

Proposed regulation

To strike a balance between concern over the risk of interest rate swaps and recognition of the valuable functions swaps serve, the bank regu-

---

[6] While swaps may improve the efficiency of financial markets, they may also increase the risk borne by the banking system by transferring credit risk from the end-users to the banks as discussed in the preceding section.

[7] Moreover, several studies suggest that long-term fixed-rate financing may create incentives for low-rated firms to underinvest and shift from low-risk to high-risk investments. Short-term floating-rate financing eliminates these adverse tendencies but exposes firms to interest rate risk. Interest rate swaps eliminate both problems. See Larry D. Wall, "Interest Rate Swaps in an Agency Theoretic Model with Uncertain Interest Rates," Federal Reserve Bank of Atlanta Working Paper 86-6.

do not consider swaps to be material and do not include them in the financial statements accessible to the general public. As a result, disclosure of the magnitude of swap activities and of the resulting risk exposure is currently lacking.[10]

Heightened reporting standards would help ensure that swaps do not cause undue risks. The Financial Accounting Standards Board's emerging issues task force is currently considering the problems posed by off-balance sheet activities, including swaps, and is expected to propose accounting modifications. Modifying standards to require that the effect of swaps on a bank's interest rate sensitivity, liquidity, and credit exposure could also help regulators and investors assess a bank's strength.[11] U.S. banks since 1983 have been required to disclose the amount of off-balance sheet activities, including swaps, in their financial statements filed quarterly with bank regulatory agencies, and many banks have voluntarily increased disclosures of swaps and other off-balance sheet activities in their annual reports. But disclosing the amount of swap activity is not in itself sufficient to determine the degree of risk associated with that activity.

Uniformity of reporting standards is, therefore, also necessary. Unless banks adhere to uniform reporting standards, increased disclosures alone may be insufficient to end the confusion regarding off-balance sheet risk. Bankers and bank regulators should agree on a set of disclosure and exposure measurement standards for swaps. An industry-sponsored dictionary of off-balance sheet risk analysis has been suggested by some. One obvious measure to be used uniformly for disclosure of swap-related exposure is the exposure measurement that will ultimately be used by bank regulatory agencies for capital adequacy purposes. Such actions would serve to reduce confusion and enhance market safety.

Self-regulation in the swap market is another complementary way of dealing with risk. The commercial banks and securities firms most actively engaged in the swap market have formed an organization to standardize the terms of swap contracts and ensure good business practices in the swap market.[12] This organization is the International Swaps Dealers Association (ISDA). While the ISDA has made substantial progress, the methods of measuring and pricing risk still vary widely among swap market participants. Moreover, internal controls, such as prompt completion of swap documentation, are inadequate at times. Continued progress by the ISDA in resolving these and other problems would further reduce the risks in the swap market and reaffirm the commitment of swap market participants to the safety of financial markets.

Conclusion

Swaps are now an integral and generally beneficial part of the financial system. These activities are the result of a number of factors, including increased competition in banking and increased demands for protection from interest rate risk. Swaps offer banks an attractive array of fee-generating and portfolio management techniques, but also expose banks to new and varied risks. The leverage capacity of swaps— and other concerns—has caused bank regulatory agencies to consider these activities for inclusion in a risk-based capital adequacy proposal.

[10] For a further discussion of accounting for interest rate swaps, see *Recent Innovations in International Banking*, Bank for International Settlements, April 1986, pp. 57-59.

[11] See Kenneth F. Cooper, "Coming to Grips with Off-Balance Sheet Risks," *The Bankers Magazine*, November-December 1985.

[12] International Swap Dealers Association, Inc., *Code of Standard Wording, Assumptions and Provisions for Swaps*, 1985.

latory agencies have proposed regulatory changes to help control the risks from swaps. The Board of Governors of the Federal Reserve System has requested public comment on a proposed risk-based capital framework for banks and bank holding companies.[8] The proposal is the result of an agreement between the U.S. bank regulatory agencies and the Bank of England. Goals of the proposal include making regulatory capital requirements more sensitive to differences in the risk of banking institutions and assessing capital requirements on certain off-balance sheet activities, such as interest rate swaps.

Under the proposal, banks will be required to hold capital against assets and certain off-balance sheet commitments in proportion to each item's credit risk. The proposed measure, which will supplement existing capital adequacy ratios, imposes a minimum ratio of adjusted primary capital to total risk-weighted assets. The face amount of off-balance sheet items is multiplied by a "credit conversion factor." The resulting amount, along with on-balance sheet assets, is assigned to one of five risk categories according to the relative risk of each asset. A designated percentage of each asset, depending on the risk category to which it is assigned, will be included in calculating risk-weighted assets, which in turn will be used to help determine the capital requirements of the bank.

Regulators are currently evaluating ways of incorporating the risk from swap activities into the proposed measure. Among the issues being considered is how best to convert the credit risk of a swap into an on-balance sheet credit equivalent that can be incorporated into the proposed framework for setting minimum capital requirements for banks.[9]

---

[8] Federal Reserve Board proposal, Docket No. R-0567.

[9] Assessing the degree of risk to banks from their swap activities is difficult, though. The amount of exposure is certainly much

Additional means of limiting risk

Cooperation among the banking regulatory agencies and the Securities and Exchange Commission, which regulates securities firms, regarding new capital guidelines is desirable for controlling the risk of swaps. In addition to commercial banks, large securities firms also play a major role in the swap market. The recent risk-based capital proposal does not apply to securities firms, however, even though the interrelationships among major swap dealers ties the safety of individual swap portfolios to one another. Consequently, regulatory changes for commercial banks alone may not be adequate to ensure that risk in the swap market is properly controlled. Moreover, more stringent requirements for banks than for securities firms raise questions about how level the playing field is for providing financial services.

More complete and more uniform disclosure of risk from swaps would also be desirable. The rules pertaining to the disclosure of banks' swap activities do not ensure adequate reporting of the risks involved. Any activity that may have a "material effect" on the financial condition of the bank should in principle be disclosed in the footnotes of the bank's financial statements. But many accountants in the United States apparently

---

less than the amount of notional principal involved in swaps. Swaps do not involve the risk of the loss of principal but only the risk of being obligated to pay a higher interest rate than is received. Moreover, most swaps are offsetting so that no risk is involved if interest rates change unless one of the end-users defaults. And banks can use interest rate swaps as a hedge against other interest-sensitive assets or liabilities. Furthermore, credit risk in the swap market may not be as extensive as some fear. Unlike default on a conventional loan, the default of an end-user may have no adverse effects on a bank at all. The default of an end-user does not generally lead to a loss for the bank if interest rates do not change, since the bank could enter into another swap on the same terms and restore the lost payment flows. And if interest rates do change, the default of an end-user is just as likely to benefit the bank—by allowing the bank to enter into a new swap on better terms—as to cause a loss.

SECTION TWO

Financial Institutions

The 1980s proved to be a turbulent decade for financial institutions, their customers, and their regulators. Interest rates not only reached record highs but also gyrated dramatically. Businesses and households were subjected to wide swings in the macroeconomy, to sizable changes in the federal tax code, and to boom and bust in major sectors like energy and agriculture. Various major financial regulations were either eased, extended, or abandoned entirely. Even more disturbing were the repercussions of all this turmoil on deposit insurance agencies: By the end of the decade, the federal savings and loan and some state deposit insurance agencies were insolvent. As if this were not enough, technological advances in information processing significantly altered the cost of providing financial services. The readings in this section address the causes and effects of these events.

George J. Benston, in "Deposit Insurance and Bank Failures," surveys the benefits and costs of the present deposit insurance arrangements. The article highlights why banks are special and shows that deposit insurance not only insures depositors against losses but also prevents bank runs, which historically are the major source of bank failures and depositor losses. Though deposit insurance reduces depositors' risks, it also allows banks to raise funds cheaply and to invest in risky projects. Until the 1980s, this practice was kept in check by regulators' restrictions on bank entry, products, prices, and capital, and by regulators' examination and supervision. Many of these regulations have become less desirable and less enforceable in recent years, however. To deal with these difficulties, Benston proposes a number of procedural improvements.

In "FDIC Policies for Dealing with Failed and Troubled Institutions," Daria B. Caliguire and James B. Thomson review both the traditional and the more recent, innovative methods that the deposit insurance agency has used to resolve the problems of failed and failing banks. In general these newer policies have had the longer-term cost of eroding the discipline provided by the financial markets. This undesirable side effect probably contributed to the magnitude of the insolvent bank problem and has led the FDIC to employ even more generous policies. These policies may cost the FDIC and perhaps its ultimate guarantor, the U.S. Treasury, more in the long run than a more market-oriented approach.

"The Thrift Industry: Reconstruction in Progress" by Thomas M. Buynak recounts how macroeconomic and regulatory forces battered the thrift industry. The combination of fixed-rate mortgage assets and short-term, and thus variable-rate, liabilities subjected the industry to heavy losses when interest rates surged in the late 1970s. The article describes how deregulation expanded thrifts' asset holding opportunities and allowed thrifts to pay market rates for their deposits. Though this deregulated environmental permits thrifts to reduce interest rate risk, many thrifts have been slow to seize this opportunity and many still seem willing to accept as much interest rate as they had a decade ago.

Edward J. Kane indicts the government for a "policy crime" in "The Dangers of Capital Forbearance: The Case of the FSLIC and 'Zombie' S&Ls." Their huge losses over the last decade have left hundreds of savings and loans with insufficient net worth to meet regulatory minimums. The policy decision to allow these institutions to continue operation without requiring that they meet the minimums—that is, forbearing the capital requirement—leads to seriously misplaced incentives for the managers and owners of such S&Ls. That policy not only will not resuscitate many of the "living dead" but also will cost taxpayers vastly more when the plug is finally pulled on these institutions. The article explains how such an army of zombies massed and what particular policy problems they pose. After arguing that the current policies are seriously flawed, Kane presents an alternative policy program.

Leonard M. Apcar vividly illustrates how some savings and loans used the expanded opportunities made available by deregulation and what the consequences have been in "Texas S&L Disasters Are Blamed, in Part, On Freewheeling Style." The tale is colorful and disturbing. One Texas institution was twisted into a "personal piggy bank" that financed lavish California homes, owned a fleet of planes, and of the loans it issued, 96 percent were in default when the government finally closed it.

It is widely thought that banks engage in excessive risk-taking because they are not forced to bear the full social costs of such behavior. "A Comparison of Risk-Based Capital and Risk-Based Deposit Insurance" by Robert B. Avery and Terrence M. Belton describes two methods of adjusting regulations for the risks that banks take. Existing regulations make no allowance in either the deposit insurance premium or in the minimum capital requirement that an individual bank faces for the riskiness of its operations. The authors find that each method tends to identify the same banks as being in danger of failing. They also find that either method would reduce bank risk-taking, and therefore is preferable to the current situation.

"Interstate Bank Mergers and competition in Banking" by Paul Calem assesses the effects on local, regional, and national banking markets of the ongoing trend toward interstate banking. The article describes and analyzes how we measure the competitiveness of these various markets. Bank regulators are especially concerned with competition in local markets, since only in those markets is there much chance of competition being reduced. To prevent this, regulators prohibit mergers that threaten local competition. Although the spread of interstate banking will reduce the number of banks, competition in the larger regional and national markets is likely to continue unabated. Bank mergers may also lead to consumers receiving more and better services at competitive prices as larger and more efficient institutions populate the local markets.

The next article, "Country Risk, Portfolio Decisions and Regulation in International Bank Lending" by Ingo Walter, advances the prescient argument that banks should more consistently apply the basic principles of portfolio theory when considering international lending. Walter concedes that the task is difficult; neither the returns nor the risks associated with loans to an individual country are easy to measure, or even to identify. Calculation of the extent to which returns are correlated across countries is also crucial but is even more problematic. Nonetheless, banks are well advised to put their assessments of the returns and risks of loans to various countries on a common footing and to make some allowance for the correlation of these returns across countries.

"Bank Risk from Nonbank Activities" by Elijah Brewer, III, Diana Fortier, and Christine Pavel reviews old evidence and presents new evidence on the amount of risk that nonbank activities imparts to banks. The authors conclude that in general nonbank activities have reduced bank risk. Some activities that are currently permitted do add more risk, however, and some that are not now permitted would reduce risk. Nonetheless the potential for reducing bank risk by diversifying into new activities is limited. One way that regulators can influence bank risk is by limiting the size of the nonbank activities that a bank is permitted to engage in.

''Banking Reform: An Overview of the Restructuring Debate'' by Mitchell Berlin points out that there is broad agreement that banking powers should be expanded, that a limited safety net for depositors be maintained, and that uniform regulations should apply to activities regardless of what institution engages in them. The primary point of disagreement concerns the extent to which a bank, which is covered by the safety net of deposit insurance, can be insulated from its affiliates. Insulation means that when trouble arises in the nonbanking portion of a banking organization, the safety net not extend, directly or indirectly, to it. Though insulation would not naturally evolve, regulations can be used to increase it. The more important issue is whether in practice regulators would refuse to hold out the safety net for a falling organization.

The current arguments over the Glass-Steagall Act, which prohibits a bank from directly conducting commercial and investment banking activities, are aired in ''Uniting Investment and Commercial Banking'' by Michael C. Keeley and Randall J. Pozdena. The article suggests that fundamental economic forces are propelling the drive toward combining these activities. The efficiency gains achieved by such integration are listed as are the relevant public policy issues. The authors discount many of the most often cited objections but contend that there are legitimate reasons for policymakers to be concerned. They dismiss some proposed solutions to the problems, which are largely engendered by the current structure of deposit insurance. They do suggest, however, that either deposit insurance reform or more stringent bank capital regulation would suffice.

''The Securitization of Housing Finance'' by Gordon H. Sellon, Jr. and Deana Van Nahmen traces the evolution of housing finance from the Great Depression until the present. First, the federal government's influential role in shaping mortgage institutions and instruments over this period is chronicled. Then the features of the various types of mortgage-backed securities are described. It is suggested that securitization has contributed to the overall size of the mortgage market and to its geographic efficiency. Securitization has also generated instruments suitable for hedging and liquidity functions. These advances have in turn enabled other institutions to make inroads on the mortgage market previously dominated by S&Ls.

''Taking the Dangers Out of Bank Deregulation'' by Robert E. Litan offers a proposal for fundamentally reorganizing the banking system. The article begins by reviewing why banks are regulated. The intensifying attempts of banks to engage in activities traditionally performed by financial institutions other than banks, and vice versa, is then documented. To resolve the difficulties that arise when banks and their competitors engage in activities that neither group was foreseen participating in, the author suggests that deposit-taking and lending be separated. The deposit-taking side of the organization would hold only extremely safe assets like Treasury bills. Loans would be funded by debt and equity issues, which would not be covered by deposit insurance. The practical details and the objections to such a dramatic recasting of the financial system, as well as the benefits that would flow from it, conclude.

Article Eight

Deposit Insurance and Bank Failures

While a business failure is painful to those whose dreams and hard work are wiped out, most people recognize failure as a necessary aspect of success. This relationship is well summed up in the aphorism, "nothing ventured, nothing gained and nothing lost." Just as important is the healthy measure of restraint provided by the prospect of failure. The possibility and cost of failure can help avert unprofitable ventures and unfortunate errors by providing a powerful incentive for the decision maker to accept the necessity of making painful choices.

Why, then, is bank failure considered to be so terrible that federal deposit insurance is required? In many important respects, a bank failure is less costly than the failure of many other enterprises. The products provided by one bank are similar to those provided by many other institutions. Checking and savings account services usually are available at scores of institutions, including other banks, savings and loan associations, credit unions and stock brokerage firms—even non-local institutions. Mortgages and consumer loans are available from an even greater number of sources, including depository institutions, mortgage companies, consumer loan companies, merchants, and individuals. Business loans are available from local and, for larger companies, non-local

banks and thrifts, insurance companies, factors, and other businesses.

While a bank's customers lose their business relationship with a bank and its knowledge of them, the loss is less than when most other suppliers fail. For example, the failure of a machinery manufacturer could make spare parts, repair and replacement services unavailable. A distributor's failure might require the development of new channels of supply and sources of information about products and reliability. Often the failed enterprise is unique. In contrast, one bank and its products are very much like another. Only for people in one-bank towns might the failure of the sole bank present a serious problem—and then only until the services are offered by another institution.

Because banks are so similar, their employees' skills are transferrable to other financial institutions. The teller in one bank needs little training to work in another. A lending officer can even benefit from a failure if she can bring her customers with her to another bank. In contrast, employees of many other enterprises often have specialized skills of little value except to their company. The only bank employees who really lose from a failure are the top officers. Not only might they be blamed for the bank's collapse,

---

With bank troubles again in the news, deposit insurance is receiving its closest scrutiny since the Depression years. This analysis questions whether a new approach to insuring deposits might be in order—with depository institutions able to choose between several public insuring agencies or even turning to private insuring organizations.

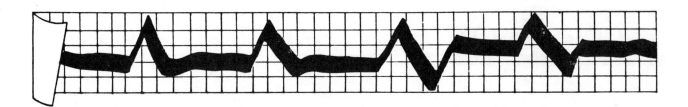

but they will forego the value of the relationships they have established. But, if fear of failure is to be beneficial, this is all to the good.

The shareholders of a failed bank, like its officers, bear costs. But, again, this can prove healthy, for the essence of a private-property, free-enterprise system is that residual owners reap the losses as well as the benefits from their investments. In any event, bank shareholders are in no different position from shareholders of other enterprises. Indeed, when one considers that a bank's fixed assets can be transferred to many other enterprises (including successor banks) at less cost than can the assets of many failed enterprises, a bank's owners face less risk with respect to a failure than most other owners.[1]

This leaves only the creditors, and here is where banks differ importantly from other enterprises. But first the similarities should be mentioned. Creditors are investors with rights over other investors. Debt instruments usually specify the amounts to be paid and the time of payment to their holders, with precedent over the equity holders. But, as with equity holders, creditors accept the risk of non-repayment, which is reflected in their contracts (debt obligations) with the equity holders. Debt holders, like other investors, put up their funds and take their chances. The possibility of failure gives them reason to monitor an enterprise's activities and to insist on a return no worse than they could get for similarly risky investments. In this regard, a bank is a safer investment than many others because its activities are relatively easy to control and comprehend and are subjected to audit. Indeed, losses to creditors (depositors) were not great before the Great Depression. Between 1900 and 1920, deposits in the 1,789 banks that suspended operations averaged 0.10 percent of total deposits each year. Over the 1921-1929 period, 5,712 banks were suspended (an annual percentage of 2.30 of the number active); deposits in these banks averaged 0.42 percent of total

deposits per year. But, after the affairs of the suspended banks were cleared up, the annual losses borne by depositors as a group were only 0.15 percent (Benston (1973), Table II, p. 12).

The Difference Between Banks and Other Enterprises

The important difference is in the demand deposits form of credit. Demand deposits and savings deposits that actually can be withdrawn on demand are much more than investments in banks. These are assets that permit depositors to effect transactions at relatively low cost while providing a means of making investments in the amounts and for the periods desired. Because deposits and withdrawals tend to offset each other, bankers learned hundreds of years ago that they could invest a large proportion of these funds in longer maturity, usually higher yielding assets. This combination of instant possible withdrawal for individual depositors and relative stability of the total of funds invested by depositors as a group gives rise to both profitability and risk in banking.

Unlike bank demand deposits, creditors of other enterprises cannot withdraw their investments when they wish. If a bondholder of an ordinary corporation believes the corporation may be unable to repay the debt as promised, the most that person can do is sell the bond before the purchaser learns the bad news. The bondholder cannot get the corporation to repay the bond until it is legally due. But a depositor who fears a bank failure can withdraw funds in person or by writing a check. A rapid withdrawal of funds by depositors may force the bank to sell assets at distress prices or to borrow at high rates. That may produce losses that exceed the stockholders' investment and have to be absorbed by remaining depositors or other debt holders. Therefore, depositors are well-advised to remove their funds if the probability of loss exceeds the cost of making another banking arrangement plus interest that would be foregone as a consequence of the withdrawal. That is why a run on

---

[1] See Tussig (1967) for a further discussion.

a bank by panicked depositors is very difficult to stop before the bank is forced to suspend withdrawals and possibly fail.

Were it not for three factors, losses from bank runs should not be considered of greater social concern than losses from other business failures. The first factor is the importance of public faith in a safe system for transferring funds. If people feared bank failures, the argument goes, they would be unwilling to accept checks in payment for goods and services, which would increase transactions costs to the detriment of society. But checks are widely and readily accepted despite the risk that the payor may not have funds on deposit when the check is presented to the bank for payment. Though a bank failure represented an additional risk, checks were widely and increasingly used as money before the advent of federal deposit insurance, even in the 1920s when over 600 banks a year suspended operations. Prior to establishment of the Federal Reserve in 1913, notes issued by individual banks were widely used as money, despite the risk that the issuing banks could fail before the notes were redeemed. Consequently, this is not a convincing argument for having a different public policy towards bank failures than towards other business failures.

The second argument for special treatment of banks relates to the depositors' costs of determining and dealing with the riskiness of their investments. Bank deposits, particularly demand deposits, often cannot be diversified efficiently among several banks. If this could be done, depositors could reduce their risk of the expected losses from bank failures generally (which was only 0.15 percent per year even during the 1920s). But such diversification would be costly to many depositors. Rather than having each depositor assessing and monitoring the operations of banks and the riskiness of their portfolios, it seems more cost-effective for a government agency to supervise the banks. But the same argument applies to many (perhaps most) other enterprises. Investors in these enterprises also must assess the risks and returns expected from their investments; in this regard, banks are likely to be easier

to analyze than are other firms. But where small deposits are involved, the depositors' costs in assessing and diversifying risk probably exceed expected benefits. Therefore, social policy could be directed toward making riskless investments and depository services available to people with relatively little to invest. But this protection could be provided by bank-purchased private insurance, rather than a government agency, much as other enterprises and individuals insure their customers and themselves against risks.

Bank Runs

The third argument, preventing multiple bank runs, is the only really strong one for considering bank deposits differently from other investments and services. Demand depositors have a great incentive to remove their funds as soon as they believe a bank **might** fail. Hence, rumors about a bank's financial condition or the failure of similar banks might touch off runs on well-managed banks. Their failures, in turn, reduce the monetary base as people exchange fractional-reserve bank deposits for 100 percent reserve currency, resulting in a multiple contraction of the money supply and the failure of more banks and other businesses. This is what happened, in part, in the 1930s.[2]

While the Federal Reserve can step in to stop this chain-reaction by making reserves available to banks to replace those withdrawn, it did not do so in the 1930s. Between 1930 and 1933, 9,096 commercial banks were suspended, representing an annual average of 11.3 percent of all banks and 4.1 percent of the deposits. The average annual loss to depositors in these banks averaged 0.81 percent. While this was less than a third of the yield on investments (the yield on prime commercial papers ranged from 3.59 percent in 1930 to 1.73 percent in 1933), it probably

---

[2]The Federal Reserve's present policy of reserve-path targeting, however, makes it likely that reserves would not be permitted to decline as they did in the 1930s. Indeed, it makes intervention automatic.
[3]Though these failures no doubt hurt the economy, most scholars agree the banks were primarily the victims rather than the cause of the Great Depression. Warburton (1966) carefully studied the relationship between bank failures by county during the Depression. He concludes: "there was a

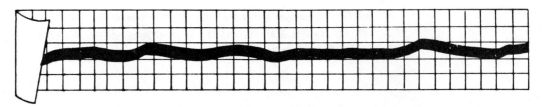

was large for affected depositors who did not hold diversified portfolios.[3]

Bank runs also played an important role in previous financial collapses before the 1930s. "Black Thursday" 1873 saw the failure of Jay Cooke's banking house and the first closing of the New York Stock Exchange. It was followed (perhaps causally) by six years of depression. The failure in 1884 of the Marine National Bank and of former President Ulysses Grant's firm, Grant & Ward, sparked runs and the consequent failure of numerous banks and brokerage houses. The Panic of 1893 was touched off by the 1890 failure of the London banking firm of Baring Brothers, which specialized in financing U.S. enterprises. Baring's European creditors demanded that Americans pay their debts in gold. As a consequence, the base money supply was depleted, a multiple contraction resulted, and 1891 saw a mini-panic. During the following 1893 panic, more than 600 banks and 13 of every 1,000 businesses failed in perhaps the nation's second deepest depression (after the depression of 1837) before 1930. The New York Clearing House suspended convertibility to specie, which ended the run. J. P. Morgan also helped by negotiating a sale in Europe of a $100 million U.S. bond issue. Panic struck again in 1907 when New York City and several corporations were unable to sell high-yielding bond issues. The Knickerbocker Trust Company failed (largely as a consequence of speculation with depositors' funds) and several major banks experienced severe runs. Again, the New York Clearing House suspended convertibility to specie and J. P. Morgan later helped increase reserves with European loans and U.S. Treasury deposits.

Creation of the Federal Reserve in 1913 was supposed to rid the country of these recurring collapses. As the lender of last resort, with great resources and the power of the printing press, it should have been able to better the Clearing House's and Morgan's record. But, when the Bank of the United States collapsed in 1930, the Fed did not prevent the failure of over a third of the banks during the next several years. Establishment of the Federal Deposit Insurance Corporation (FDIC) in 1933, though, appears to have done the job. Though 488 commercial and mutual savings banks were suspended from 1934 through 1942, most of these were leftovers from the pre-FDIC period. From 1943 through 1982, an average of only seven banks a year were closed or merged with FDIC assistance. Most importantly, bank runs appear to be a thing of the past. However, the losses incurred by large depositors when the Penn Square Bank in Oklahoma City was liquidated rather than merged into a solvent bank by the FDIC and the reported shaky condition of some very large banks with loans extended to such borrowers as Brazil, Mexico or International Harvester have provoked some concern about the possibility of runs by uninsured depositors.

Depositors in savings and loan associations, credit unions and a few mutual savings banks also are protected by government insurance agencies—the Federal Savings and Loan Insurance Corporation (FSLIC) and the National Credit Union Share Insurance Fund (NCUSIF). In recent years, unexpectedly increasing interest rates together with the specialization of savings and loans in long-term, fixed-interest assets (mortgages) have resulted in a relatively large number of failures and forced mergers. The increasing number of "troubled institutions" has renewed interest in the present deposit insurance system. This interest is expressed in the Garn-St Germain Depository Institutions Act of 1982, which calls for a study of deposit insurance and a report to the Congress by this April.

---

massive contraction of deposits nationally during the early 1930s relative to the rate of growth during the 1920s, of which less than one-fourth was accounted for by deposits in suspended banks. This indicated that the Depression of the 1930s could not be explained by the impact of balances of payment resulting from adverse conditions in particular industries or areas, but was due to, or at least associated with, some potent force operating on a national scale." (p. 2).

The Benefits From Deposit Insurance

Deposit insurance has the salutary effect of obviating bank runs by assuring insured depositors

"Deposit insurance...gives bankers an incentive to put the depositors' funds into riskier assets [than they otherwise would]."

(currently, those with less than $100,000 in an account) that their funds are safe. It also spares most depositors the cost of learning about the operation of banks. But, as a consequence, deposit insurance frees banks from the discipline and cost of those depositors' concerns. Bankers need not pay depositors a premium (in interest, "free" services, or other concessions) to compensate them for the risk of investing in the bank. Thus bank profits are increased if the reduction in their cost of deposits is greater than the cost of the deposit insurance. Such is the case for smaller banks, and was particularly so in the 1930s when the FDIC was established. Initially, FDIC insurance covered depositor accounts up to $2,500. It was raised to $5,000 in 1934, $10,000 in 1950, $15,000 in 1966, $20,000 in 1969, $40,000 in 1974 and $100,000 in 1980.

Federal insurance thus covered most of the depositors (and deposits) of small banks. It was particularly valuable to them because the public had reason to fear for the safety of their funds in small banks; 93 percent of the banks suspended in 1930-1931 had total loans and investments under $2 million, and 70 percent were under $500,000. From the beginning, the FDIC insurance premium has been assessed as a small percentage of **total** deposits, whether or not insured. Thus the large banks, which experienced much lower failure rates and which served many customers with deposit accounts exceeding $5,000 in the 1930s, have subsidized the small banks. But in return they benefited from banking legislation through the prohibition of interest on demand deposits. Golembe has estimated that in the early 1930s, the costs of deposit insurance to the large banks were offset almost exactly by savings from the interest prohibition (Golembe, 1975, p. 7). The small banks also avoided competition because national banks were denied the right to branch (except as permitted by state law).[4]

Savings and loan associations did not experience the massive number of suspensions that plagued commercial banks in the early 1930s; only 526 of the S&Ls active as of January 1930 (4.4 percent) were suspended from 1930 through 1933. The FSLIC was established by the National Housing Act of 1934 as a means of supporting the housing industry. That purpose dominated government policy towards S&Ls until, perhaps, the last few years when the institutions' survival became an important concern.

Problems With Deposit Insurance

If deposit insurance removes the concern of most depositors for the safety of their funds, it gives bankers an incentive to put the depositors' funds into riskier assets unless the FDIC or FSLIC prevents them from doing so. If a bank encounters trouble, the FDIC and FSLIC pay off the depositors; if profits are made, the shareholders get them. True, in the event of failure the bank's shareholders lose their investments (including the value of the bank charter) first. But they can lose no more. Consequently, unless the FDIC or FSLIC imposes a risk-related insurance premium, an effective minimum capital (stockholders' investment) requirement or other risk-related costs and controls, the banks' expected gains from additional risk-taking will continue to exceed the expected losses.[5]

U. S. history prior to the FDIC bears this out and also provides lessons that should be heeded. Deposit guarantee systems were established in New York (1828), Vermont (1831), Indiana (1834), Ohio (1845) and Iowa (1858).[6] The New York and Vermont systems were state run, the others

[4] See Benston (1982) for a description of the offsetting economic advantages garnered by suppliers of financial services from 1930s federal legislation.
[5] This conclusion is demonstrated analytically and rigorously in a number of papers, including Sharpe (1978), Koehn and Santonero (1980) and Hanweck (1982). Also see Flannery (1982) for a clear and concise explication and numerical example.

[6] See Federal Deposit Insurance Corporation (1952, 1953 and 1956) and Edwards (1933) for descriptions from which the following narrative was drawn.
[7] However, it should be noted that the New York State system was phased out as bank charters were granted and renewed under the free (entry) banking law. As banks left the insurance system, the premiums rose considerably.

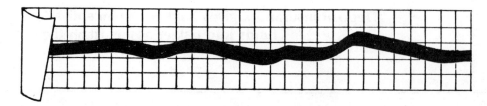

were based on mutual agreements among participating banks. They operated successfully, largely because they empowered system officials to monitor operations of the participating banks and to control excessive risk-taking.[7] Yet a second wave of deposit guarantee plans for state banks proved less successful. With one exception (Mississippi), the plans did not include effective supervision and they failed. These included the compulsory plans of Oklahoma (1908), Nebraska (1909), and South Dakota (1916) and the voluntary plans of Kansas (1909), Texas (1910), and Washington (1917). Since depositors were told that their money was safe, there was a great incentive for unscrupulous operators to take excessive risks; the record shows greater failure rates of guaranteeed banks than among similar non-guaranteed banks operating in the same areas. The Mississippi plan (1915), which included supervision and bank examinations, continued until 1930. Thus, effective supervision appears to be a necessary aspect of deposit insurance.

FSLIC deposit insurance appears to be intentionally related to risk-taking by insured savings and loan associations. Though technically the mutual associations' liabilities are shares, in actuality they are (except for time certificates) deposits withdrawable on demand by the "shareholders." Hence, were S&L deposits not insured, depositors would have reason to be concerned about the associations' concentration in long-term, local, fixed-interest mortgages. Should the market value of real estate securing the mortgages collapse, or should interest rates unexpectedly surge, the market value of an association's assets could be reduced to less than its liabilities. Fearful depositors would have the same incentive to remove their funds as would depositors in commercial banks. Thus FSLIC insurance prevents

runs on S&Ls and permits them to hold a poorly diversified portfolio, consisting mainly of mortgages.[8]

Past and Present Methods of Coping with the Problems

Restrictions on Entry and Encouragement of Mergers

The FDIC and the other regulatory agencies initially dealt with the problem of bank failures by restricting bank charters. In the 1920s, an average of 361 banks a year was chartered. But from 1935 through 1944, an average of only 53 banks was chartered annually. Understandably, few banks were chartered during World War II. But the expansionary period of 1945 through 1959 saw an annual average of only 94 newly chartered banks. Peltzman (1963, p. 48) estimated that, had the relatively unrepressed chartering policies of the 1920s continued during the 1936 through 1962 period, about 4,500 new banks would have been chartered rather than the 2,272 that were permitted. Partly as a consequence of this restrictive policy, very few banks failed, but fewer banks were established to serve the public.

Not until James Saxon became Comptroller of the Currency was this policy changed. In just four years, 1962 through 1965, he approved charters for 514 national banks, twice the number chartered in the previous 12 years. Contrary to the predictions of Saxon's detractors, neither the newly chartered banks nor their competitors failed in greater proportions than other banks. States also increased the number of bank charters issued to 124 per year over the 1962-65 period—an increase from the annual average of 86 over the previous four years. Though there have been relatively more bank failures in recent years, the number is still small and appears unrelated to the more liberal post-1960s chartering policy.

The regulatory authorities also have encouraged mergers among banks as a means of reducing the probability of failure. Until the Bank Merger Act of 1960 required the regulatory agencies and

---

[8]Federal authorities also have supported S&Ls' concentration in mortgages by imposing ceilings on deposit interest by giving them greatly reduced taxes based on their investment in mortgages, by developing a national market in mortgages with the Federal Home Loan Mortgage Corporation and by establishing Federal Home Loan Banks that lend money to S&Ls raised with government-guaranteed securities.

> "[Under previous constraints] the risks banks undertook were relatively easy to monitor and control. [Under deregulation] the possibility that greater risks will result in more failures must be considered...."

encouraged the Justice Department to evaluate and challenge mergers, their impact on competition was not considered important; safety was the primary concern.

State-enacted legal restrictions on branching have had a negative effect on bank solvency. Almost all of the banks suspended in the 1920s and 1930s were unit banks: only 10 banks with more than two branches outside their home city failed during this period. It is difficult to separate the effects of regional economic depressions and small size from unit banking as causes of the suspension of over 9,000 such banks. Still, it seems clear that the legal prohibition against banks diversifying their locations—and consequently their assets and liabilities—impaired their ability to survive liquidity or local economic crises.

In any event, reducing the number of banks—and thus competition among banks—by controlling entry and encouraging mergers is no longer a viable policy, and not just because of cost to the public. Many unchartered enterprises now offer banking services to the public: these include brokerage firms, money market funds, and specialized lenders including mortgage companies, finance companies, retail stores, factors, and insurance companies. While interstate deposit branching still is prohibited, most large banks maintain loan and customer service offices in cities around the country, as well as affiliates that specialize in such products as mortgage and personal cash loans. Smaller banks can diversify their portfolios by purchasing loans from other banks and by investing in money market instruments, such as U.S. Treasury and state and municipal obligations. Thus, reducing bank failures by controlling entry and exit appears to be neither necessary nor even possible.

The opposite policy has been applied to federal savings and loan associations, with new federal S&Ls encouraged as a means of supporting housing. Between 1933 and 1941, the number of federally chartered associations increased by 162 a year. During World War II, few federal charters were granted. But from 1946 through 1970, federally chartered S&Ls increased by 25 annually.

The recent financial problems of many S&Ls, though, do not appear attributable to excessive chartering. Rather, they are related to traditional restrictions on the portfolios they could hold and services they could offer to the public. The thrift institutions' solvency was never in doubt as long as real estate values increased, interest rates did not surge unexpectedly, and interest rate ceilings on deposits were effective in keeping their costs down but not in encouraging excessive disinter-mediation. The provisions of the Depository Institutions Deregulation and Monetary Control Act of 1980 and the Garn-St Germain Act of 1982, which permitted thrift institutions to offer most banking services and market rates of interest, came too late for many institutions to diversify their assets and liabilities successfully.

The Federal Home Loan Bank Board's policy change since the late 1970s that removed constraints on branching by federally-chartered S&Ls permitted the institutions to serve the public more effectively. Yet it was timed unfortunately from the standpoint of maintaining solvency. Branching is a means of offering depositors a return on their funds in the form of convenience. But it is often more efficient to offer them direct cash payments through interest and a wider range of services (especially checking and consumer loans). Hence, since the S&Ls can now offer these services to consumers, many branches established earlier are likely to have become financial drains on the associations. Thus, incomplete deregulation inadvertently exacerbated the S&Ls' solvency problems.

Restrictions on Products and Prices

The debacle of the 1930s gave rise to the Banking Act of 1933. This act prohibited commercial banks from underwriting and dealing in corporate securities, prohibited the payment of interest on demand deposits, and imposed a ceiling on savings and time deposits interest rates (Regulation Q). Banks and thrift institutions also were constrained over the years from competing directly and from engaging in non-traditional banking activities. One consequence of these constraints was that the risks banks undertook

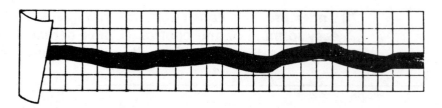

were relatively easy to monitor and control. Another was that, in the 1970s, as nominal interest rates increased and as fund transfer technologies became more efficient, unregulated institutions successfully bid for many of the regulated institutions' depositors. Banks and thrifts also attempted to enter new areas through subsidiaries, one-bank holding company affiliates, and legal expansion of powers. While the result has been greater returns and more choice for consumers, the risks undertaken by depository institutions also are likely to have increased. Nevertheless, re-regulation hardly seems possible or desirable. The possibility that the greater risks will result in more failures, then, must be considered and dealt with.

Equity (Capital) Requirements

Since the stockholders of a bank or S&L absorb losses first, a sufficiently high equity investment would inhibit them strongly from taking risks. Indeed, as long as a deposit insuring agency can step in and liquidate an institution by merger or dissolution before the value of its assets declines to less than its insured deposits, the agency assumes no risk. (Fraud, of course, can create the deceptive appearance of positive equity; therefore audits, for fraud are particularly important.) Consequently, the supervising authorities have viewed capital adequacy requirements as a means of reducing the possibility of failures.

However, the authorities' effectiveness in enforcing edicts is open to question. Mayne (1972) studied 364 randomly sampled Fourth Federal Reserve District banks to determine whether the supervisory agencies had asked them to provide additional capital over the period 1961-1968. Of the 73 percent that replied, 30 percent (81 banks) said that these requests were made, some repeatedly. But of these, only 43 percent fully complied with the authorities' requests, 27 percent partially complied, and 30 percent did

not comply at all. Mayne concluded: "The agencies do differ in their capital prescriptions, but ... these prescriptions have only a limited effect on bank capital positions because of banker resistance to supervisory pressure for more capital" (p. 47). Peltzman (1970, p. 16), who analyzed statewide aggregate data, also found that banks do not "respond to any of the regulators' standards of capital adequacy." But Mingo (1975), who used more recent individual bank data, reports that banks given lower examiner ratings subsequently tend to increase their capital.

These divergent findings may be due to the different periods or samples studied. They also may be the result of uncertainty about how much capital is adequate. Not only are the accounting numbers used to measure capital inadequate estimates of economic values, but there is reason to believe that a balance sheet ratio is not a sufficient indicator of risk.[9] Indeed, an extensive review by Lyon (1969, p. 31) led her to conclude that "the literature is voluminous but consists primarily of the prevailing opinion at any given time stated as a fact by its proponents, without benefit of analytical analysis."

In any event, the data indicate that the ratio of book capital to deposits of smaller (under $100 million in assets) banks has increased 10 percent over the 1970s from 7.6 percent in 1970 to 8.5 percent in 1980. Assuming that these accounting-based numbers reflect economic values consistently over the time period, this increase could have been the result of pressures by the regulatory authorities. Or the banks voluntarily could have increased equity relative to deposits, perhaps because the stockholders (who often are bank officers or relatives) wanted to reduce their personal income taxes by not paying dividends or officers' salaries. However, the equity/deposits percentage for very large (over $5 billion in assets) banks decreased by 13 percent over the 1970s, from 5.3 percent to 4.1 percent.

---

*See Vojta (1973), who argues that the present and future expected profitability of a bank should be taken into account. While several studies found lower capital ratios at banks that failed compared to solvent banks of similar sizes, it is unclear whether impending failures reduced their capital

or whether low capital resulted in their failures. (See Cotter (1966) for a study of West Coast banks that failed between 1921 and 1933, and Benston (1975) for an analysis of banks that failed between 1959 and 1971.)

(Over the complete range of bank sizes, the larger banks tended to have lower ratios and, over time, those ratios decreased more for the larger banks.) Again assuming that these numbers are meaningful, it would appear that the authorities have less ability to control the capital investments of large banks. One reason is suggested below.

Until about 1980, when the S&L capital problem became overwhelming, the FHLBB had somewhat greater influence in getting thrifts to maintain their book capital, primarily because many associations' capital/deposit ratios became so low that they feared cancellation of FSLIC insurance. Edward Kane (1981) points out that FSLIC insurance represents a valuable asset to most associations, since it is priced below what would be the market rate. Mutual associations, as a practical matter, cannot raise equity capital except in the form of retained earnings. Hence, Kane shows, "insured S&Ls kept their net worth from falling below the level required to stay eligible for FSLIC insurance...by not realizing capital losses on their mortgage portfolios" (p. 90), even though this would have reduced their tax liability.

Field Examinations and Supervision

Examinations constitute a principal means of reducing failures of banks and thrift institutions. National banks are examined by the Office of the Comptroller of the Currency at least twice every three years. State-chartered Federal Reserve member banks are examined by the Fed at least once a year, and other state-chartered FDIC-insured banks are examined by the FDIC and often also by state banking departments at least once a year. The Federal Home Loan Bank Board examines FSLIC-insured S&Ls annually. State-chartered S&Ls also are examined by some state banking departments.

The examiners look at the documentation and collateral for most large loans and a sample of small loans and they check the institutions' compliance with federal and state laws. Loans are classified into loss, doubtful and substandard categories. The institutions' managers and management procedures and policies also are evaluated.

If an institution is found wanting, it is characterized as a "problem" or "serious problem" and subjected to closer scrutiny and more frequent examinations.

Although it seems clear that examinations of some sort are a necessary aspect of deposit insurance (given its built-in incentive towards risk-taking), there is reason to question the usefulness of examinations for preventing many failures. The examiners' ability to uncover serious problems of fraud and insider dealings appears to be far from perfect, judging from FDIC reports and published research. Among the 56 bank failures that occurred between January 1959 and April 1971, fully 59 percent were rated as "no problem" at the examination just prior to their failures.[10] The principal reasons given for the 56 failures are: fraud and irregularities, 66 percent; brokered funds and loan losses, 27 percent; and inept management, 7 percent.[11]

A more recent study by Sinkey (1977) uses a different set of classifications but draws similar conclusions. He finds that, of 84 failures between 1960 and mid-1976, some 54 percent resulted from improper insider loans or out-of-territory loans involving brokered funds, 30 percent from embezzlement or manipulation, and 17 percent from managerial weakness in loan administration (p. 27). In an earlier failure study by the FDIC, Hill (1975) found similar proportions. It cannot be ascertained, however, whether this record is close to the best possible, in the sense that the cost of preventing more failures would have exceeded the benefit. Also, the more recent record has not been studied.

The effectiveness of the FSLIC's examiners has been studied only with respect to the relatively large number of S&Ls in Illinois that required the FSLIC's financial assistance from 1963 through 1968. These 19 losses represent 75 percent of the total losses suffered by the FSLIC over the period. Bartell (1969, p. 353), stated that he

---

[10]Benston (1975), Table XIII, p. 43.
[11]Benston (1975), Table XI, Table XI, p. 40.

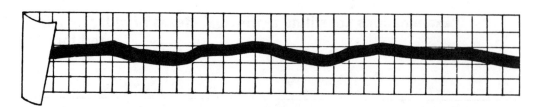

identified nine associations where failure could be attributed primarily to management deficiencies or errors of judgment. In these cases the management apparently believed that the actions which later caused failure were taken in the best interests of the association and its savers. In the second category were 10 associations where fraud, influence, defalcation, or some other criminal intent was the principal cause of failure. In all of these cases, one or more of the officers, directors, and/or major stockholders was indicted for misapplying association funds, and in most cases convictions have been obtained.

With respect to the examinations, Bartell concludes that they were well done; if anything, they were too thorough (p. 418). But, he states, "In contrast with the generally high quality of examinations, supervisory performance in the handling of failed associations leaves much to be desired" (p. 419).

Supervision of financial institutions is functionally related to, though not necessarily dependent on, field examination. To a limited extent the supervisors can specify the portfolios of assets and the nature of the liabilities that insured financial institutions can hold. Supervisors enforce a limitation on loans to any one borrower and they restrict loans to officers, directors and shareholders. They can also restrict the types of loans and investments that can be made. Field examinations to ensure that the regulations are observed would appear to be necessary, particularly where activities conducted at less than arm's length can occur. But the supervisors also can use statistical models and computers to analyze data reported by the institutions for signs of possible problems. Such systems have been used by every federal agency and several state agencies since the mid-1970s.[12] But, as Flannery

and Guttentag (1980) conclude from their analysis of the early warning systems, these systems have not been validated; hence, we do not know how well or even whether they are effective for predicting failure. In fact, the systems appear to be used primarily as a more efficient means for the examiners to look at and structure data for their reports.

The supervisory authorities also must decide when to require an institution to discontinue a criticized practice (such as acquiring brokered deposits or making high-risk loans), dismiss an inept or possibly dishonest officer, obtain more capital from shareholders, terminate insurance,[13] or close or arrange for a merger with another institution. Before the Financial Institutions Supervisory Act of 1966 gave federal supervisors authority to issue cease-and-desist orders, the principal legal sanctions available were cancellation of insurance and seizure of an institution for liquidation or reorganization. Since 1942, the principal procedure used to handle failing banks has been a sale of the bank to an institution that assumes liability for both insured and non-insured deposits.[14] Payoffs limited to insured depositors generally have involved only small institutions located in unit banking states that do not permit another bank to acquire and operate the failed institution as a branch. Recently, in the case of Oklahoma's Penn Square Bank, the poor and questionable condition of the bank's assets precluded its sale. Because they are government agencies, the FDIC, FSLIC, and NCUIF have the power to close an institution before the market value of its assets is less than its insured deposits, which can prevent losses to the insuring agencies except in cases involving rapid deterioration or fraud. But they may also be subjected to political pressure and to the reluctance of a supervisory agency to admit that one of "its" institutions has to be closed.[15]

---

[12]See paper on "Early Warning Systems for Problem Financial Institutions," in Altman and Sametz (1977, pp. 3-68) and Flannery and Guttentag (1980) for descriptions and critiques of these systems.
[13]If insurance is terminated, the institution's existing accounts continue to be insured for two years.

[14]See Barnett, Horvitz, and Silverberg 1977, pp. 308-317 for a good discussion of the advantages and disadvantages of the alternative procedures.
[15]Bartell (1969, pp. 419-421) documents the effect of prior congressional criticism of S&L closures on the reluctance of the FHLBB to follow the recommendations of its examiners expeditiously.

> **"[Since restrictions on entry also reduce competition and service], restricting entry to reduce failures, even if it were desirable, is no longer feasible."**

Some critics have argued that divided authority among regulators also has reduced the effectiveness of supervision. While the FDIC and FSLIC have responsibility for insuring the deposits of state-chartered institutions, only the state authorities have the power to close the institutions. (Bartell reports that this was an important problem for the FSLIC with respect to the failing Illinois associations.) Holding companies are regulated by the Federal Reserve but their affiliated banks are chartered by the states and/or the Comptroller of the Currency. Shull (1980) finds in his analysis of holding company failures that, "the extent of actual conflict among federal banking agencies in holding company supervision, while difficult to quantify, is important, time consuming, and diverting in problem cases" (Vol I, p. 119).

A Changing Environment for Deposit Insurance

Restrictions on entry and the encouragement of mergers have been effective in reducing failures, but at the cost of reduced competition and, therefore, less service to consumers and fewer opportunities for potential bankers. In any event, changes in technology, fueled by inflation-induced high nominal interest rates, have encouraged other, non-regulated suppliers of financial services to enter the market. Their entry no longer can be restricted. Hence, restricting entry to reduce failures, even if it were desirable, is no longer feasible.

Capital adequacy requirements are desirable. But, to be effective, they must be tailored to the asset portfolio and deposit distribution of each institution. If too much equity is required, insured depository institutions will be disadvantaged and resources allocated inefficiently. If too little capital is required, institutions will be encouraged to take greater risks and the costs to the insurance agency are likely to exceed the fees it levies. Furthermore, capital adequacy is a very blunt requirement. It is expensive for financial institutions to raise capital (in addition to retained earnings) in relatively small amounts. Closely held, usually smaller institutions, are likely to find floating equity quite difficult. Majority shareholders may lack the resources or may not wish to concentrate their wealth further, and outside investors frequently are unwilling to take minority positions except at a considerable discount. Mutual institutions also might find it expensive to market debentures.

Deposit insurance rates that vary with the riskiness of an institution's assets and liabilities have been suggested for years as a preferable means of dealing with the problem. However, the deposit insurance agencies still charge the same percentage to all institutions, partly because it is difficult to set variable premiums. (Indeed, none of those recommending this change have specified how the premiums should be determined.) But the same information is required for an equity requirement. Another reason for the resistance to change is that regulatory agencies believe the present system of field examinations and equity requirements, roughly determined and enforced though they may be, are adequate.

Finally, the present system may be politically desirable, balancing smaller institutions' benefits from having the premiums applied to all (including uninsured) deposits against large banks' benefits from an incomplete control of the risks they take. The residual risk ostensibly is borne by the deposit insurance agencies. But since the government is expected to stand behind the agencies, the general public is accepting the residual risk.

Field examinations have two major shortcomings. One is that they are expensive. Teams of examiners spend days to weeks at each bank, going over records in considerable detail. Not only do the insurance agencies and the institutions they charge for these services incur considerable costs, but the institutions bear such costs as disrupted operations and the expense of preparing and presenting requested data. The second shortcoming is the difficulty of prompt detection of problems precipitated by fraud or changes in an institution's economic environment. These are difficult to detect through periodic inspections of an institution's loan portfolio, management systems, and regulatory compliance.

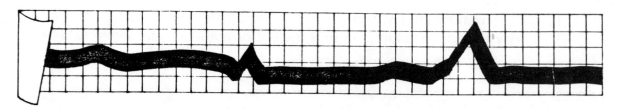

A related problem involves our system of regulation. Supervisors may not be able to control potential problem banks as well when the banks are regulated by several agencies as when they are regulated by a single agency. For many commercial banks, especially the large ones, the chartering agencies (the Comptroller or the states) and the Federal Reserve have regulatory responsibility as well as the FDIC. This divided authority may permit some banks to take greater risks than an insurance agency acting alone would have permitted. But then, the temptation for an insurance agency to reduce risk at the expense of innovation must be recognized.

Proposed Solutions

My analysis has concluded that mandatory deposit insurance is justified because deposits that are withdrawable on demand create the possibility of bank runs, which can visit considerable costs upon banks, their customers and others. The government has been charged with insuring deposits in part as a response to Depression-era political pressures by small banks, the home building industry and some depositors, and in part because the government has the power to enforce its orders on banks and cannot, itself, go bankrupt. Another reason for government intervention in insurance is that the government's control over bank reserves gives it the power to cause and the power to prevent massive numbers of bank failures.

The basic problem with government-provided mandatory deposit insurance is that it provides the insured institutions an incentive to take excessive risks. Consequently, the institutions must be examined and supervised. But there is danger that this process is conducted less efficiently and effectively because the responsible agencies are monopoly suppliers of the insurance to each group of institutions.

The following changes in current procedures, I believe, would help reduce the costs of achieving the benefits from mandatory deposit insurance.[16]

1. **All** deposits withdrawable on demand, such as checking accounts, NOW accounts, money market deposit accounts, and passbook savings accounts, should be insured by a responsible insurer. The only exceptions would occur where deposited funds are invested in assets that have almost no probability of being worth less than the deposit liability (such as money market funds that are invested in a well-diversified portfolio of short-term government obligations or bank certificates of deposit). All demand-type deposits should be insured for two reasons. One is that runs on uninsured balances can force bank failures or a massive infusion of resources by the authorities to prevent a failure (as was done for the Franklin National Bank in New York). The second reason is that **de jure** deposit insurance is preferable to **de facto** insurance. The public generally believes that large banks will not be permitted to fail, but that smaller banks may fail. Since deposit insurance premiums are imposed on deposits of all insured banks, this **de facto** difference is inequitable.

2. Time-dated deposits (such as CDs, whether negotiable or not) need not be insured, as long as the holder can withdraw funds from the financial institution only at the time stated. (Obligations that permit withdrawal of funds with an interest rate penalty would be classified as funds withdrawable on demand.) Consequently, runs cannot occur with such deposits. In this respect, time deposits are no different from the debt obligations of other companies.[17] Of course, an institution may purchase insurance coverage for these obligations if it wishes. The advantage of this

[16]Also see Barnett, Horvitz and Silverberg (1977) and Scott and Mayer (1971) for analyses of suggested changes, some of which mirror the ones presented here.

[17]Though some time-dated obligations are payable almost immediately, institutions (and the insurance agency) have incentives to ensure that the amount due at any time is not excessive.

proposal is that holders of time deposits would monitor the issuing institution. Furthermore, the interest rate paid on the deposits could provide the demand deposit insurance agency with the market's assessment of the riskiness of the institution.

3. Commercial and mutual savings banks are regulated by several agencies, which can lead to conflicting authority and a failure to act in a timely fashion. The agency with the principal interest in supervising financial institutions should be the one that must bear the cost of their failure—the insuring agency.[18] Consequently, it should have the sole authority and responsibility for supervising the financial institutions it insures.

4. The present insurance system suffers from a lack of competition among insuring agencies. As a consequence, examination procedures may be too costly and poorly focused. Because they are monopoly suppliers of deposit insurance, the present agencies have less incentive to adopt more efficient and better directed procedures, such as risk-variable insurance premiums, tests of the predictive ability of statistical models, and research on optimally diversified portfolios. Because the regulatory agencies also are subjected to severe political criticism if "their" banks fail, they may be too restrictive in some instances. They should be faced with equating the marginal costs and benefits from failures and failure-reducing measures as are other insurance providers. Consequently, the following changes should be considered:

a. The Office of the Comptroller of the Currency (OCC) should become a deposit insurance agency, initially providing insurance (and supervision) to national banks. The Federal Reserve's Division of Supervision and Regulation should also provide insurance to the member banks it examines.

These changes would continue the present examination staffs as they are presently constituted, which would minimize the cost of change. The present FDIC insurance fund could be divided among the three agencies in proportion to the total demand deposits held by the banks they insure.

b. Any deposit insured institution should then be allowed to purchase insurance at the OCC, FDIC, Fed, FSLIC or NCUSIF. Thus there would be five potential competitors. Of course, an agency need not accept applications made to it. Each agency could offer its "customers" whatever terms it wished, much as does any insurance company, so long as the terms are offered equally to all clients that present equivalent risk. An agency should, however, give at least one year's public notice before cancelling the insurance on deposit balances. It also could require an insured bank to authorize the agency to seize its assets, given designated circumstances.

c. Any demand depository institution could obtain insurance from non-government insurers, including other banks,[19] if the insurer were accepted by the chartering agency. The non-government insurer could initiate clauses into its contract with the institution that would give the insurer rights similar to (or even greater than) those held by the government agencies. These might include restrictive covenants as to dividends, specified diversification of assets, minimum equity requirements, audits by CPAs or the insurance company's examiners, pre-agreement to cease practices or to remove officers, and seizure and sale of assets after a stated "danger" point is reached.

5. The preceding proposals do not cover the difficulties of insuring deposits in the face of unpredictable problems in the financial system as a whole, problems not controllable by individual institutions. In our fractional reserve banking

---

[18]See Benston (1963) for the analysis on which this conclusion is based.
[19]The agency that insures the deposits of a bank offering deposit insurance to

other banks can adjust its premium accordingly or take other actions to control the risk.

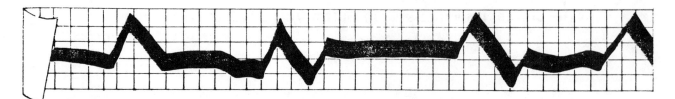

system, a substantial decline in bank reserves for any reason can cause wide-scale banking failures. Such declines in reserves also are very difficult (perhaps impossible) to predict and, thus, deposit insurance premiums cannot be set actuarially. Therefore, to make non-government supplied insurance feasible, the insurers should in some way be relieved of the cost of failures caused by substantial systemwide declines in bank reserves.

— **George J. Benston**

Professor of Accounting, Economics and Finance, Graduate School of Management, University of Rochester, and Visiting Scholar, Federal Reserve Bank of Atlanta. This article was presented at a Research Seminar at the Federal Reserve Bank of Atlanta on Jan. 6, 1983.

REFERENCES

Altman, Edward E. and Arnold W. Sametz. **Financial Crises: Institutions and Markets in a Fragile Environment,** New York: Wiley-Interscience Publication, 1977.

Barnett, Robert E., Paul N. Horvitz, and Stanley C. Silverberg. "Deposit Insurance: The Present System and Some Alternatives," **Banking Law Journal,** vol. 94, 1977, 304-332.

Bartell, H. Robert, Jr. "An Analysis of Illinois Savings and Loan Associations Which Failed in the Period 1963-68, in Irwin Friend, ed., **Study of the Savings and Loan Industry,** prepared for the Federal Home Loan Bank Board, Washington, D.C., Vol. I, 1969, 345-436.

Benston, George J. "Federal Regulation of Banking: Analysis and Policy Recommendations." **Journal of Bank Research,** Winter, 1983.

Benston, George J. "Why Did Congress Pass New Financial Services Laws in the 1930s? An Alternative View," **Economic Review,** Federal Reserve Bank of Atlanta, April, 1982, 7-10.

Benston, George J. "Bank Examination," **The Bulletin,** (New York University Graduate School of Business Administration, Institute of Finance), 1973, Nos. 89-90.

Edwards, Gurden. **The Guaranty of Bank Deposits,** Economic Policy Commission, American Bankers Association, New York, 1933.

Federal Deposit Insurance Corporation. "State Deposit Insurance Systems, 1908-30," **Annual Report,** 1956,Washington, D.C., 57-73.

Federal Deposit Insurance Corporation. "Bank-Obligation Insurance Systems, 1829 to 1866," **Annual Report,** 1953, Washington, D.C., 45-67.

Federal Deposit Insurance Corporation. "Insurance of Bank Obligations Prior to Federal Deposit Insurance," **Annual Report,** 1952, Washington, D.C., 59-72.

Flannery, Mark J. "Deposit Insurance Creates a Need for Bank Regulation," **Business Review,** Federal Reserve Bank of Philadelphia, January/February, 1982, 17-27.

Flannery, Mark J. and Jack M. Guttentag. "Problem Banks: Examination, Identification, and Supervision," in Leonard Lapidus and Others, **State and Federal Regulation of Commercial Banks,** Federal Deposit Insurance Corporation, Washington, D.C., Vol. II, 1980, 169-226.

Gibson, William E. "Deposit Insurance in the United States: Evaluation and Reform," **Journal of Financial and Quantitative Analysis,** 1972,1575-1594.

Golembe, Carter. "Memorandum re: Interest on Demand Deposits," Carter H. Golembe Associates, Inc., Volume 1975-10, 1975.

Hanweck, Gerald A. "A Theoretical Comparison of Bank Capital Adequacy Requirements and Risk Related Deposit Insurance Premia," Board of Governors of the Federal Reserve System, manuscript, September 1982.

Hill, George W. **Why 67 Insured Banks Failed—1960-1974,** Federal Deposit Insurance Corporation, Washington, D.C., 1975.

Kane, Edward J. "Reregulation, Savings and Loan Diversification, and the Flow of Housing Finance," in **Savings and Loan Asset Management Under Deregulation,** Sixth Annual Conference, December 1980, Federal Home Loan Bank of San Francisco, 1981, 80-109.

Koehn, Michael and Anthony M. Santomero. "Regulation of Bank Capital and Portfolio Risk," **Journal of Finance,** 35 (December 1980), 1235-1244.

Lyon, Sandra. "History of Bank Capital Adequacy Analysis," Federal Deposit Insurance Corporation, Working Paper No. 69-4, 1969, Banking and Economic Research Section, Division of Research.

Mayne, Lucille S. "Impact of Federal Bank Supervision on Bank Capital," **The Bulletin** (New York University Graduate School of Business Administration, Institute of Finance), 1972, Nos. 85-86.

Mingo, John J. "Regulatory Influence on Bank Capital Investment," **Journal of Finance,** 30 (September), 1111-1121.

Peltzman, Sam. "Entry in Commercial Banking," **Journal of Law and Economics,** 1 (October 1963), pp. 11-50.

Peltzman, Sam. "Capital Investment in Commercial Banking and Its Relationship to Portfolio Regulation," **Journal of Political Economy,** 78 (January-February 1970), 1-26.

Scott, Kenneth E. and Thomas Mayer. "Risk and Regulation in Banking: Some Proposals for Deposit Insurance Reform", **Stanford Law Review,** Vol. 23, 1971, 857-902.

Sharpe, William F. "Bank Capital Adequacy, Deposit Insurance and Security Value," **Journal of Financial and Quantitative Analysis** (Proceedings, November), 701-718.

Shull, Bernard. "Federal and State Supervision of Bank Holding Companies," in Leonard Lapidus and Others, **State and Federal Regulation of Commercial Banks,** Federal Deposit Insurance Corporation, Washington, D.C., Vol. II, 1980, 271-374.

Sinkey, Joseph F. Jr. "Problem and Failed Banks, Bank Examinations and Early Warning Systems: A Summary," in Edward I. Altman and Arnold W. Sametz, **Financial Crises: Institutions and Markets in a Fragile Environment,** New York: Wiley-Interscience Publication, 1977.

Tussig, Aubrey D. "The Case for Bank Failure," **Journal of Law and Economics,** Vol. 10, 1967, 129-147.

Vojta, George J. **Bank Capital Adequacy,** First National City Bank, New York, 1973.

Warburton, Clark. **Depression, Inflation and Monetary Policy, Selected Papers, 1945-1953,** Baltimore: The Johns Hopkins Press, 1952.

Article Nine

FDIC Policies for Dealing with Failed and Troubled Institutions

By Daria B. Caliguire
and James B. Thomson

Bank failures reached a post-Depression high in 1986. One hundred thirty-eight banks, including one mutual savings bank, were closed by their primary regulator; an additional seven banks needed assistance from the Federal Deposit Insurance Corporation (FDIC) to prevent them from failing.

In the first half of 1987, 100 banks failed or required assistance from the FDIC. Failures and assistance cases for 1987 are projected to reach the 200 mark by year-end. Moreover, the number of banks on the FDIC's problem bank list is at an all-time high (see figure 1), indicating that the rate of bank failures might continue at or exceed the 1986-1987 pace in the near future.

For the banking industry, the increasing incidence of troubled and failing banks reflects the changed economic environment in which they operate. Technological innovations, combined with a trend toward deregulation, have increased the competitiveness of banking markets and, consequently, have increased the degree of exposure of banks to changes in market conditions.

These factors, coupled with regulations restricting geographic and activity diversification in bank portfolios, have limited the ability of banks to protect themselves against national and regional economic shocks. In recent years, for example, depressed agricultural and energy markets have contributed to the solvency problems of an increasing number of banks in the southwest.

The FDIC has a mandate to maintain confidence in and provide stability to the commercial banking system through its regulatory and insurance functions. In addition, it is empowered to preserve that confidence and stability through the quick and efficient resolution of bank failures. The recent wave of failures has challenged the FDIC's ability to achieve these objectives. The FDIC insurance fund increasingly is threatened with illiquidity. Secondly, FDIC failure-resolution policies followed since 1984 have eroded market discipline by expanding de facto deposit insurance coverage far beyond the coverage originally intended for insured depositors.

This *Economic Commentary* examines the FDIC's policies for handling bank failures and discusses both the intended and the unintended outcomes of those policies. We conclude that the evolution of FDIC policies can be linked importantly to FDIC actions that have undermined market discipline on banks.

Background

At the lowest point in the Depression, the Banking Act of 1933 was enacted as a comprehensive reform package aimed at restoring public confidence in the stability of the banking system. Congress was concerned with eliminating the destabilizing contagion of bank runs. The banking industry was perceived as being unable to withstand "failures" in the same sense that other industries could withstand bankruptcies. Consequently, safety and soundness were placed before the "survival of the fittest" principle of market efficiency in the order of governing principles of banking. The Banking Act attempted, among other objectives, to insulate banks from some market forces by separating commercial banking from

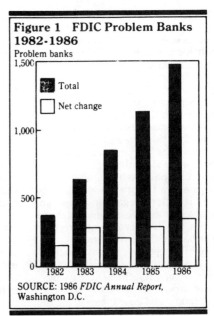

Figure 1   FDIC Problem Banks 1982-1986

Problem banks

SOURCE: 1986 *FDIC Annual Report*, Washington D.C.

investment banking. One component of the total reform package, federal deposit insurance, was put in place to enhance the long-run stability of the banking system.

Federal deposit insurance was instituted to prevent the contagion of bank runs by protecting the small depositor. Originally, the FDIC was authorized to cover insured deposits up to a $2,500 limit.[1] In this way, stability and public confidence in the banking system were to be restored at the grass-roots level. By offering insurance only to small depositors, it was intended that large depositors, general creditors, subordinated debtors, and shareholders still would be subject to the risk of financial loss that

Daria B. Caliguire was a Research Department intern and James B. Thomson is an economist at the Federal Reserve Bank of Cleveland. The authors would like to thank William Osterberg, Gary Whalen, E.J. Stevens, Charles T. Carlstrom, and William D. Fosnight for their helpful comments, and offer special thanks to Walker Todd and Lynn Downey for their valuable assistance.

1. Even in 1934, the first year the FDIC operated, $2500 was not much money, equivalent to about $22,000 today, as measured by the consumer price index. Currently, the deposit insurance ceiling is $100,000.

is a normal part of market discipline.

Even at such low levels, however, deposit insurance was controversial because it was well understood that any insulation against risk impedes the effective restraint on a bank's risk-taking ventures that is imposed by its depositors.[2] Uninsured depositors monitor a bank's risk-profile. As banks pursue riskier investment strategies, these depositors demand higher interest rates as compensation for bearing the additional risk. When deposits are insured, however, the deposit guarantor (the FDIC, for example) bears the risk of the deposits, and the depositor's incentive to monitor conduct of the bank's affairs is reduced.

Traditional Methods of Resolving Bank Failures

Deposit insurance was instituted to eliminate the contagion of bank runs, not to eliminate bank failures altogether. Given that bank failures are part of a normal functioning of the financial market, the FDIC was empowered under the Banking Act with two initial means of resolving them: payout, and purchase and assumption.

Here is how the process works. Once a bank is declared legally insolvent, and is unable to meet the demands of its depositors, the FDIC is appointed receiver by the bank's chartering agent.[3]

The FDIC operates in two capacities, as a corporation and as receiver. In its corporate capacity, the FDIC pays off insured depositors and provides necessary funding and guarantees to the receiver. As receiver, the FDIC's primary obligation is to distribute the failed bank's assets equitably, to both depositors and general creditors. Under either resolution option, the FDIC assumes a fiduciary obligation to maximize the amounts recovered from the assets and liabilities sold.

In a payout, the FDIC (in its corporate capacity) first advances funds to the receiver to pay off the insured deposit claims. The receiver, with respect to that advance, then joins the pool of uninsured depositors and general creditors as a claimant on the proceeds of the liquidation of the failed bank. Subordinated debtors and shareholders normally are subject to partial or complete losses if the proceeds of the liquidation are insufficient.

A purchase and assumption (P&A) transaction is a sale of the banking franchise, rather than a liquidation. The FDIC solicits bids for the failed institution, with the successful bidder purchasing the assets and assuming the liabilities, and with the FDIC absorbing any negative difference between the two.[4]

An attempt is made to make the bidding process as competitive as possible by attracting the maximum number of potential acquirers in order to attain the highest premium.[5] However, the pool of potential bidders can be limited severely by state branching laws, by the absence of state interstate banking laws, by federal antitrust laws, by the quality of the failed bank's assets, and by the size and 'fit' of the failed bank in relation to its potential acquirer.[6]

P&A vs. Payout

The Banking Act of 1933 did not specify exact guidelines for the FDIC to use in choosing between payout and P&A. Instead, it gave the FDIC an implicit mandate to balance two goals: to preserve market discipline and to minimize disruptions to local banking services. In view of the debate surrounding deposit insurance, market discipline concerns were given priority over service disruption considerations throughout most of the history of the FDIC.[7]

The payout better accomplishes the market discipline objective because it more closely approximates the consequences of a bank failure in an unregulated market. In a payout, only the insured depositors are guaranteed full reimbursement if the bank fails; in a P&A, both insured and uninsured depositors receive protection, as well as most general creditors. On the other hand, the P&A is less disruptive to the community because entire blocs of banking relationships are sold intact and, therefore, are preserved. By contrast, these banking services are dismantled under a payout.

The difficulty of measuring the costs of decreased market discipline, versus the community impact of a loss of banking services, initially led the FDIC to adopt a cost test for choosing between a payout or a P&A: a payout was to be performed unless a P&A was less costly to the FDIC. In practice, however, the FDIC preferred the P&A to the payout.

During the 1930s and 1940s, the P&A was employed more often because it frequently proved more cost effective. Over time, however, the political attractiveness of the P&A led to its exclusive use in resolving failures, whether or not it was the most cost-effective policy. By 1950, de facto, previous FDIC policy was reversed; a purchase and assumption was to be transacted unless it was impossible to find a buyer due to prohibitive branching or holding company laws, or if contingent liabilities or fraud were extensive enough to render the cost-test inaccurate.

The almost exclusive use of P&As in failure resolution, irrespective of cost or market discipline considerations, prompted a revision of policy in the 1950 Federal Deposit Insurance (FDI) Act. The cost test was named explicitly as the primary criterion for determining FDIC action in individual bank failures. Congress felt that such a restatement of purpose was a necessary reminder to the FDIC that its mission was not to eliminate bank failures, but to dispose of failed banks in the least costly and most efficient manner.[8]

Problems in Application

The extensive use of P&As instead of payouts, and the ensuing debate over the use of the cost test in 1950-1951, and again in recent years, highlights a fundamental flaw in the FDIC program for bank failure resolution: the assumption that the long-run impact of payouts and P&As are the same. They are not, because the payout preserves the operation of market forces while the P&A reduces market discipline by extending de facto insurance coverage to uninsured depositors and general creditors.

2. See Guy Emerson, "Guaranty of Deposits Under The Banking Act of 1933," *Quarterly Journal of Economics*, vol. 48, 1934, pp. 229-44.

3. For state-chartered banks, the FDIC does not have to be, but almost always is, appointed receiver, and it always is receiver of national banks.

4. Traditionally, the FDIC extracts all the bad assets and sells the bank on a "clean-bank basis" in order to make the offer more attractive to the bidders. As a result of placing all the bad assets on the FDIC's books, however, the liquidity of the fund increasingly is threatened. These assets now account for two-thirds of the assets in the FDIC's $18 billion fund. Operating under the philosophy that loan collection is best accomplished locally, the FDIC has begun experimenting with leaving the delinquent loans in the failed-bank package. Rescues of BancTexas Corp. and First City Bancorp in 1987 illustrate this principle.

5. Potential acquirers are willing to offer a premium for the entire bank because the value of the bank charter is preserved. See Steven A. Buser, Andrew C. Chen, and Edward J. Kane, "Federal Deposit Insurance, Regulatory Policy, and

A fundamental defect in using the cost test as the primary determinant for choosing between payouts and P&As is that the cost test considers only the short-run fiduciary costs to the FDIC fund. While the costs associated with the loss of banking services and the out-of-pocket costs of resolving failures tend to be short-run in nature, the costs associated with the erosion of market discipline occur in the future. Thus the choice of a resolution policy based on short-term cost considerations alone has a natural bias towards the use of P&As over payouts.

The second defect in the cost test is that it does not include the value of FDIC guarantees and indemnifications against unforeseen liabilities routinely given to the acquiring banks in a P&A. The seriousness of this defect is magnified by the ease at which out-of-pocket costs (counted in the cost test) can be translated into off-balance-sheet contingent claims on the FDIC (which are either not explicitly counted, or can be seriously understated in the cost test). Thus, discretion in the application of the cost test can result in actions either not consistent with the intent of the law or not consistent with sound economic practice.

By itself, the ability to redefine the costs associated with resolving bank failures would not necessarily lead to FDIC actions that systematically would favor P&As over payouts. However, it does make the resolution policy choice sensitive to political pressures and to other noneconomic considerations. These factors may be expected to operate in favor of P&As instead of payouts also because P&As create no large class of disgruntled claimants, while payouts usually leave large classes of unhappy uninsured depositors, shareholders, subordinated debtors, and general creditors who are not paid quickly, if at all.

Given the difficulty of defining failure resolution policy costs, coupled with the pressures favoring P&As, the cost test is an inherently flawed criterion for choosing between different failure resolution policies. Therefore, using the cost test to choose between payouts and P&As has had some serious unintended effects on the equity and

Table 1   Insured Deposits for the 10 Largest United States Banks

Bank	Insured deposits (billions of dollars)	Insured as a percent of	
		Domestic deposits	Total deposits[a]
Citibank	21,687	58.09	22.53
Bank of America	38,967	68.63	43.96
Chase Manhattan Bank	15,389	56.27	26.11
Morgan Guaranty Trust	1,467	12.32	3.48
Manufacturers Hanover	8,293	34.82	18.28
Chemical Bank	11,518	48.77	32.73
Bankers Trust	2,738	25.88	9.55
Security Pacific	16,677	63.56	51.37
Wells Fargo Bank	25,577	81.10	78.50
First National Bank of Chicago	4,858	43.18	19.57
10 Largest Banks	147,172	56.52	53.68
20 Largest Banks	189,014	54.26	56.36
All Insured Banks[b]	1,634,302	75.40	N/A

a. Total deposits equals the sum of domestic deposits and deposits in foreign offices.
b. Based on December 31, 1986 numbers. Source: The 1986 FDIC Annual Report, Washington, DC.
SOURCE: Federal Financial Institutions Examination Council's Consolidated Reports of Condition and Income.

efficiency of the banking system, which include a 'large-bank bias' and a decrease in market discipline on banks.

A large-bank bias, in the administrative sense, has emerged from the established pattern of FDIC bank failure resolutions. Large banks may be difficult to liquidate due to their size and to the complexity of their banking relationships. Consequently, the perception of bank regulators generally has been that large-bank failures pose a greater threat to both depositors' confidence and the safety and soundness of the financial system than do small-bank failures. In addition, the political pressures to bail out some or all parties in a bank failure are directly related to the size of the failing bank.

As a result, large-bank failures are rarely paid out. In fact, no bank over $600 million in assets has been liquidated. This is all the more striking because, at large banks, insured deposits typically constitute only a small percentage of all deposits (see table 1). The 100 percent de facto coverage of all large-bank depositors tends to produce

a fundamental inequality, a large-bank bias in the banking system.

The implicit insurance protection provided by nonpayout failure-resolution policies has led to a public perception that the FDIC provides de facto coverage of all depositors and most creditors. Over the extended period (1934-1970) when the P&A was used almost exclusively to resolve bank failures, the claims of creditors and uninsured depositors were preserved continually. Such an unintended yet pervasive public expectation of insurance coverage becomes a corrosive agent on the forces of market discipline.

The greatest danger inherent in deposit insurance coverage is its tendency to make the uninsured depositors less cautious.[9] Even when coverage is limited, insurance insulates depositors against risk and inadvertently encourages management's risk-taking behavior. Whether a bank follows a cautious or a speculative path in an insured system, the payment to insured depositors is the same in either scenario; however, the rewards are much greater for the risk-taker in management.

Optimal Bank Capital," *Journal of Finance*, vol. 36, no. 1, March 1981, pp. 51-60.

6. When a billion-dollar bank nears failure, such as the Bank of the Commonwealth in Detroit, the pool of eligible bidding banks is often very limited. See Irvine H. Sprague, *Bailout: An Insider's Account of Bank Failures and Rescues.* New York, Basic Books, Inc., 1986, pp. 53-76.

7. *Id.,* pp. 24-25.

8. See *FDIC: The First Fifty Years.* Washington, D.C.: Federal Deposit Insurance Corporation, 1984, p. 86.

9. See George G. Kaufman, "The Truth About Bank Runs," paper presented to Cato Institute Conference on the Financial Services Revolution. Washington, D.C., February 27, 1987.

The erosion of market discipline, via 100 percent de facto insurance coverage, poses a long-term threat to the FDIC's ability to close banks and slowly undermines the solvency of the FDIC's insurance fund.

New Resolution Policies

The need for reform of previous FDIC policies resulted from a changed economic environment. Interest-rate volatility and the collapse of the commodities prices in the 1980s destabilized a large number of banks. When the wave of failures began (see figure 2), there was an urgent need for new ways to cope with them. Unlike failures in previous years, the 1980s failures were concentrated geographically (see figure 3). Moreover, large banks now populate the ranks of troubled and failed banks. The development of new resolution policies, for example, began in the early 1970s as a response to the first megabank failures.

The 1980s bank failure experience has led to an accelerated series of FDIC policy initiatives producing new options that are adaptations of the earlier payouts and P&As, corrected for their more obvious shortcomings. One set of policies is designed for failed banks, another set for troubled and failing banks. Although FDIC failure-resolution policies are still in the mainstream of the FDIC's explicit statutory authority, the new assistance programs for troubled and failing banks stretch the limits of that authority. These programs include modified payout, open bank assistance, capital forbearance, and bridge banks.

Modified Payout

The FDIC devised the modified payout plan in 1983 in reaction to the 100 percent de facto coverage previously associated with widespread use of P&As. As in a straight payout, the modified payout created a receivership and liquidated the failed bank's assets. However, rather than waiting until assets were sold to begin payments, the FDIC estimated the current value of the remaining assets as the basis for an

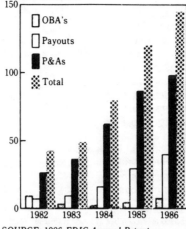

Figure 2   Bank Failures 1982-1986

Number of failures

SOURCE: 1986 *FDIC Annual Report,* Washington D.C.

immediate advance to the receiver for payments to the uninsured depositors and other claimants. In this way, the market discipline of potential losses to uninsured depositors was joined with the disruption-free timeliness of the ordinary P&A. As a result, the modified payout showed promise as a policy that could be applied equally to both large and small banks.

The modified payout first was used in 1984 as an experimental procedure with small failed banks. In the two months prior to the collapse of the Continental Illinois National Bank and Trust Company of Chicago in May 1984, nine of 17 failures involved a modified payout. Given that this procedure had been tried only on small banks, the FDIC argued that the policy was too early in its development to be applied with the requisite degree of assurance to the $33.6 billion Continental Illinois.[10] Based on its prior successful application before Continental Illinois, however, the modified payout still could be used as a possible nondiscriminatory failed-bank policy option.

Open Bank Assistance

The most significant developments in FDIC policy initiatives have come under the umbrella of the open-bank assistance program (OBA). Under the FDI Act of 1950, the FDIC obtained authority to intervene prior to a bank's failure in order to   1) facilitate the merger of a failing bank or 2) prevent failure of a bank that is deemed 'essential.' Up to this time, capital assistance to open banks to prevent failure, had been the job of the Reconstruction Finance Corporation (RFC).[11]

The first provision, section 13(e) of the FDI Act, is an extension of the P&A powers to enable conversion of a closed-bank merger into an open-bank merger when failure is imminent. The FDIC's financial assistance is predicated upon the condition that the failing bank be absorbed by another bank. The open-bank merger was an innovation intended to expedite the arrangement of a P&A and, thus, to minimize further disruption of banking services. It was not intended to save the troubled institution from failure.

The second provision, section 13(c) of the FDI Act, allows the FDIC to prevent the failure of a bank "...when in the opinion of the Board of Directors [of the FDIC] the continued operation of such bank is essential to provide adequate banking service in the community."[12] This interventionary power was intended to be restricted by the condition of essentiality attached to it. In this way, the status of such OBA as an exception rather than a rule was to be preserved.

Although authorized by statute in 1950, this essentiality doctrine was not actually used until 1971 with the "bailout" of Unity Bank of Boston. Within the span of the subsequent 10 years, however, a finding of essentiality was made, and OBA was provided four more times (the Bank of the Commonwealth in Detroit [1972], American Bank & Trust in South Carolina [1974], Farmers Bank of the State of Delaware [1976], and First Pennsylvania National Bank in Philadelphia [1980]).

The greatest logical criticism of OBA has been made on the grounds that it

---

10. See Hearings before the House Committee on Banking, Finance and Urban Affairs, Subcommittee on Financial Institutions, Supervision, Regulation and Insurance, *Inquiry into Continental Illinois Corp. and Continental Illinois National Bank,* October 4, 1984 (98th Congress,   2nd session). Washington, D.C.: Government Printing Office, 1985, pp. 466-467.

11. See Jesse H. Jones, *Fifty Billion Dollars: My Thirteen Years with the RFC, 1932-1945,* Mac-Millan, New York, 1951.

12. See Section 13(c) of the Federal Deposit Insurance Act, 12 U.S.C. Section 1823(c).

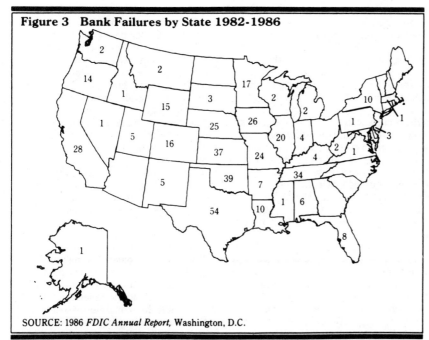

Figure 3   Bank Failures by State 1982-1986

SOURCE: 1986 *FDIC Annual Report*, Washington, D.C.

expands implicit insurance coverage to stockholders and creditors of parent bank holding companies who are not protected under a P&A or a payout.[13]

A second source of criticism surrounds the broad interpretations given to the essentiality test that arise from the vague definition of "community" and the role of opinion in assessing OBA.[14]

Third, the case-by-case basis on which the FDIC has bailed out large banks has propagated the general belief that certain banks are "too large to let fail." If depositors act on this belief, it can lead to an undesirable concentration of assets in large banks. Furthermore, such a belief has dangerous repercussions for the effectiveness of market discipline on the risk-taking of big banks. Overall, the criticisms of OBA highlight the danger that it poses to the continued efficient operation of market discipline in the long run.

As the number and complexity of bank failures has risen in recent years under deregulation, so has the adoption of new OBA programs. Within the last five years, the FDIC has revised the

OBA guidelines twice to afford greater flexibility in preventing the closure of a failing bank.[15] The 1982 Garn-St Germain Act removed essentiality as the prime consideration for OBA and replaced it with cost-efficiency: only if the cost of assistance exceeds the cost of closing and liquidating does a finding of essentiality have to be made. The underlying design is "...to lessen the (financial) risk to the Corporation posed by such insured bank under such threat of instability."[16] Since OBA enables the FDIC to accrue losses as off-balance-sheet contingent claims, there is a strong incentive for the FDIC to infuse capital into a failing institution rather than to arrange a payout or P&A, which would require immediate recognition of losses.

The replacement of essentiality with cost-efficiency as the main determinant reflects the changed role of OBA as a policy tool of the FDIC for resolving bank failures. In 1950, the OBA provision was issued as a last-resort measure, intended to save a failing bank in a rural, unit-banking area in which that bank actually did provide essential banking services. Essentiality was an

extreme condition that needed to be met in order to override the FDIC's noninterventionary role.

By 1987, however, OBA had lost its status as an exceptional measure and has become a mainstream policy. The September 10, 1987 bailout of First City Bancorp of Texas became the 41st case of OBA by the FDIC. Of the 41 OBAs, 37 have occurred in the 1980s. Although the OBA policy affords greater flexibility for the FDIC to resolve failures, such assistance packages usually have some benefit for shareholders and move the FDIC closer to 100 percent de facto coverage of all parties in a failed bank, which further insulates banks from market discipline.

Capital Forbearance
The most recent FDIC policy initiatives have been in the area of capital augmentation. Initially, a number of techniques, such as warrants and net worth certificates (before 1982, called income capital certificates) were employed to "create" capital through alterations in regulatory reporting methods. Since 1985, the FDIC has moved toward a relaxation of capital standards for troubled institutions. Regardless of which technique is used, the policy allows a troubled bank, operating with substandard capital, to remain open in the hope that the bank will eventually recover.

In March 1986, the FDIC and the Comptroller of the Currency announced a joint effort to forbear regarding the enforcement of minimum capital-asset ratios below 7 percent, but above 4 percent, for sound banks with concentrations in agriculture or energy lending.[17] A sizable proportion of recent bank failures have occurred in agriculture and energy-belt states (see figure 3). Accordingly, the capital forbearance plan is aimed at troubled banks within these regions that are seen to have been destabilized more by depressed markets than by mismanagement. The plan is designed ". . . to provide greater operational flexibility to well-managed banks" in the hope that they will recover and thus spare the FDIC considerable liquidation costs.[18]

13. See James B. Thomson, "The Use of Market Information in Pricing Deposit Insurance," *Journal of Money, Credit, and Banking*, vol. 19, no. 4 pp. 528-537 (November 1987).

14. See Sprague, *supra* note 6, p. 28.

15. See FDIC Policy Announcements of August 25, 1983 and December 8, 1986.

16. See Section 13(c), Federal Deposit Insurance Act, *supra* note 12.

17. An agriculture or energy bank is customarily defined as one in which 25 percent of its assets is in farm or energy lending.

18. See FDIC Announcement of Capital Forbearance, March 27, 1986.

Within seven months of the beginning of the forbearance plan, fewer than 20 banks had been accepted, and 17 banks had been denied acceptance into the program.[19] The FDIC and the Comptroller of the Currency then announced a revision of their guidelines, making more banks eligible for capital forbearance. According to the Comptroller of the Currency, capital forbearance is a worthwhile program, although it has not "... covered as many banks as it should have."[20]

Consequently, the program has been broadened in two significant ways: first, capital forbearance has been made available to all insured banks whose problems are seen to be the result of economic conditions, not just energy and agriculture banks; second, the minimum capital-asset ratio of 4 percent has been abolished (that is, any positive capital ratio conceivably may be enough to satisfy minimum regulatory requirements).

By broadening its availability, the FDIC made capital forbearance a more mainstream policy instrument, which is the same pattern previously noted in the development of the OBA programs. An early criticism of capital forbearance in its currently revised form is that it poses the same moral hazard problem that surfaces when troubled banks are insulated from market forces. Counter to the plan's intent, it encourages even greater risk-taking on the part of the failing institution as a last chance to gamble its way out of a weakened capital condition.[21]

Bridge Banks

The latest policy response to the increasing bank failure rate came with the August 1987 banking bill, the Competitive Equality Banking Act, which affords the FDIC more time and greater influence in the decision-making processes of troubled institutions. The FDIC is empowered to construct "bridge banks," which can run ailing institutions for up to three years. Under such a provision, the FDIC can charter a national bank with new management to guide troubled institutions to recovery. Rather than being subject to urgent time constraints, the bridge bank solution allows the FDIC expanded flexibility in pursuing many options.

Conclusion

Over the last two decades, the FDIC has assumed a more active role in the resolution of bank failures and particularly in the regulation of problem banks. Each expansion of FDIC powers has occurred in response to needs that have arisen out of a changed economic or regulatory environment. Due to the recent rise of bank failures, most of the new initiatives attempt to address the problems of troubled banks before they actually fail. Many of the programs under OBA, for example, were developed to prevent banks from failing, albeit with generous infusions of FDIC financial assistance.

In addition, capital forbearance provides banks with time to recover from problems created by depressed market conditions. Bridge banks have been created to combat the increased incentive for the management of troubled banks to "gamble" out of their problems. In this way, bridge bank arrangements could provide sufficient time for the other programs to take effect.

The greater flexibility afforded by an increased number of options allows the FDIC to meet the challenges of problem banks innovatively. However, there is a cost to the more active failure intervention by the FDIC: the erosion of market discipline in the banking system. The trend in bank failure resolution policies has reached a point of 100 percent de facto insurance for all depositors and most creditors, and at least some protection for stockholders. Some of the new FDIC policies, such as the modified payout, have tried to correct for such misallocations and inefficiencies while maintaining the economies associated with preserving ongoing banking franchises.

However, the areas in which the FDIC's failure-resolution policy is being expanded the most, such as OBAs or capital forbearance, tend to insulate problem banks even further from market forces and arguably encourage risk-taking. This could have a perverse effect on the banking system and on the ability of the FDIC to do its job. Thus, a better balance between market regulation and FDIC intervention needs to be more clearly addressed in future FDIC failure resolution policy initiatives.

19. See A. Bennett, "Regulators Report Slow Beginning For Capital Forbearance Program," *American Banker*, December 5, 1986, p. 3.

20. See B. Rehm, "FDIC Will Expand Forbearance Plan For Ailing Banks," *American Banker*, June 9, 1987, p. 1.

21. See "Thrift Industry: Forbearance for Troubled Institutions, 1982-1986," May 1987, U. S. General Accounting Office Briefing Report.

Article Ten

The Thrift Industry: Reconstruction in Progress

by Thomas M. Buynak

During the 1981-82 recession, high interest rates sparked a financial crisis in the savings and loan (thrift) industry.[1] A number of companies were liquidated; others required help from the Federal Home Loan Bank Board (FHLBB). Since then, the industry has shrunk from about 4,000 to 3,200 institutions.[2]

In this *Economic Commentary,* we discuss the problems that high and volatile interest rates have caused for thrifts, starting with the first major hint of trouble back in 1966. We show that, despite deregulation of the lending and other asset powers of thrifts since 1980, more must be done to reduce their susceptibility to high interest rates and to unfavorable economic conditions.

Setting Up Thrifts for a Crisis
The vulnerability of thrifts stems primarily from their traditionally narrow composition of assets and liabilities. Historically, thrifts specialized in offering savings deposits and mortgage loans. This special role was recognized in the 1930s with establishment of the FHLBB and the Federal Savings and Loan Insurance Corporation (FSLIC). During the 1960s and the 1970s, government policy encouraged thrift industry growth in an effort to provide a reliable source of home financing credit. It was mostly thrifts that financed the housing booms during those years.

Regulatory restrictions on thrifts traditionally limited their acquisition of assets to making mortgage loans or to purchasing mortgage-backed securities.

The regulatory restrictions were reinforced by federal tax code provisions that offer thrifts a tax deferral on current income. As recently as 1980, thrifts were still affected strongly by these historic asset restrictions. At the end of 1980, for example, FSLIC-insured thrifts held more than 77 percent of their assets in residential mortgage loans and mortgage-backed securities. Commercial mortgages and consumer loans accounted for about 7 percent and 3 percent of their assets, respectively. Prior to 1980, thrifts were barred from the corporate lending market.

Thrifts also were handicapped because they traditionally relied on personal savings deposits that were subject to interest-rate ceilings.[3] As of year-end 1980, for example, almost 79 percent of thrifts' total liabilities were retail deposits. Approximately 60 percent of these liabilities were small-denomination certificates of deposit (CDs). Until the 1980s, few thrifts attempted to manage their liabilities actively, and most thrifts had only a small number of large-denomination (over $100,000) certificates of deposit (Jumbo CDs), repurchase agreements, and borrowed funds.

The Disintermediation Problem
The first major sign of thrifts' vulnerability to high interest rates occurred during the 1966 credit crunch, when they experienced the first substantial amount of *deposit disintermediation.*

This describes a phenomenon in which depositors shifted funds into higher-yielding investments when market interest rates rose above rates that thrifts were legally allowed to pay.

In 1966, and again in 1969 and 1974, Treasury bill interest rates rose substantially above interest rates that thrifts could pay. As a result, depositors shifted funds from thrifts into higher-yielding instruments. Commercial banks also experienced fund-shifting, but they had more diversified sources of funds and could better weather deposit losses than thrifts.

One effect of fund-shifting was a disruption in the flow of credit to mortgage markets. Consequently, when there was a deposit outflow, or a slowdown in deposit inflows, many thrifts had to ration mortgage credit. Some thrifts also had to liquidate assets and to recognize capital losses on those sold assets to cover deposit withdrawals.[4]

As an alternative to asset sales, thrifts borrowed funds from outside sources, including the FHLBB, or purchased wholesale deposits. Those borrowings, and a reliance on purchased funds, enabled thrifts to avoid or minimize asset sales. However, the borrowed money hurt their earnings because market-rate liabilities were substituted for lower-cost deposit liabilities.

Thomas M. Buynak is an economist at the Federal Reserve Bank of Cleveland. The author would like to thank Mark Sniderman, Walker Todd, Daniel Littman, and Owen Humpage for their helpful comments.

1. In this article, thrifts refer to institutions that have Federal Savings and Loan Insurance Corporation (FSLIC) insurance; another segment of the thrift industry, which includes most savings banks and credit unions, are not discussed here.

2. After 1982, the frequency of FHLBB-assisted mergers decreased dramatically, in part due to the comparatively low remaining level of financial resources available to FSLIC. As of year-end 1985, FSLIC only had approximately $2 billion of its $6 billion fund available as unobligated funds to insure an industry whose assets presently exceed $1 trillion.

3. On March 31, 1986, one of the last vestiges of interest-rate ceilings was removed when passbook savings accounts were deregulated.

Initial Adjustments in the 1970s and Early 1980s

Because of a loosening of interest rate ceilings and because of more proficient liability management during the 1970s, thrifts became less vulnerable to fund-shifting. In May 1973, the Federal Reserve removed remaining interest-rate ceilings on Jumbo CDs, allowing depository institutions to pursue liability management aggressively.

With managed liabilities, thrifts could offset retail deposit outflows. When the economy was expanding, thrifts also could use liability management to accommodate growing loan demands if retail deposit inflows were sluggish or inadequate.

Greater dependence on wholesale liabilities, however, has a potentially negative aspect because such dependence subjects thrifts to sudden and large wholesale deposit withdrawals if investors lose confidence in the institutions' financial condition. This situation, for example, faced Continental Illinois of Chicago in 1984, which suffered large wholesale deposit losses and was forced to seek financial assistance from other large banks and from the Federal Reserve.

In June 1978, federal regulators authorized the 6-month money market certificate (MMC). The MMC required a $10,000 minimum deposit and its interest rate was tied to the 6-month Treasury bill rate. Armed with the MMC, depository institutions finally had a retail liability product that was competitive in a high-interest-rate environment.

At that time, thrifts began replacing liabilities that had low ceiling rates, like the passbook savings account, with market-rate deposit instruments. The MMC was a key factor that reduced thrifts' vulnerability to fund-shifting in the 1979-82 period as interest rates escalated into double digits.

Although these initial regulatory changes and steps toward liability management enabled thrifts to avert severe fund-shifting when interest rates began rising rapidly in 1978, high interest rates severely undermined the thrift industry's overall financial condition. Because of traditionally strict

asset limitations, thrifts were financing long-term, fixed-rate mortgages with rising, market-rate deposits. Thus, while MMCs prevented deposit losses, they greatly increased the cost of deposits relative to the average yield on their mortgage portfolio (see chart 1).

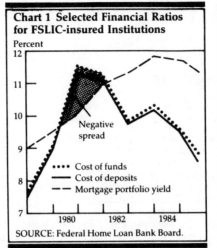

Chart 1 Selected Financial Ratios for FSLIC-insured Institutions

Percent

- •••• Cost of funds
- —— Cost of deposits
- – – – Mortgage portfolio yield

Negative spread

SOURCE: Federal Home Loan Bank Board.

In 1978 and 1979, thrifts were offering mortgages in the 9 percent to 10 percent range, while paying as much as 15 percent on their short-term, market-rate liabilities. Consequently, from 1980 through 1982, thrifts suffered severe losses (see chart 2).

As high interest rates battered thrifts' earnings, and as uncertainty grew over when interest rates would decline, some thrifts switched from low-yield, residential mortgage assets to higher yielding, but riskier, commercial mortgage assets. This strategy adds high-yielding assets at a rapid pace by purchasing high-cost wholesale or brokered deposits. Many insolvent or near-insolvent thrifts viewed this as a necessary tactic for near-term survival.

Riskier assets often indeed provided these thrifts with high returns, but also contributed to large losses when market conditions became unfavorable. An insolvent thrift, or a thrift approaching insolvency, has the incentive to take chances to improve its position because FSLIC deposit insurance

creates a "heads I win, tails the FSLIC loses" situation. If its strategy is successful, a risk-taking thrift and its stockholders profit enormously. But, if unsuccessful, the FSLIC shields depositors and bears much of the loss. This situation faces some thrifts today

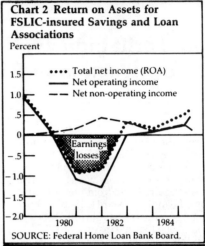

Chart 2 Return on Assets for FSLIC-insured Savings and Loan Associations

Percent

- •••• Total net income (ROA)
- —— Net operating income
- – – – Net non-operating income

Earnings losses

SOURCE: Federal Home Loan Bank Board.

Deregulating Thrifts in the 1980s

As the financial health of the thrift industry deteriorated, Congress enacted the Depository Institutions Deregulation and Monetary Control Act (DIDMCA) in 1980 and passed the Depository Institutions Act of 1982, popularly known as the Garn-St Germain Act.[6] Following DIDMCA and Garn-St Germain, many states granted *state*-chartered thrifts similar or broader asset powers.

Under DIDMCA and Garn-St Germain, federally chartered thrifts can invest up to 30 percent of their total assets in nonmortgage loans, including consumer loans, commercial paper, and corporate securities. Federally chartered thrifts also are empowered to offer up to 10 percent of their assets in non-real-estate commercial loans.

In 1982, federal regulators liberalized the adjustable rate mortgage (ARM), giving thrifts wider discretion over ARMs' terms and conditions. ARMs enabled thrifts to shorten the maturities of their mortgage portfolios, making mortgage portfolios more responsive to changing interest rates.

---

4. Capital losses occurred when market rates rose above the current mortgage yields on the loans sold. A disparity between contractual and market interest rates reduces the price of existing mortgage assets (this effect is analogous to the way in which rising market interest rates affect existing bond prices).

---

5. In 1985, the FHLBB implemented a program to control the quantity and quality of direct investments, constraining thrifts' capacity to assume an equity stake in certain real estate and other investments. There is disagreement over whether direct investments have been an important cause of thrift failures, or whether they actually have strengthened thrifts' financial condition. In another 1985 FHLBB proposal, the growth of thrifts' liabilities was tied to capital growth.

A major consequence of the 1980 deregulation acts is that the susceptibility of thrifts to fund-shifting caused by high interest rates was virtually eliminated. As a result of being permitted to offer money market deposit accounts (MMDA) and Super Nows, thrifts can now compete effectively for retail deposits.

Immunizing Thrifts' Balance Sheets

Although deregulation eliminated the fund-shifting problem and improved the sensitivity of thrifts' earnings to interest-rate changes, thrifts today still remain vulnerable to rising interest rates. Deregulation, however, has provided many of the requisite tools for thrifts to *immunize* their balance sheets, thus protecting themselves from interest-rate fluctuations.

A balance sheet is immunized if a percentage change in interest rates affects the market value of assets and the market value of liabilities by correspondingly exact amounts. Portfolio immunization relies on the concept of *duration*. A balance sheet is immunized if the duration of assets exactly equals the duration of liabilities. The duration of assets or liabilities is the weighted average maturity of cash flows from assets or payments to depositors associated with those assets or liabilities. If the duration of an asset or a liability is short, then a small change in interest rates will have a negligible impact on the prepayment of mortgages or on when depositors are paid.

The current problem faced by thrifts is that, despite deregulation and portfolio adjustment, their liability duration is still shorter than their asset duration; if interest rates rise, they could pay out money faster than they earn it. Ironically, deregulation initially aggravated thrifts' duration mismatch because the rapid growth of MMDAs, a liability of extremely short duration, came mainly at the expense of savings deposits and small CDs. This affected commercial banks as well.

Currently, thrifts' duration mismatch between assets and liabilities is narrower because they have altered the composition of their assets in several ways. During the past five years, residential mortgage assets as a percentage of thrifts' total assets has declined from over 77 percent to approximately 61 percent today. (The fixed-rate mortgage loan has the longest duration of all the assets in thrifts' asset portfolios.) In fact, the position of portfolio-held residential mortgage *loans* as a percentage of total assets has fallen from almost 73 percent in 1980 to just above 50 percent, as of 1985's third quarter. This retreat from mortgage markets by thrifts as direct lenders is being partially offset by a steady rise in their net purchases of mortgage-backed securities.

Since 1980, thrifts have gradually added consumer and commercial loans to their asset portfolios, increasing to 5.2 percent of total assets in the third quarter of l985 from 2.7 percent as of year-end l980. (These assets typically have considerably shorter durations than fixed-rate mortgage loans.) Commercial mortgage loans moreover have grown even more rapidly since 1980, rising from approximately 7 percent to 12 percent as of 1985's third quarter.

The acquisition of commercial loans by FSLIC-insured institutions has slowed considerably in recent months, owing to strong mortgage credit demand and possibly to more stringent regulations that require thrifts to hold reserve balances against poorly performing commercial loans.

Until recently, the thrift industry was actively marketing ARMs instead of fixed-rate mortgage loans. Indeed, the ARM share of new total loan originations grew rapidly in late 1983, peaking at 68 percent in August 1984. According to FHLBB estimates, ARMs presently account for about one-third of the current value of all mortgage loans held by thrifts.

Fixed-rate mortgage rates have declined substantially since mid-1985. Borrowers are demanding more fixed-rate financing of new mortgages, and are refinancing existing mortgages that have high fixed or adjustable rates. Consequently, ARMs today constitute less than one-third of all new loans.

Mortgage banking techniques are becoming an ever-growing part of the thrift business. Mortgage banking involves making mortgage loans that are sold in secondary mortgage markets to agencies such as the Federal Home Loan Mortgage Corporation. Thrifts are selling both new loans and seasoned loans—i.e., loans that are currently held in their mortgage portfolios. In the face of strong fixed-rate financing demands, some thrifts are avoiding a larger asset duration by selling their fixed-rate loans in secondary mortgage markets while retaining ARMs in their portfolios.

Financial futures contracts also are becoming more popular among thrifts as a method to protect themselves. The FHLBB broadened the ability of thrifts to use financial futures in 1981, when it eased regulations governing their use by thrifts. A financial futures or a forward contract permits thrifts to hedge interest-rate risk, particularly if they retain fixed-rate assets in their portfolios.

The Capital Adequacy Problem

Since 1983, interest rates have declined, and thrift industry profits have steadily improved. As chart 1 shows, the cost of funds to the thrift industry has fallen sharply since 1981, while the yield on mortgage portfolios has grown through 1983. After 1983, since thrifts still are liability-sensitive, their cost of funds has fallen more rapidly than the decline in their average portfolio yield.

In the third quarter of 1985, net *operating* income, which includes interest income and income from loan origination and services after deducting the cost of funds, doubled from the first half results because of even lower interest rate declines. *Non-operating* income, which results from the sale of assets, has provided thrifts with a major source of income since 1983 (see chart 2). Thus, asset sales provide a means to bolster current earnings or to minimize current losses, but do not provide a viable, long-run strategy to generate earnings because the most attractive assets are the ones sold in the market.

Thrifts' earnings losses, which were attributed to high interest rates, have

6. See, "Leveling the Playing Field — A review of the DIDMCA of 1980 and the Garn-St Germain Act of 1982," *Readings in Economics and Finance,* the Federal Reserve Bank of Chicago, December 1983, pp. 34-39.

severely eroded the industry's capital position. In the third quarter of 1985, the net worth of thrifts as an industry stood at a low 3.1 percent on the basis of generally accepted accounting principles (GAAP). Lower interest rates have improved earnings, and the industry has begun to repair net worth. However, since the level of net worth is extremely low, a sustained period of low interest rates is still required so that strong earnings can sufficiently recapitalize the industry.

Thrifts, moreover, will have to consistently generate even higher earnings if the FHLBB adopts a proposal to raise capital requirements from 3 percent to 6 percent, which is the capital ratio for commercial banks. Beginning in 1980, the FHLBB reduced capital standards, first from 5 percent to 4 percent; then, in 1982, dropped it to the current level of 3 percent. As in the banking industry, there also are proposals under discussion to impose risk-based capital standards on the thrift industry.

There is a large segment of the thrift industry that still requires low interest rates to generate the long-term earnings needed to adequately rebuild capital. According to a recent U.S. General Accounting Office (GAO) report, the number of GAAP-insolvent institutions (i.e., those with negative GAAP net worth) has risen steadily since 1979.[7] As of mid-1985, there were 461 GAAP-insolvent institutions with assets of approximately $113 billion, or 11 percent of total industry assets.

If thrifts that are poorly capitalized (i.e., those having less than 3 percent GAAP net worth) are included, the financially weak segment of the thrift industry rises to a total of 1,300 institutions, or 41 percent of all FSLIC institutions.[8] As of June 1985, these weak thrifts had assets of almost $433 billion, or nearly 43 percent of total industry assets. The GAO study also found that low net worth is correlated with low profitability. Thus, we can infer that lower interest rates have not improved the earnings of the weakest segment of the industry on any sustainable basis.

Concluding Remarks

It is evident that a large segment of the thrift industry has only marginally benefited from lower interest rates since 1983. Using the GAO's data, the financial condition of 471 thrifts, or 15 percent of the industry has, in fact, worsened or failed to improve, even as rates have fallen. It is still far from clear that marginally lower interest rates will eventually ease their financial problems.

There is even a larger thrift industry group whose long-term viability depends on a sustained period of low interest rates in the future. This group comprises about 800 thrifts (26 percent of the industry) that are currently profitable, but that have negative or extremely low net worth under GAAP.

Thrifts have made significant strides to protect themselves. The duration of their assets today is shorter than it was during the 1981-82 recession. Thrifts as a whole, however, have taken limited advantage of new asset powers under the Garn-St Germain and the DIDMCA Acts. Some observers are critical of the slow pace at which they are adjusting to their new powers. However, many thrifts apparently have adopted a moderate diversification pace because it allows them to become familiar with these powers more wisely and prudently.

Thrifts also are relying on ARMs and are adopting mortgage banking as a viable lending strategy. However, as a whole, they have made only slow progress toward portfolio immunization. The industry is still vulnerable to rising and volatile interest rates because their asset portfolios are still dominated by long-term, fixed-rate mortgage loans.

Some thrifts currently are even taking a step backwards. Indeed, history could repeat itself. The current return to fixed-rate lending by some thrifts, combined with the tendency to hold these instruments as portfolio loans, and to rely on short-term, variable-rate deposits for funding could provide all the ingredients for a case of deja vu. This could prove damaging because the duration imbalance could put some already capital-depleted thrifts in a situation of paying out more than they take in—if and when interest rates rise.

---

7. See, "Thrift Industry Problems — Potential Demands on the FSLIC Insurance Fund," United States General Accounting Office, GAO/GGD-86-48BR, February 1986.

8. As the number of insolvent institutions grew rapidly, the FHLBB liberalized its *regulatory* accounting principles (RAP) in 1982 to avoid liq-

uidating or providing financial assistance to a large number of problem cases. The purpose of RAP was to buy time so that lower interest rates could allow technically insolvent thrifts to rebuild capital. There is growing criticism of RAP in some circles because RAP has been in place for four years, has not materially improved the condition of or outlook for thrifts, and merely

conceals the true net worth of the thrift industry. The FHLBB has begun taking steps to repeal liberalized RAP rules, bringing them gradually in line with GAAP standards. Examples of this are the proposed FHLBB rule changes that would substantially limit the future use of deferred loan losses and appraised equity capital by FSLIC-insured thrifts.

Article Eleven

DANGERS OF CAPITAL FORBEARANCE:
THE CASE OF THE FSLIC AND "ZOMBIE" S&Ls

EDWARD J. KANE*

This paper portrays Federal Savings and Loan Insurance Corporation (FSLIC) forbearance and congressional unwillingness to increase the FSLIC's human or capital resources to the size necessary to handle developing economic insolvencies as a joint policy crime that has served to bifurcate the savings and loan industry into the living and the living dead. As agents for the taxpayer, Congress and the FSLIC have assumed too much discretion and have chosen to exercise that discretion myopically. An agent has a duty to represent its principal's economic interests more effectively than this. The FSLIC's policy touchstone should be to negotiate and enforce the same kind of covenant provisions that a prudent private guarantor would require.

I. INTRODUCTION

Forbearance means not requiring someone to meet an obligation that could reasonably be enforced. Deposit institution regulators engage in capital forbearance when they explicitly and asymmetrically lower their requirements for minimum net worth at a decapitalized institution. Because capital standards play an important role at insured deposit institutions in limiting managerial incentives to "bet the bank," firms qualifying for forbearance are apt to be those with the greatest need for injections of additional capital. Data compiled by Barth, Brumbaugh, and Sauerhaft (1986) show that the costs of resolving a savings and loan institution's (S&L's) insolvency rises on average with the length of time during which regulatory response is delayed. Moreover, adopting a policy of letting a capital shortfall ride in this way makes potential payoffs on risky projects more asymmetric even for a well-capitalized deposit institution.

Despite the deleterious long-run effects of capital forbearance on risk-taking incentives and on insolvency-resolution expense, federal banking regulators in March 1986 embraced a two-pronged forbearance policy for troubled farm and energy banks. The first prong of the policy consists of actively encour-

*Everett D. Reese Professor of Banking and Monetary Economics, The Ohio State University, Columbus, and Research Associate, National Bureau of Economic Research (NBER), Cambridge, Mass. The opinions expressed in this paper are the author's and should not be construed to represent those of the NBER. This paper is a revised version of a presentation at the 61st Annual Western Economic Association International Conference, San Francisco, Calif., July 1986, in a session organized by George G. Kaufman, Loyola University of Chicago, and George J. Benston, University of Rochester, N.Y.

aging these banks to use Financial Accounting Standard No. 15, which permits an institution to pump up its reported capital by charging off its de facto losses on troubled loans slowly over time. The second prong consists of reducing capital requirements for seven years from 5½ to 4 percent for banks able to gain entry into a specially instituted forbearance program.

Forbearance amounts to giving up valuable covenants in federal deposit insurance contracts without a quid pro quo. Therefore, if officers of a private fiduciary (e.g., a pension fund) were to adopt such a policy, they would risk being sued for violation of prudent-man rules. To understand why the Federal Deposit Insurance Corporation (FDIC) would turn away from its long-standing policy of enforcing its net worth covenants at commercial banks, one must look at political (especially congressional) pressures and at politicians' contention that capital forbearance by the Federal Savings and Loan Insurance Corporation (FSLIC) has served the nation well in recent years.

II. DEFINING "ZOMBIE" S&Ls

This paper's subtitle embodies a less sanguine view of the opportunity cost of FSLIC forbearance. It portrays FSLIC forbearance (which was dictated in part by congressional unwillingness to increase the FSLIC's human or capital resources to the size necessary to handle developing economic insolvencies) as a myopic policy crime that has served to bifurcate the S&L industry into the living and the living dead.

Zombie S&Ls are institutional corpses capable of financial locomotion and various forms of malefic behavior. Much as in George Romero movies, these undead entities wreak havoc in financial markets by feeding on the markets of the living, thereby turning competitors into zombies, too. Zombie firms do this in two ways: (1) They lower industry profit margins by shifting the deposit insurance subsidy they receive (this implicit subsidy grows rapidly with the riskiness of their portfolio and with the extent of their de facto insolvency) into higher deposit rates and lower loan rates. (2) They increase the annual deposit insurance premiums that surviving institutions must ultimately pay.

The number of zombies at large and the size of the government's implicit stake in undead institutions is seriously understated by accounting figures. Generally accepted accounting principles (GAAP) give managers freedom asymmetrically to defer the recognition of costs and declines in the market value of depreciated positions and to speed up the recognition of revenues and of increases in the market value of appreciated positions. At troubled institutions, mortgage points booked as current income, unbooked declines in the market value of net assets, and unrecognized layers of FSLIC commitments and indemnifications to acquirers and "consigned managers" hide real losses that deserve to flow through to the FSLIC. Eventually, the resources to resolve these losses must come from competing financial institutions and the general taxpayer (Kane 1985).

At best, accounting data can be used to bound the size of the problem from below. Given the freedom to overstate accounting income and capital, any institution with negative capital and income according to GAAP is almost certainly a zombie. General Accounting Office (GAO) figures show that in each quarter of 1984 and 1985, roughly 230 S&Ls with about $55 billion in assets failed to show either positive income or positive capital. Despite the sharp fall in market interest rates over that period, the number of firms in this condition has remained relatively steady. If zombie S&Ls are defined as those with negative capital, then the estimated number of zombies rises to 450. (More precisely, the GAO estimates that 459 S&Ls holding more than $100 billion in assets had negative GAAP net worth in September 1985.) Finally, if we increase the latter number conservatively by one-third to allow for institutions that have experienced devastating economic losses not shown under GAAP, we reach a reasonable lower-bound estimate of 600 firms with roughly $130 billion in assets. This last definition covers 18 percent of FSLIC-insured institutions and 12 percent of industry assets. Using the 14 percent ratio of explicit costs to assets that the FSLIC incurred in winding up the affairs of failing clients during 1984 and 1985 (reported in Barth, Brumbaugh, and Sauerhaft 1986) lets us bound the government's implicit equity stake in zombies as something in excess of $18 billion. If the average present value of the FSLIC's risk exposure in nonzombie institutions were only 2 percent of their assets, then the value of the FSLIC's total exposure would be $36 billion.

III. HOW DID SO MANY ZOMBIES ACCUMULATE?

Over the past 25 years, the number of S&Ls has halved and the diversity of the asset and liability sides of S&L balance sheets has increased greatly. However, the health of the S&L industry as a whole has benefited from this consolidation and reorientation. Allowing for interest-induced capital gains and losses on S&L mortgages, we estimate that the aggregate capital-to-asset ratio at S&Ls in September 1985 was in the neighborhood of 4.5 percent on a market-value basis. Of course, as we have labored to show, this net worth is distributed bimodally.

The segment of the distribution whose mode is negative owes its existence to the FSLIC's failing to bury its dead before witch doctors could get hold of the bodies. In view of the moral hazard inherent in offering a system of financial guarantees whose explicit prices are not risk-rated, FSLIC information, monitoring, and response systems have been very different from those of a self-interested private guarantor.

The FSLIC's information system consists of the accounting framework used to measure client performance and risk exposure. The agency's monitoring or targeting system has two parts: (1) the periodic reports that it collects on these matters and (2) the pattern and character of site examinations it conducts to measure changes in the risk that client operations impose on accumulated agency reserves. The FSLIC's response system comprises the policy program by which agency risk managers react to incoming analyses about unfavorable developments at client institutions. To illustrate how badly the FSLIC has administered these programs for the taxpayer, we may liken the agency to a rifleman hired to guard taxpayers from a band of marauders. This rifleman has equipped himself (1) with a set of eyeglasses whose thick lenses are misprescribed (his information system), (2) with a rifle whose telescopic sight has been mounted backwards (his monitoring system), and (3) with a pair of boxing gloves that in keeping his hands warm makes it impossible for him to pull his rifle's trigger in timely fashion (his response system).

As an agent for the taxpayer, the FSLIC has been granted too much discretion and has exercised that discretion myopically. An agent has a duty to represent its principal's economic interests more effectively than this. The FSLIC's policy touchstone should be to negotiate and enforce the same kind of covenant provisions that a prudent private guarantor would require.

Clearly, a private guarantor would define an institution's health in terms of the economic value of the institution's net assets. Its criterion for insolvency would turn on comprehensive measures of the market value of the equivalent of stockholder-contributed net worth. By contrast, the criteria that the FSLIC has used focus on market value of appreciated assets, book value of selected other assets and liabilities, and measures of the firm's liquidity. A private guarantor would require regular reports on changes in the market value of net assets. It would energetically double check these reports for possible misrepresentation and would punish misrepresentation severely. It would compile information on net asset values and on the interest rates paid by insured firms on deposits and other debts. Then it would use this information to track changes in its own risk exposure and to trigger closer examinations and regulatory penalties. Finally, a private guarantor would insist that failing firms either recapitalize themselves or be liquidated, sold off to new investors, or put into conservatorship.

IV. WHAT POLICY PROBLEMS DO ZOMBIE S&Ls RAISE?

Zombie S&Ls raise three policy issues. The first is how to resolve (i.e., how to distribute across society) the losses that zombies already have accumulated. This is the problem of how to recapitalize the FSLIC, i.e., how to give it the financial resources and bureaucratic freedom it needs to wind up expeditiously the affairs of zombie firms. The extent of the second and third problems depends on how adequately and over what time period the first problem is handled. The second problem is how to corral the zombies effectively during the windup process so that they do not accumulate even more losses. The third problem, which grows out of the second, is how to stop existing zombies from creating even more undead institutions—how to prevent these zombies from bidding down funding margins in the markets they serve and from forcing up the future level of deposit insurance premiums levied implicitly or explicitly on FSLIC-insured institutions.

In private conversation, Federal Home Loan Bank Board (FHLBB) researchers have estimated that zombies currently are paying an average 50- to 60-basis-point premium on fully insured certificates of deposit (CDs). This premium reflects a combination of two developments: (1) a portion of these institutions' deposit insurance subsidies being shifted into their deposit rates, and (2) growing public doubt that FSLIC guarantees on zombie funds will in fact be paid in timely fashion.

V. INADEQUACY OF ACTIVE POLICY PROPOSALS

The proposal currently before Congress to recapitalize the FSLIC is not making good progress. For months, the problem appeared to be merely one of finding a way to borrow funds for the FSLIC without acknowledging an impact on the federal budget. The scheme eventually agreed upon seeks to give the FSLIC access to $15 billion in new liquid resources through a shell corporation. This corporation's resources consist of a transfer of Federal Home Loan Bank (FHLB) equity and of cash flows that derive from maintaining the current supplementary deposit insurance premium of one-eighth of 1 percent of S&L deposits. In August 1986, even this too-small plan was foundering on opposition from U.S. League of Savings Association (USLSA) lobbyists concerned that its members might be required to pay the supplementary FSLIC premium indefinitely. They recognize that a semipermanent supplementary premium could put them at a disadvantage in competing with FDIC-insured firms and would, in any case, encourage their best-capitalized members to find ways to shift their insurance to the FDIC (e.g., by converting to commercial bank charters).

The irony is that even this program fails either to confront the size of the problem realistically or to deal with all three of its aspects (Ely 1986 expresses a similar view). The proposal presumes that the size of accumulated losses is relatively small ($20 billion at the outside) and will stand relatively still. The analysis fails to price the contingency elements in FSLIC guarantees. It looks only at expected cash flows from supplementary premiums and at S&Ls now known to be having difficulty. The volatility of the economic environment makes the contingency elements too important to neglect. The current interest rate environment is perhaps better perceived as merely the "eye" of interest rates' latest cyclical "storm." S&Ls are loading up on fixed-rate mortgages faster than they are selling them off into secondary markets. Across the industry, this is creating a pool of imperfectly hedged, short-funded investments. The sharp downward trend in the percentage of new mortgages made at variable rates since mid-1984 shows that S&L managers are reloading the same cannons that nearly shot so many of them out of the water the last time.

A second weakness in the proposal lies in its presumption that the S&L industry's stronger members can earn enough in the next few years to be willing and able to bail out the others with their own resources. The USLSA's lobbying activity suggests that it does not believe the FSLIC can set exit fees high enough to choke off the incentive for well-capitalized S&Ls to convert their charters either directly or indirectly as part of an acquisition by a bank holding company.

Finally, because it is undersized, the program can only thin the current zombie herd. End-game incentives facing surviving zombie managements ensure that in the aggregate, FSLIC losses will continue to grow rapidly even in a favorable interest rate environment. This is because S&Ls are now subject to important non-interest-rate forms of risk, and the FSLIC has an asymmetric share in the outcome of the risks that its clients take on. The share of client losses the FSLIC bears is much larger than the share of client gains that it is able to capture.

VI. WHAT SHOULD BE DONE TO RESTORE INCENTIVE COMPATIBILITY?

Managers of zombie institutions are exploiting the FSLIC, while political and bureaucratic incentives lead politicians and FSLIC managers to exploit taxpayers (including healthy S&Ls and healthy banks). To restore incentive compatibility, the FSLIC should be required to collect market-value performance data and to recapitalize, pay off, put into conservatorship, or liquidate all zombies as expeditiously as possible. Possibilities for regional consolidation should be exploited where this makes economic sense. This merely would rationalize current FHLBB policy, which awards acquirers up to a three-state entry license in exchange for acquiring a zombie. Implicitly, Congress already has made the political decision to cede to the FSLIC the right to sell any entry privileges it wants.

It is important that managements and stockholders of zombie firms be made to bear the costs of permitting their firms to become insolvent. Considerable long-run benefits will flow to taxpayers and to the deposit insurance system from disciplining those who abuse the system. Using an economic solvency criterion is not truly burdensome. Corporate finance theory assures us that requiring managers to raise new capital before their firms become insolvent is not heavy punishment.

If a gradual approach is to be adopted and only the worst zombies are to be culled, then the FSLIC's equity stake in other S&Ls should be made explicit. Any decapitalized firms that are mutuals should be converted to stock status and the FSLIC should be given shares or warrants to balance its claim. To keep zombies and ex-zombies from ruining the margins of healthy S&Ls, temporarily nationalized firms might be given temporary federal funding to replace the hot money currently on their books. This would remove the zombie premium from rates on insured CDs and would make the subsidy these firms receive explicit for taxpayers to see.

Congress and the administration need to face up to the long-run benefits of appropriating funds for this purpose. Because hidden subsidies are hard to control, inevitably they grow too large. That is why they are so popular with recipients. Putting off the problem increases the discounted present value of FSLIC losses.

Most importantly, the zombie problem must be resolved to clear the way for effective deposit insurance reform. We cannot design adequate pricing, information, monitoring, and response systems if we require that the burdens these systems generate not exceed the capacities of zombies to pay. Knowing that meaningful reform would place burdens on zombies that could not be collected has tended to stop serious reform proposals dead in their tracks.

APPENDIX

(The Shadow Financial Regulatory Committee has issued the statement below about the need to recapitalize the FSLIC and zombie S&Ls. The committee's purpose and membership are outined in the introduction to this symposium.)

According to estimates reported by the U.S. General Accounting Office, as of mid-1985 461 S&Ls with $113 billion of assets were operating with negative net worth, as defined by generally accepted accounting principles (GAAP). For the industry as a whole, the deficit aggregated $3½ billion. The number of economically or market-value insolvent S&L associations is underestimated by GAAP, since GAAP includes as assets goodwill and other intangibles carried at "book" values. In essence, economically insolvent S&Ls are de facto nationalized; in practice, they are appropriately described as "zombies."

The zombie development has reached its present stage for several reasons. Supervisory monitoring and information development systems for S&Ls have been inadequate. The Federal Home Loan Bank System chose to defer oversight problems; operating and valuation losses were concealed by novel and irregular regulatory accounting principles (RAP) and the use of a liquidity criterion to differentiate between the viable and zombie institutions. The availability to insolvent institutions of FSLIC guarantees of deposits has enabled most of these institutions to pass the liquidity test and continue in operation.

The presence of S&L zombies raises three issues of public policy. First, S&L zombies must be kept from absorbing additional FSLIC resources by the contamination of healthy institutions and through future operating losses. This suggests the need for expeditious recapitalization, public conservatorship, interindustry takeover, or closure of these entities, since existing regulations have been ineffective in curbing the zombie practice of bidding up deposit rates. Healthy institutions are also weakened by agency-imposed, across-the-board increases in deposit insurance premiums.

The second problem is to distribute the economic losses already imposed on FSLIC. A 1982 resolution expressed the sense of Congress that the full faith and credit of the U.S. might be available to potential claimants against FSLIC reserves. If these potential claims were now to come due, FSLIC would be unable to meet them with its present resources. An injection of substantial new capital into FSLIC would be required. Although the largest possible part of this capital injection should come in some way from the thrift industry, recent proposals for new infusions to FSLIC from advances by the Federal Home Loan Banks do not fully resolve the problem.

The third policy requirement is to prevent a repetition of this development in the future. A central element of reform must be an early elimination of well-known weaknesses. This applies to banks as well as to S&Ls. A threshold for the "wind-up" of an institution's position should be established at some level of net worth above zero. Ideally, such net worth should be defined in market terms—that is, balance sheet and off-balance sheet positions should be marked to market at frequent intervals to provide an estimate of economic net worth. Recent proposals by the Federal Home Loan Bank Board to increase capital and liquidity requirements, to move away from RAP accounting, and to strengthen oversight of credit quality represent steps in the right direction.

REFERENCES

Barth, J. R., R. D. Brumbaugh, Jr., and D. Sauerhaft, "Failure Costs of Government-Regulated Financial Firms: The Case of Thrift Institutions," unpublished manuscript, Federal Home Loan Bank Board, Washington, D.C., 1986.

Ely, B., "This Savings and Loan Mess Won't Go Away," *Wall Street Journal*, July 17, 1986, editorial page.

Kane, E. J., *The Gathering Crisis in Federal Deposit Insurance*, MIT Press, Cambridge, Mass., 1985.

Article Twelve

Loose Lending

Texas S&L Disasters Are Blamed, in Part, On Freewheeling Style

---

Some Real-Estate Developers Bought Thrifts and Used Them as Source of Funds

---

Links Among Four Bankers

By LEONARD M. APCAR

Staff Reporter of THE WALL STREET JOURNAL

DALLAS—After buying a Texas savings and loan association in 1983, Thomas M. Gaubert wasn't particularly impressed with his more-experienced competitors, comparing them to "a Rotary Club luncheon in Hamtramck, Mich."

Mr. Gaubert has never had much patience with small-town guys with small-time ideas. Citizens Savings & Loan Association of Grand Prairie, Texas, had a modest $40.5 million in assets when he bought control of it for about $1 million. He renamed it Independent American Savings Association and launched a program of explosive growth. At its zenith, the S&L had $1.86 billion in assets, and Mr. Gaubert envisioned a financial-services and real-estate empire that would provide funds for home builders like himself in good times and bad.

Instead, he was ousted from his S&L by federal regulators in 1984. Independent American is insolvent and in the hands of the Federal Savings and Loan Insurance Corp., it is operating as Independent American Savings Association, F.S.L.A.

Deregulation and a Boom

Deregulation of S&Ls in the early 1980s opened up commercial lending to the industry at a time when the Texas economy was booming. Overnight, Texas became a financial playground for Mr. Gaubert and several other Dallas real-estate high rollers. They saw the thrift business as a vehicle for their big ambitions and expensive tastes, as offering a chance to become lenders instead of borrowers.

"I am tired of playing Monopoly with my money," one developer-turned-banker confided in the early days. "This way, we can use the depositors' money."

For some developers, "owning a Texas thrift was a dream come true—a virtual printing press to provide money to develop real estate," says William K. Black, who, until July 1, was the FSLIC's deputy director. He is now a high official at the Federal Home Loan Bank of San Francisco.

Many Risky Loans

The new S&L owners often skirted the edge of regulatory propriety, and some of them, investigators say, may have committed fraud. Some S&Ls' operations were "a variant of the old pyramid scheme," Mr. Black adds. They required a steady flow of deposits, which the government insured, to pile risky loans atop others and generate quick profits from loan fees.

In effect, Uncle Sam aided the scheme. Backed by federal deposit insurance, the S&Ls paid high interest rates for big, insured deposits, which the S&Ls lent interest-free to their developer friends. The loans frequently were padded with stiff loan fees and interest charges, which the S&Ls kept on their books. When interest was due, the borrower didn't pay it; the S&L simply transferred funds to the S&L from an "interest reserve account" funded by the loan. A similar process siphoned loan fees from the loans.

The phony incomes produced wildly exaggerated profits that wound up as dividends in the pockets of some S&L owners, regulators say.

Banks may structure real-estate loans similarly, but S&L deregulation allowed only thrift institutions to make loans without any down payment by the borrower. And in Texas, where S&L powers are broader, loans could exceed the purchase price of property.

When the loans soured, the S&Ls jacked up rates to lure more deposits, cranked out

Problem Loans, Texas-Style

Thrifts' problem loans as a percentage of assets

"Texas 40"

Rest of Texas thrifts

United States

1982 '83 '84 '85 '86

*The 40 financially weakest Texas thrifts at Dec. 31, 1986

Source: Federal Home Loan Bank Board

larger long-shot loans and booked more fees to cover the losses. Now, as thrifts are collapsing in Texas, the government is protecting depositors and trying to mop up the lending mess.

"There is such a pattern there," says a former federal regulator, "that it is hard to believe that it all fell into place accidentally." At some Texas thrifts, he says, "there was clearly a looting-type situation. Some got in and started the looting," he adds, "and then others said, 'Look at those guys driving Rolls-Royces and living it up,' " and they became "copycat" S&Ls.

Today, of 280 Texas S&Ls, about 60 are insolvent. Regulators say about two-thirds of those are "brain dead," open but sustaining losses and likely to collapse. Besides Mr. Gaubert, three other leading players who piloted Texas thrifts have been removed from their S&Ls by regulators:

—Don R. Dixon, another Dallas home builder, who bought sleepy Vernon Savings & Loan Association in North Texas and converted it into a personal piggy bank with $1.3 billion in assets to finance a yacht, lavish California homes, a fleet of planes and loans to cronies. About 96% of

Vernon's loans were in default when regulators took control of it last March and accused Vernon officers of looting. He has filed for personal bankruptcy and has taken the Fifth Amendment when questioned by government investigators.

—Jarrett E. Woods Jr., a Dallas real-estate investor, who bought another small-town Texas S&L, had a fancy for million-dollar loans without borrower equity. Among them were loans to a network of other Texas S&L insiders. The seizure by federal regulators last fall of his Western Savings Association, with $2 billion in assets, was the third-largest on record. A lawsuit by Mr. Woods to regain his thrift was denied by Federal Judge Barefoot Sanders, who called Western "the story of a management oblivious to the recklessness of its policies." Mr. Woods is appealing the decision.

—Edwin T. McBirney III, a 35-year-old Dallas real-estate millionaire who merged six small, mostly unprofitable S&Ls into Sunbelt Savings Association, which at its peak was one of Texas's largest, with $3.2 billion in assets. He lent money with such eye-popping speed that would-be borrowers crowded into Sunbelt's waiting room or staked out one of his favorite restaurants. Sunbelt didn't fail, but after a string of losses and loan irregularities at the association, regulators pressured Mr. McBirney to leave, though he remains the largest shareholder. He also is the president of Tangent Corp. and Amchase Financial Corp., both of Dallas, and recently took control of Homac Inc., a small, publicly held Detroit real-estate company.

Of the four S&L executives, federal regulators have accused only Messrs. Dixon and Woods of wrongdoing in federal court.

At the local level, the Texas thrift debacle has left thousands of depositors worried about the safety of their funds, and the recession-struck real-estate market reeling from a glut of projects thrown together with easy money. Dallas has about 38 million square feet of unused office space, equivalent to 17 Empire State Buildings.

In Washington, much of the debate over the number of billions needed to bolster the FSLIC focuses on the Texas problem. Roy G. Green, the president of the Federal Home Loan Bank of Dallas, conservatively estimates that up to two-thirds of the proposed $8.5 billion bailout fund will be needed in Texas alone.

Thomas M. Gaubert
Independent Amer.

Tracking the Billions

Several weeks ago, the Federal Bureau of Investigation launched an ambitious effort to track billions of dollars in land deals throughout the Lone Star State. Many of the transactions involved Messrs. Dixon, Gaubert, McBirney and Woods and several of their borrowers. A Dallas federal grand jury subpoenaed their personal bank records as well as those of more than 250 other S&L owners, executives, borrowers and a few of their wives.

Much of what they find, it appears, also will reflect a breakdown in the federal and state S&L regulatory system. Regulators concede that the high-flying lending operations in Texas S&Ls simply spun out of their control and still aren't in hand.

"This is the biggest Keystone Kops debacle to happen to U.S. financial institutions since the Great Depression," says an experienced S&L executive hired by the FSLIC to help unravel one of Texas's weakest S&Ls. "The failure on the regulators' side is every bit equal to the failures committed by the other side."

Even though the newly minted lenders were doubling and redoubling the size of their new S&Ls, thrift examiners were taking up to two years to schedule a visit. And when the regional Federal Home Loan Bank was moved to Dallas from Little Rock in late 1983, the number of agents and supervisors shrank to 12 from 34. "We lacked bodies and experienced people," says Mr. Black, the former FSLIC official. "Turnover was pandemic."

Extra Examiners Needed

About a year ago, the situation was so grave that federal regulators summoned as many as 275 thrift examiners from around the country—more than double the Dallas examination staff at that time—to try to catch up on thrift reviews in Texas.

They found S&L owners tooling around in Rolls-Royces and private jets and lending millions interest-free to developers who put little, if any, of their own money into the projects. On paper, the thrift institutions had artificially inflated profits; in fact, they were insolvent.

As a result, 58 S&Ls, mostly in Texas, have been placed under supervisory agreements that limit certain types of lending. Also, 23 S&Ls, again mostly in Texas, were slapped with cease-and-desist orders curtailing unsafe banking practices. Officers, directors or some stockholders of four institutions have been kicked out and barred

Don R. Dixon
Vernon Savings

from ever working in a federally insured bank or S&L; regulators decline to identify them.

The problems of the high rollers went well beyond the pain induced by the collapse of the oil-based Southwest economy. They ignored problem loans, resisted foreclosing on office buildings and dug themselves even deeper into trouble by making additional loans and restructuring others. There is evidence that some S&L insiders moved troubled loans from one thrift to another, keeping one step ahead of regulators and raising questions about fraud.

Messrs. Dixon, Gaubert, McBirney and Woods, all prominent in Dallas real-estate circles, were comfortable in this go-go atmosphere. As S&L owners, they lent to some of the same customers. Some S&Ls lent to one another and often swapped land holdings and loans. "There was some incestuous trading going on," says Samuel D. Ware, a young Dallas real-estate investor who borrowed some $300 million from Texas S&Ls, including Sunbelt and Independent American.

Returning Favors

For example, Sunbelt lent money to Messrs. Woods and Gaubert, and Mr. Woods's Western and Mr. Gaubert's Independent American apparently returned the favor, lending millions to Mr. McBirney personally and buying Sunbelt loans that had gone bad. Mr. Gaubert calls it "correspondent banking" and says that bankers have done it for years. The government calls it "back-scratching" when one thrift refinances or purchases a bad loan to scrub the books prior to a federal examination or to avoid loan write-offs and losses.

Many of the highfliers' practices seem to have little to do with prudent banking. The S&Ls often didn't plan to make money by earning interest on the loans. Instead, they generated profits by charging hefty loan-origination fees—sometimes as much as 5% of the loan. And they put part of the loan on the books as interest and often invested directly in projects, hoping to cash in on the real-estate boom itself.

At most highflying Texas thrifts, a friend of the boss could get millions of dollars on a signature. Loans could exceed the purchase price of the land, thanks to some liberal Texas S&L laws and cooperative appraisers. Down payments were considered an unnecessary formality, and nobody seriously considered chasing after a borrower who didn't pay.

The flow of loan-fee income and phony interest payments allowed the Vernon S&L to avoid loan writeoffs and post impressive profits. In the first year Mr. Dixon controlled it, the S&L's reported net income tripled and loans more than doubled. Vernon, Sunbelt and Western paid hefty interest rates for "hot money" deposits offered by money brokers, who, for a commission, would make a series of deposits, each up to the federally insured $100,000 limit.

Looting Charged

A lot of that money wound up as loans to Mr. Dixon's cronies, and some of it, regulators allege, went to Mr. Dixon. In a suit filed by the FSLIC in federal court here, regulators say Vernon officers "looted, dissipated and wasted" Vernon's assets. The agency, which now is operating it as Vernon Savings & Loan Association, F.S.A., is seeking a record $540 million in damages. The FSLIC lawsuit says that Vernon's profits generated nearly $40 million in dividends to Vernon shareholders, mainly one of Mr. Dixon's companies, and that at least $8 million went to Mr. Dixon personally in dividends, bonuses and salary, though Mr. Dixon, other than serving on the loan committee, never had a formal job at the S&L.

Mr. Dixon's control of Vernon, whose assets hit a peak of $1.3 billion, paid off handsomely. His wife's diary describes "the flying house party" in October 1983, when, for 10 days, the Dixons, another Vernon couple and a host of European socialites hopscotched by private jet or Rolls-Royce to top-flight restaurants in Paris and southern France. At one marathon lunch in Lyons, complete with champagne and truffle soup, Paul Bocuse, a well-known French chef, lined up his 12 chefs in the courtyard for Mr. Dixon to review. Examiners found that Vernon paid $68,036.98 for that trip and four others.

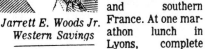

Jarrett E. Woods Jr.
Western Savings

The 250-pound Mr. Gaubert, and Mr. McBirney, who personally ran Sunbelt's lending operation, were cut from the same cloth. When young, both had their own businesses: Mr. Gaubert sawed bicycles in half in Indianapolis, modified them and rented them as tandems; Mr. McBirney rented refrigerators to students at Southern Methodist University. By the time they met, both had made millions in Dallas real estate.

Edwin T. McBirney III
Sunbelt Savings

The Midas Touch

Friends say the darkly handsome Mr. McBirney has the Midas touch in real estate: a fast mind, a retentive memory and a smooth, reassuring pitch. He ruined so many tablecloths outlining deals at Jason's Restaurant in Dallas that the management covered his table with paper.

At Sunbelt, Mr. McBirney, cigar in hand, often shuttled among two or three rooms filled with groups of borrowers, while others waited their turn in the lobby. He would huddle in a conference room to get a summary of how a multimillion-dollar deal was structured before he gave his approval. Then, he would go off to review another prospective loan. "When he walked back into the the first negotiating room," says Jack Sommerfield, a former Sunbelt vice chairman, "I'd start by bringing him up to date, and Ed would say, 'Yeah, I remember. Go from there.' "

The Gaubert-McBirney loans include about $30 million in loans for two new Dallas-area apartment projects that Mr. Gaubert is building and $6 million that Mr. Gaubert borrowed to take control of Tele-Com Corp., a diversified Dallas company that makes, among other things, heating and air-conditioning equipment, national-park souvenirs and pecan-processing equipment. Mr. Gaubert's Independent American lent Mr. McBirney personally $3 million to $4 million.

Of the four thrift executives, only Mr. Gaubert is willing to answer questions. Enmeshed in a bitter court fight with the FSLIC to regain control of Independent American, he denies that he "networked" loans between his S&L and the others.

Mr. Gaubert believes that his removal from the thrift industry is due partly to his prominent fund-raising activities for Democrats and to his willingness to supply congressional investigators with evidence about now-defunct Empire Savings & Loan Association, of Mesquite, Texas, which was involved in an earlier Texas S&L scam that he believes embarrassed federal thrift-industry regulators. The regulators also looked into his business dealings and were critical of some land transactions, but he hasn't been accused of any criminal wrongdoing.

Twice-Sold Land

Federal officials are focusing on a tract of about 6,500 acres of Dallas County land that was sold twice in 1984 in transactions involving Western Savings, Sunbelt, Independent American and Investex Savings of Tyler, Texas, a failing institution that Independent American bought. Mr. Gaubert's real-estate business found the land, Independent American Savings bought it with help from Sunbelt and later sold it to a former Sunbelt officer who got financing from Sunbelt, Independent American and Western.

Along the way, Mr. Gaubert says Independent American pocketed a tidy $30 million profit on the sale, using the money to invest in Investex Savings. He says the land deal was cleared by Dallas Federal Home Loan Bank officials because they wanted to see the failing Investex merged with another S&L. The bank won't comment.

But federal examiners and law-enforcement officials question whether the transaction wasn't a land flip—the quick sale of land at a wildly inflated price, in this case about double the purchase price—designed to generate cash for the seller and the lending S&Ls. Mr. Gaubert says the original seller of the land didn't know what it was worth.

Meanwhile, the FSLIC is paying real-estate experts to put the once-highflying thrifts back in shape. But a whiff of the freewheeling days lingers on.

The other day at Western Federal Savings, the successor S&L to insolvent Western Savings, a man dropped in unexpectedly, dressed in white tennis shorts and swirling a glass of Scotch on the rocks. He owes Western about $100 million and for three months hadn't responded to dunning letters and phone calls.

He didn't have any plans to repay the loans, he told a lending officer, adding that he will ignore further appeals. "I understand you have to take the properties away," he said, stirring his drink. "I won't answer your letters. I won't respond to subpoenas. Here's my phone number, but I won't return your calls."

A Comparison of Risk-Based Capital and Risk-Based Deposit Insurance

by Robert B. Avery
and Terrence M. Belton

Robert B. Avery is a senior economist in the Division of Research and Statistics at the Board of Governors of the Federal Reserve System. Terrence M. Belton is a senior economist at the Federal Home Loan Mortgage Corporation.

The authors would like to thank Randall W. Eberts, Edward Ettin, Gerald Hanweck, Myron Kwast, James Thomson, and Walker Todd for helpful comments and suggestions.

An earlier version of this paper was presented at the Federal Reserve Bank of Cleveland's fall seminar on the role of regulation in creating/ solving problems of risk in financial markets — November 3, 1986.

Introduction

The perception of increased bank risk-taking has raised concerns as to whether changes and improvements are needed in our system of regulatory supervision and examination. These concerns clearly underlie recent proposals for risk-based capital standards issued by all three bank regulatory agencies—the Federal Reserve Board, the Federal Deposit Insurance Corporation (FDIC), and the Comptroller of the Currency—as well as proposals by the FDIC and Federal Savings and Loan Insurance Corporation (FSLIC) for risk-based deposit insurance premiums. None of these approaches has, as yet, been implemented, and each is still under active consideration by at least one regulatory body.

As part of an ongoing evaluation of the potential effectiveness of various methods of controlling bank risk-taking, this paper presents a comparison of risk-based capital and risk-based deposit insurance premium proposals. Although these proposals may appear to represent quite different methods of controlling bank risk, the results presented below suggest that this need not be the case and that, if implemented properly, the two methods can produce a similar level of bank risk-taking.

The paper also suggests that differences that exist between the two methods lie not in the fact that one controls premiums and the other capital levels, but that one prices risk and the other sets a risk standard. This is discussed informally in section I, while evidence of how both a risk-based insurance and risk-based capital

system could be implemented using similar measures of risk is presented in the section that follows.

I. Discussion

In the current regulatory environment, commercial banks are subject to a fixed minimum level of primary capital per-dollar of assets and a fixed deposit insurance premium per-dollar of domestic deposits regardless of the risk that they present to the FDIC. As many critics have pointed out, this presents a potential problem of incentives in that banks may not bear the full social costs of increased risk-taking. Both a risk-based capital and risk-based insurance system are designed to address this problem by inducing banks to internalize the expected costs that their risk-taking imposes on the FDIC and society in general.[1] The programs appear to differ significantly, however, in how they attempt to achieve this goal.

As proposed, a risk-based deposit insurance system would explicitly price risk-taking behavior on the part of insured banks. Periodically, the FDIC would assess the risk represented by each bank and charge an insurance premium reflecting the expected social

---

[1] Another objective may be to distribute the costs of risk-taking more equitably across banks even if such differences stem from exogenous factors and if issues of moral hazard and allocative efficiency are irrelevant.

Risk Variables

Symbol	Definition
KTA	percent ratio of primary capital to total assets,
PD90MA	percent ratio of loans more than 90 days past due to total assets,
LNNACCA	percent ratio of nonaccruing loans to total assets,
RENEGA	percent ratio of renegotiated loans to total assets,
NCOFSA	percent ratio of net loan charge-offs (annualized) to total assets,
NETINCA	percent ratio of net income (annualized) to total assets.

Source: Board of Governors of the Federal Reserve System.

TABLE 1

costs attributable to it.[2] Because banks would in principle bear the full expected cost of their actions, they would either be deterred from excessive risk-taking or would pay the full expected costs to the FDIC.

A risk-based capital standard works by setting a standard that, by absorbing losses, limits the amount of risk an insured bank can impose on the FDIC, rather than by explicitly pricing risk. If the regulators determine that a bank represents a risk above the allowable standard at its current level of capital, they would require the bank to raise more capital. By adjusting capital "buffers," regulators can control the size of potential losses irrespective of bank behavior.

The regulator uses information on differences in risk-taking behavior across banks to require different amounts of capital or co-insurance, not to charge different premiums. Indeed, since adjustment of the capital buffer is used to reduce the risk represented by each bank to the same level, it is then appropriate that they be charged a flat premium rate.[3] Bank risk-taking behavior may be deterred because banks would recognize that they will incur higher expected capital costs, an implicit price, even though banks do not face explicit prices for risk. In both schemes, overall system risk-taking would be reduced because banks would take full account

of the expected consequences of their actions, either through explicit insurance premiums or implicit prices via higher capital costs.

Current Proposals on Risk-Based Deposit Insurance and Risk-Based Capital

In recent years, there have been several specific proposals made by the federal regulatory agencies for basing insurance premiums or capital requirements on the perceived risk of depository institutions. In 1986, for example, the FDIC asked for legislation authorizing the adoption of a risk-based deposit insurance system and has developed a specific proposal for implementing such a system. More recently, the Federal Reserve Board, in conjunction with the Bank of England and with other U.S. banking regulatory authorities has published for public comment a proposal for risk-based capital requirements.

The FDIC proposal for risk-based deposit insurance utilizes two measures for assessing bank risk-taking.[4] The first measure is based on examiner-determined CAMEL ratings for individual commercial banks. CAMEL ratings, which range from 1 through 5 (with 5 representing the least healthy bank) are intended to measure the bank's capital adequacy (C), asset quality (A), management skills (M), earnings (E), and liquidity (L). The FDIC's problem-bank list consists of all banks with CAMEL ratings of 4 and 5.

The second measure of bank risk employed in the FDIC proposal is a risk index developed by the FDIC that is based on publicly available Call Report data. The index is defined as:

$$(1) \quad I = .818 - .151\,KTA + .211\,PD90MA + .265\,LNNACCA + .177\,RENEGA + .151\,NCOFSA - .347\,NETINCA,$$

where all variables are defined in table 1. The weights in the index were estimated from historical data with a probit model that predicts whether or not an individual bank is on the FDIC's problem-bank list. The index can be interpreted as providing a measure of the likelihood that a bank is a problem bank. Banks with higher index values of the index are more likely to be problem institutions and therefore more likely to impose higher expected costs on the FDIC.

Premiums would be assessed, under the FDIC proposal, by defining two premium classes. Banks having a positive value of the risk index and a CAMEL rating of 3, 4, or 5, would be classified as above-normal risk. These

2 If the FDIC cannot fully assess the ex-ante risk represented by each bank, perhaps because monitoring costs would be excessive, then the "optimal" risk premium would also include "penalties" over and above the FDIC's estimate of each bank's expected social cost.

3 Assuming the risk-based capital requirement is binding so that no institution holds capital in excess of its requirement.

4 The proposal is described in "Risk-Related Program," FDIC Discussion Paper, September 20, 1985, and Hirschhorn, E., "Developing a Proposal for Risk-Related Deposit Insurance," *Banking and Economic Review*, FDIC, September/October 1986.

**Summary of Risk Weights and Major Risk Categories for State Member Banks and Bank
Holding Companies**

Category A1 (0 percent weight)
Cash—domestic and foreign
Claims on Federal Reserve Banks

Category A2 (10 percent weight)
Short-term (one year or less) claims on U.S. Government and its Agencies.

Category A3 (25 percent weight)
Cash items in process of collection.
Short-term claims on domestic depository institutions and foreign banks, including foreign
central banks.
Claims (including repurchase agreements) collateralized by cash or U.S. Government or
Agency debt.

Claims guaranteed by the U.S. Government or its Agencies.
Local currency claims on foreign central governments to the extent that bank has local cur-
rency liabilities.
Federal Reserve Bank stock.

Category A4 (50 percent weight)
Claims on U.S. Government-sponsored Agencies.
Claims (including repurchase agreements) collateralized by U.S. Government-sponsored
Agency debt.
General obligation claims on states, counties and municipalities.
Claims on multinational development institutions in which the U.S. is a shareholder or con-
tributing member.

Category A5 (100 percent weight)
All other assets not specified above, including:
Claims on private entities and individuals. Long-term claims on domestic and foreign banks.
All other claims on foreign governments and private obligators.

Source: Board of Governors of the Federal Reserve System.

TABLE 2

institutions would be charged an annual premium equal to one-sixth of one percent of
domestic deposits, or twice the current premium
level. All other institutions (that is, institutions
having either a negative value for the risk index
or a CAMEL rating of 1 or 2) would be classified
as normal-risk banks and be charged the current
premium of one-twelfth of one percent.

      The risk-based capital requirement
proposed by the Federal Reserve Board, in conjunction with other regulatory authorities, measures bank risk-taking in a somewhat different
fashion than the FDIC's deposit insurance proposal. Capital requirements would be assessed,
under the Board's proposal, as a fraction of the
on- and off-balance-sheet activity of individual
commercial banks.[5] Specifically, the proposal

. . . .

5   The proposal is described in two press releases of the Board of
Governors of the Federal Reserve System titled "Capital Maintenance: Revision to Capital Adequacy Guidelines," dated February 12,
1987 and March 18, 1987.

defines five asset categories that are shown in
table 2. These categories are intended to measure, in broad terms, assets having varying
degrees of credit risk. Cash and claims in Federal
Reserve Banks (category A1) are deemed to have
no credit risk and require no capital support.
Commercial loans to customers other than banks,
(Category A5) are deemed to have the greatest
amount of credit risk. The minimum primary capital level, K, required under the proposal would
be defined as:

$$(2) \quad K = a(0A1 + .10A2 + .25A3 + .5A4 + 1A5),$$

where a denotes the minimum required ratio (not
yet specified in the proposal) and A1 to A5
denote the asset categories defined in table 2.
      The requirement shown in equa-
tion (2) effectively imposes different minimum
capital standards on each of the five asset categories. If a is set at 7 percent, for example, all

commercial loans, except those to other banks (category A5), would effectively have minimum required capital ratios equal to 7 percent; claims on U.S. government-sponsored agencies (category A3) would have required capital ratios equal to 1.75 percent; and short-term treasury securities (category A2) would have required capital ratios of 0.7 percent.[6]

It is clear that a major difference between the risk-based capital and risk-based deposit insurance proposals just described is the type of information that is used to assess bank risk-taking. The risk-based deposit insurance proposal focuses on measures of bank performance, such as earnings and asset quality; the risk-based capital proposal focuses on the types of activities in which banks are involved. The former view is based on statistical evidence that suggests these performance measures provide the best forecast of future bank problems.[7] The latter approach to measuring bank risk-taking is based on the view that certain activities are inherently more risky than other activities and that these more risky activities should be capitalized at higher levels.

In contrasting the two approaches to measuring bank risk, it should be emphasized that the different measures used do not represent an inherent difference between risk-based capital and risk-based insurance. Indeed, both systems could, in principle, use identical information in assessing the risk of individual banks. The difference between the two systems lies not in what information the regulator collects, nor in how it uses that information to assess bank risk; rather, the difference results primarily because one system controls risk by a *standard* and the other by *explicit prices*. In the next subsection, we describe how these differences affect both banks and bank regulators.

6 In addition to imposing capital requirements on various balance-sheet asset categories, the proposal also addresses the risk from off-balance-sheet activities. Capital requirements for those activities are determined by first converting the face-amount of off-balance-sheet items to a balance-sheet equivalent. This is done by multiplying the face amount of the off-balance-sheet contract by an appropriate credit conversion factor. The resulting balance-sheet equivalent is then assigned to one of the five risk categories depending on the identity of the obligator and, in certain cases, on the maturity of the instrument.

7 In addition to the empirical work on predicting problem banks, the literature also suggests that earnings, capital and asset quality measures are important predictors of future bank failure. See J. Bovenzi, J. Marino, and F. McFadden, "Commercial Bank Failure Prediction Models," in *Economic Review*, Federal Reserve Bank of Atlanta (November 1983) and Robert B. Avery, Gerald A. Hanweck and Myron L. Kwast, "An Analysis of Risk-Based Deposit Insurance for Commercial Banks," *Preceedings of a Conference on Bank Structure and Competition (1985)*, Federal Reserve Bank of Chicago.

Differences Between Risked-based Capital and Risk-based Deposit Insurance

Because one system is based on a minimum standard and the other on a price, a number of differences are likely to exist between risk-based capital and risk-based insurance. One difference is that enforcement of a risk-based capital system is likely to offer the *regulator more flexibility* and potential for discretion than a risk-based premium system. If an annual insurance assessment appeared on a bank's income statement, and therefore was public, it would be difficult to waive or adjust the fee without alerting competing banks, financial market participants, and the public. Moreover, enforcement would likely be very mechanical. Banks would be assessed a fee, and examiners would have to deal individually only with those banks that could not or would not pay.

However, enforcement of a risk-based capital standard is likely to be of a very different nature. Enforcement might focus only on those firms close to or under the standard, and would likely entail more individual examiner input. Moreover, the judgement of whether or not a bank with a continually changing balance sheet meets the standard—and if not, how long it has to comply—is likely to offer considerable potential for discretion. Thus, in a regulatory environment based on judgement and discretionary supervision and regulation, a risk-based capital standard might be more attractive.

Another difference is that because a risk-based premium system prices risk rather than limiting it by forced capital adjustments, it is likely to offer *banks a more flexible,* and therefore potentially more efficient, means of response. Under a risk-based capital system, a risky bank facing abnormally high capital costs does not have the option of paying the FDIC for the right to take excessive portfolio risk even though this may be its most cost-effective response.[8] This feature is likely to favor a risk-based premium approach under virtually all regulatory environments. It might be argued that banks should not be allowed too much freedom as they may not properly respond to prices. However, this could be accommodated in a risk-based premium system by shutting down banks with excessive risk-taking or by altering their behavior by other supervisory means.

The two proposals are also likely to have significant differences in the amount of information that they reveal to the public. At

8 Technically, raising capital is not the only adjustment available to the bank as it can adjust any factor used in the regulator's assessment of risk. Thus, the relevant price banks face is the price of the minimum-cost method of meeting the standard. If this price is not equal to the regulator's price, there will be an inefficiency.

most, a risk-based capital standard would reveal only whether or not a bank met the standard. One could not even infer that a bank adding capital was doing so because it had become excessively risky; the extra capital might be needed because of anticipated expansion, etc. However, it would be very difficult to keep a bank's insurance premium confidential. Low-risk banks would have an incentive to advertise this fact and investors would have incentives to identify high-risk banks. This might cause particular problems in the use of confidential data to calculate premiums. Knowledge of a bank's premium could be used to draw strong inferences about values of any confidential inputs used. To the extent that this would deter the use of confidential data in a risk-based premium system, it might mean that risk assessment with a risk-based capital system would be more accurate and therefore fairer.

Moreover, even if confidential data were not used, public disclosure of a bank's premium might create the possibility of bank runs. The official declaration of the FDIC that a bank was risky, even if based on a mechanical calculation from publicly available balance sheet data, might be sufficient to induce significant withdrawals.

Yet another difference between the two methods is likely to occur in the regulatory response lag. Because it is based on a standard, a risk-based capital system may have a built-in response lag that is not present with a risk-based premium system. Under a risk-based premium system, a bank could be required to compensate the FDIC immediately for its risk exposure. In contrast, particularly if it entails raising new capital, adherence to a capital standard would likely entail some lag, thereby delaying the ability of the insurer to control its risk exposure.

Finally, even if the FDIC's assessment rate were adjusted so that it bore equivalent actuarial risk, there may be some differences in the number of bank failures under the two systems. Either system should reduce the number of bank failures from current levels because of the reduced risk-taking that should result when banks are required to bear the full costs of their risk-taking.[9] The magnitude of this reduction, however, may differ for the two systems. As noted earlier, risk-based deposit insurance systems allow banks the flexibility of holding capital levels

below those required under a comparable risk-based capital system and of offsetting the higher risk by paying larger insurance premiums. For those banks that opt to hold capital levels below those required under a capital standard and pay correspondingly larger insurance premiums, the incidence of failure would be higher under a risk-based insurance system than that observed under a risk-based capital standard.

By the same token, a risk-based insurance system would provide other banks the flexibility of holding capital levels well above those required under a risk-based capital standard and of being compensated for this increased capital by paying lower insurance premiums. For such banks, the incidence of failure will be lower under a risk-based insurance system than under a capital standard. This difference between the two systems stems from the fact that a capital standard does not reward banks for having capital greater than the minimum standard; a risk-based insurance system provides such a reward in the form of a reduced premium.

The foregoing analysis suggests that, in the aggregate, it is unclear which of the two systems would reduce bank failures by the greatest amount. Prediction of whether an individual bank's capital would be greater under a risk-based capital standard than under a risk-based premium system depends on the cost of capital faced by the bank and upon the degree to which the risk-based insurance system penalizes banks for reductions in their capital. When the cost of raising capital in the private market (or other adjustment methods) is high relative to the penalty rate charged by the deposit insurer for reductions in capital, banks will be more likely to choose lower capital levels under a risk-based insurance scheme than that required under a risk-based capital standard. Conversely, when the insurance system assigns a relatively steep penalty rate for reductions in bank capital, individual banks would be more likely to hold larger amounts of capital under a risk-based insurance system, implying a lower incidence of bank failure.

Despite these differences, if based on the same method of assessing bank risk, proposals for risk-based capital and risk-based insurance should have a similar impact on bank risk-taking. To provide a glimpse as to how such proposals might work, a practical system of risk-based deposit insurance and risk-based capital is developed and presented in the next section. Both proposals are based on the same method of

....

9 Some critics have charged that a risk-based capital or deposit insurance system might actually increase failures and incentives for risk-taking because regulators would measure risk poorly or misprice it. While this may be true, it should be pointed out that the current system assumes all banks represent the same risk. The relevant question, therefore, is not whether regulators would do a perfect job, but whether they could differentiate among banks at all.

Sample Variable Statistics

Variable	Means of Failed Banks	Means of Nonfailed Banks
KTA	6.14	9.26
PD90MA	3.41	0.77
LNNACCA	3.64	0.57
RENEGA	0.28	0.07
NCOFSA	2.89	0.43
NETINCA	-2.94	0.90

Source: Board of Governors of the Federal Reserve System.

TABLE 3

assessing bank risk. As this represents only part of an on-going effort to develop such systems, we only briefly summarize our work.[10]

II. A Model of Bank Risk

Both the risk-based capital and risk-based insurance premium proposals require an accurate method of assessing bank risk. Forming an index or rank ordering of banks by risk entails two steps. First, variables must be selected that are good predictors of risk; and second, weights must be calculated to transform values of the vector of predictor variables into a single-valued index.

Development of a good index is a substantial task and is well beyond the scope of this paper. It was decided somewhat arbitrarily, therefore, to use the same six predictor variables used by the FDIC in its risk-based insurance proposal (see table 1). One good method of forming weights for the index is to use historical data to "fit" values of the predictor variables to an observable ex-post measure of loss. Candidates for ex-post measures of bank performance might be bank failure and FDIC losses when failure occurs, or bank earnings or loan charge-offs. Although we use other measures of bank performance in other work, for the illustrative proposals developed for this paper it was decided to utilize bank failure. The basic strategy followed was to use historical data on bank failure to estimate weights that could be used to transform values of the six variables listed in table 1 into an index of risk. This

index forms the basis of both our risk-based capital and risk-based deposit insurance proposals.

In selecting data used in this study for both estimation and model evaluations, the following specific procedures were used. The sample was restricted to insured commercial banks headquartered in the United States. Mutual savings banks were excluded. Microdata were collected for each bank for each of the five semiannual call and income reports filed from December 1982 through December 1984.[11]

Each of the "calls" represented a potential observation with the following adjustments (thus each bank could appear in the sample five times). Because new banks are thought to follow a different behavioral process, all calls were eliminated whenever a bank had not been in continuous existence for three years at that point. Banks without assets, deposits, or loans were also eliminated. The sample was further reduced by eliminating all banks with assets above $1 billion (approximately two percent of all banks) because of the virtual absence of large bank failures.[12] These adjustments reduced the banks available in December 1984, for example, from 14,460 to 13,388. The actual estimation sample was further reduced by only using 10 percent (randomly selected) of the calls reported by banks that did not fail within a year of the call.

This stratification of the nonfailed banks (which was corrected for in the estimation procedure) was done to create an estimation data-set of manageable size. All calls where the bank failed within a year of the call were used (thus a failed bank could contribute two calls to the sample). The final estimation sample consisted of 6,869 observations, 160 of which represented calls for banks that failed within six months of the call and 138 for banks that failed between six months and a year after the call.

The data used for the study were taken directly from the bank's filed call report, with slight adjustment. June values for the two income variables—charge-offs and net income—were recalculated to reflect performance over the previous year rather than the 6-month period reported. Means of the variables for the estimation data are given in table 3. The data were fit using a logistic model to predict bank failure

10 See Robert B. Avery and Gerald A. Hanweck, "A Dynamic Analysis of Bank Failures," *Proceedings of a Conference on Bank Structure and Competition (1984)*, Federal Reserve Bank of Chicago; Robert A. Avery, Gerald A. Hanweck and Myron L. Kwast, "An Analysis of Risk-Based Deposit Insurance for Commercial Banks," *Proceedings of a Conference on Bank Structure and Competition (1985)*, Federal Reserve Bank of Chicago; and Terrence M. Belton, "Risk-Based Capital Standards for Commercial Banks," presented at the Federal Reserve System Conference on Banking and Financial Structure, New Orleans, Louisiana, September 19-20, 1985.

11 More time periods could have been used. However, it was decided to limit the length of the estimation period so that an "out of sample" measure of the model's performance could be computed.

12 The elimination of large banks had virtually no effect on the results.

where a bank was deemed to have failed if it failed within a year following the call. The estimated risk index is:

$$(3) \quad R = -2.42 - .501\,KTA + .428\,PD90MA +$$
$$(3.07) \quad (4.89) \quad (5.16)$$

$$.314\,LNNACCA + .269\,RENEGA$$
$$(4.31) \quad\quad\quad (1.07)$$

$$.223\,NCOFSA - .331\,NETINCA,$$
$$(1.60) \quad\quad\quad (2.68)$$

where the logistic form of the model implies that the probability that a bank will fail within a year is,

$$(3a) \quad PROB = \frac{1}{1 - exp\,(-R)}$$

T-statistics for the estimated coefficients are given in parenthesis under each weight.[13] All weights are statistically significant except those for NCOFSA (which has a perverse sign) and RENEGA.[14]

Although the overall fit of the model suggests that predicting bank failure is difficult, the failed banks in the sample had an average predicted probability of failure of 0.24, a number 69 times larger than the average predicted failure probability of nonfailed banks in the sample. Hence, the model clearly does have some ability to discriminate between high- and low-risk banks.

III. Risk-Based Deposit Insurance Premiums

Several somewhat arbitrary assumptions were used to convert the estimated risk-assessment model into a risk-based deposit insurance premium system. First, the FDIC's expected cost of

. . . .

13 Coefficients for a logistic model have a less straightforward interpretation that those in regression models. When multiplied by *PROB* (1-*PROB*) each coefficient represents the expected change in the probability of failure resulting from a one-unit change in the variable. Thus, if a bank with a probability of failure of 0.I raised its capital ratio one percentage point, the model implies that its probability of failure would fall by .045, that is, (-.501 x .1 x .9). Although they were estimated using the same variables, and with data drawn from similar time periods, the coefficients in (3) differ somewhat from those in (1). This occurs, in part, because the FDIC model was estimated using a probit rather than logistic specification, which effects the scaling of the variables (logistic coefficients should be approximately 1.8 times as large). It also stems from the fact that the FDIC used problem-bank status rather than bank failure as a dependent variable.

14 The model's log-likelihood R squared, a concept similar to the R squared in a regression model, is 0.22. The sign on the weight of NCOFSA may be not be as perverse as it appears. The coefficient on charge-offs represents the marginal impact on failure holding net income constant. Because charge-offs are also in net income, they are effectively counted twice. The positive sign on charge-offs indicates they have less impact on failure than other contributory factors toward earnings. The total impact of charge-offs (the sum of the coefficients of NCOFSA and NETINC) has the expected negative sign.

insuring each bank (per-dollar of deposits) was computed as the estimated probability of failure (from the formula in [3]) times the average FDIC loss when failure occurs (13.6 cents/ per dollar).[15] Assessment of this premium, which averaged 7.2 basis points per dollar of deposits in December 1985, would be actuarially fair if there were no monitoring or social costs. Since these factors are not known, and to provide comparability with the current system, an intercept (or flat premium) of 1.1 basis points per dollar of deposits was added to the risk-based assessment so that the total assessment would be equivalent to the FDIC's actual revenues as of December 1985 (with the current flat-rate assessment of 8.3 basis points). While certainly not a necessary ingredient of a risk-based system, the FDIC revenue constraint was adopted in order to allow the concentration of effort and discussion on estimating the risk-based component of the premium while not having to address the issue of what the appropriate level of gross revenues should be. Finally premiums were "capped" at 100 basis points because of the belief that premiums above this level would be difficult to collect.

Estimates of December 1985 risk-based premiums under this system are presented in table 4. Premiums are computed across seven asset-size classes of banks (rows [1] through [7]) and six premium-size intervals (columns [1] through [6]). It should be emphasized that while premiums for banks with over $1 billion in assets are computed and reported, these are extrapolations as no banks of this size were included in the sample used to estimate the risk index. Rows (8) and (9) show the premium distribution for banks that subsequently failed in 1986 and 1987 (through September 30), giving an idea of the system's capacity to identify and penalize risky banks. Row (10) and column (7) present totals for all banks. The first number in each cell is the average risk-based premium expressed in basis points of total domestic deposits. The second number is the average estimated (percentage) probability of failure by banks in that cell, and the third figure is the number of banks, based on the total of 13,522 banks used to compute the premium, that are predicted to fall into each size and risk-class category.

The primary conclusion to be drawn from table 4 is that the risk-based system depicted there would divide banks into three major groups. First, even with the FDIC revenue constraint imposed, the vast majority of banks

. . . .

15 This number is the average ratio of the FDIC's loss reserve to total domestic deposits calculated for banks that failed between 1981 and 1984. See Avery, Hanweck, and Kwast "An Analysis of Risk-based Deposit Insurance."

Estimated Commercial Bank Risk-based Premiums — December 1985

(Basis Points of Total Domestic Deposits)

First number is the average premium for banks in the cell. Second number is average estimated probability of failure in percent. Third number is number of banks.

Asset Size Class ($ millions)	Premium Size Class						
	(1) < 8.3	(2) 8.3-12.4	(3) 12.5-24	(4) 25-49	(5) 50-99	(6) 100	(7) All Banks
(1) < $10	2.4	10.1	17.2	32.1	61.6	100.0	6.3
	.1	.6	1.2	2.3	4.5	34.5	1.1
	933.0	29.0	23.0	16.0	9.0	25.0	1035.0
(2) $10 — $25	2.6	10.0	17.2	33.3	68.8	100.0	6.9
	.1	.7	1.2	2.4	5.0	42.7	1.2
	3135.0	109.0	131.0	61.0	44.0	78.0	3558.0
(3) $25 — $50	2.9	10.1	17.1	35.0	70.4	100.0	5.9
	.1	.7	1.2	2.5	5.1	33.6	.7
	3258.0	112.0	105.0	47.0	26.0	54.0	3602.0
(4) $50 — $100	3.1	9.9	16.8	33.9	74.3	100.0	5.9
	.2	.7	1.2	2.4	5.4	35.6	.7
	2485.0	116.0	72.0	29.0	19.0	36.0	2757.0
(5) $100 — $500	3.7	9.8	16.4	32.9	71.7	100.0	5.7
	.2	.6	1.1	2.3	5.2	71.1	.5
	1859.0	85.0	65.0	28.0	7.0	16.0	2060.0
(6) $500 — $1000	4.3	9.3	17.3	29.4	69.7	100.0	7.5
	.2	.6	1.2	2.1	5.0	54.8	.9
	171.0	14.0	9.0	3.0	3.0	2.0	202.0
(7) > $1000	5.1	9.8	15.9	37.7	78.8	0.0	7.0
	.3	.6	1.1	2.7	5.7	0.0	.4
	230.0	60.0	15.0	2.0	1.0	0.0	308.0
(8) Banks failing in 1986	4.8	10.8	17.1	38.1	71.5	100.0	68.7
	.3	.7	1.2	2.7	5.2	51.8	30.1
	17.0	8.0	9.0	12.0	12.0	75.0	133.0
(9) Banks failing in 1987	4.6	10.2	16.9	32.2	69.8	100.0	37.3
	.3	.7	1.2	2.3	5.1	35.6	9.3
	44.0	11.0	20.0	17.0	9.0	31.0	132.0
(10) All Banks	3.0	9.9	16.9	33.6	69.8	100.0	6.2
	.1	.7	1.2	2.4	5.0	37.4	.8
	12071.0	525.0	420.0	186.0	109.0	211.0	13522.0

Source: Board of Governors of the Federal Reserve System.

TABLE 4

would pay a lower insurance premium under the estimated risk-based scheme than the current gross premium of 8.3 basis points. As may be seen from the table, this is true for all size classes, with the proportion paying less ranging from a low of 75 percent to 90 percent. Overall, 89 percent of all institutions are estimated to pay less with an average premium of 3.0 basis points.

The second group of banks is composed of the 9 percent of all banks that would pay an increased premium ranging from a low of 8.3 basis points to 99 basis points (columns 2 through 5). This range of almost 92 basis points

is quite large and appears wide enough both to provide a strong incentive to alter current risk-taking behavior by banks and to deter excessive risk-taking in the future. Some perspective on the size of the estimated risk-based premium is given by noting that the average bank's return on total deposits in 1985 was only 82 basis points. The average bank's premium would have been almost 1 percent of its previous year's total capital, and somewhat over 4 percent of its net income. But in the higher risk categories (columns 4-6), the capital percentages range up to 25.5 percent.

The third group of banks is the one percent that would have been asked to pay an insurance premium of over one percent (capped at 100 basis points) of total domestic deposits in 1985 (column 6 of table 4). For these banks it is not unusual for the average expected cost imposed on the FDIC to exceed 500 basis points. Indeed, the total cost that would have been expected to be imposed on the FDIC in 1986 by the 211 banks in column 6 was $477 million, or 25 percent of the total expected cost of $1.9 billion for all 13,522 commercial banks for which premiums were computed. Clearly, because the size of the assessment might be sufficient, by itself, to force these banks into insolvency, special measures might be needed to deal with them.

The ability of the system to identify risky banks in advance is illustrated by the premiums that would have been charged in December 1985 to banks that subsequently have failed. Over 87 percent of the banks that failed in 1986 would have been required to pay higher premiums than they pay currently, a figure in sharp contrast to the overall figure of 11 percent. Over one-half of the 1986 failed banks would have been assessed premiums at the highest rate of 100 basis points. Figures for banks that failed in 1987 are somewhat less dramatic. Still, 67 percent of 1987 failed banks would have been required to pay higher premiums in 1985, and almost one-fourth would have been placed in the highest risk class.

IV. Risk-based Capital

Conversion of the bank failure model estimates into a risk-based capital system was somewhat more complicated than procedures used for the risk-based insurance premium system. To ensure comparability with the current system, it was decided to set a standard so that if all banks held exactly the required capital ratio, the expected losses to the FDIC would be identical to its expected losses under the current system. It was determined that this would occur if each bank in December 1985 were required to hold enough capital so that its probability of failure was 0.7 percent (about 95 expected bank failures per year).

A floor and ceiling were also imposed so that no bank would be required to have a capital ratio of less than 3 percent nor more than 15 percent. This particular standard was chosen in order to make the expected losses to the FDIC of the risk-based capital system as close as possible to the risk-based insurance system outlined in the previous section. Imposition of the 3 percent minimum floor was similar to the addition of an intercept term in the risk-based premium

system, and is a tacit admission that any realistic risk-based capital system would have to have a floor. The 15 maximum capital standard is similar to the cap imposed on the risk-based premium.

Solution for the amount of capital each bank would have to hold follows straightforwardly from the estimated risk index. The formula given in equation (3a) implies that a bank with a risk index value of -4.95 would have a probability of failure of precisely 0.7 percent. Equation (3), therefore, implies that the required minimum capital level, KTA^*, must satisfy

$$(4) \quad -4.95 = -2.42 - .501KTA^* + .428PD90MA + .314LNNACCA + .269RENEGA - .223NCOFSA - .331NETINCA,$$

or,

$$(5) \quad KTA^* = 5.04 + .854PD90MA + .627LNNACCA + .537RENEGA - .445NCOFSA - .661NETINCA,$$

which can be solved for each bank.[16]

Table 5 gives an indication as to how a risk-based capital system might work. It shows the December 1985 distribution of required capital by bank-size class and future failure. Rows (1) through (7) represent banks of increasing size, row (8) shows banks that failed in 1986, row (9) shows banks that failed in 1987 (through September 30), and row (10) shows the sum of all banks. The columns show the number and percent of banks in each size class that would have been assigned to various required capital classes. For each cell, the first number given is the average required capital level for banks in the cell, the second number is the percentage of banks that would have to raise capital to meet the new standard, and the third number is the number of banks in the cell.

The numbers in table 5 suggest several interesting conclusions. Eighty-six percent of all banks would have a risk-based capital assessment below 6.5 percent. A middle group would be required to hold capital ratios between 6.5 and 10 percent; and a small group (3.4 percent of the total) would have to hold capital of over 10 percent of assets. There is an indication that banks with higher risk already hold more capital than required. Thus, almost 92 percent of banks would not have to raise more capital under the risk-based standard. However, there is a small

. . . .

16 The formula implies that a bank would *reduce* its index value by 0.501 for each percentage point rise in its capital ratio. Thus, a bank with a 5.5 percent capital ratio and a risk index of -3.70 would be required to raise its capital ratio 2.5 percentage points to 8 percent, that is 2.5 = [4.95 - 3.71]/.501. Banks with risk indices below -4.95 would be allowed to divest one percentage point of capital for each 0.501 they were below -4.95.

Estimated Commercial Bank Risk-based Required Capital — December 1985

(Percent of total assets)

First number is the average capital ratio for banks in the cell. Second number is percent of banks that would have to raise capital. Third number is number of banks.

Asset Size Class ($ millions)	Required Capital Class						
	(1) < 5.5	(2) 5.5-6.4	(3) 6.5-7.4	(4) 7.5-9.9	(5) 10.0-14.9	(6) 15.0	(7) All Banks
(1) < $10	4.6	6.0	7.0	8.5	11.8	15.0	6.1
	0.0	1.0	3.3	27.7	76.1	84.6	8.5
	529.0	198.0	119.0	130.0	46.0	13.0	1035.0
(2) $10 — $25	4.7	5.9	7.0	8.5	11.6	15.0	5.9
	.1	.9	9.0	50.0	92.9	97.1	10.4
	1936.0	775.0	365.0	326.0	141.0	35.0	3558.0
(3) $25 — $50	4.8	5.9	6.9	8.5	11.8	15.0	5.7
	.2	1.1	14.0	54.0	95.7	100.0	8.3
	2158.0	749.0	336.0	252.0	92.0	15.0	3602.0
(4) $50 — $100	4.8	5.9	6.9	8.4	11.7	15.0	5.6
	.4	3.0	16.7	53.8	90.2	91.7	7.8
	1752.0	535.0	239.0	158.0	61.0	12.0	2757.0
(5) $100 — $500	4.9	5.9	6.9	8.3	11.7	15.0	5.5
	.1	4.0	24.1	69.8	100.0	100.0	7.2
	1366.0	448.0	116.0	96.0	31.0	3.0	2060.0
(6) $500 — $1000	4.9	5.9	6.9	8.7	10.9	15.0	5.5
	1.5	10.8	27.8	100.0	100.0	100.0	10.4
	137.0	37.0	18.0	6.0	3.0	1.0	202.0
(7) > $1000	5.0	5.9	6.8	8.6	10.2	0.0	5.4
	3.1	29.0	47.4	100.0	100.0	0.0	15.3
	191.0	93.0	19.0	4.0	1.0	0.0	308.0
(8) Banks failing in 1986	4.6	5.9	7.1	9.0	12.4	15.0	11.5
	0.0	33.3	53.3	86.4	98.1	100.0	86.5
	5.0	3.0	15.0	22.0	54.0	34.0	133.0
(9) Banks failing in 1987	5.0	6.0	6.8	8.8	12.1	15.0	9.2
	9.1	16.7	21.0	75.5	96.7	72.7	61.4
	11.0	12.0	19.0	49.0	30.0	11.0	132.0
(10) All Banks	4.8	5.9	6.9	8.4	11.7	15.0	5.7
	.3	2.9	13.7	51.1	91.7	94.9	8.8
	8069.0	2815.0	1212.0	972.0	375.0	79.0	13522.0

Source: Board of Governors of the Federal Reserve System.

TABLE 5

group that would have to raise a substantial amount of additional capital. The efficiency of a risk-based system is evident from the fact that aggregate bank capital would be reduced by 18 percent from the actual December 1985 total, yet expected FDIC losses would be exactly the same as under the current system. This happens because the risk-based system shifts capital to those banks most likely to fail.

The evidence of the banks that failed in 1986 and 1987 is particularly telling. All but 18 of the 133 banks that failed in 1986 would have been required to raise additional capital in December 1985. As a group, these banks would have been required to almost double their aggregate capital. Over 60 percent of the banks that failed in 1987 would have been required to raise additional capital and over 90 percent would have been assigned a capital ratio above the current standard.

V. Final Comments

The systems presented here are meant to be illustrative and would probably require substantial modification before they could be actually implemented. They do show, however, that both risk-based capital and risk-based insurance systems could be constructed that discriminate between banks in a way that would likely affect behavior.

The similarities between the distribution of banks shown in the tables summarizing the proposals is striking. This, however, should not be surprising since both systems are based on the same risk measure. Indeed, if we had arrayed banks by the amount of new capital they would have to raise, instead of by required levels, the rank orderings of banks in the two systems would have been identical. They differ in the arrangements shown only because some banks that would otherwise have higher risk hold more capital than required under the current system, and thus, would reduce their premiums.

This does not mean that the two systems would have identical impacts on bank behavior or on overall system risk. As argued earlier, the regulatory environment surrounding each system is likely to differ. If banks face prices for risk in the capital market different from those charged by the FDIC, there will be inefficiencies in a risk-based capital standard that could produce different levels of system risk.

The incentives for banks to alter their risk-taking activities are very likely to differ between the two systems. It is not clear, however, that the impact of such differences would be major. Both systems share a common basis in the principle of differentially regulating banks according to the risk they represent to society. Implementation of either type of system is likely to lead to significant progress in the battle to control bank risk.

Article Fourteen

Interstate Bank Mergers and Competition in Banking

*Paul Calem**

The interstate banking era is well under way, and the days when out-of-state banking firms cannot acquire or merge with in-state firms appear to be numbered. Only a small minority of states have yet to pass interstate banking laws. In the Third Federal Reserve District, interstate banking became a reality with the passage of legislation by New Jersey and Pennsylvania in 1986. As a

*Paul Calem is a Senior Economist in the Banking Section of the Research Department at the Federal Reserve Bank of Philadelphia.

consequence, numerous interstate mergers and acquisitions have already taken place, and many more transactions are currently pending.

It is safe to predict that a continuing wave of mergers and acquisitions will bring about consolidation in the banking industry, and there will be fewer and larger banks. But how will banking services ultimately be affected? Will all this activity lead to substantially reduced competition in banking? Will commercial and retail customers be left with too few alternatives at noncompetitive prices?

In fact, just the opposite is likely to happen.

For one thing, banking regulators will continue to guard against mergers and acquisitions that would substantially reduce competition in local banking markets. And although the market for certain banking products is national, it is unlikely that increasing nationwide consolidation in banking will have significant anticompetitive effects.

At the same time, the institutions that result from interstate mergers or acquisitions may find that because they are larger, they will be able to offer more services or provide existing services more efficiently. As a result, such institutions would be more effective competitors in their markets than the original, smaller firms.

Of equal importance in promoting competition will be the increase in the number of potential entrants into local banking markets—the more competitors who enter a banking market, the greater the competition, which translates into lower charges and better services for consumers. Entry might occur in a number of ways depending, of course, on what each state allows in its law. A new competitor may enter and gain a major share of a market; an out-of-state bank holding company may set up (or acquire) a small bank with only a minor presence in a market (so-called toehold entry); or an in-state nonbanking subsidiary of a bank holding company, such as a consumer finance or trust subsidiary, may expand its operations to provide full-service banking.

These factors will contribute towards a more competitive environment in local banking markets. Thus, given the current regulatory framework, interstate banking is more likely to enhance competition than not, which means that customers will get improved banking services at competitive prices.

THE STATUS OF INTERSTATE BANKING

In the Nation. In the last few years, state after state has opened its borders to interstate banking, and in 1986 a flurry of interstate activity took place. Several types of interstate banking laws have emerged, reflecting varying entry requirements from state to state.

The most liberal interstate banking laws are the *nationwide* laws, which allow entry by banking organizations from any state in the nation. There are five states with such a law: Alaska, Arizona, Maine, Oklahoma, and Texas. Somewhat less liberal than such laws are the *nationwide reciprocal* laws. These laws allow banking organizations from any state to acquire in-state banks, contingent on reciprocity. That is, an out-of-state organization can merge with or acquire an organization in the host state only if the acquirer's home state grants similar privileges to banking organizations in the host state. Four states have nationwide reciprocal laws: Kentucky, New York, Washington, and West Virginia.[1]

Another category of interstate banking laws includes the *specialized laws.* These laws authorize some specialized form of entry by out-of-state holding companies. This category includes the so-called "limited purpose laws," which generally prohibit entering out-of-state banks from competing with host-state organizations for retail customers. Such laws are usually intended to encourage out-of-state banks to establish special purpose facilities, such as credit card operations. Also included are "troubled institution laws," which authorize the acquisition of troubled or failing institutions within the state.[2] The last category includes the most common interstate banking laws, the *regional* laws. These laws allow only those organizations that are headquartered in a state within a specified region to acquire a

---

[1]Under Oklahoma's nationwide law, further in-state expansion of a bank acquired by an institution from a non-reciprocating state is barred for four years subsequent to the acquisition. According to the Texas law, out-of-state organizations will not be permitted to control more than a total of 25 percent of the aggregate deposits in Texas banks.

[2]States having limited purpose laws include Delaware, Maryland, Nebraska, Nevada, South Dakota, Virginia, and West Virginia. States having troubled institution laws include Illinois, New Mexico, Ohio, Oklahoma, Oregon, Utah, and Washington. (Note that many of these states also have a regional or a nationwide reciprocal law.) In addition, many states have so-called "grandfather" laws, which permit out-of-state banking organizations to expand previously existing operations.

bank or bank holding company located in the host state. Of the 28 states having such a law, all but one state (Oregon) make interstate transactions contingent on reciprocity.

Some of the laws that have been passed do not become effective until 1987 or 1988. Also, some of the regional laws include a "nationwide trigger" date, at which time the regional restriction will be eliminated. The overall effect of the diversity of interstate banking laws is that the barriers to interstate expansion are being removed rather unsystematically. But because the majority of laws are regional laws, the removal of these barriers is mainly occurring at the regional level. And roughly speaking, it is possible to delineate several regions within which the barriers to interstate banking will have been largely removed by the end of 1987. (See REGIONS WHERE INTERSTATE ACTIVITY IS LIKELY TO OCCUR.)

With the passage of interstate banking laws, numerous mergers and acquisitions are now occurring as bank holding companies move into new states. As of early October 1986, a total of 98 interstate transactions had been approved by the Federal Reserve Board, and at least 96 deals were pending. Especially active in 1986 was the Midwest region, where interstate banking laws were passed in late 1985.

The pace of interstate banking activity is likely to quicken still further in the near future. Oklahoma's nationwide law and Washington's nationwide reciprocal law will both take effect on July 1, 1987. Texas's nationwide law will take effect on January 1, 1987, and West Virginia's nationwide reciprocal law will take effect on January 1, 1988. In addition, various regional laws become effective in 1987 and 1988. And some states still without interstate banking laws may yet pass such legislation. Also, between 1987 and 1989, various states' nationwide triggers will become effective. This not only will increase the volume of interstate activity, but it also will permit more transactions involving widely separated states.

In the Third District. The "First State," Delaware, was in fact the first state in the District to pass a type of interstate banking law. Known as the Financial Center Development Act, Delaware's limited purpose law permits out-of-state bank holding companies to establish "de novo," or new, subsidiaries, provided they meet certain capital and employment conditions, limit operations to a single location, and do not compete with Delaware-based banks for retail customers. Currently, at least 24 bank holding companies from other states, including many organizations based in New York City, have taken advantage of the Delaware law to set up credit card, wholesale lending, cash management, and other operations.[3]

In 1986, New Jersey and Pennsylvania each passed regional reciprocal laws. Pennsylvania's interstate banking bill was signed on June 25, 1986, and became effective on August 25. It grants reciprocity to New Jersey, Kentucky, Ohio, and several states in the east. New Jersey's law, passed in March, 1986, also became effective on August 25. It grants reciprocity to Pennsylvania, to the same states as does Pennsylvania's law, as well as to several states in the midwest. (For more details, see NEW JERSEY AND PENNSYLVANIA GO INTERSTATE.)

Interstate activity in New Jersey and Pennsylvania is already underway. At least three interstate transactions have been approved or are currently pending between New Jersey and Pennsylvania banking organizations. In addition, some transactions are pending between Pennsylvania banking organizations and organizations in Ohio and Kentucky.

WILL COMPETITION BE KEENER IN LOCAL BANKING MARKETS?

As interstate banking legislation is passed, the urge to merge seems to be an inevitable accompaniment. When the trigger is pulled for national

---

[3]For a more detailed discussion of Delaware's law, see Janice Moulton, "Delaware Moves Toward Interstate Banking: A Look at the FCDA," this *Business Review* (July-August 1983) pp. 17-25.

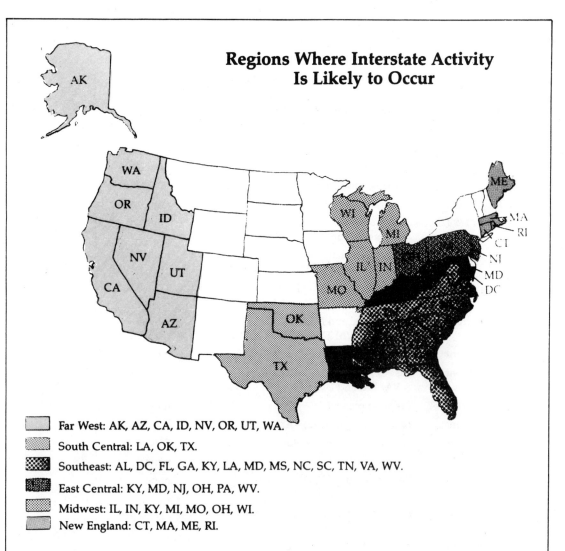

Regions Where Interstate Activity Is Likely to Occur

Far West: AK, AZ, CA, ID, NV, OR, UT, WA.

South Central: LA, OK, TX.

Southeast: AL, DC, FL, GA, KY, LA, MD, MS, NC, SC, TN, VA, WV.

East Central: KY, MD, NJ, OH, PA, WV.

Midwest: IL, IN, KY, MI, MO, OH, WI.

New England: CT, MA, ME, RI.

State with a Regional Law	Date in Effect	Specified Region[a]	Nationwide Trigger
Alabama	7/1/87	Southeast plus AR	none
California	7/1/87	Far West plus CO, TX, HI, and NM	1/1/91
Connecticut	current	New England region plus NH and VT	none
District of Columbia	current	Southeast minus KY	none
Florida	current	Southeast plus AR, minus KY	none
Georgia	current	Southeast minus WV, MD, and DC	none
Idaho	current	Contiguous states: MT, NV, OR, UT, WA, and WY	none

State with a Regional Law	Date in Effect	Specified Region[a]	Nationwide Trigger
Illinois	current	Contiguous states: IN, IA, KY, MI, MO, and WI	none
Indiana	current	Midwest minus MO and WI	none
Louisiana	7/1/87	Southeast plus AR, OK, and TX	1/1/89
Maryland[b]	7/1/87	Southeast plus AR, DE, and PA	6/30/88
Massachusetts	current	New England region plus NH and VT	none
Michigan	current	Midwest minus KY and MO, plus MN	10/10/88
Minnesota	current	Contiguous states: IA, ND, SD, and WI	none
Mississippi[c]	7/1/90	Southeast plus AR, MO, and TX, minus MD and DC	none
Missouri	current	Contiguous states: AR, IL, IA, KS, KY, NE, OK, and TN	none
Nevada[d]	current	Far West minus CA, plus CO, HI, MT, NM, and WY	1/1/89
New Jersey	current	East Central and Midwest, plus DE, VA, TN, and DC	7/1/88 (expected)
N. Carolina	current	Southeast plus AR	none
Ohio	current	East Central and Midwest, plus DE, VA, TN, and DC	10/16/88
Oregon	current	Far West plus HI	none
Pennsylvania	current	East Central plus DE, VA, and DC	3/4/90
Rhode Island	current	New England region plus NH and VT	7/1/88
S. Carolina	current	Southeast plus AR	none
Tennessee	current	Southeast plus AR, IN and MO, minus MD and DC	none
Utah[e]	current	Far West minus CA, plus CO, HI, MT, NM, and WY	12/31/87
Virginia	current	Southeast plus AR	none
Wisconsin	1/1/87	Midwest plus IA and MN	none

---

[a]For an explanation of the terms East Central, Midwest, Southeast, Far West, and New England region, see the accompanying map. Note that several regions overlap.

[b]Maryland's reciprocity law became effective in 1985 for a subregion consisting of Delaware, Virginia, West Virginia, and the District of Columbia. Maryland's nationwide trigger in effect calls for the removal of most of the restrictions inherent in the state's limited purpose law.

[c]Mississippi's law extends reciprocity to contiguous states effective 7/1/88.

[d]The reciprocity requirement in Nevada's law will be dropped on 1/1/89.

[e]Utah's reciprocity requirement will be dropped on 12/31/87.

reciprocity in a number of states, and when more states pass interstate banking laws, the Federal Reserve System and other federal regulators will be even busier than they are now, assessing the competitive effects of proposed mergers.[4]

Bank regulators are primarily concerned with competition in *local* banking markets. This is because the geographic markets for retail deposits and many other bank products tend to be local. Moreover, unless a specific product market is being examined, such as the market for large certificates of deposit, regulators view banks as providing a single composite product or cluster of services to its customers. A bank's total deposits (excluding the deposits of foreign institutions) is taken to be representative of the amount of services the bank provides. The locality within which banks respond to the pricing of one another's services is considered to be the banking market.[5]

Regulators will continue to guard against mergers that are likely to harm competition in local markets. As a result, local banking markets that are competitive will remain so, even though the structure of the banking industry is being transformed by interstate banking.

Measuring Concentration in Local Markets. To assess the effects of interstate mergers on competition, the Fed first examines the effects on banking market concentration. By definition, the greater the number of banks in a market, and the more equally divided their market shares, the less concentrated that market will be. Generally speaking, a less concentrated market is more conducive to competition. In an unconcentrated market, there will be many reliable sources of banking services, each readily available to customers. Therefore, when a market is not concentrated, banks must remain competitive in order to continue to attract customers. Only in a highly concentrated market could banks have *monopoly* power—the ability to behave noncompetitively by charging higher prices for their services. Thus, substantial increases in concentration in a banking market could signal a significant reduction in competition.

Concentration is measured by looking at each bank's market share. One measure that is often employed is the three-firm or four-firm concentration ratio. This is simply the aggregate market share of the three or four largest firms in a market. For example, if the three largest banks in a banking market control 30, 25, and 20 percent, respectively, of total market deposits, then the three-firm concentration ratio is 75 percent, indicating a concentrated market. Another concentration measure commonly used is the Herfindahl-Hirschman index (HHI). This index is simply the sum of squares of the market shares of each of the firms competing in a given market. Consider once again the preceding example. If the remaining 25 percent of the market in this example were evenly divided among five firms, then the HHI would equal $(30)^2 + (25)^2 + (20)^2 + 5(5)^2 = 2050$. Or, if the remaining 25 percent belonged to a single firm, then the HHI would equal $(30)^2 + 2(25)^2 + (20)^2 = 2550$. Generally, the fewer the number of firms in a market, and the more uneven their market shares, the higher the HHI.

The Federal Reserve Board applies Department of Justice merger guidelines in analyzing the competitive effects of a proposed merger. Specifically, if a proposed merger would increase the HHI in a market by more than 200, and lead to a post-merger HHI greater than 1800, then the

---

[4]The Federal Reserve regulates bank holding companies and state banks that are members of the Federal Reserve System. The Comptroller of the Currency regulates national banks, and the Federal Deposit Insurance Corporation regulates state nonmember banks. These regulatory agencies evaluate proposed mergers and acquisitions, and they have the authority to block transactions that are determined to be anticompetitive. In addition, the Department of Justice may challenge any bank merger or acquisition it determines to be anticompetitive, although that rarely occurs, because the banking agencies follow policies consistent with the Justice Department guidelines in evaluating the competitive effects of mergers.

[5]The size of a banking market depends upon several factors, such as local commuting patterns, which determine the degree to which banks interact.

Federal Reserve Board considers the possibility that the merger might be anticompetitive. In such cases, the Board decides whether other factors outweigh the anticipated increase in concentration; if they do not, the merger is not allowed to take place. Factors that may be taken into consideration can include, for example, competition from thrifts or other nonbank financial firms, or poor financial condition of the institution being acquired.[6]

Procompetitive Effects. While the regulatory process generally will prevent anticompetitive interstate mergers from taking place, interstate banking will often have procompetitive effects on local markets. In some cases, interstate mergers may result in more efficient institutions and, hence, in more effective competitors. In other cases, competition in a market may be enhanced by the entry of an out-of-state institution, or by the expansion of an existing nonbanking subsidiary of an out-of-state bank holding company.

Acquisition of a bank by an out-of-state holding company (or a merger involving the bank) may enable that bank to operate more efficiently, for a number of reasons. An acquirer may introduce new management procedures that reduce operating costs. Or it may share valuable information with the acquiree, such as expertise in certain types of lending. Merger or acquisition may also be a cost-effective way for a bank to expand into new lines of business; one merger partner might be providing products and services that the other partner wishes to make available to its customers.

Moreover, in some cases a merger may enable the combined organization to achieve scale or scope economies, although empirical economic research has not found much evidence to sup-

port the view that such economies are typical.[7] *Scale economies* are cost savings or efficiencies that result when two merging organizations consolidate their basic operations. For example, the partners to a merger may be able to reduce their overhead costs by combining their data processing operations at a single location. Or, because a merger results in a larger management pool, each manager may be able to oversee fewer areas of operation. More effective management can result, contributing to increased operating efficiency. Similarly, *scope economies* are cost savings that result from combining different types of financial services and activities within a single organization, which allow resources to be shared and duplication of effort to be reduced. For example, a banking organization which offers discount brokerage services can advertise these services to its depositors when mailing monthly account statements. Thus, the organization can save on advertising costs. Although bank mergers will not in general result in economies of scale or scope, some mergers may indeed yield such cost savings.

Finally, an interstate bank merger may benefit the parties involved by diversifying their risk exposure. Because the combined organization will gather deposits from a wider geographic area, deposit outflows in one market are more likely to be balanced by deposit inflows in another market, thus reducing the organization's exposure to deposit fluctuations. And on the asset side, interstate expansion may enable an organization to diversify its loan portfolio further. By reducing the degree to which its loans are concentrated within a particular industry or geographic area, an organization can reduce its vulnerability to economic downturns in that particular area.

---

[6]For a fuller discussion of the factors the Federal Reserve Board might take into consideration, see Jan Loeys, "Bank Acquisitions: The Mitigating Factors Defense," *The Banking Law Journal* (Sept./Oct. 1986) pp. 427-449.

[7]For a more detailed discussion of scale and scope economies in banking, see the studies cited in Loretta Mester, "Efficient Production of Financial Services: Scale and Scope Economies," this *Business Review.*

Each of these efficiencies that may result from a merger or acquisition would enable a merger partner to offer improved services or lower costs to its customers, and thus to be a more competitive institution. And there are at least two more ways in which interstate banking may enhance competition in local banking markets.

First, with the advent of interstate banking, many large bank holding companies may become competitors in markets outside of their home state. In many cases, they will do so via toehold entry, establishing a small, "fringe" presence in these markets. Where permissible, toehold entry may be accomplished *de novo,* (that is, by creating a new subsidiary), or by converting an existing nonbanking subsidiary into a bank. Otherwise, it may be accomplished by purchasing an existing small bank. The fringe firm thus created can have substantial ability to expand over time, because it is backed by a large holding company. That is, because of the financial support as well as the technical assistance and expertise the parent holding company can provide, the fringe firm has the *potential* to increase its deposit share and become a major player in its market. Therefore, the new fringe competitor may exert a competitive influence greater than its market share would indicate.[8]

Second, the nonbanking interstate subsidiaries of bank holding companies could have a special kind of procompetitive effect on local banking markets. Many large bank holding companies currently operate numerous nonbanking subsidiaries in markets outside of their home state.

For example, several out-of-state holding companies operate mortgage banking, consumer lending, commercial lending, as well as leasing subsidiaries in Pennsylvania. (See "OUT-OF-STATE NONBANKING SUBSIDIARIES IN PENNSYLVANIA".) Similarly, several Pennsylvania bank holding companies have a nonbanking presence in numerous other states.[9] When a bank holding company operates such an out-of-state subsidiary, providing a limited number of financial products and services, the holding company (unless prohibited by state law) can enter into other banking activities in the subsidiary's market by expanding the scope of the subsidiary's operations. This often may be easy to accomplish as the legal barriers to such interstate expansion are removed.[10] For example, consider an out-of-state holding company that operates a commercial finance subsidiary in a local market. The removal of barriers to interstate banking may enable the finance subsidiary to gather deposits, including demand deposits, for a bank affiliate. Thus, the holding company could easily become an entrant into the deposit-taking side of the market. The threat of such entry could limit the monopoly power of banks in a

---

[8]The potential procompetitive effects of toehold entry are well recognized in the economics literature. See, for instance, F. M. Scherer, *Industrial Market Structure and Economic Performance,* Boston, Houghton Mifflin Company (1980) p. 248. Evidence indicates that toehold entry into banking markets can (but not always will) have a deconcentrating effect in the long run. That such entry can be procompetitive is supported by John T. Rose and Donald T. Savage in their study "Bank Holding Company De Novo Entry and Banking Market Deconcentration," *Journal of Bank Research* (Summer, 1982) pp. 96-100.

[9]For example, Corestates Financial Corporation (Philadelphia) operates Signal Financial Corporation, a consumer finance subsidiary with offices in several states on the east coast. And Mellon Bank Corporation (Pittsburgh) operates Mellon Financial Services Corporation, a factoring, commercial and consumer lending, and leasing subsidiary, with offices in major cities nationwide. Meridian Bancorp, Inc., (Reading), operates Meridian Mortgage Corporation, a mortgage and commercial lending subsidiary with offices in Pennsylvania, New Jersey, Delaware, and Florida.

[10]In contrast, expansion into a market by a banking organization not previously present in the market would be time-consuming and difficult, due to various regulatory, technological, and physical impediments. In the language of economics, because of the existence of such impediments, banking markets are not "contestable." (In a contestable market, entry is almost costless, and established firms are induced to keep prices as low as possible so that they will not be displaced by entrants.) For a discussion of the various impediments to entry into banking markets, see Paul Calem and Janice Moulton, "Evaluating the Competitive Effects of Mergers Under Interstate Banking," Working Paper forthcoming, Federal Reserve Bank of Philadelphia, pp. 18-20.

Out-of-State Nonbanking Subsidiaries in Pennsylvania

The following is a partial listing of the out-of-state bank holding companies having a nonbanking presence in Pennsylvania, and the types of subsidiaries they own.

Holding Company	Mortgage Banking	Consumer Lending	Commercial Lending	Leasing	Representative Offices
Fleet Financial Group - Rhode Island	√	√	√	√	
Chase Manhattan Corp. - New York	√		√		√
First Maryland Bancorp. - Maryland	√		√		√
Security Pacific Corp. - California	√	√	√	√	
BankAmerica Corp. - California	√	√	√		
Manufacturers Hanover Corp. - New York	√	√	√		
NorWest Corp. - Minnesota	√		√		
Beneficial Corp. - Delaware		√			
BarclaysAmerican Corp. - North Carolina			√		
Bank of Boston Corp. - Massachusetts			√		
Citicorp - New York			√	√	
First Interstate Bancorp - California			√	√	
Marine Midland Banks, Inc. - New York			√		√
Midlantic Banks - New Jersey					√

concentrated banking market. It might not be worthwhile for those banks to maintain monopoly prices for their services, because that could induce the potential entrant to become a more active competitor in the market.

INTERSTATE BANKING AND COMPETITION IN REGIONAL MARKETS

Whereas local banking markets typically encompass a metropolitan area or rural county, the markets for some specific bank products may comprise a region consisting of several states or even, in some cases, the entire nation. In regional markets, banks compete for large or medium-sized corporate customers, engage in syndicated lending to corporations and governments, underwrite or deal in government securities and money market instruments, act as correspondent banks, and engage in such nonbanking activities as data processing and leasing. As the barriers to interstate banking fall, and the banking industry consolidates regionally and nationally, concentration in these markets is increasing. What effect will this have on competition in these markets?

In regional banking markets, a variety of factors affecting competition come into play. On balance, it appears very unlikely that consolidation in these markets will have anticompetitive effects. First, in terms of deposit shares, the banking industry is currently quite unconcentrated nationwide. The four-firm concentration ratio for the banking industry nationally is only 5.8 percent. Moreover, the share of domestic deposits of the top ten firms is only 10.4 percent, and that of the top fifty only 37.9 percent. Although these figures cannot be equated with the level of concentration in specific bank product markets, concentration in regional product markets tends to reflect these low levels. Increases in concentration that are large enough to be a matter of concern are not likely to happen as interstate mergers occur. For instance, according to a recent survey, the top ten correspondent banks nationwide hold less than 28 percent of total domestic correspondent balances.[11] In a region consist-

ing of the Second and Third Federal Reserve Districts (New York, New Jersey, Delaware, eastern Pennsylvania, and southern Connecticut), the four-firm concentration ratio in correspondent banking is about 54 percent.

Second, nonbank financial firms, nonbank subsidiaries of out-of-market banks, and foreign banks provide a substantial degree of competition in many of these regional banking markets. This acts as a mitigating factor, limiting the anticompetitive effects of increasing concentration. For instance, in lending to middle market businesses (businesses that are too large to be considered small businesses, but that are not major national or multinational corporations), regional banks generally compete with the commercial loan subsidiaries of money center banks, foreign banks, and other nonbank financial institutions. And since instruments such as commercial paper and publicly issued bonds can be substitutes for commercial bank loans, banks compete with investment banking firms in the market for large corporate customers. Competition from securities firms is also significant in Treasury bill dealing and municipal bond underwriting. And banking organizations that offer data processing services must compete with many large nonbanking firms such as NCR.[12]

Third, the Federal Reserve System, in evaluating the competitive effects of proposed mergers or acquisitions, considers in particular the nonbanking subsidiaries of the merging organizations. A proposed merger that would substantially reduce competition in some nonbanking activity (an unlikely occurrence to begin with) would face a possible denial or forced divestiture.

The last kind of procompetitive factor to mention here involves customer bargaining power.

---

[11]See "1984 Correspondent Banking Survey," *American Banker* (November 30, 1984) pp. 27-33, and (March 18, 1985) pp. 26-35.

[12]For a listing of the largest providers of data processing services to financial institutions, see *Savings Institutions*, Special Supplement (September 1984) pp. 43-44.

It is difficult for a bank to behave noncompetitively in dealing with high volume, sophisticated customers, even in a concentrated market. If a bank were to raise its fees too high, these customers could threaten to take their business to a major competitor or to a fringe competitor of the bank, or to withdraw from the market completely, and the loss of such a customer could have a significant impact on bank earnings. Large borrowers, whether middle market businesses or larger corporations, as well as local government bond issuers, may often have bargaining power. This factor also mitigates the effect of increasing concentration in regional markets.

CONCLUSION

Interstate bank mergers and acquisitions are already commonplace events in some parts of the country, and within a few years they are likely to become common occurrences nationwide. Although regional and nationwide concentration in banking will increase as a result, competition in banking is likely to remain vigorous. The current regulatory framework prevents mergers that would substantially reduce competition in local markets. And regional and national markets, which are generally unconcentrated to begin with, are likely to remain competitive. Various factors, such as competition from nonbank financial firms, will mitigate the effects of increasing concentration in those markets.

Of course, while competition will probably be strong, there exists some concern that interstate banking will have undesirable consequences on other fronts. For instance, it is feared that a banking industry that is highly concentrated nationwide (or within a particular state) might wield too much political clout. Also, banks will grow in size due to mergers and acquisitions. This increasing size of banks may be viewed as a threat to the safety and soundness of the banking system, on the grounds that the failure of a very large bank could have a serious impact on the financial sector and other sectors of the economy. Further, many small community banks may be acquired by large organizations, and it is feared that these organizations will take away local control from the community banks and will be less apt to support the local economies.[13] These are issues that legislators and regulators will address as need be.

At the same time, the need for restrictions on interstate banking should not be exaggerated, because such restrictions would place a limitation on competition in banking. In many local markets, competition is actually being enhanced as a result of interstate banking. Local markets are experiencing entry by new competitors that are subsidiaries of out-of-state holding companies, including "fringe" competitors. In addition, nonbanking interstate subsidiaries of bank holding companies are becoming potential entrants into full service banking, and as such may be exerting a greater competitive influence on local markets. Competition in a local market is also enhanced when the acquisition of a bank in the market transforms that bank into a more efficient, more dynamic institution. So on balance, bank customers will reap the benefits of more and better bank services at competitive prices as banks expand interstate.

---

[13]It is likely, however, that many small banks will survive, unscathed by the new interstate banking environment. In fact, a body of evidence indicates that community banks will by no means disappear. See, for instance, Dave Phillis and Christine Pavel, "Interstate Banking Game Plans: Implications for the Midwest," Federal Reserve Bank of Chicago *Economic Perspectives* (March/April 1986) pp. 23-39, or Dean F. Amel and Donald T. Savage, "The Structural Effects of Interstate Banking: Evidence from Changes in State Banking Laws," draft, (1986) Board of Governors of the Federal Reserve System.

New Jersey and Pennsylvania Go Interstate

New Jersey's interstate bill establishes an interstate banking region comprising Delaware, Illinois, Indiana, Kentucky, Maryland, Michigan, Missouri, Ohio, Pennsylvania, Tennessee, Virginia, West Virginia, Wisconsin, and the District of Columbia. To be eligible to enter New Jersey, bank holding companies must have at least 75 percent of their total domestic deposits within the region; this restriction prohibits leapfrogging, that is, entry into New Jersey by a bank holding company from outside the region that has established a small presence in some state in the region. The law originally required that New Jersey banking organizations be allowed reciprocal entry into at least three states in the region (other than West Virginia or Delaware) before New Jersey extended reciprocity to any state in the region. As Ohio, Kentucky, and Pennsylvania have offered reciprocity to New Jersey, the law is now effective.

The New Jersey law also contains a trigger to nationwide reciprocity. The law will extend nationwide when at least ten more states allow bank holding companies located in New Jersey to acquire bank holding companies or banks located in those states; four of those states must be among the ten largest, by total commercial deposits, in the country. It appears that New Jersey's trigger date for nationwide reciprocity will fall on July 1, 1988, given the current status of interstate legislation.

Pennsylvania's interstate banking bill establishes an interstate banking region consisting of Delaware, Kentucky, Maryland, New Jersey, Ohio, Virginia, West Virginia, and the District of Columbia. Like New Jersey, Pennsylvania's law contains an anti-leapfrogging provision. The law also establishes a nationwide trigger date: March 4, 1990, when reciprocity will be extended nationwide. Pennsylvania's law also requires that certain criteria be met concerning the availability of banking services to individuals and businesses. The Pennsylvania Department of Banking must certify that Pennsylvania bank holding companies and out-of-state bank holding companies involved in interstate deals offer basic account transaction services and promote investment and employment in their communities.

Article Fifteen

COUNTRY RISK, PORTFOLIO DECISIONS AND REGULATION IN INTERNATIONAL BANK LENDING*

Ingo WALTER**

New York University, New York, NY 10006, USA

This paper examines the concept of 'country risk' and relates it to the construction of efficient loan portfolios in international banking. Applicability of conventional portfolio-theoretic concepts to the management of country lending exposure is examined, as are the requisites of country review systems for national exposure management. The issue of international banking regulation is assessed in this context, focusing on the dangers inherent in national and international regulatory initiatives for optimum global capital allocation.

1. Introduction

In the growing literature on 'country risk', one finds relatively little discussion of what is, or ought to be, management's ultimate objective — incorporating country-specific risk characteristics into the design of asset portfolios that are in some sense 'efficient'. We shall attempt to develop in this article some of the issues involved in closing this gap, both within the asset management decision process of individual banks and in the context of bank regulation.

Modern portfolio theory suggests that there are two types of risk facing any asset manager — unsystematic (diversifiable) risk, and systematic (non-diversifiable) risk. Using a stock market analogy, unsystematic risk is associated with factors affecting individual asset (share) returns. This kind of risk can be reduced, and even eliminated, by diversifying a portfolio across shares subject to different return movements in the market. Systematic risk, on the other hand, is associated with factors affecting the stock market as a whole; it influences all shares in a portfolio and is therefore non-diversifiable. The relative riskiness of a particular stock can be measured by its 'beta' coefficient, the ratio of its own return volatility to the overall return volatility

*Based on a more extensive paper presented at a conference on 'Internationalization of Financial Markets and National Economic Policy', held at the Graduate School of Business Administration, New York University on 10–11 April 1980. Helpful comments by Kaj Areskoug, Ernest Bloch, Larry Brainard, Peter Gray, Dennis Logue, Noralyn Marshall, Arturo Porzecanski, Richard Stapleton, and Clas Wihlborg are gratefully acknowledged, as is research support during the summer of 1980 by the Deutsche Forschungsgemeinschaft under a grant to the Universität Mannheim (Forschungsbereich 5).

**Visiting Professor of Economics, Universität Mannheim, D-68 Mannheim, Federal Republic of Germany.

of the stock market as a whole. Its value to the investor depends not only on its expected returns, but also on how it would affect the riskiness of the entire portfolio. Such concepts permit a skilled investor to build an 'efficient' stock portfolio which maximizes returns subject to risk, given his own personal risk preferences.

Instead of stocks, banks involved in international lending have 'portfolios' of cross-border exposures in different politically-sovereign states. In a global context, much of this exposure is in the nature of unsystematic 'country' risk and thus is diversifiable, resulting in reduced riskiness of the entire portfolio. Systematic risk, on the other hand, derives from factors affecting a number of countries simultaneously, and is less readily reduced through diversification of country exposures. Change in cross-border exposure in a particular country must be evaluated in terms of both its implications for returns and its impact on the riskiness of the bank's overall asset portfolio. An 'efficient' international loan portfolio of a given risk might then be constructed once management's degree of risk aversion is known, returns on country exposures have been correctly assessed, and an attempt has been made to identify something similar in concept to individual country 'betas'. The risk premium associated with exposures in a particular country will tend to reflect the implicit 'beta' associated with the country in question.

It is easy (and dangerous) to push this analogy too far in any mechanistic attempt to develop the principles underlying 'efficient' portfolios of international bank exposures. There are a number of factors that limit the applicability of conventional portfolio theory in this particular context. For one thing, unlike the case of the stock market, the measurement of risks and returns relating to country exposures is extraordinarily difficult. It is here that the 'science' of portfolio management shades into the 'art' of international banking.

Still, as with any other portfolio management problem, the task facing managers of international banks is to maximize the real, economic value of their assets subject to various types of risks. One of these is linked to the political and economic fortunes of countries in which they have cross-border exposures. Returns on these assets depend on competitive factors facing a bank in the market-place for its services. What needs to be evaluated is the expected value of these returns in the future, together with elements that may influence their variance (reflecting the degree of risk).

We can express this in the form of a conventional present value equation such as the following:

$$PV_j^0 = \sum_{t=0}^{n} \frac{E(F_t)}{(1 + i_t + \alpha_t)^t} \, ,$$

where PV_j^0 is the present value of the future stream of returns to the bank related to exposure in a particular country j, $E(F_t)$ denotes the expected value of that future returns stream at time t, i_t is the risk-free discount factor representing the bank's cost of funds, and α_t represents a country risk premium, which depends on the variance of the expected future returns associated with country j relative to β_j (the beta coefficient associated with the institution involved). Prospective future developments in countries in which a bank has cross-border exposures will be reflected in the means as well as the variances of the probability distributions associated with these returns, and hence will influence both $E(F_t)$ and α_t.

2. Expected returns in international lending

If rational portfolio decisions in international lending depend on defensible assessments of risks and returns, it is important to develop first an accurate picture of the expected returns side $E(F_t)$. One important component is, of course, repayment of principal. A second component covers the interest returns which, in the case of floating-rate syndicated loans (comprising perhaps 40–50% of medium and long-term international financings in recent years), usually involves the spread over the three- or six-month London Interbank Offered Rate (LIBOR), or a similar floating base rate of interest. Changes in LIBOR itself tend to show up as shifts in both $E(F_t)$ and i_t, and thus cancel out, although a bank does face some residual interest-rate risk through negotiated spreads, generally fixed for the life of the loan, which may narrow or widen with future market conditions. A recent innovation, 'floating spreads', eliminates this residual risk as well. But principal and interest returns, properly adjusted in a time context for maturities, drawn-down schedules, and the like, represent only a part of the picture.

First, and most obvious in the case of lead managers, co-managers, agents, and others involved in the process of international loan syndication, there is a share of fees agreed upon with the borrower. These may be quite substantial, perhaps well in excess of the incremental costs involved in providing syndication services and — especially since they represent a relatively certain and immediate 'front-end' payment — may add materially to the overall returns of banks engaged in syndicate management. On occasion, borrowers unwilling to incur higher published spreads for prestige or future market-access reasons may inflate front-end fees in order to compensate international lenders.

Second, banks often lend to a particular borrower at terms that might otherwise be considered unattractive in order to develop or maintain a 'relationship'. This involves existing and past ties, and focuses on the expectation of future earnings from a variety of activities that include continued private and public-sector lending activities, foreign exchange transactions, deposit balances, advisory services, custodial business, and the like. There is ample evidence of the importance of the 'relationship' factor in international lending behavior, with regular scrambles by banks to get 'close to' the borrower within syndicates, and in the tendency for losers of syndication mandates to participate anyway in the loans in order to maintain a relationship with the borrower. Similarly, borrowers can sometimes 'encourage' banks to participate in loans that would not otherwise be attractive by suggesting that failure to do so may lead to a loss of collateral business or pressure on their operations in host countries — thereby requiring the addition to apparent returns, in effect, of an insurance premium against possible future earnings losses elsewhere in the relationship. Particularly where the country relationship has been highly profitable in the past, and/or promises to be so in the future, such anticipated 'indirect' returns can be an important part of the total, characterized by their own profile of expected earnings.

Third, a bank's lending to a particular borrower may generate future returns with third parties that might not otherwise materialize. A major syndication may create opportunities for future trade financing or letter of credit business with home or third-country suppliers, for example. Or a particular loan can cement a relationship with a particular domestic or foreign client ('do-good') in a way that promises additional future earnings. Once again, the ultimate returns from this source to the bank may be quite indirect and their assessment quite speculative.

It is clear, therefore, that return of principal and interest, fees, and the remaining less tangible earnings components form a many-sided, probabilistic picture. Each element has its own time-profile and expected value, so that $E(F_t)$ in our formula is itself a highly complex composite. Each element also has its own measure of variability, so that the associated risk premium α_t is similarly complex. And often there are tradeoffs, as when the terms of loan agreements (legal documentation) are relaxed at the insistence of the borrower, thereby possibly exchanging higher expected returns in some of the aforementioned earnings components for greater risk in others. Partly for such reasons, profit attribution in international banking tends to be extraordinarily difficult, and in most banks is considered quite imperfect. For such reasons as well, the returns facing individual banks that are members of lending syndicates may well differ substantially from one to the other, particularly between banks in the management group and the rest.

3. Value of assets exposed to country risk

What kinds of eventualities associated with conditions in countries where a bank has cross-border exposure would tend to influence the real (economic) value of the exposed assets? First, the borrowing country may ultimately be unwilling or unable to effect debt service in full, the default resulting in realized accounting losses of principal and/or accrued interest which the bank must book against earnings, capital or reserves after recovering what it can through the 'right of offset' or other means. The consequences of default for the borrower's access to international capital markets and normal channels of trade are such that this event tends to be triggered by a unique and relatively rare set of circumstances — consequences that are magnified by cross-default clauses commonly written into international loan agreements.

Second, the borrowing country may be unable to meet its external debt obligations on contractual terms and be forced to stretch-out repayment. By definition, the necessary refinancing or rescheduling under such circumstances cannot be accomplished at market terms and occurs under duress, and so the original lenders are forced to extend further credit in the hope of avoiding accounting losses in the end. This may involve an extension of maturities, a new grace period, negotiation of new facilities, an adjustment in interest spreads, or other modifications. Even if this ultimately results in increased accounting returns, if the lender under free-market conditions would have restructured his portfolio out of the exposed assets in question at any point, but cannot do so because he is locked-in, he has in fact incurred an economic loss. The real value of this particular component of his asset portfolio, in effect, has declined. The difference between *economic* and *accounting* shifts in asset values under such circumstances is not always accepted by bankers, and this may influence their reaction to the causative debt service problems and their portfolio decisions in the future.

Third, the borrowing country may be perfectly able and willing to service its external debt — successfully avoiding both default and problems leading to reschedulings or forced refinancings — yet something happens that raises the riskiness of the exposed assets from the perspective of the foreign lender. Assassination of the head of state, for example, may mean nothing at all from a debt service point of view, or it may mean eventual debt repudiation and default, or any of a number of eventualities in-between. Even though neither of our first two types of losses has been incurred by the lender, he has suffered a decline in the value of his assets insofar as he cannot immediately reallocate them in a manner consistent with his new perception of the constellation or relative risks and returns. Some such reallocation may be possible at the margin by running down exposures beginning with the very short maturities. This process, however, is usually far from the kind of instantaneous adjustment — characteristic of efficient financial markets — that is needed to avoid longer-run downward adjustment in the value of the bank's loan portfolio. Once again, bankers are reluctant to recognize such shifts, and they often ignore them in portfolio valuation and decision-making. Yet international lending to South Korea after the assassination of President Park Chung Hee, Thailand after the Vietnamese invasion of Cambodia, and Eastern Europe after the Soviet invasion of Afghanistan seems to suggest that markets are in fact responsive to shifts in 'risk-classes' of countries. Thus, relative rates of change in (net) new loans in effect become a substitute for market-type portfolio adjustments.

In terms of our formula, a number of events may reduce PV_j^0. Prospective defaults can be viewed as reductions in $E(F_t)$, anticipated rescheduling or refinancing losses as forced introduction of higher-valued t's that are less than compensated for by negotiated increases in $E(F_t)$, and losses from risk-class shifts as increases in α_t. Reschedulings or forced refinancings may additionally have the effect of increasing α_t if, as a result, the country is viewed by the market as being more risky.

4. Diversification and risk

The purpose of 'country risk assessment' is, of course, to get a fix on $E(F_t)$ and α_t — usually (as we have previously argued, mistakenly) focusing exclusively on possible threats to interest and principal. Its application to the construction of international loan portfolios is in part related to the objective of diversification, under the presumption that the α_t values for individual countries are essentially independent. If there is indeed zero correlation among returns on the country exposures in a bank's asset portfolio, it is possible for management through diversification to virtually eliminate variability in returns on international lending. The greater the degree of this correlation, the more difficult it is to do so. Yet even with some correlation in earnings variability, bank managers are in principle free to choose how much unsystematic risk to incorporate into their portfolios through the extent of diversification and the kinds of exposures incurred. Our discussion of risk and returns indicates how difficult it is to apply conventional financial theory to international bank lending. Neither the risks associated with individual country exposures nor the returns are easy to measure or identify, nor are the conventional efficient market assumptions satisfied, although movement toward 'efficient' loan portfolios is at least conceptually possible. There are, moreover, some additional problems as well.

For one thing, risk-aversion and hence portfolio preference may be quite different as viewed by (a) an undiversified bank owner or manager, (b) a diversified stock market investor, and (c) the regulatory authorities. The first of these is well served by conventional measures of the dispersion of expected portfolio returns. The second would also have to worry about the covariance of returns on the bank's international portfolio with returns on other assets in his own portfolio — indeed, some of the affected shareholders might possibly reside outside of the bank's country of domicile. The difference between the two perspectives could be attributed to gaps in management's information about (or response to) the market's valuation of the bank's equities. The regulatory authorities, for their part, would tend to focus on the 'bankruptcy tail' associated with different asset portfolios, given the limits of their own liability. When a bank adds a particular loan to its portfolio, therefore, its impact on the riskiness of that portfolio will depend on which of these three specific perspectives is being applied. We shall return to this point later.

A second problem, already mentioned in our earlier discussion, is that international banks are to a significant extent unable to 'buy' and 'sell' assets exposed to country risk. This important option, as envisaged in conventional portfolio theory, is limited to short-term exposure, which can be 'run down' in a relatively short period of time and the assets deployed elsewhere. But the 'term exposure' that makes up a good deal of total international lending is basically locked-in for the duration, with management unable to react through portfolio adjustment to changes in the variance of expected returns. As a result, the lender is not independent of the factors that generate the ultimate returns, as might be the case if a secondary market existed for such assets.

A third problem is that the principal and interest component of $E(F_t)$ in international loan portfolios, unlike stock or bond portfolios, may be subject to asymmetrical variance. That is, the variance of these returns may be entirely on the down-side. In conventional stock or bond portfolios, the investor can win or lose with changes in prices and interest rates. In international loan portfolios, assuming the borrower bears the interest-rate risk as in LIBOR-based loans, prospects of the bank for up-side variance in returns do not exist. As in the case of mortgage and other types of lending subject to asymmetrical variance, such truncated returns distributions tend to induce among bankers a reluctance to recognize changes in the value of their assets until losses are essentially certain. It encourages lenders to take extra care in the assessment of the down-side risks involved, design of loan documentation, assembly of syndicates, and management of 'problem' situations. It may also give added bargaining leverage to 'problem' borrowers in dealing with the international banks, which can itself ultimately accentuate the downside variance of returns. The idea of asymmetrical variance, however, has to be modified if we go beyond the interest and principal components of $E(F_t)$ to take a broader view of expected returns, the prospects for which can improve significantly with a more favorable country outlook.

A fourth problem is that changes in country exposure may be 'lumpy' in the case of banks faced with large loans representing discrete jumps in cross-border exposure, so that portfolios may be difficult to adjust at the margin. And the fact that American and certain other banks are subject to capital-based or similar lending constraints may give rise to additional limits on building efficient portfolios.

Despite such difficulties, some of the basic lessons of portfolio theory can be applied. One of these is the effects of the ability of banks to diversify· and its impact on the value of their overall international loan portfolios. In one sense, the whole purpose of country risk assessment is to ascertain the covariance of expected returns on a portfolio of loans *within* a particular country. But individual country exposures in a bank's global loan portfolio may also have *in common* certain sources of risk, and this moves us closer to an application of the concept of 'systematic' risk, or limits to the value of diversification in international lending.

One source of non-diversifiable risk relates to conditions in the Euromarkets as a whole. Countries requiring rollover financing may face difficulties under tight market conditions. Similarly, since the interest cost of much of the external debt of countries to international banks is linked to LIBOR, tighter international credit conditions may raise the borrowers' respective debt service (balance of payments) burdens, and thereby increase the risk associated with exposed assets in a number of countries at once. Moreover, the Euromarkets tend to be highly sensitive to the fortunes of individual countries, and serious problems in the case of one borrower may impede the ability of others to secure access to credit.

Other sources of possible covariance in returns on country exposures include conditions facing them in major export markets. This is quite clear in the case of commodity markets, where cyclical price weakness can seriously affect the terms and balances of trade of a number of countries at once — e.g., sugar, coffee, copper, and rubber. It also holds for manufactured exports, where a variety of countries may be adversely affected simultaneously by recessions and declines in import demand in principal markets, and by protectionist pressures affecting particular industry segments. Similarly, on the import side a large number of countries are clearly affected by changes in petroleum supplies and costs, and perhaps somewhat narrower analogies may be drawn for other categories of imports (food, raw materials) as well. Such risks are not totally non-diversifiable, however, since care can be taken in constructing international loan portfolios to incorporate such covariances in banks' exposure decisions.

Finally, there is the matter of the geographic distribution of country exposures. Countries in a particular region, such as Southeast Asia, may be subject to common economic or political threats. Portfolio diversification can still be achieved within such constraints. But the degree of difficulty increases when the commonalities become more prevalent, as in the case of geopolitical shocks, perceived 'domino' effects, and the like.

5. Lending decisions and approaches to country risk assessment

Despite the difficulties in measuring risks and returns, in recognizing and reacting to changes in values of country exposure in international loan portfolios, and in developing and implementing approaches to effective diversification, there is little doubt that the core lessons of portfolio theory are of substantial value in international banking. Yet exposure limits in international bank lending often seem to be set in the absence of such an overriding philosophy, and on the implicit assumption that there is zero correlation among countries, or between country conditions and the various other sources of risk we have identified. The reason may have something to do with the difficulties encountered in the country risk assessment process itself and a natural tendency to focus intensively on country-by-country analysis. A great deal has been written about this problem, and it is not necessary to review that literature once again here. The problem essentially breaks down to a matter of forecasting expected returns $E(F_t)$ and the specific sources of risk that load into our α_t variable, risk that arises out of structural (supply-side) elements, demand-side and monetary elements, external economic and political developments, as well as the quality of the national economic management and the domestic political constraints bearing upon decision-makers.

In the absence of an efficient market whose data can be analyzed, the delivery of effective country risk assessment ideally requires the employment of a true 'renaissance person' — exceedingly intelligent, a holder of doctorates from respectable institutions in economics, political science, sociology, psychology and perhaps a few other fields as well, totally objective, with a great deal of common sense. In addition to being rather well-traveled, he or she is up-to-date on developments in all countries of interest to the bank (and in other countries that might affect them), and personally acquainted with key policymakers. Obviously, there are few such individuals wandering around these days. And so the question is whether international banks, *as institutions*, can in some way put together all of these qualities, using relatively 'ordinary' individuals and traditional organizational linkages to assemble a superior ability to forecast the future of countries, its bearing on the real value of exposed assets, and its implications for portfolio management. Low quality estimates of $E(F_t)$ and α_t yield low quality portfolio decisions and, ultimately, second-rate performance of the bank in the competitive marketplace.

In the design of a country analysis function aiming at high-quality $E(F_t)$ and α_t estimates for use in portfolio decisions, the emphasis clearly must be on the fact that it is the beginning, not the end, of the task. Approaches that try to be overly precise risk triggering arguments among users over irrelevant points. Those that are too general may fail to concentrate on the true sources of risk in country exposure, and on the specific concerns facing a particular bank. Risk to medium- and long-term exposure requires a far more complex analysis than risk in short-term lending, yet one that is still much simpler than risk to any foreign direct investment exposure that a bank may have in a particular country.

The twin temptations of 'quick and dirty' and 'overloaded' country risk assessments constantly seem to confront international banks. The first approach promises mechanical short-cuts and the use of low-priced talent to grind out results at reasonable cost, but often appears to succeed only in producing nonsense — there really is no substitute for high-quality analysis, flexibility, judgement, and familiarity. The second approach may rely on well qualified internal personnel at high cost, yet encounter a dangerous narrowing of country expertise, possibly cause dissention, and create bottlenecks in the decision-making process.

The conflicting demands of country assessment — ranging from high levels of usability, auditability and comparability, and the need to capture exceedingly complex and country-specific qualitative judgments over extended periods of time, to the need to avoid abuse of the results in decision-making — probably means that there is no such thing as an 'ideal' system.

'Appropriate' systems will certainly differ for different banks. The key may reside as much on the 'human resources' side as on the 'technology' side. To train line bankers in using reasonably unsophisticated yet sensible country assessments properly, and in being sensitive to changing country risk profiles and sources of covariance as they go about their business, may in the end contribute more to sound portfolio decisions than comparable resources devoted to the design and implementation of more elegant systems. This would appear to follow from the view of multinational banks' general competitive advantage as 'information factories', to which their global operations and headquarters-affiliate links are ideally suited. Whether in systems-design or in the training function, resources devoted to the assessment of country risk clearly are subject to constraints, and there is some implicit optimum where the incremental costs in country assessment begin to outweigh the economic losses implicit in inefficient international loan portfolios.

To get the best possible fix on the critical $E(F_t)$ and α_t variables that have been the core of our discussion, the exercise of country risk assessment should be an integrated managerial process that focuses the network of information and actively involves individuals with different functions and perspectives. The exercise will thus have intangible portfolio benefits all its own, quite apart from its more visible output in the form of defensible country-by-country evaluations. Mechanization and decentralization of the country review process will tend to cut down and perhaps eliminate this benefit, and may thereby help to stifle an environment conducive to sound portfolio decisions.

Each bank's institutional information-flow and decision-making setup has its own profile, depending on such factors as the organization's size and structure. Some banks incorporate country assessments into portfolio decisions quite flexibly and informally, while others seem to rely on rigid and formalized review procedures. In some cases the review process is closely tied as well to the annual budget cycle and the allocation of lending authority to countries and regions. These again may be quite rigid in some banks, while in others they are relatively easily altered as perceived market and risk conditions change. In some banks, the determination of 'loan loss provisions' is an integral part of the process, and affects the anticipated net profitability of loans by adjusting for risk and presumably permits improved performance evaluation within the bank's organizational framework.

While few international banks fail to maintain adequate cross-border exposure measurement, allocation, and monitoring, there seems to be far greater variability in the state of the country assessment systems themselves. Some are carefully thought through, while others are largely cosmetic or pseudo-scientific. Some are well integrated into the life of the organization, while others seem separate and even isolated. Until fairly recently, smaller U.S. banks, particularly when participating in loan syndications, tended to rely on the country evaluations of the larger money center banks. Besides being unsatisfactory from a regulatory point of view (see below), we have already noted that the appropriate risk-return calculus of lead banks is not necessarily the same as that of the smaller banks. Banks in Europe and Japan so far do not appear to have placed a great deal of emphasis on the design of formal approaches to country assessment or to incorporate them into international lending decisions, preferring instead to rely much more informally on the collective experience and wisdom of senior bank officers.

Whatever the approach, rational portfolio decisions demand that forecasts of country futures be maintained on a comparable basis — and modified in the light of covariances arising out of common export markets or sources of supply, conditions in and access to international financial markets, and regional as well as global political developments. It should also be clear that, in assessing the impact of a particular change in country exposure on the value of a bank's asset portfolio as a whole, it is not only the specific country-related variance of returns that is of importance, but also the intercountry covariance of returns, and this can easily be masked by an exclusive focus on country-specific sources of risk. And so it is possible to envision the application of the portfolio context we have developed — with risk aversion dictated by top management, correctly attributed returns estimated by line bankers, carefully defined risks to these returns estimated by formal or informal approaches to country evaluation, and covariances therein brought into the picture in the setting of exposure limits and term sublimits.

6. Regulatory influence on portfolio decisions

With the growth in international lending during the 1970s came increasing concern on the part of those responsible for bank regulation and supervision that sound banking practice be maintained, including adequate information on exposure, country risk assessment, loan diversification and pricing. In terms of our earlier discussion, the regulatory function focuses exclusively on the expected value of interest and principal recovery and its variance — usually with reference to potential impairment of capital — without regard to the other types of returns relevant to bank portfolio decisions. One might therefore envision a scenario whereby influence of regulators on bank lending decisions could well move them *away from* efficient international loan portfolios, particularly since different banks have different sets of returns, access to information, perceptions of risk, and risk preferences. In the process, certain borrowers could be closed out of international credit markets who would otherwise have continued access. Is this a danger?

For American banks, losses in international lending have consistently been below domestic losses. Yet in the late 1970s, a borrower's market characterized by declining, compressed averaged spreads and lengthening average maturities 'has caused concern among bankers about an erosion of documentation and lending standards. Some borrowers will no longer provide financial accounts that were standard loan documentation a couple of years ago.... Borrowers are demanding less stringent conditions in their loans' legal documentation, including less use of cross-default clauses'.[1] Such implicit concerns about the α_t values in the equation we have been using were instrumental in moving U.S. bank regulators toward a uniform system of segregating country risks from other lending risks, and dealing with them separately in their examination reports. The emphasis has been on diversification of country exposure within a bank's international loan portfolio based on capital ratios, and on an assessment of the bank's own country risk analysis and monitoring capabilities. This new supervisory aspect necessitated agreement in November 1978 on a uniform country risk screening procedure by the U.S. regulatory authorities themselves, undertaken in the form of a joint effort by the Federal Reserve System, the Comptroller of the Currency, and the Federal Deposit Insurance Corporation for use by bank examiners.

In current practice, a nine-member committee of international bank examiners representing the three supervisory authorities meets several times each year to reach a consensus on the riskiness of exposure in selected countries based on a set of 'briefing notes' generated by Federal Reserve economists. These, together with oral supplements, form the basis of 'comments' and of the examiners' discussions with senior bank management. Although the purpose is explicitly *not* to preclude certain countries from additional U.S. bank lending, or to suggest 'superior' international loan portfolios, one would suspect that the inherent 'second guessing' function of the examination process is bound to have an affect on international lending decisions by influencing our α_t variable. There is the undeniable advantage of forcing the less well-managed banks to conduct independent country risk monitoring in order to justify individual exposure positions, and to pay careful attention to risks and returns in international lending. But beyond this, aversion of banks to having particular country exposures subject to 'listing' or 'comment' in examination reports may well drive them away from optimum loan portfolios that still meet acceptable standards of risk from a public-policy point of view by influencing relative risk premiums used in making portfolio decisions. This could involve implicit imposition of the supervisory authorities' own views of risk and diversification on the banks. Whether this consideration — together with possible flaws in the supervisory application of country analyses by bank examiners — leads to significant distortions in the international allocation of credit remains to be seen.

So far, the United States is alone in making country risk assessment an integral part of the bank examination process. Most other countries make no distinction among international lending risks pertaining to different countries, and rely almost entirely on uniform capital-asset ratios. Nor is supervisory pressure on banks to develop defensible, independent country risk

[1]*IMF Survey*, 3 September 1979, p. 277.

assessment and monitoring systems very much in evidence outside the U.S. On the other hand, there may be a good deal of moral suasion present in the informal discussions between banks and their supervisory authorities that is an important part of the regulatory process in a number of countries. Clearly, international differences in the supervisory function, as it embodies elements of country risk, have the potential of influencing both the flow of international credit and competitive relationships in international banking.

The best recent example occurred in October 1979, when the Japanese Ministry of Finance clamped an embargo on further overseas foreign-currency lending by Japanese banks, exempting only export credits and loans for energy imports. The authorities apparently feared the vulnerability of the banks, 80% funded in the interbank market, to a repetition of the 1974 Euromarket credit squeeze. A return of the Japanese banks to the market in June 1980 was accompanied by ceilings on Euroloans, American-type lending limits, and far sharper surveillance even to the point, apparently, of imposing Ministry of Finance judgments on loan size and borrower qualifications.

There is also some movement to achieve a greater degree of international regulatory uniformity with respect to country exposure. The supervisory authorities in the United States have pushed hard to expand and refine data on cross-border exposure of American banks, and to some extent this has been paralleled by similar improvements elsewhere, including international efforts to compile and publish the relevant data. For instance, the Bank for International Settlements has assembled a great deal of information on country debt and provides guidance for national supervisory authorities on how to interpret it. The emerging consensus seems to be that authorities should apply bank supervision on a consolidated balance sheet basis, as is done in the U.S. The view is taking hold that, even though foreign subsidiaries are legally independent entities, in case of debt service problems the liabilities would nevertheless fall due to the parent bank. Both Switzerland and the United Kingdom have moved in this direction. The idea of minimum capital-asset ratios is also catching on. There is, however, no consensus on formal, systematic guidelines for diversification of loan portfolios exposed to country risk.

Besides the supervisory role at the national level, there is the possibility that country evaluations on the part of international organizations may influence the management of loan portfolios by private banks. Among the international institutions concerned with this issue are the BIS Cooke Committee of national bank supervisors, the Berne Union focusing on government export credit guarantees, and the so-called Paris Club involved in rescheduling official debt of countries in trouble. All are concerned in one way or another with assessment of country risk. While no direct links yet exist, attitudes emerging in such forums have the potential of influencing bank regulators at the national level and, through them, bank portfolio decisions.

Of possibly greater importance is the International Monetary Fund, and to a lesser extent the World Bank, which maintain detailed country evaluations used in their respective decisions on balance of payments and project financing. While these assessments are nominally confidential, important elements are available to member governments and there is the possibility that IMF opinion will gradually add a certain degree of uniformity to bank lending decisions via its links to national regulators. A strong argument can of course be made for the widest possible dissemination of data collected and analyzed by international institutions. But this hardly justifies, on either competence or portfolio grounds, undue influence of IMF staff assessments of country risk on the private banks' international lending decisions.

At the same time, in actual or potential problem situations there is great value in coordinated lending by the IMF and the banks — assuming reasonably thoughtful application of IMF conditionality. If the problems are serious enough, the banks are naturally more than anxious to have a country approach the IMF, and have been known to await the outcome of such negotiations before committing themselves to further financing. Indeed, additional bank loans may be dependent on successful discussions with the IMF, and drawdowns under such facilities carefully tied to the borrower's observance of conditions attached to parellel drawings on its IMF standby facility. In this way, added weight can be given to the IMF's influence in pressing for effective adjustment and economic discipline in deficit countries, while the implicit value of the banks' exposed assets is supported. Such parallelism, however, has so far appeared only in serious problem situations. Its extension to ordinary country lending situations could superimpose IMF country assessments upon the private banks, distorting loan portfolios by influencing risk perceptions and affecting the direction and volume of international bank lending.

7. Conclusions

Whereas assessment of country risk is itself an exceedingly difficult task, building country evaluations into the design of international loan portfolios that are in some sense 'efficient' is even more complicated. Neither the risks nor the returns are clearly definable, and the assumptions underlying conventional financial theory are hardly satisfied. Nevertheless, it is important for banks to realize what they ought to be doing when they make international lending decisions, and when they throw scarce human and financial resources into country risk assessment. Portfolio theory can contribute importantly in clarifying the risks. It also helps to identify the dangers inherent in externally-imposed risk evaluations for rational portfolio decisions, particularly when they emanate from the regulatory system. At the same time, the development of informational and interactive networks within banks as part of the country evaluation process can itself lead to improved international lending decisions that implicitly embody some of the elusive portfolio concepts we have tried to focus on here.

Application of the portfolio concepts we have suggested will also help pin down the link between risk and pricing. Portfolio theory says that the riskiness of any single loan is not what is important, but rather the effect of that loan on the riskiness of the overall bank or shareholder portfolio. So, for example, loans by different banks for similar maturities to a single country might well have quite different pricing, dependent on both the nature of the 'indirect' returns accruing to the lending banks and on the covariances with the total market return.

References

Caldwell, J. Alexander and J. Antonio Villamil, 1979, U.S. lenders are learning to discriminate, Euromoney, May.

Donaldson, T.H., 1979, Lending in international commercial banking (Halsted-Wiley, New York).

Eaton, Jonathan and Mark Gersovitz, 1979, Debt with potential repudiation: Theoretical and empirical analysis, Mimeo. (Princeton University, Princeton, NJ).

Kobrin, Steven J., 1979, Political risk: A review and reconsideration, Journal of International Business Studies, Sept.

Kubarych, Roger M., 1980, Portfolio approaches to managing country risk: The view from the Federal Reserve Bank of New York, Federal Reserve Bank of New York, Mimeo., Jan.

Nagy, Panchras, 1979, Quantifying country risk: A system developed by economists at the bank of Montreal, Columbia Journal of World Business, Jan.

Porzecanski, Arturo C., 1980, The assessment of country risk: Lessons from the Latin American experience, in: J.C. Garcia-Zamor and S. Sutin, eds., Financing development in Latin America (Praeger, New York).

Sargen, Nicholas, 1977, Use of economic indicators and country risk appraisal, Federal Reserve Bank of San Francisco, Economic Review, Fall.

Van Agtmael, Antoine, 1976, Evaluating the risks of lending to developing countries, Euromoney, April.

Volcker, Paul A., 1980, The recycling problem revisited, Federal Reserve Board, Mimeo., March.

Walter, Ingo, 1981, International capital allocation, in: R.G. Hawkins, R.M. Levich and C. Wihlborg, eds., Internationalization of financial markets and national economic policy (JAI Press, Greenwich, CT).

Article Sixteen

Bank risk from nonbank activities

Elijah Brewer, III, Diana Fortier, and Christine Pavel

Banking organizations are permitted to engage in more than 50 nonbank activities, including commercial and consumer finance, mortgage banking, and leasing. However, they are precluded from engaging in some other financial activities. These include insurance, securities underwriting and real estate, which many believe are essential to banking firms if they are to compete effectively in the financial services industry (see Table 1).[1] However, it is feared that the removal of the legal barriers that prevent the entry of banks and bank holding companies (BHCs) into these activities will increase bank risk.

This article reviews previous studies and presents new information on the riskiness of various permissible and impermissible nonbank activities. The first section discusses the issues concerning nonbank risk. The second section describes the current regulatory framework within which banking firms must operate in expanding their nonbank activities. The third section reviews the various economic and methodological issues that arise when analyzing the risk implications of nonbank activities. The fourth section examines the track record of regulators by looking at the risk implications of currently permissible nonbank activities of bank holding companies. The fifth section looks to the future and examines the risk implications of currently impermissible activities. New evidence, as well as previous research, regarding the riskiness of nonbank activities are presented in the latter two sections. A summary and the policy implications are presented in the final section.

In brief, we find that the potential for bank holding companies to reduce overall risk through diversification into individual nonbank activities is limited. We also find that regulations and laws have permitted BHCs to engage in activities that are likely to increase BHC risk, while they have not permitted BHCs to engage in a few activities that would likely reduce BHC risk or at least not increase it as much as some currently permissible activities.

But, the regulatory process is designed to control the risk of nonbank activities. The impact of this process can only be judged by ex-amining actual nonbank activities that have been undertaken by BHCs. We find that overall investment in nonbank activities has reduced the volatility of BHC returns even though the potential for risk reduction seems limited when individual nonbank activities are examined separately.

Issues concerning nonbank risk

Banks and other federally insured depository institutions have access to a unique "safety net." The safety net has three components: the ability to borrow on a collateralized basis from the Federal Reserve's discount window; the ability to issue federally insured deposits; and occasional eligibility for open bank assistance and forbearance programs. These elements of the safety net give banks an advantage in holding risky assets and can, in some instances, create incentives for banks to take on undesirable amounts of risk.

New powers for banking organizations can be granted either to the bank itself or to an affiliate of the bank under the umbrella of a BHC. The concern about risk is quite clear when the question is whether to grant additional powers to banks. Granting additional powers directly to banks can result in an increase in the risk of the bank and in the FDIC's exposure.

When the issue is whether to grant powers to a subsidiary of a BHC, the reasons for concern about risk are less clear. If the bank can be financially insulated from the rest of the holding company, then the risk of the holding company should not be an issue. However, there are several reasons why this insulation may be less than perfect.

It may be difficult to financially insulate the bank from activities elsewhere in the holding company.[2] Problems may arise if high-risk assets of a nonbank are transferred to a bank affiliate or if a bank provides an excessive amount of funds to its affiliate. Problems also

Elijah Brewer, III, Diana Fortier, and Christine Pavel are economists at the Federal Reserve Bank of Chicago. The authors thank Herbert Baer, Douglas Evanoff, and Randall Merris for their comments.

161

Table 1
Status of nonbank activities*

Permissible Activities

  By regulation

Mortgage banking
Finance company: general, consumer, commercial,
    insurance premium, mobile homes, agriculture
Factoring
Industrial banking
Investment, financial, and economic adivsory services
Leasing
Community development
Data processing
Insurance agency or broker per Garn St. Germain
Insurance underwriting for credit life, credit
    accident, and health
Fiduciary and trust
Courier services
Management consulting for depository institutions
Travelers checks, issuance or sale
Payment instruments, issuance or sale
Real estate and personal property appraisals
Arranging equity financing
Discount broker
Underwriting government and other securities
Arrange and advise foreign exchange transactions
Futures commission merchant
Consumer financial planning
Tax planning and preparation
Collection agency
Credit bureau

  By order

Savings and loan (limited)
Savings bank
Pool reserve plan
Precious metal (buy and sell for customers)
Securities agent
Offshore commercial banking
New York investment company
Employee benefits consulting
Nonbank bank
Cash management services
Underwrite and deal in commercial paper
Underwrite and deal in municipal revenue bonds,
    commercial paper, mortage related securities,
    and consumer receivable related securities
Other

Impermissible Activities

  Not closely related

Travel agency
Sale or underwriting of insurance other
    than the seven exemptions under
    Garn St. Germain
Contract key entry services
Property and casualty insurance
Commodities dealing
Independent actuarial services

  Closely related but not
  proper incident

Savings and loan
Foreign exchange options specialist
Underwriting mortgage guarantee insurance
Investment note activity

  Not closely related and
  not proper incident

Management consulting
Pit arbitrage
Public credit ratings on bonds, preferred stock,
    and commercial paper
Real estate brokerage, investment, development,
    and syndication
Life insurance
Equity funding
Property management, generally

---

*Prohibited activities are those proposed or those applied for but denied as not being closely related to banking and/or not being a proper incident thereto (as of November 1987). Additional information on specific *Federal Reserve Bulletin* citations and applications may be found in Special Reference Section: "Permitted and Prohibited 4(c)(8) Activities." *Bank Expansion Quarterly.* Golembe Associates, Inc., Washington, DC.

may develop when a nonbank is a major provider of services to its affiliated banks; if the nonbank fails, services to the banks may be disrupted. Furthermore, loss of public confidence in affiliated banks and consequent social costs may occur when a bank's affiliated nonbank firm fails.[3]

In addition to the risk implications of nonbank activities, regulators must also be careful not to confer unfair competitive advantages on the nonbank activities of bank holding companies. By allowing banking firms to engage in nonbank activities that compete with nonbank firms, BHCs may be given a competitive advantage over other financial services providers through deposit insurance and the discount window. In that case, the playing field has not been leveled; the bumps have merely been moved from one side of the field to the other.

The regulation of nonbank activities

The rationale for restricting nonbank activities of bank holding companies centers on three concerns: 1) safety and soundness of the banking system; 2) undue concentration of financial power and conflicts of interest; and 3) extensions of deposit insurance and the discount window to banks' uninsured affiliates.

The Bank Holding Company Act of 1956 and its 1970 amendments, as well as the Glass-Steagall Act of 1933, which separates investment from commercial banking, are the primary laws that prescribe permissible nonbank activities for banking organizations. The intent of these laws seems to be to limit concentration of power and conflicts of interest more than to ensure the safety and soundness of the banking system.[4]

Sections 5(c), 16, 20, 21, and 32 of the Glass-Steagall Act prescribe what securities activities are permissible for banks and bank holding companies. The sum of these sections, in brief, is that a bank that is a member of the Federal Reserve System and any affiliate of such a bank cannot be "principally engaged in" the dealing or underwriting of "ineligible" securities.[5]

Section 4(c)(8) of the Bank Holding Company Act defines and regulates all nonbank activities in which BHCs may engage, including securities-related activities, directly or indirectly through a subsidiary. For the Federal Reserve Board to deem a new activity permissible either by regulation or Board order, it must be proven to be "closely related to banking or managing or controlling banks as to be a proper incident thereto."[6] That is, it must pass 1) the closely related and 2) the proper incident (public benefits) tests.

In finding an activity to be closely related to banking, the Board considers three criteria: 1) banks engage in the proposed activity; 2) banks generally provide services that are operationally or functionally so similar to the proposed activity as to equip them particularly well to provide the proposed activity; or 3) banks generally provide services that are so integrally related to the proposed activity as to require their provision in a specialized form. The Board also has the discretion to consider other criteria when evaluating an activity. This provides a reasonable basis for determining whether a particular nonbank activity has a close relationship to banking.[7]

Using the proper incident test, the Board considers whether or not the performance of the activity by the BHC can reasonably be expected to produce benefits to the public. The Board looks for benefits such as greater convenience, increased competition, and gains in efficiency that outweigh possible adverse effects, such as undue concentration of resources, decreased or unfair competition, conflicts of interest, and unsound banking practices. Because the BHC is to serve as a source of strength to its banking subsidiaries, the Board also takes into account the financial and managerial resources of the BHC, its affiliates, and, in the case of an acquisition, the company to be acquired, as well as the effect of the proposed acquisition on those resources.[8]

Many of the activities in which bank holding companies would like to engage have already been found to be "closely related to banking" (Table 1). We concentrate here on one aspect of the "proper incident" test for nonbank activities. Specifically, we focus on the riskiness of nonbank activities.

Economic and methodological issues

In analyzing the implications of nonbank activities for BHC risk, two questions must be addressed. First, is banking less risky than nonbanking activities? Second, does the combination of a nonbanking activity with banking, or with banking and other nonbanking activities in which BHCs currently engage, significantly increase BHC risk?

If the returns from banking are perfectly correlated with the returns from a particular nonbank activity, then banking and that nonbank activity are identical based on rates of return. In such a case, risk will be reduced only if the nonbank activity is less risky than banking. Otherwise, the BHC would be, in effect, putting more eggs in one basket: diversification would be decreased and risk increased. The "closely related to banking" test seems to imply that any nonbank activity deemed permissible would be highly, although not necessarily perfectly, positively correlated with banking. But, an activity might be riskier than banking, and reduce the overall risk of the

Table 2
Review of selected studies of the risk of nonbank activities*

Study	Time Period	Methodology**	Do nonbank activities reduce BHC risk?
Accounting Industry data Heggestad(1975)	1953-67	COV	Yes. Impermissible activities: insurance agents, and brokers and real estate agents, brokers, managers, holdings and investment companies, and lessors of R.R., oil and mining properties. Banking is among the riskiest activities based on the coefficient variation in profits. (Studied activities of one-BHCs prior to 1970 BHC Act amendments.)
Johnson and Meinster(1974)	1954-1969 (annual data)	COV and portfolio analysis	Yes. Impermissible activities: insurance agents and brokers, holding and investment companies, and real estate agents, brokers and managers. Studies 13 activities. Portfolio analysis based on earnings and cash flow conclude there are diversification benefits into nonbank activities but that the benefits are sensitive to the percentage of assets in each activity.
Wall and Eisenbeis (1984)	1970-80	COV	Yes. Impermissible activities: S&Ls, security brokers and dealers, life insurance, general merchandise stores, lessor of R.R. property. Permissible activities: personal and business credit agency. Banking neither highest nor lowest risk based on coefficient of variation. Results are sensitive to time period.
Firm data Jessee and Seelig (1977)		COV	No. Risk reduction is not related to share of nonbank investment.
Meinster and Johnson(1979)	1973-77	ROF	Yes. BHCs effectively diversified but slightly increased probability of capital impairment with debt financing. (Sample of only 2 BHCs in 7 permissible activities of leasing, consumer finance, mortgage banking, bank management consulting, financial services, and foreign bank services.)
Litan(1985)	1978-83	COV	As likely to reduce volatility of BHC income as to increase it. (Sample of 31 large BHCs.)
Wall(1986)	1976-84	ROF	Nonbank activity either decreases BHC risk slightly or has no impact. The positive relationship between nonbank risk and BHC risk, BHC leverage, and bank risk is consistent with the possibility that management preferences influence the riskiness of the BHC's subsidiaries and determine the use of leverage to influence overall risk.
Boyd and Graham (1986)	1971-83, (1971-77 and 1978-83)	ROF	Entire period: no significant relationship between nonbank activity and any risk or return measures. Less stringent policy period (1971-77): no, nonbank activity is positively related to risk. More stringent policy period (1978-83): weak negative relationship between nonbank activity and risk.
Boyd and Graham (1988)	1971-84 (annual data)	COV/ROF/MS	Study covers six impermissible activities. Yes for life insurance. The standard deviation and bankruptcy risk measures indicate risk is likely to increase for real estate development, securities firms, and property/casualty insurance activities, and increase slightly for other real estate and insurance agency and brokerage activities. BHC is lowest risk activity.
Brewer(1988)	1979-1985	COV	Yes. One standard deviation increase in investment in nonbank subsidiaries leads to 6 basis point drop in BHC risk (approximately 7 percent).

Study	Time Period	Methodology**	Do nonbank activities reduce BHC risk?
Industry and firm data Stover(1982)	1959-68	Wealth maximization; debt capacity	Yes. Impermissible activities: S&Ls, investment banking, land development, fire and casualty insurance. Measures equity returns and diversification benefits of 14 permissible and impermissible activities in wealth maximization model.
Boyd, Hanweck and Pithyachariyakul (1980)	1971-77	COV/ROF	Yes, but limited. Permissible activities: mortgage banking, factoring, consumer finance, credit card, loan servicing, investment advisors, leasing(except auto), community welfare, data processing, credit life, accident and health insurance agents and underwriters, and management consulting.
			No (any investment increases probability of bankruptcy). Permissible activities: commercial and sales finance, industrial banks, trust services, auto leasing. (Study only covered permissible activities.)
Market data **Industry data** Eisemann(1976)	1961-68 (monthly data)	Industry (portfolio) selection model (COV)	Yes. Banking is minimum risk activity. Lowest risk BHC includes permissible activity of sales finance and impermissible activities of insurance investment banking. Highest risk BHC includes permissible activity of data processing. Studies 20 activities.
Firm data Wall(1984)	Select dates	Bond returns	No significant effect.
Wall and Eisenbeis(1984)	Select dates (monthly data)	Bond returns	No. (Study only covered permissible activity of discount brokerage).
Boyd and Graham (1988)	1971-84 (annual data)	COV/ROF/MS	Studies six impermissible activities. Yes for life insurance, insurance agency and brokerage, and property/ casualty insurance. Risk likely to increase for real estate development and securities firms, and increase slightly for other real estate. Based on standard deviation, bankruptcy, and beta risk measures BHC is not lowest risk activity. Insurance agency and brokerage, and property and casualty insurance are lowest risk activities.
Brewer(1988)	1979-85 (daily data)	COV	Yes. One standard deviation increase in investment in nonbank subsidiaries leads to an 8-11 percent basis point drop in BHC risk. Results are sensitive to the time period studied.
Brewer, Fortier and Pavel(1988)	1980, 1982 and 1986 and 1979-1983	COV/MS	Yes. Impermissible activities of insurance agents and brokers, property and casualty and life insurance underwriting. Investment of 5 percent or less for any of the tested activities would not increase the variance of the BHC significantly, but investment of 25 percent or more for all but the above listed activities would increase the riskiness of the BHC significantly. Examination of the impact of total investment in nonbank activities regardless of the specific activities finds increases in nonbank activity tends to lower BHC risk significantly.

* Permissible activities refer to those nonbank activities currently permissible (May 1988), whether or not they were permissible at the time of the study.
Impermissible activities also include activities not yet ruled upon by the Board at the time of the study.

** COV—analysis of coefficient of variation of rates of return of banking and nonbanking activities,
ROF—risk of failure (bankruptcy) analysis; MS—simulated merger analysis.

organization when combined with banking if the correlation between the returns is negative or imperfect.

Numerous studies have addressed the question of the riskiness of selected nonbank activities (see Table 2).[9] A review of these studies indicates that the methodology, type of data (i.e., accounting or market), level of aggregation (i.e., firm or industry), and the sample period significantly affect the results. Nevertheless, most of the studies conclude that diversification of risk through nonbank activities is limited.

In addition, studies on nonbank risk generally do not account for synergies from BHC affiliations. There may be systematic differences in the operations of certain nonbank activities as conducted in unaffiliated firms and BHC-affiliated companies.[10] Additionally, the impact of financing alternatives for acquisitions and the managerial and financial characteristics associated with specific acquisitions have been ignored. While it may be difficult to account for these factors, it is important to note that failure to consider their effects may influence the results.

Previous studies have employed different methods to analyze the impact of nonbank activities on BHC diversification. The two most frequently used statistical methods are variance/covariance analysis and risk-of-failure analysis. Variance/covariance studies use the variability of returns from banking and various nonbank activities and the correlations among those activities to assess risk-return characteristics of nonbank activities alone and in combination with each other and with banking. BHCs may benefit from diversification into nonbank activities if they can increase their returns while decreasing the variability of those returns. Risk-of-failure studies analyze the impact of engaging in nonbank activities on the variability of the BHCs' cash flow. A reduction in cash flow variability should improve debt capacity and reduce failure probabilities.

Although various methods have been used in prior studies, they have all employed one of two types of data to measure the riskiness of activities—accounting data and market data. Either type of data has its problems.

Stock market returns as a measure of BHC value are limited to a relatively small sample of banking firms. Such returns are not available for smaller, untraded or less frequently-traded, BHCs. In addition, most of the stock data available are for holding companies that are involved in activities other than banking, and it is not possible to obtain data on many bank stocks alone. Using these data leads to upwardly biased correlations between the returns to permissible activities and those of bank holding companies that already engage in the permissible activities. The variances of the BHC returns will also be biased—upward if the nonbank activity increases risk and downward if it decreases risk. Another problem with using stock data is that SIC classifications may not allow sufficient disaggregation of activities. This problem also arises with accounting data.

Other problems arise from the use of consolidated accounting data for BHCs and their subsidiaries. Accounting data reflect historical costs and values, rather than current market values. Furthermore, the pricing of interaffiliate transactions, which may or may not be at market prices, affects the reported income of both the bank and the nonbank affiliates. In addition, for subsidiaries acquired by the purchase method of accounting, the reported income and equity may not be the same on the books of the parent BHC and subsidiaries. BHC double leverage policies and BHC parent activities will also influence reported consolidated income and equity, leading to accounting data with reduced volatility of returns.[11] In using these data, studies make an explicit or implicit assumption that reported income is a true reflection of the organization's economic income.

Using either accounting or market data, the choice between data at the individual level or industry level is also important. Industry data reveal cyclical variations in profitability but conceal intra-industry variability, whereas firm-level data capture firm-specific profit variations. Industry data almost always lead to underestimation of the riskiness of activities by biasing the variance of returns downward and the correlation between returns away from zero. Several authors have also found that correlations of returns were substantially different when firm and industry data were used.[12]

Almost all of the studies using accounting data conclude that investment in some nonbank subsidiaries tends to reduce BHC risk. The few studies using market data generally find no significant discernible impact of prod-

Table 3
The relationship between BHC risk and BHC nonbank activity (1979-1983)

	Market data	Accounting data
	(Cross-section time series)	(Cross-section)
Intercept	0.0141 (2.889)	0.0239 (4.521)
Capital	−0.0595 (2.581)	−0.0960 (2.810)
Total Assets	0.0005 (1.716)	−0.0010 (3.936)
Nonbank	−0.0175 (2.217)	−0.0138 (2.093)
1979*	−0.0059 (5.139)	—
1980*	−0.0030 (2.572)	—
1981*	−0.0039 (3.411)	—
1982*	−0.0009 (0.818)	—
	$R^2 = 0.2174$ N = 200	$R^2 = 0.3216$ N = 40
Sample mean	0.1173	0.1173
Sample standard deviation	0.0494	0.0417

*Dummy variable.

uct diversification by BHCs into nonbank activities as measured by the market's perceived value of the BHC or the level of BHC risk.

No previous study using market data was so similar to an accounting data study as to make it clear whether or not the results were driven solely by the choice of data. However, a recent study by Boyd and Graham (1988) as well as our own research used both accounting data and market data to examine the effects of investments in nonbank activities on BHC risk.

We examined the impact of total investment in nonbank activities, regardless of the specific activities involved. We pooled data on 40 large bank holding companies for the years 1979 through 1983. Using these pooled data, we first estimated the relationship between the standard deviation of stock returns and the proportion of a BHC's assets devoted to nonbank activities, controlling for the BHC's capital-to-asset ratio. The results, shown in

Table 3, indicate that increases in nonbank activity tend to lower BHC risk significantly

We also estimated our model after replacing the dependent variable, the standard deviation of stock returns, with the standard deviation of returns on assets. This second model was virtually identical to that employed by Boyd and Graham (1986).[13] Unlike the other authors, we found, a strong negative correlation between nonbank activities and bank holding company risk.

A more recent study by Boyd and Graham (1988) used both annual accounting data and market data for the 1971-1984 period to discern the impact of individual nonbank activities on BHC risk. They conducted a simulation study of hypothetical mergers of banking and nonbank organizations over the period 1971 to 1984. Their results were similar but not identical when accounting data were used and when market data were used. For example, their results from both accounting data and market data indicate that BHC diversification into life insurance would reduce BHC risk. However, their market data results also indicate that property and casualty insurance underwriting would also reduce BHC risk, while the accounting data indicate quite the contrary.

The merits of accounting data relative to market data in assessing the likely impact of nonbank diversification, therefore, are still undetermined. Our results suggest that when total nonbank investment is analyzed, both data sources produce similar results. Boyd and Graham (1988), however, indicate that this is not the case when individual nonbank activities are considered.

Track record

In attempting to predict the impact of further expansion of bank powers, it may be useful to examine the track record of regulatory policy on existing bank powers. If activities that are likely to increase BHC risk have been approved, then BHC risk would be expected to increase unless supervision and regulation of those activities minimized the impact, or economic efficiencies that were not considered in assessing the impact of nonbank activities were significant.

As shown in Table 2, several studies examined whether or not bank holding company

Table 4
Riskiness of banking vs.
nonbank activities: 1980, 1982, and 1986

	Variances of average daily returns	Correlations of average daily returns
Banking	0.220	1.000
Permissible nonbank activities		
Consumer finance	2.068	.345
Commercial finance	1.510	.380
Mortgage banking	4.575	.245
Consumer credit reporting	1.918	.379
Leasing	1.367	.457
Impermissible nonbank activities		
Savings and loan associations	1.409	.647
Securities brokers and dealers	9.449	.296
Insurance agents and brokers	0.654	.419
Life insurance underwriters	1.392	.274
Health and accident insurance underwriters	3.671	.284
Property/casualty insurance underwriters	0.659	.668
Real estate	1.515	.477
Management consulting	1.711	.445

Table 5
Ranks of nonbank activities according
to risk and correlation with banking:
1980, 1982, and 1986

	Risk	Correlation
Permissible nonbank activities		
Consumer finance	4	9
Commercial finance	8	7
Mortgage banking	2	13
Consumer credit reporting	5	8
Leasing	11	4
Impermissible nonbank activities		
Savings and loan associations	9	2
Securities brokers and dealers	1	10
Insurance agents and brokers	12	6
Life insurance underwriters	10	12
Health and accident insurance underwriters	3	11
Property/casualty insurance underwriters	13	1
Real estate	7	3
Management consulting	6	5

diversification into permissible activities reduced risk. While these studies differ with respect to methodology, data, and sample period, they all generally conclude that there is limited potential for risk reduction via diversification into nonbank activities. In addition, those that found risk-reduction opportunities generally did not find them in the same places. Nevertheless, more than one study found that consumer credit and commercial finance reduced BHC risk.

To determine which nonbank activities are likely to reduce risk and which are likely to increase it, we examined the variances of market returns, the correlations of those returns with banking returns, and the impact of hypothetical mergers on BHC risk. Our study differs from that of Boyd and Graham (1988) in that we used only daily stock market data for individual BHCs and nonbank firms; we examined 13 nonbank activities, whereas Boyd and Graham examined only six; our hypothetical mergers are between a "repesentative BHC" and a "representative nonbank firm" rather than between actual BHCs and actual nonbank firms; and we analyzed the impact of a BHC engaging in more than two nonbank activities at a time.

The data used are from Interactive Data Services, Inc. for an average of 325 nonbank firms and 170 banking firms, which were ac-

tively traded, for each of three time periods (1980, 1982, and 1986).[14] These time periods were chosen to represent different phases of the business cycle. Each nonbank firm is categorized into one of 13 activity categories. (If a firm engaged in more than one activity with no one dominating, then the firm was excluded.) Daily stock market returns were calculated for each firm.[15] The daily returns were then averaged across firms within each category to yield average daily returns for each activity group.

Of the nonbank activities studied, five are currently permissible. As shown in Table 4, all five permissible nonbank activities are riskier than banking. Risk is defined as the variance of the average daily returns. The riskiness of banking, however, reflects the fact that banks are federally insured and, therefore, the riskiness of banking firms is biased downward. The same is true for the results for savings and loan associations.

As mentioned earlier, an activity can be riskier than banking, but when combined with banking it could, depending on the proportions, reduce the overall riskiness of the organization if the correlation between the returns is less than unity. Some activities that are risky have very low correlations with banking and could therefore increase the diversification of the bank holding company enough to reduce its risk (Tables 4 and 5). For example, mortgage banking is the riskiest among the five permissible nonbank activities, but it has the lowest correlation with banking.

Table 6
The risk effects of hypothetical nonbank acquisitions

	Variance w/ 5% nonbank	Variance w/ 10% nonbank	Variance w/ 25% nonbank
Permissible nonbank activities			
Consumer finance	.226	.241	.340
Commercial finance	.223	.233	.300
Mortgage banking	.233	.268	.502
Consumer credit reporting	.227	.242	.336
Leasing	.226	.237	.303
Impermissible nonbank activities			
Savings and loan associations	.236	.257	.347
Securities brokers and dealers	.263	.350	.874
Insurance agents and brokers	.217	.217	.231
Life insurance underwriters	.216	.219	.268
Health and accident insurance underwriters	.232	.261	.449
Property/casualty insurance underwriters	.224	.231	.260
Real estate	.227	.240	.315
Management consulting	.229	.244	.333

Leasing is the least risky of the permissible activities, but it is more highly correlated with banking than mortgage banking is.

Table 6 gives the variances that would result if the representative BHC were combined with each of the representative nonbank firms in our sample. If the correlation of the returns between banking and a given nonbank activity is greater than the ratio of the standard deviations of the returns to banking and the nonbank activity, then even very small proportions of the nonbank activity will increase the riskiness of the banking firm. Only one permissible nonbank activity—commercial financial—does not fall into this category. Nevertheless, as shown in the first column of Table 6, an acquisition of any of the average permissible nonbank firms that would result in nonbank activity accounting for 5 percent or less of the equity of the resulting organization would not increase the variance of the bank holding company to any significant extent. Similarly, an acquisition of any of the permissible nonbank firms would not appreciably increase the banking firm's risk even if the nonbank activity accounted for 10 percent of the resulting organization. At 25 percent, all of the permissible nonbank activities would increase the riskiness of the new banking organization considerably.

One problem with hypothetical-merger studies is that they do not recognize the possibility that managers and regulators may be biased towards choosing and approving acquisitions that are risk-reducing. For instance, it is probably possible to find a combination of a bank and a securities firm that would be risk-reducing, and it is probably also possible to find such a combination that would be risk-increasing. Managers and regulators would be more likely to choose the risk-reducing combination; therefore, hypothetical random or "representative" combinations may overstate the potential for increased risk. Furthermore, current regulatory and supervisory policies may affect the way that a BHC manages its nonbank actitivies such that increases in risk are minimized.

A recent study by Brewer (1988) deals with this problem by examining the impact of total investment in nonbank activities, regardless of the specific activities involved. Using a market-based measure of risk and pooled cross-section and time series data on 40 large BHCs for the 1979-1985 period, Brewer finds that increases in nonbank activity tend to lower BHC risk. His results indicate, as did ours using a different time period, that BHCs with above-average investments in nonbank activities will have below-average risk. Furthermore, the implied differences in risk are not trivial. A one-standard-deviation increase in a BHC's investment in nonbank subsidiaries would translate into a 8 to 11 basis point drop (about 5 to 7 percent) in BHC risk. Therefore, even though some permissible activities, when examined in isolation, seem likely to increase BHC risk, they appear, in reality, to have actually decreased risk. Whether the drop in risk can be attributable to regulation, management, efficiency gains, or pure diversification is not clear.

A look ahead

Some previous studies have assessed the risk-reduction potential of allowing bank holding companies to engage in currently impermissible activities. These studies do not concur that allowing BHCs to enter new activities would reduce risk. However, those studies that do find potential for risk reduction find it most often with insurance agency and brokerage, real estate, life insurance, and securities activities.

The reasons for this finding can be seen from data on the average returns for nonbank financial firms engaged in the eight activities that are currently impermissible for BHCs. Using the variances of market rates of return as our measure of risk, we find that banking is less risky than at least eight impermissible nonbank activities. However, as shown in Table 4, for every permissible activity, there exists an impermissible one that is less risky. Securities activities are the riskiest of all nonbank activities, but securities activities are not as highly correlated with banking as are several other less risky activities (Table 5).

As shown in Table 4, of the permissible activities, leasing has the highest correlation with banking. Five impermissible activities had lower correlations during the three periods studied. These include securities brokerage and dealing, life insurance, health and accident insurance, insurance agents and brokers, and management consulting.

Among the eight impermissible activities listed in Table 6, life insurance underwriting and insurance agency and brokerage would reduce BHC risk when combined with the representative BHC in our sample. A combination of a BHC and any of the other six activities would likely increase risk, although not significantly as long as the nonbank activity accounted for less than 5 percent of the resulting organization. An investment in securities activities of 10 percent would increase BHC risk significantly, and an investment of 25 percent or more would increase BHC risk drastically.

BHCs will not necessarily engage in only one nonbank activity, and large BHCs usually operate many nonbank subsidiaries that engage in many permissible activities. Correlations among activities, therefore, are as important to BHC risk as the correlations between banking and nonbank activities.

We analyzed the impact on risk when a BHC engaged in more than one nonbank activity. We allowed a BHC to engage in all 13 of the nonbank activities we studied. Using the variances and covariances of the average nonbank firm in each category, we solved for the least risky bank holding company over the years studied. This holding company would invest 87.6 percent of its equity in banking, an additional 7.5 percent in insurance agents and brokers, and 4.9 percent in life insurance underwriting. This would reduce the risk of the BHC by about 3 percent. At the same time, the average return would fall by 3 percent.

Summary and policy implications

Banks claim that they are gradually losing market share in their traditional areas of lending and deposit taking and therefore need to expand into several nonbank activities that are currently impermissible. One of the concerns of the regulators, however, is that these nonbank activities would increase the riskiness of bank holding companies and therefore expose their bank affiliates as well as federal deposit insurance and the discount window to increased risk.

Previous research has been inconclusive on the impact that nonbank subsidiaries have on the overall riskiness of the BHC. Furthermore, prior studies have not been entirely consistent in determining the relative risk of banking and individual activities. Recent research, however, indicates that individual nonbank activities either have no or little impact on risk. We found that a very small investment in a few nonbank activities—insurance agents and brokers and property and casualty and life insurance underwriting—would reduce risk. Further, a 10 percent investment in most activities, other than securities-related activities, would not increase risk significantly.

Most researchers have concluded that some permissible activities are riskier than some impermissible ones. We found this also. If the riskiness of permissible activities reflects the risk tolerance of regulators, then it can be argued that BHCs should be allowed to engage in all impermissible activities that are less risky than permissible ones. The potential costs and benefits from competitive effects and efficiency gains and losses must also be weighed. We found that investment in nonbank activities reduces BHC risk overall; therefore, regulation, efficiency, or diversification must be at work. Nevertheless, careful consideration must be made before permitting BHCs to engage in new activities even if they are less risky than some permissible ones.

We found, as have others, that some nonbank activities could reduce BHC risk, but we found that there is limited potential for risk reduction via diversification into nonbank activities when activities are considered separately. However, an important element in risk determination is the percentage of BHC assets devoted to each nonbank activity. This implies that, by restricting the relative size of nonbank investments, regulators could expand the laundry list of permissible activities without fear of significantly increasing BHC risk.

Previous studies, as well as our own research, have examined the risk associated with investing in nonbank activities, but they do not consider the potential synergies or the potential drains on banking subsidiaries that may result from interaffiliate transfers. Therefore, in addition to the restrictions on the size of investments in nonbank activities, restrictions on transactions between banks and nonbank affiliates would probably be necessary, but such restrictions should not destroy potential synergies. Although additional regulatory reform may be needed to ensure that deposit insurance and the discount window are not indirectly used to protect nonbank subsidiaries, the current system may be able to handle much of the impact of increased bank holding company risk and potential concentration of financial power.

Sections 23A and 23B of the Federal Reserve Act place restrictions on banks' transactions with affiliates. Section 23A limits the amount any member bank can lend to an affiliate to 10 percent of the bank's capital, and the sum of all extensions to affiliates by a member bank cannot exceed 20 percent. In enforcing Section 23A, the Fed has the ability to initiate cease-and-desist orders and cash penalties and to remove directors if it feels the organization is operating in an unsafe and unsound manner. However, these measures are not currently used to the fullest extent.

Regulators, therefore, will actually need to impose the penalties that they have at their disposal now. Further restrictions, such as limits on the relative size of nonbank investments, may also be needed before BHCs are allowed to engage in new activities.

---

[1] It should be noted that the banking industry is divided on the issue of expanded powers. The Independent Bankers Association has opposed such expansion, due in part to the issue of functional regulation and the preemption of states rights regarding activities of state-chartered nonmember banks. For another view on nonbank activities, see also Robert E. Litan. "Taking the Dangers out of Bank Deregulation." *The Brookings Review* (Fall 1986).

[2] For a general discussion of this issue, see Robert A. Eisenbeis. "How should bank holding companies be regulated?" *Economic Review,* 69, Federal Reserve Bank of Atlanta, (January 1983) pp. 42-47.

[3] Anthony Cornyn, and others. "An Analysis of the Concept of Corporate Separateness in BHC Regulation from an Economic Perspective." *Proceedings of a Conference on Bank Structure and Competition,* Federal Reserve Bank of Chicago, 1986, pp. 174-212.

[4] Larry D. Wall, and Robert A. Eisenbeis. "Risk Considerations in Deregulating Bank Activities." *Economic Review,* Federal Reserve Bank of Atlanta, (May 1984) p. 9.

[5] Recently, there has been much debate over what constitutes "principally engaged in" and "eligible" securities.

[6] See Bank Holding Company Act, Section 4—Interests in Nonbanking Organizations, (12 USC 1843); and Regulation Y, Section 225.24—Factors Considered in Acting on Nonbanking Applications.

[7] These guidelines were established in *National Courier Association v. Board of Governors,* 516 F.2d 1229 (D.C. Cir., 1975); *Securities Industry Ass'n v. Board of Governors,* 468 U.S. 207, 210-11 n.5 (1984); *Board of Governors v. Investment Company Institute,* 450 U.S. 46, 56-58 nn. 20-23 (1981); and *Association of Data Processing Service Organizations, Inc. v. Board of Governors,* 745 F.2d 677 (D.C. Cir. 1984).

[8] See, for example, Security Pacific Corporation, Vol. 73 *Federal Reserve Bulletin* (1987) p. 815. It is also noteworthy that eighty-six percent of the 11,162 4(c)(8) applications and notifications filed from January 1, 1971 to June 30, 1987 have been *de novo* notifications (9,686), and the remainder have been applications for acquisitions of existing concerns (1,476). (Numbers are unoffical estimates

from *Bank Expansion Quarterly,* Second Quarter 1987, Vol. XXXVII Num.2, Golembe Associates, Inc., Washington, DC.)

[9] Most early studies analyzed the activities of one-bank holding companies. One-bank holding companies were not covered under the original Bank Holding Company Act, thus they were able to engage in activities that were impermissible for multibank holding companies under Regulation Y, until the 1970 amendments to the BHC Act.

[10] See, for example, Stephen A. Rhoades, and Gregory Boczar. "The Performance of Bank Holding Company-Affiliated Finance Companies." *Staff Economic Studies,* Board of Governors of the Federal Reserve System, 1976; Stephen A. Rhoades. "The Performance of Bank Holding Companies in Equipment Leasing." *Staff Economic Studies,* Board of Governors of the Federal Reserve System, 1978; and Samuel H. Talley. "Bank Holding Company Performance in Consumer Finance and Mortgage Banking." *The Magazine of Bank Administration* (July 1976) pp. 42-44.

[11] Larry D. Wall. "Nonbank Activities and Risk." *Economic Review,* Federal Reserve Bank of Atlanta (October 1986) pp. 19-33.

[12] See Arnold A. Heggestad. "Riskiness of Investments in Nonbank Activities by Bank Holding Companies." *Journal of Economics and Business,* Vol. 27 (Spring 1975) pp. 219-223; and John H. Boyd, Gerald A. Hanweck, and Pipat Pithyachariyakul. "Bank Holding Company Diversification." *Proceedings of a Conference on Bank Structure and Competition,* Federal Reserve Bank of Chicago, 1980 pp. 102-121.

[13] In our study the values of the financial variables for each year were obtained by averaging quarterly Reports of Condition data. These estimated dollar amounts were then averaged over the 1979-1983 period. The financial ratios were calculated from these averages. In the Boyd and Graham (1986) study, the data were averaged only over the annual observations.

[14] An "actively traded" stock is defined as one that traded, on average, at least 3 times per week.

[15] Daily market return is the percentage change in price after correcting for dividends and stock splits.

References

Brewer III, Elijah. "A Note on the Relationship Between Bank Holding Company Risk and Nonbank Activity." Federal Reserve Bank of Chicago, Staff Memorandum 88-5 (1988).

Boyd, John H., and Stanley L. Graham. "Risk Regulation, and Bank Holding Company Expansion into Nonbanking." Federal Reserve Bank of Minneapolis, *Quarterly Review,* Vol. 10 (Spring 1986), pp. 2-17.

Boyd, John H., and Stanley L. Graham. "Bank Holding Company Diversification into Nonbank Financial Services: A Simulation Study." Federal Reserve Bank of Minneapolis, Working Paper 378 (January 1988).

Boyd, John H., Gerald A. Hanweck, and Pipat Pithyachariyakul. "Bank Holding Company Diversification." *Proceedings of a Conference on Bank Structure and Competition,* Federal Reserve Bank of Chicago, 1980, pp. 102-121.

Chase, S. "The Bank Holding Company as a Device for Sheltering Banks from Risk." *Proceedings of a Conference on Bank Structure and Competitition,* Federal Reserve Bank of Chicago, 1971, pp. 38-49.

Cornyn, Anthony, and others. "An Analysis of the Concept of Corporate Separateness in BHC Regulation from an Economic Perspective." *Proceedings of a Conference on Bank Structure and Competition,* Federal Reserve Bank of Chicago (1986), pp. 174-212.

Corrigan, Gerald E. *Financial Market Structure: A Longer View.* New York: Federal Reserve Bank of New York, 1987.

Eisemann, P.C. "Diversification and the Congeneric Bank Holding Company." *Journal of Bank Research* (Spring 1976), pp. 68-77.

Eisenbeis, Robert A. "How Should Bank Holding Companies Be Regulated?" *Economic Review,* Federal Reserve Bank of Atlanta (January 1983), pp. 42-47.

Eisenbeis, Robert A., Robert S. Harris and Josef Lakonishok. "Benefits of Bank Diversification: The Evidence from Shareholder Returns." *The Journal of Finance,* Vol. 39 (July 1984), pp. 881-894.

Heggestad, Arnold A. "Riskiness of Investments in Nonbank Activities by Bank Holding Companies." *Journal of Economics and Business,* Vol. 27 (Spring 1975), pp. 219-223.

Huertas, Thomas F. "Redesigning Regulation: The Future of Finance in the United States." Federal Reserve Bank of Kansas City Symposium on Restructuring the Financial System, August 22, 1987.

Jessee, M., and S. Seelig. *Bank Holding Companies and the Public Interest,* Lexington, MA: Lexington Books, 1977.

Johnson, Manual H., Jr. "Banking Regulatory Options and the Implications for Supervision." Paper presented to the Federal Reserve System Spring Management Conference, March 19, 1987.

Johnson, Rodney D., and David R. Meinster. "Bank Holding Companies: Diversification Opportunities in Nonbank Activities." *Eastern Economic Journal*, Vol. 1 (October 1974), pp. 1453-1465.

Litan, Robert E. "Assessing the Risks of Financial Product Deregulation." Paper presented to the American Economics Association in New York, December 1985.

Litan, Robert E. "Taking the Dangers out of Bank Deregulation." *The Brookings Review* (Fall 1986).

Meinster, David R., and Rodney D. Johnson. "Bank Holding Company Diversification and the Risk of Capital Impairment." *The Bell Journal of Economics*, Vol. 10 (Autumn 1979), pp. 683-694.

Rhoades, Stephen A., and Gregory Boczar, "The Performance of Bank Holding Company-Affiliated Finance Companies." *Staff Economic Studies*, Board of Governors of the Federal Reserve System, 1976.

Rhoades, Stephen A. "The Performance of Bank Holding Companies in Equipment Leasing." *Staff Economic Studies*, Board of Governors of the Federal Reserve System, 1978.

Rhoades, Stephen A. "Interstate Banking and Product Line Expansion: Implication From Available Evidence." *Loyola of Los Angeles Law Review*, Vol. 18 (1985), pp. 1115-1164.

Rose, John T. "Bank Holding Companies as Operational Single Entities." In *Bank Holding Company Movement to 1978: A Compendium.* Washington DC: Board of Governors of the Federal Reserve System, 1978(1), pp. 69-93.

Rose, John T. "The Effect of the Bank Holding Company Movement on Bank Safety and Soundness." In *Bank Holding Company Movement to 1978: A Compendium.* Washington DC: Board of Governors of the Federal Reserve System, 1978(2), pp. 137-184.

Talley, Samuel H. "Bank Holding Company Performance in Consumer Finance and Mortgage Banking." *The Magazine of Bank Administration* (July 1976), pp. 42-44.

Stover, Roger D. "A Reexamination of Bank Holding Company Acquisitions." *Journal of Bank Research*, Vol. 13 (Summer 1982), pp. 101-108.

Wall, Larry D., and Robert A. Eisenbeis, "Risk Considerations in Deregulating Bank Activities." *Economic Review*, Federal Reserve Bank of Atlanta (May 1984), pp. 6-18.

Wall, Larry D. "Insulating Banks from Nonbank Affiliates." *Economic Review.* Federal Reserve Bank of Atlanta, (September 1984), pp. 18-28.

Wall, Larry D. "Has BHC's Diversification Affected Their Risk of Failure?" Federal Reserve Bank of Atlanta, Working Paper 85-2 (1985).

Wall, Larry D. "Nonbank Activities and Risk." *Economic Review*, Federal Reserve Bank of Atlanta (October 1986), pp.19-34.

Article Seventeen

Banking Reform:
An Overview of the Restructuring Debate

*Mitchell Berlin**

Proponents of banking reform, whether they be bankers, nonbank bankers, would-be bankers, or bank regulators, all agree on one thing: our current regulatory system is out of sync with the financial marketplace. Proponents of reform point out that regulatory restrictions prevent a firm that might be able to provide a financial service to customers at lowest cost from competing for customers' business, and that services that fill

the same customer needs and pose very similar risks—like making short-term loans and underwriting commercial paper—often cannot be provided by the same firm. They also have argued that as customer demand shifts from one product to another, financial firms frequently face a dilemma: to seek out ways to evade regulations or else to lose business.

Policymakers have tinkered with regulations and patched loopholes in response to marketplace changes, but this piecemeal approach always seems to leave regulators one repair behind, because financial changes have been so rapid. And each repair is time-consuming, both because

*Mitchell Berlin is a Senior Economist in the Banking Section of the Research Department of the Federal Reserve Bank of Philadelphia.

of the amount of time required to analyze the issues being raised in each case and because many industry groups seek to influence the final outcome. There is a growing feeling that it is time for a more fundamental financial restructuring, guided by a longer-term blueprint. Reform would be made more coherent if public debate could be focused on a longer-term vision of a workable and efficient regulatory framework.

There is no shortage of complicated restructuring plans (see A BIBLIOGRAPHIC GUIDE TO THE RESTRUCTURING PROPOSALS), and evaluating the merits of the different proposals may seem like a daunting task. A helpful first step is to identify and explain the broad areas of agreement and disagreement among the various plans. Indeed, most participants in the debate agree that bank powers should be expanded and that a limited safety net for banks should be retained. There is, however, much disagreement about what powers banking organizations should have, what types of holding company structures — if any — are desirable, and how holding companies should be regulated. While the disagreements are far-ranging, they stem primarily from disagreement about a single issue: can a bank be insulated from its affiliates?

THREE BROAD AREAS OF AGREEMENT

Bank Powers Should Be Expanded. All the restructuring proposals agree that some expansion of bank powers would not only enhance the competitiveness of banks in financial markets but would also benefit consumers and businesses.

A Bibliographic Guide to the Restructuring Proposals

To illustrate the various points of view on restructuring the banking system, this article focuses on the following proposals made by bank regulators:

Comptroller of the Currency-The main elements of the Comptroller's views are contained in the Statement of Robert L. Clarke, Comptroller of the Currency, before the Committee on Banking, Housing, and Urban Affairs, United States Senate, May 21, 1987.

FDIC-The views of the FDIC are contained in a staff study, *Mandate for Change: Restructuring the Banking Industry*, August 18, 1987, and L. William Seidman, *Perspectives on Financial Restructuring*, Remarks to an Economic Policy Conference, Federal Reserve Bank of Kansas City, Jackson, Wyoming, August 21, 1987.

Federal Reserve System-Although the Fed has not presented a formal long-term plan, the consensus viewpoint can be gleaned from testimony by Alan Greenspan, Chairman, Board of Governors of the Federal Reserve System, before the Committee on Banking, Housing, and Urban Affairs, United States Senate, December 1, 1987. E. Gerald Corrigan's, *Financial Market Structure: A Longer View*, Federal Reserve Bank of New York, January 1987, while not an official statement of the Fed, is a good illustration of Fed thinking on many points.

Bank regulators are not the only participants in the debate. Other restructuring proposals include:

Association of Bank Holding Companies, "Financial Services Holding Company Act of 1988," draft IV, May 15, 1987.

Association of Reserve City Bankers, Emerging Issues Committee, "Proposals for a Financial Services Holding Company," May 1987.

Committee on Government Operations, "Modernization of the Financial Services Industry: A Plan for Capital Mobility Within a Framework of Safe and Sound Banking," House Report 100-324, U.S. Government Printing Office, Washington D.C., 1987.

Other useful summaries of the restructuring debate include:

Thomas F. Huertas, "Redesigning Regulation: The Future of Finance in the United States," *Issues in Bank Regulation*, Fall 1987.

Manuel H. Johnson, Statement before the Committee on Banking, Housing, and Urban Affairs, U.S. Senate, May 21, 1987.

While there is no universal agreement about which products and services banks should be permitted to sell, the possibilities include financial services—such as investment banking, underwriting and selling insurance, and real estate investment and brokerage—and even nonfinancial products. The reasons for proposing expanded bank powers are varied, but tend to focus on efficiencies that might be realized.

Under the current regulatory framework, customers for financial services have to use different types of firms even though the services being purchased are closely related. Proponents of expanded powers argue that aside from facing the simple inconvenience of dealing with more than one firm, the customer might be able to purchase several services at lower cost from a single firm. For example, the credit analysis performed by a bank processing a loan request will include information that would also be useful in determining the customer's insurance needs— what economists call an economy of scope.[1] Regulations that restrict the bank from providing both loans and insurance may increase the costs of producing both services and, in turn, the price that customers must pay for them. It should be noted, however, that the empirical evidence for significant scope economies is actually rather scanty.

Bank loans and commercial paper illustrate another potential benefit of an expanded menu of services for banks that has been proposed by proponents of reform: expanded powers would ease the flow of resources between markets as customer demand changes. Many large and medium-size firms have switched from bank loans to the commercial paper market as their primary source of short-term funds. But when a firm makes the switch, the bank's accumulated knowledge about the firm is effectively destroyed

as a valuable resource, because it is difficult to sell or transfer knowledge to another firm. Thus, the firm must pay the investment banker to develop the expertise that was lost. If the commercial bank were permitted to underwrite commercial paper, this added expense to the customer could be saved and the shift to satisfy the new customer demand would be facilitated.

While the case for expanded powers is most convincing for financial services, proponents of expanded powers also argue that economies of scope between financial and nonfinancial services may also exist. All of the major auto firms have finance subsidiaries, which were initially set up to coordinate the marketing and financing of new car purchases. And the successful entry by these finance subsidiaries into the expanding markets for other types of consumer loans— such as mortgages—illustrates the potential benefits of a free flow of resources between financial and nonfinancial sectors.

Functional Regulation Is Desirable. If banks are granted powers to sell insurance or underwrite securities, policymakers must make sure that regulatory rules do not favor banks over their competitors, or vice versa. All restructuring proposals agree, at least in principle, that different types of firms providing the same service—or function—should be subject to similar regulatory rules. This principle is called *functional regulation.* Although functional regulation does not necessarily mean that all providers of a particular service should be governed by the same regulator, it may be difficult to ensure uniform regulatory treatment when different regulators are involved. And while all proposals agree that functional regulation is desirable, there is no such agreement about who should regulate which services.

Functional regulation promotes competitive equity and invites firms to use their ingenuity to satisfy customer needs rather than to evade regulations. In the competitive battle for customers, the firm with the lowest costs and best products is supposed to win. But we cannot be sure that the well-run firm will win if it is saddled with more burdensome regulatory rules than its

[1]For a more thorough discussion of economies of scope, see Loretta J. Mester, "Efficient Production of Financial Services: Scale and Scope Economies," this *Business Review* (January/February 1987) pp.15-25.

poorly run competitor. In fact, the well-run firm is not likely to take this situation lying down. Instead, the firm will spend much of its time figuring out legal ways to evade the regulations that place it at a competitive disadvantage. From society's standpoint, all this time and effort are sheer waste.

A Strictly Limited Safety Net for Banks Is Needed. Deposit insurance and access to the discount window are the two main ways in which the federal authorities provide a safety net for banks and their customers. The safety net is designed to guarantee stability in the payments system and to ensure that banks can play their special role in providing liquid funds to businesses and consumers, especially in times of financial stress. But since the safety net provides government guarantees to banks and their customers, it must be supplemented by regulations to make sure that the government is not writing bankers a blank check to take on risky activities. These regulations include capital requirements and periodic bank examinations.

Most proposals agree that firms providing deposits on demand should be protected by a safety net, yet no one wishes to see government guarantees and regulations extended willy-nilly to other types of activities and services; that is, the safety net should be limited in scope. But this is easier said than done. If banks' powers are expanded, how can the government hold the safety net under the bank when it provides "banking" services without extending the net to all the other services provided by the bank? This question raises a host of vexing issues concerning how bank holding companies should be organized and regulated. Here, agreement ends and the proposals part ways.

RESTRUCTURING PROPOSALS DIFFER ON THREE MAJOR ISSUES

The institutions at issue are bank holding companies, which are firms that own one or more banks. Current law defines a bank as either a firm that offers federally insured deposits or one that offers demand deposits and makes com-

mercial loans. It is easier to see the differences among the restructuring proposals using just the first definition.

What Activities Can Be Carried out within Bank Holding Companies? Much of the immediate controversy over banking reform has been about the desirability of adding particular financial services to the bank holding company's menu of permitted activities. And, as a practical matter, only financial powers—underwriting and dealing securities, real estate investment and brokerage, and selling and underwriting insurance—are under serious consideration by federal legislators for the near future.[2] Each and every financial power has been hotly contested, partly because of opposition from entrenched firms who are unhappy with the prospect of new competitors, partly because of differences of opinion about the potential risks to bank safety, and partly because of different interpretations about the range of permissible powers under current banking laws. In particular, the federal bank regulators do not all agree about which of these financial services banks should be permitted. (See HOW THE REGULATORS LINE UP ON BANK POWERS.)

In the long term, however, perhaps the most important issue is whether bank holding companies should be permitted to offer just financial services or whether they should also be permitted to offer nonfinancial services and products, like automobiles. The example of a bank holding company selling cars is not unrealistic. General Motors already sells cars and also makes consumer loans. If it were permitted to offer insured deposits through its finance subsidiary, it would be a bank holding company that also produces cars.

Proposals coming from the Federal Reserve System take a narrow view of the issue of separating banking and commerce. Speaking for the

---

[2]For a summary of banking legislation before Congress, see Federal Reserve Bank of Philadelphia, *Banking Legislation and Policy*, Vol. 7, No. 1 (January/March 1988).

How the Regulators Line Up on Bank Powers

REGULATOR	FINANCIAL					NON-FINANCIAL
	Investment Banking	Real Estate		Insurance		
		Investment	Brokerage	Underwriting	Sale	
Comp-troller	yes	yes with restrictions	yes	yes	yes	no formal position
FDIC	yes	yes	yes	yes	yes	yes
Federal Reserve	yes	no with exceptions	yes	no formal position	no formal position	no

Fed, Chairman Alan Greenspan has argued that banking should be separated from commerce, which is just another way of saying that bank holding companies should not be permitted to offer nonfinancial services.[3] Gerald Corrigan, President of the New York Fed, has presented his own detailed restructuring plan that restricts bank holding companies to offering financial services. On the other hand, the Federal Deposit Insurance Corporation (FDIC) has proposed that bank holding companies be free to offer a full range of financial and nonfinancial services. Under that plan, General Motors could own a bank subsidiary or Citicorp could own an automobile factory.

Where Can Nonbank Activities Be Carried Out Inside the Bank Holding Company? Anyone who has examined the organizational chart of a large company knows that internal organizational structures can be quite complex. (See AN IMAGINARY HOLDING COMPANY, p. 8.) With expanded powers, bank holding companies might choose a number of different ways to provide nonbanking services. Take the hypothetical example of a holding company that wishes to provide both commercial banking services and underwriting of securities. The holding company could create two separate subsidiaries, a commercial bank subsidiary and an investment bank subsidiary. Each subsidiary would be separately capitalized and have its own management. Or, the holding company could set up a commercial bank subsidiary which provides investment banking activities through its own investment bank subsidiary. That is, the holding company owns the commercial bank, which in turn, owns the investment bank. Finally, the holding company could simply create a single subsidiary that provides both services, perhaps in separate departments.

Although there are some analysts who would

---

[3]Actually, "banking" and activities "closely related to banking" as defined by regulators are not all financial services. The distinction between financial and nonfinancial activities, however, is a close approximation to the distinction between banking and commerce.

An Imaginary Holding Company

BHC Inc. illustrates a holding company structure that might arise if bank holding companies were permitted to offer underwriting and insurance services and if they were free to choose their own internal organization. The *parent company*, BHC, owns stock in its two subsidiaries: a *bank subsidiary*, Megabank National, and a *nonbanking subsidiary*, Two Hands Insurance. Normally, BHC will hold a large share of its subsidiaries' equity, because there are substantial tax benefits if the parent owns at least 80% of a subsidiary's stock. Megabank also has its own subsidiary, an investment banking firm, Salmon Brothers. The bank owns stock in Salmon Brothers, just as BHC owns stock in the bank and the insurance company. BHC and Two Hands Insurance are both *nonbanking affiliates* of Megabank. Megabank's own subsidiary, Salmon Brothers, is also considered a nonbanking affiliate of the bank.[a]

---

[a] Megabank might also have affiliates outside of the holding company. Under Section 23a of the Federal Reserve Act, the Federal Reserve System has substantial discretion in defining an affiliate. If business dealings between a bank and another firm are not "at arm's length," the Fed considers that firm an affiliate of the bank.

leave the bank holding company free to make any of these choices, none of the major restructuring proposals advocates the third possibility.[4] The major proposals are, however, divided between those which would permit banks to own nonbanking subsidiaries and those which would require that nonbanking services be provided through subsidiaries that are managed and capitalized separately from bank subsidiaries. President Corrigan, in his own proposal, and Chairman Greenspan, speaking for the Fed, have taken the approach that banking and nonbanking activities should be housed in separate subsidiaries of the holding company. The Comptroller of the Currency has taken the less restrictive stance that bank holding companies should be free to choose either organizational form. The FDIC, while nearer to the Comptroller's position, has agreed that separate subsidiaries might be required for some activities that regulators deem to be especially risky.

What Parts of the Bank Holding Company Should Be Regulated By Bank Regulators? On this question, the proposals are divided between those that advocate consolidated regulation of the bank holding company and those that would have bank regulators oversee just the bank subsidiaries of the holding company.

Consolidated regulation can mean different things to different people. In the official Fed position, consolidated regulation, at the minimum, would permit the bank regulator to set capital requirements for the parent company as well as for its bank subsidiaries.[5] The Corrigan proposal takes a more expansive view of the supervisory powers of the holding company's regulator. In his proposal, the holding company's regulator could also set capital requirements for and exercise "prudential supervision" over each component part of the holding company. Thus, a separately capitalized investment banking subsidiary of the holding company would be subject to direct oversight by a bank regulator.

Both the FDIC and the Comptroller take a narrower view of bank regulators' oversight role. Specifically, bank regulators would set standards—like capital requirements and portfolio restrictions—for the bank, but not for the holding company or for any of the nonbanking subsidiaries of the holding company. The bank's regulators would, however, set and enforce rules governing relations *between* the bank and its nonbanking affiliates: the parent company, the nonbanking subsidiaries of the holding company, and the subsidiaries of the bank. For example, bank regulators would set rules limiting lending by the bank to an insurance affiliate or to the parent company.

The Root of the Differences. If we step back for a minute, we can see that the proposals' answers to each of the questions are linked. Proposals requiring strictly separate nonbanking affiliates also call for consolidated supervision of the holding company—the Corrigan view and the Fed view. Proposals granting bank holding companies more freedom to choose how to offer nonbanking activities do *not* call for consolidated supervision—the Comptroller and the FDIC view. And those who demand tighter restrictions on holding company organization and require consolidated supervision would also permit bank holding companies to offer fewer nonbanking services.

But how are the answers to these very different questions linked? The most important reason why President Corrigan and the Fed answer one

---

[4] Analysts who advocate the third possibility believe that existing restrictions on interaffiliate transactions are a feasible alternative to restrictions on organizational choice. See, for instance, Anthony Saunders, "Bank Holding Companies: Structure, Performance, and Reform," in William Haraf (ed.) *Restructuring the Financial System,* American Enterprise Institute, Washington, D.C. (forthcoming).

[5] The recent Fed interpretation of its traditional position that the holding company should act as a "source of strength" to its bank subsidiaries implies an even stronger role for the consolidated capital of the bank holding company. Under the source of strength doctrine, regulators can require the holding company to provide financial support to a weakened or failing bank subsidiary when the holding company is in a position to do so.

way and the FDIC and the Comptroller another is that they have different views about the possibility of insulating the bank from non-banking affiliates within the holding company. Both President Corrigan and the Fed believe that insulation of the bank is quite difficult to guarantee, while both the FDIC and the Comptroller are more optimistic about the feasibility of insulating the bank.

INSULATION OF THE BANK: THE KEY TO THE DEBATE

What Does Insulation Mean? In the debate over regulatory reform, the idea of insulating the bank has paraded under a number of colorful phrases such as the creation of "Chinese walls" or "fire walls" between the bank and its non-banking affiliates. Whichever term is used, the basic idea is that the safety net, which necessarily includes government guarantees to the bank and its depositors, should not be extended to nonbanking affiliates within the holding company.

In normal times, when the bank and its affiliates are financially healthy, insulation means that the holding company cannot use the bank to subsidize nonbanking activities. For instance, the bank might conceivably pay out "excessive" dividends to the parent company, which then reinvests these funds in an insurance subsidiary. These transfers may weaken the bank financially, but some of the increased risk is borne by the FDIC, which generally guarantees the bank's depositors against loss. This type of policy, in effect, transfers the benefit of the government guarantees for bank depositors to the insurance affiliate.

In times of crisis, when either the parent company or a nonbanking firm in the holding company is financially troubled, insulation means that neither the bank nor bank regulators will prop up the affiliate. Suppose a real estate investment affiliate's investments have shaky foundations and are beginning to fall in value. The parent company might direct the bank to make loans to the real estate affiliate, even though

these loans would normally be considered excessively risky. Should these loans threaten the health of the bank, bank regulators might step in to save the bank, effectively passing on losses from the real estate affiliate to the FDIC. An insulated bank would neither subsidize its affiliates nor prop up affiliates in trouble.[6]

Why Is Insulation the Key? Suppose banks can be insulated effectively from their non-banking affiliates. In that case, a whole host of problems disappear. There is little danger in permitting bank holding companies to offer a wide range of nonbanking activities. For example, regulators need not worry that the highly cyclical demand for automobiles could lead to periodic problems for the bank subsidiary of a holding company that also produces cars. The parent company can also be given substantial freedom in choosing its own internal organizational structure. If loans and other types of financial transfers between a bank and a real estate subsidiary of the bank can be easily monitored and controlled, then it makes little sense to force the holding company to house banking and real estate activities in separately managed subsidiaries. The holding company can choose the most efficient organizational form without endangering the banking system or extending the safety net to the real estate industry. Finally, bank regulators will not need to supervise the holding company or its nonbanking subsidiaries. Regulators can direct their attention to the bank alone

---

[6]Although this account stresses the importance of the behavior of holding company management and regulators for ensuring insulation, the beliefs of the public—investors and customers of the bank and its affiliates—and the willingness of the courts to enforce the doctrine of corporate separateness are also important. The debate over insulation is closely related to the debate over so-called conflicts of interest. Both among regulators and academics, there is substantial disagreement about the incentives for holding companies to weaken the financial condition of the bank, even in the absence of regulatory safeguards to ensure insulation. See Anthony Saunders, "Securities Activities of Commercial Banks: The Problems of Conflicts of Interest," this *Business Review* (July/August 1985) pp.17-27, for a complete discussion of these issues.

and permit the nonbanking affiliates to make unfettered business decisions, risky or otherwise. Insulation guarantees that risky or imprudent decisions by a nonbanking affiliate will not increase the bank's risk or the regulator's exposure. None of this is true, however, if the bank cannot be insulated or if the regulatory costs of ensuring insulation are too large.

IS INSULATION POSSIBLE?

If Bank Holding Companies Are Highly Integrated, Insulation Is a Bigger Problem. The organizational chart of a holding company provides only a partial picture of the way the business is actually run. Consider the example of a hypothetical holding company, BHC Inc., which owns just two subsidiaries, a bank and an insurance company. This organization might be run in many different ways. One extreme possibility is that BHC Inc. leaves the two subsidiaries alone to make all important business decisions, such as how profits are to be used, which investments should be made, and which new markets should be entered. In this case, BHC Inc.'s managers act like passive investors owning a two-firm portfolio. They might act this way if the sole reason for investing in both the bank and insurance companies were to diversify, that is, to reduce fluctuations in the returns on their total investment.

At the other extreme, BHC might centralize all decisionmaking at the holding company level. BHC might decide how all profits made by the bank and the insurance company should be reallocated between the two companies, which types of investments should be made by each, and which new markets should be entered. In this case, the entire holding company is operated as a single consolidated organization.

While these extreme cases are unrealistic, they help to illustrate the connection between the level of integration of the holding company and the possibility of insulating the bank. If a bank holding company is merely a portfolio of completely independent firms, then the bank is clearly insulated from both the parent and the

insurance affiliate. Without direction from BHC, the bank acts exactly like a bank without any affiliates. If, however, all decisionmaking is centralized, then situations may arise where BHC's management views the profitability and safety of its bank subsidiary as a secondary concern, less important than the profitability of the holding company as a whole. Also, bank regulators will find it difficult to separate the affairs of the bank and its affiliates should the holding company experience financial difficulties.

The empirical evidence about how bank holding companies are actually run suggests that they are not merely portfolios of independently run firms.[7] For instance, banks inside holding companies normally pay out more dividends and hold less capital than independent banks.[8] Survey evidence shows that parent companies centralize some decisions but not others. Gary Whalen finds that parent companies often set dividend payments by bank subsidiaries and make other capital management decisions like how external funds should be raised.[9] In

---

[7]See Anthony Cornyn, Gerald Hanweck, Stephen Rhoades, and John Rose, "An Analysis of the Concept of Corporate Separateness in BHC Regulation from an Economic Perspective," *Proceedings of A Conference on Bank Structure and Competition*, Federal Reserve Bank of Chicago (May 1986); Timothy Hannan, "Safety, Soundness, and the Bank Holding Company: A Critical Review of the Literature," Working Paper, Board of Governors (1984); and Anthony Saunders, "Bank Holding Companies: Structure, Performance, and Reform," for reviews of the empirical literature.

[8]This does not necessarily mean that banks inside holding companies are being used to subsidize affiliates or that they have a greater risk of failure. In part, dividend payments are used to retire holding company debt used to purchase the bank. While lower capital, by itself, tends to increase the bank's risk of failure, the bank's expected profits and the variability of profits must also be considered. Empirical studies of the risk of failure for banks in holding companies have reached varying conclusions.

[9]Gary Whalen, "Operational Policies of Multibank Holding Companies," Federal Reserve Bank of Cleveland, *Economic Review* (Winter 1981/82). For the most part, empirical studies have concentrated on the relationships between the parent company and its bank subsidiaries. Evidence about the degree of coordination of banking and nonbanking activities by the parent company is scanty and anecdotal.

addition, parent companies often have the final say over major investment decisions by bank subsidiaries. On the other hand, Whalen finds that the parent company is likely to leave portfolio management decisions and pricing decisions to its bank subsidiary.

Since the degree of integration of bank holding companies appears to be substantial, insulation of the bank may be a problem. But bank regulators need not be, and are not, helpless observers, whose only tools for influencing the behavior of bank holding companies are a wish and a prayer. And strict limitations on permissible products and services, extensive restrictions on organizational structure, and consolidated supervision are not the only regulatory alternatives.

Existing Regulatory Safeguards Enhance Insulation . . . Among the safeguards that are already in place, perhaps the two most important are the restrictions on interaffiliate transactions written into Section 23 of the Federal Reserve Act, and regulatory capital requirements for banks. The FDIC proposal, in particular, lays great stress on these regulatory safeguards as a workable alternative to more extensive regulation of bank holding companies.

Sections 23a and 23b of the Federal Reserve Act are designed to limit a bank's exposure to its nonbanking affiliates and to prevent a bank holding company from using its bank subsidiary to subsidize nonbanking activities. Section 23a places quantitative limits on financial transactions between a bank and its affiliates, including loans, equity investments, and certain types of guarantees such as letters of credit.[10] To see how these limits work, consider BHC Inc. again and imagine, for simplicity, that the only types of internal financial transactions are loans from the bank to BHC Inc. and its insurance subsidiary. Under Section 23a, bank loans to either affiliate could not exceed 10 percent of the bank's capital. Further, the total loans made by the bank to both its affiliates together could not exceed 20 percent of the bank's capital. Thus, in the extremely unlikely event that both the parent company and the insurance company were unable to repay any of their loans, the most the bank would stand to lose is 20 percent of its capital, a painful, but not necessarily fatal, loss as long as the rest of the bank's portfolio is healthy. Of course, a 20 percent decline in the bank's capital is no trivial matter, but recent evidence from a study at the Board of Governors of the Federal Reserve System suggests that, in practice, banks do not approach the regulatory limits.[11] In fact, the Board study shows that net financial flows from banks to their affiliates tend to be negative; that is, funds flow from the affiliates to the bank rather than the other way around.

Section 23b requires that any transactions between the bank and the insurance affiliate must be on terms at least as favorable to the bank as a similar transaction with an insurance company outside the holding company. Thus, if the bank would demand a 10 percent rate of interest on a one-year loan to a nonaffiliated insurance company, it could demand no less from the insurance subsidiary of BHC Inc.

Of course, regulations are only as good as the information available to regulators. Unless bank regulators have timely and accurate information about financial flows between banks and affiliated companies, they cannot be sure that attempts to breach restrictions will be caught in time. All of the restructuring plans agree that more stringent and detailed reports from banks about transactions with affiliates are a necessary price to pay for

---

[10]See "The Banking Affiliates Act of 1982: Amendments to Section 23a," *Federal Reserve Bulletin* (November 1982) for a more detailed description of Section 23a.

[11]See John Rose and Samuel Talley, "Financial Transactions Within Bank Holding Companies," Staff Study #123, Board of Governors (May 1983). Their results are only suggestive, because they do not include all types of financial flows. Also Section 23a limits do not net out offsetting financial transactions between the bank and its affiliates. It is possible for the bank to make loans to affiliates equal to 20% of its capital yet still have a *net* inflow of funds.

permitting bank holding companies to offer more nonbanking services.

Minimum capital requirements for banks also insulate the bank from its affiliates' financial losses, because capital serves as a cushion against potential losses. In fact, capital standards serve a double duty in this regard, because the quantitative limitations in Section 23a are all expressed as fractions of the bank's capital. A bank without much capital faces severe limits on the dollar value of loans or guarantees to its affiliates. If the bank is pressing against its limits, yet wishes to expand financial transactions with affiliated firms, it must increase its capital, perhaps by selling new equity.

If bank capital cushions the bank and the FDIC against losses, won't additional capital requirements for the parent company or nonbanking subsidiaries of the holding company work even better? It is true that the FDIC's potential losses are smaller if the consolidated organization has a larger capital cushion. However, it doesn't necessarily follow that any additional capital should be held by the parent company or other nonbank subsidiaries, as long as bank regulators enforce capital requirements for each bank stringently. Requiring holding company capital to serve as a backup for bank capital only makes sense if regulators believe that banks in holding companies are riskier than independent banks. But if there is reason to believe that banks inside holding companies should hold more capital than independent banks, then an alternative is for regulators to impose a supplemental requirement on the banks directly, rather than on the parent company or nonbanking subsidiaries. This alternative approach would not only be more direct but would also be more consistent with the principle of functional regulation.

. . . But Insulation Is Possible Only if Regulators Will Keep the Bank Separate. Inevitably, situations will arise where the parent company or a nonbanking affiliate is in serious financial trouble, while the bank is financially healthy. Much of the debate about the feasibility of insulation has focused on the behavior of the holding company's management in these situations. Equally important—maybe more so—is the behavior of bank regulators. If regulators feel compelled to extend guarantees to troubled affiliates out of fear that the public will lose confidence in the bank when an affiliate fails, then insulation is not feasible.[12]

The regulator might reason that since a troubled nonbanking subsidiary and the bank are part of the same organization, the public will interpret troubles in the nonbanking company as evidence of weak management of the holding company and, in turn, of the bank. If regulators, who by nature take a wary and conservative view of the dangers of financial instability, do reason this way, then public pronouncements that the safety net will not be extended to nonbank activities are not credible. And if regulators cannot credibly commit to separate the bank from its troubled affiliates, then the holding company management won't take as seriously regulatory restrictions designed to keep the bank separate.

The credibility of regulators' commitment not to extend guarantees to nonbanking affiliates also will depend on how the financial and regulatory system is restructured. A bank regulator who supervises the holding company on a consolidated basis may have considerable power to intervene to save a struggling nonbanking affiliate. The consolidated supervisor of the holding company might be sorely tempted to devise complicated recovery plans involving transfers between the firms in the holding company to save the organization from failure. On the other hand, a regulator whose supervisory role is limited to setting standards for the bank alone will have fewer options to extend guarantees to nonbank affiliates.

One likely effect of expanded powers for bank

---

[12]See Anthony Cornyn, et. al., "An Analysis of the Concept of Corporate Separateness...," pp.185-191, and Anthony Saunders, "Bank Holding Companies: Structure, Conduct and Reform," pp. 32-37, for contrasting readings of the empirical evidence about public attitudes.

holding companies is the emergence of larger organizations, which will also affect the options facing regulators. This development cuts two ways. In general, regulators are much more concerned about the potential failure of a large banking organization than a small one, because the disruptive effects to the financial system of the failure of a large organization are more widespread. Commitments to keep the bank separate when a very large bank holding company is on the edge of collapse may be very difficult to honor. But the emergence of larger banking organizations may also mean that there will be more firms that could purchase a bank from a financially troubled holding company. The greater the number of firms that can afford to purchase the bank, the more credible regulators' commitment to keep the bank separate from the holding company's problems.

CONCLUSION

Diverse as the recent proposals for restructuring the financial system are, they agree on some basic principles: bank holding company powers should be expanded, functional regulation is desirable, and a strictly limited safety net for banks should be maintained. How far powers should be expanded, how bank holding companies should be organized, and how much of the bank holding company should be supervised by bank regulators are the major sources of disagreement. These disagreements flow in large part from different beliefs about the possibility of insulating the banks from their affiliates.

Whether banks can be insulated is a complicated, and unresolved, issue. The effectiveness of Section 23a and 23b restrictions have yet to be tested in an environment where bank holding companies engage in a wide range of financial, and perhaps nonfinancial, services. Whether regulators can keep the bank separate and avoid extending the safety net to nonbanking affiliates in large bank holding companies is another open question. Bank regulators' behavior since the rescue of Continental Illinois Bank, however, does provide some evidence on this issue. In recent years, regulators have gained substantial experience in dealing with large troubled banking organizations, especially in Texas and Oklahoma. For the most part, regulators have avoided bailing out parent companies when the troubled banks were reorganized or sold.[13]

Ultimately, debates over economic issues inform but don't dominate the course of legislative reform. Self-interested industry groups will all have their say, and legislators and regulators are unlikely to ignore their pleas. As the banking bills now winding their way through the House and Senate show, restructuring will occur in fits and starts and will not be as coherent as the formal plans that have been presented. Public debate over the economic issues, however, can only improve the coherence of regulatory reform as it unfolds.

---

[13]See FDIC, "Mandate for Change..." for a summary of regulators' experience with bank failures since Continental Illinois' rescue.

Article Eighteen

Uniting Investment and Commercial Banking

Banking organizations in the U.S. face obsolete legal prohibitions on the products and services they can provide. In particular, the Glass-Steagall and the Bank Holding Company Acts limit the ability of banks to underwrite corporate securities and to hold investments in the equity of nonbank enterprises.

Nevertheless, banks have had some success at circumventing legal barriers. For example, because state-chartered banks that are not members of the Federal Reserve are not covered by Glass-Steagall, they or their subsidiaries are allowed in some states to provide many investment banking services, including securities underwriting and direct equity investment. Likewise, subsidiaries of U.S. bank holding companies are able to perform some investment banking activities in offshore markets.

In addition, the interpretation of Glass-Steagall by regulators has evolved over time. For example, on April 30, the Federal Reserve approved applications that gave limited authority to bank holding companies to underwrite certain securities through subsidiaries "not principally engaged" in underwriting. (The Fed approved underwriting and dealing in municipal revenue bonds, mortgage-backed securities, and commercial paper.)

Full-fledged integration of commercial and investment banking would require changes in existing statutes. As Congress considers a one-year moratorium on any new banking powers legislation, the immediate prospect of such change has dimmed. Nevertheless, we discuss some of the policy issues involved in integrating commercial and investment banking.

Forces for change
It is apparent from the vigor with which banks and nonbanks are seeking to realign their traditional functions that the underlying economic forces stimulating change are strong. One of the forces has been the high degree of instability of interest rates, prices, and exchange rates that has characterized the world economy in recent years. This instability has not only stimulated the demand for specific risk-management products, such as options and futures, but also increased the complexity of traditional financial instruments and heightened the need for institutions to diversify their activities and portfolios.

The declining cost of gathering, managing, transmitting, and analyzing the data required to produce financial services has enhanced the feasibility of diversifying and realigning financial activities. Innovation in electronic data processing and communication makes new financial services feasible and makes it possible to repackage old financial services into more convenient combinations.

To a large extent, regulations separating commercial and investment banking have long been in conflict with economic forces. In the absence of prohibitive regulations, banking and investment banking traditionally have been affiliated both in this country and abroad. In the United States, for example, commercial banks began forming securities affiliates before World War I, and, within two decades, underwrote almost 60 percent of new corporate security issues. Even now, U.S. commercial banks are major providers of those investment banking services they are allowed to offer, such as underwriting general obligation municipal bonds.

In Great Britain, the historical regulatory practice of separating commercial and investment banking has eroded and it is common for the large commercial banks (the "clearing banks") to perform investment banking functions through subsidiaries. More recently, the ability of organizations (including banks) to own securities brokerage houses in Britain was expanded, enhancing integration of banking and brokerage. In West Germany and Austria, so-called "universal banking" is practiced — commercial banking organizations perform not only investment banking and brokerage functions but also take major equity positions in commercial enterprises.

Benefits

The tendency for commercial and investment banking services to be integrated when allowed is partly due to the complementarity of their functions. Virtually all of the functions performed by investment banks have a counterpart in commercial banking operations. In evaluating borrowers, or in originating, syndicating, and selling loans, commercial banks perform the component activities involved in underwriting corporate securities and distributing them in the marketplace. Similarly, the payments services that banks provide are a valuable adjunct to the business of investing in corporate securities. Indeed, nonbanks have found that providing payments services (checkable accounts) is crucial in marketing money market mutual funds, cash management brokerage accounts, and other retail investment products.

If these potential synergies between commercial and investment banking activities could be realized, the economies of operation that would result would benefit customers and the economy as a whole. The cost of raising or investing in corporate capital also would decline, in part, because the competitiveness of the investment banking market would increase. Presently, 12 firms generate over 50 percent of all U.S. investment banking revenue. "Deepening" the investment banking market may be particularly important in light of the rapid growth of primary securities markets.

Conflicts of interest

Resistance to the integration of commercial and investment banking stems in large part from turf considerations of the now separate industries. In addition to these private concerns, there are important public policy concerns. Glass-Steagall has been defended, and, in fact, was enacted primarily on the grounds that it prevents conflicts of interest and thereby protects banks and the securities market against excessive risk.

Many have argued that conflicts of interest might occur if banks were both major lenders to corporations and also underwriters, and possibly even major purchasers, of corporate securities. The concern is that banks would fraudulently misrepresent the securities underwritten on behalf of firms to which they were creditors, or lend preferentially to those entities in which they had equity or underwriting stakes.

Most independent observers, however, discount such concerns. Although the activities of bank securities affiliates were cited at the time for contributing to the bank failures of the Great Depression, recent research by Mark Flannery and others has been unable to find an association between the securities underwriting activities of banking firms in the 1920s and 1930s and subsequent bank failures. Similarly, concerns over conflict of interest in West German banking also were reviewed extensively and rebutted by the Gessler Commission in 1979. In addition, economist Richard Dale, in a more recent examination of the West German banking system, finds no association between the securities activities of that country's universal banks and their stability.

Conflicts of interest also are relatively easy to monitor and to control directly if necessary. In fact, such conflicts could arise today in the activities of banks and their trust departments, but are uncommon. This suggests that bank regulatory powers and the protections against securities abuse afforded by the Securities Act of 1933 and the Securities Exchange Act of 1934 are adequate to the task. Moreover, competitive market forces should provide a check on self-dealing in securities. Institutions that engaged in such activities, and thus failed to act in the best interests of their customers, might soon find themselves with many fewer customers.

Moral hazard

A more legitimate public policy concern in the debate over integrating securities activity and commercial banking is whether such integration would lead to an undesirable propagation of the deposit insurance guarantee and its corresponding moral hazard. Deposit insurance, which can prevent bank runs, is a central, and, many believe, essential feature of our present banking system. However, it can create an undesirable side effect — an incentive for excessive risk-taking because an insured bank can attract funds at a risk-free rate regardless of the riskiness of the bank's portfolio.

Under these circumstances, only regulation will restrain an insured institution, acting in the best interest of its shareholders, from assuming more risk than is socially desirable. If bank powers were expanded, such as through the integration of investment and commercial banking, it might become increasingly difficult for regulators to assess and limit a banking organization's level of risk-taking. Put differently, the "subsidy" provided by deposit insurance would propagate to the nonbanking activities of the organization, where any problems that develop could be an additional source of instability for banking.

Corporate separateness

One method proposed to prevent the undesirable effects of deposit insurance from propagating is the strict enforcement of "corporate separateness". Corporate separateness entails putting all nontraditional financial functions in subsidiaries of bank holding companies and then trying to insulate the bank from the risks of the nonbank subsidiaries.

There are several reasons corporate separateness is unlikely to work very well. Most important is the very strong profit incentive for a corporation (in this instance, a bank holding company) to manage its various subsidiaries as a single entity. While it might be possible to enforce corporate separateness strictly, and thereby truly insulate the bank, doing so might severely restrict or even eliminate any synergies the consolidated organization might otherwise enjoy. Thus, from a purely organizational viewpoint, the erection of legal barriers between banks and their securities affiliates, in itself, would be unlikely to remove incentives for the propagation of deposit insurance guarantees.

In fact, there is abundant empirical evidence that bank holding companies in the U.S. are run as consolidated enterprises. For example, such companies tend to use affiliate relationships to avoid capital and other regulatory constraints imposed on banking activities, and are reluctant to let their nonbank affiliates fail. Indeed, even from a purely legal standpoint, it is unclear whether the liability of a subsidiary can be effectively separated from that of its parent.

Capital regulation

While the enforcement of corporate separateness is not the solution to the problems presented by the integration of investment and commercial banking to the deposit insurance system, there are a number of ways in which the insurance system itself could be restructured to prevent the same problems. Perhaps most promising would be a move toward much more stringent capital regulation, whereby banks would always be closed when they could not or would not maintain sufficient capital as valued on a current market basis.

Such reform would require fundamental changes in the rules governing the valuation of banks' capital and those determining when institutions would be declared legally insolvent. Specifically, it would require a shift from measuring capital on a historical book-value basis, as is done now, to a current or market-value basis and closing banks before their market value of capital could fall below zero. If both could be accomplished, bank powers could be expanded and nonbank financial firms allowed access to the payments system without threatening the viability of the deposit insurance fund.

To be effective, such an approach might require increased and more frequent supervision of insured institutions to monitor closely the market values of their equity. One major practical difficulty in doing so lies in assigning market values to nontraded assets and liabilities. However, many investment banking functions entail holding traded assets and liabilities whose market values are readily ascertainable. Moreover, valuation procedures could be structured conservatively to avoid overevaluation of an organization's net worth.

One way such a system could be phased in would be to require banks that wished to offer investment banking services to submit to stringent market-value capital regulation of the sort outlined above. Thus, banks actually expanding their services would do so because they expected to realize the efficiencies involved, not because they wished to exploit the deposit insurance system.

Michael C. Keeley and Randall J. Pozdena

Article Nineteen

The Securitization of Housing Finance

By Gordon H. Sellon, Jr. and Deana VanNahmen

Prior to 1970, the system of housing finance in the United States suffered from a number of deficiencies. A principal concern was the lack of a national secondary market for mortgage loans. The absence of a secondary market resulted in geographic imbalances in the flow of mortgage funds and prevented housing from tapping into the growing supply of savings managed by institutional investors, such as pension funds, mutual funds, and life insurance companies. These problems were exacerbated by regulations on loan and deposit rates that distorted the flow of savings into the housing industry and contributed to boom and bust cycles in mortgage lending.

Since 1970, however, housing finance has undergone a radical transformation. The securitization of mortgage loans and financial deregulation have revolutionized the nature of housing finance. The first stage of securitization

Gordon H. Sellon, Jr. is an assistant vice president and economist at the Federal Reserve Bank of Kansas City. Deana VanNahmen is a research associate at the bank.

occurred in the early 1970s as the introduction of government-insured mortgage securities provided the basis for a national secondary market in mortgage lending that helped eliminate geographic imbalances in mortgage flows and attract new investors to housing. A second wave of securitization occurred in the early 1980s as unprecedented interest rate volatility and financial deregulation spawned a variety of new mortgage contracts and a plethora of complex mortgage securities.

While transforming housing finance, securitization has also raised a number of important public policy issues. Among these issues are the proper scope of government involvement in the securitization process, the future role of traditional housing lenders, and the relationship between securitization and the riskiness of the financial system.

This article provides an overview of the impact of securitization on housing finance and discusses some of the important public policy issues. The article is divided into three sections. The first section describes the nature of housing finance prior to 1970 and the important part played by government in the housing process. The second section discusses the development of mortgage-backed securities and their impact on housing finance. The final section explores some of the implications of securitization for public policy.

Housing finance prior to 1970

Government policy has played a key role in the evolution of the system of housing finance. Extensive government involvement in housing began in the 1930s as the government attempted to restore stability to a system of housing finance that had been dangerously weakened during the Depression. Government continued to have an active role in the postwar period as housing policy emphasized the provision of an expanding supply of affordable housing to meet the needs of a growing population.

The role of government in housing finance

During the Depression, the system of housing finance suffered considerable damage as the flow of funds into housing was reduced and foreclosures became widespread. Among the many government programs enacted in the 1930s to assist housing, four developments stand out as playing a key role in the subsequent evolution of housing finance. They are the establishment of the Federal Home Loan Bank System and the insurance of savings deposits, the development of government mortgage insurance, the creation of the Federal National Mortgage Association, and the adoption of the long-term, fixed-rate mortgage contract.[1]

Prior to the 1930s, savings and loan associations were the primary source of funds to housing. During the Depression, government pro-

---

[1] Much of this discussion is motivated by James L. Pierce, *Monetary and Financial Economics*, John Wiley and Sons, New York, 1984, pp. 275-295.

grams to create the Federal Home Loan Bank System and to provide federal insurance on savings deposits helped stabilize the flow of funds into housing. Deposit insurance provided stability to housing by reducing the risks of financial loss for depositors in S&Ls. At the same time, the Home Loan Bank System promoted stability by providing liquidity to S&Ls, allowing them to invest more funds in home mortgages. Thus, the effect of these programs was to reinforce the traditional role of S&Ls in housing finance.

A second important government program was the creation of federal mortgage insurance under the FHA and, later, VA programs. Direct government insurance of mortgages had a number of consequences for housing. First, mortgage insurance allowed investors other than savings and loan depositors to commit funds to housing with reduced credit risk. Second, with the government assuming credit risk, mortgage investors were willing to accept a lower yield on their investment, which translated into reduced costs for borrowers. Third, the government mortgage insurance program required standardization of the underlying mortgage contract. Standardization is crucial both to the development of a wider primary market for mortgage lending and to the creation of a secondary mortgage market.

The third key government housing program during the 1930s was the creation of the Federal National Mortgage Association (FNMA) or "Fannie Mae." A principal function of FNMA was to improve liquidity in housing finance by providing secondary market services to the housing industry. FNMA was authorized to purchase mortgages from originators, to hold these mortgages in its portfolio, and to finance its purchases of mortgages with debt issues in the capital market. Thus, in principle, FNMA could provide stability to housing by purchasing mortgages in periods of strong credit demand and selling mortgages in periods of weak credit demand. In practice, because it was limited to purchasing government-insured loans, FNMA was severely restricted in its secondary mortgage market activities. Later, however, FNMA and other similar federally created housing agencies became the vehicle for the securitization of housing finance.

The fourth government initiative introduced in the 1930s was support for a long-term, fixed-rate mortgage contract as the standard of the housing industry.[2] Prior to the 1930s, mortgage loans were typically short-term, 3 to 5 year, nonamortizing loans. During the Depression, the characteristics of this type of loan contributed to the housing crisis as mortgage lenders became unwilling to roll over existing loans and borrowers were unable to repay the principal. To reduce these problems, the government required the housing industry to adopt the familiar long-term, fixed-rate mortgage contract. This contract was attractive to housing lenders because deposit insurance provided a stable source of mortgage funds. At the same time, borrowers found the terms of this type of loan to be more affordable. This form of mortgage contract had important implications later, however, both for the health of the savings and loan industry and for the types of institutions providing funds to the housing industry.

The structure of housing finance

In the postwar period, the demand for housing grew rapidly and the supply of investment funds flowing into housing expanded. The government programs enacted in the 1930s helped shape the way housing was financed.[3]

The programs enacted in the 1930s to strengthen the savings and loan industry helped S&Ls emerge as the dominant provider of housing funds in the 1950-70 period. Indeed, as shown in Chart 1, S&Ls generally gained market share versus alternative mortgage lenders, such as commercial banks, life insurance companies, and mutual savings banks.

Government mortgage insurance also played a significant part in postwar housing finance by effectively creating separate markets for government-insured and conventional mortgage loans. The conventional mortgage market was essentially a local market with lending dominated by S&Ls. That is, conventional mortgage loans were generally made by S&Ls to borrowers in their local market using locally generated deposits.[4]

The market for government-insured loans operated very differently. The largest lenders for government-insured mortgages were life insurance companies and mutual savings banks.[5] Unlike S&Ls, these lenders generally did not originate the loans in their portfolios. Instead, they purchased the loans from mortgage banking companies who originated and serviced the loans. Also, in contrast to the conventional mortgage market, the government-insured market tended to be national in scope, with life insurance companies and mutual savings banks purchasing loans from around the country.

The dominance of the S&Ls in the conventional market but not in the government-insured market can be traced at least in part to the insurance guarantee and to the nature of the mortgage contract. Life insurance companies and mutual savings banks were attracted to the government market largely because of the insurance guarantee and the associated standardization of the loans.

---

2 Pierce, p. 284.

3 For a detailed discussion of post-war housing finance to 1965, see J.A. Cacy, "Financial Intermediaries and the Post-war Home Mortgage Market," *Monthly Review*, Federal Reserve Bank of Kansas City, January/February 1967, pp. 12-21.

4 Cacy, pp. 13-14.

5 Cacy, pp. 13-14.

CHART 1

Market share: mortgage debt as a percentage of total residential mortgage debt

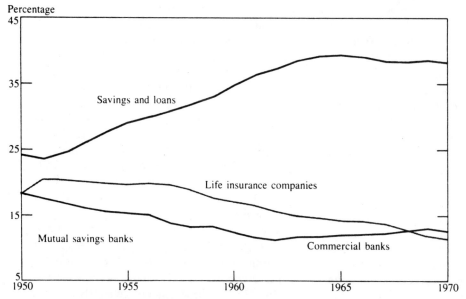

Source: Board of Governors, Federal Reserve System, Macro Data Library.

Thus, S&Ls faced significant competition for government-insured mortgages, which tended to reduce the profitability of these loans for S&Ls.[6]

In contrast, S&Ls faced less competition in the conventional market. Partly, this reflected the greater credit risks and costs of monitoring uninsured loans that excluded nonlocal lenders. In addition, other local lenders such as commercial banks were not generally attracted to the mortgage market because of the long maturity of mortgage loans.

The nature of the mortgage contract also posed difficulties for other potential mortgage lenders, such as pension funds. Although the standard mortgage contract had a long stated maturity of 30 years, the ability of homeowners to prepay the mortgage reduced the effective maturity of

these loans. In addition, the possibility of prepayment was quite uncertain and depended upon a variety of factors such as interest rates and demographic variables. Thus, potential housing lenders with a preference for a debt instrument of a long maturity and/or a certain maturity tended to avoid mortgage loans.

The final government housing initiative of the 1930s, "Fannie Mae," played a limited role in the 1950-70 period. Originally envisaged as a means of promoting a secondary market for mortgage loans, FNMA's lending activities were greatly restricted. Until 1970, FNMA was prohibited from holding conventional mortgage loans in its portfolio. Thus, its mortgage market support activities were confined to the government-insured market. Additional restrictions on its ability to purchase older loans or to sell loans from its portfolio limited FNMA's efforts in the government market.

---

[6] Cacy, p. 19.

CHART 2

Conventional vs. government-insured mortgage loans as a percentage of total residential mortgage debt

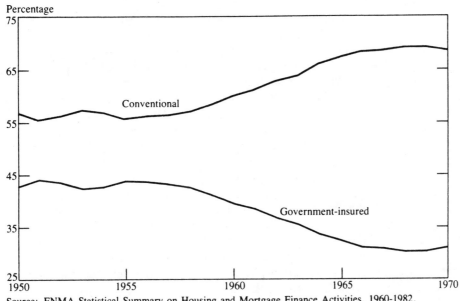

Source: FNMA Statistical Summary on Housing and Mortgage Finance Activities, 1960-1982.

The need for housing finance reform

Despite the rapid growth of housing in the postwar period, policymakers were increasingly concerned that the supply of affordable housing was not keeping pace with society's needs. Academics and policymakers identified a number of problems with the structure of housing finance whose resolution would require significant reform in the government's housing program.[7]

The principal problems with housing finance stemmed from the fact that most of the growth in housing in the postwar period occurred in the conventional mortgage market.[8] The relative shares of the conventional and government-insured markets are shown in Chart 2. Because conventional mortgage markets were local in their scope, the allocation of funds to housing was marred by geographic inefficiencies. That is, with a series of unconnected local markets for conventional loans, housing funds did not flow from areas with surplus savings to areas with excess demands for housing loans.

In addition to the lack of integration of local housing markets, there was a lack of integration of these markets with national capital markets. This problem had two dimensions. On the one hand, housing was periodically affected by credit

---

[7] See, for example, Oliver Jones and Leo Grebler, *The Secondary Mortgage Market: Its Purpose, Performance, and Potential,* University of California, Los Angeles, 1961; and J.A. Cacy, "Specialized Mortgage Marketing Facilities," *Monthly Review,* Federal Reserve Bank of Kansas City, July/August 1967, pp. 3-13.

[8] The differential growth in the two markets can be traced to restrictions on eligibility for government-insured loans and to factors such as liberalized terms on conventional mortgages and the development of private mortgage insurance.

crises when high market interest rates led to an outflow of deposits from S&Ls. The credit crisis in 1966 was a prime example of this "disintermediation," and it had an important effect on the push for housing reform. On the other hand, the enormous growth in savings controlled by institutional investors, such as pension funds, mutual funds, and life insurance companies, was seen as a source of funds that potentially could be tapped for housing needs.

In contrast to the conventional market, the market for government-insured loans did not suffer from the same difficulties. The role of government insurance was particularly important in developing a national market for these loans. For example, with the protection of insurance guarantees, mutual savings banks in the Northeast could channel surplus savings to other parts of the country. Moreover, government-insured loans proved to be attractive to national institutional investors, such as life insurance companies. Finally, the government-insured market had access to capital markets through FNMA debt issues.

The development of mortgage-backed securities

To create an active secondary market for both conventional and government-insured loans and to improve the linkages between mortgage and capital markets, the government made radical changes in its housing program from 1968 to 1970. The key features of this new program were a restructuring and expansion of the role of the federal housing agencies and the creation of a new type of debt instrument, the mortgage-backed security.

Since the early 1970s, the market for mortgage-backed securities has undergone tremendous growth and change. Financial deregulation and interest rate volatility have played an important part in the development of the market as new types of securities have been created and private financial institutions have begun to assume a limited role in the market.

The role of government agencies

To implement changes in its housing program, the government changed the role of FNMA and created two new housing finance agencies, the Government National Mortgage Association (GNMA) or "Ginnie Mae," and the Federal Home Loan Mortgage Corporation (FHLMC) or "Freddie Mac." The three agencies differ in their structure and ownership and in the functions that they perform in the mortgage market.[9]

In 1968, FNMA was turned into a private corporation with private management and publicly held stock.[10] GNMA was created at the same time to assume FNMA's credit market support functions and to administer mortgage guarantee programs. GNMA operates as a government agency, under the supervision of the Secretary of Housing and Urban Development. FHLMC was created in 1970 in order to develop a secondary market for conventional mortgage loans. FHLMC is owned by savings and loan associations and the Federal Home Loan Banks.

A principal function of all three agencies in support of the housing market is their provision of a guarantee for mortgage-backed securities. Thus, GNMA guarantees full and timely payment of interest and principal on its securities and its guarantee is backed by the "full faith and credit"

---

[9] A more detailed discussion of the agencies and their programs can be found in Kenneth G. Lore, *Mortgage-Backed Securities: Developments and Trends in the Secondary Mortgage Market,* Clark Boardman Co. Ltd., New York, 1987-88 edition, pp. 2-1 to 2-58.

[10] FNMA continues to be subject to a number of federal constraints and so is not an entirely private corporation. See Lore, p. 2-19 to 2-20.

of the government. FNMA provides a similar guarantee and, while it is no longer a government agency, is viewed in the capital markets as having "agency status." FHLMC guarantees full and timely payment of interest and ultimate payment of principal and, it too, is viewed as having agency status. Having agency status allows FNMA and FHLMC to obtain AAA credit ratings and thus incur lower borrowing costs.[11]

GNMA's principal role in the market for mortgage-backed securities is to act only as a guarantor of securities issued by thrifts, mortgage bankers, and other mortgage originators. That is, GNMA does not issue mortgage-backed securities or purchase mortgage loans. In contrast, both FNMA and FHLMC provide insurance guarantees, issue mortgage-backed securities, and buy and sell mortgage loans. More recently, FHLMC and FNMA have been actively involved in the design of new types of mortgage-backed securities.

GNMA guaranteed securities, backed by FHA and VA loans, were first issued in 1970. FHLMC first issued securities backed by conventional loans in 1970, while FNMA-issued mortgage-backed securities began in 1981.[12]

Types of mortgage-backed securities

In generic form, a mortgage-backed security is a debt instrument whose interest and principal payments are either derived from the cash flows of an underlying pool of mortgages or are collateralized by the mortgage pool. The market for mortgage-backed securities has evolved in several stages of increasing complexity. Despite structural differences, however, all mortgage-backed securities share a common goal: to create a security that is similar to and competitive with other debt instruments in the capital market. This subsection examines three important types of mortgage-backed securities and summarizes some of the more recent market developments.

Pass-through securities. Pass-throughs were the first mortgage-backed security and are still the most important type in the market. Their importance derives from the fact that they are widely held in investment portfolios and are also used as backing or collateral for other, more complex types of mortgage securities.[13]

The basic features of a pass-through security can be seen in a typical GNMA security. To create a GNMA pass-through, an approved mortgage originator will assemble a pool of government-insured mortgages that conform to criteria set by GNMA. The originator will then issue a security whose interest and principal represent an undivided interest in the cash flow of the underlying mortgages. That is, each investor receives a pro-rata share of the underlying cash flow. GNMA guarantees timely payment of interest and principal for securities backed by this mortgage pool and charges a fee for this guarantee. The interest rate on the GNMA security is lower than the rate on the underlying mortgages due to the GNMA guarantee fee and to payments to the servicer of the mortgage pool.

The pass-through security has a number of characteristics, both positive and negative, that

---

11 For a more detailed discussion of these guarantees, see Lore, p. 9-21 to 9-28.

12 GNMA guarantees are confined to government-insured mortgages. FHLMC and FNMA are not restricted but operate mainly in the conventional market. Both FHLMC and FNMA have upper limits on the size of the mortgage that can be included in their mortgage pools. This limit is linked to housing prices and so has generally increased over time.

13 Additional information of pass-through securities can be found in Kenneth H. Sullivan, Bruce M. Collins, and David A. Smilow, "Mortgage Pass-through Securities" in *The Handbook of Fixed Income Securities*, Frank J. Fabozzi and Irving M. Pollack (eds.), Dow Jones-Irwin, Homewood, Ill., 1987, pp. 382-403.

CHART 3
Agency pass-throughs outstanding

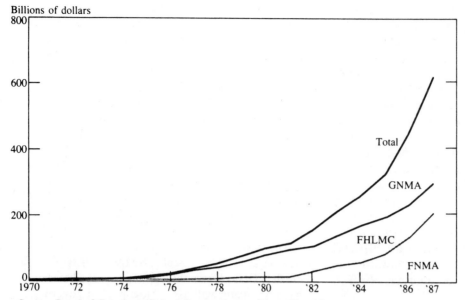

Source: Board of Governors, Federal Reserve System, Macro Data Library.

influence its acceptance by investors. First, because of the government guarantee, the pass-through security is free of credit risk. Second, unlike the underlying individual mortgages, the security can be issued in large denominations and is highly liquid. Third, its cash flow is monthly, unlike the cash flows of corporate or government debt. Fourth, the pass-through security is subject to the same prepayment risk as the underlying mortgages so that the size and timing of payment is uncertain. Fifth, the sale of a pass-through is treated as sale of assets; that is, ownership of the underlying mortgages is transferred to the owner of the security.

The pass-through market was created by the government housing agencies and continues to be dominated by these agencies. There have been relatively few privately issued and guaranteed pass-throughs.[14] The growth of GNMA,

FHLMC, and FNMA pass-throughs is shown in Chart 3. At the end of 1987, approximately $627 billion of agency pass-through securities were outstanding.

The development of the pass-through security has had a number of beneficial effects on housing finance. Its principal impact has been to improve the liquidity of the mortgage market, helping to eliminate the geographic inefficiencies that characterized mortgage markets prior to 1970. For example, a lender with surplus funds because of a lack of local housing demand can

---

[14] For the most part, private pass-throughs have involved

so-called "jumbo" loans, which exceed agency ceilings. In 1987, $11.1 billion of private pass-through securities were issued. Generally speaking, privately guaranteed pass-through securities have not been cost-competitive with government-guaranteed securities. In addition, the development of a private market has been hindered by favorable tax and regulatory treatment of government securities. See Lore, pp. 1-37 to 1-49.

purchase pass-through securities. Alternatively, a lender with local mortgage demand exceeding local funding can sell pass-through securities and use the funds generated to make additional loans. A second positive effect is the ability to use pass-throughs as collateral for borrowing. Thus, institutions holding pass-through securities as assets find that the credit guarantees and liquidity make these securities better and cheaper sources of collateral than whole mortgage loans. Finally, pass-throughs improve the integration of mortgage and capital markets because they appeal to investors desiring to purchase securities rather than individual loans.

Despite these advantages, pass-through securities have not proved to be the solution to all housing finance problems. First, while pass-throughs have some of the characteristics of traditional debt securities, they also have limitations. The chief limitation is the presence of prepayment risk and the lack of certainty about interest and principal payments. In addition, monthly payment streams are less attractive to many institutional investors who are accustomed to quarterly payments. Unfortunately, for many years tax laws prevented the modification of pass-throughs to remedy these difficulties. Any change in the structure or timing of pass-through payments was sufficient to change the pass-through to a debt instrument for tax and accounting purposes.[15]

Second, because of their treatment as a sale of assets, pass-throughs proved to be unattractive to many thrift institutions whose loan portfolio consisted of mortgages with below-market yields. If securitized using a pass-through, these loans would have to be sold at a loss. As a result of these limitations, other types of mortgage-backed securities were developed by financial institutions and the federal agencies.

Mortgage-backed bonds. A second type of mortgage-backed security is the mortgage-backed bond. Mortgage-backed bonds are debt instruments that are collateralized by mortgage loans or pass-through securities. Unlike pass-through securities, the owners of mortgage-backed bonds do not have an ownership interest in the underlying mortgage instruments and there is no automatic pass-through of cash flow from the mortgages to the bond holder. As a debt instrument, mortgage-backed bonds are a liability of the issuing institution and the underlying collateral remains on the balance sheet of the issuer.[16]

Mortgage-backed bonds were developed by thrift institutions and investment bankers in the mid-1970s as a way for thrift institutions to obtain funds without having to sell mortgages with below-market yields from their portfolios. Like corporate bonds, the timing of interest and principal payments on mortgage-backed bonds are not directly related to the cash flow of the collateral. As a result, the cash flows of the mortgage-backed bond are not subject to prepayment risk, and payments can be made quarterly or semi-annually. Thus, in principle, mortgage-backed bonds solve many of the difficulties of pass-through securities.

However, mortgage-backed bonds have their own limitations that have hindered their development. The chief problem with mortgage-backed bonds is the lack of a government credit guarantee. Even though the collateral may have government insurance, the cash flow of the collateral is not directly connected to the cash flow of the bond. Thus, to be competitive with other securities, mortgage-backed bonds must have

---

[15] For a detailed discussion of tax and accounting issues related to mortgage-backed securities, see Lore, pp. 6-1 to 6-109 and pp. 7-1 to 7-28.

[16] Additional information on mortgage-backed bonds can be found in Barbara Pauley and Richard Brennan, ''Mortgage-Backed Bonds: Evolution Creates Opportunity,'' *Memorandum to Portfolio Managers*, Salomon Brothers, Inc., New York, March 10, 1988.

CHART 4
Mortgage-backed bonds issuance

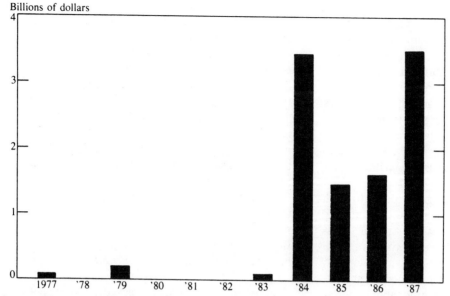

Billions of dollars

Source: Salomon Brothers: *Mortgage-backed Bonds: Evolution Creates Opportunity*, Barbara Pauley, March 10, 1988

substantial credit enhancement, typically in the form of a high degree of overcollateralization. As a consequence, mortgage-backed bonds can be an expensive way of raising funds. In addition, the absence of government insurance and lack of standardization of the bonds issues imply that these bonds have very little secondary market liquidity.

The development of the market for mortgage-backed bonds is shown in Chart 4. Initially issued in small amounts in 1977 and 1979, mortgage-backed bonds did not become popular again until 1984. Although issuance has risen in recent years, these bonds make up a very small part of the market for mortgage-backed securities. Thus, the total amount of mortgage-backed bonds outstanding at the end of 1987 was about $12 billion, an amount that is dwarfed by the $627 billion of outstanding federally related pass-throughs. The increase in recent years is partly due to an increased demand for funds by thrifts and partly due to the development of new types of bonds with characteristics appealing to specific investor niches.[17]

Collateralized mortgage obligations. Collateralized mortgage obligations (CMOs) represent an important advance in the growing market for mortgage-backed securities. Introduced in 1983 by FHLMC and First Boston Corporation, CMOs are multi-class bonds backed by a pool of mortgages or by pass-through securities. CMOs share characteristics of both pass-throughs and mortgage-backed bonds. Like pass-throughs, CMOs are backed by collateral whose cash flows are dedicated to the bond. Thus, CMOs do not require as much overcollateralization as

---

[17] Thus, some issues have been in the eurobond market and others have involved new features such as yields fixed in real terms.

CHART 5
CMO's issuance

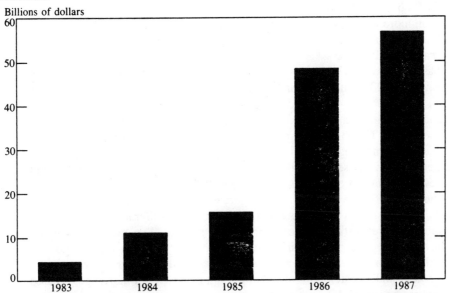

Billions of dollars

Source: Salomon Brothers: Review of Housing and Mortgage Markets, August 1987, *Weekly Mortgage Market Update*, June 3, 1988.

mortgage-backed bonds. Like mortgage-backed bonds, CMOs are treated as debt instruments and so remain on the balance sheet of the issuer. Moreover, while the mortgages or pass-through securities backing a CMO may be insured, the CMO bonds have no government insurance guarantees.[18]

The basic objective in the design of a CMO was to transform mortgage cash flows into bond classes of different maturities so as to reduce the uncertainty about the timing of cash flows caused by prepayment. In this way, CMOs overcame the main limitations of pass-throughs. This goal was

accomplished by allocating principal payments and prepayments to different bond classes according to a predetermined schedule. For example, in its simplest form, a CMO might have two bond classes. The first class is a fast-paying class that receives scheduled interest payments and all principal payments and prepayments until the class is paid off. The second or slow-paying class receives interest payments, but no principal payments, until the first class is retired. In effect, the cash flows of the mortgages are transformed into two bonds, one with a relatively short maturity and one with a longer maturity.

Unlike pass-throughs, which have been the province of the federal housing agencies, CMOs have been issued by federal agencies and by investment banks, thrifts, home builders, mortgage bankers, insurance companies, and commercial banks. CMOs have been issued in a variety of formats with as few as three classes and as many

---

[18] Additional discussion of CMOs can be found in Richard Roll, "Collateralized Mortgage Obligations: Characteristics, History, Analysis," in *Mortgage-Backed Securities: New Strategies, Applications and Research*, Frank J. Fabozzi (ed.), Probus Publishing, Chicago, Ill., 1987, pp. 7-44; and Gregory J. Parseghian, "Collateralized Mortgage Obligations," in *The Handbook of Fixed-Income Securities*, pp. 404-421.

as ten classes. As shown in Chart 5, issuance of CMOs expanded gradually from 1983 to 1985 and then increased dramatically in 1986 and 1987. In relative terms, CMOs are much more important than mortgage-backed bonds and are growing in relation to the pass-through market. In 1987, $57 billion of CMOs were issued as compared to $3.5 billion of mortgage-backed bonds and $235 billion of agency pass-throughs.

CMOs have advantages and disadvantages as compared with pass-through securities. The chief attraction of CMOs is the creation of mortgage-backed securities with distinct maturity classes. Thus, CMOs may attract new investors to the housing market, investors who did not find pass-through securities attractive.[19]

In fact, there is some limited evidence that CMOs are accomplishing the objective of attracting new investors. In 1986, thrifts, commercial banks, life insurance companies, and pension funds were the largest purchasers of CMO classes. Pension funds who have traditionally committed few funds to housing were the largest purchasers of all of the classes. Moreover, pension funds and life insurance companies mainly bought the longer-maturity classes while thrifts and commercial banks tended to purchase the shorter maturities.[20]

CMOs also have disadvantages which may limit their appeal. The chief disadvantage is that CMO classes are relatively illiquid securities. In sharp contrast to pass-throughs, CMO classes are issued in relatively small amounts, by a variety of issuers, with little standardization among issuers.

CMOs also lack government guarantees. Thus, CMO classes do not have a well-established secondary market and so are not nearly as liquid as pass-throughs.

Recent developments in mortgage-backed securities. The market for mortgage-backed securities has undergone considerable evolution in recent years. While the market originally developed as a government initiative, many recent developments have been market-driven in response to financial deregulation and greater interest rate volatility. Significant changes have been made in the structures of pass-through securities and CMOs.

An important development in the pass-through market has been the proliferation of new types of mortgage contracts. The high and volatile interest rates in the early 1980s led to important changes in the standard mortgage contract. Some of the important new types of mortgages created are adjustable rate mortgages, graduated payment mortgages, shorter term mortgages, and mortgages that are convertible from variable to fixed rates. New types of pass-through securities have been developed by the federal agencies to conform to the new mortgage contracts and to provide secondary market support for these mortgages.

A second development is the creation of pass-through securities which, like CMOs, transform the cash flows of the mortgage pool. An important factor in this development was the 1986 change in tax laws, which created the Real Estate Mortgage Investment Conduit (REMIC). A REMIC is a legal entity for issuing mortgage-backed securities without the tax and accounting difficulties that plagued their early development.[21]

---

[19] With a CMO, the timing of the payments can be different from the underlying mortgages. This may make CMOs attractive to investors who want a quarterly or semi-annual payment stream.

[20] See Lore, p. 3-21. Similar information is provided in Parseghian, pp. 420-421.

---

[21] For an overview of REMICS, see Panos Konstas, "REMICS: Their Role in Mortgage Finance and the Securities Market," *Banking and Economic Review,* Federal Deposit Insurance Corporation, May/June 1987, pp. 11-18. For a more comprehen-

As a result of these changes, multi-class pass-through securities have been developed in the past two years. One of the more notable examples is the stripped mortgage-backed security in which one class receives only interest payments from the mortgage pool while a second class receives only principal payments.[22]

CMOs have also evolved in more complex ways. One early development was the creation of a so-called Z-bond. The Z-bond class of a CMO is a zero-coupon bond that receives neither interest nor principal payments until prior classes are paid off. Thus, the Z-bond has an extremely long maturity and also has the effect of shortening the maturities of the other classes. More recent developments in CMO structures have included floating-rate and inverse floating rate classes.[23]

These recent developments in both the pass-through and CMO markets have helped expand the investor pool for mortgage lending by protecting investors from increased interest rate volatility. Thus, for example, the interest-only portion of a stripped mortgage-backed security can be used as a hedging device for investors in mortgage-backed securities. Certain CMO classes also have useful hedging properties while floating rate classes directly protect the investor from interest rate volatility. At the same time, however, many of these new securities have unusual price and interest rate behavior as compared to stan-dard pass-through securities. Thus, they pose considerable risks for unsophisticated investors.[24]

Mortgage-backed securities and housing finance

Evaluating the impact of mortgage-backed securities on housing finance involves answering two questions. What is the magnitude of mortgage securitization since 1970 and is the trend likely to continue? Have mortgage-backed securities contributed to solving the problems that plagued housing finance prior to 1970?

By most measures, securitization has had a large and growing influence on the mortgage market. One gauge of this impact is the fraction of mortgage debt that has been securitized. Chart 6 shows the amount of agency pass-through securities outstanding as a percent of residential mortgage debt. By this measure, the fraction of mortgage debt securitized has increased steadily since 1970, reaching 30 percent in 1987.[25]

An important determinant of the future trend of securitization is the rate at which new mortgage loans are being securitized. Chart 7 shows the fraction of new mortgages that have been turned into agency pass-through securities from 1970 to 1987. Although variable from year to

---

sive treatment see Kenneth G. Lore and Kyllikki Kusma, *Mortgage-Backed Securities—Special Update: REMICS*, Clark Boardman Co. Ltd., New York, 1987.

[22] Stripped securities are discussed in more detail in Sean Becketti, ''The Role of Stripped Securities in Portfolio Management,'' *Economic Review*, Federal Reserve Bank of Kansas City, May 1988, pp. 20-31.

[23] See Lore, pp. 3-40 to 3-43. For a more technical discussion, see Gail M. Belonsky and Steven D. Meyer, ''Floating Rate CMOs: The Floater, the Inverse Floater, and the Residual,'' *Mortgage-Backed Securities Research*, Drexel Burnham Lambert, December 1986.

[24] These dangers are illustrated by the estimated $275 million loss suffered by Merrill Lynch in 1987 on a position in stripped securities. See Lore, *Mortgage-Backed Securities: Developments and Trends*, pp. 3-38 to 3-40.

[25] This is not a perfect measure for a number of reasons. While some CMOs are backed by pass-throughs, others are backed by whole loans that do not conform to agency guidelines. Those CMOs backed by whole loans should be included in a measure of securitization, but this data is not available. Also, this measure does not include the more traditional debt issues by FNMA and FHLMC to finance loans held in their portfolios. Adding this debt to pass-throughs would raise the share of mortgage debt securitized. The reported measure also does not include non-agency pass-throughs.

CHART 6

Agency pass-through securities as a percentage of total residential mortgage debt

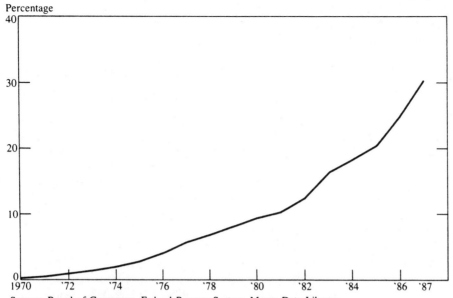

Source: Board of Governors, Federal Reserve System, Macro Data Library.

year, the rate of securitization has recently approached 60 percent. If this rate continues, the stock of securitized mortgage debt will continue to grow.[26]

Mortgage-backed securities also appear to have helped improve the geographic efficiency of housing finance and to have strengthened the linkage between housing and capital markets. Evidence supporting this conclusion comes from recent studies that point to reduced variation in mortgage rates across regions and to increased sensitivity of mortgage interest rates to changes in capital market rates.[27] Additional evidence is provided by data showing that institutional investors, such as pension funds and mutual funds have been significant purchasers of mortgage securities.

The various types of mortgage-backed securities have made different contributions to this process. Pass-through securities have played the most important role by creating a liquid, national secondary market for conventional and government-insured loans. In addition, pass-throughs have appealed to nontraditional housing investors with a preference for investment securities rather than whole mortgage loans.

Mortgage-backed bonds and CMOs have served a different function. They overcame some of the problems of the traditional mortgage contract by reducing the uncertainties of cash flows caused by mortgage prepayments. Thus, these types of mortgage securities appeal to a wider

[26] Part of the reason for this variability is that adjustable-rate pass-throughs are relatively recent. Before these new pass-throughs were created, an increase in the market share of ARMs versus fixed-rate loans would reduce the fraction of originations securitized.

[27] See, for example, Howard L. Roth, "Volatile Mortgage Rates—A New Fact of Life?" *Economic Review,* Federal Reserve Bank of Kansas City, March 1988, pp. 16-28. Also, see Stuart A. Gabriel, "Housing and Mortgage Markets: The Post-1982 Expansion," *Federal Reserve Bulletin,* December 1987, pp. 893-903.

CHART 7
Agency pass-through issuance as a percentage of total mortgage originations

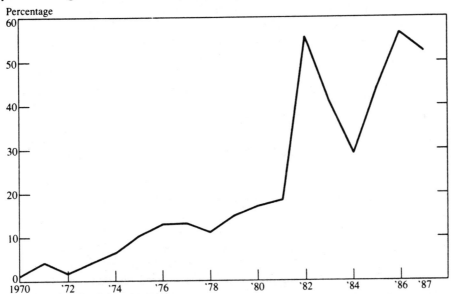

Source: *The Mortgage-Backed Securities Market, Statiscal Annual-1988,* Guy D. Cecala (ed.), Probus Publishing Company, Chicago, IL.

Board of Governors, Federal Reserve System, Macro Data Library, Statistics from the Department of Housing and Urban Development.

range of potential investors than do pass-throughs. At the same time, without the government guarantees or standardization of pass-throughs, these securities do not have much of a secondary market so that the investor may sacrifice considerable liquidity.

Securitization and housing finance: policy issues

Despite its beneficial effects, the securitization of housing finance has raised a number of questions about the proper scope of government involvement in housing finance and the future structure and stability of the financial system. This section discusses the implications of securitization for three public policy issues: the relative roles of government and the private sector in

housing, the viability of the S&L industry, and the implications of securitization for financial system risk.

Government's role in housing finance

The expanding role of government in housing finance since the 1930s has led to increasing concern about the desirability and economic efficiency of government programs. This issue has been a particularly important topic of debate during the term of the Reagan administration. The administration has promoted the privatization of housing finance, that is, the reduction of the role of government in housing. This view runs counter to most of the housing legislation passed since the 1930s, which uses government programs to expand the availability and affordability of housing.

Proponents of privatization question the cost and effectiveness of federal housing policy. They argue that too many resources are devoted to housing and that government subsidies crowd out more productive forms of investment. In contrast, opponents of privatization argue that, in the absence of federal programs, too little housing would be produced and housing would not be affordable.

The privatization issue directly involves the federal housing agencies and their role in the securitization process. Critics of government housing policy point out that the scope of agency activities has expanded far beyond their original intent of providing affordable housing to low income families and supporting the development of the secondary market. These critics note that as much as 80 percent of single-family mortgages conform to FNMA and FHLMC guidelines and so are eligible for securitization by the agencies. Thus, critics contend, federal housing subsidies extend to moderate and upper income families. In addition, critics argue that rather than supporting the secondary market, agency activities dominate the market and prevent the development of a private secondary market.

Most proponents of privatization focus their displeasure on the "agency status" of FNMA and FHLMC. They contend that the agencies have a competitive advantage because of the implicit government guarantee of their activities. Thus, agency competition reduces the profitability of private participants in housing finance who are without government guarantees. Generally speaking, supporters of privatization advocate turning FNMA and FHLMC into private institutions without government guarantees supporting their activities.[28]

In contrast, supporters of current housing policy are generally opposed to a major change in government programs or a change in the status of the agencies. They argue that in the absence of government support, housing availability and affordability would suffer. In this view, scaling back government guarantees would raise housing costs and might impair the liquidity of the secondary market and the integration of housing and capital markets.[29]

Securitization and the viability of S&Ls

A policy concern related to the privatization issue is the future role of S&Ls in housing finance. As discussed earlier, from 1930 to 1970, government housing programs gave S&Ls a central role in housing finance. Since 1970, however, the government-sponsored securitization of housing finance has tended to erode the dominant position of S&Ls. As securitization has broken down geographic barriers to the flow of housing funds and linked housing and capital markets, S&Ls have forced increased competition in mortgage lending. This increased competition has lowered the returns to mortgage lending. In addition, deposit rate deregulation has raised the cost of funds for S&Ls. As a result of these two forces, the spread or profit that S&Ls can earn on their mortgage portfolio has declined.[30]

---

[28] See, for example, Terry R. Mendenhall, "Setting New Boundaries," *Secondary Mortgage Markets*, FHLMC, Fall 1987,

pp. 7-10; and Dennis Jacobe, "Federal Agencies Are Taking Over," in *Savings Institutions*, January 1984, pp. S-41 to S-45.

[29] See Michael J. Lea, "Dueling Guarantees," *Secondary Mortgage Markets*, Fall 1986, pp. 22-27.

[30] To put this issue into perspective, it must be recognized that this issue is not confined to the thrift industry. Similar concerns have been raised about the impact of securitization on the future of commercial banks both in their domestic and international markets. Thus, the viability of S&Ls is really part of a broader question about the implications of securitization for traditional depository intermediaries. See, *Recent Trends in Commercial Bank Profitability*, Federal Reserve Bank of New York, 1986, and *Recent Innovations in International Banking*, Bank for International Settlements, April 1986.

The adverse effects on S&L profitability can be seen more clearly by looking at the variety of functions or services provided by S&Ls. Historically, S&Ls have originated mortgage loans; serviced these loans; assumed the credit, interest rate, and prepayment risk of these loans; and provided liquid savings and transactions accounts to depositors. Securitization and deregulation have combined to alter the profitability of many of these activities. Thus, for example, government insurance of pass-through securities has transferred credit risk responsibilities to the government, reducing S&L earnings. Interest rate risk has been transferred to borrowers through adjustable rate loans and to purchasers of mortgage-backed securities. Deposit rate deregulation and the growth of savings alternatives have eroded any local competitive advantage of thrifts in raising funds.

These changes have led some to speculate that the primary function of S&Ls in the future may be to provide mortgage banking activities such as loan origination and servicing. While this may be an extreme view of the impact of securitization on S&Ls, there is no question that the exclusive focus of S&Ls on mortgage lending is diminishing. This reality is reflected in recent legislation expanding thrift powers beyond mortgage lending and reducing the tax incentives for S&Ls in mortgage lending.

At the same time, however, securitization has had positive effects on thrifts. Holding mortgage-backed securities can provide geographic diversification that makes S&L loan portfolios less sensitive to local economic conditions. In addition, holdings of mortgage-backed securities can provide liquidity to thrift investment portfolios as well as serving as an efficient form of collateral for borrowing. Finally, mortgage-backed securities and derivative securities can help S&Ls manage interest rate risk more effectively by providing hedging instruments or by providing sources of funds that allow better matching of asset and liability maturities.

Risks to the financial system

A third policy concern is the impact of housing securitization on the stability of the financial system. One issue is the effect of securitization on thrift institution incentives to take risk. That is, if the returns to mortgage lending are reduced, thrifts may have incentive to undertake more risky investments with adverse effects on the deposit insurance system. If so, regulatory policies may have to be adjusted to allow for greater supervision or to change thrift incentives through risk-based deposit insurance or capital requirements.

A broader question concerns the relationship between interest rate risk and financial stability. In the past, S&Ls held much of the outstanding mortgage debt and absorbed a good deal of the associated interest rate risk. This proved to be disastrous for many thrifts in the volatile interest rate environment of the early 1980s. With a part of the potential interest rate risk of mortgage lending transferred to borrowers and to other lenders, S&Ls may have less risk exposure but the impact of interest rate volatility on the health of the financial system is unclear. A particular concern to policymakers is investors' understanding of the behavior of the more exotic derivative mortgage securities in an adverse interest rate environment.[31]

A final aspect of risk related to mortgage securities is counterparty risk or fraud. There have been well-publicized instances in recent years in government securities markets where collateral turned out to be inadequate or nonexis-

---

[31] Federal regulators of banks and thrifts have recently questioned the appropriateness of investments by these institutions in derivative mortgage securities.

tent. In addition to sizable financial loss for individual investors, these events may cause disruptions in the normal functioning of financial markets or the payments system. Since mortgage securities are frequently layered in complex ways, the presence and adequacy of collateral may be difficult to determine in many situations. This problem could be compounded by investors lulled into complacency by the assumption of a government guarantee where none exists.

Summary

The development of mortgage-backed securities has revolutionized housing finance. These securities have allowed the creation of a national secondary market for mortgage loans that has improved the geographic flow of mortgage funds. In addition, these securities have served to improve the linkages between mortgage markets and capital markets and have attracted new investors to mortgage lending.

At the same time, however, the continuing growth and development of the market for mortgage securities has raised important questions about the appropriate role of the government in the securitization process, the viability of traditional housing lenders, and the impact of mortgage securitization on risk and stability in the financial system.

SECTION THREE

The Money Supply

The benefit of the typical textbook treatment of the money supply process is its simplicity. Conceptually simple formulas, analogous to those for the Keynesian income multiplier, use readily grasped ratios (excess reserves to deposits, checkable to time deposits, required reserve ratios, and so on) to account for the size of the money supply. The cost of this approach is that most students lack an appreciation of how variable such "constants" can be. The readings in this section document that variability over the past few years, investigate some possible causes for it, and illustrate why that variability affects the relation between the money supply and the economy. The surprising, continuing prevalence of currency transactions is then probed. Historically, currency drains during financial panics have led to dramatic changes in the money supply. Finally, the nature of bank runs, and the role of deposit insurance in preventing them, is detailed.

Howard L. Roth opens this section by asking "Has Deregulation Ruined M1 as a Policy Guide?" Depository institutions are now free to set the interest rates they pay on all accounts except for demand deposits. Contrary to initial expectations, these rates do not follow short-term market interest rates quickly or closely. Coupled with the as-yet-unknown response of the public to shifting interest rate spreads across various types of accounts, this sluggishness has led to unpredictable movements of the various measures of the money supply. Theory and evidence to date suggest that this sluggish adjustment is likely to persist, as are unforecastable shifts in the public's desire to hold funds in various accounts. Together, these factors probably preclude using M1 as an effective policy guide for some time to come.

In "M1A-M.I.A.?" William T. Gavin and Michael R. Pakko investigate whether a narrower measure of the money supply bears a more consistent relation to GNP than does the M1 measure. The Fed may have more success in achieving its goals for economic growth and price stability by targeting M1A, which consists solely of currency, travelers checks, and demand deposits, rather than M1, which also includes interest-bearing checking accounts. To the extent that M1A contains only transaction balances and that M1 is composed of an ever-shifting mixture of transaction and savings balance, M1A may be more reliably related to economic activity. Arguing against relying on M1A is the more recent empirical evidence: M1A now seems plagued by much the same unpredictability in relation to the economy that tarnished M1 earlier.

Michael C. Keeley reports on the use of currency, checks, and electronic payments in "A Cashless Society?." During the 1980s the incentive to undertake transactions in cash in order to evade income taxes has been reduced and the increased use of credit cards has likewise reduced the demand for currency. Yet cash transactions remain surprisingly common, accounting for more than a third of all consumer expenditures. Indeed, the advent of automatic teller machines and other factors have apparently made cash more, not less, popular in recent years. Keeley argues that the time savings for households and expense savings for institutions relative to checks and electronic payments are apt to preserve currency's attraction as a means of carrying out transactions. As of 1984, however, only about 1/6 of outstanding currency was held by domestic residents for transaction purposes and ATM users had lower average cash balances. The rapid growth of currency holdings since then may be due more to the increase in other, less admirable activities.

"Bank Runs, Deposit Insurance, and Bank Regulations" by Charles T. Carlstrom describes the nature of bank runs and their relation to deposit insurance. In addition to its major benefit of stemming bank runs and the associated disruption of the financial system, deposit insurance has other benefits and costs. Other benefits of deposit insurance include insulation of uninformed depositors and of otherwise solvent banks during panics. One of the major costs is the lessening of market discipline on banks, leading them to hold excessively risky portfolios. This subjects the deposit insurance fund, and ultimately taxpayers, to uncompensated burdens. The government can compensate for the lack of market discipline with additional regulatory discipline, like restrictions on portfolios and imposition of minimum capital requirements. It can also seek to reintroduce some market discipline by charging risk-based deposit insurance premiums.

Article Twenty

Has Deregulation Ruined M1 As a Policy Guide?

By Howard L. Roth

The apparent breakdown in the relationship between M1 and the economy that began in late 1981 triggered a heated debate. Although most economists agreed that the breakdown had been brought on by the nationwide introduction of NOW accounts, they were divided on the implications of the breakdown for the use of M1 as a policy guide. Some argued that the breakdown would only be temporary, that M1 would again be stably related to the economy once deregulation of deposit rates was complete. Others doubted this prognosis, believing that the deregulated M1 would remain so sensitive to developments other than the course of the economy that it would no longer be useful as a policy guide.

The behavior of M1 since 1981 has supported the pessimists' view. Although the deregulation of M1 has been completed, a reliable relationship between M1 and the economy has not reappeared. Uncertain about M1's relationship to the economy, the Federal Reserve decided not to establish a target range for M1 in 1987. Meanwhile, intense efforts are being made to understand the behavior of M1.

Some of these efforts to understand M1 have focused on the rates paid on M1 deposits. These rates have not behaved as was generally expected. The conventional wisdom a few years ago was that deregulated deposit rates would move in step with short-term market interest rates. As a result, it was thought that M1's appeal would be little affected by changes in market rates because spreads between the rates on the interest-paying deposits in M1 and the rates on other financial assets would remain relatively constant. Thus, it could be argued that deregulation would make M1 a better policy guide. Demand for M1 would vary less with market rates and would reflect to a greater extent developments in the goal variables of monetary policy—income and prices.

Contrary to what was expected, deregulated deposit rates have not moved in step with short-term market rates. Even though deregulation of rates on other checkable deposits (OCD's) was completed in January 1986, rates paid on OCD's

Howard Roth is an economist at the Federal Reserve Bank of Kansas City. Michael J. Grace, a research associate at the Bank, assisted in the preparation of the article.

did not decline as much as the higher rates paid on market instruments in 1986, causing spreads between OCD rates and short-term market rates to narrow.

Unexpectedly rapid growth of M1 during that time did not reflect the true state of the economy and raised the question of whether M1 might have become sensitive to changing portfolio preferences. If M1 did become sensitive to changing portfolio preferences, the sluggish adjustment of deregulated deposit rates was likely instrumental.

The likelihood that M1 might again become a useful policy guide would be increased if rates on deregulated deposits were to begin adjusting more rapidly. This article looks for evidence that deregulated rates are becoming more responsive to market rates. Finding none, it concludes that M1 will continue to be subject to changing portfolio preferences, particularly when market rates are trending in one direction or the other and that, as a result, conditions are not favorable for a quick return of M1 as a policy guide.

The remainder of the article is structured as follows. The first section argues that sluggish deposit rate behavior could impair M1's usefulness as a policy guide. The second section points out that in theory the sluggish behavior of OCD rates could continue. The third section shows that if Super NOW rates are indicative, sluggish adjustment of OCD rates is likely to continue.

Deregulated M1— not what was expected

An essential property of a policy guide is that it be closely related to the economic variables in which the goals of policy are specified. M1 has had this property in the past, but it appears to have lost this property in recent years. The deregulation of deposit rate ceilings and the subsequent behavior of deregulated deposit rates have likely contributed to the deterioration of M1's performance as a policy guide.

How deposit rate deregulation could impair M1 as a policy guide

To be useful as a policy guide, M1 must be closely related to income and the general level of prices in the economy. Without such a close relationship, the Federal Reserve cannot determine the level of growth in M1 that is consistent with sustainable, noninflationary economic growth.

Except for a few well-documented instances, M1 growth before the deregulation of deposit rates mainly reflected economic growth and inflation. This behavior was consistent with a transactions motive for holding M1—the holding of M1 balances in anticipation of spending. Growth of M1 was also influenced by short-term market interest rates, which affect the opportunity cost of holding transactions balances. But except for short-term market rates, growth of M1 depended primarily on economic growth and inflation. As a result, M1 was a good policy guide.

But M1 might not reflect economic growth and inflation so closely with the deregulation of rates on M1 deposits. Inflows of savings balances resulting from deregulation of deposit rates could weaken M1's relationship with the goal variables of policy because savings balances likely have different characteristics than transactions balances. For example, savings balances are likely to reflect decisions on how wealth is allocated among alternative financial and real assets—decisions that would not be heavily influenced by developments in income and prices. Rather, interest rate spreads between financial assets, and possibly between financial and real assets, are important considerations in allocating wealth as are inflation expectations and the relative riskiness of the assets in which wealth can be held. Therefore, if M1 became attractive as a repository for savings balances, it could be influenced more by changes in wealth, by interest rate spreads between OCD's and other financial assets, and by spreads between

OCD rates and returns on real assets—none of which are closely related to income and the general price level. In assessing a change in M1 over a period of time, policymakers are interested in determining how much of the change is due to changes in income and prices. Accurately estimating and subtracting out any changes in M1 due to changing portfolio preferences would make such a determination much more difficult.

Sluggish adjustment of rates on M1 deposits increases the likelihood that changes in portfolio preferences would affect M1 when short-term market rates trend upward or downward. The reason is simple. If other short-term rates change and the rate on OCD's does not keep pace, spreads between OCD rates and the other rates would change. Because M1's appeal as a savings vehicle depends on these spreads, demand for M1 as a savings vehicle would change when short-term rates change.

If instead, rates on OCD's followed market rates closely, M1's appeal as a savings vehicle would vary less with changes in market rates. M1 could still be appealing as a savings vehicle. But changes in market rates would have little effect on rate spreads involving OCD's and thus would have little effect on M1's appeal as a savings vehicle.

Rate spreads that change with market rates are problematic because much less is known about how the demand for M1 as a savings vehicle responds to changes in interest rate spreads than how the demand for M1 as a transactions medium responds. For example, it could be that M1 is appealing as a savings instrument only when the relevant interest rate spreads are less than some critical value. Demand for M1 as a transactions medium, on the other hand, is generally believed to vary continuously with interest rate spreads, at least for individuals. Moreover, the interest sensitivity of the demand for M1 as a transactions medium has been estimated in numerous empirical studies.

The problem is uncertainty about how M1's appeal as a savings vehicle varies with short-term market rates, not uncertainty about the sluggish adjustment of OCD rates. The adjustment of OCD rates could be perfectly understood and perfectly predictable, and uncertainty about how the demand for M1 as a savings vehicle responds to changes in rate spreads would remain if OCD rates responded sluggishly to changes in market rates.

Sluggish adjustment of rates on OCD's could pose problems in two other ways even if the demand for M1 were purely a transactions demand. First, slow adjustment of OCD rates can increase the sensitivity of M1 to changes in short-term market interest rates. Interest sensitivity increases when the OCD rate responds so sluggishly to changes in other short-term rates that spreads involving the OCD rate change proportionally more than the other short-term rates. When this happens, the effect of a change in short-term rates on demand for M1 is magnified, whether the demand for M1 is as a transactions medium, or as a savings vehicle.

An increase in the sensitivity of M1 to changes in short-term market interest rates increases the importance of being able to predict movements in short-term market rates in setting targets for M1. An unexpected change in short-term market rates could cause M1 to depart significantly from its targeted value. Unfortunately, interest rates have proven very difficult to forecast.

The second problem arises when there is uncertainty about the adjustment process. The problem is that the rate on OCD's has to be predicted in setting targets for M1. If the rate on OCD's closely followed other short-term rates, demand for M1 would likely be quite insensitive to changes in short-term rates, including the OCD rate, because the spreads between the OCD rate and other short-term rates would remain relatively unchanged when short-term rates changed. Predicting short-term market rates, including the

OCD rate, would be relatively unimportant in predicting M1. But when the OCD rate responds sluggishly to changes in other short-term rates, as it has since the beginning of deposit rate deregulation, changes in spreads can have an important effect on M1. In this case, accurately predicting short-term market rates, including the OCD rate, is important, and uncertainty regarding the precise nature of the sluggish adjustment of the OCD rate becomes a problem. The results of the empirical study of Super NOW rates in the last section of this article suggest that the adjustment of the OCD rate is a source of uncertainty.

Thus, there are a number of ways in which the deregulation of deposit rates might impair M1's usefulness as a policy guide. Although sluggish adjustment of the OCD rate to changes in other short-term rates can create a number of problems, the remainder of the article focuses on the problems posed by variability in the amount of savings balances held in OCD's that results when rates on OCD's adjust sluggishly. Thus, it is assumed for simplicity that changes in wealth, inflation expectations, and the returns on real assets have no effects on the demand for M1 as savings vehicle. That is, the demand for M1 as a savings vehicle depends only on rate spreads between OCD's and other short-term financial assets that are substitute repositories for savings balances.

The experience in 1985 and 1986

For a number of reasons, it appears that inflows of savings balances contributed to M1's growth in 1985 and 1986. First, growth of M1 was very strong relative to economic growth. While M1 grew 12.2 percent in 1985 and 15.6 percent in 1986, nominal GNP grew only 6.3 percent in 1985 and 4.2 percent in 1986. Chart 1 shows M1 velocity—nominal GNP divided by M1—on a quarterly basis since 1970. From 1970 to 1981, M1 velocity grew at an average annual rate of 3.7 percent, with growth ranging from 1.5 percent in 1979 to 6.1 percent in 1978. In sharp contrast, M1 velocity fell almost 6 percent in 1985 and more than 9.5 percent in 1986. This deviation of M1 velocity from its behavior in the 1970s was the latest manifestation of the apparent breakdown in the relationship between M1 and the economy in late 1981. From 1982 to 1986, the velocity of M1 fell at an annual average rate of 3.4 percent.

Experience suggests that the declines in short-term market rates during the past two years contributed to the decline of M1's velocity. Three-month Treasury bill rates fell from about 8.2 percent in the first quarter of 1985 to 5.3 percent in the fourth quarter of 1986 (Chart 1). But, previously reliable empirical models of money demand underpredict M1 growth even when simulated with actual levels of short-term interest rates, prices, and income over the two-year period. If declining short-term market rates are the answer, demand for M1 must have become more interest sensitive in recent years.

A second reason for suspecting that inflows of savings balances contributed to M1's growth the past two years is that the growth was strongest in OCD's, the component of M1 that is most attractive as a repository for savings balances. These accounts are liquid; that is, they can be exchanged quickly for other assets with no loss in value. Protected by deposit insurance, OCD's are virtually free of default risk. And of course, OCD's earn interest. As shown in Table 1, OCD's grew 22 percent in 1985 and nearly 29 percent in 1986, more than twice as fast as demand deposits and currency.

A third reason for suspecting that savings flowed into M1 is that rates on some savings alternatives fell relative to the rates on OCD's in 1985 and 1986, and growth of these alternatives slowed as growth of OCD's quickened. For example, as shown in Chart 2, the rate spread between small time deposits and OCD's fell from about 3.2

CHART 1
M1 velocity and the Treasury bill rate

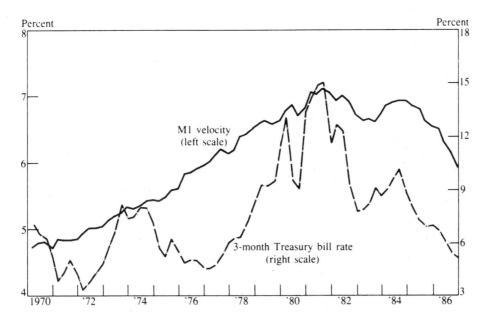

percentage points in the first quarter of 1985 to about 1.0 percentage point in the fourth quarter of 1986. As a result, NOW accounts became more attractive as a repository for savings balances transferred from maturing small time deposits. And, as can be seen in Chart 2, growth of small time deposits slowed sharply while growth of OCD's picked up.

The rate spread between small time deposits and OCD's narrowed over the two-year period because rates on small time deposits matched declines in short-term market rates more closely than OCD rates did. As shown in Chart 3, rates on OCD's have displayed considerable inertia when short-term market rates, as represented by the federal funds rate, have changed.

TABLE 1
Growth of M1 and its components—1985 and 1986
(percent)

	Currency plus Travelers Checks	Demand Deposits	Other checkable Deposits	M1
1985:Q4/1984:Q4	7.8	8.9	22.2	12.1
1986:Q4/1985:Q4	7.5	11.6	28.6	15.2

CHART 2
Growth of small time deposits and OCD's
(percent change from a year earlier)

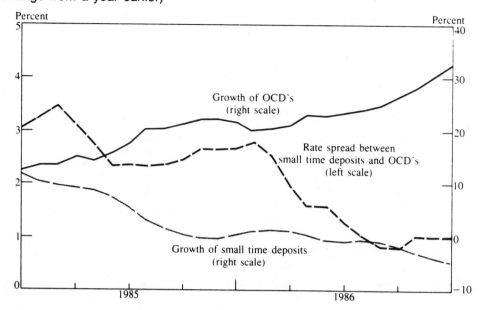

CHART 3
Sluggish adjustment of OCD rates

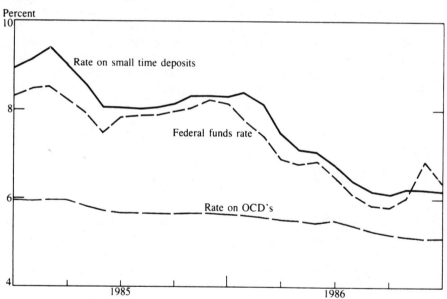

The sluggish response of OCD rates to changes in short-term market rates came as a surprise. The conventional wisdom in the early 1980s was that rates on deregulated deposits would closely follow short-term market rates. As a result, demand for M1 was expected to become insensitive to changes in short-term market rates. Yet, OCD rates have not followed short-term market rates closely. And this failure to follow other short-term rates closely could explain why recent empirical work and the behavior of M1 in the past two years indicate that demand for M1 has become more sensitive to changes in short-term market rates, not less sensitive.[1]

One important question is, Why have rates on OCD's exhibited so much inertia? Another important question is, Will this behavior be a lasting phenomenon?

Why rates on OCD's adjust sluggishly

Past regulation explains much of the sluggishness in OCD rates since deregulation of M1 began in 1981. Before January 1, 1986, rates on NOW accounts were subject to a ceiling of 5.25 percent. Many banks and thrifts had paid this rate since the nationwide authorization of NOW's in late 1980. Much of the sluggishness in NOW rates in 1986 may thus have been due to reluctance by banks and thrifts to lower rates on NOW's below the old regulatory ceiling. By the second half of the year, short-term market interest rates had declined to levels that made NOW rates higher than 5.25 percent artificially high. But banks and thrifts were concerned that pushing the rate below the old ceiling might antagonize customers accustomed to earning 5.25 percent on their NOW balances. Ironically, what had been a regulatory ceiling rate became a floor when NOW's were deregulated.

But regulation does not totally explain the phenomenon. Super NOW's were not subject to a ceiling since their introduction in January 1983, although they were subject to minimum balance requirements until January 1986. Yet their rates also displayed considerable inertia during this period. And rates on NOW's responded sluggishly to changes in short-term market rates after their ceiling was lifted in January 1986, even before their old ceiling began to have an effect. Thus, something in addition to banks and thrifts' concern about maintaining long-term customer relationships must give rise to the phenomenon.

A number of explanations have been offered. One possibility is that large banks and thrifts might be able to lower total funding costs by slowly adjusting OCD rates. Most large institutions have a relatively smaller presence in the national money markets than in the local OCD market.[2] Such an institution might be able to satisfy additional funding needs by buying funds in the money market at the rates prevailing there but would have to raise the rate it offers on existing OCD's if it tries to raise funds by attracting more OCD's. Under these conditions, changing the rate offered on OCD's to reflect fully changes

[1] See, for example, Richard D. Porter, Paul A. Spindt, and David E. Lindsey, "Econometric Modeling of the Demands for the U.S. Aggregates: Conventional and Experimental Approaches," Board of Governors of the Federal Reserve System (mimeo), November 1986, or Michael C. Keeley and Gary C. Zimmerman, "Deposit Rate Deregulation and the Demand for Transactions Media," *Economic Review*, Federal Reserve Bank of San Francisco, Summer 1986, pp. 47-62. For an alternative view, see Robert H. Rasche, "M1-Velocity and Money Demand Functions: Do Stable Relationships Exist?" *Carnegie-Rochester Conference Series*, forthcoming.

[2] Evidence of local and statewide Super NOW markets in the Twelfth Federal Reserve District was found by Michael C. Keeley and Gary C. Zimmerman in "Determining Geographic Markets for Deposit Competition in Banking," *Economic Review*, Federal Reserve Bank of San Francisco, Summer 1985, pp. 25-45.

in short-term market rates might result in higher funding costs. A second possible explanation also involves bank funding behavior. In this explanation, banks and thrifts respond to changes in loan demand by adjusting the rates they offer on managed liabilities and deposits with fixed terms—small time deposits, large CD's, term repurchase agreements—rather than the rates on nonterm deposits like OCD's. When loan demand weakens and banks' funding needs fall, banks lower their rates on deposits with fixed terms. At these times, the spread between term deposits and OCD's narrows, making OCD's relatively more attractive.[3] A third possible explanation is that depository institutions are taking a cautious approach to pricing OCD's as they try to learn how sensitive the public's demand for OCD's is to the rate offered on the accounts.

The first two proposed explanations suggest that the sluggishness of OCD rates will be a continuing phenomenon. But experience with deregulated deposits is too limited to determine which of these explanations best accounts for the sluggishness.

Even though the underlying cause of the sluggish adjustment of OCD rates has not been identified, it should be possible to measure the extent of the sluggishness. A number of researchers have done this.[4] Generally, they have found that Super NOW rates match only about 10 to 15 percent of a change in short-term market rates in one

month. The extent of longer run adjustment varies across the studies and depends on the specification used in modeling the relationship between OCD rates and short-term market rates. But in some studies, complete adjustment takes as long as a year.

Although little is known about why rates on deregulated deposits adjust slowly to changes in short-term market rates, the staff of the Federal Reserve Board has shown that taking account of the sluggish adjustment of rates is beneficial in trying to account for the strong growth of M1 in 1985 and 1986.[5] When this behavior is explicitly modeled in the Board's quarterly econometric model, the interest sensitivity of M1 is considerably higher—approximately twice as high when market rates are 5 percent. Increased interest responsiveness of demand for OCD's is attributable for most of the increased interest sensitivity. The interest rate sensitivity of this component averages four times higher in absolute value in the respecified model. The increased interest rate sensitivity allows the respecified model to explain the growth of M1 in 1985 and 1986 more closely than most models that do not explicitly allow for sluggish adjustment of OCD rates.

Although rates on deregulated deposits in M1 were sluggish in adjusting to declining short-term market rates last year, this does not necessarily imply that rates on deregulated deposits did not adjust more rapidly to changes in market rates in 1986 than in, say, 1983. And it does not preclude more rapid adjustment of deregulated rates in coming years. If rates on deregulated deposits are moving toward more rapid adjustment, the likelihood of M1 again becoming a useful policy guide is greater.

---

[3] This rate spread behavior is an implication of an explanation for the rapid growth of M1 in 1985 and early 1986 proposed by Bharat Trehan and Carl E. Walsh in "Portfolio Substitution and Recent M1 Behavior," *Contemporary Policy Issues*, January 1987, pp. 54-63.

[4] See Paul F. O'Brien, "Deregulated Deposit Rate Behavior," Federal Reserve Board, processed, April 1986; George Moore, Richard Porter, and David Small, "Forecasting Retail Deposit Rates in the Long Run and the Short Run," Board of Governors of the Federal Reserve System (mimeo), July 1986; and John Wenninger, "Responsiveness of Interest Rate Spreads and Deposit Flows to Changes in Market Rates," *Quarterly Review*, Federal Reserve Bank of New York, Autumn 1986, pp. 1-10.

---

[5] See Richard D. Porter, Paul A. Spindt, and David E. Lindsey, "Econometric Modeling . . . ."

Slow adjustment of OCD rates— merely transitional?

The limited experience with deregulated deposits makes it difficult to predict whether the sluggish adjustment of OCD rates will be merely a transitional phenomenon that will abate over time. The account that would be the most likely to shed light on whether OCD rates will become less sluggish is the Super NOW account, which has not been subject to ceiling rates since its introduction.

The experience with Super NOW's

An immediate problem in studying the behavior of deregulated rates is a scarcity of data. OCD's became an appreciable part of M1 only with the nationwide introduction of NOW accounts in 1981. These accounts, eventually referred to as regular NOW's to distinguish them from the Super NOW account introduced later, were subject to a regulatory ceiling until January 1986. The rate most banks and thrifts paid on these accounts varied little from the regulatory ceiling of 5.25 percent over the five-year period. Thus, rates on regular NOW's have little to say about how ceiling-free deposit rates might behave.

The behavior of rates on Super NOW's, however, should be more representative of deregulated deposit rates. Super NOW's have never been subject to a rate ceiling. Experience with these accounts is limited, though, as Super NOW accounts were not introduced until January 1983. A change in the relationship between Super NOW rates and short-term market rates would not show up in quarterly or even monthly data on Super NOW rates unless the change was quite dramatic.

The *Bank Rate Monitor,* however, has been collecting weekly data on Super NOW rates since their introduction. With more than 200 weekly observations, a change in the relationship of these rates to short-term market rates should be more apparent.

When the Super NOW rate is viewed alongside short-term market interest rates, inertia in the Super NOW rate is evident. Chart 4 shows the Super NOW rate and the federal funds rate from 1983 through 1986. Three episodes of sluggish adjustment of the Super NOW rate stand out. Between January and August of 1984, the federal funds rate rose over 200 basis points, while the Super NOW rate rose only about 20 basis points. Between August 1984 and June 1985, the federal funds rate fell about 400 basis points, while the Super NOW rate eased less than 150 basis points. More recently, between December 1985 and October 1986, the federal funds rate fell about 230 basis points, while the Super NOW rate declined only about 80 basis points.

There is little indication in Chart 4 that Super NOW rates have become more responsive to changes in the federal funds rate. A gradual change might not be apparent, however. A test of this hypothesis requires the specification and statistical testing of a general model relating Super NOW rates to the federal funds rate.

A model relating changes in the Super NOW rate to changes in the federal funds rate is described in detail in the appendix. The model allows the Super NOW rate to adjust gradually to changes in the federal funds rate, with one rate of adjustment when the Super NOW rate is adjusting upward and another when it is adjusting downward. There are some indications that banks and thrifts adjust deposit rates more quickly when market rates fall to keep interest rate spreads from becoming too small or even negative, and the model allows for an asymmetrical response. The model also imposes complete long-run adjustment on the Super NOW rate so that the marginal cost to the bank or thrift of an additional dollar of Super NOW's is the same in the long run as the marginal cost of borrowing an additional dollar of federal funds.

CHART 4
Federal funds rate and the yield on Super NOW accounts

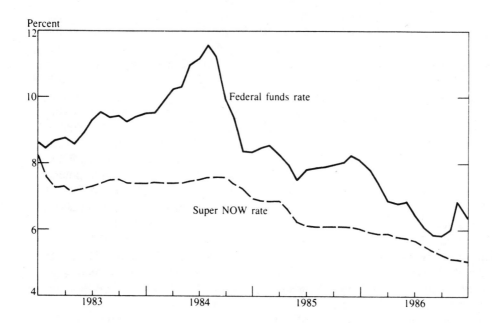

To test whether the relationship between the Super NOW rate and the federal funds rate has changed over the last four years, the model was estimated over three periods: July 6, 1983 to December 26, 1984; January 2, 1985 to December 31, 1985; and January 8, 1986 to February 4, 1987. Data from the first half of 1983 were excluded as Super NOW's were being promoted then with rates that were high relative to prevailing market rates. The breakpoint between the first and second periods is somewhat arbitrary, although it coincides with a reduction in the minimum balance requirement on Super NOW's. The breakpoint between the second and third periods marks the elimination of minimum balance requirements on Super NOW's and the lifting of the ceiling rate on regular NOW's.

Statistical tests of the model reveal no significant change in the relationship between the Super

NOW rate and the federal funds rate in the first and second periods but a significant change in the third period.[6] The model is so complex, however, that it cannot be determined directly from the regression results whether the Super NOW rate adjusted more or less quickly in the third period. Simulating the estimated models establishes which was the case.

The model as estimated for each of the three periods was simulated for a once-and-for-all change in the federal funds from 6 percent to 5 percent. Estimated with data from the earliest period, the model of Super NOW rates adjusts completely in one year. The adjustment is about the same when the model is estimated with data

---

[6] The results of the statistical tests are given in the appendix.

from the second period, about 96 percent complete at the end of a year. But in the most recent period, the adjustment is only 64 percent complete at the end of a year. Thus, the adjustment of Super NOW rates was considerably slower in 1986 and early 1987 than in the two earlier periods.

A ceiling becomes a floor

Super NOW rates thus are apparently becoming less responsive to changes in short-term market rates. But this reduced responsiveness may not represent a trend but rather a special situation. As discussed earlier, banks and thrifts were reluctant to lower their NOW rates below the old regulatory ceiling of 5.25 percent in the second half of 1986 for fear of losing long-time customers. Another reason banks and thrifts were reluctant to lower rates on NOW accounts was fear that customers who previously held NOW accounts subject to the ceiling would come to expect the rate on their accounts to move above 5.25 percent when market rates warranted. The reluctance of banks and thrifts to lower rates below the old ceiling may thus account for some of the increased sluggishness in the Super NOW rate in the most recent period.

To test this hypothesis, the model was estimated over the entire sample period from July 6, 1983 to February 4, 1987 with an allowance for the possibility that banks and thrifts were reluctant to lower Super NOW rates below 5.25 percent. The results of the estimation support the hypothesis.[7] Thus, the slowdown in the adjustment of Super NOW rates in the most recent period results to some extent from a special circumstance. Be that as it may, however, the statistical tests show

no signs of a transition to more rapid adjustment of Super NOW rates.

Conclusions

The finding that Super NOW rates are not becoming more responsive to changes in short-term market rates casts doubt on a quick return of M1 as a useful policy guide. Sluggish adjustment of rates on OCD's is likely to continue to create problems in using M1 as a policy guide.

This article has focused on one problem stemming from the sluggish adjustment of OCD rates. Because OCD rates adjust sluggishly, changes in short-term market rates affect rate spreads between OCD's and other financial assets and, as a result, increase the likelihood of M1 being affected by portfolio choices. Unfortunately, little is known about how the demand for M1 as a savings vehicle responds to changes in rate spreads. And, of course, changes in M1 resulting from changes in portfolio preferences shed little or no light on economic growth or inflation.

Strictly speaking, M1 has not necessarily become less closely related to income and prices. Rather, the relationship appears to have changed, and the new relationship is not well understood. Under these circumstances, determining the level of M1 growth that is consistent with attaining the goals of policy is difficult, particularly when the trend of short-term market rates changes unpredictably. This point can be restated in terms of velocity. Velocity growth does not have to be constant for M1 to be a useful policy guide. What is necessary is that velocity be predictable.

If rates on deregulated deposits had followed market rates more closely, changes in the relationship between M1 and the goal variables would likely have been more predictable. Spreads between OCD's and other financial assets would have been less affected by changes in short-term market rates. Therefore, M1's appeal as a repository for savings balances would likely have been

---

[7] See the appendix.

less affected. The relationship between M1 and the economy would have been less affected by changes in portfolio preferences.

Although the empirical results reported in this article suggest that M1 is not likely to return soon as a useful policy guide, two developments could speed M1's recovery. First, to the extent that flows of savings balances into OCD's in the past two years have been a one-time phenomenon, the relationship between M1 and the goal variables of policy could be more stable in the future. More specifically, the relationship will be more stable if the volume of savings balances in OCD's is not sensitive to future changes in rate spreads. If this is the case, changes in M1 will primarily reflect changes in spending intentions.

A second development that might speed M1's recovery as a policy guide would be continued progress toward price stability. Changes in rate spreads and, in turn, changes in portfolio preferences will be less likely if improved price stability can be maintained. Falling inflation expectations

appear to have been a significant factor behind declining interest rates and rapid M1 growth in recent years. Changing rate spreads complicate the relationship between M1 and the goal variable of policy primarily when short-term interest rates are trending in one direction or the other. One of the policy victories of the 1980s has been a dramatic reduction in the rate of inflation. Consolidating the gains made against inflation would promote more stable inflation expectations and, in turn, more stable interest rates.

Has deregulation ruined M1 as a policy guide? It is too early to conclude that M1 has been permanently ruined. But M1's usefulness as a guide clearly has been damaged. And there is little reason now to believe that the flows of savings balances into M1 were a one-time phenomenon or that inflation expectations will have less effect on interest rates in the future. A reasonable assumption for now is that M1 will continue to be less closely related to economic growth and inflation, at least for a while.

Appendix

This appendix describes the model of Super NOW rate behavior used in the study, lists the estimated values for the parameter in the model, and documents the results of statistical tests conducted with the model.

Model of Super NOW rate behavior

For statistical reasons, the behavior of Super NOW rates was not modeled in this study as following market rates according to a partial adjustment mechanism. Rather, an error-correction model was used to relate Super NOW rates to a representative short-term market rate, the federal funds rate.[1] The model consists of two equations. The first is a long-run equilibrium rela-

tionship between the Super NOW rate and the federal funds rate based on cost minimizing behavior by banks operating in a competitive environment. This relationship, as estimated by researchers at the Federal Reserve Board, is

$$(1) \quad R_t^{SN} = -1.014 + 0.88 \, R_t^{FF} + e_t$$

where R_t^{SN} is the Super NOW rate, R_t^{FF} is the federal funds rate, and e_t is the residual in

---

[1] The approach taken here is the same as that taken by George Moore, Richard Porter, and David Small in "Forecasting Retail Deposit Rates in the Long Run and the Short Run," Federal Reserve Board (mimeo), July 1986. See the references therein on the error-correction model.

period t.[2] This relationship was estimated using data from a monthly survey of deposit rates conducted by the Federal Reserve. The coefficient on the federal funds rate was constrained to equal 1 minus the marginal reserve requirement on Super NOW's, 12 percent, after unconstrained estimation yielded almost identical results.

The second equation specifies short-run dynamic adjustment of Super NOW rates, that is, how Super NOW rates behave when not in equilibrium. This behavior is given by

$$(2) \quad \Delta R_t^{SN} = a \cdot e_{t-1}^P + b \cdot e_{t-1}^N$$

$$+ \sum_{i=0}^{4} c_i \cdot \Delta R_{t-i}^{FF} + \sum_{i=1}^{4} d_i \cdot \Delta R_{t-i}^{SN}$$

$$+ f \cdot D1 \cdot e_{t-1}^P + u_t$$

where $\Delta R_t^{SN} = R_t^{SN} - R_{t-1}^{SN}$; e_t^P is the residual from Equation 1 when that residual is positive—that is, the amount the Super NOW rate exceeds its long-run equilibrium value—and is zero otherwise; e_t^N is the residual from Equation 1 when that residual is negative and is zero otherwise; and D1 is a dummy variable which equals 1 if the long-run equilibrium value of the Super NOW rate is less than 5.25 percent.

When a and b are negative, the first two terms on the right-hand side of Equation 2 force an out-of-equilibrium expected value of the Super NOW rate to return to its long-run equilibrium. Separate terms for positive and negative residuals allow the speed of adjustment of the Super NOW rate to depend on whether it is greater than or less than its long-run equilibrium value. The third and fourth terms allow for a very general reaction of the Super NOW rate to changes in the federal funds rate. The fifth term, incorporating the dummy variable D1, allows the speed of adjustment of the Super NOW rate to slow when the

equilibrium rate is below 5.25 percent and the Super NOW rate exceeds the equilibrium rate.

Table A1 lists estimates of the parameters in Equation 2 when estimated over five periods.

Testing the stability of the relationship

To test whether the relationship changed over the three subperiods—January 6, 1983 to December 26, 1984, January 2, 1985 to December 31, 1985, and January 8, 1986 to February 4, 1987—the error correction model was estimated separately over each of these subperiods (columns 1, 2, and 4 of Table A1) and also over combinations of these subperiods (columns 3 and 5). An F-test conducted with the residuals of the regressions listed in columns 1, 2, and 3 of Table A1 indicate no evidence of statistically significant change in the relationship between the first two periods. But an F-test conducted with the residuals of the regressions listed in columns 3, 4, and 5 strongly rejects the hypothesis of no change in the relationship in period 3. The results of the F-tests are given in Table A2.

Effect of old regulatory ceiling

Simulations conducted with the model as estimated in each of the three subperiods demonstrated that Super NOW rates adjusted considerably slower in the most recent subperiod. To test whether this finding was due to the reluctance of banks and thrifts to lower their rates on Super NOW's below the old 5.25 percent regulatory ceiling on NOW's, a dummy variable accounting for this possibility was incorporated into the model and the model was reestimated over the entire sample period. The results of the regression, column 6 of Table A1, show the dummy variable to be a significant explanatory variable (f is significantly different from 0). If the equilibrium Super NOW rate is below 5.25 percent, the response to positive errors is a+f and is smaller in absolute value than a.

---

[2] See George Moore, Richard Porter, and David Small, "Forecasting Retail Deposit Rates . . . ."

TABLE A1
Short-run dynamic adjustment of the Super NOW rate

Estimated Parameters	Estimation Period					
	July 6, 1983 to Dec. 26, 1984	Jan. 2, 1985 to Dec. 31, 1985	July 6, 1983 to Dec. 31, 1985	Jan. 8, 1986 to Feb. 4, 1987	July 6, 1983 to Feb. 4, 1987	July 6, 1983 to Feb. 4, 1987
a	−0.033	−0.020	−0.024	−0.037	−0.013	−0.031
	(−2.743)	(−1.353)	(−2.876)	(−4.685)	(−2.829)	(−3.721)
b	−0.001	−0.049	−0.001	0.001	−0.001	−0.003
	(−0.371)	(−0.538)	(−0.302)	(0.056)	(−0.294)	(−0.669)
Σc_i	0.044	0.146	0.066	0.002	0.034	0.026
	(1.839)	(2.054)	(2.938)	(0.073)	(1.911)	(1.880)
Σd_i	0.564	0.547	0.518	−0.888	0.539	0.645
	(3.435)	(3.123)	(4.820)	(−2.629)	(5.471)	(3.856)
f						0.021
						(2.579)
Summary Statistics						
R^2	0.52	0.64	0.57	0.44	0.42	0.45
$R^2{}_{adj}$	0.43	0.54	0.53	0.29	0.39	0.41
Standard error (percentage points)	0.021	0.028	0.024	0.026	0.026	0.026

Note: t-statistics in parentheses

TABLE A2
Stability tests

Periods of Comparison	F-statistic	Critical Value	Conclusion
July 6, 1983 to Dec. 26, 1984 and Jan. 2, 1985 to Dec. 31, 1985	1.24	1.88 (5%) 2.43 (1%)	No evidence of change in the relationship
July 6, 1983 to Dec. 31, 1985 and Jan. 8, 1986 to Feb. 4, 1987	6.83	1.85 (5%) 2.37 (1%)	Strong evidence of change in the relationship

Article Twenty-One

M1A — M.I.A.?   by William T. Gavin and Michael R. Pakko

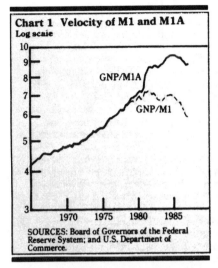

Chart 1   Velocity of M1 and M1A
Log scale

GNP/M1A

GNP/M1

SOURCES: Board of Governors of the Federal Reserve System; and U.S. Department of Commerce.

sensitivity to a variety of economic and financial circumstances ...."[1]

The uncertainty about M1's behavior is often described in terms of a break-down in the growth trend of its *velocity*—the ratio of nominal GNP to M1 (see chart 1). M1 velocity rose at roughly a 3 percent annual rate for most of the post-World War II era, fluc-tuating slightly in response to changes in nominal interest rates. Since 1982, however, the velocity of M1 has shown much greater volatility and has, on average, *declined* at a 3.2 percent annual rate.

In light of M1's weakened status, economists inside and outside the Fed-eral Reserve System have searched for an alternative policy target. One pro-posed solution is for the Federal Reserve to target an aggregate that would exclude interest-bearing check-ing accounts from the present defini-tion of M1 (see table 1). The Federal Reserve reported statistics for this monetary measure from 1980 until 1983, referring to it as M1A.[2]

From 1982 through 1984, the velocity of M1A seemed to follow a growth trend similar to that which had pre-viously characterized M1 velocity, pro-viding support for the idea of an M1A target. During 1985 and 1986, however, M1 and M1A each grew much faster than expected given the rates of inflation and economic growth, resulting in unanticipated velocity declines for both measures. Despite this departure, sup-port for greater reliance on M1A in the conduct of monetary policy has per-sisted.[3] In this *Economic Commentary*, we examine the behavior of M1 and M1A in the 1980s and discuss some

Table 1   The Composition of M1 and M1A

	Levels in Dec. 1986*
Currency and Traveler's Checks	$189.9
+ Demand Deposits	308.3
= M1A	498.2
+ Other Checkable Deposits	232.3
= M1	730.5

*Billions of dollars, seasonally adjusted.
SOURCE: Board of Governors of the Federal Reserve System.

issues relevant to the possibility of replacing M1 with M1A.

Most analysts who question the use of M1 as a policy target have focused on the contamination of M1 by savings-related balances in interest-bearing checking accounts. However, we sug-gest that the characteristics of demand deposits have also been altered by deregulation; specifically, that demand deposits are now dominated by com-mercial accounts. All else being equal, this change would tend to raise the growth rate of M1A velocity above that of pre-deregulation M1.

The similarity of M1A velocity growth in the 1980s to pre-1980 M1 velocity growth may, therefore, reflect a coinci-dence of offsetting influences. Thus,

For many years, monetary policy has been implemented largely through the pursuit of monetary aggregate targets. The Federal Open Market Committee (FOMC), the policymaking arm of the Federal Reserve System, sets target ranges for the growth of various mone-tary aggregates, which are intended to be consistent with the broader objec-tives of policy.

While the Federal Reserve has main-tained the need for multiple monetary targets, business and research econo-mists have considered the M1 aggregate to be the most important of these var-ious monetary targets. The Federal Reserve did not set a target range for M1 in 1987, however, citing "uncertain-ties about its underlying relationship to the behavior of the economy and its

William T. Gavin is an economic advisor at the Federal Reserve Bank of Cleveland, currently on leave of absence at the U.S. Department of State. Michael R. Pakko is an economic analyst at the Federal Reserve Bank of Cleveland.

1. See "Monetary Policy Report to Congress," *Federal Reserve Bulletin*, vol. 73, no. 4 (April 1987), pp. 239-254.

2. See Thomas D. Simpson, "The Redefined Monetary Aggregates," *Federal Reserve Bulletin*, vol. 66, no. 2 (February 1980), pp. 97-114.

3. See John Paulus, "Monetarism: If It Ain't Broke, Don't Fix It," *Economic Perspectives*, Mor-gan Stanley, May 7, 1986, pp. 1-9; and more recently, Michael R. Darby, Angelo R. Mascaro, and Michael L. Marlow, "The Empirical Reliabil-ity of Monetary Aggregates as Indicators: 1983-1986," Research Paper No. 8701, U.S. Depart-ment of the Treasury, 1987.

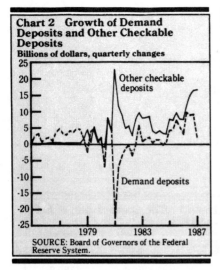

Chart 2 Growth of Demand Deposits and Other Checkable Deposits
Billions of dollars, quarterly changes

SOURCE: Board of Governors of the Federal Reserve System.

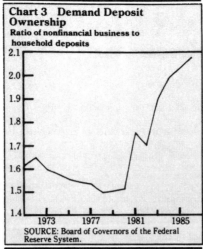

Chart 3 Demand Deposit Ownership
Ratio of nonfinancial business to household deposits

SOURCE: Board of Governors of the Federal Reserve System.

the source of the declines in M1A velocity in 1985 and 1986 is likely to be the same as for the earlier breakdown in M1's velocity: a fundamental realignment of the relationship between transactions deposits and nominal GNP in the new disinflationary environment.

M1 vs. M1A

M1 was previously considered the most important of the monetary targets for a variety of reasons. For many analysts, M1 was preferable on theoretical grounds, as the Federal Reserve's attempt to construct a comprehensive measure of assets that were held primarily for transactions. To others, M1 seemed to be the most controllable of the targeted aggregates. Finally, many economists preferred M1 because it seemed to be most predictably related to economic activity.

Since the deregulation of deposit rates in the early 1980s, it is increasingly difficult to argue that M1 represents a theoretically pure measure of transactions balances. It appears likely that at least a portion of the funds in new interest-bearing transactions accounts represent savings. Furthermore, many money market funds and accounts allow limited check-drafting privileges, making it probable that some transactions-related funds are in these non-M1 instruments.

Proponents of M1A as a policy target

have not generally claimed that M1A provides a comprehensive measure of transactions money, but that it is preferable to M1 because it excludes accounts contaminated by savings balances. Furthermore, because M1A is a subset of the relatively controllable M1, it might also be more controllable than either the broader aggregates or proposed weighted-average aggregates.

The most important rationale for an M1A target, though, is that its relationship to economic activity seems to have changed less than that of M1. However, recent declines in M1A velocity indicate that M1A is not as immune to velocity instability as the 1982 to 1984 experience suggested. If we are to consider M1A as a policy guidepost, it is important that we understand what has happened to the growth patterns of transactions deposits—interest-bearing and non-interest-bearing—in this era of deregulation and disinflation.

Deposit Rate Deregulation

The proposal to replace M1 with M1A may be appropriate if the deregulation of deposit-rate ceilings underlies the breakdown in M1 velocity. One of the important, and easily distinguishable, effects of deregulation has involved the flow of funds into newly authorized types of accounts. In fact, this type of distortion was behind the FOMC's 1982 decision to de-emphasize the M1 target temporarily.[4]

The element of deposit deregulation most relevant to M1 was the introduction of negotiable orders of withdrawal (NOW) accounts and automatic transfer services (ATS) accounts. These interest-bearing checking accounts—referred to as other checkable deposits or OCDs—were introduced on an experimental basis in Massachusetts and New Hampshire in 1974. OCDs spread to the rest of New England in 1976, to New York in 1978, and to New Jersey in 1979. They became available nationwide in 1981. While the behavior of M1 was measurably affected by early, limited introduction of NOW accounts, the effect on M1 velocity was not outside the range of uncertainty normally associated with velocity forecasts.

The nationwide authorization of NOW accounts at the end of 1980, however, triggered large transfers of funds into the new accounts. Although evidence suggests that a complex pattern of flows among various account types took place, chart 2 illustrates that the net effect was a large transfer of funds from demand deposits to OCDs.[5] This phenomenon is reflected in the velocity measures shown in chart 1 primarily as a sharp upward shift in the level of M1A velocity.

The introduction of Super-NOW accounts in 1983 and the elimination of rate ceilings and minimum balance requirements in 1986 did not seem to cause the same type of initial net deposit flows observed for the nationwide introduction of NOW accounts. One important reason may be simply that the ceilings had become nonbinding before they were eliminated. That is, rates were already below the maximum, so the elimination of that constraint did not result in deposit rate increases that would have attracted new funds.

Regardless of their initial effects, the new regulations have affected how people manage their savings and transactions balances. OCD growth has proved to be higher and more variable than demand deposit growth, past or present, given rates of economic growth and inflation.

Because the major difference in the two types of transactions accounts is the explicit interest rates paid on OCDs, it is often concluded that OCDs are unlike demand deposits because they have characteristics of savings accounts. To the extent this is true, an M1A aggregate might, in fact, represent a truer measure of the transactions role of money than M1.

4. See "Remarks on Monetary Policy" by Paul A. Volcker in the *Federal Reserve Bulletin*, vol. 68, no. 11 (November 1982), pp. 691-692.

5. For a detailed analysis of the flows among alternative accounts, see Thomas D. Simpson and John R. Williams, "Recent Revisions in the Money Stock," *Federal Reserve Bulletin*, vol. 67,

no. 7 (July 1981), pp. 539-544. An alternative view can be found in John A. Tatom, "Recent Financial Innovations: Have They Distorted the Meaning of M1?" *Review*, Federal Reserve Bank of St. Louis, vol. 64, no. 4 (April 1982), pp. 23-32.

Inflation

M1A may not resolve the problem with the monetary targeting process, however, if the drop in M1 velocity can be traced to recent disinflation, which has led to a prolonged and substantial drop in interest rates. The new interest-bearing transactions accounts would be expected to show a more pronounced response to the large changes in nominal interest rates, but the opportunity costs of all financial assets—including demand deposits—should be affected.

Between 1947 and 1979, the average level of inflation and interest rates doubled about every decade. As interest rates rose, both households and businesses looked for ways to reduce the relative amount of funds held in non-interest-bearing accounts. This behavior is reflected in the steadily rising velocity of M1.

As inflation and interest rates fell beginning in 1982, M1 generally grew more rapidly than expected. The incremental deregulation of deposit ceilings and somewhat sluggish response of the new floating-rate accounts resulted in gradual shifts into some of the newer accounts; but as interest rates continued to decline, the spread between rates paid on transactions deposits and alternative savings instruments narrowed.

This situation has reduced the incentive for careful economizing on transactions balances. As interest rates—and thus the opportunity cost of holding OCDs—have continued to fall, more and more people have changed banking habits; passbook accounts have been closed, and ever-larger balances have been allowed to accumulate in OCDs. If this accumulation in interest-bearing OCDs was the only source of M1 velocity declines, however, we would not expect non-interest-bearing demand deposits to follow the same pattern.

Hence, the declines in M1A velocity during 1985 and 1986 suggest that at least part of the upward trend in M1 velocity from 1947 to 1979 was related to the upward trend in inflation and interest rates. In the new period of declining interest rates, the impact of interest rate trends on demand deposits—and money demand in general—has been more clearly revealed.

The Changing Composition of M1A

The M1A velocity declines of 1985 and 1986 would seem to negate the assumption that the "purer" M1A aggregate can adequately fill the role that M1

once had as a policy target. Rather, an explanation that includes the effects of disinflation on the opportunity costs of financial assets seems necessary to explain the velocity behavior of both aggregates. This point becomes even more apparent when one considers how deregulation has altered the composition and characteristics of M1A.

Because OCDs can be owned by households but not by businesses, demand deposits have become increasingly dominated by business accounts. Chart 3 illustrates the stark change in the composition of demand deposits. After declining gradually through the 1970s, the ratio of business to household demand deposits has risen sharply since 1980.

Businesses tend to manage their transactions accounts much more intensively than do most households, so the increase in the share of demand deposits held by businesses has been reflected in a rise in the average turnover rate of demand deposits. This, in turn, affects the nature of M1A's behavior and will probably affect the velocity trend of M1A.

The turnover rate of an account is conceptually similar to velocity because it defines the relative intensity with which a particular type of account is used. As would be expected from the above discussion, the turnover rates compared in the upper panel of chart 4 show that an increase in the growth rate of regular demand-deposit turnover (as in M1A) has accompanied the change in ownership composition. Interestingly, though, the average turnover rate of total transactions deposits (as in M1) appears to have increased at roughly the same trend rate of growth as during the 1970s.

However, the turnover rates in the upper panel of chart 4 represent the use of deposits in ways unrelated to GNP, including intermediate and financial transactions. The lower panel of chart 4 shows turnover measures adjusted to reflect only transactions associated with final sales.[6] With this adjustment, sharp declines are evident for both demand deposits and total transactions deposits, although demand-deposit turnover remains higher than OCD turnover. After the adjustment has been made to turnover rates, neither the demand deposits measure nor the total transactions deposits measure appears very similar to the demand deposit component of M1 before 1980.

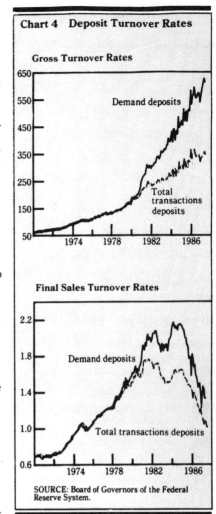

Chart 4   Deposit Turnover Rates

Gross Turnover Rates

Demand deposits

Total transactions deposits

Final Sales Turnover Rates

Demand deposits

Total transactions deposits

SOURCE: Board of Governors of the Federal Reserve System.

Similar evidence on the effects of M1A's compositional change can be seen in ratios of currency to deposits. The currency/deposit ratio is important because it reflects the relative usefulness of financial assets for financing transactions. Currency is primarily—if not exclusively—a transactions asset, so a stable trend in the currency/deposit ratio might indicate that the relative usefulness of the deposit measure was unchanged. On the other hand, if an increasing proportion of deposits are held for reasons unrelated to their usefulness as transactions, then the currency ratio should show a downward

---

6. The adjusted turnover rates shown in the lower panel of chart 4 are derived in Appendix C of David E. Lindsey and Paul Spindt, "An Evaluation of Monetary Indexes," Special Studies Paper 195, Board of Governors of the Federal Reserve System.

Chart 5 Currency/Deposit Ratios

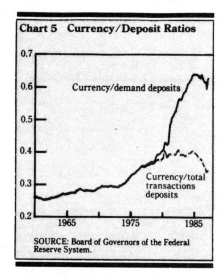

SOURCE: Board of Governors of the Federal Reserve System.

shift as the deposit measure increases (and vice versa).

Chart 5 shows currency/deposit ratios for demand deposits and total transactions deposits. Like the turnover rates in chart 4, a striking feature of chart 5 is that total transactions deposits appear to be behaving more like pre-deregulation demand deposits than do demand deposits themselves.

The ratio of currency to demand deposits shows a protracted rise, which begins at about the same time as the introduction of NOW accounts, but which goes far beyond the period usually identified with initial flows from demand deposits to OCDs.

Putting this evidence together, an interesting possibility emerges. As households switched transactions accounts from regular demand deposits to the new interest-bearing type, the demand deposits component was transformed. Both the turnover rates and currency/deposit ratios suggest that demand deposit behavior has changed dramatically since deregulation.

Within this scenario, we would expect to see the velocity of M1A rising faster during the early 1980s than did M1 velocity before deregulation. But, as noted earlier, the rate of M1A velocity growth from 1982 through 1984 was roughly comparable to that of pre-deregulation M1. This corresponds with the period in which the velocity of M1 was experiencing sharp declines. It seems possible that the relative stability of M1A velocity in the early 1980s merely reflected a coincidence of offsetting forces on the rate of velocity growth. While the changing composition of demand deposits would have tended to raise the average growth rate of M1A velocity through higher turnover rates, this tendency was offset by the velocity-depressing effects of disinflation. Thus, it is not the composition of transactions deposits that matters most, but the relationship of those deposits to nominal GNP.

Conclusion

In 1981, the nationwide introduction of NOW accounts caused a large shift of funds from demand deposits to OCDs, distorting the measured growth rates of both M1 and M1A. Since then, no other regulatory changes have had such distortive effects. Nevertheless, the velocity of M1 has departed from its previous growth trend to such an extent that the FOMC chose not to set an explicit target for M1 in 1987.

The apparent stability of M1A's velocity from 1982 through 1984 led some observers to suggest that this narrower measure of transactions money could be substituted for M1 as a target. However, data on demand deposit ownership shares, turnover rates, and currency/deposit ratios suggest that the observed stability of M1A's velocity in the early 1980s may represent a coincidence of offsetting forces.

In the long run, the behavior of M1A velocity could be expected to be quite different from that of M1 prior to the 1980s. The same factors that have affected M1's behavior have also affected M1A, diminishing its usefulness as a potential policy target. The recent decline in M1A velocity provides preliminary evidence that its velocity may not, in fact, follow a growth pattern as predictable as M1's previous velocity trend.

Article Twenty-Two

A Cashless Society?

For years analysts have been predicting that the U.S. will become a cashless society in which most payments will be made electronically. Such predictions might seem reasonable in light of rapid advances in computer and telecommunications technology and the growth of electronic funds transfers.

However, less technologically sophisticated means of payments stubbornly refuse to go away. Most individuals still rely primarily on checks, cash, and credit cards to make payments. A fully electronic payment system apparently remains a far distant development. In fact, trends in cash usage and holdings suggest that cold, hard cash is becoming an even *more* popular means of payment. This *Letter* examines trends in the use of cash, checks, and electronic payments to assess the likely evolution of the payment system over the next few years.

Means of payment
In the U.S., *households'* primary means of payment (in dollar volume) are checks, followed by cash (currency and coin), and then credit cards. According to a 1984 Federal Reserve survey, 57 percent of a typical family's expenditures are made by check, a surprisingly large 36 percent are made by cash, and the remaining 7 percent are made by credit card. Very few households make payments via electronic wire transfers.

Detailed data on trends in the use of various means of payments are not readily available. However, trends in the Federal Reserve's provision of various payments services may give a useful indication of underlying trends. The Federal Reserve is a major provider of check clearing services, electronic funds transfers, and cash services. Trends in both dollar volumes and numbers of items processed suggest that although electronic payments are growing, traditional means of making payments are well entrenched.

In terms of dollar volume, electronic wire transfers are by far the most important type of payments processed by the Fed. Over $142 trillion dollars were transferred over the Federal Reserve's electronic transfer system in 1987, more than twelve times the dollar volume transferred by check. Most of these transactions occurred among large corporations, depositories, and financial companies. Moreover, electronic transfers mainly involved federal funds trades and securities purchases and sales, not purchases and sales of final goods and services. Individual electronic transfers tended to be large, averaging $2.7 million each. Thus, the *number* of these "wholesale" electronic transfers was minuscule in relation to the total check volume processed by the Federal Reserve.

The growth in electronic transfers has been rapid, with a 62 percent increase in dollar value and a 39 percent increase in transfer volume between 1983 and 1987. In contrast, checks grew only 16 percent in dollar value and 16 percent in volume over the same period. Thus, electronic transfers apparently are gaining in popularity over checks. But checks still handle over 300 times the number of payments that electronic transfers do, so it is unlikely that electronic funds transfers will displace checks as the most popular mode of payment anytime soon.

Cash still is king
It is not surprising that electronic funds transfers are used for large-dollar transfers and that they have become increasingly popular, but it is surprising how popular currency still is. In fact, contrary to predictions of a cashless society, currency is becoming increasingly popular as a means of payment.

The dollar volume of currency outstanding in the hands of the public has been growing for a long time. In keeping with this trend, currency grew from $148 billion in 1983 to $200 billion in 1987, a 35 percent increase. Moreover, currency's share of the Fed's M1 monetary aggregate — a measure of transaction balances — declined only slightly from 27 percent in 1977 to 26.5 percent in 1987, even though interest-earning NOW and Super-NOW checking accounts for individuals were introduced during this period. In theory, the introduction of such accounts should have increased the popularity of checking accounts and reduced the attractiveness of cash balances. Interest-paying checking accounts, in fact, have been very popular (over 35 percent of households had them by 1985), but their popularity did not diminish that of currency. Rather, they attracted funds mainly from non-interest bearing checking accounts and other interest bearing accounts.

Federal Reserve cash processing

Another sign of the growing popularity of cash as a means of payment is the rapid growth in the volume of currency and coin processed by the Federal Reserve. As part of their central bank services, the 12 regional Federal Reserve Banks and their branches count, sort, store, and ensure that the quality of currency in circulation is maintained. Banks can deposit excess or unfit currency at a Federal Reserve Bank or branch and can withdraw sorted, fit currency from their reserve accounts upon request. Typically, the total volume of cash withdrawals from reserve accounts follows deposit volume fairly closely over time, but withdrawals run slightly higher than deposits as a result of the growing volume of cash held by the public. (New currency is printed by the Bureau of Engraving and Printing.)

The volume of currency received by all Federal Reserve Banks has been growing rapidly for some time. During the 1983-1987 period, unit volume increased 47 percent and dollar volume 52 percent — approximately triple the corresponding percentage increases for check volumes and in line with the percentage increases in electronic transfer volumes. Moreover, the 1986-87 growth rate in unit volume was about 9.5 percent, considerably greater than the 6.6 percent average annual growth rate since 1974.

In 1987, the Federal Reserve System processed about 17 billion notes of various denominations, representing a dollar value of more than $216 billion. Thus, slightly more than the entire dollar volume of currency outstanding ($200 billion) circulates through the Federal Reserve during a typical year.

These figures understate the extent to which cash is used as a means of payment, however. According to the 1984 Federal Reserve survey, only 15 percent of all currency (or about $30

billion in 1987), is held for transaction purposes by domestic residents. (The rest is held outside the U.S., or possibly within the U.S. in hoards for illegal purposes.) Apparently, each dollar held by a U.S. resident for transaction purposes circulated through the Federal Reserve System several times, probably after being used in several transactions. Thus, the $30 billion held domestically for transaction purposes probably supports transactions valued at several times the $216 billion that the Fed receives annually in currency deposits. In view of these estimates, the cashless society is far from reality.

Reasons for cash's popularity

There are several reasons why cash as a means of payment is likely to remain popular. There are even some reasons why it is likely to become *more* popular. For one thing, cash is a convenient means of payment, especially for small purchases. It takes much less time to make a cash payment than it does to make a check or credit card payment, and cash is more widely acceptable. The time involved in making a transaction is a very real cost, which increases with the value of alternative uses of an individual's time. These values have increased along with real wages and the proportion of the population employed. As a result, convenience has become a more important determinant of the choice of method of payment.

Another reason for using currency is that cash transactions are anonymous, making them widely used in illegal transactions or for tax evasion. In fact, several economists have relied on patterns of cash usage to try to estimate the size of the "underground" economy. However, the recent reductions in federal marginal tax rates, in theory, should have reduced the incentives for tax evasion and therefore, reduced the popularity of cash transactions.

Growth in ATMs

Perhaps a more important reason for the growing popularity of cash is the introduction and rapid growth of automatic teller machines (ATMs), a trend that is also related to the convenience demand for cash. The number of these machines has grown from 10,000 nationwide in 1977 to over 80,000 today.

By offering virtual around-the-clock availability from many locations, ATMs make it possible for individuals to obtain cash frequently and at their

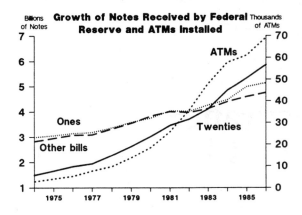

Growth of Notes Received by Federal Reserve and ATMs Installed

convenience, thereby reducing the time costs involved in obtaining cash. Moreover, individuals do not have to risk possible loss, theft, or loss of interest on large cash balances. Instead, they can obtain cash frequently and in amounts more closely related to the size and timing of planned expenditures. In fact, the 1984 Federal Reserve survey confirms that ATM users hold smaller average cash balances and obtain cash more frequently than do non-ATM users. Also, ATMs are used more frequently by high-income persons with high time costs and thus larger incentives to economize on the time involved in making payments.

The chart shows a correlation between the growth of ATMs and the demand for cash. Since most ATMs use $20 bills, it is interesting to note that the growth in the volume of $20 bills has been greater than that of other denominations since 1977 — about the same time that the number of ATMs installed started to grow rapidly nationwide. Moreover, the volume of

$20 bills processed by the Federal Reserve has exceeded that of other denominations since 1983. Surveys by the Bank Administration Institute in 1979 and 1986 also show that the fraction of the number of all debits from checking accounts arising from ATM cash withdrawals increased 336 percent while the number of debits associated with checks actually declined about 4 percent.

One final reason that cash has been and likely will continue to be so popular is that the Federal Reserve's cash services are not priced. (However, institutions pay the full costs of transporting cash to and from the Federal Reserve.) Check services and wire transfers, in contrast, are both priced at levels intended to recover processing costs. Because Federal Reserve cash services are underpriced compared to checks and electronic transfers, cash payments are more economical than if users had to pay the full costs of the Federal Reserve's services. This, in turn, may help to explain the rapid growth of ATMs, since ATMs require sorted and fit currency — two services banks can obtain without cost from the Federal Reserve.

Cash is here to stay
Far from becoming a cashless society, the U.S. appears to be relying *more* on currency as a means of payment. The reasons for this trend include increased time costs, the innovation of ATMs and the underpricing of Federal Reserve cash services. Thus, it seems unlikely that electronic payments will replace cash anytime in the near future.

Michael C. Keeley

Bank Runs, Deposit Insurance, and Bank Regulation, Part I

by Charles T. Carlstrom

As long as there have been banks, there have been bank runs. Unlike the failure of mom-and-pop grocery stores (or Lockheed, for that matter), bank failures are frequently viewed as contagious—able to cause other bank runs and lead to failures of otherwise solvent banks.

A rumor or a hunch that a bank is in trouble can lead to its demise. Thus, the fear that a bank "might" be in trouble can be a self-fulfilling prophecy.

Haunted by the contagion of bank failures that occurred during the Great Depression, regulators are still wary of letting banks fail. Large banks in particular are a cause of concern, because the potential spillover effects are thought to be excessive.

Along with other bank regulators, the Federal Deposit Insurance Corporation (FDIC) has an implicit mandate to maintain confidence in, and provide stability to, the commercial banking system. A principal method of achieving this mandate is by insuring depositors for losses up to a current maximum of $100,000.[1]

The justification for FDIC insurance is simply that insured depositors will no longer have an incentive to pull their money out of a bank that is merely rumored to be insolvent. Unfortunately, federal deposit insurance provides little incentive for insured depositors to withdraw their funds from a bank that actually is insolvent.

For nearly 50 years after its inception in 1934, the FDIC was considered successful in fulfilling its mandate. The banking system grew rapidly with few bank failures, and none widespread enough to threaten the entire system. Since 1981, however, the number of bank failures has increased sharply. In 1987 there were 184 bank closings, and an additional 19 required FDIC assistance to stay afloat.[2] Bank failures are currently at their highest level since the Great Depression.

This *Economic Commentary*, presented in two parts, discusses whether federally provided deposit insurance is necessary to prevent widespread bank runs by exploring some of the myths and folklore associated with bank runs. Adam Smith argued that the invisible hand of self-interest leads men to effectually promote the interests of society. We attempt to analyze whether this invisible hand extends into the banking industry by examining both the causes and cures of bank runs.

Widespread bank failures are often thought to be a possible consequence of a banking system without federal deposit insurance. This article considers whether federal deposit insurance is necessary to prevent bank runs. Part I describes some of the costs of providing deposit insurance and then introduces its justification and benefits. Part II, presented in the upcoming February 15 *Economic Commentary*, concludes with an examination of contagious bank runs and a discussion of how the market handled banking panics prior to the Federal Reserve System and the Federal Deposit Insurance Corporation.

■ **The Nature of Bank Runs**
A bank run can occur when some of a bank's depositors perceive the bank to be insolvent or expect insolvency to occur.

If banks are like other businesses, then a bank run would be quite acceptable as a source of market discipline. For example, if the public thought that a bank's manager had embezzled a substantial portion of the bank's capital, depositors would have an incentive to withdraw their money. If a substantial portion of a bank's deposits were withdrawn, the bank would then be forced to close.

The threat of being run on and closed down provides the incentive for stockholders to spend the necessary resources to monitor their employees. The potential for bank runs also creates the incentive necessary to stop banks from undertaking excessively risky investments: those in which there is a high probability of failure as well as success.[3]

■ **The Costs of Providing Deposit Insurance**
Deposit insurance circumvents the market discipline of insured depositors. Because their funds are guaranteed, insured depositors (those with deposits less than or equal to $100,000) have little incentive to place their money in a safe, well-managed bank. Similarly, if they discover that a bank is not financially viable, they have no incentive to withdraw their money from the bank. Therefore, unless regulators promptly close insolvent institutions, it is up to the shareholders and the uninsured depositors to impose discipline on troubled banks.

The role of uninsured depositors may be quite small under the present system, however. Since a depositor can have several accounts of $100,000, the de facto maximum of deposit insurance is many times greater than the stated legal limit of $100,000. And, because of the failure-resolution policies that have been applied to some large banks (for example, Continental Illinois, First City, and First Republic), the perception exists that some banks are too big to fail and that all depositors in these banks are, in effect, insured.[4] Both of these factors work to reduce the disciplinary action of depositors.

Deposit insurance provides banks with a no-risk source of funding. Without the threat of bank runs, stockholders and senior management in the existing regulatory environment have reduced incentive to monitor their employees to minimize insider dealing, bank fraud, and simple incompetence.

It may not be a surprise that fraud and embezzlement have been the primary causes of bank failures.[5] According to a recent study by the Office of the Comptroller of the Currency, since 1979 "poor management, either by the bank officers, the board of directors, or both, played a significant role in 89 percent of the failures."[6]

Deposit insurance also reduces the amount of capital a bank chooses to maintain. A higher capital-to-asset ratio enables a bank to borrow money more easily in case of financial difficulty. By guaranteeing insured depositors against losses, the risk of bank runs, as well as the amount of capital that is necessary to protect a bank from withdrawals, is lessened.

At the turn of the century, capital-to-asset ratios were 20 percent; by the 1930s, they had declined to about 15 percent. Today the capital-to-asset ratio is approximately 7 percent—substantially less than the capital ratios of other industries.[7] Concern about the decrease in bank profitability and the increase in bank failures during the 1970s led to increased concern about capital adequacy and, in 1983, to enactment of a law that provided bank regulators with the legal authority to enforce minimum capital standards.

Along with limited liability, deposit insurance creates an incentive for banks to hold more risky investment portfolios. Bank owners reap the rewards when a bank's investment succeeds, but because of limited liability, the FDIC—and perhaps the taxpayers as well—shares in the losses when an investment fails.

Deposit insurance further reduces the incentives for banks to avoid risky investments, because a bank does not have to compensate its depositors (by paying them a higher interest rate) when it undertakes substantial risks. This problem is aggravated by the recent failure-resolution policies applied to some large banks. Such policies have served to erode the market's discipline further and to subsidize these banks just because they are large.

■ **Bank Regulation and Deposit Insurance**
Bank regulators are aware of these problems. Not only can regulators impose minimum capital requirements on banks, but they are empowered to close down banks that are not solvent and to assist banks that are becoming insolvent.

Traditionally, bank regulators did not have the power to close a bank when its market value reached zero. Instead, they could close a bank only after its book value became negative.[8] Even then, however, a bank was not necessarily closed down, as the recent FDIC-assisted merger of Alaska Mutual and United Bankcorporation of Alaska indicates.[9] With the Competitive Equality Banking Act of 1987, chartering authorities can now close a bank when book insolvency appears imminent.

This forbearance occurs even though the FDIC may spend more money later to bail out such banks. While it is true that an insolvent bank may later become financially viable, the Alaskan situation illustrates that financial health may not be regained.[10]

The incentive to take on more risk is especially prevalent for a bank that is close to being shut down. The threat that regulators might close a bank can lead a bank's manager to make investments that have a small chance of a large payoff and a larger chance of expected loss. In the outside chance that the gamble pays off, the manager saves the bank and hence his job; if the gamble fails, the bank goes out with a bang instead of a whimper. Although this scenario is not firmly established in banking, the precedent has been set in the thrift industry.

The longer the FDIC waits to close a bank, the greater the incentive for the bank to undertake risky investments. If an insolvent bank is not closed promptly, then the losses to shareholders are postponed. Because a dollar in the future is worth less than a dollar today, postponing shareholders' losses provides an extra indirect subsidy.

Besides closing banks when they first become insolvent, another way to lessen the negative aspects of deposit insurance is for regulators to charge banks an insurance premium based on the riskiness of their portfolios. Risk-taking would be punished by requiring the bank to pay higher premiums. However, Congress has long been opposed to any plan that would allow the FDIC to charge different premiums to different banks.

Absent these measures, the best ways to strengthen market discipline are to sharply reduce the legal limit of deposit insurance, to limit insurance to one account per person, to assist only insured depositors, and to send a signal to the market that no banks are too large to let fail.

■ **The Case for Deposit Insurance**
Supporters of the current deposit insurance and regulatory system generally respond to these criticisms on two fronts. First, while the FDIC is interested in economic efficiency, it is also interested in equity considerations, that is, in protecting the interests of the small or less-informed depositor. Second, while inefficiencies and moral hazards are the costs of providing deposit insurance, the benefits of deposit insurance are even

greater than the costs, because a bank is unlike other forms of business.

Unfortunately, using deposit insurance to protect the less-informed diminishes the incentives for them to become informed. If the objective is to protect the small depositors, one might question the need to insure depositors up to a current maximum of $100,000, to extend coverage to more than one account, or to protect uninsured depositors.

Society should ask itself not only whether it wants to protect certain depositors who lose money in bank runs, but also how much protection to provide in the most cost-effective way. For example, the federal government could allow an income tax credit so that depositors could deduct their losses, up to a legislated maximum.

Justifying deposit insurance because depositors lost money due to bank failures prior to the FDIC is also tenuous, because these losses were generally small. From 1930 to 1933, depositors of failed banks lost only 0.81 percent on average. During noncrisis years, losses to depositors averaged only 0.07 percent.[11]

Losses have typically been small because rational depositors run on a bank when they first perceive it to be insolvent. Given that depositors in failed institutions generally receive more than 99 cents on the dollar even during bad times, one might well question whether deposit insurance is necessary to protect the vast majority of depositors.

The most important argument in support of deposit insurance is that banks are not like other businesses. They are potentially special because 1) bank failures can cause undue economic hardship in a community, 2) the economy depends on the safety and security of the banking system, which could potentially be upset

if some larger banks were to fail, and 3) bank failures can be contagious and can cause otherwise solvent banks to fail.

The first argument, that banks are special because bank failures could impose a hardship in a particular geographical area, is not unique to banking. The closing of a mill in a one-mill town would be at least as devastating as the closing of the town's only bank.

In the absence of laws against branch banking, a bank failure would typically result in the transfer of ownership from a poorly managed banking firm to a banking company that is potentially better managed. It is the presence of regulations against branch banking and the restrictive policies of bank chartering agencies that can cause economic hardships when a bank closes in a small town.

Another potential reason for protecting banks is the argument that a well-functioning market economy depends on the security of the banking system. Because banks facilitate savings and investment, a large number of bank failures can have real effects.

The potential for a series of bank runs to threaten the banking system is limited, however, because the failure of a few banks would tend to strengthen the remaining banks. This is because large depositors who have a high opportunity cost of holding their assets in cash would redeposit their money in sound banks.[12] The exception to this rule is when a bank failure causes a run on otherwise sound banks.

A series of bank runs may also hamper economic activity because widespread bank failures can cause a significant drop in the money supply. The money supply contracted during the Great Depression because individuals decided to hold their money in currency instead of depositing it in banks. Because such a reduction in the money supply can be offset by supplying additional reserves to the banking system, justifying deposit insurance to eliminate a bank-run-induced multiple contraction of the money supply is not warranted.

In order to justify deposit insurance, one must understand not only the costs associated with its administration, but also the benefits of having deposit insurance. The preceding discussion indicates that an analysis of contagious bank failures is necessary in order to understand these benefits.

Part II of this article, presented in the upcoming February 15 *Economic Commentary,* concludes with an examination of contagious bank runs and a discussion of how the banking system prior to the Federal Reserve System handled such problems.

Charles T. Carlstrom is an economist at the Federal Reserve Bank of Cleveland. The author wishes to thank Walker Todd, James Thomson, John Scadding, William Gavin, and Mark Sniderman for their helpful comments.

The views stated herein are those of the author and not necessarily those of the Federal Reserve Bank of Cleveland or of the Board of Governors of the Federal Reserve System.

■ Footnotes

1. In 1934, the first year the FDIC operated, depositors were insured up to a maximum of $2,500 (which amounts to approximately $22,000 today). This maximum increased slowly until 1982, when it increased from $40,000 to its current level of $100,000.

2. See "1987 Bank Failures Set Post-Depression Record," *The Washington Post,* January 6, 1988.

3. See George G. Kaufman, "The Truth About Bank Runs," Staff Memoranda SM-87-3, Federal Reserve Bank of Chicago, April 1987.

4. See Daria B. Caliguire and James B. Thomson, "FDIC Policies for Dealing with Failed and Troubled Institutions," *Economic Commentary,* Federal Reserve Bank of Cleveland, October 1, 1987.

5. See George J. Benston, Robert A. Eisenbeis, Paul M. Horvitz, Edward J. Kane, and George G. Kaufman, *Perspectives on Safe and Sound Banking: Past, Present, and Future,* Cambridge, MA: The MIT Press, 1986, pp. 1-4.

6. See "Study Says Bad Management Had Key Role in Bank Failures," *The Washington Post,* January 21, 1988.

7. See George J. Benston and George G. Kaufman, "Risk and Solvency Regulation of Depository Institutions: Past Policies and Current Options," Staff Memoranda SM-88-1, Federal Reserve Bank of Chicago, 1988. This is not meant to imply that deposit insurance is the only reason for the decline in banks' capital-to-asset ratios.

8. See Edward J. Kane, *The Gathering Crisis in Federal Deposit Insurance,* Cambridge, MA: The MIT Press, 1985, p. 20.

9. See "Two Big Alaska Banks Unveil Rescue Plan," *The American Banker,* October 8, 1987.

10. In fact, in the thrift industry, financial health is usually not regained. See "Thrift Industry: Forbearance for Troubled Institutions, 1982-1986," U.S. General Accounting Office Briefing Report, May 1987.

11. See Benston, et al., op. cit., p. 64. Some investors did not receive their money until years later. If capital markets are efficient, however, depositors would have been able to borrow against a portion of their likely settlement.

12. This same argument has been used to contend that deposit insurance should cover deposits only up to a maximum of $5,000 to $10,000.

SECTION FOUR

Central Banking and Monetary Policy

The readings in this section address various aspects of conducting monetary policy in the short run. The first two articles speculate about and assess how current Federal Reserve chair Alan Greenspan views the economy and how he is likely to steer monetary policy. The next selections describe how the Fed actually operates its open market desk and its discount window to counteract typical and atypical variations in the relation between the monetary base and the money supply. This section concludes with a proposal for Federal Reserve policy operation given that there are unpredictable variations in the relation between the money supply and the macroeconomy.

"The Impact of a New Federal Reserve Chairman" by Edward J. Kane presents an analysis of the trade-offs President Reagan may have been considering in deciding to select Alan Greenspan as Federal Reserve chair, instead of re-appointing Paul Volcker. Kane then speculates on the repercussions of the change in Fed leadership on monetary policy choices, on financial restructuring, and on the institution of the Federal Reserve itself.

"Happy Anniversary, Alan Greenspan" by former Fed Governor Lyle E. Gramley details the events leading up to, and the Fed's response to, the stock market plunge of October 19, 1987. The Fed and its leader are given accolades for quick, decisive, and appropriate reactions to that potential disaster. Next Greenspan's leadership style is described. More collegial than his predecessor, Greenspan is judged to be able to effectively mold a consensus for his inflation-reducing policy.

Open market operations are the Federal Reserve System's primary method of implementing monetary policy. The lead article in this section, Howard L. Roth's "Federal Reserve Open Market Techniques," shows how the Fed uses open market operations to produce changes in the supply of reserves and to prevent factors beyond its direct control from producing undesired changes in the supply of reserves available to banks and other depository institutions. These latter, defensive operations may be required to offset either temporary or permanent changes in the sources and uses of reserves. The vast majority of the Fed's activities attempt to offset temporary fluctuations in the reserves market. The author describes how repurchase agreements are used to reduce this variability in the amount of reserves available to depository institutions.

In "The Discount Window," David L. Mengle gives several examples of why and how financial institutions come to the Fed to borrow reserves. These examples highlight the conditions under which the Fed approves borrowing at the discount window. The Fed does not look kindly on all requests for discount borrowing, however, and it rations loans to prevent inappropriate use of the window. Also discussed is the differential access small and large institutions are granted to the window.

"Looking Forward" by John P. Judd points out the size and timing of the effects of direct monetary policy actions on the macroeconomy are unreliable. That leads policymakers to search for leading indicators of the effects of changes in open market operations or discount rates. Unfortunately, the connections between the macroeconomy and traditional feedback variables like the money supply have also proven to be unreliable in recent years. One alternative is to assess the appropriateness of current policies by looking at their impact on forecasts of the economy itself, instead of on the money supply. Though models of the economy are less than perfect, and thus will sometimes provide incorrect signals to the policymaker, the breakdown of the relation between the money supply and economy argues for the superiority of this alternative.

Article Twenty-Four

THE IMPACT OF A NEW FEDERAL RESERVE CHAIRMAN

EDWARD J. KANE*

This paper treats appointing a Federal Reserve Chairman as a portfolio investment made by the United States President. It models Ronald Reagan's 1987 choice between Paul Volcker and other candidates as a trade-off between a potentially unfavorable short-term market response to replacing Volcker and various long-term political benefits from installing Reagan's own man. The paper discusses possible effects of Alan Greenspan's chairmanship on the trajectory of future monetary policy, on the Fed's preferences for financial reform, and on the Fed's corporate culture.

I. INTRODUCTION

During one of his last days as Chairman of the Federal Reserve Board, Paul Volcker is reputed to have treated the rest of the Governors to lunch. So as not to waste the Governors' valuable time, a waiter arrived quickly to take their orders. Ordering first, Volcker said that he would have the prime rib, which happened to be the restaurant's blue-plate special that day. Presuming that a trained economist such as Volcker would not want to order a la carte, the waiter asked, "What about the vegetables?" Paul replied, "*They* can order for themselves."

This story underscores the primacy of the Federal Reserve Chairman over the rest of the Board. It also illustrates the lack of public standing of the relatively inexperienced Governors currently in place: Manuel Johnson, Martha Seger, Wayne Angell, H. Robert Heller, and Edward Kelley. The Governors' relatively low salaries have caused personnel turnover which has made a mockery of the stability in Board composition Congress supposedly assured by establishing a system of staggered 14-year terms.

Like any other incoming chief executive, a new Chairman is expected to place his personal stamp on his firm's goals, strategies, tactics, and organizational structure. In producing public confidence and resolving important Federal Reserve System problems, a strong Chairman can reduce the other Governors' function largely to window dressing. Moreover, efforts by heads of other financial regulatory agencies to influence public opinion and elected politicians are often dwarfed by those of the Federal Reserve Chairman.

*Everett D. Reese Professor of Monetary and Banking Economics, The Ohio State University, and Research Associate, National Bureau of Economic Research (NBER). The author thanks Anna Schwartz, Kenneth Guenther, and Thomas Mayer for valuable comments on an earlier draft. Opinions expressed are those of the author and should not be construed as those of the NBER. An earlier version of this paper was presented at the 62nd Annual Western Economic Association International Conference, Vancouver, B.C., July 1987, in a session organized by William Poole, Brown University.

George Kaufman has remarked acidly that other financial regulators' relative weakness imparts a nasty implication to the hackneyed phrase "policy tools."

This unbalanced structure of shared responsibility creates opportunities for a Fed Chairman to act heroically. Volcker, after apparently exercising such opportunities to spectacular effect, leaves office with the enviable reputation of an inflation fighter extraordinaire. However, in a polity devoted to interposing checks and balances, the freedom to become an individual hero is not necessarily regarded as an unalloyed good—either for elected politicians or for the U.S. financial system. Hence, important limits to a Chairman's freedom of action exist in: (i) his need to get along with other members of the Federal Open Market Committee (FOMC); (ii) his interest in participating in formulating the Administration's overall economic plan, in participating in appointing new Board members, and in being reappointed to a new four-year term; and (iii) his sensitivity to criticism delivered through congressional hearings, Presidential pronouncements, and strategic leaks to the press.

Economists' dominant paradigm for individual decision making is constrained maximization. To predict what changes Alan Greenspan may make in the Fed's operative goals and constraints, one must understand his personality, his tastes for various policies, his special talents, and especially the constraints under which he must operate. To clarify the role of political constraints and connections, it is helpful to model the choice process leading the President to choose Greenspan over all other candidates.

II. MODELING THE PRESIDENT'S DECISION PROCESS

My model is a personal and introspective analysis. It treats appointing a Federal Reserve Chairman as the President's making a portfolio investment. What matters is the expected value and variance of "political profits" to Reagan and the Republican Party from the President's choice. In turn, political profits arise from paying off or establishing political debts and from developing opportunities to influence favorably the trajectory of selected economic goal variables.

An appointee's post-appointment policy choices are controlled *ex ante* in two ways: (i) by narrowing the set of candidates to those whose views of the nation's policy needs match closely those of the President and his advisers, and (ii) by laying a groundwork for future give and take on policy matters with the eventual appointee.

This analysis summarizes my attempt to shadow the President's thought processes during roughly the first six months of 1987. I first tried to define the opportunity set, and so developed tables 1 and 2. Table 1 sets forth some basic facts about the all-male universe of previous Chairmen: their ages, tenures, and professional backgrounds. I consider two facts particularly significant. First, the average tenure of Federal Reserve Chairmen has been only six years. This means that Volcker's eight years in office is an above-average run. I see this as telling the President that the length of Volcker's prior service makes it feasible to replace him. Reagan need not feel constrained—as he may have

TABLE 1
Age, Background, and Tenure of Past Federal Reserve System Chairmen

Name	Birthdate	Date of Accession	End of Chairmanship	Age at Accession (in years)	Length of Tenure (in years)	Listed Professions	Nonhonorary Postgraduate Degrees
Hamlin	Aug. 30, 1861	Aug. 10, 1914	Aug. 9, 1916	52	2	Lawyer; also ran for various state offices	A.M., L.L.B.
Harding	May 5, 1864	Aug. 10, 1916	Aug. 9, 1922	52	6	Banker	A.M.
Crissinger	Dec. 10, 1860	May 1, 1923	Sept. 15, 1927	62	4.4	Lawyer	L.L.B.
Young	May 17, 1882	Oct. 4, 1927	Aug. 31, 1930	45	2.9	Banker	*
Meyer	Oct. 31, 1875	Sept. 16, 1930	May 10, 1933	54	2.6	Newspaper executive	—
Black	Jan. 7, 1873	May 19, 1933	Aug. 15, 1934	60	1.2	Banker	*
Eccles	Sept. 9, 1890	Nov. 15, 1934	Jan. 31, 1948	44	13.2	Financier, business executive	*
McCabe	July 11, 1893	April 15, 1948	March 31, 1951	54	3.0	Business executive, banker	—
Martin	Dec. 17, 1906	April 2, 1951	Jan. 31, 1970	44	18.8	Broker	—
Burns	April 27, 1904	Jan. 31, 1970	Feb. 1, 1978	65	8.0	Economist	Ph.D.
Miller	March 9, 1925	March 8, 1978	Aug. 6, 1979	52	1.4	Merchant banker, business executive	J.D.
Volcker	Sept. 5, 1927	Aug. 6, 1979	Aug. 5, 1987	51	8.0	Banker, economist	M.A.
Greenspan	March 6, 1926	Aug. 11, 1987		61	—	Economist	Ph.D.

Sources: Who's Who in America, various editions. List of dates of service for Chairmen compiled by Edward J. McCarthy.

*Did not graduate from college.

TABLE 2

Republican or Nonpartisan Financial Experts with Enough
Government and Political Experience to Be Potential
Candidates for Federal Reserve Chairman in 1987

1. Paul Volcker
2. Alan Greenspan
3. George Shultz
4. Donald Regan
5. E. Gerald Corrigan
6. Jerry Jordan
7. Beryl Sprinkel
8. George Gould

Note: An alternative—and politically unconstrained—slate was compiled in a Drexel Burnham Lambert survey of 200 institutional investment managers reported in the *Wall Street Journal,* February 27, 1987. Respondents were asked to state "in whom they would have the most confidence" as a replacement for Volcker. The top three approval ratings were (1) Corrigan, 26.2 percent of the vote; (2) Greenspan, 18.4 percent; and (3) James Baker, 8.9 percent.

felt in 1983—to reappoint Volcker just because the public believes that Volcker has done a good job. The second fact I consider important is that two of the previous three Chairmen had advanced training in economics and a record of significant federal service. Moreover, the last Chairman who had neither these attributes nor significant experience as a financier was Volcker's economically undertrained and politically adroit, though self-effacing, predecessor—and he is perceived to have performed disastrously. Given the breadth and depth of the nation's current financial stresses, mean–variance efficiency requires that if the President is to appoint a Republican as Chairman, the latter had better be a professionally close substitute for the outgoing Chairman. By this, I mean a Republican who the U.S. financial community recognizes is economically competent, has political savvy, and possesses enough government experience to take up the reins without much on-the-job training. Were it not for his party affiliation and personal independence, Volcker would meet these standards better than anyone else.

Table 2 lists individuals whom I consider to be experienced and knowledgeable economists or financiers who had enough recognition in the financial community to be marketed as another Volcker. This also happens to be an all-male list. I found that introducing only a little risk aversion into the Presidential mindset reduced the list to Volcker and Greenspan. The other candidates either hadn't been tested politically (Corrigan), had been eliminated during the Iran–Contra scandal (Schultz and Regan), or were insufficiently magisterial to quiet international and domestic financiers' transitional fears of renewed inflation and increased chances for financial disaster (Sprinkel, Jordan, and Gould).

The next step is to model the choice between Volcker and Greenspan. I view this as a trade-off between accepting some market disapproval—especially from financiers in other countries—by replacing Volcker with Reagan's own man and improving the President's opportunities to develop unspecified partisan political benefits over the rest of his term. I postulate that, other things equal, a President prefers to proffer a key appointment such as the Fed chairmanship as a reward for past services performed for him or other party members. Politically, such an appointment creates positive incentives all around. Moreover, a grateful Chairman with grateful sponsors should be marginally more malleable as a policymaker whenever and wherever such malleability may be helpful. In this respect, the non-Republican Volcker, like the non-Democrat Arthur Burns before him, had come to enjoy too much stature for his own good. Volcker viewed his continued service at $89,500 a year as his doing the President a favor rather than the other way around. This led me to suppose two things. First, the President would replace Volcker with Greenspan unless a developing crisis or scandal compressed Reagan's tolerance for market disapproval seriously enough to make him beg Volcker to stay on. Second, the economic summit meeting last June allowed the President to clear the appointment with the international financial and regulatory community, creating a go/no-go point for implementing this strategy.

I saw partial confirmation of this analysis in organizational events that suggested that a transition was already underway at the Fed. In assigning leadership to Gerald Corrigan for shaping the Fed's future role in financial regulation, Volcker appeared to be positioning himself for a gracious departure and to be grooming Corrigan as a potential successor. In addition, the behavior of Reagan appointees on the Board suggested that their appointments had not been cleared carefully with Volcker. As long ago as February 1986, Volcker began experiencing problems in commanding the support of other Board members on specific issues. These Governors also were working to force top research staff reporting arrangements to be decentralized. (I viewed this as an effort to reduce the Chairman's power to set the System's policy agenda.) If the President and other Governors perceived Volcker as a lame duck, such events would be far more likely to occur.

III. EFFECTS OF A NEW CHAIRMAN ON THE TRAJECTORY OF FUTURE MONETARY POLICY

Like any decision makers, Fed officials operate within an information and incentive system. At the Fed, goals and constraints are both political and economic in origin. Because meaningful shifts in monetary policy redistribute income temporarily, they create political interests in extending or curtailing these policies. Congress and the President are attuned to these effects. In a nonstationary fashion, they help Fed policymakers define the operational specification of the public interest that governs the trade-offs actually made between the national economy's short- and long-run performances and between alternative patterns of various special interests' costs and benefits. Rationality requires Fed officials not only to recognize alternative policies' political, bureaucratic, and economic consequences, but also to accept the task of selling the policies they adopt to elected politicians and to society at large. In the last analysis, how a given Chairman performs as a policy salesman largely determines how much of a difference he makes. As noted in Kane (1980), Sherlock Holmes' musings on Scotland Yard detectives' undeserved reputation apply equally well to Fed officials: What you do in this world is a matter of no consequence; the question is, what can you make people believe you have done?

Any public institution must build and maintain a political base of support. In a democracy, determining what is the public interest is recognized as a political task. Therefore, Fed targets are variables for which well-placed and vocal segments of the public hold Fed officials responsible. Deviations from the target growth rates for monetary aggregates—published by the Fed since 1975—show that the central bank's relative concern for fighting inflation and fighting unemployment varies over the business cycle. So do popular rankings of these same goals in opinion polls directed at what may be conceived as the body politic (Fischer and Huizenga, 1982).

Whether a Fed Chairman can influence the evolving political consensus on prioritizing the nation's conflicting economic goals, and whether he openly acknowledges what political compromises the System makes on divisive economic policy issues, makes a considerable difference. Matters of style as much as substance made the Volcker era special. It was widely understood that in accepting his initial appointment, Volcker negotiated for the Fed a reduced need to compromise its long-run goals of inflation fighting and financial stability by yielding to short-run political pressures for monetary stimulus. This enhanced Volcker's stature. During his regime, popular interpretations of the Fed's traditional stop-and-go approach to monetary growth were notably less politicized than they had been for years.

Every important political appointment inherently is a two-way street. Just as the President has expressed confidence in Greenspan's judgment and policymaking skills, Greenspan has expressed confidence in the future thrust of the President's economic policies. Both sides have assumed a political debt to support each other, at least implicity.

Still, Greenspan has strong incentives to cooperate also with congressional Democrats. First, his term of office runs 2⅔ years beyond the end of Reagan's presidency, and the next President might well be a Democrat serving in Congress today. Second, Democrats chair the banking committees with which he must contend regularly.

Volcker supposedly received a special mandate prioritizing the Fed's fight against inflation. Without this mandate, these obligations and incentives render the Fed somewhat less independent politically than it has seemed since August 6, 1979. They do this by making the Federal Reserve Chairman at least temporarily a more integrated member of the Reagan and congressional economic policy teams. So long as he remains a team player, Greenspan may reach beyond the confines of the Fed to help articulate national policies on the trade and budget deficits and on financial reform. Volcker's "Lone Ranger" attitude made him look like a force that other federal policymakers had to adjust to rather than work with. His priority was slowing inflation in the long run while suppressing any short-run financial crises in confidence that might develop in the wake of this effort. These all-too-frequent interim crises included threats to public confidence raised by continuing thrift institution weakness, the Hunt Brothers' silver speculation, less developed countries' (LDCs) loan repayment problems, sectoral declines in energy and agriculture, the run on Continental Illinois, a spate of repurchase agreement defaults, and deposit insurance fund failures in Ohio and Maryland. This pattern of priorities made Volcker willing to accept a series of dangerously stop-gap repairs designed only to forestall the spectre of a long-run breakdown in the inherited financial regulation system. He also was willing to limit his opposition to budget and payments deficits almost exclusively to the advisory and verbal plain, regardless of how heartfelt this opposition seemed.

The upside of improved relations between the Fed and elected politicians is the prospect of a more fully integrated policy mix. The downside is: (i) a less open process of forming macroeconomic policy and (ii) irrespective of actual monetary growth rates, an almost certain acceleration in the average inflation rate. In the public's mind, monetary policy decisions promise to be at least marginally more responsive to short-run political calls for monetary expansion to shore up sectoral and regional economic weaknesses, and perhaps to brighten election-year economic conditions. Ironically, during the past two years, sectoral vulnerability to interest rate increases had constrained Volcker's monetary policy options noticeably. While interest rate increases massively threatened the solvency of savings and loan institutions (S&Ls) and an array of troubled borrowers in agriculture, real estate, energy, and LDCs, Volcker allowed substantial monetary growth to occur in an attempt to prevent short-term rates from backing upward. He could not stop this rapid monetary growth from feeding an increase in long-term interest rates. However, keeping it from rekindling short-run inflation is among Volcker's most impressive marketing accomplishments and is strong testimony to the public's faith in his political incorruptibility.

To win any such public standing for himself, Greenspan must scrupulously avoid at least the appearance of political doubletalk. He must also appear willing to sacrifice his good relations with the White House and Congress to protect the Fed's credibility. This means giving high priority to preserving the domestic purchasing power of the dollar. In turn, this probably means arresting the decline in the dollar's foreign purchasing power by accepting higher short-term interest rates. It is ironic that if Greenspan succeeds merely in pushing Fed policies slightly below the monetary trajectories achieved during Volcker's last two years, he must expect to be perceived as fostering rather than fighting inflation.

IV. EFFECTS OF GREENSPAN ON THE FED'S POSITION ON FINANCIAL REFORM

Blessed as it was by Volcker, Corrigan's (1987) detailed blueprint for financial restructuring has been central to the debate over the shape of financial reform. However, during the late 1980s, Volcker, Corrigan, and perhaps the Senate Banking Committee Chairman, William Proxmire, may have become the last high-ranking policymakers to believe that banks truly are "special." Greenspan's public statements indicate not only that he does not fear geographic and product-line deregulation of the financial industry, but also that he sees continuing this process as "essential to the health of both banking and financial services" (Greenspan, 1985). He attributes the "deterioration and general turmoil that we are seeing" to "inadequate bank capital" and "the deterioration of other balance sheet fundamentals" (Greenspan, 1985). A desire by the Administration to reorient the Fed's microeconomic philosophy in this way may have been a major factor in deciding to replace Volcker. In any case, the difference in philosophy implies that one of Greenspan's first orders of business will be to oversee drafting a new blueprint for the Fed's future role in setting regulatory and supervisory policies. This new blueprint should render Corrigan's blueprint a nonstarter.

Unlike Corrigan or Volcker, Greenspan is not a veteran Fed employee. Because he possesses only an outsider's view of the Fed's institutional self-interest, he does not share his predecessor's determination to keep banking and commerce separate generally or to close what may now be called the nonthrift–thrift loophole in particular. For bankers, the new Chairman's advocating financial deregulation is both good news and bad news. The good news is that it will present opportunities for expanded powers by which banks and bank holding companies can pursue nontraditional profit opportunities. The bad news is that it probably will enhance opportunities for large bank and nonbanking firms—particularly nonfinancial entities such as Sears—to invade banks' traditional markets. For many large banks, the good news outweighs the bad news. For small banks, the bad news might be interpreted as a mandate for educating the new Chairman quickly about the political value of keeping small banks' lobbying power squarely in the Fed's corner.

V. EFFECTS OF A NEW CHAIRMAN ON THE FEDERAL RESERVE ITSELF

Policy responsibility within the Fed is formally shared across a lattice of System committees and boards, but the Fed is fundamentally a hierarchical organization. Within such an organization, one's status is tied not only to his own job performance, but also to his superiors' job performance. For this reason, most Fed researchers come to see that an important part of their jobs is to make their bosses and their bosses' bosses look good.

To the extent that the constituent elements of a leader's personality influence what he perceives as making him look good, a leader's personality helps define the perceived missions of his subordinates. The leader's internal and external activity sends signals about what the organization values, and these signals implicitly redefine the organization's structure and strategy.

In this sense, the structure of Federal Reserve policymaking responds not merely to changes in economic problems that the Fed faces over time. They respond also to changes in the character of Fed Chairmen (Meltzer, 1982) and in the nature of a Chairman's interaction with the President, Congress, and the press on the one hand and with other Governors, Reserve Bank Presidents, and top research staff on the other. Fed leaders and employees want the power and freedom to achieve a favorable impact on System policies and for their contributions to be reinforced by formal confirmation of their achievements. This makes it a bureaucratically divisive strategy to engage in disguised—as opposed to open—political compromises. A Chairman whom the press perceives as masking the political adjustments made in Fed policies is led to worry excessively about his subordinates' loyalty to him. Such worries make demonstrating loyalty more important internally than communicating honest dissent. This set of values tends to sap colleagues' and staff's self-esteem and to create a corporate culture in which only those sharing common views and common foes can prosper. One of Volcker's more subtle accomplishments was ridding the System of some of the institutional paranoia created by disguised politics under Burns and by public relations incompetence under G. William Miller.

Volcker restored the Fed's self-image as a confident and politically tough fighter of inflation and defender of financial stability set largely outside the short-run chain of Presidential and congressional command. Rather than pretending to juggle the nation's many economic goals simultaneously, he claimed to put fewer objects into the game. He narrowed the Fed's perceived mission to controlling inflation in the long run while avoiding financial instability in the short run. If Greenspan can define his priorities with equal clarity and communicate them even half as persuasively, the tasks of restoring the Fed's credibility and of refocusing its corporate culture should continue to progress.

REFERENCES

Corrigan, E. G., "Financial Market Structure: A Longer View," *Annual Report, 1986*, Federal Reserve Bank of New York, 1986.

Fischer, S., and J. Huizenga, "Inflation, Unemployment, and Public Opinion Polls," *Journal of Money, Credit and Banking*, February 1982, 1–19.

Greenspan, A., "The Case for Deregulation of the Banking Industry," 1985; reprinted in *American Banker*, June 4, 1987, 4, 16.

Kane, E. J., "Politics and Fed Policymaking: The More Things Change the More They Remain the Same," *Journal of Monetary Economics*, 1980, 199–211.

Meltzer, A. H., "Discussion" in R. E. Lombra and W. E. Witte, eds., *Political Economy of International and Domestic Monetary Relations*, Iowa State University Press, Ames, 1982, 233–235.

Article Twenty-Five

REGULATION

The new chairman confronted the worst crash in history during his first year, and that was just the beginning. Here is an assessment by MBA's chief economist, a former governor of the Federal Reserve.

Happy Anniversary, ALAN GREENSPAN

When Alan Greenspan accepted President Reagan's nomination to become chairman of the Federal Reserve Board in mid 1987, he knew he was taking on a tough assignment. Previous occupants of that position had given him ample warning.

William McChesney Martin, chairman of the Board from 1951 to 1970, said that the Federal Reserve had the unenviable task of removing the punch bowl just when the party was becoming interesting. The late Arthur F. Burns, Martin's successor, must have agreed, because he gave a lecture called "The Anguish of Central Banking" soon after his departure from the chairman's post in 1979. And Paul A. Volcker, who gained worldwide fame as chairman from 1979 through mid 1987, wryly observed that "a central banker is a person who worries that there might be someone, somewhere, who is happy."

The chairman of the Federal Reserve Board is continuously on trial with financial markets, the Congress, the administration and the general public. He cannot please everyone.

Memories are short for what he does that goes right; what goes wrong is never forgotten.

Alan Greenspan has occupied this lofty post for the past year. He has proven amazingly adept at dealing with formidable problems. Yet, critics still question his antiinflation credentials, and administration officials periodically grumble that his monetary policies are too erratic or too restrictive.

The Federal Reserve was confronted with the most serious financial crisis in modern times just two months after Greenspan took office. The stock market's crash on October 19 threatened a total financial meltdown and a potential collapse of the economy. The fact that the worst did not happen in no way diminishes the gravity of the problem that confronted the Federal Reserve. On the contrary, without the Fed's skillful handling of that crisis, the damage to financial markets and the economy could well have been frighteningly large.

The Fed's adroit management of the problem was facilitated by the contingency planning for a variety of potential crises that Greenspan initi-

Lyle E. Gramley

246

ated immediately after his arrival at the Board. On the morning after the stock market's plunge, Greenspan issued a statement saying: "The Federal Reserve, consistent with its responsibilities as the nation's central bank, affirmed today its readiness to serve as a source of liquidity to support the economic and financial system."

That statement told the nation and the world that the Federal Reserve had no intention of letting 1987 become 1929 all over again. To emphasize the point, the Fed made its presence in financial markets highly visible by conducting open market purchases of government securities in substantial amounts. To underscore the Fed's intentions, these purchases were often made earlier in the day than usual.

Behind the scenes, the Federal Reserve went into high gear to monitor ongoing developments and offer assistance where needed. Federal Reserve System examiners were placed in major banking institutions; credit relationships between banks and securities dealers were closely watched to ensure adequate funding of brokers and dealers in stress; daily monitoring of primary government securities dealers was intensified. Through these and other steps, the Federal Reserve successfully walled off the stock market's crash and prevented a flood of financial problems from cascading through the economy.

If Greenspan's contribution to the Federal Reserve and the nation were confined solely to the management of the crisis posed by the crash, that alone would warrant a hero's medal. Oddly enough, along with the words of praise he so genuinely deserves, Greenspan has been curiously *blamed* in some quarters for causing the stock market's crash by tightening monetary policy and raising interest rates in August and September of last year.

As I see it, such an accusation is sheer drivel. Greenspan stated it better than I could. Said he: "Stock prices finally reached levels which stretched to incredulity expectations of rising real earnings and falling discount factors . . . The market plunge was an accident waiting to happen."

No one can deny that rising interest rates in August, September and early October contributed to a sobering of attitudes among equity investors. But

the Fed's contribution to the interest rate rise was cause for praise, not condemnation.

Here is why. Economic growth had begun to accelerate in the summer of 1987, as activity in the industrial sector responded strongly to a markedly improved competitive position in world markets and to increased domestic demands for new equipment. Coming late in the fifth year of the expansion, the economy's renewed vigor threatened economic overheating, with a concomitant worsening of inflation later on.

Clearly, steps were needed to curb the growth of money and credit, and the Fed quite properly took them. Downward pressures on the dollar's exchange value also were a worrisome development. The alacrity with which the Fed under Greenspan's guidance

---

"Greenspan has been curiously *blamed* for causing the stock market's crash. Such an accusation is sheer drivel."

---

moved to ward off inflation in the summer of 1987 should have gone a long way toward strengthening the confidence of financial markets in Greenspan and the Federal Reserve. Unfortunately, that has not happened, and for a variety of reasons.

First, worries abound that the Federal Reserve will play election-year politics in the conduct of monetary policy for the rest of 1988. Charges that such practices have been followed in the past are without substance, but their tenacity shows that myths are hard to dispel. The truth is that the Fed tightened substantially in the latter half of 1980 and again in the first half of 1984, both election years. In 1988, tightening actions began in early April, and further steps toward restraint occurred around mid May.

Second, markets worry about the division of views among Board members. Diversity of analytic approaches does exist, but it always has. The dif-

ference now is principally that individual Board members' views become public more frequently. That is partly a consequence of Greenspan's style. He encourages lively internal debate and does not try to suppress public expression of individual views of everything from bank regulatory policy to monetary policy.

From my vantage, this is not a significant problem. It might be if Greenspan were unable to build an effective consensus to conduct and implement Federal Reserve policy. But Greenspan is a strong leader, and the history of his first year in office indicates that when the chips are down, he can carry with him a majority of his Board and of the voting presidents on the Federal Open Market Committee.

Third, the market yearns for a more simplistic world than we now have. In particular, there is a strong desire to return to the days when monetary policy was guided and judged by the growth of the monetary aggregates. Returning to targeting the monetary aggregates, it is thought, would make it easier to determine whether the Fed is truly concerned with holding down inflation over the long run or whether its priorities have changed.

I sympathize with market participants who have difficulty interpreting monetary policy in today's environment. I would strongly support a return to closer targeting on the monetary aggregates as soon as possible, and I suspect that most policymaking officials in the Federal Reserve would, too. But the fact is that the Federal Reserve really has no alternative to an eclectic approach. Relationships between the monetary aggregates and GNP and prices are simply not as stable or predictable as they used to be, and Greenspan and his fellow policymakers can do nothing about that.

As far as financial markets are concerned, the acid test of Greenspan's qualities as a Federal Reserve chairman lies just ahead. Fears of higher inflation have mounted this year as the economy has continued to show relatively strong growth despite the crash and the inventory correction necessitated by a buildup of excess stocks late in 1987. Skilled labor resources have become scarce after five and a half years of solid economic expansion, and capacity has become strained in a number of manufacturing industries, particularly those that have benefited from a booming export business. This is the kind of environment in which inflationary pressures have flourished in the past, and there is concern that it could happen again.

Greenspan is well known for believing that inflation seriously damages the economy. Moreover, in his term as chairman of Gerald Ford's Council of Economic Advisers, Greenspan strongly supported Federal Reserve efforts to limit the inflationary effects of rising oil prices during 1973 and 1974. He did it when political sentiment was running the other way.

So why has Greenspan yet to establish his credentials as a staunch supporter of antiinflation policies? A friend of mine put it this way: "Financial markets worry that Greenspan may be more like Arthur Burns than Paul Volcker." Volcker told the world that he planned to bring inflation down, and he did it. Burns made tough public statements on the need to reduce inflation, but inflation increased on his watch, whether it was his fault or not.

My own judgment is that a moderate upturn in inflation this year is almost inevitable. Specifically, I expect consumer prices to be increasing at an annual rate of 5 to 5.5 percent by the fourth quarter—compared with the 4 to 4.5 percent rate that has prevailed during the expansion to date. This worsening of inflation is regrettable, and it might have been avoided if the October crash had not deflected the Federal Reserve from the more restrictive monetary policy course on which it had embarked last summer.

Greenspan's credentials as Fed chairman will not be made or destroyed by this moderate upturn in inflation, but rather by the way he and his colleagues in the Federal Reserve respond to it. If participants in financial markets complain early in 1989 about tight money threatening to stall the economy's expansion, Alan Greenspan will have successfully led the Fed through its first major test in fighting inflation since he took office. I, for one, am betting that he makes it.
MB

Lyle E. Gramley joined MBA as a senior staff vice president and chief economist in 1985 after serving five years as a Federal Reserve Board governor. He also was on Jimmy Carter's Council of Economic Advisers from 1977 to 1980.

Article Twenty-Six

Federal Reserve Open Market Techniques

By Howard L. Roth

Open market operations are the Federal Reserve's primary monetary policy instrument for promoting noninflationary economic growth and other policy goals. Through open market operations—the buying and selling of U.S. government securities—the Federal Reserve influences interest rates and the supply of money and credit. Changes in financial conditions lead in turn to movements in economic activity and the general level of prices in the economy.

In conducting open market operations, the Federal Reserve uses a number of different techniques, ranging from outright transactions with U.S. government security dealers to self-reversing transactions with foreign central banks. The particular technique used depends, among other things, on the Federal Reserve's operating procedures and changes in factors other than open market operations that affect reserve availability.

Howard Roth is an economist at the Federal Reserve Bank of Kansas City. Richard Roberts, a research associate at the bank, assisted in the preparation of the article.

This article describes the different techniques that are used in conducting open market operations and identifies some changes that have occurred in recent years in their relative importance. The first section provides background material on the role open market operations play in the conduct of monetary policy. The open market operating techniques are described in the second section, while the third section examines the changes that have occurred in the usage of these techniques in recent years.

Open market operations and monetary policy

Open market operations by the Federal Reserve lead initially to changes in the supply of reserves that depository financial institutions have available to meet their reserve requirements. Changes in reserves—which are held either as deposits at Federal Reserve banks or as vault cash—lead in turn to changes in interest rates and the supply of money and credit. For example, when reserves increase, depository institutions are able to increase their loans and investments, and thereby increase the deposit accounts held by borrowers. The attendant rise in the supply of money and credit tends, in turn, to be accompanied by a decline in interest rates. Alternatively, a reduction in reserves leads to a decline in money and credit and upward pressure on interest rates.

The linkage between open market operations and reserves is made clear by the accounting transaction that occurs when the Federal Reserve pays for the securities it buys or is paid for securities it sells. When the Federal Reserve buys securities, it pays for them by crediting the reserve accounts held at the Federal Reserve by the sellers' depository institutions.[1] The sellers' accounts at depository institutions, in turn, are credited. Conversely, sales of securities by the Federal Reserve are handled through debits to depository institutions' reserve accounts at the Federal Reserve. Thus, when the Federal Reserve purchases securities, reserves increase; and when the Federal Reserve sells securities, reserves decline.

The Federal Reserve's portfolio of securities is one of several sources of reserves, as shown in Table 1. Other sources include Federal Reserve loans to depository institutions and Federal Reserve float. Table 1 also shows how the total source of reserves can be used. In general, sources of reserves can be used three ways: they can be used as reserves, be used by the public as currency, or be used to increase other nonreserve liabilities of the Federal Reserve.[2]

_____

[1] The Federal Reserve engages in security transactions with about three dozen large securities dealers. About a third of the dealers are departments in large money center banks. To buy or sell securities from a bank, the Federal Reserve simply credits or debits the bank's reserve account.

[2] The Federal Reserve capital accounts and the Treasury's monetary net worth make up the remaining uses.

As indicated in Table 1, total sources of reserves equal total uses of reserves.[3] Also, as the table shows, reserves equal total sources minus the uses other than reserves. The following reserve equation is similarly constructed and provides a breakdown of sources and nonreserve uses of reserves along the lines of Table 1.

$$
\begin{aligned}
\text{Reserves} = \;& \text{Securities} + \text{Loans} \\
& + \text{Float} + \text{Other Sources} \\
& - \text{Currency in Circulation} \\
& - \text{Treasury Deposits} \\
& - \text{Foreign and Other Deposits} \\
& - \text{Other Uses.}
\end{aligned}
$$

The sources and uses on the right hand side of the equation are more generally referred to as factors affecting reserves. The most important factor is the Federal Reserve's portfolio of securities. Loans to depository institutions are also a factor affecting reserves because reserves increase when the Federal Reserve credits the accounts of borrowing institutions for the amounts of their loans. Float—cash items in the process of collection minus deferred availability cash items—arises when the scheduled credit-deferral period on a check presented to the Federal Reserve for collection elapses before the Federal Reserve can collect

_____

[3] Table 1 is a condensed version of a table published weekly in Federal Reserve publication H.4.1, "Factors Affecting Reserve Balances of Depository Institutions and Condition Statement of Federal Reserve Banks," and monthly as Table 1.11 in the *Federal Reserve Bulletin*. The consolidated balance sheet of the 12 Federal Reserve banks is published in the *Federal Reserve Bulletin* every month as Table 1.18. Information about the Treasury's monetary accounts is printed in the *Treasury Bulletin*.

For a description of the items appearing in these tables, see *The Federal Reserve System: Purposes and Functions*, Board of Governors of the Federal Reserve System, Washington, D.C., 1984, *Statfacts: Understanding Federal Reserve Statistical Reports*, Federal Reserve Bank of New York, November 1981, or any of a number of undergraduate money and banking textbooks.

TABLE 1
Sources and uses of reserves
November 20, 1985
(millions of dollars)*

Sources

Federal Reserve portfolio of securities	180,341
Loans to depository institutions from the Federal Reserve	1,178
Float†	1,483
Other sources	47,122
Total sources	230,124

Uses

Currency in circulation	191,471	
Minus vault cash used to satisfy reserve requirements	20,117	171,354
Treasury deposits		3,036
Foreign and other deposits held with Federal Reserve banks		800
Other uses		8,575
Total nonreserve uses		183,765
Reserves		46,359
Total uses		230,124

Source: *Federal Reserve Bulletin*, Tables 1.11 and 1.12, February 1986

*Biweekly averages of daily averages for two-week period ended November 20, 1985

†Cash items in the process of collection minus deferred availability cash items

from the depository institution on which the check was drawn. When this happens, both the presenting institution and the paying institution have credit for the funds, a development that adds reserves to the financial system until the Federal Reserve collects.

Another factor affecting reserves is currency in circulation, which consists of paper currency and coin held outside the Treasury and Federal Reserve banks. As the negative sign in the equation indicates, when currency in circulation increases, reserves of depository institutions decline. Deposits held with the Federal Reserve banks, other than reserve deposits, also affect reserves. These deposits include accounts that the Treasury, foreign central banks, and international institutions hold at Federal Reserve banks. The Treasury uses its account for depositing tax revenues and other receipts and for making expenditures. Foreign central banks and international institutions hold accounts at the Federal Reserve Bank of New York to facilitate international settlements. When the Treasury, foreign central banks, or international institutions transfer funds from domestic depository institutions to accounts at the Federal Reserve, reserves of depository institutions decline. Increases in these deposits are associated with decreases in reserves.

The factors affecting reserves can be divided into two categories—controllable and uncontrollable—according to whether the Federal Reserve has close control over them. The only factor the Federal Reserve can control closely is its portfolio of securities. All of the other factors cannot be closely controlled.

Within this framework of factors affecting reserves, the Federal Reserve follows a three-step procedure in conducting monetary policy. The first step is to determine a target level of reserves consistent with the objectives of monetary policy.[4] The second step is to estimate the net change in reserves that will occur due to movements in uncontrollable factors. The third step is to undertake open market operations that increase or decrease security holdings enough to bring about the targeted level of reserves. Reserves are targeted over two-week maintenance periods that correspond to periods during which depository institutions are required to hold specified average levels of reserves.

A simplified example helps illustrate the three-step reserve-targeting procedure. Suppose the Federal Reserve determines that the target level of reserves for a reserve maintenance period is $41 billion. Also, suppose reserve projections show that when estimated developments of uncontrollable factors are taken into account, reserves would average $40 billion if the Federal Reserve took no action. In this case, therefore, the Federal Reserve would seek to supply depository institutions with an average of $1 billion in reserves by increasing its holdings of securities through open market operations. If, on the other hand, reserve projections showed reserves would exceed the targeted level, the Federal Reserve would absorb reserves by reducing its holdings of securities.

---

[4] More precisely, reserve targets are formulated in terms of non-borrowed reserves—reserves net of adjustment and seasonal borrowing by depository institutions.

Open market techniques

Open market operations are carried out by a unit in the Securities Department of the Federal Reserve Bank of New York.[5] This unit, known as the Desk, operates according to directives from the Federal Open Market Committee (FOMC).

The operations available to the Desk for managing reserves fall into two broad categories—outright or permanent transactions and temporary or self-reversing transactions. Buying, selling, or redeeming securities are outright transactions, while engaging in repurchase agreements (RP's) or engaging in matched sale purchase agreements (MSP's) are temporary transactions. With RP's, the Federal Reserve buys securities but agrees to sell them at a specified future date at a specified price.[6] Under MSP's, it sells securities but agrees to buy other securities at specified future dates and terms.

Outright transactions

The Desk uses outright transactions when it wants to provide or absorb reserves over relatively long time spans. Outright transactions typically are used when projections show a shortage or excess that is likely to persist longer than a single two-week maintenance period.

---

[5] Lucid descriptions of these operations are provided by Paul Meek, *U.S. Monetary Policy and Financial Markets*, Federal Reserve Bank of New York, 1982, and in *Open Market Operations*, Federal Reserve Bank of New York, 1985. See also William Melton, *Inside the Fed: Making Monetary Policy*, Dow Jones-Irwin, Homewood, Ill., 1985.

[6] The Federal Reserve's use of "RP" is opposite that of securities dealers. When the Federal Reserve says it is undertaking RP's, it is putting out money and taking in securities, thereby increasing reserves. When securities dealers undertake RP's, they are effectively borrowing money. The conventional definition of an RP, then, is a sale of securities with an agreement to repurchase the securities on a fixed date.

Long-lasting needs to add or drain reserves arise for a variety of reasons—to meet the needs of a growing economy, to offset long-lasting seasonal movements in uncontrolled factors, and to accommodate permanent changes in the demand for reserves.

A growing economy requires a growing money supply. Depository institutions must hold additional reserves to support growth in checkable and nonpersonal time deposits. And growth in currency in circulation must also be supported by additional reserves if reserve availability is to be maintained. Outright purchases supply the reserves needed for monetary expansion.

Seasonal movements in factors affecting reserves for more than a two-week maintenance period also may call for outright transactions. For example, currency in circulation rises before holidays as consumers prepare to make additional purchases, and then returns to more normal levels after the holidays. If not offset, the rise and fall of currency in circulation would first drain reserves from the financial system and then supply reserves. The seasonal pattern for the Christmas holiday season spans several weeks. By purchasing securities outright before Christmas and selling securities outright after Christmas, the Desk can offset much of the seasonal effect of currency in circulation on reserves.[7]

---

[7] Recent changes in the long-run demand for reserves by depository institutions have been met with outright transactions. The Depository Institutions Deregulation and Monetary Control Act of 1980 mandated reserve requirements for nonmember banks and thrift institutions. The reserve requirement of these institutions has been phased in over six years. Demand for reserves by these institutions increases on the dates that their reserve requirements increase. The act also provided a schedule for reducing the reserve requirements of member banks. The phasing down, completed in 1984, reduced member banks' demand for reserves. Because they affected the demand for reserves, the phase-ups and phase-downs had to be accounted for in implementing policy. Since a phase-down permanently reduces demand for reserves, its effect on reserves is offset by an outright transaction

The Desk engages in outright transactions with U.S. government security dealers and with foreign central banks and other institutions that maintain accounts at the Federal Reserve Bank of New York. The Desk acts either as an intermediary between the foreign accounts and the securities market or deals directly with the foreign accounts in buying securities from them or selling securities to them. Foreign central banks and international institutions maintaining accounts at the Federal Reserve Bank of New York usually also hold accounts at domestic depository institutions. When the deposits of foreign institutions rise above the levels needed for ordinary transactions purposes, the surplus funds are normally invested in interest-earning assets. In many instances, foreign institutions ask a depository institution or a securities dealer to invest the funds in the securities market. In other instances, the institutions ask the Desk to invest the surplus funds. Depending on its perception of the need to add or drain reserves from the financial system, the Desk either invests the funds in the market or sells securities from its own account to absorb the funds.

The effects of outright transactions on reserves are illustrated in Table 2. Entry 1 shows the effect of an outright purchase of $1 billion in securities from a security dealer. The Federal Reserve's security portfolio (an asset of the Federal Reserve) is increased by $1 billion. The reserve account of the securities dealer's depository institution (a liability of the Federal Reserve and an asset of the depository institution) is correspondingly increased. The securities dealer's demand deposit at the financial institution (an asset of the securities dealer and a liability of the

---

reducing the supply of reserves. Similarly, a phase-up is offset by an outright purchase of securities.

TABLE 2
Reserve accounting
(billions of dollars)

Federal Reserve

	Assets		Liabilities	
(1)	Securities	+1	Reserves	+1
(2)			Reserves	−1
			Foreign deposits	+1
(3)	Securities	−1	Foreign deposits	−1
(4)			Reserves	+1
			Foreign deposits	−1
(5)	Securities	+1	Reserves	+1
(6)	Securities	−1	Foreign deposits	−1
(7)			Reserves	+1
			Foreign deposits	−1
(8)	Securities	−1	Reserves	−1

Depository Institutions

	Assets		Liabilities	
(1)	Reserves	+1	Demand deposits	+1
(2)	Reserves	−1	Demand deposits	−1
(3)				
(4)	Reserves	+1	Demand deposits	+1
(5)	Reserves	+1	Demand deposits	+1
(6)				
(7)	Reserves	+1	Demand deposits	+1
(8)	Reserves	−1	Demand deposits	−1

Public

	Assets		Liabilities	
(1)	Demand deposits	+1		
(1)	Securities	−1		
(2)				
(3)				
(4)	Securities	−1		
(4)	Demand deposits	+1		
(5)	Demand deposits	+1	RP's	+1
(6)				
(7)			RP's	+1
(7)	Demand deposits	+1		
(8)	Demand deposits	−1		
(8)	RRP's	+1		

Foreign

	Assets		
(2)	Demand deposits	−1
(2)	Deposit at FRB	+1
(3)	Securities	+1
(3)	Deposit at FRB	−1
(4)	Securities	+1
(4)	Deposit at FRB	−1
(6)	RRP's	+1
(6)	Deposit at FRB	−1
(7)	RRP's	+1
(7)	Deposit at FRB	−1

depository institution) is increased. And the securities dealer's portfolio of securities (an asset of the securities dealer) is reduced. Thus, the outright purchase injects reserves into the financial system. Conversely, an outright sale drains reserves from the financial system, and the associated accounting entries are the reverse of those for an outright purchase.

The effects of outright transactions with foreign accounts are illustrated by entries 2 and 3 in Table 2. The illustration assumes that the Desk sells securities to a foreign account. To see the effect on reserves, it is useful to break the transaction into two components. One is the transfer of excess funds by the foreign institution from its account at a domestic depository institution to its account at the Federal Reserve Bank of New York. The other is the subsequent investment of these funds in securities from the Federal Reserve's portfolio. In entry 2 of Table 2, the foreign institution transfers funds from its account at a depository institution account to its account at the Federal Reserve, a transfer that drains reserves from the financial system. In entry 3, the Federal Reserve sells securities from its own account to the foreign account. The net effect of entries 2 and 3 is that securities are transferred from the Federal Reserve to foreign institutions, demand deposits of foreign institutions are reduced, and reserves are drained from the financial system. Conversely, when the Federal Reserve purchases securities offered for sale by foreign accounts, reserves are injected into the financial system.

When the Desk acts as agent for a foreign account in the securities markets, the level of total reserves in the financial system is not affected. When the Desk buys securities in the market for a foreign account, entry 2 is still appropriate but entry 3 is not. Instead, entry 4 records the investment of the funds in the market by the Federal Reserve acting as agent. When the seller of the securities deposits the check drawn on the foreign institution's account at the Federal Reserve Bank of New York, reserves (and demand deposits) increase to their original level. The net result of the two transactions shown in entries 2 and 4 is that the public has fewer securities and higher demand deposits while foreign institutions have lower demand deposits and fewer securities. Reserves are unchanged.

When the Federal Reserve redeems maturing securities held in its portfolio, the effect is to drain reserves in a similar manner as an outright sale of securities. The Desk redeems maturing securities by subscribing for a smaller amount of the issues offered in a Treasury or federal agency refunding than the Federal Reserve's current holdings of maturing issues. The accounting entries for a redemption are not shown in Table 2.

Temporary transactions

The Desk uses temporary transactions when it wants to provide or absorb reserves for relatively short time periods. Temporary transactions typically will be used when projections show a shortage or excess that is likely to persist no longer than a single two-week maintenance period.

Short-run needs to add or drain reserves typically arise from changes in uncontrollable factors. Temporary transactions are arranged to limit the effects on reserves of anticipated changes in uncontrollable factors and to offset the effects on reserves of unanticipated changes in these factors.

The Desk engages in two kinds of repurchase agreements and two kinds of matched sale-purchase transactions. System RP's are arranged for the account of the Federal Reserve Bank of New York. Customer-related

RP's are arranged for foreign and international institutions holding accounts at the Federal Reserve. MSP's in the market are between the Federal Reserve and securities dealers. The other kind of MSP is between the Federal Reserve and official foreign and international accounts.

The Desk makes available a daily investment facility in which foreign account funds are pooled. This arrangement allows the Desk either to invest the entire pool in the market in one transaction (customer-related RP's), to meet these investment needs from its own portfolio of securities (MSP's with the foreign investment pool), or to engage in a combination of the two. This pooling of foreign funds simplifies Desk operations and enables the Desk to serve the investment needs of more foreign accounts than it could otherwise.

The reserve effects of temporary transactions are also shown in Table 2. As entry 5 shows, the accounting for a System RP is similar to that for an outright purchase. One difference is that the securities dealer considers the transaction as having increased one of its liabilities, repurchase agreements. The securities dealer has borrowed funds from the Federal Reserve with an agreement to repay with interest on an agreed-on date, at most 15 days later. The other difference from an outright purchase is that the transaction is later reversed. Most often, the funds are loaned only overnight. In that case, reserves are increased for only one day. When the transaction is reversed, the accounting entries are reversed and reserves return to their original level.

Customer-related RP's and MSP's with the pool are alternative ways of investing the pool. The Desk does not consider MSP's with the pool a reserve management technique even though the MSP's drain reserves. Instead, when the Federal Reserve forecasts the level of reserves that will be available in the financial system, it assumes that the funds in the pool will be invested with the system as MSP's. That is, the pool is treated as an uncontrolled factor that regularly absorbs reserves, like currency in circulation.

The accounting entries for doing MSP's with the foreign pool are shown in entry 6 of

The use of temporary transactions has changed significantly in the past few years.

Table 2. Making MSP's with the pool does not offset the initial reserve drain when foreign and international accounts transfer their excess funds from depository institutions to the Federal Reserve Bank of New York. The net effect on reserves from lines 2 and 6 is a drain of reserves.

Because the prospective drain on reserves from doing MSP's with the pool is factored into reserve projections, customer-related RP's reduce the drain and increase reserves relative to the level that was projected. In this respect, both customer-related RP's and System RP's supply reserves to the financial system. However, like the outright purchase of securities for foreign or international account illustrated in entries 2 and 4, customer-related RP's have no net effect on reserves when the initial buildup of funds in foreign institutions' accounts at the Federal Reserve is taken into account. The accounting entries recording the investment of funds in the market are shown in entry 7. The foreign institution invests in reverse repurchase agreements (RRP's), an asset. The public, most likely a securities dealer, incurs an increase in RP's, a liability. There is no net effect on reserves when entries 2 and 7 are combined. The entries are reversed as the RP unwinds the next day.

Both System RP's and customer-related RP's increase reserves relative to reserve projections. The choice between the two depends largely on the magnitude of the reserve need that the Desk wants to meet. Customer-related RP's are limited by the amount of funds in the pool. System RP's can be used to meet larger reserve needs. Another consideration can be the duration of the reserve need. Reserve needs extending more than one day can be easily handled with multi-day System RP's. Designing a customer-related RP for this task would be difficult because the future size of the pool cannot be known precisely.

The accounting entries for a MSP in the market are given in entry 8 of Table 2. From the securities dealer's point of view, it has made a short-term loan to the Federal Reserve. The loan is recorded on the dealer's books as a debit to RRP's and a credit to demand deposits, another asset. When the MSP matures, the accounting entries are reversed. Thus, reserves are lower for the duration of the MSP and then return to their original level.

Use of the techniques

In conducting open market operations, the Desk relies more on temporary transactions than on outright transactions. The use of temporary transactions has changed significantly in the past few years. Their use declined sharply in 1980 and 1981, but has increased somewhat since 1981.

The dollar volume of total temporary transactions typically has been ten times the volume of total outright transactions. For example, temporary transactions totaled $310 billion in 1985, compared with $34 billion for outright transactions (Table 3). [8]

The reason for the much heavier use of temporary transactions is that uncontrolled factors are highly volatile in the short run. For example, while total reserves showed a net change of around $80 million a week in 1985, absolute week-to-week changes in uncontrolled factors averaged $1.4 billion during the year. To prevent this short-run variability in uncontrolled factors from leading to weekly variability in reserves, the Desk provided and absorbed reserves through temporary transactions.

The dollar volume of total temporary transactions dropped $63 billion in 1980, fell another $101 billion in 1981, and then increased $41 billion in 1982. From 1983 to 1985, total temporary transactions averaged

---

Changes in operating procedures contributed to the sharp drops in temporary transactions in 1980 and 1981.

---

almost precisely their 1982 level. Much of the pattern since 1979 can be attributed to changes in day-to-day operating procedures and changes in the variability of uncontrolled factors.

Changes in operating procedures contributed to the sharp drops in temporary transactions in 1980 and 1981. Until October 1979, the Desk had used its reserve management techniques in day-to-day operations to hold the federal funds rate to a narrow band around a level thought to be consistent with the desired growth of money and credit. Heavy use of temporary transactions was required. Under the operating procedures instituted in October 1979, the Desk targeted nonborrowed reserves—reserves net of adjustment plus seasonal borrowing by

---

[8] The source of most of the dollar figures in Table 3 is a series of articles published yearly by the staff of the Federal Reserve Bank of New York, "Monetary Policy and Open Market Operations," *Quarterly Review*, Federal Reserve Bank of New York.

TABLE 3
Volume of open market operations
(billions of dollars)

	1978	1979	1980	1981	1982	1983	1984	1985
Outright transactions								
Purchases								
In market	15.0	7.1	8.5	8.8	10.5	10.7	14.1	17.1
From foreign accounts	9.9	14.1	4.4	8.4	9.4	11.8	9.7	9.4
Sales								
In market	0.2	2.3	2.8	2.6	1.5	0	1.1	1.5
To foreign accounts	13.7	5.6	4.5	4.1	7.1	3.4	7.6	2.7
Redemptions	2.3	3.0	3.5	1.9	3.2	2.8	8.0	3.7
Total outright	41.1	32.1	23.7	25.8	31.7	28.7	40.5	34.4
Temporary transactions								
Repurchase agreements								
System	221.5	185.5	167.2	110.9	179.1	124.0	144.8	156.4
Customer-related	47.3	53.0	64.3	79.5	89.1	159.9	126.7	116.7
Matched sale purchases								
in market	140.2	194.6	138.6	78.4	42.0	11.9	55.0	36.6
Total temporary	409.0	433.1	370.1	268.8	310.2	295.8	326.5	309.7

depository institutions from the Federal Reserve. Because the federal funds rate was allowed to vary over a much wider range, fewer temporary transactions were needed.[9]

Another change in operating procedures occurring in the fall of 1982 is consistent with the increased use of temporary transactions after 1981. The nonborrowed reserves operating procedure was modified in late 1982 when a breakdown in the relationship between M1 and economic activity forced the Federal Reserve to rely more on judgments of mone-

tary and economic developments in deciding on the appropriate level of reserves in the financial system. The new procedure has been described as being between a nonborrowed reserves operating procedure and a federal funds operating procedure. As such, the use of temporary transactions might be expected to be more frequent than under the nonborrowed reserves procedure used from late 1979 to late 1982 but less frequent than under the federal funds rate procedure used until late 1979.

A decline in the variability of uncontrollable factors also contributed to the decline in the use of temporary transactions in 1980 and 1981. Chart 1 plots the dollar volume of total temporary transactions and the variability of total uncontrolled market factors for 1978 through 1985. Variability is measured by the average absolute week-to-week change in total uncontrolled market factors. Chart 1 shows that uncontrolled factors became less variable during the years that the use of temporary

---

[9] A study of the new operating procedures revealed that the number of market entries to conduct temporary transactions in the first year under the new operating procedures was about a third less than in the preceding year. See Fred J. Levin and Paul Meek, "Implementing the New Operating Procedures: The View from the Trading Desk," *New Monetary Control Procedures*, Federal Resere Staff Study, Vol. I, Board of Governors of the Federal Reserve System, February 1981. See also Neil G. Berkman, "Open Market Operations Under the New Monetary Policy," *New England Economic Review*, Federal Reserve Bank of Boston, March/April 1981, pp. 5-20.

Relationship between temporary transactions and the variability of uncontrolled factors

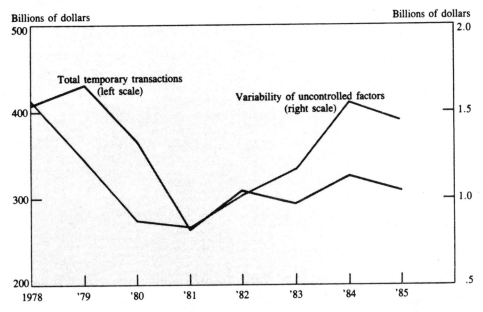

transactions was declining. The average absolute change declined from $1,202 million in 1979 to $850 million in 1981.

An upward movement in the variability of uncontrolled factors appears to be in part responsible for the increased use of temporary transactions after 1981. As shown by Chart 1, the variability of uncontrolled factors reached

---

An upward movement in the variability of uncontrolled factors appears to be in part responsible for the increased use of temporary transactions after 1981.

---

a low in 1981, then rose steadily from 1982 through 1984 before declining slightly in 1985.

The factor contributing most to changes in

variability in recent years has been Treasury deposits with the Federal Reserve. The variability of these deposits and their average level fell dramatically in 1979, remained low for three years, and then rose sharply in 1982 (Table 4). Since 1982, these deposits have been quite variable, although not as variable as they were in 1978.

The 1979-81 decline in the variability of Treasury deposits was due to changes in Treasury cash management techniques. In 1978, Congress authorized commercial banks to pay interest on tax and loan (T&L) accounts and charge the Treasury for services. The Treasury returned to a practice followed before 1967 of transferring funds from T&L accounts to Federal Reserve accounts only in anticipation of expenditures. In this way, the Treasury could maintain a fairly constant balance at the Federal Reserve, and the Treasury account at the

TABLE 4
**Variability of uncontrolled factors
affecting reserves held at Federal Reserve banks**
(millions of dollars)

	Period							
	1978	**1979**	**1980**	**1981**	**1982**	**1983**	**1984**	**1985**
Uncontrolled factors providing reserves								
Loans	278	305	339	333	246	319	579	511
	(867)	(1,338)	(1,441)	(1,358)	(1,046)	(1,039)	(3,721)	(1,313)
Float	972	1,155	948	722	556	438	465	357
	(5,430)	(6,616)	(4,685)	(3,337)	(2,540)	(1,787)	(830)	(801)
Other sources*	226	284	248	286	283	235	347	323
Uncontrolled factors absorbing reserves								
Currency in circulation	471	522	573	649	737	741	818	828
Treasury deposits with the Federal Reserve	1,665	410	559	365	807	937	1,214	1,097
	(8,034)	(3,238)	(3,018)	(3,163)	(3,800)	(2,164)	(4,399)	(4,071)
Foreign and other deposits with the Federal Reserve	100	156	114	115	128	79	78	155
Other uses†	232	238	110	180	151	101	241	166

Note: Variability is measured as the mean absolute week-to-week change in the weekly averages of daily data for each factor indicated. The yearly average of weekly averages of daily data is shown in parentheses for selected factors.

*Includes other Federal Reserve assets, gold stock, the special drawing rights certificate account, and Treasury currency outstanding (lines 11 through 14 of Table 1.11 in the *Federal Reserve Bulletin*). For a description of these items, see "Statfacts: Understanding Federal Reserve Statistical Reports," Federal Reserve Bank of New York, November 1981.

†Includes other Federal Reserve liabilities and capital, service-related balances and adjustments, and Treasury cash (lines 21, 19, and 16, respectively, of Table 1.11 in the *Federal Reserve Bulletin*).

Federal Reserve became a much less variable factor affecting reserves.

The rise in the variability of Treasury deposits after 1981 has been due to a shortage of collateral to back T&L accounts. Funds in T&L accounts must be backed by U.S. securities owned by the commercial bank. When available collateral is depleted, additional receipts must be transferred to the Federal Reserve.

Float has also contributed to changes in the variability of uncontrolled factors. The variability of float declined substantially, beginning in 1980. The Federal Reserve has taken sev-

eral steps to reduce float in recent years. The most significant step was to begin charging depository institutions for float in 1983. Float is, in effect, an extension of credit to depository institutions presenting checks. This credit was interest-free until 1985. Pricing of float and improvements in transporting and processing checks have led to the reduction of float indicated by the averages appearing in parentheses in Table 4.[10]

---

[10] The Federal Reserve has designed its credit deferral schedule so that presenting institutions generally receive credit no later than when the check clears. Thus, float is seldom negative, on

tors have not changed dramatically. The variability of currency in circulation grew steadily over the period, about in line with growth in currency.[11] The variability of loans nearly doubled in 1984, primarily because of Continental Illinois' need to borrow heavily on an extended basis. Extended borrowing resulted in more variability of loans than normal again in 1985, although to a less extent than in 1984. The higher variability of loans is most likely temporary.

---

average, during a week. Because of this, the decline in the weekly average of float since 1978 has been accompanied by a decline in the variability of float.

[11] The variability of currency in circulation is partially predictable, making it less troublesome in formulating policy than if it were totally unpredictable.

The Federal Reserve uses a number of techniques when conducting open market operations to control the supply of reserves available in the financial system. Open market operating techniques include outright and temporary transactions with U.S. government security dealers and foreign official institutions. Due to the need to prevent undue short-run variability in reserve availability, temporary transactions are used more heavily than outright transactions. In recent years, though, the use of temporary transactions has declined somewhat, due in part to a change in the Federal Reserve's operating procedures. Changes in the variability of factors affecting reserves other than open market operations have also affected the relative usage of temporary transactions.

Article Twenty-Seven

THE DISCOUNT WINDOW*

David L. Mengle

The discount window refers to lending by each of the twelve regional Federal Reserve Banks to depository institutions. Discount window loans generally fund only a small part of bank reserves. For example, at the end of 1985 discount window loans were less than three percent of total reserves. Nevertheless, the window is perceived as an important tool both for reserve adjustment and as part of current Federal Reserve monetary control procedures.

Mechanics of a Discount Window Transaction

Discount window lending takes place through the reserve accounts depository institutions are required to maintain at their Federal Reserve Banks. In other words, banks borrow reserves at the discount window. This is illustrated in balance sheet form in Figure 1. Suppose the funding officer at Ralph's Bank finds it has an unanticipated reserve deficiency of $1,000,000 and decides to go to the discount window for an overnight loan in order to cover it. Once the loan is approved, the Ralph's Bank reserve account is credited with $1,000,000. This shows up on the asset side of Ralph's balance sheet as an increase in "Reserves with Federal Reserve Bank," and on the liability side as an increase in "Borrowings from Federal Reserve Bank." The transaction also shows up on the Federal Reserve Bank's balance sheet as an increase in "Discounts and Advances" on the asset side and an increase in "Bank Reserve

Accounts" on the liability side. This set of balance sheet entries takes place in all the examples given in the Box.

The next day, Ralph's Bank could raise the funds to repay the loan by, for example, increasing deposits by $1,000,000 or by selling $1,000,000 of securities. In either case, the proceeds initially increase reserves. Actual repayment occurs when Ralph's Bank's reserve account is debited for $1,000,000, which erases the corresponding entries on Ralph's liability side and on the Reserve Bank's asset side.

Discount window loans, which are granted to institutions by their district Federal Reserve Banks, can be either advances or discounts. Virtually all loans today are advances, meaning they are simply loans secured by approved collateral and paid back with interest at maturity. When the Federal Reserve System was established in 1914, however, the only loans authorized at the window were discounts, also known as rediscounts. Discounts involve a borrower selling "eligible paper," such as a commercial or agricultural loan made by a bank to one of its customers, to its Federal Reserve Bank. In return, the borrower's reserve account is credited for the discounted value of the paper. Upon repayment, the borrower gets the paper back, while its reserve account is debited for the value of the paper. In the case of either advances or discounts, the price of borrowing is determined by the level of the discount rate prevailing at the time of the loan.

Although discount window borrowing was originally limited to Federal Reserve System member banks, the Monetary Control Act of 1980 opened the

---

* An abbreviated version of this article will appear as a chapter in **Instruments of the Money Market,** 6th edition, Federal Reserve Bank of Richmond, 1986 (forthcoming December 1986).

Figure 1

BORROWING FROM THE DISCOUNT WINDOW

Ralph's Bank		Federal Reserve Bank	
Assets	**Liabilities**	**Assets**	**Liabilities**
Reserves with Federal Reserve	Borrowings from Federal Reserve Bank	Discounts and Advances	Bank Reserve Accounts
+ $1,000,000	+ $1,000,000	+ $1,000,000	+ $1,000,000

Examples of Discount Window Transactions

Example 1 — It is Wednesday afternoon at a regional bank, and the bank is required to have enough funds in its reserve account at its Federal Reserve Bank to meet its reserve requirement over the previous two weeks. The bank finds that it must borrow in order to make up its reserve deficiency, but the money center (that is, the major New York, Chicago, and California) banks have apparently been borrowing heavily in the federal funds market. As a result, the rate on fed funds on this particular Wednesday afternoon has soared far above its level earlier that day. As far as the funding officer of the regional bank is concerned, the market for funds at a price she considers acceptable has "dried up." She calls the Federal Reserve Bank for a discount window loan.

Example 2 — A West Coast regional bank, which generally avoids borrowing at the discount window, expects to receive a wire transfer of $300 million from a New York bank, but by late afternoon the money has not yet shown up. It turns out that the sending bank had due to an error accidentally sent only $3,000 instead of the $300 million. Although the New York bank is legally liable for the correct amount, it is closed by the time the error is discovered. In order to make up the deficiency in its reserve position, the West Coast bank calls the discount window for a loan.

Example 3 — It is Wednesday reserve account settlement at another bank, and the funding officer notes that the spread between the discount rate and fed funds rate has widened slightly. Since his bank is buying fed funds to make up a reserve deficiency, he decides to borrow part of the reserve deficiency from the discount window in order to take advantage of the spread. Over the next few months, this repeats itself until the bank receives an "informational" call from the discount officer at the Federal Reserve Bank, inquiring as to the reason for the apparent pattern in discount window borrowing. Taking the hint, the bank refrains from continuing the practice on subsequent Wednesday settlements.

Example 4 — A money center bank acts as a clearing agent for the government securities market. This means that the bank maintains book-entry securities accounts for market participants, and that it also maintains a reserve account and a book-entry securities account at its Federal Reserve Bank, so that securities transactions can be cleared through this system. One day, an internal computer problem arises that allows the bank to accept securities but not to process them for delivery to dealers, brokers, and other market participants. The bank's reserve account is debited for the amount of these securities, but it is unable to pass them on and collect payment for them, resulting in a growing overdraft in the reserve account. As close of business approaches, it becomes increasingly clear that the problem will not be fixed in time to collect the required payments from the securities buyers. In order to avoid a negative reserve balance at the end of the day, the bank estimates its anticipated reserve account deficiency and goes to the Federal Reserve Bank discount window for a loan for that amount. The computer problem is fixed and the loan is repaid the following day.

Example 5 — Due to mismanagement, a privately insured savings and loan association fails. Out of concern about the condition of other privately insured thrift institutions in the state, depositors begin to withdraw their deposits, leading to a run. Because they are not federally insured, some otherwise sound thrifts are not able to borrow from the Federal Home Loan Bank Board in order to meet the demands of the depositors. As a result, the regional Federal Reserve Bank is called upon to lend to these thrifts. After an extensive examination of the collateral the thrifts could offer, the Reserve Bank makes loans to them until they are able to get federal insurance and attract back enough deposits to pay back the discount window loans.

window to all depository institutions, except bankers' banks, that maintain transaction accounts (such as checking and NOW accounts) or nonpersonal time deposits. In addition, the Fed may lend to the United States branches and agencies of foreign banks if they hold deposits against which reserves must be kept.

Finally, subject to determination by the Board of Governors of the Federal Reserve System that "unusual and exigent circumstances" exist, discount window loans may be made to individuals, partnerships, and corporations that are not depository institutions. Such lending would only take place if the

Board and the Reserve Bank were to find that credit from other sources is not available and that failure to lend may have adverse effects on the economy. This last authority has not been used since the 1930s.

Discount window lending takes place under two main programs, adjustment credit and extended credit.[1] Under normal circumstances adjustment credit, which consists of short-term loans extended to cover temporary needs for funds, should account for the larger part of discount window credit. Loans to large banks under this program are generally overnight loans, while small banks may take as long as two weeks to repay. Extended credit provides funds to meet longer term requirements in one of three forms. First, seasonal credit can be extended to small institutions that depend on seasonal activities such as farming or tourism, and that also lack ready access to national money markets. Second, extended credit can be granted to an institution facing special difficulties if it is believed that the circumstances warrant such aid. Finally, extended credit can go to groups of institutions facing deposit outflows due to changes in the financial system, natural disasters, or other problems common to the group (see Box, Example 5). The second and third categories of extended credit may involve a higher rate than the basic discount rate as the term of borrowing grows longer.

In order to borrow from the discount window, the directors of a depository institution first must pass a borrowing resolution authorizing certain officers to borrow from their Federal Reserve Bank. Next, a lending agreement is drawn up between the institution and the Reserve Bank. These two preliminaries out of the way, the bank requests a discount window loan by calling the discount officer of the Reserve Bank and telling the amount desired, the reason for borrowing, and the collateral pledged against the loan. It is then up to the discount officer whether or not to approve it.

Collateral, which consists of securities which could be sold by the Reserve Bank if the borrower fails to pay back the loan, limits the Fed's (and therefore the taxpaying public's) risk exposure. Acceptable collateral includes, among other things, U. S. Treasury securities and government agency securities, municipal securities, mortgages on one-to-four family

dwellings, and short-term commercial notes. Usually, collateral is kept at the Reserve Bank, although some Reserve Banks allow institutions with adequate internal controls to retain custody.

The discount rate is established by the Boards of Directors of the Federal Reserve Banks, subject to review and final determination by the Board of Governors. If the discount rate were always set well above the prevailing fed funds rate, there would be little incentive to borrow from the discount window except in emergencies or if the funds rate for a particular institution were well above that for the rest of the market. Since the 1960s, however, the discount rate has more often than not been set below the funds rate. Figure 2, which portrays both adjustment credit borrowing levels and the spread between the two rates from 1955 to 1985, shows how borrowing tends to rise when the rate spread rises.

The major nonprice tool for rationing discount window credit is the judgment of the Reserve Bank discount officer, whose job is to verify that lending is made only for "appropriate" reasons. Appropriate uses of discount window credit include meeting demands for funds due to unexpected withdrawals of deposits, avoiding overdrafts in reserve accounts, and providing liquidity in case of computer failures (see Box, Example 4), natural disasters, and other forces beyond an institution's control.[2]

An inappropriate use of the discount window would be borrowing to take advantage of a favorable spread between the fed funds rate and the discount rate (Example 3). Borrowing to fund a sudden, unexpected surge of demand for bank loans may be considered appropriate, but borrowing to fund a deliberate program of actively seeking to increase loan volume would not. Continuous borrowing at the window is inappropriate. Finally, an institution that is a net seller (lender) of federal funds should not at the same time borrow at the window, nor should one that is conducting reverse repurchase agreements (that is, buying securities) with the Fed for its own account.

The discount officer's judgment first comes into play when a borrower calls for a loan and states the reason. The monitoring does not end when (and if)

---

[1] For more detailed information on discount window administration policies, see Board of Governors of the Federal Reserve System, **The Federal Reserve Discount Window** (Board of Governors, 1980). The federal regulation governing the discount window is Regulation A, 12 C.F.R. 201.

[2] In order to encourage depository institutions to take measures to reduce the probability of operating problems causing overdrafts, the Board of Governors announced in May 1986 that a surcharge would be added to the discount rate for large borrowings caused by operating problems unless the problems are "clearly beyond the reasonable control of the institution." See "Fed to Assess 2-Point Penalty on Loans for Computer Snafus," **American Banker**, May 21, 1986.

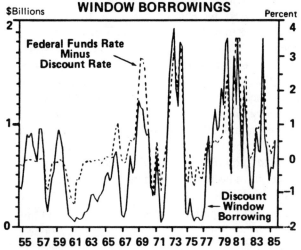

Figure 2

THE SPREAD BETWEEN THE FEDERAL FUNDS RATE AND DISCOUNT RATE COMPARED WITH DISCOUNT WINDOW BORROWINGS

the loan is approved, however. The discount officer watches for patterns in borrowing and may look at such summary measures as discount window loans as a percentage of deposits and of reserves, and duration and frequency of past borrowing. In addition, special circumstances and efforts to obtain credit elsewhere receive attention. Finally, discount window borrowings are compared with fed funds market activity to make sure banks are not borrowing from the Fed simply to lend at a higher rate in the fed funds market.

If the discount officer suspects that borrowing by an institution has possibly gone beyond what is appropriate, he or she makes an "informational" call in order to find out the particular problems and circumstances of the case (Example 3), as well as how the institution plans to reduce its reliance on the discount window. If little or nothing changes, it may be time for counseling as well as a more direct effort to help the borrower find new sources of credit. It is conceivable that an institution's credit could be terminated if counseling were to fail, but this is rarely if ever necessary.

The Borrowing Decision

When deciding whether and how much to borrow from the discount window, a bank's funding officer can be expected to compare the benefit of using the discount window with the cost. The benefit of an additional dollar of discount window credit is the savings of the rate on federal funds, which is normally the next best alternative to the window. The marginal cost contains two elements. The first is the price of discount window credit, that is, the discount rate. The second is the cost imposed by nonprice measures used by the Fed to limit the amount of borrowing. An equilibrium level of borrowing would be reached when the marginal benefit of savings of the fed funds rate is balanced by the marginal cost including both the discount rate and the cost imposed by nonprice measures.[8]

Antecedents

In the United States in the late nineteenth and early twentieth centuries, establishment of a central bank was urged in order to provide an "elastic" currency. The central bank's task would be to expand discount window loans as production (and demand for money) expanded over the business cycle. The loans would then be repaid as goods finally went to market. Such a view of the central bank's role was based on the "real bills" or "commercial loan" school, which asserted that expansion of the money supply would not be inflationary so long as it was done to meet the "needs of trade." In other words, loans made by rediscounting commercial loans (which were considered to be made for "productive" purposes) would be self-liquidating since they would be paid back as the goods produced were sold on the market. The money supply increase would consequently be extinguished.[4] Reflecting the influence of the real bills doctrine, the Preamble to the Federal Reserve Act of 1913 included as a stated purpose "to furnish an elastic currency." Accordingly, the Act contained provisions for the rediscounting of bank loans "arising out of actual commercial transactions" and defining what paper was eligible for rediscount.

Although the real bills doctrine had the most practical influence on the development of central bank lending, some nineteenth century writers argued that the most important function of a central bank was to act as lender of last resort to the financial system. The first major writer to detail the role of a lender of last resort was Henry Thornton at the beginning of the nineteenth century.[5] In today's terms, Thornton described a lender acting as a "cir-

---

[8] See Marvin Goodfriend (1983).

[4] For a demonstration of the fallaciousness of this doctrine, see Thomas M. Humphrey (1982).

[5] For a more detailed treatment of the material in this and the following paragraph, see Thomas M. Humphrey and Robert E. Keleher (1984).

cuit breaker," pumping liquidity into the market in order to prevent problems with particular institutions from spreading to the banking system as a whole. He emphasized that the lender of last resort's role in a panic is precisely opposite that of a private banker in that the former should expand lending in a panic while the latter contracts it. At the same time, Thornton did not advocate lending in order to rescue unsound banks, since that would send the wrong message to bankers, namely, that imprudent management would be rewarded with a bailout. Rather, he urged that loans be made only to banks experiencing liquidity problems due to the panic. In other words, the central bank has a responsibility to protect the banking system as a whole, but not to protect individual banks from their own mistakes.

The other important architect of the lender of last resort idea was Walter Bagehot, who detailed his beliefs in *Lombard Street* in 1873. Generally, Bagehot agreed with Thornton, but developed the lender's role in far greater detail. His contribution is best summed up in the venerable Bagehot Rule: Lend freely at a high rate. This implies three points. First, the public should be confident that lending will take place in a panic, so that there is no question as to the central bank's commitment. Second, lending should go to anyone, not just banks, who presents "good" collateral. In addition, collateral should be judged on what it would be worth in normal times, and not on the basis of its temporarily reduced value due to a panic. Finally, borrowers should be charged a rate higher than prevailing market rates. The justifications for a high rate are several, namely, ensuring that central bank credit goes to those who value it highest, encouraging borrowers to look first to other sources of credit, giving borrowers incentives to pay back such credit as early as possible, and compensating the lender for affording borrowers the insurance provided by a lender of last resort.

The ideas set forth by both Thornton and Bagehot emphasized emergency lending rather than adjustment credit. In actual practice, the Bank of England did act as lender of last resort several times during the late nineteenth century, but such lending was done in addition to its normal practice of providing adjustment credit at the "bank rate." In the United States, the real bills doctrine was more influential in shaping the central bank than were the ideas of Thornton or Bagehot.[6]

---

[6] The lender of last resort idea did surface in the practice of some American clearinghouses acting as emergency lenders during panics. See Gary Gorton (1984).

Evolution of Discount Window Practices

The only type of lending allowed Federal Reserve Banks by the Federal Reserve Act of 1913 was discounting. In 1916 the Act was amended to add the authority for Federal Reserve Banks to make advances, secured by eligible paper or by Treasury securities, to member banks. Advances replaced discounts in practice during 1932 and 1933, when the volume of banks' eligible paper fell precipitously due to the general banking contraction taking place at the time. Emphasis on lending on the basis of "productive" loans gave way to concern with whether or not collateral offered to secure an advance, be it commercial or government securities, was sound enough to minimize risk to the Fed. Since then, advances have been the predominant form of discount window lending.

Nonprice rationing of Federal Reserve credit became firmly established as a matter of practice during the late 1920s. Use of the discount window to finance "speculative" investments was already discouraged due to the real bills doctrine's stress on "productive" uses of credit, but other reasons for lending also received the Board's disapproval. For example, in 1926 the Board adopted a policy of discouraging continuous borrowing from the discount window. In 1928, it specifically stated that banks should not borrow from the window for profit. Since then, the Federal Reserve has emphasized nonprice measures along with the discount rate to control borrowing.

Because market rates were well below the discount rate, banks used the discount window sparingly between 1933 and 1951. From 1934 to 1943, daily borrowings averaged $11.8 million, and only $253 million from 1944 to 1951. For the most part, banks held large amounts of excess reserves and were under little pressure to borrow. Even after the business recovery of the early 1940s, borrowing remained at low levels. Banks held large quantities of government securities, and the Federal Reserve's practice of pegging the prices of these securities, instituted in 1942, eliminated the market risk of adjusting reserve positions through sales of governments.

The pegged market for government securities ended in 1947, and the subsequent increased fluctuations of these securities' prices made buying and selling them a riskier way for banks to change reserves. As a result, the discount window began to look more attractive as a source of funds. By mid-1952, borrowings exceeded $1.5 billion, a level not seen since the early 1930s. Given the new importance of the window, Regulation A, the Federal Reserve regulation governing discount window credit, was revised in 1955 to incorporate principles that had developed over the past thirty years. In particular, the General Principles at the beginning of Regulation A stated that borrowing at the discount window is a privilege of member banks, and for all practical purposes enshrined nonprice rationing and the discretion of the discount officer regarding the appropriateness of borrowing as primary elements of lending policy.

The new version of Regulation A notwithstanding, the discount rate was for the most part equal to or greater than the fed funds rate during the late 1950s and early 1960s. As a result, there was not much financial incentive to go to the window. By the mid-1960s, however, the difference between the fed funds rate and the discount rate began to experience large swings, and the resulting fluctuations in incentives to borrow were reflected in discount window credit levels (see Figure 2).

In 1973, the range of permissible discount window lending was expanded by the creation of the seasonal credit program. More significantly, in 1974 the Fed advanced funds to Franklin National Bank, which had been experiencing deteriorating earnings and massive withdrawals. Such an advance was made to avoid potentially serious strains on the financial system if the bank were allowed to fail and to buy time to find a longer term solution. This particular situation was resolved by takeover of the bulk of the bank's assets and deposits by European American Bank, but the significant event here was the lending to a large, failing bank in order to avert what were perceived to be more serious consequences for the banking system. The action set a precedent for lending a decade later to Continental Illinois until a rescue package could be put together.

Reflecting a discount rate substantially below the fed funds rate from 1972 through most of 1974, discount window borrowings grew to levels that were high by historical standards. A recession in late 1974 and early 1975 drove loan demand down, and market rates tended to stay below the discount rate until mid-1977. During the late 1970s, the spread was positive again, and borrowing from the window increased. Borrowing then jumped abruptly upon the adoption of a new operating procedure for day-to-day conduct of monetary policy (described in the following section), which deemphasized direct fed funds rate pegging in favor of targeting certain reserve aggregates. Because this procedure generally requires a positive level of borrowing, the gap between

the fed funds rate and the discount rate has frequently remained relatively high during the first half of the 1980s.

The Monetary Control Act of 1980 extended to all banks, savings and loan associations, savings banks, and credit unions holding transactions accounts and nonpersonal time deposits the same borrowing privileges as Federal Reserve member banks. Among other things, the Act directed the Fed to take into consideration "the special needs of savings and other depository institutions for access to discount and borrowing facilities consistent with their long-term asset portfolios and the sensitivity of such institutions to trends in the national money markets." Although the Fed normally expects thrift institutions to first go to their own special industry lenders for help before coming to the window, private savings and loan insurance system failures in 1985 led to increased use of extended credit.

The Role of the Discount Window in Monetary Policy

As a tool of monetary policy, the discount window today is part of a more complex process than one in which discount rate changes automatically lead to increases or decreases in the money supply. In practice, the Federal Reserve's operating procedures for controlling the money supply involve the discount window and open market operations working together.[7] In the procedures, there is an important distinction between borrowed reserves and nonborrowed reserves. Borrowed reserves come from the discount window, while nonborrowed reserves are supplied by Fed open market operations. While nonborrowed reserves can be directly controlled, borrowed reserves are related to the spread between the funds rate and the discount rate.

During the 1970s, the Fed followed a policy of targeting the federal funds rate at a level believed consistent with the level of money stock desired. Open market operations were conducted in order to keep the funds rate within a narrow range, which in turn was selected to realize the money growth objective set by the Federal Open Market Committee. Under this practice of in effect pegging the fed funds rate in the short run, changes in the discount rate only affected the spread between the two rates and therefore the division of total reserves between borrowed and nonborrowed reserves. In other words,

---

[7] These are described in more detail by R. Alton Gilbert (1985) and Alfred Broaddus and Timothy Cook (1983).

if the discount rate were, say, increased while the fed funds rate remained above the discount rate, borrowing reserves from the Fed would become relatively less attractive than going into the fed funds market.[8] This would decrease quantity demanded of borrowed reserves, but would increase demand for their substitute, nonborrowed reserves, thereby tending to put upward pressure on the funds rate. Given the policy of pegging the funds rate, however, the Fed would increase the supply of nonborrowed reserves by purchasing securities through open market operations. The result would be the same fed funds rate as before, but more nonborrowed relative to borrowed reserves.[9]

After October 6, 1979, the Federal Reserve moved from federal funds rate targeting to an operating procedure that involved targeting nonborrowed reserves. Under this procedure, required reserves, since they were at the time determined on the basis of bank deposits held two weeks earlier, were taken as given. The result was that, once the Fed decided on a target for nonborrowed reserves, a level of borrowed reserves was also implied. Again assuming discount rates below the fed funds rate, raising the discount rate would decrease the fed funds-discount rate spread. Since this would decrease the incentive to borrow, demand would increase for nonborrowed reserves in the fed funds market. Under the new procedure the target for nonborrowed reserves was fixed, however, so the Fed would not inject new reserves into the market. Consequently, the demand shift would cause the funds rate to increase until the original spread between it and the discount rate returned. The upshot here is that, since discount rate changes generally affected the fed funds rate, the direct role of discount rate changes in the operating procedures increased after October 1979.

In October 1982, the Federal Reserve moved to a system of targeting borrowed reserves.[10] Under this procedure, when the Federal Open Market Committee issues its directives at its periodic meetings, it specifies a desired degree of "reserve restraint." More restraint generally means a higher level of borrowing, and vice versa. Open market operations are then conducted over the following period to provide the level of nonborrowed reserves consistent with desired borrowed reserves and demand for total reserves. A discount rate increase under this procedure would, as in nonborrowed reserves targeting, shrink the spread between the fed funds and discount rates, and shift demand toward nonborrowed reserves. In order to preserve the targeted borrowing level, the fed funds rate should change by about the same amount as the discount rate so that the original spread is retained. As a result, discount rate changes under borrowed reserves targeting affect the funds rate the same as under nonborrowed reserves targeting.

Discount Window Issues

As is the case with any instrument of public policy, the discount window is the subject of discussions as to its appropriate role. This section will briefly describe three current controversies regarding the discount window, namely, secured versus unsecured lending, lending to institutions outside the banking and thrift industries, and the appropriate relationship between the discount rate and market rates.

The risk faced by the Federal Reserve System when making discount window loans is reduced by requiring that all such loans be secured by collateral. William M. Isaac, who chaired the Federal Deposit Insurance Corporation from 1981 to 1985, has suggested that this aspect of discount window lending be changed to allow unsecured lending to depository institutions.[11] Mr. Isaac's main objection to secured lending is that, as uninsured depositors pull their money out of a troubled bank, secured discount window loans replace deposits on the liability side of the bank's balance sheet. When and if the bank is declared insolvent, the Fed will have a claim to collateral that otherwise may have been liquidated by the FDIC to reduce its losses on payouts to insured depositors. Sensing this possibility, more uninsured depositors have an incentive to leave before the bank is closed.

Mr. Isaac's proposed policy is best understood by considering how risks would shift under alternative policies. Under the current policy of secured lending

---

[8] Broaddus and Cook (1983) analyze the effect of discount rate changes if the discount rate is kept above the fed funds rate.

[9] Although under this procedure discount rate changes did not directly affect the funds rate, many discount rate changes signaled subsequent funds rate changes.

[10] See Henry C. Wallich (1984). In addition, since February 1984 required reserves have been determined on an essentially contemporaneous basis.

[11] **Deposit Insurance Reform and Related Supervisory Issues,** Hearings before the Senate Committee on Banking, Housing, and Urban Affairs, 99th Cong. 1 Sess. (Government Printing Office, 1985), pp. 27-8, 40. As an alternative, Mr. Isaac has suggested that if the policy of making only secured loans at the window is continued, only institutions that have been certified solvent by their primary regulators should be eligible.

at the discount window, if the Fed lends to a bank that fails before the loan is paid back, the fact that the loan is secured makes it unlikely that the Fed will take a loss on the loan. Losses will be borne by the FDIC fund, which is financed by premiums paid by insured banks. Thus, risk in this case is assumed by the stockholders of FDIC-insured banks.[12] Under Mr. Isaac's alternative, the Fed would become a general rather than a fully secured creditor of the failed bank. As a result, losses would be borne by both the Fed and the FDIC fund, depending on the priority given the Fed as a claimant on the failed bank's assets. Since losses borne by the Fed reduce the net revenues available for transfer to the United States Treasury, the taxpaying public would likely end up bearing more of the risk than under current policy. The attractiveness of moving to a policy of unsecured discount window lending thus depends on the degree to which one feels risks should be shifted from bank stockholders to the general public.[13]

A second discount window issue involves the exercise of the Fed's authority to lend to individuals, partnerships, and corporations. Although such lending has not occurred for over half a century, major events such as the failure of Penn Central in the mid-1970s and the problems of farms and the manufacturing sector of the 1980s raise the question of whether or not this authority should be exercised. On the one hand, one might argue that banking is an industry like any other, and that lending to nonfinancial firms threatened by international competition makes just as much sense as lending to forestall or avoid a bank failure. On the other hand, the Federal Reserve's primary responsibility is to the financial system, and decisions regarding lending to assist troubled industries are better left to Congress than to the Board of Governors.[14]

A final issue regarding the discount window is whether to set the discount rate above or below the prevailing fed funds rate.[15] Figure 2 shows that both policies have been followed at different times during the last thirty years. One could make several arguments in favor of a policy of setting the discount rate above the funds rate. First, as mentioned earlier, placing a higher price on discount window credit would ensure that only those placing a high value on a discount window loan would use the credit. Since funds could normally be gotten more cheaply in the fed funds market, institutions would only use the window in emergencies. Second, it would remove the incentive to profit from the spread between the discount rate and the fed funds rate. As a result, the process of allocating discount window credit would be simplified and many of the rules regarding appropriate uses of credit would be unnecessary. Finally, it might simplify the mechanism for controlling the money supply, since borrowed reserves would not likely be a significant element of total reserves. Indeed, setting targets for borrowed or nonborrowed reserves would probably not be feasible under a penalty rate. Targeting total reserves, however, would be possible, and open market operations would be sufficient to keep reserve growth at desired levels.[16]

Despite the possible advantages of keeping the discount rate above the fed funds rate, it is not clear what would be an effective mechanism for setting a discount rate. Should the discount rate be set on the basis of the previous day's funds rate and remain fixed all day or should it change with the funds rate? Letting it stay the same all day would make it easier for banks to keep track of, but incentives to profit from borrowing could result if the funds rate suddenly rose above the discount rate. Further, what is an appropriate markup above the fed funds rate? Too high a markup over the funds rate might discourage borrowing even in emergencies, thus defeating the purpose of a lender of last resort.[17] Finally, some banks that are perceived as risky by the markets can only borrow at a premium over market rates. Even if the discount rate were marked up to a penalty rate over prevailing market rates,

---

[12] Since Congress has pledged the full faith and credit of the United States government to the fund, it is also possible that the public may bear some of the losses.

[13] Fed Chairman Paul Volcker has characterized the proposal as changing the Fed from a provider of liquidity to a provider of capital to depository institutions. Ibid., pp. 1287-8.

[14] Ibid., pp. 1315-6. For a discussion of the possibility of discount window lending to the Farm Credit System, see **The Problems of Farm Credit**, Hearings before the Subcommittee on Economic Stabilization of the House Committee on Banking, Finance, and Urban Affairs, 99th Cong. 1 Sess. (GPO, 1985), pp. 449-55, 501-4.

[15] For a more complete summary of arguments regarding the appropriate use of the discount rate, see Board of Governors (1971), vol. 2, pp. 25-76.

[16] For further arguments in favor of total reserves targeting, see Goodfriend (1984). For arguments against, see David E. Lindsey et al. (1984).

[17] Lloyd Mints (1945), p. 249, argues that a higher price for discount window credit would discourage borrowing precisely at the time when the central bank should be generous in providing liquidity.

such banks might attempt to borrow at the discount window to finance more risky investments. In such a case, certain administrative measures might be necessary to ensure that, as under present policy, discount window credit is not used to support loan or investment portfolio expansion.

Choosing between policies of keeping the discount rate either consistently above or consistently below the fed funds rate involves a decision not only on how best to manage reserves but also on the relative merits of using prices or administrative means to allocate credit. Administrative limits on borrowing may help to brake depository institutions' incentives to profit from rate differentials, but will not remove them. Pricing would take away such incentives, but there are difficulties with setting an optimal price. As in most policy matters, the choice comes down to two imperfect alternatives.

References

Board of Governors of the Federal Reserve System. *Reappraisal of the Federal Reserve Discount Mechanism*, vol. 2. Washington: Board of Governors, 1971.

Broaddus, Alfred and Timothy Cook. "The Relationship between the Discount Rate and the Federal Funds Rate under the Federal Reserve's Post-October 6, 1979 Operating Procedure." Federal Reserve Bank of Richmond, *Economic Review* 69 (January/February 1983): 12-15.

Gilbert, R. Alton. "Operating Procedures for Conducting Monetary Policy." Federal Reserve Bank of St. Louis, *Review* 67 (February 1985): 13-21.

Goodfriend, Marvin. "Discount Window Borrowing, Monetary Policy, and the Post-October 6, 1979 Federal Reserve Operating Procedure." *Journal of Monetary Economics* 12 (September 1983): 343-56.

—————. "The Promises and Pitfalls of Contemporaneous Reserve Requirements for the Implementation of Monetary Policy." Federal Reserve Bank of Richmond, *Economic Review* 70 (May/June 1984): 3-12.

Gorton, Gary. "Private Clearinghouses and the Origins of Central Banking." Federal Reserve Bank of Philadelphia, *Business Review* (January/February 1984), pp. 3-12.

Humphrey, Thomas M. "The Real Bills Doctrine." Federal Reserve Bank of Richmond, *Economic Review* 68 (September/October 1982): 3-13. Reprinted in Thomas M. Humphrey, *Essays on Inflation*, 5th Edition, Federal Reserve Bank of Richmond, 1986, pp. 80-90.

————— and Robert E. Keleher. "The Lender of Last Resort: A Historical Perspective." *Cato Journal* 4 (Spring/Summer 1984): 275-318.

Lindsey, David E., Helen T. Farr, Gary P. Gillum, Kenneth J. Kopecky, and Richard D. Porter. "Short-Run Monetary Control: Evidence Under a Non-Borrowed Reserve Operating Procedure." *Journal of Monetary Economics* 13 (January 1984): 87-111.

Mints, Lloyd W. *A History of Banking Theory*. Chicago: University of Chicago Press, 1945.

Wallich, Henry C. "Recent Techniques of Monetary Policy." Federal Reserve Bank of Kansas City, *Economic Review* (May 1984), pp. 21-30.

Article Twenty-Eight

Looking Forward

Most analysts agree that excessive money growth causes inflation and that a primary goal of any central bank should be to promote price stability. Since the 1970s, the Federal Reserve has focused on growth in monetary aggregates to fight inflation. Unfortunately, the recent deregulation of the financial system and innovations in financial practices have made it more difficult to assess the implications of growth in these aggregates for future rates of inflation. As a consequence, both last year and this year the Fed declined to specify a target range for M1, the narrow transaction aggregate it once emphasized in formulating policy. The Fed also widened the target ranges for M2 and M3 in 1988 to reflect the greater uncertainty in interpreting movements in these broader savings-type aggregates.

This *Letter* discusses the problems that deterioration in the reliability of the monetary aggregates poses for the Fed in pursuing its objective of moving the economy toward price stability. As a second-best solution to these problems, a conditional forecast from an econometric model of the U.S. economy could serve as an indicator of the impact of policy actions. Such economic forecasts could be used in much the same way that monetary aggregates and other intermediate targets have been used in the past in designing policies.

Intermediate targets
Monetary-policy actions—open market-operations and discount rate changes—do not have an immediate impact on the economy, but instead, influence it with a lag. Thus, if policymakers intend to follow a discretionary policy, as opposed to a fixed growth-rate rule, they need a tool, or "intermediate target," that gives them feedback on the future effects of today's actions. To be helpful in this way, the intermediate target should meet three conditions. First, it should have a reliable (predictable) relationship to the ultimate goals of policy, such as future economic activity and the price level. It also should have a leading relationship with these variables—that is, changes in the intermediate target should precede changes in the price level, for example.

Finally, the intermediate target should be subject to control by the Federal Reserve both in the short run and the long run.

Real interest rates, for example, do not satisfy the last of these criteria since the levels of real rates vary along with changes in fundamental saving and investment characteristics of the economy and are only temporarily affected by monetary policy. If the Fed were to try to hold a given interest rate below (or above) its long-run equilibrium value, the economy would become dynamically unstable, swinging into accelerating inflation (or deflation). In contrast, the Fed *can* determine the level of the money supply in the long run, and this will have long-run implications for the price level and nominal GNP.

To measure the money supply, the Fed has employed three monetary aggregates—M1, M2, and M3. M1, in particular, satisfied the criteria for an intermediate target reasonably well until recently. Its relationship with prices was relatively stable most of the time, and it was subject to a reasonable degree of control. Moreover, its movements led movements in important macroeconomic variables. The lag from changes in M1 growth to changes in the growth of real GNP was around six months, while the lag to inflation was about 1½ to 2 years.

These lags from M1 growth to inflation meant that a policy oriented around M1 automatically looked forward. Changes in *current* values of M1 provided a forecast of *future* developments in the economy. With respect to inflation, a change in the rate of M1 growth of one percent, for example, generally led to an equal change in the rate of inflation 1½ to 2 years later. Thus a policy that focused on *current* deviations between M1 and its targeted values, in effect, also was focusing on deviations between *future* inflation and an objective for future inflation.

Unfortunately, in recent years the relationship between M1 and future economic developments has deteriorated. The velocity of M1—the rate at which it is spent and re-spent each year in generating GNP (measured at current prices)—grew at a relatively steady 3 percent rate in the 1960s and 1970s. But beginning in 1982, M1's velocity became much less predictable, and has ended up declining on balance since then. It appears that the deregulation of deposit interest rates and the introduction of new deposit instruments, among other things, have changed the nature of M1, and made it a less reliable intermediate target.

Today, the broader aggregates—M2 and M3—appear to be more reliable than M1, but still less reliable than M1 once was. Recently, a number of alternative indicators have been discussed, including, for example, commodity prices, the monetary base (which includes reserves held at the Federal Reserve banks and currency in circulation), and M1A (which includes currency and non-interest-bearing transaction deposits). But while these indicators provide useful information for monetary policy, it has not been demonstrated that any of them has sufficient reliability to be the sole, or even primary, focus of Fed policy.

Current data
In the absence of a highly reliable intermediate target, it would be dangerous for policy to be judged mainly on the basis of the current condition of the economy. Primary reliance on current data would be risky and could allow policy inadvertently to wander off course. Assume, for example, that over the course of a year incoming data on the economy suggested increasing strength, and that the Fed in response gradually tightened reserve availability, thereby raising interest rates. Although the tightening of policy in this situation might be appropriate, current economic developments would not provide a gauge for the correct *degree* of tightening needed over the year. By the time the year was over, policy might have been tightened too much or too little. Since the feedback from real GNP and inflation is slow to emerge, large mistakes can be made before they are discovered.

A current-data approach also can lead to policy mistakes because the timing of the effects of policy actions is likely to be inappropriate. For example, if policy were eased in response to a weak current quarter, the effects might not be felt until the economy already had begun to strengthen. These timing problems are acute in the case of inflation. For example, by the time the actual data on inflation begin to show an increase, the underlying inflationary pressures already have been present for a year or more. Thus, it would be too late to turn the inflationary trend around without severe tightening and the attendant high costs of lost output and employment.

"Targeting" a conditional forecast
Given the problems with the current-data approach, it is clear that an alternative approach to policy needs to be forward-looking to take account of the lags in the effects of monetary policy on the economy. In addition, a wide variety of information on current and expected future economic developments should be taken into account to compensate for the deterioration in the information content of the monetary aggregates.

In lieu of a reliable monetary aggregate target, these criteria may be best met by explicitly orienting policy around information obtained from conditional forecasts of inflation and other goal variables. Using an econometric forecasting model of the economy, growth paths can be estimated for the monetary-policy instruments—open-market operations and the discount rate—to achieve the inflation objective.

Given the lags in policy, this objective would need to be defined over a period covering one to two years into the future. If the ultimate goal were price stability, one most likely would want to aim at gradual year-by-year reductions in inflation to mitigate adverse effects on employment and output.

Of course, a forward-looking econometric model can be used to estimate paths for the policy instruments that are consistent with achieving any other policy objective, such as nominal income, as well.

Once an inflation objective is chosen, an econometric model could be used to make a number of forecasts using different assumptions about the paths for the policy instruments. The path that generated the forecast consistent with the inflation objective would be the appropriate path for policy. The chosen estimates then would define policy actions until the next policy meeting. The conditional forecasts would need to be updated as new information emerged, and thus the policy setting would change over time.

Several types of models potentially could be used. Models that process a wide variety of information seem the most useful today. Neo-Keynesian-style structural models and vector autoregressions fall into this category, since both types of models are capable of processing a wide variety of information and attempt to represent or mimic the dynamic structure of the economy. No matter what type of model is used, though, policy makers still could adjust model forecasts according to their own best judgments, just as they could when policy was oriented around an intermediate target.

This conditional forecasting approach, in fact, is conceptually similar to using an intermediate monetary target. The intermediate target in this instance is the conditional forecast of inflation, which in turn, is a function of all of the data that are processed by the model. In effect, the method involves targeting a forecast of future inflation, and requires the policy instrument to be adjusted to keep the forecast of inflation equal to the objective for inflation. If the forecast were reasonably accurate, the change in inflation forecasted today would lead actual changes in inflation in the future, in the same way that changes in the growth of M1 used to lead changes in inflation.

Accuracy of forecasts

It is well known that economic forecasting is not an exact science—inevitably, errors are made. Why, then, should the design of monetary policy be entrusted to one- to two-year-ahead forecasts? First, it is by no means obvious that forecasts into the future are less accurate than current-quarter estimates. Current-quarter data contain a lot of "noise"—movements not related to changes in economic fundamentals—that cancels out over time. Thus the fundamentals tend to show through more clearly over longer forecast horizons.

A recent article in *Challenge Magazine* examined the accuracy of forecasts obtained from a

regular survey of forecasters conducted by *Blue Chip Economic Indicators* from 1977 to 1986. The one-year-ahead consensus forecasts of real GNP growth were significantly more accurate than the forecasts of current-quarter growth. For current-quarter growth, the average (absolute) error for GNP was a huge 2.6 percentage points (at an annual rate), whereas the forecasts made in October for real GNP growth in the following year had an error of only 1.0 percent. For inflation, the error one-year ahead was 1.2 percent. Unfortunately, the current-quarter errors for inflation were not presented. However, forecasting experience at this Bank suggests that the inflation forecast errors over these two horizons are about equal.

Second, and more importantly, short of basing policy on a fixed rule, there is no choice but to forecast, either implicitly or explicitly, because of the lags in monetary policy. Since actions today have little or no effect on results today, there is no way to judge the thrust of today's policy by looking at current economic performance. Reliance on current numbers implicitly makes the questionable assumption that today's performance is a good forecast of tomorrow's performance. Thus the issue of forecast accuracy must be considered in relative, not absolute terms. No matter how large a model's forecast errors, if they are smaller than the errors that would be made using current data only, or intermediate monetary targets, then the model should be used.

This discussion is not intended to downplay the size of forecast errors that inevitably will be made using econometric models. However, the long lags from monetary-policy actions to inflation make forecasting an essential part of effective inflation control. Given that simple forecasting models (such as those based on intermediate targets like the money supply) have deteriorated in recent years, the best alternative appears to be econometric models that process a wide range of information and attempt to predict the future effects of policy changes on the economy.

John P. Judd

SECTION FIVE

Monetary Theory

The readings in this section focus on long run policies and performance of the economy. They consider how the existing policy institutions can be improved, what longrun effects monetary and fiscal policies have on the economy, why policies change over time in the way they do, and how optimal policies and the performance of the economy itself are affected by the way that the private sector forms its expectations about those policies and performance.

In the first article, Daniel L. Thornton answers the question, "Why Does Velocity Matter?" He begins by explaining that velocity definitionally links money, which the Fed can control, to income, which it hopes to influence indirectly. This task is complicated by the fact that velocity is not only variable but, to an important extent, unpredictable. Among the factors that affect velocity, either temporarily or permanently, are interest rates, financial innovation, and the business conditions. Since the connection between these factors and velocity is not always reliable, and since these factors are themselves difficult to predict, monetary policy is often forced to react to rather than anticipate velocity shifts.

Milton Friedman follows with "The Case for Overhauling the Federal Reserve." He begins by offering suggestions for improving the short-run conduct of monetary policy. These modifications preserve the basic institutional features of monetary policy, seeking only to fine-tune Fed operations. More drastic proposals follow. Among them are to legally require the Fed to increase the money supply by some amount each year and to end the Fed's independence by converting it into a bureau of Treasury. These suggestions culminate in the proposal to freeze the amount of high-powered money.

Herb Taylor explains why, as time passes, the Fed is often tempted to abandon policies that it has set for itself in "Time Inconsistency: A Potential Problem for Policymakers." He argues that unbreakable rules and credibility generated by experience are valuable to policymakers. The reason is that unless policymakers stick to long-run policies and pass up the short-run benefits of changing policies, people will anticipate such policy shifts. This anticipation puts the Fed in the position of then almost certainly changing policy and not following its original intent, since the terms of the public's financial and labor market contracts will require the Fed to change policy to achieve its economic goals.

"Maintaining Central Bank Credibility" by Anne Sibert and Stuart E. Weiner points out that central banks can create credibility problems for themselves by trying to convince the public to believe the unbelievable. To avoid this problem, it has been suggested that central banks abandon discretionary policy and adhere consistently to a pre-announced policy rule, like a constant growth rate rule for the money supply, that they can credibly pursue. The authors demonstrate why there will be costs associated with any such inflexible policy rule. Rules that are more complex but still rigid are likely to better respond to certain kinds of shocks to the economy. Such rules are also likely to re-introduce credibility problems, since not all shocks that a rule might respond to are observable to the public. The public then may not believe that the rule is being rigidly followed in response to an unobservable shock, but instead presume that the policymaker is claiming there has been an unobservable shock as a ruse to allow policy to be changed.

"Rules Versus Discretion: Making a Monetary Rule Operational" by John B. Carlson continues the evalution of policy carried out through precommitment to publicly-known rules versus policy carried out through policymaker discretion. Carlson begins by reviewing the history of this debate, paying particular attention to the problems associated with actually carrying out a rule-constrained monetary policy. He points out that the Fed's choice of the money supply or interest rates as its short run operating target to achieve a longer run goal is a type of discretion. As such, changing which operating target to aim at is not generally allowed by rules. In the early 1980s, changing uncertainty about the workings of the economy itself led to a switch in targets. In this case, a change in operating policy seems to have been exercised in order to maintain a constant, longer run, anti-inflation policy.

Article Twenty-Nine

Why Does Velocity Matter?

DANIEL L. THORNTON

THE significant decline in the income velocity of money during 1982 and in the first quarter of 1983 has engendered confusion and controversy.[1] Amid this controversy, little attention has been paid to the more fundamental role velocity plays in macroeconomics and, hence, about its potential and actual importance in the conduct of monetary policy. This article sets forth the concept of income velocity and illustrates the potential effects of a change in velocity for monetary policy.

INCOME VELOCITY: A BRIEF OVERVIEW

Irving Fisher's famous "equation of exchange" primarily was responsible for the prominent role of income velocity in macroeconomic analysis.[2] In its most rudimentary form, the equation of exchange can be written as the identity given by equation 1 in table 1. Here, M and Y denote the nominal money stock (however defined) and nominal GNP, respectively, and V represents income velocity, the average number of times each unit of nominal money is used to support nominal GNP. Nominal GNP, in turn, can be represented by the average level of prices, P, times real

GNP, X. In this form, the equation of exchange is an accounting identity equating the nominal money stock multiplied by the number of times each unit turns over to nominal output, that is, $V = Y/M$. In this form, the equation is of little practical use since there is one equation and four unknown quantities, M, V, P and X.

Making the Equation of Exchange Useful

Fisher argued, however, that the level of velocity is determined by a number of social and economic factors.[3] He argued further that these factors tend to be relatively stable so that velocity could be treated as a constant, $\bar{V}$.[4] Under this assumption, equation 1 ceases to be an identity and becomes Fisher's useful equation of exchange (equation 2, table 1).[5] If V is constant and M is controlled exogenously by the monetary authority, nominal GNP can be determined — indeed, con-

---

Daniel L. Thornton is a senior economist at the Federal Reserve Bank of St. Louis. John G. Schulte provided research assistance.

[1]The decline in velocity was a persistent concern of the Federal Open Market Committee (FOMC) in the conduct of monetary policy during 1982 and contributed to the Committee's decision to suspend the use of M1 as an intermediate policy target in October 1982. See Daniel L. Thornton, "The FOMC in 1982: Deemphasizing M1," this *Review* (June/July 1983), pp. 26–35.

[2]Irving Fisher (assisted by Harry G. Brown): *The Publishing Power of Money: Its Determination and Relation to Credit, Interest and Crises* (MacMillan, 1911).

[3]Money was viewed primarily as a medium of exchange necessitated by the lack of synchronization between the sale of one good and the purchase of another. Thus, the proportion of income held (on average) in the form of money balances was determined by institutional factors that determined the pattern of payments and receipts. A discussion of this can be found in most macroeconomics textbooks.

[4]Actually, the classical economists never considered V to be a constant in the sense of unchangeable. Indeed, they recognized the effects of interest rates and price expectations on velocity; however, they generally believed that such factors would be relatively unimportant over the long run. For a good discussion of these issues, see Laurence Harris, *Monetary Theory* (McGraw-Hill, 1981), chapter 6.

[5]Although they stem from different theoretical approaches, Fisher's equation of exchange is similar to the "Cambridge cash balance equation" of Marshall and Pigou. See Alfred Marshall, *Money, Credit and Commerce* (MacMillan, 1923); and A. C. Pigou, "The Value of Money," *Quarterly Journal of Economics* (November 1917), pp. 38–65.

Table 1
Various Forms of the Equation of Exchange

$$(1) \quad MV = PX$$
$$(2) \quad M\overline{V} = Y$$
$$(3) \quad M\overline{V} = P\overline{X}$$
$$(4) \quad \dot{M} + \overline{\dot{V}} = \dot{Y} = \dot{P} + \overline{\dot{X}}$$
$$(5) \quad \dot{P} = \dot{M} + (\overline{\dot{V}} - \overline{\dot{X}})$$

Table 2
Growth Rates of Real Output and Velocity: II/1954–IV/1981

Country	$\dot{M}1$	$\dot{P}$	$\dot{V}$	$\dot{X}$
United States	4.5%	4.5%	3.4%	3.4%
Germany[1]	7.9	4.4	0.5	3.7
Japan[2]	15.3	5.6	−0.5	8.2
United Kingdom[3]	8.8	10.3	4.0	2.1
Canada	6.9	5.2	3.4	4.6

[1]Data covers period II/1960–IV/1981.
[2]Data covers period II/1957–IV/1981.
[3]Data covers period III/1963–IV/1981.

trolled — through monetary policy.[6] That is, for any $\overline{V}$, the monetary authority can obtain any Y it desires simply by setting M at the appropriate level. If a primary goal of policy is to stabilize nominal income growth, a constant velocity would give the monetary authority the means to achieve this goal by controlling money growth.[7] Of course, it is impossible from this relationship to determine the separate effects of changes in M on real output and prices.

The Quantity Theory of Money

If real output is determined independently of the stock of nominal money in the long run, selecting the money stock is tantamount to determining the price level. This is essentially the position of the classical economists, who argued that the amount of real output is determined by the "real" side of the market (e.g., factors of production, technology and relative prices). In the most elementary form of the equation, output is fixed at the full-employment level, $\overline{X}$. With this added assumption, Fisher's equation of exchange becomes the so-called crude quantity theory of money, given by equation 3 of table 1. With V and X constant, there is a direct, proportional link between money and the price level: if the money stock doubles, the price level will double.[8]

This version of the quantity theory, while appealing because of its simplicity, is of limited use because real output is not constant at the full-employment level; instead it varies over business cycles.

Thus, a more sophisticated quantity theory of money is a long-run (secular) theory of the relationship between money and prices. Under this more general theory, changes in the money stock may result in changes in real output or prices (or both) in the short run, but result primarily in price level changes in the long run (i.e., over business cycles).[9] Within this expanded framework, the quantity theory conclusion of the close correspondence of money growth and price level movements holds in the long run.

Velocity Is Not a Numerical Constant

Frequently, velocity is treated erroneously as a numerical constant; however, this restriction is both unnecessary and incorrect. Equation 1 can be written in the useful growth rate form as equation 4 of table 1. The dots over the variables denote compounded annual growth rates. Velocity need not be constant for

---

[6]Money is assumed to be largely exogenous. Both classical and neoclassical writers acknowledged the feedback of prices to money. Modern writers like Friedman and Schwartz consider money to be "for all practical purposes" exogenous in the sense that it can be controlled by the monetary authority. See Milton Friedman and Anna J. Schwartz, *Monetary Statistics of the United States* (National Bureau of Economic Research, 1970), p. 124.

[7]The goals of economic policy as set forth in the Full-Employment Act of 1946 are (1) full employment, (2) price level stability, (3) equilibrium in the balance of payments and (4) a high rate of economic growth. The first two of these are reiterated in the Humphrey-Hawkins Act. Since Y = P · X, the first two objectives amount to stabilizing nominal GNP.

[8]This is the "neutrality of money." Also, there was the closely related "classical dichotomy" between money and output. For a discussion of these points, see Harris, *Monetary Theory*, chapters 4 and 6; and Don Patinkin, *Money, Interest and Prices* (Harper and Row, 1965), chapter 8.

[9]Furthermore, full employment does not necessarily mean zero unemployment, but is merely a level consistent with stable prices given the structural characteristics of the labor and output markets, including market imperfections. See Milton Friedman, "The Role of Monetary Policy," *American Economic Review* (March 1968), pp. 1–17, for his concept of the natural rate of unemployment.

Chart 1
Rate of Price Change minus Rate of Money Growth [1]

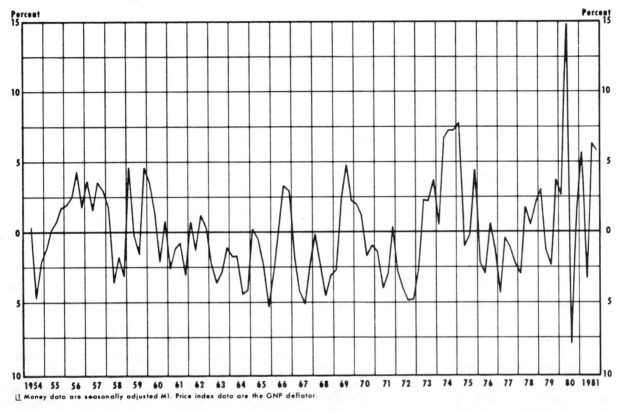

[1] Money data are seasonally adjusted M1. Price index data are the GNP deflator.

nominal GNP to be controlled through monetary policy; all that is required is that its growth rate be relatively stable. Equation 4 can be rewritten as equation 5 to show that the rate of increase in prices (inflation) is related to money growth. Thus, in the long run, the relative growth rates between money and prices reflect the relative difference between the growth rates of velocity and real output. The slower velocity growth is relative to real output growth, the faster the growth in nominal money can be consistent with stable prices or a low rate of inflation.

If $\dot{V}$ and $\dot{X}$ are approximately equal on average, then the rate of inflation will equal approximately the growth rate of money. Basically, this situation has existed in the United States for roughly the past three decades. The average quarter-to-quarter compounded annual rates of growth of M1 velocity and real output from II/1954 to IV/1981 were both 3.4 percent. As a result of the equality between $\dot{V}$ and $\dot{X}$, $\dot{M}1$ and $\dot{P}$ were equal over this period. Both the implicit price deflators for GNP and M1 increased at an average compounded annual rate of 4.5 percent over this same period. In the

short run, however, $\dot{X}$ and $\dot{V}$ deviate from each other; thus, so do $\dot{M}1$ and $\dot{P}$. This is illustrated in chart 1, which shows the difference between $\dot{P}$ and $\dot{M}1$ for the period.

This long-run, near-equality between $\dot{P}$ and $\dot{M}1$, however, does not hold for all countries. This is shown in table 2, which shows the average growth of $\dot{V}$, $\dot{X}$, $\dot{P}$ and $\dot{M}1$ for five countries, including the United States.

VELOCITY AND MONETARY POLICY

If one goal of monetary policy is to stabilize nominal GNP growth, policymakers must incorporate velocity considerations into their decisions. There are, however, a variety of ways in which velocity can change. These complicate the analysis of velocity movements for policy decisions.

Permanent Vs. Temporary Changes

If a change in velocity is known and is permanent, the appropriate policy response is a compensatory

Figure 1

Level shift in velocity at t_0 with no change in growth rate

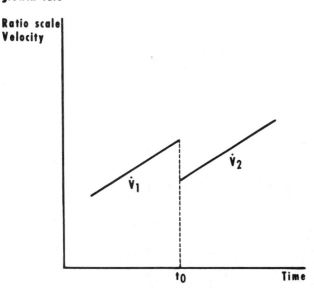

Decrease in the growth rate of velocity at t_0

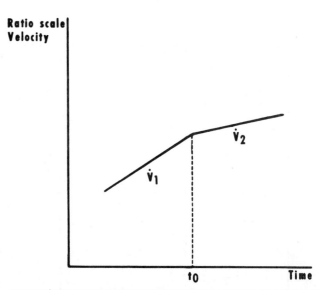

change in money to offset the effects of a velocity change on Y.[10]

If a change is temporary, however, policymakers may decide not to respond to the change because their response may increase rather than reduce the instability of nominal income. For example, suppose that policymakers observe a decline in velocity that they anticipate will reverse itself in the course of a quarter or two. If policymakers want to neutralize the effect of this temporary change on nominal income, they will increase the rate of money growth to keep nominal income growth on course, then reduce money growth later when the velocity change reverses.

Because policymakers are generally uncertain about the timing and extent of such a shift, they may be too aggressive for too long, producing larger swings in nominal income growth than would have occurred otherwise. Such instability need not result inevitably from policy responses to temporary changes in velocity; nevertheless, the danger is there. Thus, if policymakers suspect that the velocity change they observe is temporary, they may choose to ignore it.[11]

Level Vs. Growth Rate Shifts

Policymakers also must distinguish between changes in the levels of velocity and changes in its growth rate; the policy response will be different in the two cases. To illustrate this, consider the cases depicted in figure 1.[12] In both, $\dot{V}_1$ and $\dot{V}_2$ represent the growth rate of velocity before and after the hypothetical change at time t_0.

In the case of a permanent decline in the *level* of velocity that leaves the growth rates unaffected ($\dot{V}_1 = \dot{V}_2$), a policy response that accelerated the growth of money temporarily until the higher desired level is obtained and then returned money growth to its previous rate would produce an unvarying rate of growth in GNP. In the second case ($\dot{V}_2 < \dot{V}_1$), a compensatory and permanent increase in the growth rate of money at time t_0 is necessary to maintain the growth rate of GNP.

If policymakers failed to respond to the velocity changes depicted in figure 1, the consequences would

---

[10]This statement and much of the discussion that follows assumes a long-run neutrality of money; that is, changes in the growth rate of money have no lasting effect on the growth rate of real output. If money is not neutral in the long run, both the policy prescriptions and the effects of a failure to respond to velocity changes would differ accordingly.

[11]For example, at its meeting of November 16, 1982, the Federal Open Market Committee anticipated that M1 might grow due to a

temporary buildup of balances in M1 components for eventual placement in the new money market deposit accounts (MMDAs), which would become effective on December 14, 1982. Thus, the Committee anticipated a short-run decline in velocity resulting from this potential buildup. See "Record of Policy Actions of the FOMC," *Federal Reserve Bulletin* (January 1983), p. 19.

[12]A ratio scale for the natural log of velocity is presented in figure 1 so that the growth rates can be represented by the slopes of straight lines.

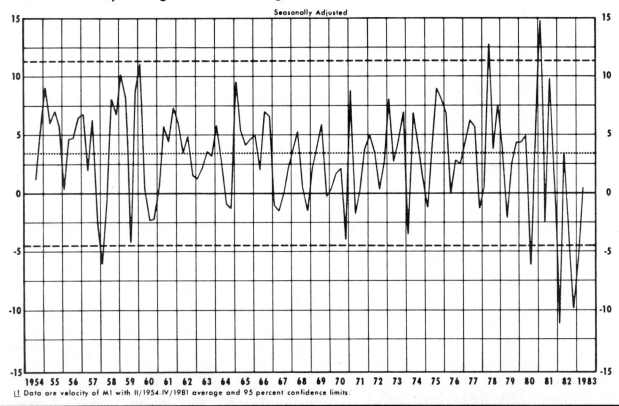

Chart 2

Rate of Velocity Change and its Average ⊔

Seasonally Adjusted

⊔ Data are velocity of M1 with II/1954-IV/1981 average and 95 percent confidence limits.

be different in the two cases. In the first (level-shift) case, there would be a *temporary* reduction in the rate of change of prices or real output, or both. In the long run, however, velocity would return to its former growth rate and, hence, so would the growth of nominal output. In the second case, the growth rate of prices would be lowered *permanently*; in addition, the growth rate of real output may be lowered temporarily if the monetary authority failed to adjust the growth rate of money in response to a permanent decline in velocity growth.

THE VARIABILITY OF VELOCITY

The timing of the policy response to the velocity change, of course, is very important. Unfortunately, it is difficult to determine whether there has been a significant change in velocity, let alone to foresee such a change. Furthermore, it is difficult to differentiate between level and growth rate shifts, and to differentiate between temporary and permanent changes.

In order to see why this might be the case, consider the historical movements in the growth rate of M1

velocity presented in chart 2. This chart shows the quarter-to-quarter growth rate of M1 velocity, a horizontal line showing the average growth rate of M1 velocity for the period II/1954–IV/1981, and dashed lines representing plus or minus two standard deviations of the quarter-to-quarter growth rate of velocity from its mean over this period.[13]

It is obvious that the quarter-to-quarter growth rate of velocity is highly variable. Nevertheless, it falls outside the range of plus or minus two standard deviations in four of the 111 quarters from II/1954–IV/1981. More recently, there have been three occasions during the last six quarters when the growth rate of velocity has fallen outside of this range. A priori, it is difficult to determine whether these apparent shifts are simply temporary movements in the growth rate associated with a permanent change in the level of velocity, a permanent change in the growth rate, or a temporary change in the growth rate associated with a temporary change in the level. Indeed, it is difficult to know

---

[13]If $\dot{V}$ is normally distributed, then approximately 95 percent of its observed values should fall within ±2 standard deviations.

whether these changes represent a significant change in velocity. It could be that other factors that affect velocity may have caused it to change. Thus, in order to determine whether a policy response is called for, it is necessary to examine the factors that determine velocity.

FACTORS THAT AFFECT VELOCITY

There are a number of factors that can cause velocity to change.[14] Since increased velocity is simply the ratio of nominal GNP to the stock of money, any factor that causes the stock of money to change relative to nominal output, or vice versa, can produce a change in the level of velocity. Likewise, any factor that causes the growth rate of money to change relative to the growth rate of nominal GNP, or vice versa, will cause the growth rate of velocity to change. Furthermore, since the growth rate of velocity is defined as the percentage change in the *level* of velocity per unit of time, factors that affect the level of velocity affect the growth rate if they likewise change through time. Thus, the following discussion will be carried out in terms of the level of velocity, unless otherwise stated.

Many of the factors that affect velocity can be analyzed easily by recognizing that velocity changes whenever people alter their holdings of money relative to their income. Factors that cause people to hold less money relative to their income increase velocity, while factors that cause people to increase their money holdings reduce it. For example, if two households have the same income and monthly expenditure patterns but one receives its income once a month while the other receives it twice a month, the latter, all other things constant, will hold less money on average than the one that receives income once a month. Thus, changes in the pattern of receipts and expenditures can produce changes in society's holdings of money relative to income.

Economizing on Money Balances

Other factors that cause individuals to economize on their holdings of money relative to income increase velocity. For example, the increased use of credit cards could reduce individuals' desires to hold money balances and, thus, increase velocity. In particular, these and other lines of credit may lessen individuals' desires to hold money as a contingency against uncertainty.[15]

Two of the most commonly cited factors that can cause changes in velocity are changes in real interest rates and expectations of inflation. Increases in the real interest rate tend to cause individuals to hold less money relative to their real income. The same generally will be true of an increase in the expected rate of inflation. Higher expected inflation will cause individuals to economize on their money holdings, raising velocity.

Financial Innovations

Financial innovations also can produce velocity changes. In general, innovations that reduce the implicit or explicit cost, or both, of transferring funds from non-transaction to transaction forms (perhaps by giving transaction characteristics to assets not included in M1) tend to increase the velocity of M1. Therefore, innovations such as money market deposit accounts and money market mutual funds would increase the velocity of M1 to the extent that they lower these costs.

In contrast, innovations that lower the cost of holding M1 relative to non-M1 assets tend to reduce the velocity of M1. This could be the case with automatic transfer of savings, negotiable order of withdrawal (NOW), and Super-NOW accounts.[16] Such innovations, however, may produce a temporary decline in velocity that lasts only until individuals realign their portfolios.

Cyclical Factors

Finally, there are a number of factors that can cause velocity to change with cyclical movements in real income (see appendix). They suggest that velocity tends to rise during periods of rising real income and fall during periods of declining real income.

Furthermore, there is considerable evidence that a change in money growth affects nominal income with a

---

[14]For discussions of some of these, see John A. Tatom, "Was the 1982 Velocity Decline Unusual?" this *Review* (August/September 1983), pp. 5–15; and William T. Gavin, "Velocity and Monetary Targets," *Economic Commentary*, Federal Reserve Bank of Cleveland (June 6, 1983).

[15]For a more detailed discussion, see Mack Ott, "Money, Credit and Velocity," this *Review* (May 1982), pp. 21–34. To date, however, there is little empirical support for this proposition about credit cards.

[16]John A. Tatom, "Recent Financial Innovations: Have They Distorted the Meaning of M1?" this *Review* (April 1982), pp. 23–35; and John A. Tatom, "Money Market Deposit Accounts, Super-NOWs and Monetary Policy," this *Review* (March 1983), pp. 5–16.

lag that is distributed over several quarters. Thus, an acceleration in money growth will produce a temporary decline in velocity as nominal output temporarily grows at a slower rate than does money. Thus, a decline in velocity associated with a recession can be exacerbated if the monetary authority expands money rapidly in order to stimulate a sluggish economy.

Permanent Vs. Temporary Effects

While all the factors mentioned above can affect velocity, they need not produce a lasting effect on its level or on its growth rate. For example, it is commonly recognized that, in a noninflationary environment, interest rates tend to be procyclical — rising during the expansion phase of the business cycle and declining during the contraction phase. Although the level of velocity and its growth rate can be affected by movements in interest rates, neither need change permanently; they, like such cyclical movements in interest rates, simply will average out over the course of a business cycle.

Also, financial innovations can have a permanent effect on the level of velocity but, perhaps, only a temporary effect on its growth rate. An innovation that lowers the cost of holding M1 relative to non-M1 assets induces a shift out of non-M1 into M1 assets, permanently lowering M1 velocity but reducing the growth rate only temporarily. Once the portfolios are realigned, the growth rate of velocity simply may resume its previous path.[17] Nevertheless, financial innovations can affect the extent to which velocity responds to changes in some of the other factors mentioned above.[18]

Forecasting Velocity Changes

Indeed, several economists have suggested recently that the seemingly unusual changes in velocity shown in chart 2 can be accounted for by cyclical movements in velocity and by changes in the inflation rate and interest rates.[19] This section does not attempt to evaluate these claims. Instead, the purpose here is to show that even when these factors are accounted for, it is difficult to forecast short-run changes in velocity.

To illustrate this point, the in-sample standard deviation of a model of velocity growth which recently appeared in this *Review* will be used as an estimate of the true one-quarter-ahead forecast error. The in-sample standard deviation is used to be conservative, and this model was selected because it incorporates many of the factors discussed above and because it performs well in forecasting velocity growth.[20] The in-sample standard deviation is about 2.0 percentage points. Thus, after accounting for factors that significantly influence velocity growth, the approximate 95 percent confidence interval for the forecast of velocity growth, $\dot{V}_f$, will be $\dot{V}_f \pm 2(2.0)$ or $\dot{V}_f \pm 4$.[21] This implies a fairly large margin for error. For example, if the forecast for velocity growth is 5 percent, then, loosely interpreted, actual velocity growth can be expected to be between 1 and 9 percent with high probability. This sizable margin for error demonstrates that the monetary authority will generally find it difficult to stabilize nominal output growth in the short run by offsetting short-run changes in velocity.[22]

Furthermore, the sizable error makes it difficult to determine whether a significant change in velocity has taken place. It takes a fairly large change in velocity growth to be significant enough to be considered unusual. Of course, the problems of discriminating between permanent and temporary shifts and between level and growth rate changes remain.

---

[17]For example, if individuals held expectations of inflation over a long period of time because of, say, excessive money growth, they might attempt to realign their portfolios continually in order to economize on money holdings and, as a result, the growth rate of velocity would be positive over this period.

[18]The availability of more and better substitutes for a commodity tends to increase its own and cross elasticities of demand. Thus, financial innovations affect velocity to the extent that they alter velocity's response to the above factors.

[19]See Tatom, "Was the 1982 Velocity Decline Unusual?"; John P. Judd, "The Recent Decline in Velocity: Instability of Money Demand or Inflation?" Federal Reserve Bank of San Francisco *Economic Review* (Spring 1983), pp. 12–19; and Milton Friedman, "Why a Surge of Inflation is Likely Next Year," *Wall Street Journal*, September 1, 1983. Though these economists generally agree on the factors affecting velocity, they disagree on the relative importance of the factors cited.

[20]The Tatom model has a smaller root-mean-squared error than the best univariate time series model recently reported by Hein and Veugelers, as well as a model which explains velocity growth with movements in real interest rates and the expected rate of inflation alone. See Tatom, "Was the 1982 Velocity Decline Unusual?"; and Scott E. Hein and Paul T. W. M. Veugelers, "Velocity Growth Predictability: A Time Series Perspective," this *Review* (October 1983), pp. 34–43.

[21]That is, approximately 95 percent of the intervals so constructed in one quarter would contain the value of velocity in the next. This simplified interpretation of the forecast interval tends to understate the margin of forecast error. See Robert S. Pindyck and Daniel L. Rubinfeld, *Econometric Models and Economic Forecasts* (McGraw-Hill, 1976), chapter 6.

[22]This result implies that recent suggestions that the Federal Reserve use nominal GNP as an intermediate target are ill-advised.

SUMMARY AND CONCLUSIONS

This article outlines the meaning of income velocity and reviews its important role as the link between money growth and nominal GNP growth. It demonstrates the problems that the monetary authority faces if it attempts to offset short-run (quarter-to-quarter) changes in velocity growth. Indeed, it appears that, even if a conservative estimate of the one-quarter-ahead forecast standard deviation is used, the forecast errors are large for policy purposes. Thus, while it might seem desirable for the monetary authority to respond to permanent changes in the level or growth rate of velocity, it is difficult to predict such changes, or to verify them quickly *ex post*.

Appendix:
Cyclical Factors That Affect Velocity

The purpose of this appendix is to illustrate four factors that can produce movements in velocity associated with cyclical swings in GNP.

Measured Vs. Theoretical Velocity

Velocity as it is usually measured may differ from its theoretical counterpart. As a result, not all changes in measured velocity indicate true changes in velocity. To illustrate this, consider the common specification of the demand for nominal money,

$$(A.1) \quad M^d = f(P, \dot{p}^e, r, r^e, Y_p, Z),$$

where

P = the current price level

$\dot{p}^e$ = the expected future price level

r = the current real interest rate

r^e = the expected future real interest rate

Y_p = current nominal *permanent income*

Z = all other factors that affect money demand.[1]

It is usually assumed that individuals do not suffer from a money illusion (i.e., equation A.1 is homogenous of degree one in P and Y_p) so that equation A.1 can be written as

$$(A.2) \quad M^d/P = f(\dot{P}^e, r, r^e, Y_p/P, Z)$$

or

$$(A.3) \quad m^d = f(\dot{P}^e, r, r^e, y_p, Z),$$

where m^d denotes the demand for *real* money balances and y_p denotes real permanent income. Now assume that A.3 is homogenous of degree s in real permanent income so that A.3 can be written as

$$(A.4) \quad m^d/(y_p)^s = f(\dot{P}^e, r, r^e, Z).$$

Further assume that s = 1, so that the theoretical measure of velocity, V*, is

$$V^* = Y_p/M = 1/f(\dot{P}^e, r, r^e, Z).$$

Thus, if velocity is measured as Y/M, changes in measured velocity can occur that do not reflect changes in V*. Of course, estimates of Y_p could be used to get a better estimate of V*; however, this problem will continue to the extent that there are estimation errors. Moreover, the most commonly watched measure of velocity is Y/M.

Economies of Scale

Another problem arises when s ≠ 1. It is sometimes argued that the elasticity of the demand for real money balances with respect to real permanent income is less than one. If this is the case, the percentage change in real money balances will be less than the percentage change in real income. An increase in real income will result in a less than proportionate increase in the holding of real money and, hence, an increase in velocity. Thus, if there are cyclical movements in permanent income, velocity would rise during the expansion phase of the cycle and fall during the contraction phase. This would occur even if permanent income

---

[1]See Milton Friedman, "The Quantity Theory of Money: A Restatement," in *Studies in the Quantity Theory of Money* (University of Chicago Press, 1956).

were measured precisely. This factor also could account for a secular rise in velocity as real output expands. For example, if real output is growing at a 4 percent rate and the real income elasticity of the demand for real money is about one-half, then velocity would grow secularly at about a 2 percent rate.

Short-Run Adjustments of Money Demand

Another factor that can account for cyclical movements in velocity is the possibility of short-run adjustments of money demand. A change in one of the factors in f (·) alters an individual's demand for real money while leaving his actual holdings of real money unchanged. As a result, the individual must adjust actual money holdings to his new desired holdings. Such an adjustment is costly, so the adjustment may progress (perhaps slowly) over time. Theoretically, the speed at which this portfolio adjustment takes place depends on the cost of moving to the new equilibrium relative to the cost of being out of equilibrium: the higher the former cost relative to the latter, the slower the speed of adjustment.[2] If these adjustment costs are small, the adjustment will be rapid; however, most empirical estimates suggest a very slow adjustment.[3] In any event, if money demand does not adjust immediately,

an increase in real income can produce a smaller increase in the demand for money in the short run and, hence, a short-run increase in velocity. As the demand for money adjusts towards the new equilibrium, velocity will approach the level implied in A.4.

The above analysis rests in a disequilibrium between actual and desired money holdings. If such disequilibria exist, they also could be caused by real-side shocks, such as natural disasters, oil price shocks and the like.

Lags in the Effect of Money on Nominal Income

Another possibility is a lag effect from money to income.[4] That is, changes in the current money stock produce changes in nominal income with a lag that is distributed over several quarters. If this is the case, a change in the current money stock produces a less than proportional change in current nominal income and, hence, an initial decline in velocity. Thus, periods of relatively rapid money growth tend to be associated initially with declining velocity, while periods of relatively slow money growth tend to be associated initially with rising velocity. Taking this factor and previously mentioned factors into consideration, it could be argued that the decline in velocity during 1982 was precipitated by the decline in real economic activity and exacerbated by the rapid growth of M1 beginning III/1982.

---

[2]See Zvi Griliches, "Distributed Lags: A Survey," *Econometrica* (January 1967), pp. 16–49.

[3]For a discussion of this problem and some estimates of the speed of adjustment, see Daniel L. Thornton, "Maximum Likelihood Estimates of A Partial Adjustment-Adaptive Expectations Model of the Demand for Money," *Review of Economics and Statistics* (May 1982), pp. 225–29.

---

[4]If money were exogenous, then this lag would only result from a lagged response of money demand, such as that discussed above. In this instance, this and the previous factor would be identical.

Article Thirty

MILTON FRIEDMAN

The Case for Overhauling the Federal Reserve

Changing the Fed's monetary tactics may help, but the System needs basic reform. We should end its money-creating powers, make it a bureau of the Treasury, and freeze the quantity of high-powered money.

Monetary policy can be discussed on two very different levels: the tactics of policy—the specific actions that the monetary authorities should take; and the strategy or framework of policy—the ideal monetary institutions and arrangements for the conduct of monetary policy that should be adopted.

Tactics are more tempting. They are immediately relevant, promise direct results, and are in most respects easier to discuss than the thorny problem of the basic framework appropriate for monetary policy. Yet long experience persuades me that, given our present institutions, a discussion of tactics is unlikely to be rewarding.

The temptation to concentrate on tactics derives in considerable part from a tendency to personalize policy: to speak of the Eisenhower, Kennedy, or Reagan economic policy and the Martin, Burns, or Volcker monetary policy. Sometimes that approach is correct.

The particular person in charge may make a major difference to the course of events. For example, in *Monetary History of the United States, 1867-1960*, Anna Schwartz and I attributed considerable importance to the early death of Benjamin Strong, first governor of the Federal Reserve Bank of New York, in explaining monetary policy from 1929 to 1933. More frequently, perhaps, the personalized approach is misleading. The person ostensibly in charge is like the rooster crowing at dawn. The course of events is decided by deeper and less visible forces that determine both the character of those nominally in charge and the pressures on them.

Monetary developments during the past few decades have, I believe, been determined far more by the institutional structure of the Federal Reserve and by external pressures than by the intentions, knowledge, or personal characteristics of the persons who appeared

MILTON FRIEDMAN, a 1976 Nobel laureate, is a senior research fellow at the Hoover Institution, Stanford University, and Paul Snowden Russell Distinguished Service Professor of Economics at the University of Chicago. This article is adapted from "Monetary Policy for the 1980s" in *To Promote Prosperity*, edited by John H. Moore and published by the Hoover Institution Press. © 1984 by the Board of Trustees of the Leland Stanford Jr. University.

to be in charge. Knowing the name, the background, and the personal qualities of the chairman of the Fed, for example, is of little use in judging what happened to monetary growth during his term of office.

If the present monetary structure were producing satisfactory results, we would be well advised to leave it alone. Tactics would then be the only topic. However, the present monetary structure is not producing satisfactory results. Indeed, in my opinion, no major institution in the United States has so poor a record of performance over so long a period yet so high a public reputation as the Federal Reserve.

The conduct of monetary policy is of major importance; monetary instability breeds economic instability. A monetary structure that fosters steadiness and predictability in the general price level is an essential precondition for healthy noninflationary growth. That is why it is important to consider fundamental changes in our monetary institutions. Such changes may be neither feasible nor urgent now. But unless we consider them now, we shall not be prepared to adopt them when and if the need is urgent.

The tactics for avoiding a crisis

Three issues are involved in the tactics of monetary policy: adopting a variable or variables as an intermediate target or targets; choosing the desired path of the target variables; and devising procedures for achieving that path as closely as possible.

• *The intermediate targets.* The Fed has vacillated between using one or more interest rates or one or more monetary aggregates as its intermediate targets. In the past decade, however, it joined monetary authorities in other countries in stressing monetary growth. Since 1975, it has been required by Congress to specify explicit numerical targets for the growth of monetary aggregates. Although many proposals have recently surfaced for the substitution of other targets—from real interest rates to sensitive commodity prices to the price of gold to nominal GNP—I shall assume that one or more monetary aggregates remains the intermediate target.

In my opinion, the selection of a target or of a target path is not and has not been the problem. If the Fed had consistently achieved the targets it specified to Congress, monetary growth would have been highly stable instead of highly variable, inflation would never have become the menace it did, and the United States would have been spared the worst parts of the punishing re-

cession (or recessions) from 1979 to 1982.

The Fed has specified targets for several aggregates primarily, as I have argued elsewhere, to obfuscate the issue and reduce accountability. In general, the different aggregates move together. The exceptions have essentially all been due to the interest-rate restrictions imposed by the Fed under Regulation Q and the associated development of new forms of deposit liabilities. And they would not have arisen if the Fed had achieved its targets for any one of the aggregates.

The use of multiple intermediate targets is undesirable. The Fed has one major instrument of monetary control: control over the quantity of high-powered money. With one instrument, it cannot independently control several aggregates. Its other instruments—primarily the discount rate and reserve requirements—are highly defective as instruments for monetary control and of questionable effectiveness in enabling it to control separately more than one aggregate.

It makes far less difference which aggregate the Fed selects than that it selects one and only one. For simplicity of exposition, I shall assume that the target aggregate is M_1 as currently designed. Selection of another aggregate would alter the desirable numerical targets but not their temporal pattern.

• *The target path.* A long-run growth rate of about 1 to 3 percent per year for M_1 would be roughly consistent with zero inflation. That should be our objective. Actual growth in M_1 was 10.4 percent from fourth quarter 1982 to fourth quarter 1983; 5.2 percent from fourth quarter 1983 to fourth quarter 1984. A crucial question is how rapidly to go from such levels to the 1 to 3 percent range. In my opinion, it is desirable to proceed gradually, over something like a three- to five-year period, which means that the rate of growth should be reduced by about 1 to 1.5 percentage points a year—a very different pattern from the erratic ups and downs of recent years.

The Fed has consistently stated its targets in terms of a range of growth rates. For example, its initial target for M_1 for 1983 was a growth rate of 4 to 8 percent from the fourth quarter of 1982 to the fourth quarter of 1983. That method of stating targets is seriously defective: it provides a widening cone of limits on the absolute money supply as the year proceeds and fosters a shift in base from year to year, thereby frustrating accountability over long periods. This is indeed what happened. In July 1983, Chairman Volcker announced a new target of 5 to 9 percent for the second quarter of 1983 to the second quarter of 1984 but from the second-quarter 1983 base, which is 3 percent (6 percent at an annual rate) above the top of the earlier range.

A better way to state the targets is in terms of a central target for the absolute money supply plus or minus a band of, say, 1.5 percent on either side—about the range the Fed has specified for annual growth rates. [Since this was written and initially published, the Council of Economic Advisers has made the same suggestion, and Chairman Volcker has expressed support for such a change.]

• *Procedures for hitting the target.* There is widespread agreement both inside and outside the Federal Reserve System that current procedures and reserve regulations make accurate control of monetary growth over short periods difficult or impossible. These procedures and regulations do not explain such long sustained departures from the targets as the monetary explosions from April 1980 to April 1981 or July 1982 to July 1983 or the monetary retardations from April 1981 to October 1981 or January 1982 to July 1982. However, they do explain the wide volatility in monetary growth from week to week and month to month, which introduces undesirable uncertainty into the economy and financial markets and reduces Fed accountability for not hitting its targets.

There is also widespread agreement about the changes in procedures and regulations that would enable the Fed to come very much closer to hitting its targets over fairly short periods. The most important such change was the replacement of lagged reserve accounting, introduced in 1968, by contemporaneous reserve accounting comparable to that prevailing from 1914 to 1968. The obstacle to controlling monetary growth posed by lagged reserve accounting has been recognized since 1970 at the latest. Unfortunately, the Fed did not act until 1982, when it finally decided to replace lagged by contemporary reserve requirements. However, it delayed implementation until February 1984—the longest delay in implementing a changed regulation in the history of the Fed. There was no insuperable technical obstacle to implementing the change more promptly.

The other major procedural changes needed are:

1. Selection by the Fed of a single monetary target to end the Fed's juggling between targets;

2. Imposition of the same percentage reserve requirements on all deposit components of the selected target;

3. The use of total rather than nonborrowed re-serves as the short-term operating instrument;

4. Linking of the discount rate to a market rate and making it a penalty rate (neither this change nor the preceding was feasible for technical reasons under lagged reserve accounting; they are now feasible, but neither has been adopted);

5. Reduction of the churning in which the Fed engages in the course of its so-called defensive open-market operations.

Even without most of these changes, it would be possible for the Fed to put into effect almost instantaneously a policy that would provide a far stabler monetary environment than we have at present, even though it would by no means be ideal. The obstacle is not feasibility but bureaucratic inertia and the preservation of bureaucratic power and status.

A simple example will illustrate. Let the Fed continue to state targets for M_1 growth. Let it estimate the change in its total holdings of U.S. government securities that would be required in the next six months, say, to produce the targeted growth in M_1. Divide that amount by 26. Let the Fed purchase the resulting amount every week on the open market, in addition to any amount needed to replace maturing securities, and make no other purchases or sales. Finally, let it announce this schedule of purchases in advance and in full detail and stick to it.

Such a policy would assure control over the monetary aggregates, not from day to day, but over the longer period that the Fed insists is all that matters. It would enable the market to know precisely what the Fed would do and adjust its own actions accordingly. It would end the weekly guessing game that currently follows each Thursday's release of figures on the money supply. The financial markets have certainly demonstrated that they have ample flexibility to handle whatever day-to-day or seasonal adjustments might be needed. It is hard to envisage any significant adverse effects from such a policy.

A few numbers will show how much difference such a policy would make to the Fed's open-market activities. In 1982, it added an average of $176 million a week to its total holdings of government securities—an unusually high amount. In the process of acquiring $176 million, it purchased each week an average of $13 *billion* of securities and sold nearly as much. About half of these transactions were on behalf of foreign central banks. But that still leaves roughly $40 of purchases or $80 of transactions for every one dollar added to its portfolio—a degree of churning of a customer's account that would send a private stockbroker to jail, or at least to limbo.

Increased predictability, reduced churning, the loss of inscrutability—these are at the same time the major reasons for making so drastic a change and the major obstacles to its achievement. It would simply upset too many comfortable dovecotes.

A framework for basic reform

The chief problem in discussing the framework of monetary policy is to set limits. The subject is old, yet immediately pertinent; numerous proposals have been made, and few, however ancient, do not have contemporary proponents. In view of my own belief that the important desiderata of structural reform are to reduce the variability of monetary growth, to limit the discretion of the monetary authorities, and to provide a stable monetary framework, I shall limit myself to proposals directed at those objectives, proceeding from the least to the most radical.

• *Imposing a monetary rule on the Fed.* I have long argued that a major improvement in monetary policy could be achieved without any significant change in monetary institutions simply by imposing a monetary rule on the Fed. From an economic point of view, it would be desirable to state the rule in terms of a monetary aggregate such as M_1 that has a close and consistent relation to subsequent changes in national income. However, recent years have demonstrated that the Fed has been unable or unwilling to achieve such a target, even when it sets it itself, and that it has been able to plead inability and thereby avoid accountability. Accordingly, I have reluctantly decided that it is preferable to state the rule in terms of a magnitude that has a somewhat less close relation to national income but that unquestionably can be controlled within very narrow limits within very brief time periods, namely, the Fed's own non-interest-bearing obligations, the monetary base.

In *Free to Choose*, my wife, Rose, and I proposed a specific form of rule as a constitutional amendment: "*Congress shall have the power to authorize non-interest-bearing obligations of the government in the form of currency or book entries, provided that the total dollar amount outstanding increases by no more than 5 percent per year and no less than 3 percent.*

"It might be desirable to include a provision that two-thirds of each House of Congress, or some similar qualified majority, can waive the requirement in case of a declaration of war, the suspension to terminate annually unless renewed."

A constitutional amendment would be the most effective way to establish confidence in the stability of the rule. However, it is clearly not the only way to impose the rule. Congress could equally well legislate it, and, indeed, proposals for a legislated monetary rule have been introduced in Congress.

I remain persuaded that a monetary rule that leads to a predictable long-run path of a specified monetary aggregate is a highly desirable goal—superior either to discretionary control of the quantity of money by a set of monetary authorities or to a commodity standard. However, I am no longer so optimistic as I once was that it can be effected by either persuading the monetary authorities to follow it or legislating its adoption. Congressional attempts in the past decade to push the Fed in that direction have repeatedly failed. The Fed has rhetorically accepted monetary targets but never a firm monetary rule. Moreover, the Fed has not been willing even to match its performance to a rhetorical acceptance of monetary targets. All this suggests that a change in our monetary institutions is required in order to make such a rule effective.

• *Separating regulatory from monetary functions.* A modest institutional reform that promises considerable benefits is to separate the regulatory from the monetary functions of the Fed. Currently, regulatory functions absorb most of the Fed's attention. Moreover, they obscure accountability for monetary control by confusing the two very separate and to some extent inconsistent functions.

As has recently been proposed in a study of the Federal Deposit Insurance Corporation, the Fed should be stripped of its regulatory functions, which would be combined with the largely overlapping functions of the FDIC, the Federal Savings and Loan Insurance Corporation, and the comptroller of the currency. Such a combined agency should have no monetary powers. It also might well include the operating functions of the Federal Reserve Banks—the monitoring of reserve requirements, issuance of currency, clearing of checks, reporting of data, and so forth.

A separate monetary-control agency could be a very small body, charged solely with determining the total quantity of high-powered money through open-market operations. Its function would be clear, highly visible, and subject to effective accountability.

• *Ending the independence of the Fed.* An approach that need involve relatively little institutional change—

although it is far more drastic than the preceding—and that could be implemented by legislation would be to end the independence of the Fed by converting it into a bureau of the Treasury Department. That would end the present division of responsibilities for monetary and fiscal policy that leads to the spectacle of chairmen of the Fed blaming all the nation's ills on the defects of fiscal policy and secretaries of the Treasury blaming them on the defects of monetary policy—a phenomenon that has prevailed for decades. There would be a single locus of authority that could be held responsible.

The immediate objection that arises is that it would make monetary policy a plaything of politics. My own examination of monetary history indicates that this judgment is correct, but that it is an argument for, not against, eliminating the central bank's independence.

I examined this issue at length in an article published more than two decades ago entitled "Should There Be an Independent Monetary Authority?" I concluded that it is "highly dubious that the United States, or for that matter any other country, has in practice ever had an independent central bank in [the] fullest sense of the term. . . . To judge by experience, even those central banks that have been nominally independent in the fullest sense of the term have in fact been closely linked to the executive authority.

"But of course this does not dispose of the matter. The ideal is seldom fully realized. Suppose we could have an independent central bank in the sense of a coordinate constitutionally established, separate organization. Would it be desirable to do so? I think not, for both political and economic reasons.

"The political objections are perhaps more obvious than the economic ones. Is it really tolerable in a democracy to have so much power concentrated in a body free from any kind of direct effective political control? . . .

"One [economic] defect of an independent central bank . . . is that it almost inevitably involves dispersal of responsibility. . . .

"Another defect . . . is the extent to which policy is . . . made highly dependent on personalities. . . .

"A third technical defect is that an independent central bank will almost inevitably give undue emphasis to the point of view of bankers.

"The three defects I have outlined constitute a strong technical argument against an independent central bank."

The experience of the past two decades has led me to alter my views in one respect only—about the importance of personalities. They have on occasion made a

great deal of difference, but additional experience and study has impressed me with the continuity of Fed policy, despite the wide differences in the personalities and backgrounds of the persons supposedly in charge.

For the rest, experience has reinforced my views. Anna Schwartz and I pointed out in *Monetary History* that subservience to congressional pressure in 1930 and 1931 would have prevented the disastrous monetary policy followed by the Fed. That is equally true for the past fifteen years. The relevant committees of Congress have generally, though by no means invariably, urged policies on the Fed that would have produced a stabler rate of monetary growth and much less inflation. Excessively rapid and volatile monetary growth from, say, 1971 to 1979 was not the result of political pressure—certainly not from Congress, although in some of these years there clearly was pressure for more rapid growth from the Administration. Nonetheless, no political pressures would have prevented the Fed from increasing M_1 over this period at, say, an average annual rate of 5 percent—the rate of increase during the prior eight years—instead of 6.7 percent.

Subordinating the Fed to the Treasury is by no means ideal. Yet it would be a great improvement over the existing situation, even with no other changes.

• *Competitive issue of money.* Increasing interest has been expressed in recent years in proposals to replace governmental issuance of money and control of its quality by private market arrangements. One set of proposals would end the government monopoly on the issuance of currency and permit its competitive issue. Another would eliminate entirely any issuance of money by government and, instead, restrict the role of government to defining a monetary unit.

The former set of proposals derives largely from a pamphlet by F. A. Hayek entitled *Choice in Currency: A Way to Stop Inflation.* Hayek proposed that all special privileges (such as "legal tender" quality) attached to government-issued currency be removed, and that financial institutions be permitted to issue currency or deposit obligations on whatever terms were mutually acceptable to the issuer and the holder of the liabilities. He envisaged a system in which institutions would in fact issue obligations expressed in terms of purchasing power either of specific commodities, such as gold or silver, or of commodities in general through linkage to a price index. In his opinion, constant-purchasing-power moneys would come to dominate the market and largely replace obligations denominated in dollars or pounds or other similar units and in specific commodities.

The idea of a currency unit linked to a price index is an ancient one—proposed in the nineteenth century by W. Stanley Jevons and Alfred Marshall, who named it a "tabular" standard—and repeatedly rediscovered. It is part of the theoretically highly attractive idea of widespread indexation. Experience, however, has demonstrated that the theoretical attractiveness of the idea is not matched by practice.

I approve of Professor Hayek's proposal to remove restrictions on the issuance of private moneys to compete with government moneys. But I do not share his belief about the outcome. Private moneys now exist—traveler's checks and cashier's checks, bank deposits, money orders, and various forms of bank drafts and negotiable instruments. But these are almost all claims on a specified number of units of government currency (of dollars or pounds or francs or marks). Currently, they are subject to government regulation and control. But even if such regulations and controls were entirely eliminated, the advantage of a single national currency unit buttressed by long tradition will, I suspect, serve to prevent any other type of private currency unit from seriously challenging the dominant government currency, and this despite the high degree of monetary variability many countries have experienced over recent decades.

The recent explosion in financial futures markets offers a possible new road to the achievement, through private market actions, of the equivalent of a tabular standard. This possibility is highly speculative—little more than a gleam in one economist's eye. It involves the establishment of futures markets in one or more price indexes—strictly parallel to the markets that have developed in stock-price indexes. (The Commodities Futures Trading Commission has authorized the Coffee, Sugar, and Cocoa Exchange to begin futures trading in the Consumer Price Index as of June 21, 1985.) Such markets, if active and covering a considerable range of future dates, would provide a relatively costless means of hedging long-term contracts against risks of changes in the price level. A combination of an orthodox dollar contract plus a properly timed set of futures in a price level would be the precise equivalent of a tabular standard, but would have the advantage that any one party to a contract, with the help of speculators and other hedgers in the futures market, could have the benefit of a tabular standard without the agreement of the other party or parties.

Recent changes in banking regulations have opened another route to a partial tabular standard on a substantial scale. The Federal Home Loan Bank has finally authorized federally chartered savings and loan associations to offer price-level-adjusted mortage (PLAM) loans. Concurrently, the restrictions on the interest rate that can be paid on deposits by a wide range of financial institutions have been eased and removed entirely for deposits of longer maturities.

This would permit financial institutions simultaneously to lend and borrow on a price-level-adjusted basis: to lend on a PLAM and borrow on a price-level-adjusted deposit (PLAD), both at an interest rate specified in real rather than nominal terms. By matching PLAM loans against PLAD deposits, a bank would be fully hedged against changes in inflation, covering its costs by the difference between the interest rate it charges and pays. Similarly, both borrowers and lenders would be safeguarded against changes in inflation with respect to a particular liability and asset.

As yet, I know of no financial institutions that have proceeded along these lines. I conjecture that no major development will occur unless and until inflation once again accelerates. When and if that occurs, PLAMs and PLADs may well become household words and not simply mysterious acronyms.

• *Freezing high-powered money.* The final proposal combines features from most of the preceding. It is radical and far-reaching, yet simple.

The proposal is that, after a transition period, the quantity of high-powered money—non-interest-bearing obligations of the U.S. government—be frozen at a fixed amount. These non-interest-bearing obligations now take two forms: currency and deposits at the Federal Reserve System. The simplest way to envisage the change is to suppose that Federal Reserve deposit liabilities were replaced dollar for dollar by currency notes, which were turned over to the owners of those deposits. Thereafter, the government's monetary role would be limited to keeping the amount constant by replacing worn-out currency. In effect, a monetary rule of zero growth in high-powered money would be adopted. (In practice, it would not be necessary to replace deposits at the Federal Reserve with currency; they could be retained as book entries, so long as the total of such book entries plus currency notes was kept constant.)

This proposal would be consistent with, indeed require, the continued existence of private institutions issuing claims to government currency. These could be regulated as now, with the whole paraphernalia of required reserves, bank examinations, limitations on lending, and the like. However, they could also be freed from all or most such regulations. In particular, the need for reserve requirements to enable the Fed to control the quantity of money would disappear.

Reserve requirements might still be desirable for a different though related reason. The new monetary economists argue that only the existence of such government regulations as reserve requirements and prohibition of the private issuance of currency explains the relatively stable demand for high-powered money. In the absence of such regulations, they contend, non-interest-bearing money would be completely dominated by interest-bearing assets, or, at the very least, the demand for such money would be rendered highly unstable.

I am far from persuaded by this contention. It supposes a closer approach to a frictionless world with minimal transaction costs than seems to me a useful approximation to the actual world. Nonetheless, it is arguable that the elimination of reserve requirements would introduce an unpredictable and erratic element into the demand for high-powered money. For that reason, although personally I would favor the deregulation of financial institutions, thereby incorporating a major element of Hayek's proposed competitive financial system, it would seem prudent to proceed in stages: first, freeze high-powered money; then, after a period, eliminate reserve requirements and other remaining regulations, including the prohibition on the issuance of hand-to-hand currency by private institutions.

Why zero growth? Zero has a special appeal on political grounds that is not shared by any other number. If 3 percent, why not 4 percent? It is hard, as it were, to go to the political barricades to defend 3 rather than 4, or 4 rather than 5. But zero is—as a psychological matter—qualitatively different. It is what has come to be called a Schelling point—a natural point at which people tend to agree, like "splitting the difference" in a dispute over a monetary sum. Moreover, by removing any power to create money it eliminates institutional arrangements lending themselves to discretionary changes in monetary growth.

Would zero growth in high-powered money be consistent with a healthy economy? In the hypothetical long-long-run stationary economy, when the whole economy had become adjusted to the situation, and population, real output, and so on were all stationary, zero growth in high-powered money would imply zero growth in other monetary aggregates and mean stable

velocities for the aggregates. In consequence, the price level would be stable. In a somewhat less than stationary state in which output was rising, if financial innovations kept pace, the money multiplier would tend to rise at the same rate as output, and again prices would be stable. If financial innovations ceased but total output continued to rise, prices would decline. If output rose at about 3 percent per year, prices would tend to fall at 3 percent per year. So long as that was known and relatively stable, all contracts could be adjusted to it, and it would cause no problems and indeed would have some advantages.

However, any such outcome is many decades away. The more interesting and important question is not the final stationary-state result but the intermediate dynamic process.

Once the policy was in effect, the actual behavior of nominal income and the price level would depend on what happened to a monetary aggregate like M_1 relative to high-powered money and what happened to nominal income relative to M_1—that is, on the behavior of the money multiplier (the ratio of M_1 to high-powered money) and on the income velocity of M_1 (the ratio of nominal income to M_1).

Given a loosening of the financial structure through continued deregulation, there would be every reason to expect a continued flow of innovations raising the money multiplier. This process has in fact occurred throughout the past several centuries. For example, in the century from 1870 to 1970, the ratio of the quantity of money, as defined by Anna Schwartz and me in *Monetary History*, to high-powered money rose at the average rate of 1 percent per year. In the post-World War II period, the velocity of M_1 has risen at about 3 percent per year, and at a relatively steady rate. This trend cannot, of course, continue indefinitely. Above, in specifying a desirable target for the Fed, I estimated that the rise in velocity would slow to about 1 or 2 percent per year. However, a complete end to the rapid trend in velocity is not in sight.

There is no way to make precise numerical estimates, but there is every reason to anticipate that for decades after the introduction of a freeze on high-powered money, both the money multiplier and velocity would tend to rise at rates in the range of historical experience. Under these circumstances, a zero rate of growth of high-powered money would imply roughly stable prices, though ultimately, perhaps, slightly declining prices.

What of the transition? Over the three years from 1979 to 1982, high-powered money grew an average of 7.0

percent a year. It would be desirable to bring that rate to zero gradually. As for M_1 growth, about a five-year period seems appropriate—or a transition that reduces the rate of growth of high-powered money by about 1.5 percentage points a year. The only other transitional problem would be to phase out the Fed's powers to create and destroy high-powered money by open-market operations and discounting. Neither transition offers any special problem. The Fed, or its successor agency, could still use part of the existing stock of high-powered money for similar purposes, particularly for lender-of-last-resort purposes, if that function were retained.

The great advantage of this proposal is that it would end the arbitrary power of the Federal Reserve System to determine the quantity of money, and would do so without establishing any comparable locus of power and without introducing any major disturbances into other existing economic and financial institutions.

I have found that few things are harder even for knowledgeable nonexperts to accept than the proposition that twelve (or nineteen) people sitting around a table in Washington, subject to neither election nor dismissal, nor close administrative or political control, have the power to determine the quantity of money—to permit a reduction by one-third during the Great Depression or a near-doubling from 1970 to 1980. That power is too important, too pervasive, to be exercised by a few people, however public-spirited, if there is any feasible alternative.

There is no need for such arbitrary power. In the system I have just described, the total quantity of any monetary aggregate would be determined by the market interactions of many financial institutions and millions of holders of monetary assets. It would be limited by the constant quantity of high-powered money available as ultimate reserves. The ratios of various aggregates to high-powered money would doubtless change from time to time, but in the absence of rigid government controls—such as those exemplified by Regulation Q, fortunately being phased out—the ratios would change gradually and only as financial innovations or changes in business and industry altered the proportions in which the public chose to hold various monetary assets. No small number of individuals would be in a position to introduce major changes in the ratios or in the rates of growth of various monetary aggregates—to move, for example, from a 3 percent per year rate of growth in M_1 for one six-month period (January to July 1982) to a 13 percent rate of growth for the next six months (July 1982 to January 1983).

Conclusion

Major institutional change occurs only at times of crisis. For the rest, the tyranny of the status quo limits changes in institutions to marginal tinkering—we muddle through. It took the Great Depression to produce the FDIC, the most important structural change in our monetary institutions since at least 1914, when the Federal Reserve System began operations, and to shift power over monetary policy from the Federal Reserve Banks, especially that in New York, to the Board in Washington. Since then, our monetary institutions have been remarkably stable. It took the severe inflation of the 1970s and accompanying double-digit interest rates—combined with the enforcement of Regulation Q—to produce money-market mutual funds and thereby force a considerable measure of deregulation of banking.

Nonetheless, it is worth discussing radical changes, not in the expectation that they will be adopted promptly but for two other reasons. One is to construct an ideal goal, so that incremental changes can be judged by whether they move the institutional structure toward or away from that ideal.

The other reason is very different. It is so that if a crisis requiring or facilitating radical change does arise, alternatives will be available that have been carefully developed and fully explored. International monetary arrangements provide an excellent example. For decades, economists had been exploring alternatives to the system of fixed exchange rates—in particular, floating exchange rates among national currencies. The practical men of affairs derided proposals for floating rates as unrealistic, impractical, ivory-tower. Yet when crisis came, when the Bretton Woods fixed-rate system had to be scrapped, the theorists' impractical proposal became highly practical and formed the basis for the new system of international monetary arrangements.

Needless to say, I hope that no crises will occur that will necessitate a drastic change in domestic monetary institutions. The most likely such crisis is continued monetary instability, a return to a roller coaster of inflation about an upward trend, with inflation accelerating to levels of 20, 30, or more percent per year. That would shake the social and political framework of the nation and would produce results none of us would like to witness. Yet, it would be burying one's head in the sand to fail to recognize that such a development is a real possibility. It has occurred elsewhere, and it could occur here. If it does, the best way to cut it short, to minimize the harm it would do, is to be ready not with Band-Aids but with a real cure for the basic illness.

As of now, I believe the best real cure would be the reform outlined above: abolish the money-creating powers of the Federal Reserve, freeze the quantity of high-powered money, and deregulate the financial system.

The less radical changes in policy and procedures suggested in the section on tactics seem to me to offer the best chance of avoiding a crisis. These tactical changes are feasible technically. However, I am not optimistic that they will be adopted. The obstacle is political: as with any bureaucratic organization, it is not in the self-interest of the Fed to adopt policies that would render it accountable. The Fed has persistently avoided doing so over a long period. None of the tactics that I have proposed is new. The proposed changes would have made just as much sense five or ten years ago—indeed, if adopted then, the inflation and volatility of the past ten years would never have occurred. The proposals have had the support of a large fraction of monetary experts outside the Fed. The Fed has resisted them for bureaucratic and political, not technical, reasons. And resistance has been in the Fed's interest. By keeping monetary policy an arcane subject that must be entrusted to "experts" and kept out of politics, incapable of being judged by nonexperts, the Fed has been able to maintain the high public reputation of which I spoke at the outset of this article, despite its poor record of performance.

One chairman after another, in testimony to Congress, has emphasized the mystery and difficulty of the Fed's task and the need for discretion, judgment, and the balancing of many considerations. Each has stressed how well the Fed has done and proclaimed its dedication to pursuing a noninflationary policy and has attributed any undesirable outcome to forces outside the Fed's control or to deficiencies in other components of government policy—particularly fiscal policy. The testimony of the four most recent chairmen of the Fed documents their pervasive concern with avoiding accountability—a concern with which it is easy to sympathize in view of the purely coincidental relation between their announced intentions and the actual outcome.

Clearly the problem is not the person who happens to be chairman, but the system.

Article Thirty-One

Time Inconsistency:
A Potential Problem for Policymakers

*Herb Taylor**

Many industrialized countries, including the United States, experienced high rates of inflation throughout the 1970s. In most of these countries prices have risen at more modest rates over the last several years, but concern over the long-term inflation outlook lingers. The fear usually expressed is that after a few years of low inflation everyone will forget how costly and disruptive high rates of inflation are, and that as industrial economies slow, their central banks will be tempted to pursue inflationary monetary policies to boost real growth. But the difficulty with maintaining a low-inflation monetary policy over the long-term may be more fundamental than that. Using simple examples, economists have demonstrated that even when a central bank recognizes that inflationary monetary policies cannot stimulate real growth and it wants to achieve a low rate of inflation, it may *still* wind up pursuing a high-inflation policy. The problem is that low-inflation policies suffer from what has been called time inconsistency. As a result, even though low-inflation policies always seem best when the central bank lays its plans for the future, they never seem best when the time comes to act on them, and consequently they are not implemented.

Time inconsistency is not unique to monetary policy; the problem often arises in other policy-making situations. But the idea that time inconsistency keeps central banks, such as the Federal Reserve, from sustaining low-inflation monetary policies has generated a great deal of interest among monetary economists recently.

This article presents the basic elements of the current debate: What is time inconsistency? How does it arise in the monetary policy context? Does it create a significant problem for monetary policymakers?

TIME INCONSISTENCY: AN UNFAMILIAR NAME FOR A COMMON PROBLEM

The "time inconsistency of optimal plans" is not a concept with which many are familiar, but the problem itself is very common.[1] In fact, time inconsistency problems are, as the game show host used to say, "something often found in the home." Those exasperating situations in which parents find themselves with their children, for instance, frequently arise because parents' policies are time inconsistent and their children know it. An example best illustrates the point.

The Case of George and Martha. George and Martha's daughter, Betsy, is graduating from high school and wants to go to college in the fall. Betsy is willing to work in order to help pay her college expenses, but she cannot earn enough over the summer to pay all of them. So George and Martha discuss the situation and devise a plan.

After the high school graduation ceremony, George and Martha call Betsy into the living room and say to her, "Betsy, we want you to go to college and further your education, but we also want you to get a job and learn some responsibility. So if you get a job for the summer and save your pay, we will make up the difference between your savings and your college expenses in the fall. But if you don't

*Herb Taylor is a Senior Economist in the Macroeconomics Section of the Research Department of the Federal Reserve Bank of Philadelphia. The author would like to acknowledge his intellectual debt to Gary Gorton, while absolving him from any responsibility for errors.

[1] Kydland and Prescott (1977) introduced the notion of time inconsistency. The paper provides a mathematical characterization of the problem as it confronts policymakers, and a number of examples, including a version of the monetary policy example discussed later in this article.

get a job and save this summer, you'll get nothing from us for college in the fall."

George and Martha are happy with the way they have handled the situation. They know that their daughter wants to go to college and is willing to work for it, so they are confident that she will work and save all summer, start college in September, and emerge from the whole experience a more responsible and better educated person. But things do not go according to plan. First, Betsy does not get a job that summer. In fact, she doesn't even try very hard to find one. Second, when the fall comes, Betsy starts college anyway, and George and Martha pick up the tab.

What went wrong? Did George and Martha misjudge Betsy's desire to go to college and her willingness to work? Did they then simply lose interest in developing Betsy's sense of responsibility? No, it is not that George and Martha misunderstood Betsy, or that their commitment to certain principles suddenly weakened. George and Martha's plan came apart because it was not time consistent—that is, it was not the plan that would serve their best interest when the time came for them to act—and because Betsy realized this from the beginning.

Dissecting George and Martha's Plan. Right after Betsy's parents explained their policy to her, Betsy went to her room and rationally assessed the situation. As a member of the Pac-Man generation, she recognized that her parents had set up a kind of game. In this game, Betsy would make the first move, choosing either to get a summer job or not to get a summer job. Her parents would get their turn in the fall, when they would choose whether or not to pay her college expenses. The game had four possible outcomes. Betsy knew her parents' goals, so she knew how each outcome would measure up in their eyes. Figure 1 summarizes the situation.

Betsy's parents had just told her how they *planned* to play the game and Betsy could see that the plan was optimal from their perspective. If Betsy chose "Get a Job" on her turn, her parents planned to choose "Pay Betsy's Expenses" on their turn. If Betsy chose "Do Not Get a Job" on her turn, her parents planned to choose "Do Not Pay Betsy's Expenses" on their turn. Thus, the plan, if followed, would force Betsy to choose between two possible paths: she could either get a job and go to college or not get a job and not go to college. Given that choice, she would take the former, producing what George and Martha saw as the optimal outcome: a responsible, well-educated daughter.

But Betsy realized that it did not matter how her parents *planned* to play the game in June. What mattered is how they would *actually* play the game

in September. And since Betsy knew what her parents' goals were, she could figure out how they would actually respond when it came time for them to make their move. She thought:

> Suppose I get a job over the summer. When the fall comes, will George and Martha better serve their goals by paying my college expenses or by not paying them? Well, I will already have worked and learned some responsibility, whether they pay my expenses or not. But by paying my expenses, they will enable me to become well-educated too. So they will choose to pay.

> Now suppose I don't get a summer job. When fall comes, will George and Martha better serve their goals by paying my college expenses or by not paying? Well, I will have been without work all summer and I will not have learned any responsibility. But whether they pay my expenses or not will not change that. It will be too late; the summer will be over. And if they do pay my college expenses, then at least I will get an education, which is better than nothing. So they will choose to pay.

Thus Betsy deduced that whether she chose "Get a Job" or "Do Not Get a Job" on her turn, her parents would find it best to choose "Pay Betsy's Expenses" on their turn. So Betsy's choice was really between getting a job before going to college, and taking a vacation before going to college. Given this pair of alternatives, her decision was easy—she took the vacation.

The Perennial Problem of Time Inconsistency. Time inconsistency in George and Martha's optimal plan kept them from achieving their goal of getting Betsy to work for the summer. But the problem can affect anyone trying to influence the behavior of others—and that includes anyone making social or economic policy. For instance, the FDIC wants to maintain a sound financial system, so it tries to discourage people from depositing their funds with banks that undertake risky investments by announcing that it will not insure large deposits (those over $100,000) in the event of a bank failure. But the public realizes that once a bank does fail, the FDIC's desire to maintain confidence in the financial system is likely to dictate that it insure the deposits, so they deposit their funds with risky banks. Similarly, national governments want to protect their citizens from terrorists, so they announce that they will not negotiate with skyjackers. But

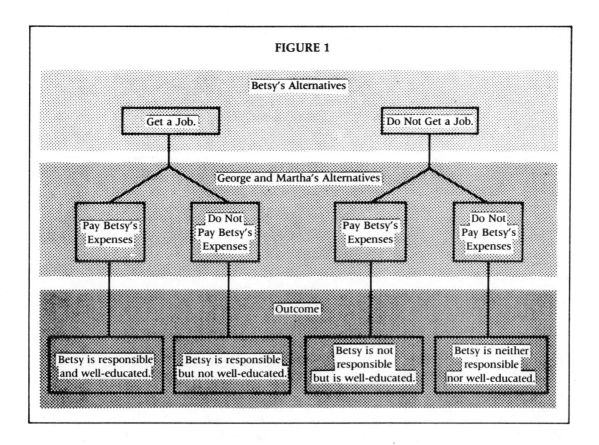

FIGURE 1

Betsy's Alternatives

Get a Job.

Do Not Get a Job.

George and Martha's Alternatives

Pay Betsy's Expenses

Do Not Pay Betsy's Expenses

Pay Betsy's Expenses

Do Not Pay Betsy's Expenses

Outcome

Betsy is responsible and well-educated.

Betsy is responsible but not well-educated.

Betsy is not responsible but is well-educated.

Betsy is neither responsible nor well-educated.

terrorists realize that once they have seized an airliner, the government's concern for the hostages is likely to dictate that the government negotiate, so the terrorists take the plane. Whatever the particulars of the situation, the problem created by time inconsistency follows the same pattern.[2]

A policymaker sets out to achieve goals which involve getting other individuals to behave in certain ways. The policymaker realizes that how these individuals choose to behave depends on how they expect him to react to their choices, and he takes this into account in formulating his optimal plan of action. (George and Martha want Betsy to get a summer job. They realize that how Betsy decides to spend her summer depends on how she expects them to react at tuition time, so they tell her that they plan to link what she does about a summer job with what they will do about her college expenses.)

But there is a difficulty. When it comes time to act, the policymaker will be free to reassess the situation and decide what course of action seems best *at that time*. And generally he will find that following the original plan is no longer in his best interest. Why? Because when the original plan was formulated, it took into account the impact of the policymaker's planned actions on the individuals' behavior. But when it comes time to act, taking the planned actions can no longer influence individuals' behavior. They have already chosen how to behave. Now the policymaker must choose the course of action that brings him closest to achieving his goals *given* the individuals' previous behavior. (So when the fall comes, George and Martha will abandon the plan designed to *influence* Betsy's summer behavior and select the original plan of action which best meets their goals *given* her summer behavior.)

Unfortunately for the policymaker, individuals realize from the beginning that the policymaker will take the time consistent plan of action—the plan which seems best *at the time the action is to be taken*—rather than the one which seemed optimal to the policymaker initially. So from the beginning,

---

[2]Kydland and Prescott (1977) develop a tax policy example. Newberg (1981) discusses the problem of maintaining the oil cartel in the context of dynamic inconsistency.

individuals' behavior deviates from that called for by the policymaker's optimal plan. (Betsy knows in June that her parents will pay her expenses in September no matter what, so she takes the summer off.)

In sum, time inconsistency is a general problem facing policymakers of all types. And recently economists have been giving serious consideration to the way in which time inconsistency can undermine central banks' abilities to contain inflation. But to appreciate how the problem arises for the makers of monetary policy, it is useful to consider what motivates central banks' choice of monetary policy actions and how the economy responds to them.

HOW TIME INCONSISTENCY CAN FOIL POLICYMAKERS' LOW INFLATION PLANS

Monetary policy is widely acknowledged to have a direct impact on the rate of inflation, but central banks are also held responsible, to varying degrees, for the level of real economic activity in their countries. Consequently, a central bank's goals generally include not only maintaining a low rate of inflation, but maintaining a low rate of unemployment as well. In the United States, for example, the Full Employment and Balanced Growth Act of 1978 requires that the Fed testify before Congress annually, indicating how its plans fit into Congress' long-term objectives of achieving zero inflation and a 4 percent unemployment rate.

Until about ten years ago, discussions of monetary policy were often predicated on the notion that the central bank faced a fairly stable tradeoff between achieving its inflation and unemployment goals: rapid growth of the money supply would bring low unemployment but high inflation; slow money growth would bring a low rate of inflation but a high rate of unemployment. However, the anomalous behavior of inflation and unemployment in the 1970s—high and even increasing inflation accompanied by high and sometimes increasing unemployment in most industrialized countries—prompted macro-economists to reformulate their views about the economy's response to monetary policy. Perhaps the two most important ideas to emerge from the recent reformulation are the so-called "natural rate" and "rational expectations" hypotheses. Taken together, these two ideas imply that the growth rate of the money supply directly affects the rate of inflation in the economy, but it has no systematic impact on the unemployment rate. Consequently, to the extent that these two hypotheses are correct, there is no tradeoff

between inflation and unemployment for the central bank. Its choice of a monetary policy influences only the inflation rate, not the unemployment rate.[3]

For some time now macroeconomists have been stressing the obvious implication of the natural rate and rational expectations hypotheses: regardless of the central bank's concerns about unemployment, the monetary policies which produce low inflation are generally optimal. It is only recently that economists have paid much attention to a more subtle implication of the two hypotheses: because of the central bank's concerns about unemployment, monetary policies which produce low inflation may also be time inconsistent.

Choosing the Optimal Monetary Policy. According to the natural rate hypothesis, the economy tends toward a natural rate of unemployment which is independent of the stance of monetary policy. It may be possible for monetary policymakers to keep the actual unemployment rate from settling at its natural rate, at least temporarily, but only if they are able to create rates of inflation that the public had not been expecting.

For instance, the monetary authority might consider the natural rate of unemployment too high, and so decide that it will stimulate the economy by increasing the growth rate of the money supply. More rapid money growth increases the growth in private sector demand for goods and services. The increased demand puts upward pressure on prices, and the inflation rate rises. But will the higher inflation rate bring a lower unemployment rate? Not necessarily, according to the natural rate hypothesis. It depends on the public's inflation expectations. If firms and workers had been expecting the central bank to generate a high inflation rate and had figured this into their current wage agreements, then the higher inflation will not induce firms to hire any more workers than they intended to, so unemployment will remain at its natural rate. It is only if firms and workers had been expecting the central bank to generate low inflation and had signed contracts for low wage increases that the high-inflation policy would give firms the incentive to

---

[3]Criticisms of the standard "Phillips Curve" tradeoff between inflation and unemployment, and development of the alternative notions of the natural rate hypothesis and rational expectations have become nearly standard components of textbooks in macroeconomics and monetary theory. See, for example, Ritter and Silber (1983), Chapter 2, for a good summary.

hire additional workers, and thus push unemployment below its natural rate.

Conversely, if the monetary authority considered the current inflation rate too high, and so decided to reduce the growth rate of the money supply, the response of unemployment would likewise depend on inflation expectations. As long as firms and workers had expected a slowdown in money growth and inflation when they forged current wage agreements, unemployment will remain at its natural rate. Lower inflation would be accompanied by an increase in the unemployment rate only if labor market participants had signed contracts for high wage increases and the lower inflation took them by surprise.[4]

The natural rate hypothesis leaves the door open for the central bank to affect the unemployment rate, if it can generate an inflation rate which the public does not expect. Proponents of the rational expectations hypothesis slam the door shut by arguing that the central bank cannot systematically engineer any inflation "surprises." According to rational expectations, the public knows as much about the way the central bank conducts monetary policy as the central bank does, so the central bank cannot count on doing anything that participants in the economy did not expect. Consequently, the central bank cannot plan on using monetary policy to drive the unemployment rate away from its natural rate.[5]

If the natural rate and the rational expectations hypotheses were perfectly accurate descriptions of the way the economy worked, then monetary policy would not affect the unemployment rate, and it clearly would be optimal for the central bank to concentrate its efforts on keeping the inflation rate low. Yet even in these circumstances the central bank may wind up pursuing a high-inflation monetary policy. How can this be? Because as long as the central bank would be willing to trade high inflation for low unemployment, the low-money-growth, low-inflation policy is not time consistent. A simple example demonstrates the central bank's predicament.

---

[4]Analyses of the impact of surprise inflation on the unemployment rate based on the wage rigidity introduced by labor contracts are presented by Fischer (1977) and J. Taylor (1980). An alternative analysis based on a firm's initial inability to distinguish between general inflation and an increase in the demand for its product is developed by Lucas (1973).

[5]The conclusion that monetary policy systematically affects the inflation rate but has no systematic influence on real output or unemployment was given a clear exposition in Sargent and Wallace (1975).

Dissecting the Optimal Plan For Monetary Policy. Suppose that at the beginning of the year all of the workers and firms in an economy are in the process of negotiating their annual wage agreements. Before the agreements are signed, the central bank announces that it intends to follow a low-money-growth, low-inflation monetary policy during the year. Having received the central bank's statement, the firms and workers in the labor market must decide whether to sign contracts for low wage increases or for high wage increases. What should they do?

Labor market participants realize they are locked into a game with the central bank. In this game, they get the first move, at the beginning of the year, when they choose between signing labor contracts with low wage increases or signing contracts with high wage increases. The central bank takes its turn next, during the year, when it chooses between creating a low rate of money growth or creating a high rate of money growth. The game will produce one of four possible outcomes for the economy (see Figure 2).

The firms and workers in the economy understand that the central bank's announced plan seems optimal under the circumstances. The blanket statement that it will pursue a low-money-growth policy seems to leave labor market participants with the choice between signing contracts for low wage increases which will match the rate of inflation and put unemployment at its natural rate, or signing contracts for high wage increases which will outstrip inflation and push unemployment above its natural rate. Since labor market participants will settle on wage increases which just keep pace with expected inflation, the central bank anticipates they will choose low wage increases. So, if all goes according to plan, workers and firms will sign for low wage increases, and the central bank will then follow with the low-money-growth policy which they had expected. As a result, inflation will come in low and unemployment will come in at the natural rate—the optimal outcome.

Of course, the question in the mind of labor market participants is "Will the central bank still see the low-money-growth, low-inflation policy as best after the contracts are signed and it is time for the central bank to carry out its policy?" And in this case, the answer is "No," because the central bank is willing to trade off higher inflation for lower unemployment.

Suppose, for instance, that the firms and workers in the economy were to agree on contracts specifying low wage increases. Now the monetary authority can choose between the low-inflation

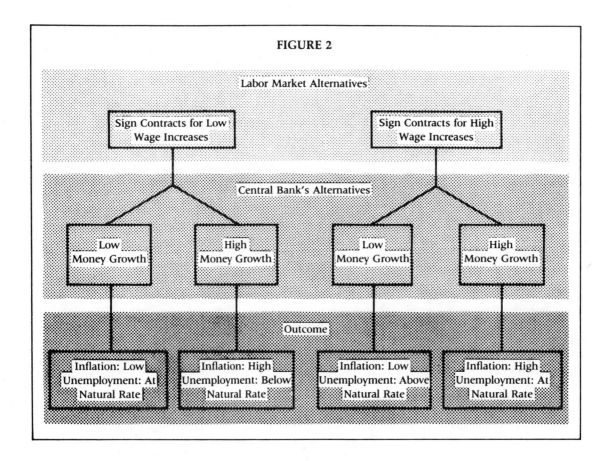

FIGURE 2

Labor Market Alternatives

| Sign Contracts for Low Wage Increases | | Sign Contracts for High Wage Increases | |

Central Bank's Alternatives

| Low Money Growth | High Money Growth | Low Money Growth | High Money Growth |

Outcome

| Inflation: Low Unemployment: At Natural Rate | Inflation: High Unemployment: Below Natural Rate | Inflation: Low Unemployment: Above Natural Rate | Inflation: High Unemployment: At Natural Rate |

policy called for by the optimal plan and a high-inflation policy which will drive the unemployment rate below its natural rate. The central bank is presumed to be willing to pursue a high-inflation policy if it would reduce unemployment, and with low wage increases already locked in, the central bank would have its chance. So it would pursue the high-inflation policy.

On the other hand, suppose that labor market participants signed contracts specifying high wage increases for the year. Again, the monetary authority has to choose between the low-inflation policy called for by the optimal plan and a high-inflation policy. But this time the low-inflation policy would drive unemployment above its natural rate. And if the monetary authority is willing to run a high-inflation monetary policy to push unemployment below the natural rate, it is surely willing to do so in order to keep unemployment from rising above it. So the monetary authority would again pursue the high-inflation policy.

In short, the firms and workers of the economy enter into their wage negotiations with the realization that pursuing a high-money-growth,

high-inflation policy is the only time consistent plan for the central bank to follow. So their choice is obvious—they sign contracts for high wage increases at the beginning of the year. During the year, the central bank pursues the high-money-growth policy that they expected, so inflation comes in high. And with both wage increases and inflation running high, unemployment settles at its natural rate. So, as a result of the time inconsistency of the optimal low-inflation policy, the central bank winds up creating a high rate of inflation even though it gains nothing on the unemployment front.[6]

A POSSIBLE SOLUTION: CREDIBLE PRECOMMITMENTS TO THE OPTIMAL PLAN

One weakness with the analysis thus far is that it seems to imply that individuals understand the policymaker's situation better than the policymaker does. But surely if Betsy can figure out that her parents' original plan is time inconsistent, so

---

[6]A mathematical presentation of the dynamic inconsistency in low-inflation monetary policies along these lines is carefully developed by Barro and Gordon (1983a).

can her parents. Likewise if the workers and firms in the economy recognize that a low inflation policy is not time consistent, so must the central bank. And if policymakers are aware of the time inconsistency in their original optimal plans, isn't there something they can *do* about it? At least in principle, it seems there is—they can take measures to make their original plans time consistent.

In order for the original optimal plan to work it must be time consistent. Everybody must recognize *at the outset* that when the time comes for the policymaker to act, following the original optimal plan will still represent the policymaker's best course of action. The policymaker can ensure this by making some additional arrangements which will make deviating from the optimal plan very costly to him—so costly that he will not choose to deviate from the plan when he acts. Once the policymaker has established this *credible precommitment* to the original optimal plan, so that individuals (rightly) expect him to follow it in the future, they too will behave according to the optimal plan when they make their decisions.

George and Martha might apply this approach to overcoming the time inconsistency in their optimal plan: before talking to Betsy they can have all of their savings put into a trust account with the provision that the trust manager not disburse funds to finance Betsy's education unless she can document that she has worked a summer job. Then when they tell Betsy that they will help her with her college expenses only if she gets a summer job, Betsy will get the job, because she knows that they are committed to the optimal policy and they will not pay her expenses if she does not get a job.

Similarly, one solution to the time inconsistency problem in our simple economic example is for the central bank to begin the year, not simply by announcing that it considers a low-inflation policy optimal, but by establishing a credible commitment to the low-inflation policy. For example, the central bankers themselves may agree to forfeit their position or their personal wealth if money growth or the inflation rate exceeds some announced percent for the year. Once firms and workers realize that it will still be in the central bank's best interest to run a low-inflation monetary policy during the year, they will sign contracts for low wage increases at the beginning of the year, and the economy can achieve the natural rate of unemployment at a low inflation rate.[7]

---

[7]The role of the monetary authority's credibility in the disinflation process is discussed in J. Taylor (1982).

While arrangements establishing a credible precommitment to low inflation monetary policies can be devised, such arrangements are not likely to be implemented. Governments seem to be unwilling to impose the necessary system of penalties on their central banks, and central bankers are unlikely to do so themselves (see Donald J. Mullineaux's "Monetary Rules and Contracts: Why Theory Loses to Practice" in this issue of the *Business Review*). But all is not lost. Even in the absence of formal arrangements, there are forces at work to push the time consistent policy closer to the original optimal low-inflation rate.

THE ADVANTAGE OF HAVING A GOOD REPUTATION

Both the family example and the monetary policy example consider only a single interaction between the policymakers and the individuals they were trying to influence. But parents try to influence their offsprings' behavior, and central banks try to influence economies' performances, every day. And this repeated interaction itself may help bridge the gap between the optimal plan and the time consistent one.

When the encounter between the policymaker and other individuals is part of a long sequence of encounters, the policymaker becomes concerned about how the present encounter will affect his "reputation"—others' expectations about how he will act in the future. Adhering to the optimal plan in the current encounter presumably will enhance the policymaker's reputation, so that in future encounters, when he announces that he intends to follow the optimal plan, people are more likely to believe him and behave in accordance with that plan. On the other hand, deviating from the optimal plan in the current encounter will impair the policymaker's reputation, so that his announcement of an intent to follow the optimal plan in the future will be less credible, and people will be more likely to act on the assumption that he will deviate from it. In short, adhering to the announced optimal policy today improves the policymaker's prospects for obtaining optimal outcomes tomorrow. Thus, building a reputation functions in the same way as an explicit precommitment to the optimal policy; it raises the relative cost of deviating from the optimal policy, and so keeps the policymaker to the original optimal policy when the time comes to act. Individuals realize this, anticipate the policymaker following the optimal plan, and so behave in accordance with the optimal plan from the beginning.

For example, suppose George and Martha realize that by adhering to their optimal plan and refusing to pay for Betsy's freshman year in college unless she gets a summer job, they will reap the benefit that Betsy will find that policy credible during the summers before her sophomore, junior, and senior years. She may even find similar policies credible on other occasions. And maybe Betsy's younger brothers and sisters will do the same. On the other hand, by abandoning the optimal plan after that first summer and paying Betsy's tuition bill when she does not work, George and Martha forgo all the benefits of having a reputation for adhering to their optimal plans. If the long-run benefits of sticking with the optimal plan and maintaining a reputation outweigh the short-run benefits of sending Betsy to college on schedule, George and Martha will stick to their optimal plan. Betsy will realize this, she will find their optimal policy credible, and she will get a summer job.

Similarly, in the case of monetary policy, suppose that by sticking with the optimal low-inflation policy one year, the central bank reaps the benefit of convincing the public that it will stick with this policy in future years. As long as the central bank weighs this future benefit more heavily than any current benefits from a high-inflation policy, it will stick to its optimal plan. Firms and workers realize this, and, seeing the announced low-inflation policy as credible, sign contracts for low wage increases at the beginning of the year.

There is no guarantee that the central bank's concern about preserving its reputation will work as well as an explicit precommitment to keep the central bank to low-inflation policies. The central bank in our example has a simple choice: high inflation or low inflation. Either the perceived benefits of building its reputation are sufficient to make the low-inflation policy time consistent or they are not. In reality, the central bank chooses from a continuum of possible inflation rates and the greater the benefits of building its reputation the closer the inflation rate associated with the time consistent policy will be to the inflation rate associated with the optimal policy. For instance, if the central bank takes a long-run view of its policies' impacts and sees prospects of high inflation in the future as a serious problem, then it will value its reputation more highly. Similarly, if the central bank knows that the public's confidence is easy to lose and hard to regain, then it will weigh reputation considerations more heavily in its policy decisions. Such considerations will push the time consistent monetary policy closer to the optimal one, and hence push the actual inflation rate closer to the optimal one. A central bank might consider that adherence to the optimal monetary policy today pays a rich enough dividend in terms of lower inflation tomorrow to warrant sticking with that policy, but that would be the extreme case.[8]

CONCLUSION

Decisionmakers charged with setting social policy, from parents to Presidents, often face the problem that their optimal plans are time inconsistent—the plans will no longer seem optimal when the time comes for the policymaker to act. The individuals whose behavior the plans are supposed to affect realize this and, as a result, behave in a way that keeps the policymakers from achieving their original goals.

Some economists are now exploring the notion that the Fed's efforts to reduce inflation are plagued by time inconsistency problems. Simple examples have been developed to show how a central bank that is willing to use inflationary monetary policies to drive unemployment below its natural rate may find itself producing chronic high inflation and never reducing unemployment.

No one is quite ready to argue that time inconsistency spells an inevitable return to double-digit inflation. There are ways around the problem. First of all, time inconsistency can be overcome if the central bank can establish a credible precommitment to follow a low-inflation policy. Admittedly, this solution has yet to be adopted by any country today, but a more practical solution or near-solution may be at work already. A central bank which realizes that its current policy actions influence the public's expectations about the future course of monetary policy will find it nearly as much in its self-interest to pursue a low inflation policy as it would if an explicit precommitment had been made. Viewed from this perspective, the recent emphasis that preserving the central bank's reputation has been given in monetary policy discussions, both in the United States and abroad, represents a substantive step forward in containing inflation over the long term.

---

[8]Barro and Gordon (1983b) emphasize the role of reputation in helping to reduce the impact of dynamic inconsistency problems on inflation.

BIBLIOGRAPHY

Barro, Robert J., and David B. Gordon (1983a), "A Positive Theory of Monetary Policy in a Natural Rate Model," *Journal of Political Economy*, pp. 589-610.

_____, and _____ (1983b), "Rules, Discretion and Reputation in a Model of Monetary Policy," *Journal of Monetary Economics*, pp. 101-121.

Fischer, Stanley (1977), "Long Term Contracts, Rational Expectations and the Optimal Money Supply Rule," *Journal of Political Economy*, pp. 191-206.

Kydland, Finn E., and Edward C. Prescott (1977), "Rules Rather Than Discretion: The Inconsistency of Optimal Plans," *Journal of Political Economy*, pp. 473-491.

Lucas, Robert E., Jr. (1973), "Some International Evidence on Inflation-Output Tradeoffs," *American Economic Review*, (June), pp. 326-334.

Newberg, D.M.G., (1981), "Oil Prices, Cartels, and the Problem of Dynamic Inconsistency," *Economic Journal* (September), pp. 617-645.

Ritter, Lawrence S., and William Silber (1983), *Principles of Money, Banking and Financial Markets*, Fourth Edition, (NY: Basic Books).

Sargent, Thomas J., and Neil Wallace (1975), "Rational Expectations, the Optimal Monetary Instrument, and the Optimal Money Supply Rule," *Journal of Political Economy*, pp. 241-254.

Taylor, John B. (1980), "Aggregate Dynamics and Staggered Contracts," *Journal of Political Economy*, pp. 1-23.

_____ (1982), "Establishing Credibility: A Rational Expectations Viewpoint," *American Economic Review, Papers and Proceedings*, (May), pp. 81-85.

Article Thirty-Two

Maintaining Central Bank Credibility

By Anne Sibert and Stuart E. Weiner

Central banks throughout the world have increasingly recognized the importance of maintaining public confidence in the commitment of governments to controlling inflation. This recognition has resulted in part from the worldwide inflation in the 1970s. Whether because of oil supply shocks, excessive wage demands, or unduly expansionary government policies, inflation ratcheted upward throughout the 1970s in most industrial countries. As a result of this experience, households and businesses may have become skeptical about the ability and willingness of governments to maintain a reasonably stable price level.

Recent economic research has focused on the implications of such skepticism and what can be done to keep the public's confidence in monetary policy. One major conclusion of this research is that the credibility of a central bank's commitment to price stability can be undermined by public perceptions that keeping unemployment at an unrealistically low level is an overriding goal of monetary policy. Such perceptions can lead the public to expect an inflationary monetary policy even when the central bank announces its commitment to price stability.

Moreover, the public's fear of an inflationary policy may be particularly acute if the central bank does not conduct policy according to a fixed rule but instead exercises judgment depending on a variety of economic variables. Exercising judgment in this way is often referred to as a discretionary policy procedure. A possible problem with this procedure is that what a central bank promises to do in the future may be inconsistent with what it in fact does when the time comes for it to act. For that reason, the problem arising from discretionary monetary policies is referred to as the time-inconsistency problem, which causes a related credibility problem for a central bank in convincing the public of its commitment to price stability.

Some economists have concluded from this line of reasoning that central banks should avoid discretion and be required to adopt monetary

Anne Sibert is an assistant professor of economics at the University of Kansas and a visiting scholar at the Federal Reserve Bank of Kansas City. Stuart E. Weiner is a research officer and economist at the bank.

growth rules that will relieve the public's anxiety about the prospect of inflationary monetary policy in the future. Recognizing the possible shortcomings of these monetary growth rules, other economists have proposed alternative solutions to the time-inconsistency and credibility problems faced by central banks.

This article argues that neither monetary growth rules nor other proposed solutions to the time-inconsistency problem are costless. The first section explains why discretionary conduct of monetary policy may make it difficult to establish the credibility of a central bank's commitment to price stability. The second section shows why monetary growth rules are not a costless solution to the credibility problem. And the third section demonstrates why alternative proposals are also problematical.

Time inconsistency and central bank credibility

The credibility problem arises if the public is skeptical about a central bank's intention to pursue noninflationary monetary policies. Individuals and businesses might be skeptical, for example, if they perceive that the central bank would like to lower unemployment temporarily below the rate that can be achieved in a noninflationary environment. Even if the public and the central bank understand that attempting to temporarily lower unemployment may not be successful and will result in permanently higher inflation that will damage the economy, the public may distrust a central bank's assertions that it will not succumb to this temptation to inflate. Ironically, the public's skepticism arises in large part because private citizens realize that they might well pursue such an inflationary policy if placed in the position of central bankers.[1]

---

[1] The seminal paper in the time-inconsistency literature is Finn Kydland and Edward Prescott, "Rules Rather Than Discretion:

The tradeoff between unemployment and inflation

Society and central banks would like to achieve both low inflation and low unemployment. Inflation is considered undesirable because it contributes to social strains by creating the perception that a market economy can lead to arbitrary and unfair redistribution of wealth. Moreover, inflation imposes real economic costs by causing an inefficient allocation of society's scarce resources.[2] Unemployment is considered undesirable because it means that an important scarce resource, labor, is being underutilized. Consequently, both unemployment and inflation reduce society's overall economic welfare.

But lowering unemployment and inflation simultaneously may not be possible in the short run. An unexpected expansionary monetary policy, for example, not only leads firms to hire more workers but also causes inflation to worsen as demand for output increases. The level of inflation is thus inversely related to the level of unemployment in the short run. This inverse relationship is embodied in the short-run Phillips curve, which shows that lowering unemployment is typically associated with higher inflation.

Over longer run periods, trying to keep unemployment low through expansionary macroeconomic policies also leads to higher inflation. Not only do prices of goods rise throughout the

---

The Inconsistency of Optimal Plans," *Journal of Political Economy,* June 1977, pp. 473-492. The idea was popularized by Robert Barro and David Gordon in "A Positive Theory of Monetary Policy in a Natural Rate Model," *Journal of Political Economy,* August 1983, pp. 589-610. Shortcomings of this literature are examined by Torsten Persson, "Credibility of Macroeconomic Policy: An Introduction and a Broad Survey," *European Economic Review,* 1988, pp. 519-532.

[2] For further discussion of the costs of inflation see Stanley Fischer, "The Benefits of Price Stability," *Price Stability and Public Policy,* proceedings of an economic symposium sponsored by the Federal Reserve Bank of Kansas City, 1984.

economy, but wages rise as well as labor contracts are renegotiated.

The amount of unemployment that is consistent with stable inflation is called the natural level of unemployment. Some unemployment is inevitable in a market economy in which workers are free to change jobs and take time off between jobs. The natural level of unemployment is thus positive.

The natural level of unemployment may nonetheless be above the socially optimal level of unemployment because of labor market distortions. Income taxes and social security taxes provide an example. Such taxes reduce workers' after-tax wages. By driving a wedge between what employers pay and what employees receive, income and social security taxes keep some workers from working as much as they otherwise would. As a result of such distortions, the level of unemployment that is consistent with stable inflation in the long run may well be higher than is socially desirable in a broader sense.[3]

Central banks and society thus face the dilemma of accepting undesirably high unemployment or lowering unemployment through inflationary monetary policies. The dilemma arises because

society cannot achieve both of its major macroeconomic objectives simultaneously. One or the other must be sacrificed unless labor market imperfections are eliminated.

Moreover, a central bank cannot lower unemployment by pursuing inflationary policies that are fully anticipated by firms and workers. Firms decide how many workers to hire based on the real, or inflation-adjusted, wage they must pay. Similarly, workers decide whether to take a job based on the real purchasing power of the wages they are offered. Inflation that is fully anticipated would thus not alter employment decisions. Instead, anticipated inflation merely lowers social welfare because of the associated inefficiencies without any compensating reduction in unemployment.

The only way for a central bank to lower unemployment is to pursue monetary policies that cause inflation to rise unexpectedly.[4] If workers and firms initially expect no inflation and enter into long-term wage contracts based on this expectation, an unexpected rise in inflation can change the real wage and thus the level of employment. To see how a central bank can lower unemployment by generating surprise inflation, consider the labor market diagram in Figure 1. The real wage is measured along the vertical axis, and the employment level is measured along the horizontal axis. The real wage is the nominal wage (W) deflated by the price level (P). The labor demand curve, D_1, shows the amount of labor that firms want to hire at any given real wage. It slopes downward and to the right because firms want to hire more workers as the real wage falls, that is, as labor becomes cheaper. The labor supply curve, S_1, shows the amount of labor that workers want to supply at any given real wage. It slopes upward and to the right because more individuals

---

[3] Income taxes reduce the amount of pay that workers take home but also provide revenue for government services. Given a certain tax level, workers will collectively choose to supply labor along a given labor supply curve, and overall employment will be at its natural level. Any individual worker, however, would prefer that overall employment be greater than this natural level because tax revenues, and hence government services, would be correspondingly higher. Individual workers will not increase their work effort, however, because they would view the increased government services resulting from this effort as negligible. Consequently, the higher level of "optimal" employment will not be achieved.

Other labor market features that impede the attainment of optimal employment (though not necessarily strictly within the context of the above model) include skill mismatches, location mismatches, institutional barriers, imperfect information flows, and transfer payment disincentives. For discussion, see Stuart E. Weiner, "The Natural Rate of Unemployment: Concepts and Issues," *Economic Review,* Federal Reserve Bank of Kansas City, January 1986, pp. 11-24.

[4] This description follows Kydland and Prescott, "Rules Rather Than Discretion . . . ."

FIGURE 1
The labor market

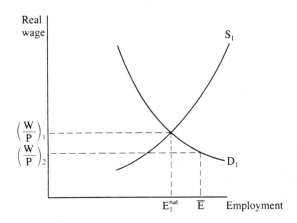

want to work as the real wage rises, that is, as workers are paid more.

Assume that workers and firms enter into a contract in which workers are paid a fixed nominal wage over a certain period of time. Workers and firms agree on this nominal wage without knowing the future price level. Once the actual price level is known, firms decide how much labor to employ based on the resulting real wage. By assumption, workers are obligated to supply this labor according to the terms of the labor agreement. Thus, the level of employment is determined by the demand for labor by firms.[5]

Suppose that the nominal wage agreed on and the associated price level yield a real wage of $(\frac{W}{P})_1$. At this real wage, the labor demand and labor supply curves intersect, so the amount of

labor demanded is equal to the amount of labor supplied. Firms are on their labor demand curve, and workers are on their labor supply curve. The resulting employment level, denoted E_1^{nat}, is called the "natural level of employment." It is the employment counterpart to the natural level of unemployment discussed above.

A central bank that is allowed discretion in conducting policy can temporarily raise employment by generating surprise inflation through an unexpected increase in the money supply. Suppose that some labor market distortion, such as income taxes, causes the natural level of employment to be below the optimal level of employment (and, correspondingly, causes the natural level of unemployment to be above the optimal level of unemployment). A central bank could increase employment to the optimal level by unexpectedly pursuing an inflationary monetary policy. The unexpected rise in the price level would lower real wages because nominal wages are assumed to be fixed. In Figure 1, the real wage would decline from $(\frac{W}{P})_1$ to $(\frac{W}{P})_2$, and employment would rise from E_1^{nat} to $\bar{E}$.

The rise in employment will only be temporary, however, because workers are supplying more labor than they want to. Workers are not on their labor supply curve. If workers believe that higher prices will continue, they will compensate by negotiating higher nominal wages in the next contract negotiation. The real wage will eventually retrace its path, settling again at $(\frac{W}{P})_1$. In the end, the price level will be higher, nominal wages will be higher, and employment will be back at the natural level.

The temptation to inflate

The discussion above demonstrates that a central bank can temporarily increase employment by generating surprise inflation. This possibility causes a credibility problem for the central bank and can introduce an inflationary bias into

5 This assumption that employment is demand-determined is reasonable for unionized U.S. labor markets and follows that of Jo Anna Gray, "Wage Indexation: A Macroeconomic Approach," *Journal of Monetary Economics*, April 1976, pp. 221-235.

monetary policy.[6] Even if a central bank announces a strict anti-inflation policy and has every intention of adhering to it, the central bank has an incentive to renege once nominal wages are fixed. This temptation to inflate once nominal wages are set is the essence of the time-inconsistency problem. Workers and firms understand the central bank's incentives and are thus skeptical about its policy announcements. Lacking credibility, the central bank is unable to increase employment and, indeed, must tolerate higher inflation to maintain existing employment.

To understand this argument, consider again the firms and workers depicted in Figure 1. Suppose the central bank announced that it would not inflate and that workers and firms negotiated a nominal wage expected to yield a real wage of $(\frac{W}{P})_1$ and a corresponding employment level of E_1^{nat}. With the nominal wage fixed, the central bank would now have an incentive to renege on its anti-inflation promise. By driving prices higher and real wages lower, the central bank is able to attain a higher level of employment, say $\bar{E}$. Workers and firms recognize this ability, however, and in fact would not agree to a nominal wage that permits it to happen. Rather, expecting inflation, workers and firms will negotiate a higher nominal wage that compensates for the expected inflation. The central bank will then have to inflate just to ensure that the real wage does not go *above* $(\frac{W}{P})_1$ and employment go *below* E_1^{nat}. The end result is higher inflation with no compensating reduction in unemployment.

In summary, the time-inconsistency and credibility problems arise when the public comes to doubt a central bank's commitment to price stability. The doubt arises when the public believes the central bank can and will sacrifice price stability in order to lower unemployment, even if only temporarily. A central bank can do so if it conducts monetary policy using discretion rather than rules and if real wages and thus employment are affected by unexpected inflation. A central bank may be willing to make the trade-off if labor market distortions make it impossible to achieve the socially desirable level of employment without creating unexpected inflation. Recognizing the incentive to promise low inflation but deliver high inflation, the public could become skeptical of a central bank's commitment to price stability. Such skepticism would lead workers and firms to expect inflation in the future and seek to protect themselves by building an inflation premium into wage contracts. When this occurs, the inflation expectations become a self-fulfilling prophecy. This process may be reversed if the central bank follows a monetary policy restrictive enough to cause unemployment to remain high long enough to change the public's expectations.[7] Lack of central bank credibility can thus result in either higher inflation, higher unemployment, or both. For this reason, it is important to analyze how monetary policy can be conducted to maintain public confidence in the central bank's commitment to price stability.

Caveats

The assumption that a central bank is perceived as wanting to keep unemployment artificially low is a critical element in the argument that central banks face a serious credibility problem. If,

[6] A government might also be tempted to inflate for reasons other than generating employment gains. See, for example, Kenneth Rogoff and Anne Sibert, "Elections and Macroeconomic Policy Cycles," *Review of Economic Studies,* February 1988, pp. 1-16, and Guillermo Calvo, "On the Time Consistency of Optimal Policy in a Monetary Economy," *Econometrica,* November 1978, pp. 1411-1428.

[7] This is the conclusion reached by David Backus and John Driffill, "Rational Expectations and Policy Credibility Following a Change in Regime," *Review of Economic Studies,* April 1985, pp. 211-222. If the private sector is uncertain of the preferences of the central bank, it may revise its beliefs about the credibility of the bank after observing the bank carrying out an anti-inflation policy.

instead, it is assumed that the public believes monetary policy is directed toward maintaining price stability and keeping the unemployment rate near the natural level, the conclusion that central banks face a serious credibility problem is much weaker. Indeed, one study in the professional literature shows that the credibility problem vanishes if the public believes the central bank's objectives do not include keeping the unemployment rate below the natural level.[8]

The authors of this important study do not attempt to provide a compelling case for why a central bank would try to reduce unemployment below the natural level. Rather, they conjecture that the socially desirable unemployment level is probably below the natural level due to labor market distortions of the type described above. That the unemployment level is kept above the socially desirable level by various microeconomic distortions does not in itself prove, however, that the central bank would be perceived as trying to remedy the problem through macroeconomic policy. It might be argued, for example, that the public and the central bank would both recognize the advisability of using policies other than monetary expansion to compensate for distortions in labor markets.

The extent to which central banks do try to keep unemployment below the natural level may well vary. The institutional arrangements of and legislative mandates for central banks vary widely. Such variation may lead some central banks to have different priorities than others. Moreover, the central bank of any particular country may emphasize certain goals more in some circumstances than in others, leading the public's skepticism about the central bank's commitment to control inflation to vary accordingly.

For these and other reasons, the conclusions of the time-inconsistency literature have by no

means been universally accepted. No consensus has emerged on the practical importance of the time-inconsistency problem in explaining inflation in industrial countries. In addition, some ambiguities remain in the fundamental analysis, and several theoretical issues are unresolved.[9] Nevertheless, this literature does provide insight into the potential inflationary bias of a society and its central bank. And it provides insight into the importance of credibility.

Monetary growth rules

The principal conclusion of the central bank credibility literature is that central banks will tend

---

[8] See Barro and Gordon, "A Positive Theory . . . . "

[9] One unresolved issue involves the compatibility of social welfare with individual preferences. The time-inconsistency problem assumes that social welfare depends negatively upon deviations from optimal levels of employment and inflation. Thus, social welfare must be increasing in unanticipated inflation (until the optimal level of employment is reached) and decreasing in actual inflation. However, it is not obvious that this is the case. One reason is that unanticipated inflation may be costly as well as beneficial. Suppose, for example, that suppliers see their own prices rise before they observe that the general price level has risen. Then they may incorrectly conclude that the demand for their product has increased, and they may produce more than they would if their information was perfect. Another problem is that it is not clear that economic welfare is decreasing in actual inflation. The usual arguments for why this is the case are that the tax system must be changed and individuals must hold higher money balances. However, in the above arguments, it is expected inflation rather than actual inflation that is costly. For discussion, see Robert Lucas, "Expectations and the Neutrality of Money," *Journal of Economic Theory*, April 1972, pp. 103-124, and Herschel Grossman, "A General Model of Monetary Policy, Inflation, and Reputation," mimeo, 1987.

A second unresolved issue involves labor market distortions. The root of the time-inconsistency problem is the tax-induced distortions in the labor market that keep employment below its socially optimal level. But these distortionary taxes finance public goods. Suppose that at the natural level of employment tax revenue is below the socially optimal amount. Then the government will want to increase revenues. Should it do this by increasing or decreasing employment? It may be that less employment at a higher real wage leads to increased tax revenues. Thus, the government may not wish to inflate. See Alex Cukierman and Allan Drazen, "Do Distortionary Taxes Induce Policies Biased Towards Inflation? A Macroeconomic Analysis," Tel-Aviv University, August 1986.

to adopt inflationary policies unless a way can be found to limit their discretion. A rule that limits the central bank's discretion might seem an obvious solution to the credibility problem. And, indeed, rules placing constraints on monetary growth have been proposed. Unfortunately, some of the features of such rules are themselves problematical.[10]

One proposed solution to the central bank credibility problem is for the central bank to adopt a strict constant growth rate rule. Under such a rule, the central bank would be required to keep the money supply growing at a constant rate every year. The central bank could never exercise discretion to vary this growth rate.

The principal appeal of the strict constant growth rate rule is that it does in fact solve the central bank credibility problem. Although the central bank still has an incentive to inflate when nominal wages are fixed, it can no longer act on that incentive. The central bank does not have the discretion to make policy changes. Because workers and firms know the central bank must adhere to the rule, they know that the central bank cannot generate surprise inflation. Thus, the credibility problem is solved.

The principal drawback of the strict constant growth rate rule is that it prevents a central bank from responding to various shocks that occasionally disrupt the economy. These shocks—either to the supply of goods and services (supply shocks) or to the amount of money that individuals wish to hold (money demand shocks)—lead firms to employ fewer workers, causing employment to decline below its natural level. An example of a supply shock is a drought. An example of a money demand shock is a financial crisis that increases the demand for liquid assets. (See box on page 11.) Such shocks impose a cost on an economy because they reduce employment, and adherence to a constant growth rate rule would not allow monetary policy to be eased to offset these costs. The results of a strict constant growth rate rule are summarized in row 1 of Table 1.[11]

An alternative to this strict constant growth rate rule is a more flexible rule that permits the central bank to respond to supply shocks but not to money demand shocks. Under such a rule, the central bank would be required to keep the money supply growing at a constant rate unless the economy experienced a supply shock. If a supply shock occurred, the central bank could accommodate it by increasing the rate of monetary growth. If a money demand shock occurred, in contrast, the central bank could not exercise such discretion.

Liberalizing the strict constant growth rate rule in this way does not reintroduce the credibility problem. Supply shocks such as droughts can be recognized by workers and firms. As a result, the central bank could never falsely claim that it had expanded the money supply to accommodate a supply shock when its real intention was to generate surprise inflation. It is assumed that the public can discriminate between actual and alleged supply shocks.[12] Hence, the credibility problem remains solved, and there are no costs incurred because of the inability to accommodate supply shocks. The costs of not accommodating money demand shocks remain, however. The results of this constant growth rate rule adjusted for supply shocks are summarized in row 2 of Table 1.

---

[10] These rules are described by Matthew Canzoneri in "Monetary Policy Games and the Role of Private Information," *American Economic Review,* December 1985, pp. 1056-1070.

[11] These results extend to more complicated average targeting and feedback rules. See Anne Sibert, "Notes on Time-Inconsistency," unpublished notes, 1988.

[12] Supply shocks cannot always be easily identified. Productivity shocks, for example, are difficult to detect.

TABLE 1

Monetary growth rule solutions to the central bank credibility problem

Solution	Economy is shock free	Economy is subject to supply shocks	Economy is subject to both supply shocks and money demand shocks
	(1)	(2)	(3)
1. Strict constant growth rate rule	Problem solved Solution costless	Problem solved Solution costly	Problem solved Solution costly
2. Constant growth rate rule adjusted for supply shocks	Problem solved Solution costless	Problem solved Solution costless	Problem solved Solution costly
3. Constant growth rate rule adjusted for supply and money demand shocks	Problem solved Solution costless	Problem solved Solution costless	Problem remains

A third approach, of course, is to adopt a growth rate rule that permits the central bank to accommodate both supply shocks and money demand shocks. Under such a rule, the central bank would be forced to keep the money supply growing at a constant rate unless the economy experienced a supply shock or a money demand shock. The central bank would have the freedom to accommodate whatever shock occurred by altering the growth of money. The chief appeal of this rule is that it would eliminate the employment and output losses associated with not reacting to money demand shocks. The chief drawback of this rule is that the credibility problem reappears.

The credibility problem reappears because, unlike supply shocks, money demand shocks cannot typically be identified by the public.[13] An increase in the preference of individuals for more

liquid assets, for example, cannot easily be inferred except from empirical estimation of money demand functions. As a result, the central bank and the public must forecast money demand. Assuming that the central bank's forecast is not publicly available, the central bank will once again have an incentive to generate surprise inflation, claiming that it expanded the money supply on the mistaken belief that money demand had increased. And awareness on the part of workers and firms of this incentive may cause them to be skeptical of the central bank's claim that its empirical estimates indicate that the money demand function has shifted.

In effect, this constant growth rate rule adjusted for supply and money demand shocks is not really a rule at all. It is rather an arrangement that permits considerable discretion to the central bank. The central bank is free to change monetary growth in response to whatever real or imagined shock. There are no effective limitations on the central bank's actions. The results of such a rule are shown in row 3 of Table 1.

---

[13] Canzoneri makes this point in "Monetary Policy Games . . . ."

Economic Shocks

An economy is typically subjected to a variety of random shocks. Two common shocks are supply shocks and money demand shocks. How monetary policy reacts to such shocks is the focus of much attention in the credibility literature.*

A supply shock, as the name would indicate, is some development that disrupts the supply of goods and services. Examples of supply shocks include an oil embargo, a crop failure, or a decline in labor productivity. When an economy experiences a supply shock, employment typically declines. How far it declines depends in part on how the central bank responds.

Figure 2 shows the labor market in the presence of a supply shock. Before the shock, workers and firms are assumed to be on their labor supply (S_1) and labor demand (D_1) curves, respectively, with the real wage at $(\frac{W}{P})_1$ and employment at its natural level, E_1^{nat}. Now a shock occurs—OPEC, for example, institutes an oil embargo that forces the price of oil much higher. As the price of oil rises, the demand for labor will fall because firms will want to scale back production. This decline in the demand for labor is represented in Figure 2 as a leftward shift in the labor demand curve, from D_1 to D_2.

What happens to employment? Employment falls to $\bar{\bar{E}}$, and workers are forced off their supply curve. Note that $\bar{\bar{E}}$ is below the new natural level of employment, E_2^{nat}. Employment will remain at $\bar{\bar{E}}$ until the real wage declines.

As new contracts are negotiated, the real wage will decline because workers will come to realize that nominal wage restraint is necessary if employment is to rise. However, the process could be long and hard. An alternative way to get employment at its new natural level is for the central bank to "accommodate" the supply shock. It does this by increasing the money supply, which in turn causes a rise in prices and a decline in

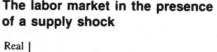

FIGURE 2

The labor market in the presence of a supply shock

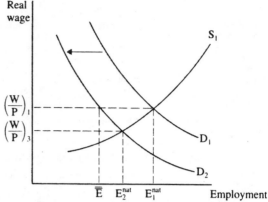

the real wage. The right amount of accommodation will lower the real wage to $(\frac{W}{P})_3$ and raise employment to E_2^{nat}.

A money demand shock is different. Such a shock occurs when—for reasons unrelated to changes in income or inflation—the public decides to hold more or less of its assets in the form of money.

Figure 3 shows the labor market in the presence of a money demand shock. Before the shock, workers and firms are assumed to be on their labor supply (S_1) and labor demand (D_1) curves, respectively, with the real wage at $(\frac{W}{P})_1$—and employment at its natural level, E_1^{nat}. Now a money demand shock occurs—households, for example, decide to sell some stocks and want to hold the proceeds in checking accounts. Because the supply of money has not changed, the amount of money now available to facilitate everyday transactions has declined. As a result, the price level falls and the real wage rises, to $(\frac{W}{P})_4$. At this higher real wage, firms want to hire fewer workers, so employment falls to $\tilde{E}$ and workers

FIGURE 3
The labor market in the presence
of a money demand shock

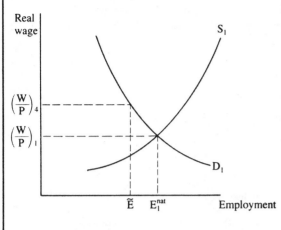

are again forced off their labor supply curve. Note that $\tilde{E}$ is below the natural level of employment, E_1^{nat}. Employment will remain at $\tilde{E}$ until the real wage declines.

As in the supply shock case, when an economy experiences a money demand shock, the central bank can take steps to ensure a speedy return to the natural level of employment. Specifically, it can increase the money supply, which causes a rise in prices and a decline in the real wage. The right amount of such accommodation will lower the real wage back to $(\frac{W}{P})_1$ and raise employment back to E_1^{nat}. Thus given some discretion, the central bank can offset disruptive shocks.

*The discussion here and in the text focuses on negative shocks; that is, shocks that potentially cause output and employment losses. Positive shocks, in contrast, potentially cause output and employment gains.

The main message of this discussion of monetary growth rules is summarized in column 3 of Table 1: In a realistic economic environment, one subject to both supply shocks and money demand shocks, either a credibility problem will remain or a solution will be costly.

Alternative solutions

Because of the problems inherent in monetary growth rules, alternative solutions to the central bank credibility problem have been proposed. These proposals do not limit the degree of central bank discretion but, rather, alter the environment in which the bank operates. Such proposals include wage indexation, a conservative central bank, and long-term relationships. A common feature of all is that they, too, are problematical.

Wage indexation

One possible solution to the credibility problem is to rely on wage indexation. Wage indexation ties nominal wages to the price level, so that nominal wages rise in line with the overall price level. Wage indexation typically takes the form of cost-of-living allowances (COLAs) in labor agreements.

Wage indexation can be either complete or partial. Complete indexation offers workers full protection against price increases: If prices rise 1 percent, nominal wages rise 1 percent, leaving the real wage unchanged. Partial indexation offers workers partial protection: If prices rise 1 percent, nominal wages rise less than 1 percent, causing some reduction in the real wage. As potential solutions to the central bank credibility problem, complete indexation and partial indexation possess different attributes.

Complete wage indexation would solve the credibility problem. A central bank would have no incentive to generate surprise inflation because expansionary monetary policy could not lower unemployment, even temporarily. Any increase in prices brought on by the central bank would be fully reflected in higher nominal wages. The

TABLE 2
Alternative solutions to the central bank credibility problem

Solution	Economy is shock free (1)	Economy is subject to supply shocks (2)	Economy is subject to both supply shocks and money demand shocks (3)
1. Complete wage indexation	Problem solved Solution costless	Problem solved Solution costly	Problem solved Solution costly
2. Partial wage indexation	Problem remains	Problem remains	Problem remains
3. Conservative central bank	Problem solved Solution costless	Problem solved Solution costly	Problem solved Solution costly
4. Long-term relationships	Problem solved Solution costless	Problem solved Solution costless	Problem solved Solution costly

real wage and the level of unemployment would remain unchanged. The central bank would thus have no incentive to pursue inflationary policies. Accordingly, the public would find a central bank's assurances of its commitment to price stability entirely credible.

Complete wage indexation would leave workers vulnerable to supply shocks, however. As noted in the previous section, a supply shock causes employment to fall below its natural level, and employment will remain below its natural level until the real wage is permitted to fall. With complete wage indexation, the real wage cannot fall. Thus, as noted in row 1 of Table 2, complete wage indexation would be costly because it would lead to higher unemployment by preventing real wages from adjusting to supply shocks.[14]

Partial wage indexation, in contrast, would allow greater flexibility of real wages but would not solve the credibility problem. Because the real wage would decline somewhat whenever prices rose, a central bank could temporarily raise employment by generating surprise inflation.

Recognizing the ability of the central bank to affect real wages and thus employment, the public would be skeptical about the central bank's commitment to price stability. This point is noted in row 2 of Table 2.

Conservative central bank

A second proposed solution to the credibility problem is that of a conservative central bank. A conservative central bank can be defined as one that dislikes inflation more than society does. Such a central bank will be less inclined to generate surprise inflation in an attempt to increase employment beyond its natural level. Thus, the credibility problem will be solved. However, this solution is not costless because this same central bank might also be less willing to accommodate supply shocks by increasing the rate of monetary growth. If so, employment and output would be lost.[15]

---

[14] For further discussion, see Gray, "Wage Indexation . . . . "

[15] See Kenneth Rogoff, "The Optimal Degree of Commitment to an Intermediate Monetary Target," *Quarterly Journal of Economics,* November 1985, pp. 1169-1189.

This discussion is moot, however, if inflation-averse central bankers cannot be appointed. The only way to ensure that they can be appointed is to have the central bank independent of the rest of government. That is, an institutional framework needs to be established that allows the central bank to operate free of political pressure. To some extent, such a framework is in place in the United States as well as other industrialized countries. The results of this conservative central bank solution are shown in row 3 of Table 2.

Long-term relationships

A final proposed solution to the credibility problem involves long-term relationships. The central bank credibility problem might be avoided or at least reduced if the relationship between a central bank and the private sector is a lasting one. Specifically, if the actions of the central bank affect the expectations of the private sector about the future, the central bank must weigh not only the direct costs and benefits of inflation but also the impact of such inflation on inflationary expectations. If current inflation leads to a sufficient worsening of inflationary expectations, the central bank may not have an incentive to inflate in the current period.[16]

Economists have developed formal models to capture the effect of central bank actions on inflation expectations. Suppose that the private sector has the following beliefs. If the central bank has never inflated more than the socially optimal amount, excess inflation is not expected. But if the central bank ever does generate surprise inflation, excess inflation will be expected for a certain amount of time in the future. Given these beliefs, the central bank can increase employment in the short run. But the cost of doing so is higher inflation—with no accompanying employment gain—for some time in the future. If society and the central bank care enough about the future, these long-run costs may deter the central bank from generating surprise inflation.[17]

In a world free of money demand shocks, this deterrent effect of the public's inflation expectations would solve the credibility problem. Unfortunately, the world is not free of money demand shocks. Moreover, such shocks are not directly observable and, hence, must be forecasted by the central bank. As a result, when the private sector observes excess inflation, it does not know whether the central bank inadvertently inflated by incorrectly forecasting money demand or deliberately inflated in an attempt to increase employment.

But the credibility problem may still be solved, albeit at a cost. Suppose, for example, that as long as inflation remains below a certain trigger level the private sector will not expect inflation but that if inflation rises above this trigger level inflation will be expected for some time in the future. As in the previous scenario, if society and the central bank care enough about the future, the central bank may decide not to deliberately generate surprise inflation. However, because of unobserved money demand shocks, accidental inflation could arise. And if this accidental inflation exceeds the target level, the public will raise its inflation expectations. One would thus observe periods of costly excess inflation interspersed with

---

[16] For further discussion, see William Fellner, *Towards a Reconstruction of Macroeconomics*, American Enterprise Institute, 1976, and William Fellner, "The Credibility Effect and Rational Expectations: Implications of the Gramlich Study," *Brookings Papers on Economic Activity*, 1:1979, pp. 167-178.

[17] This model is due to Robert J. Barro and David Gordon, "Rules, Discretion, and Reputation in a Model of Monetary Policy," *Journal of Monetary Economics*, July 1983, pp. 101-121, and based on a game theory model developed by James W. Friedman, "A Noncooperative Equilibrium for Supergames," *Review of Economic Studies*, January 1971, pp. 1-12. Strictly speaking, in the Barro and Gordon model, the credibility problem is not fully solved but rather lessened.

periods of little or no inflation.[18] The characteristics of this long-term relationship are summarized in row 4 of Table 2.

This framework of a long-term relationship appears to provide some insight into developments in the United States in the 1970s and 1980s. Some economists would argue that the Federal Reserve pursued an overly expansionary monetary policy in the 1970s in an attempt to keep unemployment below its natural level. Others would argue that monetary policy was inadvertently expansionary because the Federal Reserve had imprecise information about supply shocks, money demand shocks, and changes in the natural level of unemployment.[19] For whatever reason, inflation and inflation expectations rose dramatically. By announcing a strict anti-inflation policy in 1979 —and then following through in the 1980s—the Federal Reserve has been able to reduce inflation and inflation expectations equally dramatically. The Federal Reserve in recent years has thus reestablished a good deal of credibility by recognizing that bringing inflation down can be worthwhile in the long run despite the short-run costs of doing so. Conducting monetary policy in a way that takes account of the long-term relationship between a central bank and the private sector may therefore be the best hope for maintaining the credibility of the central bank's commitment to price stability.[20]

Summary

Some economists believe that one important cause of higher inflation in the 1970s was central banks' attempt to keep unemployment at unrealistically low levels. If so, central banks' credibility in convincing the public of their commitment to price stability was tarnished. This article has explored the options available to central banks in maintaining their credibility.

The article has argued that, to the extent a credibility problem exists, solutions to the problem are themselves problematical. There are no costless ways to maintain the credibility of a central bank's commitment to price stability. Monetary growth rules remove too much discretion from a central bank operating in an environment in which financial innovation and deregulation create uncertainty about money demand and in which supply shocks can intermittently cause employment losses that perhaps should be offset by monetary policy. Nor are wage indexation and conservative central banks panaceas.

Perhaps the most promising approach is for the central bank to conduct policy in a way that takes account of the long-term nature of its relationship with the public. Even this approach has problems, however. Once inflation expectations have become imbedded in economic decisions as in the late 1970s, disinflation is likely to be accompanied by a temporary rise in unemployment until inflation expectations abate. Despite the proliferation of research analyzing the time-inconsistency and credibility problems, therefore, economists have not been able to discover a foolproof substitute for vigilance against inflation for maintaining central bank credibility.

[18] This model is due to Canzoneri, "Monetary Policy Games . . . ," and based on a model developed by Edward Green and Robert Porter in "Noncooperative Collusion Under Imperfect Price Information," *Econometrica*, January 1984, pp. 87-100.

[19] For further discussion of supply shocks, money demand shocks, and changes in the natural level of unemployment in the 1970s and 1980s, see Robert J. Gordon, *Macroeconomics*, 4th edition, Little, Brown and Company, 1987, pp. 295-301; Stanley Fischer, "Monetary Policy and Performance in the U.S., Japan, and Europe, 1973-86," NBER Working Paper No. 2475, December 1987, and Stuart E. Weiner, "The Natural Rate of Unemployment . . . ," respectively.

[20] Herb Taylor comes to a similar view in "Time Inconsistency: A Potential Problem for Policymakers," *Business Review*, Federal Reserve Bank of Philadelphia, March/April 1985, pp. 3-12.

Article Thirty-Three

Rules Versus Discretion: Making a Monetary Rule Operational

by John B. Carlson

John B. Carlson is an economist at the Federal Reserve Bank of Cleveland. The author would like to thank Charles Carlstrom, Edward Gambier, William Gavin, James Hoehn, Mark Sniderman, and E.J. Stevens for their helpful comments.

Introduction

The rules-versus-discretion debate is the most enduring, if not the most central, issue in monetary policy. It concerns whether monetary policy should be conducted by rules known in advance to all or by policymaker discretion.

For many years, the case for a monetary rule was associated with a particular proposal by Milton Friedman (1959). Building on a tradition initiated by Henry Simons (1936), Friedman introduced the idea that the effects of monetary policy were uncertain, occurring with long and variable lags. In short, he argued that discretionary management of the money supply in the face of such uncertainty actually amplified economic fluctuations. Hence, Friedman argued for a constant-money-growth rule.

The case for rules has changed fundamentally since an important paper by Kydland and Prescott (1977). They show that precommitment to a rule could have beneficial effects that discretionary policies cannot. Unlike Friedman's argument, the Kydland-Prescott case was not specific to any one view of the world, but could be applied to a very general class of models. In principle, one cannot deny that a policy rule can have potentially stabilizing effects.

The example of Kydland and Prescott, however, trivialized an important concern of policymakers: how to account for uncertainty in the link between policy instruments and ultimate objectives. Once one allows for uncertainty, there is a potential role for flexibility to deal with variability in the links. To the extent that some variation is systematic and can be predicted, it is possible to incorporate feedback into a rule. However, some contingencies cannot be foreseen. When such events are potentially destabilizing, discretion may not be ruled out a priori.

This suggests that it is reasonable to consider the idea of rules with discretion. Fischer (1988) has concluded that the dichotomy between rules and discretion should be seen as a continuum, in which the extent of the monetary authority is determined by the immediacy of the link between its actions and the attainment of the objectives.

The actual practice of monetary policy can be viewed as a point on the continuum. Moreover, the rise of monetary targeting in the 1970s, which led to alternative operating procedures with differing degrees of commitment, illustrates that the degree of commitment to any rule can vary over time. Changes in the degree of commitment are best understood when one confronts the difficulties in making rules operational.

This paper reviews the historical development of the rules-versus-discretion debate and examines the problems associated with making rules operational. Section I traces the evolution of rule advocacy from the time of the Federal Reserve Act. Section II describes the actual operating procedures from the early 1970s to the present. The operational problems facing rule advocates are highlighted in Section III, and Section IV discusses how two recently proposed rules address the operational problems. Section V offers some concluding comments.

I. Rule Advocacy in the United States After the Federal Reserve

The original Senate bill to create the Federal Reserve System in 1913 contained a provision that the system should *promote a stable price level.* This provision was stricken by the House Committee on Banking and Currency and was not included in the original Federal Reserve Act, reflecting the dominant influence of the real bills doctrine at that time. By the late 1920s, however, several bills had been proposed to amend the Federal Reserve Act explicitly to include a provision for price stability.[1] Advocates of these bills essentially sought to legislate a rule establishing the primacy of the price-level objective.

These efforts culminated in the Strong Hearings, held by the House Banking Committee in 1926-1927.[2] The hearings initially considered a bill by Representative James G. Strong including a provision that "all the powers of the Federal Reserve System should be used for promoting a stable price level." Specifically, Congressman Strong did not want the Federal Reserve to have the discretion to vary the price level for the pursuit of any other objective.

While the bill instructed that the Federal Reserve's discount-rate policy was to be determined with "the view of promoting price stability," no formula was specified. Thus, there was a certain vagueness about how the rule would be implemented.[3] It left open the role for discretion in determining how much the discount rate should be altered when the price level deviated

from its objective. A subsequent version of the bill was even more ambiguous about the objective of price stability. Eventually, Congressional interest in establishing the primacy of the objective of price stability faded.

The Simons Tradition

In a widely celebrated article of 1936, Henry Simons initiated a case for rules that was to become known as the Chicago view. Specifically, Simons contrasted two sharply distinct ways to conduct monetary policy: one, to assign in advance specific responsibilities to a monetary authority to be carried out in accordance with well-defined operational rules; the other, to specify a general goal while allowing the monetary authority wide discretionary powers to achieve the goal. The essential distinction is that the first regime defines the authority's objective in terms of the means, while the second defines the objective in terms of the ends.

Simons argued for rules in terms of means. His case was predicated on liberal (19th-century sense) principles. "The liberal creed demands organization of our economic life largely through individual participation in a game *with definite rules.* It calls upon the state to provide a stable framework of rules within which enterprise and competition may effectively control and direct the production and distribution of goods." (Simons [1936], p. 1)

The essential notion is that government is necessary for establishing laws that would define the rules for a "game" in which competitive free enterprise could flourish, but that government should not be a player in the game. The idea that government would manage the currency to manipulate aggregate economic outcomes meant that government would be a player and thus violated the liberal creed.

An ideal rule according to Simons would be one that fixed the quantity of the money supply. He did not believe, however, that such a rule could be made operational without radical reform of the financial structure. Essentially, he believed that an unregulated financial sector was a source of great instability in money demand. This instability was reflected in the perverse behavior of velocity which, he argued, necessitated a role for discretionary actions. Simons

---

1 For a thorough review of the debate, see Fisher (1934). It should be noted here that a provision for purchasing power was eventually incorporated in the Employment Act of 1946. However, the price-stability goal was not included as the primary objective as most advocates of price stability in the 1920s had sought.

2 For an excellent discussion of the background and events surrounding the Strong hearings, see Hetzel (1985).

3 Hetzel (1985) notes that Congressman Strong and his supporters wanted to institutionalize the policy of Governor Strong (no relation) of the New York Federal Reserve Bank, which they credited for the considerable price stability that existed after 1922.

therefore suggested a number of ideal reforms to reduce the variability of velocity to levels conducive to successful implementation of a fixed-money-supply rule. That is, government would need to redefine the rules of the game to avoid having to manage the money supply.

One proposed reform was the elimination of fractional-reserve banking. By requiring 100-percent reserves on all demand deposits, Simons sought to reduce greatly the threat of bank runs and the consequent effects on hoarding money (velocity changes). Such a reform would also give the monetary authority direct control over the total money supply by making it equivalent to the monetary base.

Simons recognized, however, that fixing the supply of deposits might merely serve to encourage the creation of effective money substitutes that would also affect velocity. Thus, another "ideal" (but even more radical) reform would be to prohibit fixed-money contracts. Restricting claims to residual equity or common-stock form would essentially drive a wedge between money and other assets and would tend to minimize the variability of velocity. In sum, Simons believed that a monetary rule in terms of means could be made operational only under a highly regulated financial system.

Simons was not naive about the kind of assent that could be gained for such radical reforms in modern democratic societies. He thought that adoption of an appropriate framework could be implemented only after decades of "gradual and systematic reordering of financial practices." Ironically, liberal principles also seem to support the notion that financial institutions should be largely unregulated and free to offer any instruments they choose. Indeed, institutional reform has moved in the opposite direction of Simons's ideal.

Recognizing the practical difficulties of sharp changes in velocity and that his ideal reforms might be unattainable, Simons argued for a rule for price stability in the interim. Because this is a rule of ends rather than means, the operational procedures were not well defined. His basis for this practical solution was that it was the "least illiberal" of the alternatives he considered. Thus, he recognized that for immediate purposes a certain amount of discretionary latitude was necessary. While Simons may have misjudged society's willingness to adopt his ideal reforms (new rules), his liberal view of economic agents participating in a game was prescient about the future state of the debate.

The Simons tradition was subsequently modified and popularized by Milton Friedman (1948, 1959, 1969). Initially, Friedman offered detailed proposals much in the spirit of Simons. They included the 100-percent reserves reform applied to both time and savings deposits at banks.

Subsequently, however, Friedman changed tack, taking the position that the behavior of velocity, particularly the velocity of the M2 aggregate, was not so perverse in a relative sense, even under a fractional-reserve banking system. He argued that the discretionary actions of the Federal Reserve (albeit well-intentioned) were likely to be a more perverse source of economic instability. Thus, adherence to a constant-money-growth rule would lead to greater economic stability than would a rule with feedback, with or without discretion. In essence, Friedman maintained the idea that the monetary authority should not be a player in the game, but he eventually rejected the need for wholesale reform of the financial system.

Friedman's case for a constant-growth rule was based less on the liberal creed and more on pragmatism. His premise was that the economic impact of monetary policy occurs with a long and variable lag. Feedback, especially of the discretionary type, would have effects at the inappropriate time more often than not. Moreover, Friedman argued that political pressures and accountability problems under discretion are likely to exacerbate the problem.

While Friedman's case has intuitive appeal, it is difficult to justify in principle. Potentially stabilizing effects of policy feedback could be ruled out a priori only if money were the exclusive determinant of nominal GNP in the short run. If other identifiable factors also have significant explanatory power, then judicious use of feedback can, in principle, reduce the variability of nominal GNP, even if the coefficients on lagged money are stochastic. On the other hand, the stabilizing effects of policy feedback with parameter uncertainty are smaller than when parameters are nonstochastic (see Brainard [1967]).[4]

By eventually abandoning 100-percent reserves, Friedman also allowed a control problem: how to make a constant-growth rule operational for measures of inside money. Under 100-percent reserves there would be virtually no distinction between money and monetary base. Since Friedman also proposed closing the discount window, all money would essentially be outside money, and hence directly controlled by the Fed.

■ **4** When effects of monetary policy occur with a lag, there is a potential for instrument instability. The prospect of dynamic instability can be reduced with appropriate modifications to the objective function.

As advocates for constant money growth dropped the idea of 100-percent reserves, however, the issue of monetary control became relevant. When the measure of money is endogenous, the problem of making a constant-money-growth rule operational is far from trivial. Such was an important lesson of monetary targeting in the early 1980s. Perhaps recognizing this fact, advocates for money-growth rules now typically propose closing the discount window and adopting a constant-growth rule for the monetary base.

Arguments for a monetary rule in the Simons tradition remain highly controversial in principle. One cannot rule out the possibility that an intelligent policymaker could effectively take account of incomplete information when deciding optimal monetary policy. As Barro (1985) notes, "if the policymaker were also well-meaning, then there was no obvious defense for using a rule in order to bind his hands in advance." Moreover, Fischer argues, "At a formal level Friedman's analysis suffered from the logical weakness that discretion seemed to dominate rules: if a particular rule would stabilize the economy, then discretionary policymakers could always behave that way—and retain the flexibility to change the rule as needed."

Kydland and Prescott

The idea that discretion could always replicate a preferred policy rule seemed to provide a highly influential argument in which intelligent, well-meaning policymakers should not be bound by rules. However, in a widely recognized paper, Kydland and Prescott (1977) demonstrate a fallacy in this argument. It is now well understood that if economic outcomes depend on expectations about future policies, then credible precommitment to a rule could have favorable effects on the economic outcomes that discretionary policies cannot have.

Applications of the Kydland and Prescott result to monetary policy are often developed in familiar (and highly abstract) models of output and inflation.[5] These models assume that wage-setters and the monetary authority are engaged in a noncooperative game. In this game, wage-setters must specify the nominal wage rate in a

contract (their play) *before* prices are determined (the policymaker's play). Firms' decisions to hire are made after prices are determined, so that the real wage is known. Since firms are assumed to be profit maximizers, the real wage determines the level of output for the economy.

An essential feature of the game is that by determining the price level, the policymaker's play determines the real wage and level of real output. Moreover, expectational errors of wage-setters determine the deviation of output from its full employment levels. Thus, the game yields the familiar output supply function

$$(1) \quad y = y^* + b(\pi - \pi^e),$$

where y and π are output and inflation, y^* is full employment output, and π^e is the expected inflation rate.

The policymaker is assumed to have a loss function quadratic in the deviations of inflation and output from target levels. Here, desired inflation is assumed to be zero.

$$(2) \quad L = a\pi^2 + (y - ky^*)^2$$

The target rate of output is assumed to be above the natural rate, that is, $k > 1$. One motivation for this assumption is that tax distortions and unemployment policy cause the natural rate to be too low from a social point of view. Alternatively, one might argue that the labor market is dominated by large unions (see Canzoneri [1985]). He assumes that the labor supply curve includes only union members and that wage-setters' behavior systematically excludes other workers. By contrast, the loss function includes all workers. Others have argued that equation (2) is not really a measure of social utility, but reflects the bias of policymakers to underestimate the natural rate of unemployment.

To illustrate the advantage of a rule, consider the case in which the policymaker has discretion in a one-period game. Because the policymaker chooses policy *after the wage-setters specify the wage rate,* the wage-setters know that the policymaker has the incentive to take the *expected inflation rate as given* and to induce higher employment with additional inflation, if possible. Given the known loss function, there is only one strategically rational expectation (that is, Nash solution) for inflation:

$$(3) \quad \pi^e = a^{-1}b(k - 1)y^*.$$

Under this solution, the policymaker has no incentive to choose an inflation rate higher than

■ 5 The particular example presented here is the compact static model in Fischer (1988). The use of a *static* model to illustrate *dynamic* inconsistency has been criticized as inadequate. The basic concept, however, has been developed in the context of a dynamic model (see Roberds [1986]). Since it is the concept we want to convey here, the static model suffices.

expected. The gains from the additional output would be more than offset by the loss of the additional inflation. Note also that if the policymaker had an objective for the inflation rate less than the expected inflation rate *before* wage-setters acted, it would be inconsistent *afterward*. That a zero-inflation objective is not credible with discretion is an example of the problem of *time inconsistency*.

The value of the loss function evaluated at the solution is denoted as L_d and is given by

$$(4) \quad L_d = (k-1)^2 y^{*2} [1 + a^{-1} b^2].$$

If the policymaker could credibly precommit to a policy of zero inflation, that is, a dynamically consistent inflation objective, the loss function would be

$$(5) \quad L_p = (k-1)^2 y^{*2}.$$

Since $L_p < L_d$, precommitment to a zero-inflation objective affects expectations in a way that leads to a more favorable outcome than pure discretion would allow. Essentially, discretion buys nothing in terms of output, which is the same under both policies, but leads to an inflationary bias.

To be sure, the basic result of Kydland and Prescott demonstrates in a very precise way a benefit to precommitment to a policy rule. Although developed in a highly abstract model, the result has been widely influential in academic research. A major shortcoming of the analysis, however, is that it trivializes the control problem. Specifically, it presumes that the policymaker has a deterministic operating procedure that enables precise control of inflation. Once disturbances are introduced into the model, the precommitment solution does not necessarily dominate the discretion solution.

To analyze the control problem, Canzoneri considers a stochastic disturbance to money demand such that velocity follows a random walk. In his game, wage-setters cannot see the disturbance at the time they specify their wage, but the Federal Reserve has some forecast of money demand before it chooses its policy for money growth. If the Fed is left with some flexibility, it can accommodate the predictable component of the change in velocity. As Canzoneri notes, this practice benefits both wage-setters and society as a whole. Thus, the policy problem becomes one of trading off flexibility needed for stabilization with the constraint needed for eliminating the inflation bias.[6]

The discussion thus far has been in the context of a one-period framework. In reality, however, the central bank has a horizon that extends beyond one period. Indeed, this may explain why central banks are typically isolated from political pressures by design. It is now widely understood that in a multiperiod context, the Fed may be able to establish a reputation that serves the same purpose as a monetary rule. This possibility has been investigated by Barro and Gordon (1983a, 1983b). They find that under certain conditions, reputation-building can lead to a result that is superior to pure discretion, although not as good as precommitment to a rule.

Barro and Gordon assume, however, that wage-setters eventually have access to the same information as the Fed. Canzoneri shows that when the Fed has its own private forecast of money demand, it has an incentive to misrepresent its intentions.[7] He further demonstrates that no stable resolution of the credibility problem can rely on the Fed's own announcement of its forecast. When the Barro and Gordon model is modified to account for asymmetric information, the Fed cannot build sufficient credibility by simply running a noninflationary policy for a few periods.

Rogoff (1985) has shown that other solutions may mitigate the problem of dynamic inconsistency. One such solution is that society can benefit by choosing a "conservative" central banker—one that places a high cost on inflation. In the context of the simple model above, this means that the central bank places a high value on parameter a in its loss function. Equation (4) reveals that as a gets large, the value of the loss function diminishes, ultimately approaching the value of the precommitment solution given in equation (5).

Like Barro and Gordon, Rogoff assumed symmetric information. When the Fed has private information, it has the incentive to appear more conservative than it actually is; the wage-setters have no way of telling. The implication is that there could be periodic inflationary breakdowns followed by sustained periods where credibility builds and wage-setters learn the true intentions of their central bank. Unfortunately, Canzoneri shows that it is no simple matter to legislate incentive-compatible rules that would remedy the problem posed by private information.

■ **6** Fischer (1988) demonstrates in a formal model that when control error exists, the ordering of the loss functions under precommitment and discretion is ambiguous.

■ **7** If the money demand forecast were predicated on a stable model over time, it would be preferable for the Fed to commit to a contingent rule based on that model forecast. Thus, while the rule would allow flexibility, it would not admit discretion. Given the absence of evidence of stability in money demand, such a rule seems infeasible.

Rogoff also demonstrates that under certain conditions, intermediate targeting may also provide a reasonable solution to the problem of dynamic inconsistency. By providing the central bank with incentives to hit an intermediate target, it is possible to induce fewer inflationary wage bargains in the context of his model. While the Rogoff result demonstrates some a priori basis for intermediate targeting, his analysis abstracts from many problems the policymaker faces in practice. Nevertheless, the literature since 1977 suggests there is a reasonable basis for some precommitment—if not to a rule for all time—to some monetary policy on a continuum between a pure rule and pure discretion.

II. The Operating Strategy of the Federal Reserve

The operating strategy of the Federal Reserve can be viewed as a commitment to a policy on the continuum between a pure rule and pure discretion. The rule-like elements are embedded in the Fed's monetary targeting procedure. Monetary targets are not ends in themselves, but are intermediate variables between the instrument variables that the Fed directly controls, such as the federal funds rate or nonborrowed reserves, and ultimate goals, such as price stability and stable output growth. Thus, intermediate target variables must be closely linked to both ultimate objectives and instruments.

The use of intermediate targets has been criticized as redundant and inefficient from a control-theoretic perspective (see B. Friedman [1975]). These objections, however, are based on the assumption that policymakers have precise, reliable knowledge about the relationships between instruments and final objectives. In practice, policymakers see great uncertainty in these links and doubt that such relationships could be captured by econometric models accurately enough to be operationally useful (see Black [1987]). In contrast, intermediate target variables are seen as relatively more controllable than ultimate variables.

Moreover, policy decisions are made by majority rule. It is therefore difficult, if not impossible (Arrow's theorem) to obtain a consensus for adopting a particular social objective function, which is necessary under direct targeting of final objectives. Under an intermediate targeting strategy, the Fed does not need to specify numerical objectives for goal variables.

Intermediate targeting strategies can vary sub-

stantially in degree of flexibility or commitment. In principle, intermediate targets may or may not be designed to allow feedback. For example, a target could be specified for a five-year horizon without allowing for revisions, or for a three-month horizon to accommodate frequent adjustments based on new information. Also, the operating procedure used to control the target variable may or may not allow for a high degree of discretion. Thus, operating rules could be highly automatic with infrequent discretionary input or be judgmentally modified day-to-day, based on the latest information.

Actual practice of monetary targeting indicates that the degree of flexibility and discretion incorporated into the strategy is influenced by two key factors. The first is evidence concerning the stability of the relationship on which the strategy is based. If there is a broad consensus about the reliability of the relationship between the intermediate target and ultimate goals, then it is more likely that a central bank would be willing to commit to closer targeting of the variable with less feedback from other sources, whether discretionary or not. The other key factor is the central bank's credibility or reputation in containing inflationary expectations. If the central bank establishes its credibility by avoiding inflationary policies, then the public and Congress are generally more willing to accept a greater degree of discretion in strategy and tactics.

The interplay of these factors may well account for the increased reliance on monetary aggregates as intermediate targets during the early 1970s. Before the mid-1960s, there was scant evidence that discretion exercised by the Federal Reserve provided a substantive basis for inflationary expectations. Nominal interest rates were, on average, too low to indicate expectations of rising inflation. The public apparently believed that the Fed would "take the punchbowl away just as the party got going," a perception consistent with Rogoff's notion of a conservative central bank. Although the Federal Reserve had intermediate targets for interest rates—a strategy that is now widely viewed as potentially defective for avoiding inflation—the Fed seemed to use its discretion judiciously in avoiding inflation and hence in assuaging public doubt about the efficacy of its operating strategy.

By the early 1970s, however, a basis for doubt was beginning to emerge, as inflation had accelerated to new and persistently high levels. Over that decade the Fed gradually strengthened its reliance on monetary aggregates as a source of information about its ultimate objectives. While the process was initially internal only, the

Fed began to announce publicly its desired annual growth ranges for selected monetary aggregates in response to a Congressional resolution in 1975. Evidence in the early 1970s convinced many that the relationship between money and nominal GNP—as summarized by velocity—was sufficiently reliable to choose monetary targets over annual, or even longer, horizons. Also, the parallel rise in the price level offered simple but persuasive evidence that inflation could be slowed by slowing growth of the monetary aggregates. In 1979, the Fed adopted a strategy for disinflation by gradually reducing the rate of money growth from year to year.

The strategy was coupled with an automatic feedback rule to enhance monetary control and demonstrate a commitment to the strategy. Over most of the 1970s, the Fed used the federal funds rate—the interest rate banks charge one another on overnight loans of reserves—as its operating target for controlling money growth. Specifically, it sought to influence the quantity of money the public demanded by altering the opportunity cost of money. For example, if money growth was too rapid, it attempted to raise the federal funds rate, and thereby raise other short-term rates.

The higher rates were expected to slow money growth by inducing the public to shift from monetary assets to other financial assets. Over longer horizons, higher interest rates might also be expected to slow spending growth and hence the transactions demand for money. In practice, however, there is always substantial pressure for the Fed to minimize interest-rate movements, particularly interest-rate increases. For this reason and others, the Federal Reserve did not respond sufficiently promptly or intensively to keep monetary growth from accelerating in the 1970s.

By late 1979, the inflation rate had accelerated to double-digit levels. Financial markets, especially foreign markets, began reacting strongly to the inflationary developments. The dollar was falling rapidly as foreign investors appeared to doubt the Fed's resolve to contain inflation. In response to the evident inflationary pressures, the Federal Reserve adopted a new set of tactics "as a sign of its commitment to longer-run restraint on money growth" (Lindsey [1984], p. 12). These tactics in effect eliminated a substantial degree of discretion that the Fed had used to smooth short-term interest-rate movements.

The new procedures sought to control money growth by maintaining a short-run target path for nonborrowed reserves. As Lindsey describes, "holding to a nonborrowed reserves path essen-

tially introduces in the short run an upward sloping money supply curve on interest rate and money space" (p. 12). In effect, the nonborrowed reserves target created an *automatic* self-correcting mechanism that would partially resist all deviations of money from target. If money growth in a given week moved above target, the prespecified level of nonborrowed reserves virtually assured that the federal funds rate would move upward. In sum, the Federal Reserve gave up its discretion to minimize federal funds rate movements to assure financial markets of its commitment to the disinflation strategy.

While the new procedure involved substantial commitment at the tactics level, it permitted significant discretionary feedback at the strategy level. Under the strategy, the FOMC was free to change its short-term monetary target to take account of new information—a practice that led to significant deviations of money from announced annual targets. Such discretionary feedback was deemed necessary as evidence mounted that the velocity of money was not as reliable as expected.

It was well understood at the time that deregulation in financial markets, changes in transactions technology, and disinflation were having a substantial impact on individual portfolios and hence on the velocity of money. While such factors could account for the target misses in a qualitative sense, policymakers lacked means to predict the impact on money growth in order to specify reliable target values. By August 1982 the evidence was compelling that the behavior of velocity had been altered in some permanent way. Because time was needed to identify the new patterns of velocity behavior, attempts to control monetary aggregates closely appeared futile.

Consequently, the Fed abandoned its operating procedure and hence its commitment to a fixed path of nonborrowed reserves in the short run. It de-emphasized the role of M1 and adopted a more flexible operating strategy. Since the fall of 1982, the Fed's operating target has been the aggregate level of seasonal plus adjustment borrowings at the discount window. Under this procedure, the FOMC specifies a short-term objective for this variable at each of its regularly scheduled meetings (at approximately five- to six-week intervals).

Unlike with the nonborrowed reserves operating target, the current procedure does not produce automatic self-correcting federal funds rate responses to resist divergences of money from its long-run path. Substantial changes in the federal funds rate are largely a consequence of judgmental adjustments to the borrowings target. Thus, the Fed has regained much of the leeway to smooth short-term interest rate changes that it had prior to 1979.

It is important to note that by the end of 1982 the disinflation process had become credible to most of the public. Financial markets, particularly those for fixed-income securities, reacted favorably to the procedural change. Long-term interest rates continued to decline substantially after the Fed announced abandonment of the nonborrowed-reserves procedure. Moreover, over the long term, wage demands moderated to pre-1970s levels and have been persistently moderate to this day.[8] Such would seem strong evidence that wage-setters haven't suspected the Fed of "cheating" on its goal of reducing and maintaining lower inflation.

The evolutionary cycle of the Federal Reserve's operating procedure provides a useful illustration of how the degree of discretion has varied in response both to evidence concerning the reliability of the money-income relationship and to the reputation of the Fed. As the Fed's credibility on inflation appeared to wane in the 1970s, it adopted procedures that increased reliance on monetary aggregates as intermediate targets and limited its discretion to smooth interest rates. As evidence suggested a breakdown in the behavior of velocity, the degree of commitment to monetary control diminished to allow the necessary operational flexibility. By that time the Fed's commitment to maintaining lower rates of inflation had become credible. While the actual strategy can be characterized as a monetary rule with varying degrees of discretion, it never incorporated the degree of commitment that most monetarists had hoped for—one that would have not altered monetary targets at all.

III. Problems with Making Rules Operational

The review of the Federal Reserve's actual operating strategy also serves to highlight a number of potential problems with making rules operational. Poole (1988), a longtime monetary rule advocate, recently concludes that "there is a serious and probably insurmountable problem to designing a predetermined money growth path to reduce inflation." Essentially, he argues that it is not possible to reliably quantify the effects of disinflation on money demand and, hence, on velocity.[9] Thus, managed money is

unavoidable during the transition to lower inflation. While Poole accepts the eventual efficacy of a constant-growth rule, he believes there is no formula to determine when the discretionary mode should terminate. Presumably, it would only be after inflation has been eliminated.

Even if the transition to lower inflation were no longer operationally relevant, the experience of the early 1980s makes it clear that money demand and velocity have also been independently affected by regulatory change and by developments in transactions technology. McCallum (1987) has recently argued that a rule should not rely on the presumed absence of the effects of such changes. This principle of rule design precludes simple, fixed rules like the constant growth rate of money (or monetary base). Operational feasibility demands that a monetary rule should at least be flexible enough to accommodate the effects of such changes on velocity.

Recognizing a need for some form of flexibility, some pure-rule advocates now propose nondiscretionary feedback rules. Nondiscretionary feedback requires specification of a formula linking goal (or target) variables to policy instruments. The formula presumes the existence of some reasonably stable and hence reliable model, that is, one that characterizes sufficiently well the relationship between instruments and objectives.

The absence of a consensus in macroeconomics about an appropriate model poses a serious obstacle for gaining assent for any *particular* feedback rule in practice. While most economists adopt *a* perspective, few seem willing to accept the notion that a particular (especially simple) characterization of the economy would be sufficiently reliable for long periods. Even among rule advocates sharing a common perspective, there are likely to be subtle differences about the formula specification that may splinter support for a given rule.

This problem of model uncertainty is compounded by the important demonstration by Lucas (1976) that "structural" models are in general not invariant to the way in which policy is implemented. Since this critique, there has been no widely accepted means of evaluating operationally concrete policy proposals.[10] While many large-scale econometric models have met the market test, few economists seem convinced by policy evaluations based on particular econometric models.

■ **8** For evidence concerning moderation in compensation demands, see Groshen (1988).

■ **9** This point is an example of a more general result of Lucas (1976), which is discussed below.

■ **10** Advocates of rules sometimes argue that if a nondiscretionary rule were to be implemented, relationships would stabilize, leading to more favorable outcomes than suggested by simulations based on historical relationships. While this purely a priori theoretical argument is consistent, it does not appear to be convincing to most economists.

Without a consensus about how monetary policy affects aggregate economic outcomes, it is not compelling to argue that expectations of economic agents (for example, wage-setters) are based on any one model of the economy. Any given rule could possibly be perceived as unsustainable by a sufficient number of agents such that the rule would not be credible in an aggregate sense. If agents believed the rule was unsustainable, the game between agents and policymakers would become extremely complicated, with no apparent solution. Thus, it would not be clear that commitment to a rule would be beneficial. It would seem useful that a rule advocate demonstrate that favorable consequences of a proposed rule would be robust to alternative models of the economy.

IV. Two Recently Proposed Rules

Two recently proposed rules by McCallum (1987, 1988) and Hall (1984) illustrate how the debate over rules versus discretion has evolved to a more operationally concrete level. Both authors appeal to the result of Kydland and Prescott as a justification for implementing their rules. Both also recognize a need for flexibility and address operational problems. In sharp contrast, however, is the way they incorporate flexibility.

McCallum proposes a nondiscretionary feedback rule for nominal income using the monetary base as the instrument. The target path of nominal income is fixed and grows at a prespecified rate of 3 percent per year. The feedback formula is

$$(6) \quad \Delta b_t = 0.00739 - (1/16)[v_{t-1} - v_{t-17}] + \lambda(x_t^* - x_{t-1}),$$

where b_t = log of monetary base (for period t), v_t = log of base velocity, x_t = log of nominal GNP, and x_t^* = target path for nominal income.

The constant term 0.00739 is simply a 3 percent annual growth rate translated into quarterly logarithmic units. The second term subtracts the average growth rate of velocity, approximated by the average difference in the logarithm of velocity over the previous four years. This term can be thought of as a simple time-series estimate of trend velocity growth. The third term specifies how policy is to respond to deviations of nominal income from its target path.

The moving average of velocity growth is a simple statistical filter designed to detect permanent changes in velocity growth. As such, it provides a mechanism to maintain a long-term

correspondence between the current base growth path and the long-term nominal objective to account for changes in transactions technology. Given the length of the moving-average period (four years) and the absence of any systematic feedback from interest rates, however, the rule provides virtually no adjustment in response to the current state of the business cycle or to financial conditions.[11]

The third term provides feedback to assure that nominal income ultimately returns to its trend path. The choice of parameter λ incorporates some degree of flexibility to deal with the potential problem of instrument instability. This problem arises when effects of policy occur over time as they do in actual economies, particularly those with sticky prices. Large responses to maintain a target path in the near term could lead to longer-term effects in the opposite direction, requiring even greater offsetting policy responses in later periods. This sequence would be unstable if responses and effects were to become ever increasing. The value of λ (presumably less than zero) should be chosen to minimize the potential for this dynamic instability, under the constraint that it be sufficiently large to provide adequate responsiveness of base growth to target misses. McCallum suggests that a value of 0.25 appears to be somewhat robust for this objective over alternative models of the economy.

If velocity growth were constant, and if nominal GNP were on its target path for a sustained period, the policy prescribed by McCallum's rule would be the same as a 3 percent growth rule for the monetary base. Thus, McCallum's rule is essentially a generalization of the constant-money-growth rule. Because it is more general, it allows for flexibility to deal with some of the problems of making monetarist rules operational.

Moreover, McCallum claims that because the monetary base is "controllable," the rule can be accomplished with no operational discretion.[12]

■ **11** Recent evidence suggests that velocity has become increasingly interest-sensitive in the 1980s. To the extent that systematic effects of interest rates could be reliably estimated, additional flexibility could be introduced into the rule as feedback to compensate for short-run variability in velocity. McCallum expresses doubt, however, that economists know enough to base policy on any one short-run empirical model. In this sense he defends, if only indirectly, the monetarist dictum of Friedman, in which monetary policy affects the economy with long and variable lags.

■ **12** Under current institutional arrangements, the total monetary base can be controlled only indirectly, working through effects of changes in interest rates on the demand for base components. Advocates of base targeting often call for institutional reforms—such as exactly contemporaneous reserve accounting and closure of the discount window—to enable direct control of the base. Alternatively, McCallum's rule can be applied to the nonborrowed base, which is directly controllable under existing institutions.

In this sense McCallum's proposal is a flexible version of a rule for means. The flexibility is extremely limited, however, involving only feedback from simple statistical models to maintain long-run relationships. No role is given to structural models that might allow feedback for short-term economic stabilization. Such a rule shows little faith in macroeconomic models or in discretionary decisions of the Fed.

Some rule advocates, on the other hand, propose a much greater role for economic models and judgment of the Fed. An example is an ends-oriented rule advanced by Hall (1984). Under Hall's strategy, the Federal Reserve is instructed to stabilize the price level around a constant long-run average value. To make this strategy elastic in the short run, Hall proposes giving the Fed some prespecified leeway in achieving the target depending on the amount of unemployment. The permissible deviation of the actual price level, p, from its target, p^*, is defined by the simple numerical rule linking it to the deviation of the unemployment rate, u, from its normal rate, presumed to be 6 percent:

$$(7) \quad 100(p - p^*)/p^* = A(u - 6).$$

The coefficient A is to be specified by the Federal Reserve. Based on simulations, Hall tentatively recommends that it equal eight.

Specifically, this relationship is to be imposed as a constraint on policy instrument settings. In formal terms: "Monetary policy is on track when the deviation of the price level from its constant target is eight times the deviation of unemployment times its normal level [*presumed to be 6 percent*]. Policy is too tight if the price deviation is less than eight times the employment deviation; it is too expansionary when the price deviation is more than eight times the employment deviation. The elasticity of 8 in this statement is a matter for policymakers to choose." (Hall [1984], p. 140)

Policy formulation under this approach would be prospective. Thus, the Fed would need to employ a model that links instrument variables to the price level and to the unemployment rate over the criterion period.[13] It would be free to use whatever model and instruments it chooses. Instrument settings would be determined by an iterative process. To begin, an initial forecast for the unemployment rate and price level would be compared against the rule formula to be judged for appropriateness—for example, too tight, too easy, or on track. This process would thereby determine the direction in which instrument settings should be changed, if necessary. A second round of forecasts would then be obtained and compared. The process would continue until the instrument settings yielded price-level and unemployment forecasts consistent with the rule.

To impose discipline, Hall would require the Fed to be explicit about its forecasts, defending them publicly at the semiannual Congressional review and in comparison with private forecasts. Hall argues that forecasting errors of good private forecasters would provide a sufficiently reliable standard to maintain unbiased outcomes. If the Fed's forecasts were consistently different from reputable private forecasts, and if the outside forecasts were more often correct, then the Fed would be under public pressure to modify its way of setting policy instruments. For Hall, the problem with discretion lies not with the use of faulty econometric models but with the absence of a commitment to an explicit rule for the price level.

Both Hall and McCallum employ small empirical models to generate simulations under their rules. McCallum uses a variety of models based on competing views to examine the robustness of his rule's performance. His simulations suggest that his rule would have produced a root mean square error (RMSE) of nominal income of around 2 percent from 1954 to 1985. This is approximately one-third the RMSE of actual GNP around its trend over the same period. He concludes that his rule would have worked relatively well in the United States.

To address the criticism that his simulations are subject to the Lucas critique, McCallum notes that his rule relates nominal demand to nominal policy instruments. He argues that the sensitivity of parameters to policy regime changes is likely to be quantitatively less important for such rules than for rules that relate real to nominal variables, for example, based on Phillips curve models. Hall's simulations, on the other hand, are based on the presumption that there is a reliable (policy invariant) relationship between the *variability* of the inflation rate and the *variability* of the price level.[14] His simulation results suggest that *both* price level variability and unemployment variability would have been less than actually experienced from 1952 to 1983 under the elastic-price rule.

---

13 Based on the assumption that monetary policy affects the unemployment rate reliably only after a yearlong lag, Hall argues that the criterion period should be the forecast horizon for the year beginning six months ahead.

14 The analysis of policy in terms of the *variability* of unemployment and price level was developed by Taylor (1980, 1981). It is important to note that there is no implied trade-off in this model between the inflation rate and *trend* output growth.

While the results presented under both rules appear favorable, few analysts seem convinced by small-model simulations. Experience with large-scale econometric models, for example, suggests that interest rates would vary sharply under McCallum's rule. His models, which do not allow for interest-rate interactions, cannot account for the economic consequences of such interest-rate variation. Fischer (1988) argues that the natural vehicles for studying policy rules are the large-scale econometric models, many of which have met the market test. Nevertheless, he notes that it would be difficult to justify legislating any nondiscretionary rule given the variety and inadequacies of existing models. On the other hand, existing models may be no more reliable for discretionary decisions, particularly when policymakers may use them selectively to support their own prior beliefs.

V. Some Concluding Comments

The success of the U.S. disinflation strategy early in this decade helped reestablish the Federal Reserve's credibility as an inflation fighter. Much of the reputational capital surely persists today. Recently, however, some analysts have questioned whether the current strategy is adequate to extend and maintain the progress against inflation (see Black [1987]).

A key concern is that the strategy may lack sufficient institutional discipline to assure that short-term objectives—such as interest-rate smoothing—do not interfere with the achievement of longer-term price stability. This fear has led to a renewed interest in alternative strategies that are closer to a pure rule on the continuum between a pure rule and pure discretion.

Ideally, a policy strategy should perform adequately well under alternative views about aggregate economic relationships so that sufficient numbers of agents believe that the rule could be credibly implemented. Rule advocates might well follow the example of McCallum and examine the robustness of their rule's performance, simulating with alternative models of the economy. The choice of criteria for "adequate performance" is of course a difficult and controversial matter. We conclude here, as does Fischer (1988), that the discussion of alternative policies is too important to be suppressed by the econometric evaluation critique.

References

Barro, Robert J. "Recent Developments in the Theory of Rules Versus Discretion." *Conference Papers: Supplement to the Economic Journal.* 96(1985): 23-37.

————, and David B. Gordon. "A Positive Theory of Monetary Policy in a Natural Rate Model." *Journal of Political Economy.* 91(1983a): 598-610.

————, and David B. Gordon. "Rules, Discretion, and Reputation in a Model of Monetary Policy." *Journal of Monetary Economics.* 12(1983b): 101-21.

Black, Robert P. "The Fed's Anti-inflationary Strategy: Is It Adequate?" Federal Reserve Bank of Richmond. *Economic Review* (September/October 1987): 1-9.

Brainard, William. "Uncertainty and the Effectiveness of Policy." *American Economic Review Papers and Proceedings.* 57(May 1967): 411-25.

Canzoneri, Matthew B. "Monetary Policy Games and the Role of Private Information." *American Economic Review.* 75(December 1985): 1056-70.

Fischer, Stanley. "Rules Versus Discretion in Monetary Policy." National Bureau of Economic Research Working Paper No. 2518 (February 1988).

Fisher, Irving. *Stable Money: A History of the Movement.* New York: Adelphi Company, 1934.

Friedman, Benjamin M. "Targets, Instruments, and Indicators of Monetary Policy." *Journal of Monetary Economics.* 1(October 1975): 443-73.

Friedman, Milton. "The Lag in Effect of Monetary Policy." *Journal of Political Economy.* 69(October 1961): 447-66. Reprinted in *The Optimum Quantity of Money and Other Essays.* Chicago: Adeline Publishing Company, 1969: 237-60.

————. *A Program for Monetary Stability.* New York: Fordham University Press, 1959.

————. "A Monetary and Fiscal Framework for Economic Stability." *American Economic Review.* 38(June 1948): 245-64. Reprinted in *Essays in Positive Economics.* Chicago: The University of Chicago Press, 1953.

Groshen, Erica L. "What's Happening to Labor Compensation?" Federal Reserve Bank of Cleveland. *Economic Commentary,* May 15, 1988.

Hall, Robert E. "Monetary Strategy with an Elastic Price Standard." *Price Stability and Public Policy.* A symposium sponsored by the Federal Reserve Bank of Kansas City, August 1984: 137-59.

Hetzel, Robert L. "The Rules Versus Discretion Debate Over Monetary Policy in the 1920s." Federal Reserve Bank of Richmond. *Economic Review* (November/December 1985): 3-14.

Kydland, Finn E., and Edward C. Prescott. "Rules Rather than Discretion: The Inconsistency of Optimal Plans." *Journal of Political Economy.* 85(June 1977): 473-91.

Lindsey, David E. "The Monetary Regime of the Federal Reserve System." Conference on Alternative Monetary Regimes sponsored by Ellis L. Phillips Foundation and Dartmouth College (August 1984).

Lucas, Robert E. "Econometric Policy Evaluation: A Critique." *Journal of Monetary Economics.* Supplementary Series 1(1976): 19-46.

McCallum, Bennett T. "Robustness Properties of a Rule for Monetary Policy." *Carnegie-Rochester Conference Series on Public Policy.* Carnegie Mellon University and National Bureau of Economic Research (February 1988).

_____ . "The Case for Rules in the Conduct of Monetary Policy: A Concrete Example." Federal Reserve Bank of Richmond. *Economic Review* (September/October 1987): 10-18.

Poole, William. "Monetary Policy Lessons of Recent Inflation and Disinflation." *The Journal of Economic Perspectives.* 2(Summer 1988): 73-100.

Roberds, William. "Models of Policy Under Stochastic Replanning." Federal Reserve Bank of Minneapolis Research Department Staff Report 104 (March 1986).

Rogoff, Kenneth. "The Optimal Degree of Commitment to an Intermediate Monetary Target." *Quarterly Journal of Economics.* C4(November 1985): 1169-89.

Simons, Henry C. "Rules Versus Authorities in Monetary Policy." *Journal of Political Economy.* 44(February 1936): 1-30.

Taylor, John B. "Stabilization, Accommodation, and Monetary Rules." *American Economic Review Papers and Proceedings.* 71(May 1981): 145-49.

_____ . "Output and Price Stability: An International Comparison." *Journal of Economic Dynamics and Control.* 2(February 1980): 109-32.

SECTION SIX

International Finance

Over the past decade, the international economy has witnessed increasingly open and developed markets; massive shifts in income and wealth across countries due to changes in prices of raw materials like oil; and large movements in individual countries' regulatory and macroeconomic policies, current account positions and exchange rates. As a consequence, there have been dramatic increases in activity in international financial markets and in calls for international cooperation to even out the effects of these events. The readings in this section discuss various aspects of international financial markets and policies.

The first article in this section, ''A Guide to Foreign Exchange Markets'' by K. Alec Chrystal, identifies who deals in the markets for foreign currencies and why. It also explains how trading in these markets takes place, noting the sizable differences between the large-bank-dominated wholesale market and the much-smaller-scale retail market foreign exchange. The use of futures and options contracts to hedge exchange rate risk is then outlined. Finally, Chrystal discusses the central role that the U.S. dollar plays in foreign exchange trading.

''Distinguished Lecture on Economics in Government: Thinking About International Economic Coordination'' by Martin S. Feldstein argues that attempting to link macroeconomic policies across countries is difficult, largely diversionary, risky, and ultimately infeasible. This is especially true for the United States, whose interdependence is not so great and whose policies cannot effectively be pledged by policymakers in any event. Though coordination may sometimes prove fruitful, pinning hopes on the benevolent actions of other countries is bound to disappoint, since in the end each country will pursue its own self-interest instead of self-sacrifice. Contending that international coordination is a prerequisite for domestic economic success also inappropriately increases apprehension when it is not achievable and decreases pressure for the appropriate domestic policy.

''Louvre's Lesson—The World Needs a New Monetary System'' by C. Fred Bergsten indicts the current system of floating exchange rates for several, serious failings: permitting the drastic overvaluation of the dollar, breeding protectionism, and removing shorter term constraints on domestic policies. It is proposed that a system of target zones for exchange rates would suffer much less from these maladies. One way it would do so is by generating pressure, quickly and identifiably, on individual economies to pursue policies that ultimately are more beneficial to themselves and to others.

''Understanding International Debt Crisis'' by James R. Barth, Michael D. Bradley, and Paul C. Panayotacos, examines the importance of international debt to the world economy. After explaining how cross-country lending facilitates economic growth, the problems peculiar to international debt are discussed. The magnitude of and potential solutions to the current crisis are then explored. Finally, the prospects for avoiding a recurrence of this crisis are assessed.

"Financial Markets in Europe: Toward 1992" by Morgan Guaranty Trust Company outlines the opportunities and obstacles presented by the European plan to integrate their financial markets. In the next few years, that plan seeks to achieve vast changes, largely reductions, across the entire Common Market in regulations affecting taxes, capital, tariffs, market access, and other major aspects of finance. Drawing upon the somewhat limited American experience, the implications for geographical, product, and size attributes of financial firms are explored. Pitfalls in the financial integration of Europe abound, however. Some of the more predictable difficulties are raised and appraised.

Article Thirty-Four

A Guide to Foreign Exchange Markets

K. Alec Chrystal

THE economies of the free world are becoming increasingly interdependent. U.S. exports now amount to almost 10 percent of Gross National Product. For both Britain and Canada, the figure currently exceeds 25 percent. Imports are about the same size. Trade of this magnitude would not be possible without the ability to buy and sell currencies. Currencies must be bought and sold because the acceptable means of payment in other countries is not the U.S. dollar. As a result, importers, exporters, travel agents, tourists and many others with overseas business must change dollars into foreign currency and/or the reverse.

The trading of currencies takes place in foreign exchange markets whose major function is to facilitate international trade and investment. Foreign exchange markets, however, are shrouded in mystery. One reason for this is that a considerable amount of foreign exchange market activity does not appear to be related directly to the needs of international trade and investment.

The purpose of this paper is to explain how these markets work.[1] The basics of foreign exchange will first

be described. This will be followed by a discussion of some of the more important activities of market participants. Finally, there will be an introduction to the analysis of a new feature of exchange markets — currency options. The concern of this paper is with the structure and mechanics of foreign exchange markets, not with the determinants of exchange rates themselves.

THE BASICS OF FOREIGN EXCHANGE MARKETS

There is an almost bewildering variety of foreign exchange markets. Spot markets and forward markets abound in a number of currencies. In addition, there are diverse prices quoted for these currencies. This section attempts to bring order to this seeming disarray.

Spot, Forward, Bid, Ask

Virtually every major newspaper, such as the *Wall Street Journal* or the *London Financial Times*, prints a daily list of exchange rates. These are expressed either as the number of units of a particular currency that exchange for one U.S. dollar or as the number of U.S. dollars that exchange for one unit of a particular currency. Sometimes both are listed side by side (see table 1).

For major currencies, up to four different prices typically will be quoted. One is the "spot" price. The others may be "30 days forward," "90 days forward,"

K. Alec Chrystal, professor of economics-elect, University of Sheffield, England, is a visiting scholar at the Federal Reserve Bank of St. Louis. Leslie Bailis Koppel provided research assistance. The author wishes to thank Joseph Hempen, Centerre Bank, St. Louis, for his advice on this paper.

[1]For further discussion of foreign exchange markets in the United States, see Kubarych (1983). See also Dufey and Giddy (1978) and McKinnon (1979).

Table 1
Foreign Exchange Rate Quotations

Foreign Exchange

Wednesday, September 7, 1983
The New York foreign exchange selling rates below apply to trading among banks in amounts of $1 million and more, as quoted at 3 p.m. Eastern time by Bankers Trust Co. Retail transactions provide fewer units of foreign currency per dollar.

Country	U.S. $ equiv. Wed.	U.S. $ equiv. Tues.	Currency per U.S. $ Wed.	Currency per U.S. $ Tues.
Argentina (Peso)	.09652	.09652	10.36	10.36
Australia (Dollar)	.8772	.8777	1.1340	1.1393
Austria (Schilling)	.05296	.0560	18.88	17.84
Belgium (Franc)				
Commercial rate	.01851	.01855	54.01	53.90
Financial rate	.01844	.01846	54.21	54.15
Brazil (Cruzeiro)	.001459	.00149	685.	671.00
Britain (Pound)	1.4910	1.5000	.6707	.6666
30-Day Forward	1.4915	1.5004	.6704	.6664
90-Day Forward	1.4930	1.5010	.6697	.6662
180-Day Forward	1.4952	1.5028	.6688	.6654
Canada (Dollar)	.8120	.8123	1.2315	.2310
30-Day Forward	.8125	.8128	1.2307	1.2303
90-Day Forward	.8134	.8137	1.2293	1.2289
180-Day Forward	.8145	.8147	1.2277	1.2274
Chile (Official rate)	.01246	.01246	80.21	80.21
China (Yuan)	.50499	.50489	1.9802	1.9806
Colombia (Peso)	.01228	.01228	81.4	81.40
Denmark (Krone)	.10362	.10405	9.65	9.6100
Ecuador (Sucre)				
Official rate	.02082	.02082	48.03	48.03
Floating rate	.010917	.010917	91.60	91.60
Finland (Markka)	.17424	.17485	5.7390	5.7190
France (Franc)	.1238	.1238	8.0750	8.0750
30-Day Forward	.1235	.1230	8.0955	8.1300
90-Day Forward	.1224	.1223	8.1695	8.1725
180-Day Forward	.1203	.1202	8.3100	8.3150
Greece (Drachma)	.01075	.01078	93.	92.70
Hong Kong (Dollar)	.1297	.13089	7.71	7.6400
India (Rupee)	.0980	.0980	10.20	10.20
Indonesia (Rupiah)	.001015	.001015	985.	985.
Ireland (Punt)	1.1715	1.1775	.8536	.8493
Israel (Shekel)	.0173	.0173	57.80	57.80
Italy (Lira)	.000624	.0006255	1602.	1598.50
Japan (Yen)	.004072	.004067	245.55	245.85
30-Day Forward	.004083	.004079	244.88	245.15
90-Day Forward	.004107	.004102	243.48	243.75
180-Day Forward	.004147	.004142	241.10	241.39
Lebanon (Pound)	.20618	.20618	4.85	4.85
Malaysia (Ringgit)	.42462	.42489	2.3550	2.3535
Mexico (Peso)				
Floating rate	.00665	.00666	150.25	150.00
Netherlands (Guilder)	.33288	.3333	3.0040	3.000
New Zealand (Dollar)	.6497	.6505	1.5397	1.5327
Norway (Krone)	.13368	.1340	7.48	7.4625
Pakistan (Rupee)	.07518	.07518	13.30	13.30
Peru (Sol)	.0005105	.0005105	1958.89	1958.89
Philippines (Peso)	.09085	.09085	11.007	11.007
Portugal (Escudo)	.00804	.00807	124.35	123.90
Saudi Arabia (Riyal)	.28735	.28735	3.48	3.48
Singapore (Dollar)	.46609	.4664	2.1455	2.1440
South Africa (Rand)	.8870	.8900	1.1273	1.1236
South Korea (Won)	.001285	.001285	778.20	778.20
Spain (Peseta)	.00655	.00658	152.60	151.90
Sweden (Krona)	.12635	.12666	7.9140	7.8950
Switzerland (Franc)	.4596	.4591	2.1755	2.1780
30-Day Forward	.4619	.4615	216.46	2.1666
90-Day Forward	.4662	.4657	2.1449	2.1470
180-Day Forward	.4728	.4723	2.1150	2.1172
Taiwan (Dollar)	.02489	.02489	40.17	40.17
Thailand (Baht)	.043459	.043459	23.01	23.01
Uruguay (New Peso)				
Financial	.02798	.02798	35.73	35.73
Venezuela (Bolivar)				
Official rate	.23256	.23256	4.30	4.30
Floating rate	.07194	.07272	13.90	13.75
W. Germany (Mark)	.3726	.3726	2.6835	2.6835
30-Day Forward	.3740	.3741	2.6731	2.6728
90-Day Forward	.3767	.3768	2.6540	2.6538
180-Day Forward	.3808	.3808	2.6260	2.6259
SDR	1.04637	1.04903	.955685	.953625

Special Drawing Rights are based on exchange rates for the U.S., West German, British, French and Japanese currencies. Source: International Monetary Fund.
z-Not quoted.

The Dollar Spot and Forward

Sept 7	Day's spread	Close	One month	% p.a.	Three months	% p.a.
UK†	1.4860-1.4975	1.4910-1.4920	0.02-0.07c dis	-0.36	0.17-0.22dis	-0.52
Ireland†	1.1665-1.1720	1.1710-1.1720	0.36-0.30c pm	3.39	0.88-0.78 pm	2.84
Canada	1.2305-1.2320	1.2310-1.2315	0.09-0.06c pm	0.73	0.24-0.21 pm	0.73
Nethind.	3.0050-3.0150	3.0050-3.0070	1.12-1.02c pm	4.26	3.00-2.90 pm	3.92
Belgium	54.06-54.20	54.06-54.08	7-6c pm	1.44	14-11 pm	0.92
Denmark	9.6400-9.6800	9.6400-9.6450	2-2¹⁄₂ore dis	-2.79	par-¹⁄₂ dis	-0.10
W. Ger.	2.6850-2.6980	2.6865-2.6875	1.07-1.02pf pm	4.66	3.00-2.95 pm	4.42
Portugal	124.20-125.00	124.40-124.70	115-290c dis	-19.51	330-790dis	-17.98
Spain	152.40-152.70	152.50-152.60	170-220c dis	-15.33	675-775dis	-18.99
Italy	1604-1608	1605-1606	10-10¹⁄₂lire dis	-7.65	29¹⁄₂-31 dis	-7.53
Norway	7.4730-7.4940	7.4730-7.4780	1.90-2.20ore dis	-3.29	5.90-6.20ds	-3.23
France	8.0775-8.1225	8.0825-8.0875	2.02-2.12c dis	-3.07	9.85-9.85ds	-4.81
Sweden	7.9120-7.9265	7.9120-7.9170	0.90-1.10ore dis	-1.51	2.25-2.45ds	-1.19
Japan	245.50-246.50	245.65-245.75	0.69-0.64y pm	3.24	2.11-2.03 pm	3.36
Austria	18.89-18.95¹⁄₂	18.89-18.90	7.50-6.70gro pm	4.50	21.00-18.50 pm	4.17
Switz.	2.1770-2.1875	2.1800-2.1810	1.10-1.05c pm	5.91	3.10-3.05 pm	5.63

†UK and Ireland are quoted in U.S. currency. Forward premiums and discounts apply to the U.S. dollar and not to the individual currency.

Belgian rate is for convertible francs. Financial franc 54.40-54.45.

London Financial Times, September 8, 1983

Wall Street Journal, September 8, 1983

and "180 days forward." These may be expressed either in "European Terms" (such as number of $ per £) or in "American Terms" (such as number of £ per $). (See the glossary for further explanation.)

The spot price is what you must pay to buy currencies for immediate delivery (two working days in the interbank market; over the counter, if you buy bank notes or travelers checks). The forward prices for each currency are what you will have to pay if you sign a contract today to buy that currency on a specific future date (30 days from now, etc.). In this market, you pay for the currency when the contract matures.

Why would anyone buy and sell foreign currency forward? There are some major advantages from having such opportunities available. For example, an exporter who has receipts of foreign currency due at some future date can sell those funds forward now, thereby avoiding all risks associated with subsequent adverse exchange rate changes. Similarly, an importer who will have to pay for a shipment of goods in foreign currency in, say, three months can buy the foreign exchange forward and, again, avoid having to bear the exchange rate risk.

The exchange rates quoted in the financial press (for example, those in table 1) are not the ones individuals would get at a local bank. Unless otherwise specified, the published prices refer to those quoted by banks to other banks for currency deals in excess of $1 million. Even these prices will vary somewhat depending upon whether the bank buys or sells. The difference between the buying and selling price is sometimes known as the "bid-ask spread." The spread partly reflects the banks' costs and profit margins in transactions; however, major banks make their profits more from capital gains than from the spread.[2]

The market for bank notes and travelers checks is quite separate from the interbank foreign exchange market. For smaller currency exchanges, such as an individual going on vacation abroad might make, the spread is greater than in the interbank market. This presumably reflects the larger average costs — including the exchange rate risks that banks face by holding bank notes in denominations too small to be sold in the interbank market — associated with these smaller exchanges. As a result, individuals generally pay a higher price for foreign exchange than those quoted in the newspapers.

Table 2
Dollar Price of Deutschemarks and Sterling at Various Banks

	Deutschemark		Sterling	
	Buy	Sell	Buy	Sell
Retail				
Local (St. Louis) banks (avg.)	.3572–.3844		1.4225–1.5025	
Wholesale				
New York banks	.3681–.3683		1.4570–1.4580	
European banks (high)	.3694–.3696		1.4573–1.4583	
European banks (low)	.3677–.3678		1.4610–1.4620	
Bankers trust	.3681		1.4588	

Note: These prices were all quoted on November 28, 1983, between 2:00 p.m. and 2:45 p.m. (Central Standard Time). Prices for local banks were acquired by telephoning for their price on a $10,000 transaction. The prices quoted were reference rates and not the final price they would offer on a firm transaction. Figure for Bankers Trust is that given in the *Wall Street Journal*, November 29, 1983, as priced at 2:00 p.m. (Central Standard Time) on November 28, 1983. Other prices were taken from the Telerate information system at 2:35 p.m. New York prices were the latest available (Morgan and Citibank, respectively). European prices were the last prices quoted before close of trading in Europe by various banks. Deutschemark prices were actually quoted in American terms. The sell prices above have been rounded up. The difference between buy and sell prices for DM in the interbank market actually worked out at $0.00015.

An example of the range of spot exchange rates available is presented in table 2, which shows prices for deutschemarks and sterling quoted within a one-hour period on November 28, 1983. There are two important points to notice. First, all except those in the first line are prices quoted in the interbank, or wholesale, market for transactions in excess of $1 million. The sterling prices have a bid-ask spread of only 0.1 cent (which is only about 0.07 percent of the price, or $7 on $10,000). On DM, the spread per dollars worth works out to be about half that on sterling ($4 on $10,000).[3]

Second, the prices quoted by local banks for small, or retail, transactions, which serve only as a guide and do not necessarily represent prices on actual deals, involve a much larger bid-ask spread. These retail spreads vary from bank to bank, but are related to (and larger than) the interbank rates. In some cases, they

---

[2]Notice the *Wall Street Journal* quotes only a bank selling price at a particular time. The *Financial Times* quotes the bid-ask spread and the range over the day.

[3]In practice, the spread will vary during the day, depending upon market conditions. For example, the sterling spread may be as little as 0.01 cents at times and on average is about 0.05 cents. Spreads generally will be larger on less widely traded currencies.

may be of the order of 4 cents or less on sterling, though the prices quoted in St. Louis involved average spreads of 8 cents on sterling. The latter represents a spread of about 5½ percent (about $550 per $10,000 transaction). The equivalent spread for DM was 7 percent ($700 per $10,000 transaction).

The spread on forward transactions will usually be wider than on spot, especially for longer maturities. For interbank trade, the closing spread on one and three months forward sterling on September 8, 1983, was .15 cents, while the spot spread was .10 cents. This is shown in the top line of the *Financial Times* report in table 1. Of course, like the spot spread, the forward spread varies with time of day and market conditions. At times it may be as low as .02 cents. No information is available for the size of spread on the forward prices typically offered on small transactions, since the retail market on forward transactions is very small.

HOW DOES "THE" FOREIGN EXCHANGE MARKET OPERATE?

It is generally not possible to go to a specific building and "see" the market where prices of foreign exchange are determined. With few exceptions, the vast bulk of foreign exchange business is done over the telephone between specialist divisions of major banks. Foreign exchange dealers in each bank usually operate from one room; each dealer has several telephones and is surrounded by video screens and news tapes. Typically, each dealer specializes in one or a small number of markets (such as sterling/dollar or deutschemark/dollar). Trades are conducted with other dealers who represent banks around the world. These dealers typically deal regularly with one another and are thus able to make firm commitments by word of mouth.

Only the head or regional offices of the larger banks actively deal in foreign exchange. The largest of these banks are known as "market makers" since they stand ready to buy or sell any of the major currencies on a more or less continuous basis. Unusually large transactions, however, will only be accommodated by market makers on more favorable terms. In such cases, foreign exchange brokers may be used as middlemen to find a taker or takers for the deal. Brokers (of which there are four major firms and a handful of smaller ones) do not trade on their own account, but specialize in setting up large foreign exchange transactions in return for a commission (typically 0.03 cents or less on the sterling spread). In April 1983, 56 percent of spot transactions by value involving banks in the United States were channeled through brokers.[4] If all interbank transactions are included, the figure rises to 59 percent.

Most small banks and local offices of major banks do not deal directly in the interbank foreign exchange market. Rather they typically will have a credit line with a large bank or their head office. Transactions will thus involve an extra step (see figure 1). The customer deals with a local bank, which in turn deals with a major bank or head office. The interbank foreign exchange market exists between the major banks either directly or indirectly via a broker.

FUTURES AND OPTION MARKETS FOR FOREIGN EXCHANGE

Until very recently, the interbank market was the only channel through which foreign exchange transactions took place. The past decade has produced major innovations in foreign exchange trading. On May 16, 1972, the International Money Market (IMM) opened under the auspices of the Chicago Mercantile Exchange. One novel feature of the IMM is that it provides a trading floor on which deals are struck by brokers face to face, rather than over telephone lines. The most significant difference between the IMM and the interbank market, however, is that trading on the IMM is in futures contracts for foreign exchange, the typical business being contracts for delivery on the third Wednesday of March, June, September or December. Activity at the IMM has expanded greatly since its opening. For example, during 1972, 144,336 contracts were traded; the figure for 1981 was 6,121,932.

There is an important distinction between "forward" transactions and "futures" contracts. The former are individual agreements between two parties, say, a bank and customer. The latter is a contract traded on an organized market of a standard size and settlement date, which is resalable at the market price up to the close of trading in the contract. These organized markets are discussed more fully below.

While the major banks conduct foreign exchange deals in large denominations, the IMM trading is done in contracts of standard size which are fairly small. Examples of the standard contracts at present are £25,000; DM125,000; Canadian $100,000. These are actually smaller today than in the early days of the IMM.

Further, unlike prices on the interbank market, price movements in any single day are subject to specific

---

[4]See Federal Reserve Bank of New York (1983).

Figure 1
Structure of Foreign Exchange Markets

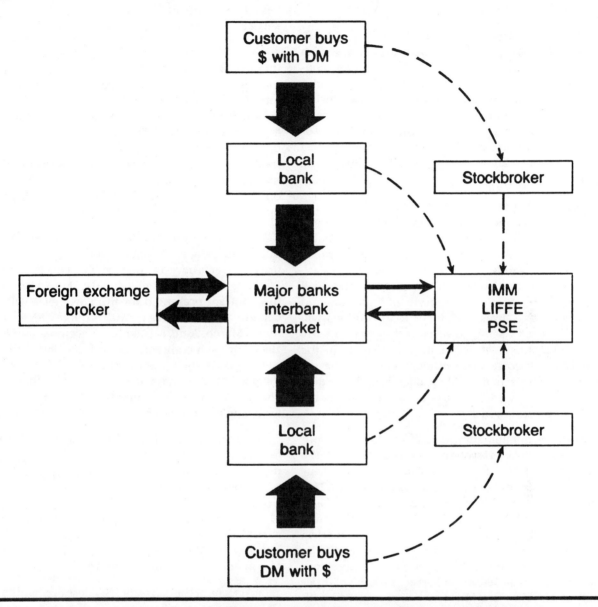

NOTE: The International Money Market (IMM) Chicago trades foreign exchange futures and DM futures options.
The London International Financial Futures Exchange (LIFFE) trades foreign exchange futures.
The Philadelphia Stock Exchange (PSE) trades foreign currency options.

limits at the IMM. For example, for sterling futures, prices are not allowed to vary more than $.0500 away from the previous day's settlement price; this limit is expanded if it is reached in the same direction for two successive days. The limit does not apply on the last day a contract is traded.

Unlike the interbank market, parties to a foreign exchange contract at the IMM typically do not know each other. Default risk, however, is minor because contracts are guaranteed by the exchange itself. To minimize the cost of this guarantee, the exchange insists upon "margin requirements" to cover fluctuations in the value of a contract. This means that an individual or firm buying a futures contract would, in effect, place a deposit equal to about 4 percent of the value of the contract.[5]

Perhaps the major limitation of the IMM from the point of view of importers or exporters is that contracts cover only eight currencies — those of Britain, Canada, West Germany, Switzerland, Japan, Mexico, France and the Netherlands — and they are specified in standard sizes for particular dates. Only by chance will these conform exactly to the needs of importers and exporters. Large firms and financial institutions will find the market useful, however, if they have a fairly continuous stream of payments and receipts in the traded foreign currencies. Although contracts have a specified standard date, they offer a fairly flexible method of avoiding exchange rate risk because they are marketable continuously.

A major economic advantage of the IMM for non-bank customers is its low transaction cost. Though the brokerage cost of a contract will vary, a "round trip" (that is, one buy and one sell) costs as little as $15. This is only .04 percent of the value of a sterling contract and less for some of the larger contracts. Of course, such costs are high compared with the interbank market, where the brokerage cost on DM 1 million would be about $6.25 (the equivalent-valued eight futures contracts would cost $60 in brokerage, taking $7.50 per single deal). They are low, however, compared with those in the retail market, where the spread may involve a cost of up to 2.5 percent or 3 percent per transaction.

A market similar to the IMM, the London International Financial Futures Exchange (LIFFE), opened in September 1982. On LIFFE, futures are traded in sterling, deutschemarks, Swiss francs and yen in identical bundles to those sold on the IMM. In its first year, the foreign exchange business of LIFFE did not take off in a big way. The major provider of exchange rate risk coverage for business continues to be the bank network. Less than 5 percent of such cover is provided by markets such as IMM and LIFFE at present.

An entirely new feature of foreign exchange markets that has arisen in the 1980s is the existence of option markets.[6] The Philadelphia Exchange was the first to introduce foreign exchange options. These are in five currencies (deutschemark, sterling, Swiss franc, yen and Canadian dollar). Trades are conducted in standard bundles half the size of the IMM futures contracts. The IMM introduced an options market in German marks on January 24, 1984; this market trades options on futures contracts whereas the Philadelphia options are for spot currencies.

Futures and options prices for foreign exchange are published daily in the financial press. Table 3 shows prices for February 14, 1984, as displayed in the *Wall Street Journal* on the following day. Futures prices on the IMM are presented for five currencies (left-hand column). There are five contracts quoted for each currency: March, June, September, December and March 1985. For each contract, opening and last settlement (settle) prices, the range over the day, the change from the previous day, the range over the life of the contract and the number of contracts outstanding with the exchange (open interest) are listed.

Consider the March and June DM futures. March futures opened at $.3653 per mark and closed at $.3706 per mark; June opened at $.3698 per mark and closed at $.3746 per mark. Turn now to the Chicago Mercantile Exchange (IMM) futures options (center column). These are options on the futures contracts just discussed (see inset for explanation of options). Thus, the line labeled "Futures" lists the settle prices of the March and June futures as above.

Let us look at the call options. These are rights to buy DM futures at specified prices — the strike price. For example, take the call option at strike price 35. This means that one can purchase an option to buy DM 125,000 March futures up to the March settlement date for $.3500 per mark. This option will cost 2.05 cents per mark, or $2,562.50, plus brokerage fees. The June option to buy June futures DM at $.3500 per mark will cost 2.46 cents per mark, or $3,075.00, plus brokerage fees.

---

[5]A bank may also insist upon some minimum deposit to cover a forward contract, though there is no firm rule.

[6]For a discussion of options in commodities, see Belongia (1983).

Table 3
Futures and Options Markets

Futures Prices

Tuesday, February 14, 1984.
Open Interest Reflects Previous Trading Day.

	Open	High	Low	Settle	Change	Lifetime High	Low	Open Interest
BRITISH POUND (IMM)—25,000 pounds; $ per pound								
Mar	1.4150	1.4400	1.4150	1.4370	+ .0170	1.6010	1.3930	17,694
June	1.4175	1.4435	1.4175	1.4395	+ .0170	1.5520	1.3950	3.251
Sept	1.4285	1.4410	1.4220	1.4410	+ .0160	1.5240	1.3980	157
Dec	1.4280	1.4435	1.4245	1.4435	+ .0160	1.4650	1.3990	75
Mar85	1.4280	1.4460	1.4270	1.4470	+ .0170	1.4625	1.4000	65
Est vol 10,651; vol Mon 1,987; open int 21,242, +78.								
CANADIAN DOLLAR (IMM)—100,000 dlrs.; $ per Can $								
Mar	.8010	8024	8010	8020	....	8169	7979	4.033
June	.8014	8029	8013	8023	....	8168	7983	740
Sept				8026		8147	7988	312
Dec	.8021	8031	8021	8029	....	8040	8021	152
Mar85	.8035	8035	8035	8032	....	8035	8023	50
Est vol 1,087; vol Mon 535; open int 5,287, −103.								
JAPANESE YEN (IMM) 12.5 million yen; $ per yen (.00)								
Mar	.4276	.4297	4276	4294	+ .0011	4396	.4125	25,730
June	.4315	4337	4312	4334	+ .0011	4435	4180	3.908
Sept	.4354	4375	4354	4374	+ .0012	4450	4354	974
Dec	.4416	4420	4400	4415	+ .0012	4493	4395	271
Est vol 9,133; vol Mon 3,306; open int 30,883, +534.								
SWISS FRANC (IMM)—125,000 francs; $ per franc								
Mar	4495	4556	4486	4549	.0047	5230	.4470	24,164
June	4564	4629	4557	4622	+ .0051	5045	4536	3.165
Sept	4632	4692	4632	4688	+ .0052	5020	4598	153
Dec	.4705	4780	4705	4747	+ .0049	4880	4665	71
Mar85				4830	+ .0050	4840	.4755	5
Est vol 30,610; vol Mon 8,466; open int 27,558, +296.								
W. GERMAN MARK (IMM)—125,000 marks; $ per mark								
Mar	3653	3713	3650	3706	.0036	4100	3537	30,974
June	3698	3754	3688	3746	+ .0037	4002	3568	4.911
Sept	3743	3790	3743	3780	+ .0034	4030	3602	362
Dec	.3780	3825	3780	3825	+ .0043	3825	3640	204
Mar85				3838	+ .0035	3699	3699	1
Est vol 30,248; vol Mon 9,045; open int 36,452, +680.								

Futures Options

Chicago Mercantile Exchange

W. GERMAN MARK—125,000 marks, cents per mark

Strike Price	Calls—Settle Mar	Jun	Puts—Settle Mar	Jun
34	...	...	0.01	0.01
35	2.05	2.46	0.01	0.09
36	1.11	1.66	0.06	0.25
37	0.38	1.00	0.33	0.57
38	0.10	0.54	1.00	1.02
39	0.01	0.27	...	...
Futures	.3706	.3746		

Estimated total vol. 2,187.
Calls: Mon vol. 180; open int. 2,416.
Puts: Mon vol. 73; open int. 1,841.

Foreign Currency Options

Philadelphia Exchange

Option & Strike Underlying Price		Calls—Last Mar	Jun	Sep	Puts—Last Mar	Jun	Sep
12,500 British Pounds-cents per unit.							
BPound	140	3.40	r	5.70	0.40	1.85	r
143.00	.145	0.70	2.40	r	3.40	r	r
50,000 Canadian Dollars-cents per unit.							
CDollar	.80	r	r	0.68	−r	r	r
62,500 West German Marks-cents per unit.							
DMark	.34	2.67	r	r	r	r	r
36.88	.35	1.99	2.18	r	r	r	r
36.88	.36	1.04	1.59	r	0.05	0.35	r
36.88	.37	0.38	1.00	r	0.37	0.56	r
36.88	.38	0.10	0.62	0.85	r	r	r
36.88	.39	r	0.28	s	r	r	s
36.88	.40	0.01	0.11	s	r	r	s
6,250,000 Japanese Yen-100ths of a cent per unit.							
JYen	.42	0.95	1.49	2.04	r	r	r
42.75	.43	0.30	0.90	r	0.50	0.60	r
42.75	.44	0.04	0.45	0.99	r	r	r
62,500 Swiss Francs-cents per unit.							
SFranc	.44	r	r	3.15	r	0.24	r
45.18	.45	0.65	r	r	0.26	r	r
45.18	.46	0.28	1.09	1.82	r	1.00	r
45.18	.47	0.06	r	r	r	r	r
45.18	.48	0.02	0.28	r	r	r	r
Total call vol.	2,271		Call open int.	37,349			
Total put vol.	799		Put open int.	26,173			

r—Not traded. s—No option offered. o—Old.
Last is premium (purchase price).

***Wall Street Journal*, February 15, 1984**

The March call option at strike price $.3900 per mark costs only 0.01 cents per mark or $12.50. These price differences indicate that the market expects the dollar price of the mark to exceed $.3500, but not to rise substantially above $.3900.

Notice that when you exercise a futures call option you buy the relevant futures contract but only fulfill that futures contract at maturity. In contrast, the Philadelphia foreign currency options (right column) are options to buy foreign exchange (spot) itself rather than futures. So, when a call option is exercised, foreign currency is obtained immediately.

The only difference in presentation of the currency option prices as compared with the futures options is that, in the former, the spot exchange rate is listed for comparison rather than the futures price. Thus, on the Philadelphia exchange, call options on March DM 62,500 at strike price $.3500 per mark cost 1.99 cents per mark or $1,243.75, plus brokerage. Brokerage fees here would be of the same order as on the IMM, about $16 per transaction round trip, per contract.

We have seen that there are several different markets for foreign exchange — spot, forward, futures, options on spot, options on futures. The channels through which these markets are formed are, however, fairly straightforward (see figure 1). The main channel is the interbank network, though for large interbank transactions, foreign exchange brokers may be used as middlemen.

FOREIGN EXCHANGE MARKET ACTIVITIES

Much foreign exchange market trading does not appear to be related to the simple basic purpose of allowing businesses to buy or sell foreign currency in order, say, to sell or purchase goods overseas. It is certainly easy to see the usefulness of the large range of foreign exchange transactions available through the interbank and organized markets (spot, forward, futures, options) to facilitate trade between nations. It is also clear that there is a useful role for foreign exchange brokers in helping to "make" the interbank market. There are several other activities, however, in foreign exchange markets that are less well understood and whose relevance is less obvious to people interested in understanding what these markets accomplish.

Foreign Exchange Options

An option is a contract specifying the right to buy or sell — in this case foreign exchange — within a specific period (American option) or at a specific date (European option). A call option confers the right to buy. A put option confers the right to sell. Since each of these options must have a buyer and a seller, there are four possible ways of trading a single option: buy a call, sell a call, buy a put, sell a put.

The buyer of an option has the right to undertake the contract specified but may choose not to do so if it turns out to be unprofitable. The seller of the option *must* fulfill the contract if the buyer desires. Clearly, the buyer must pay the seller some premium (the option price) for this privilege. An option that would be profitable to exercise at the current exchange rate is said to be "in the money." The price at which it is exercised is the "exercise" or "strike" price.

Consider a call option on £1000 (although options of this size are not presently available on organized exchanges, it is used to present a simple illustration of the principles involved). Suppose this costs $0.03 per pound or $30 and the exercise price is $1.50 per pound. The option expires in three months. This means that the buyer has paid $30 for the right to buy £1000 with dollars at a price of $1.50 per pound any time in the next three months. If the current spot price of sterling is, say, $1.45, the option is "out of the money" because sterling can be bought cheaper on the spot market. However, if the spot price were to rise to, say, $1.55, the option would be in the money. If sold at that time, the option buyer would get a $50 return (1000 × $0.05), which would more than cover the cost of the option ($50 − $30 = $20 profit). In contrast, a put option at the same terms would be in the money at the current spot price of $1.45, but out of the money at $1.55.

Figure 2 presents a diagrammatic illustration of how the profitability of an option depends upon the relationship between the exercise price and the current spot price.[1] Figure 2a illustrates the profit avail-

<hr />

[1]The pricing of options has been the subject of a large theoretical literature with a major contribution being made by Black and Scholes (1973). The Black-Scholes formula has been modified for foreign exchange options by Garman and Kohlhagen (1983) [see also Giddy (1983)], but the Black-Scholes formula is complex and beyond the scope of the present paper.

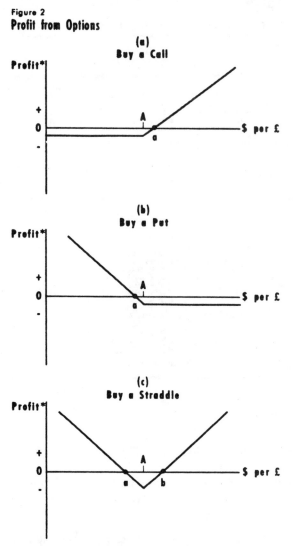

Figure 2
Profit from Options

(a)
Buy a Call

(b)
Buy a Put

(c)
Buy a Straddle

*Profit from exercise of option at current spot exchange rate.

One simple relationship which is of interest may be called "option price parity." This arises because arbitrage will ensure that the difference between a call option price (per unit) and a put option price (per unit) at the same exercise price will be equal to the present value of the difference between the exercise price and the forward exchange rate at maturity of the options (if the options are marketable, it will also hold for any date to maturity). The relationship may be expressed:

$$C - P = \frac{F - E}{1 + r},$$

when C and P are the call and put option prices at exercise price E. F is the forward exchange rate and r is the interest rate per period of the contracts. This arises because the simultaneous buying of a call and selling of a put is equivalent to buying currency forward at price E. The forward contract, however, would be paid for at the end of the period, whereas the options are transacted at the beginning. Hence, the forward contract has to be discounted back to the present.

able from buying a call option at exercise price A. At spot exchange rate A and anything lower, the option will not be exercised so the loss will equal the price of the option. At a spot exchange rate above a, the option is sufficiently in the money to more than cover its cost. Between A and a, the option is in the money but not by enough to cover cost. The profit from *selling* a call could be illustrated by reversing the + and − signs in figure 2a, or by flipping the profit line about the horizontal axis.

Figure 2b illustrates the profit from buying a put option. At spot exchange rates below a, the option with exercise price A will show a profit.

Figure 2c illustrates the profit from a simultaneous purchase of a put and call at the same exercise price. This combination will show a profit at exercise price A if the spot price goes *either* above b or below a. It is known as a "straddle." The straddle is of special interest because it makes clear the role of options as a hedge against risk. The price of a straddle can be regarded as the market valuation of the variability of the exchange rate. That is, the buyer of the straddle will show a profit if the spot price moves from some central value (the exercise price) by more than plus or minus some known percentage. The seller of the straddle accepts that risk for a lump sum. More complicated "multiple strategies" are also possible.[2]

---

[2]See Giddy (1983).

Two major classes of activity will be discussed. First, the existence of a large number of foreign exchange markets in many locations creates opportunities to profit from "arbitrage." Second, there is implicitly a market in (foreign exchange) risk bearing. Those who wish to avoid foreign exchange risk (at a price) may do so. Those who accept the risk in expectation of profits are known as "speculators."

Triangular Arbitrage

Triangular arbitrage is the process that ensures that all exchange rates are mutually consistent. If, for example, one U.S. dollar exchanges for one Canadian dollar, and one Canadian dollar exchanges for one British pound, then the U.S. dollar-pound exchange rate should be one pound for one dollar. If it differs, then there is an opportunity for profit making. To see why this is so, suppose that you could purchase two U.S. dollars with one British pound. By first buying C$1 with U.S.$1, then purchasing £1 with C$1, and finally buying U.S.$2 with £1, you could double your money immediately. Clearly this opportunity will not last for long since it involves making large profits with certainty. The process of triangular arbitrage is exactly that of finding and exploiting profitable opportunities in such exchange rate inconsistencies. As a result of triangular arbitrage, such inconsistencies will be eliminated rapidly. Cross rates, however, will only be roughly consistent given the bid-ask spread associated with transaction costs.

In the past, the possibility of making profits from triangular arbitrage was greater as a result of the practice of expressing exchange rates in American terms in the United States and in European terms elsewhere. The adoption of standard practice has reduced the likelihood of inconsistencies.[7] Also, in recent years, such opportunities for profit making have been greatly reduced by high-speed, computerized information systems and the increased sophistication of the banks operating in the market.

Arbitrage of a slightly different kind results from price differences in different locations. This is "space" arbitrage. For example, if sterling were cheaper in London than in New York, it would be profitable to buy in London and sell in New York. Similarly, if prices in the interbank market differed from those at the IMM, it would be profitable to arbitrage between them. As a result of this activity, prices in different locations will be brought broadly into line.

Interest Arbitrage

Interest arbitrage is slightly different in nature from triangular or space arbitrage; however, the basic motive of finding and exploiting profitable opportunities still applies. There is no reason why interest rates denominated in different currencies should be equal. Interest rates are the cost of borrowing or the return to lending for a specific period of time. The relative price (exchange rate) of money may change over time so that the comparison of, say, a U.S. and a British interest rate requires some allowance for expected exchange rate changes. Thus, it will be not at all unusual to find

---

[7]All except U.K. and Irish exchange rates are expressed in American terms. Futures and options contracts are expressed in European terms.

interest rates denominated in dollars and interest rates denominated in, say, pounds being somewhat different. However, real returns on assets of similar quality should be the same if the exchange rate risk is covered or hedged in the forward market. Were this not true, it would be possible to borrow in one currency and lend in another at a profit with no exchange risk.

Suppose we lend one dollar for a year in the United States at an interest rate of r_{us}. The amount accumulated at the end of the year per dollar lent will be $1 + r_{us}$ (capital plus interest). If, instead of making dollar loans, we converted them into pounds and lent them in the United Kingdom at the rate r_{uk}, the amount of pounds we would have for each original dollar at the end of the year would be $S(1 + r_{uk})$, where S is the spot exchange rate (in pounds per dollar) at the beginning of the period. At the outset, it is not known if $1 + r_{us}$ dollars is going to be worth more than $S(1 + r_{uk})$ pounds in a year's time because the spot exchange rate in a year's time is unknown. This uncertainty can be avoided by selling the pounds forward into dollars. Then the relative value of the two loans would no longer depend on what subsequently happens to the spot exchange rate. By doing this, we end up with $\frac{S}{F}(1 + r_{uk})$ dollars per original dollar invested. This is known as the "covered," or hedged, return on pounds.

Since the covered return in our example is denominated in dollars, it can reasonably be compared with the U.S. interest rate. If these returns are very different, investors will move funds where the return is highest on a covered basis. This process is interest arbitrage. It is assumed that the assets involved are equally safe and, because the returns are covered, all exchange risk is avoided. Of course, if funds do move in large volume between assets or between financial centers, then interest rates and the exchange rates (spot and forward) will change in predictable ways. Funds will continue to flow between countries until there is no extra profit to be made from interest arbitrage. This will occur when the returns on both dollar- and sterling-denominated assets are equal, that is, when

(1) $\quad (1 + r_{us}) = \frac{S}{F}(1 + r_{uk})$.

This result is known as covered interest parity. It holds more or less exactly, subject only to a margin due to transaction costs, so long as the appropriate dollar and sterling interest rates are compared.[8]

Speculation

Arbitrage in the foreign exchange markets involves little or no risk since transactions can be completed rapidly. An alternative source of profit is available from outguessing other market participants as to what future exchange rates will be. This is called speculation. Although any foreign exchange transaction that is not entirely hedged forward has a speculative element, only deliberate speculation for profit is discussed here.

Until recently, the main foreign exchange speculators were the foreign exchange departments of banks, with a lesser role being played by portfolio managers of other financial institutions and international corporations. The IMM, however, has made it much easier for individuals and smaller businesses to speculate. A high proportion of IMM transactions appears to be speculative in the sense that only about 5 percent of contracts lead to ultimate delivery of foreign exchange. This means that most of the activity involves the buying and selling of a contract *at different times* and possibly different prices prior to maturity. It is possible, however, that buying and selling of contracts before maturity would arise out of a strategy to reduce risk. So it is not possible to say that all such activity is speculative.

Speculation is important for the efficient working of foreign exchange markets. It is a form of arbitrage that occurs across time rather than across space or between markets at the same time. Just as arbitrage increases the efficiency of markets by keeping prices consistent, so speculation increases the efficiency of forward, futures and options markets by keeping those markets liquid. Those who wish to avoid foreign exchange risk may thereby do so in a well-developed market. Without speculators, risk avoidance in foreign exchange markets would be more difficult and, in many cases, impossible.[9]

Risk Reduction

Speculation clearly involves a shifting of risk from one party to another. For example, if a bank buys for-

---

[8]Since there are many different interest rates, it obviously cannot hold for all of them. Where (1) does hold is if the interest rates chosen are eurocurrency deposit rates of the same duration. In other words, if for

r_{us} we take, say, the three-month eurodollar deposit rate in Paris and for r_{uk} we take the three-month eurosterling deposit rate in Paris, then (1) will hold just about exactly. Indeed, if we took the interest rate and exchange rate quotes all from the same bank, it would be remarkable if (1) did not hold. Otherwise the bank would be offering to pay you to borrow from it and lend straight back! That is, the price of borrowing would be less than the covered return on lending. A margin between borrowing and lending rates, of course, will make this even less likely so that in reality you would lose.

[9]This is not to say that all speculative activity is necessarily beneficial.

Covered Interest Parity: An Example

The following interest rate and exchange rate quotations are taken from the *London Financial Times* of September 8, 1983 (table 1).

Closing Exchange Rate: dollars per pound	Spot	3-Month Forward
	1.4910–1.4920	.17–.22 discount

Interest Rates: 3-Month Offer Rate	Eurosterling	Eurodollar
	$9^{13}/_{16}$	$10^{1}/_{4}$

The interest rate on the three-month eurodollar deposit is a little higher (.7 percent) than that on an eurosterling deposit. If the exchange rate remains unchanged, it would be better to hold dollars; if the exchange rate falls, the eurosterling deposit would be preferable. Suppose you decide to cover the exchange risk by selling the dollars forward into pounds. Let us compare the return to holding a sterling deposit with the return to holding a dollar deposit sold forward into sterling (assuming that you start with sterling).

Two important points need to be clarified about the above data. First, the interest rates are annualized so they are not what would actually be earned over a three-month period. For example, the three-month rate equivalent to an annual rate of $10^{1}/_{4}$ percent is 2.47 percent.

Second, the forward exchange rates need some explanation. The dollar is at a discount against sterling. This means the forward dollar buys less sterling. So we have to *add* the discount onto the spot price to get the forward price (because the price is the number of dollars per pound, not the reverse). Notice also that the discount is measured in fractions of a cent, not fractions of a dollar! So the bid-ask spread on the forward rate would be 1.4927 – 1.4942.

Now let us see if we would do better to invest in a three-month eurosterling deposit or a three-month eurodollar deposit where the dollars to be received were sold forward into sterling. The return per £100 invested in eurosterling is £2.369 (annual interest rate of $9^{13}/_{16}$), whereas the return on a covered eurodollar deposit is

$$£2.251 = (100 \times \frac{1.4910}{1.4942} \ 1.0247) - 100.$$

Thus, we could not make a profit out of covered interest arbitrage. Despite the fact that dollar interest rates are higher, the discount on forward dollars in the forward market means they buy fewer forward pounds. As a result, there is no benefit to the operation. Transaction costs for most individuals would be even greater than those above as they would face a larger bid-ask spread than that quoted on the interbank market.

Consequently, there is no benefit for the typical investor from making a covered or hedged eurocurrency deposit. The return will be at least as high on a deposit in the currency in which you start and wish to end up. That is, if you have dollars and wish to end up with dollars, make a eurodollar deposit. If you have sterling and wish to end up with sterling, make a eurosterling deposit. If you have sterling and wish to end up in dollars, there is likely to be little or no difference between holding a eurosterling deposit sold forward into dollars or buying dollars spot and holding a eurodollar deposit. Of course, if you hold an "uncovered" deposit and exchange rates subsequently change, the result will be very different.

ward foreign exchange from a customer, it increases its exposure to risk while the customer reduces his. However, there is not a fixed amount of risk that has to be "shared out." Some strategies may involve a net reduction of risk all around.

As a general rule, financial institutions (or other firms), operating in a variety of currencies, will try to minimize the risk of losses due to unexpected exchange rate changes. One simple way to do this is to ensure that assets and liabilities denominated in each operating currency are equal. This is known as "matching." For example, a bank that sells sterling forward to a customer may simultaneously buy sterling forward. In this event, the bank is exposed to zero exchange rate risk.

Banks often use "swaps" to close gaps in the maturity structure of their assets and liabilities in a currency. This involves the simultaneous purchase and sale of a currency for *different* maturity dates. In April 1983, 33 percent of U.S. banks' foreign exchange turn-

Why Is the Dollar the "Money" of Foreign Exchange Markets?

One interesting aspect of the organization of the foreign exchange markets is that the "money" used in these markets is generally the U.S. dollar. This is generally true for spot markets and universally true for forward markets. "Cross-markets" between many currencies are very thin, and future cross markets are virtually nonexistent. For example, the bulk of foreign exchange trading between £s and cruzeiro will involve dollar-£ and dollar-cruzeiro transactions instead of direct £-cruzeiro trading. The only exception to this is the transactions involving the major Organization for Economic Cooperation and Development (OECD) currencies, especially within Europe. Of the $702.5 billion turnover in foreign exchange reported by U.S. banks in April 1983, only $1.5 billion did not involve U.S. dollars.

There are two explanations for this special role of the dollar in foreign exchange markets. Both rely upon the fact that transaction costs are likely to be lower if the dollar is used as a medium. Krugman shows that the clearing of foreign exchange markets requires some "intermediary" currency.[1] Even if ev-

ery country is in payments balance vis a vis the rest of the world, it will not necessarily be in bilateral balance with each other country. Because some currency has to be used to cover this residual finance, it is natural to choose the currency that has the lowest transaction costs. Chrystal shows there are economic reasons why cross-markets between many currencies do not exist.[2] It typically will be easier and cheaper to set up a deal in two steps via the dollar than in a single step (cruzeiro-dollar, dollar-drachma rather than cruzeiro-drachma). This is because these cross-markets, if they existed, would be fairly thin and hence relatively costly for such transactions. The two markets with the dollar, on the other hand, are well developed.

These analyses refer to the role of the dollar in the interbank market. In the development of the trading places such as the IMM in Chicago and LIFFE in London to date, it is also true that all currency futures are traded against the dollar.

[1]See Krugman (1980).

[2]See Chrystal (1982).

---

over involved swaps as compared with 63 percent spot contracts and only 4 percent outright forward contracts.[10]

Suppose a bank has sold DM to a customer three months forward and bought the same amount of DM from a different customer six months forward. There are two ways in which the bank could achieve zero foreign exchange risk exposure. It could either undertake two separate offsetting forward transactions, or it could set up a single swap with another bank that has the opposite mismatch of dollar-DM flows whereby it receives DM in exchange for dollars in three months and receives back dollars in exchange for DM in six months. Once the swap is set up, the bank's net profits are protected against subsequent changes in spot exchange rates during the next six months.

Within the limits imposed by the nature of the contracts, a similar effect can be achieved by an appropriate portfolio of futures contracts on the IMM. Thus, a

[10]See Federal Reserve Bank of New York (1983).

bank would buy and sell futures contracts so as to match closely its forward commitments to customers. In reality, banks will use a combination of methods to reduce foreign exchange risk.

Markets that permit banks, firms and individuals to hedge foreign exchange risk are essential in times of fluctuating exchange rates. This is especially important for banks if they are to be able to provide efficient foreign exchange services for their customers. In the absence of markets that permit foreign exchange risk hedging, the cost and uncertainty of international transactions would be greatly increased, and international specialization and trade would be greatly reduced.

CONCLUSION

The foreign exchange markets are complex and, for the outsider, hard to comprehend. The primary function of these markets is straightforward. It is to facilitate international transactions related to trade, travel or investment. Foreign exchange markets can now accommodate a large range of current and forward transactions.

Given the variability of exchange rates, it is important for banks and firms operating in foreign currencies to be able to reduce exchange rate risk whenever possible. Some risk reduction is achieved by interbank swaps, but some is also taken up by speculation. Arbitrage and speculation both increase the efficiency of spot and forward foreign exchange markets and have enabled foreign exchange markets to achieve a high level of efficiency. Without the successful operation of these markets, the obstacles to international trade and investment would be substantial and the world would be a poorer place.

REFERENCES

Belongia, Michael T. "Commodity Options: A New Risk Management Tool for Agricultural Markets," this *Review* (June/July 1983), pp. 5–15.

Black, Fisher, and Myron Scholes. "The Pricing of Options and Corporate Liabilities," *Journal of Political Economy* (May/June 1973), pp. 637–54.

Chrystal, K. Alec. "On the Theory of International Money" (paper presented to U.K. International Economics Study Group Conference, September 1982, Sussex, England). Forthcoming in J. Black and G. S. Dorrance, eds., *Problems of International Finance* (London: Macmillan, 1984).

Dufey, Gunter, and Ian H. Giddy. *The International Money Market* (Prentice-Hall, 1978).

Federal Reserve Bank of New York. "Summary of Results of U.S. Foreign Exchange Market Turnover Survey Conducted in April 1983" (September 8, 1983).

Garman, Mark B., and Steven W. Kohlhagen. "Foreign Currency Option Values," *Journal of International Money and Finance* (December 1983), pp. 231–37.

Giddy, Ian H. "Foreign Exchange Options," *Journal of Futures Markets* (Summer 1983), pp. 143–66.

Krugman, Paul. "Vehicle Currencies and the Structure of International Exchange," *Journal of Money, Credit and Banking* (August 1980), pp. 513–26.

Kubarych, Roger M. *Foreign Exchange Markets in the United States.* (Federal Reserve Bank of New York, 1983).

McKinnon, Ronald I. *Money in International Exchange: The Convertible Currency System* (Oxford University Press, 1979).

Glossary

American option — an option that can be exercised any time up to maturity.

American terms — an exchange rate expressed as number of currency units per dollar.

arbitrage — the simultaneous purchase and sale of currency in separate markets for a profit arising from a price discrepancy between the markets.

bid-ask spread — the difference between the buying (bid) and selling (ask) price.

covered interest arbitrage — buying a country's currency spot, investing for a period, and selling the proceeds forward in order to make a net profit due to the higher interest rate in that country. This act involves "hedging" because it guarantees a covered return without risk. The opportunities to profit in this way seldom arise because covered interest differentials are normally close to zero.

covered interest parity — the gap between interest rates in foreign and domestic currencies will be matched by the forward exchange rate differential, such that the "covered" interest rate differential will be close to zero.

eurodollar deposits — bank deposits, generally bearing interest and made for a specific time period, that are denominated in dollars but are in banks outside the United States. Similarly, euro-sterling deposits would be denominated in sterling but outside the United Kingdom.

European option — an option that can be exercised only on a specified date.

European terms — an exchange rate expressed as number of dollars per currency unit.

floating exchange rate — an exchange rate that is allowed to adjust freely to the supply of and demand for foreign exchange.

foreign exchange speculation — the act of taking a net position in a foreign currency with the intention of making a profit from exchange rate changes.

forward exchange rate — the price of foreign currency for delivery at a future date agreed to by a contract today.

futures market — a market in which contracts are traded to buy or sell a standard amount of currency in the future at a particular price.

hedging — or covering exchange risk, means that foreign currency is sold forward into local currency so that its value is not affected by subsequent exchange rate changes. Say an exporter knows he will be paid £10,000 in two months. He can wait until he gets the money and convert it into dollars at whatever the spot rate turns out to be. This outcome is uncertain as the spot rate may change. Alternatively, he can sell £10,000 two months forward at today's two-month forward price. Suppose this is $1.5 per £. In two months, he will receive £10,000, fulfill his forward contract and receive $15,000. This export contract has been hedged or covered in the forward market.

matching — equating assets and liabilities denominated in each currency so that losses due to foreign exchange rate changes are minimized.

options market — a market in which contracts are traded that gives a purchaser the right but no obligation to buy (call) or to sell (put) a currency in the future at a given price.

spot exchange rate — the price paid to exchange currencies for immediate delivery (two business days in the interbank market, or over the counter in the retail and travelers check market).

swap — the simultaneous purchase and sale of a currency for different maturity dates that closes the gaps in the maturity structure of assets and liabilities in a currency.

Article Thirty-Five

Distinguished Lecture on Economics in Government: Thinking About International Economic Coordination

Martin S. Feldstein

I should perhaps begin these remarks by emphasizing that I am not opposed to international cooperation in economic affairs. We as economists recognize that conflict in international trade and the development of protectionist policies would reduce the standard of living around the world. Moreover, the immediate effect of a shift to protectionism could be a major worldwide recession.

The quiet exchange of macroeconomic forecasts and policy plans among government officials that occurs within the framework of the Bank for International Settlements, the OECD, the Group of 7 (the United States, Great Britain, France, Germany, Japan, Italy and Canada) and elsewhere plays an important role in the formulation of domestic economic policies. It is also important for maintaining friendly working relationships among governments that senior officials are not surprised by major policy shifts abroad.

I start with these obvious remarks and with the assertion that I am not opposed to international cooperation in all economic matters because I do not want to be misunderstood when, as in this lecture, I stress the counterproductive consequences of the international coordination of macroeconomic policy.

I do not deny that the economies of the world are linked in a way that makes the monetary and budget policies adopted in one country affect the economic performance of other countries. But I believe that many of the claimed advantages of cooperation and coordination are wrong, that there are substantial risks and disadvantages to the types of coordination that are envisioned, and that an emphasis on international coordination can distract attention from the necessary changes in domestic policy. Moreover, the attempt to pursue coordination in a wide range of macroeconomic policies is likely to result in disagreements and disappointments that

■ *Martin Feldstein is Professor of Economics, Harvard University, and President, National Bureau of Economic Research, both in Cambridge, Massachusetts.*

reduce the prospects for cooperation in those more limited areas of trade, defense and foreign assistance where international cooperation is actually necessary.[1]

In stressing the limited scope for the international coordination of macroeconomic policy and exchange rates, I do not wish to imply that such action is never appropriate. Far from it. There are some small and very interdependent countries where such coordination should undoubtedly be the general rule. There are also some conditions when the potential gains from coordination are such that all countries could expect to benefit from participation. But the active coordination of the macroeconomic policies and of exchange rates among the United States, Japan and Germany will generally be inappropriate. Moreover, as I shall explain in these remarks, the United States is particularly unsuited to participate in an ongoing process of economic coordination.

The Management of Exchange Rates

After less than a decade of floating exchange rates, the sharp rise in the value of the dollar during the early 1980s caused a renewed interest in the possibility of the international management of exchange rates and even of a return to a system of fixed exchange rates. The rise in the real value of the dollar was the primary reason why the United States shifted from a trade surplus in 1981 to a massive trade deficit by 1986. It is not surprising, therefore, that American businesses and their workers in the wide range of industries hurt by the strong dollar called for government action to stop and reverse the dollar's rise.

Until September 1985, the Reagan Administration argued that the value of the dollar should be left to the market and that it was inappropriate to shift U.S. domestic economic policy or to intervene in currency markets in an attempt to alter the dollar's value. This was a continuing source of conflict with the European and Japanese governments that did not like the dollar's rise because of the inflationary pressures that it imparted to their own economies, the rising real interest rates that resulted from the capital outflow to the United States, and the increased support for protectionist trade policies that was developing in the United States because of the surging U.S. trade deficit.

---

[1] My criticisms of international macroeconomic coordination were sketched first in an article that I wrote for the Economist magazine ("The World Economy Today," June 11, 1983). Earlier versions of the current lecture were presented as one of my two 1986 Horowitz Memorial Lectures of the Bank of Israel and as a lecture on the fiftieth anniversary of Nuffield College, Oxford (see Feldstein, forthcoming). The general subject of international economic cooperation (in macroeconomic policy, exchange rate policy, international trade and developing country debt management) was unexplored at an April 1987 conference of the National Bureau of Economic Research. The conference volume presents valuable survey papers, personal comments by individuals who have had significant experience in government and business, and an extensive bibliography that makes it unnecessary to provide such references in the current talk; my own views are summarized in an introductory chapter. The interested reader may also wish to see Feldstein (1987b; forthcoming a, b).

The Plaza Hotel meeting of the finance ministers of the G-5 countries (United States, Great Britain, France, Germany and Japan) in September 1985 was a political watershed in this process. Faced with the reality that the dollar had been declining for more than six months, Treasury Secretary James Baker abandoned the previous Treasury position that the strong dollar was a measure of foreign investors' approval of the economic policies of the United States. He acknowledged publicly that the high value of the dollar was a serious problem for American industry. And, most surprisingly and significantly of all, he agreed to participate in coordinated exchange market intervention aimed at lowering the dollar's value.

Immediately after the Plaza meeting the United States did join with other countries in a major exchange market intervention, selling dollars and buying other currencies. The Japanese central bank also raised short-term interest rates temporarily in order to make yen denominated bonds a more attractive investment and thereby to stimulate the demand for the yen.

Exchange rate targeting and economic policy coordination aimed at achieving desired levels of the exchange rates have been a frequent theme of intergovernmental meetings since that time. The finance ministers of the G-7 countries met at the Louvre in February 1987 to assert their belief in macroeconomic coordination and to call for exchange rate stability. They reaffirmed this call at the June 1987 Venice summit and the September 1987 IMF-World Bank meeting. In more recent days (November and December 1987), European and Japanese government officials have repeated their case for coordinated actions to achieve a stable value of the dollar and a new G-7 communique calling for a stable dollar has been issued.

In contrast to these assertions, I believe that the dollar must continue to decline because the future trade deficit implied by the dollar's current level would be too large to finance otherwise. Experts estimate that without a further decline of the dollar the U.S. trade deficit will remain at more than $100 billion a year and the current account deficit will grow explosively because of the interest and dividends owed on the U.S. net borrowing from abroad. Only a decline of the dollar can achieve the change in the relative prices of American and foreign goods that can induce American consumers to import less and foreign consumers to buy more American-made goods. The more rapid growth in Japan and Europe that the finance ministers continually stress as an alternative to a dollar decline simply cannot be powerful enough to make a significant dent in the U.S. trade deficit. Similarly, while a decline of the American budget deficit would help to shrink the U.S. trade deficit, it would do so by lowering U.S. interest rates which in turn would reduce the value of the dollar; a decline in the budget deficit, while essential for other reasons, is not an alternative to a decline in the dollar as a means of shrinking the trade deficit. (A longer nontechnical discussion of why the dollar must decline is presented in Feldstein, 1987a.)

I believe that the pursuit of exchange rate goals is likely to be both futile and economically damaging, not just in the current circumstances but more generally as well. In the short term, as the experience of October 1987 painfully demonstrated, the expectation that monetary policy would tighten to defend artificial exchange rate levels can destabilize financial markets. The fear that the Fed would push rates even higher than they were in early October—to offset the downward pressure on the dollar that resulted from the unfavorable trade news of October 14th—was one of the key factors that triggered the stock market crash. Over an extended period of time, the primary risk in the pursuit of exchange rate targets is an increase in the rate of inflation in every country. A policy of targeting exchange rates can also hurt the process of capital formation, weaken the capital goods and construction industries, and delay the recovery of the manufacturing industries that are hurt by an overvalued exchange rate.

Nominal and Real Exchange Rates

To understand the likely effects of an exchange rate policy, it is crucial to distinguish between changes in nominal exchange rates and changes in real exchange rates. The change in the nominal exchange rate between two countries is the change in the actual exchange rate that prevails in the market. The change in the real exchange rate is equal to the change in nominal exchange rate adjusted for differences in the inflation rates in the two countries. It is, of course, the real value of the currency that influences the competitiveness of the country's products and thus its exports and imports. This point is worth emphasizing for two reasons.

First, the political discussion about exchange rate targets, target zones and exchange rate management are always in terms of the nominal exchange rates. Therefore even if the politically agreed upon exchange rate targets were achieved and maintained, the relative competitiveness of the countries could change substantially because differences in inflation rates would cause the real exchange rates to change. In short, exchange rate management is likely to be misguided because it focuses on the wrong target.

Second, economic policies that change a country's rate of inflation can easily alter nominal exchange rates without changing the real exchange rates. Therefore, there is a serious danger that an agreement to stabilize exchange rates would lead to increased inflation without any change in the real exchange rates that influence imports and exports.

Consider, for example, the sharp rise in the real value of the dollar that began in 1980 because of the massive increase in current and projected U.S. budget deficits. Reversing the budget deficit could have prevented the dollar's rise or caused it to decline at an earlier time. But on the basis of my experience as a participant in the making of American economic policy at that time, I do not believe that an exchange rate agreement would have produced such a change in budget policy. The Reagan administration was already trying to reduce the budget deficit by a strategy that combined major domestic spending cuts with a conditional tax increase. There is no reason to think that it would have taken a more conciliatory position with Congress in order to deal with the high dollar. Treasury Secretary Regan apparently believed that the budget deficit had no effect on the dollar. In addition, many experts both inside and outside the government argued that the strong dollar showed only that monetary policy was too tight and therefore argued in favor of depressing the dollar by a monetary expansion.

If the United States had agreed in 1983 to stop the dollar's rise, the easiest way would have been for the Federal Reserve to ease monetary policy. The easier monetary policy would have temporarily lowered real interest rates and that in turn would have caused a temporary decline in the real value of the dollar. More importantly, the easier monetary policy would produce inflation and the inflation would cause the dollar's nominal value to decline. In the end, there would have been no change in the real exchange rate or the trade deficit but a higher price level and a high rate of inflation.

Of course, there are two sides to every exchange rate and the relative value of the dollar could have been depressed by a tightening of monetary policy in Europe and Japan that lowered the inflation rates in those countries. There was in fact some tightening of monetary policy in Europe in response to the rising dollar, but that process was inevitably limited by the increased unemployment that resulted from such a monetary contraction. Political reality would inevitably have required that a change in monetary policy to stabilize the dollar be an inflationary easing by the United States rather than a deflationary tightening in the other countries of the world.

The current attempts to slow the rise of the yen and the German mark provide a further example of the risk that exchange rate coordination is likely to be inflationary. The process of intervention in both Germany and Japan has led to very rapid increases in the money supply and in overall liquidity. This had increased the fear of inflation and raised long-term interest rates in both countries. Although the governments of Germany and Japan have asked the United States to raise interest rates as an alternative way of maintaining the value of the dollar, the U.S. has been reluctant to do so in the context of a recovery that has already lasted five years and with an election this year. Although the German and Japanese intervention has not yet produced any significant rise in inflation, a continuation of the associated increases in money and overall liquidity for an extended period would undoubtedly begin to do so.

Gains and Losses of an Overstrong Dollar

There are of course some who believe that the real value of the dollar can be influenced by exchange market intervention alone. Before considering whether such a policy could be expected to work, it is useful to ask whether stabilizing the dollar would in itself have been desirable in today's world economy.

Stopping the rise in the dollar's real value in early 1983 would have reduced the subsequent U.S. trade deficit. Output and employment would have deteriorated less in our export industries and in those firms that compete with imports from abroad. But that is only half of the story. The reduced trade deficit would automatically have meant a reduced capital inflow from abroad. Real interest rates would have been higher in the United States. Investment in plant and equipment and housing construction would have been depressed. The pattern of employment would have been different, but there is no reason to suppose that total employment and output would have been higher. Moreover, the lower rate of capital formation would have reduced the growth of productivity.

In short, stopping the dollar's rise earlier would have had both good and bad effects on the American economy. There is no way to know whether the favorable effects on the export industries and firms that compete with imports would have outweighed the adverse effects on capital investment. I believe that in the absence of clear evidence or analysis to the contrary, it is best to assume that the market produces a better solution than government intervention. That is as true about exchange market intervention as it is about so many other aspects of government interference with the market economy.

The same principle is relevant today. If intervention per se could stop the dollar's fall at the present time, that would contribute to U.S. price stability and would maintain a flow of capital from abroad that dampens real interest rates and provides the funds to finance additional investment in housing and in plant and equipment. But the high dollar would also limit the improvement in the trade deficit, depressing activity in export industries and those that compete with imports from abroad. Ultimately, moreover, the dollar's adjustment would have to occur and would have to be larger because the dollar had contributed to a greater accumulation of net debt from the United States to the rest of the world.

Exchange Market Intervention

Although substantial past experience and economic logic both imply that sterilized exchange market intervention (i.e., currency intervention with no change in domestic monetary policy) cannot be expected to have a sustained effect on exchange rates, the fall of the dollar in the year after the G-5 finance ministers meeting at the Plaza Hotel in September 1985 and the relative stability of the dollar in the seven months after the Louvre meeting in February 1987 have led some government officials and others to attribute significant power to coordinated exchange rate intervention. I believe that conclusion is a misreading of the recent experience.

There is in fact no evidence that the G-5 Plaza meeting or the subsequent coordinated intervention had any lasting effect on the dollar's rate of decline. In the days immediately after the G-5 meeting there was a four percent decline in the dollar's value. But the rate of decline of the dollar during the subsequent year was no greater than it had been in the six months before the G-5 meeting.

Immediately after the Louvre meeting the central banks were able to prevent the dollar's continued decline by a combination of massive intervention and the threat of even more intervention in the future. But after a short time, continued stabilizing of the dollar required a significant rise in U.S. interest rates relative to interest rates in Japan and Germany. The resulting tight monetary policy in the United States and the fear of further Fed tightening in response to market pressure for a lower dollar were important causes of the stock market crash. As soon as the United States declared that monetary policy would no longer be directed at stabilizing the dollar, the dollar's value responded to market pressures and began to decline sharply. The experience in 1987 thus again demonstrates the inability of intervention to shift currency values for more than a very short time.

The Coordination of Macroeconomic Policies

Coordinated exchange rate intervention is only one aspect of the potential coordination of macroeconomic policies. Indeed there are many who accept that exchange rate intervention per se is powerless and who therefore argue for a more general coordination of monetary and budget policies. The Tokyo summit in May 1986 emphasized such macroeconomic coordination and called for a new "multilateral surveillance" procedure managed by the International Monetary Fund.

The first such multilateral surveillance session was held in conjunction with the IMF annual meetings in September 1986. The agenda was predictable. The United States called on Japan and the European countries to expand their economies more rapidly in order to increase their imports from the United States. The Europeans and Japan called on the United States to reduce its budget deficit and to slow the decline of the dollar relative to their currencies, an inherently self-contradictory request. No serious agreements were reached. The Germans explained that their economy was expanding rapidly, that their monetary policy was if anything too loose already, and that a tax cut was scheduled for 1988. The Japanese noted that they were moving gradually toward fundamental changes in their economy and Treasury Secretary Baker said the United States was committed to eliminating the budget deficit over the next five years as promised in the Gramm-Rudman-Hollings legislation. In short, every country said it would go on doing just what it had been doing. And, despite the subsequent pronouncements at the Louvre meeting and the Venice summit, each country continued to pursue what it saw as its own interest, generally unaffected by the "international coordination" process.

Only when the government of Japan became convinced in early 1987 that the sharp rise in the yen-dollar rate during 1986 would create a serious downturn for the Japanese economy did Japan abandon its goal of budget deficit reduction and adopt a package of fiscal and monetary stimulus. In contrast, Germany, despite its high unemployment and zero inflation rate, has not adopted any significant expansionary policies because of a government decision to give primacy to preventing inflation and to reducing domestic labor market rigidities. And the $70 billion decline in the U.S. budget deficit between 1986 and 1987 was not the result of international actions but of domestic politics and the peculiarities of budget accounting. This failure of the summit and other international coordination discussions to achieve any changes in domestic economic policies should not be seen as a surprise or as a reflection of the fact that the process of explicit coordination only began in 1986. It should be seen as the most likely outcome of all such meetings. The experience at and immediately after the September 1987 IMF-World Bank meetings again demonstrated the emptiness of the coordination process and the inclination of major governments to pursue their own self interests.

Constitutional Limits on American Participation

A primary reason why macroeconomic policy coordination cannot work as envisioned by its advocates is that the United States is constitutionally incapable of participating in such a negotiation. The separation of powers in the American form of government means that the Secretary of the Treasury cannot promise to reduce or expand the budget deficit or to change tax rules. This power does not rest with the president or the administration but depends on a legislative agreement between the president and the Congress. In this sense, the United States' participation in any macroeconomic coordination process is fundamentally different from the participation of a country with a parliamentary system in which the prime minister or the prime minister's representative can commit to a change in the nation's economic policy.

It is sometimes suggested that an American Treasury secretary or president, although incapable of promising the enactment of specific budget legislation, could promise that the American government would support a particular legislative proposal. Such a suggestion ignores the negotiating nature of the relation between the president and the Congress. The president cannot propose the legislative package that he expects Congress to enact and he cannot disclose the extent to which he is willing to compromise on specific issues.

Because it is impossible for the United States to reach an international agreement on specific budget, tax or spending policies, any actual agreement would have to call for a change in U.S. monetary policy. International economic coordination could thus be a recipe for the wrong policy change in the United States. For example, if the United States had entered into an agreement in 1983 or 1984 to shift policy in a way that reduced the value of the dollar, the agreement would have required an inflationary increase in the supply of money. At the present time, the finance ministers of other major industrial countries are urging the United States to defend the dollar by a tight monetary policy that could push the U.S. economy into an unnecessary recession. Moreover, even agreements on monetary policy would be beyond the legal authority of the Treasury secretary or the president since it would require the concurrence of the independent Federal Reserve.

Even if the United States could participate effectively in international macroeconomic coordination, I believe that the incentive for the United States and other major industrial countries to do so is more apparent than real. Uncertainties about the actual state of the international economy and uncertainties about the effects of one country's policies on the economies of other countries make it impossible to be confident that coordinated policy shifts would actually be beneficial. The Germans still remember and regret their agreement to serve as a "locomotive" for worldwide expansion after the 1978 Bonn summit meeting. Today the Germans argue that foreign pressure for more expansionary German policy exaggerates the potentially favorable effects of such a change on foreign economies and ignores both the underlying strength of German demand and the need to achieve structural reforms in the German labor market as a precondition for reduced unemployment. A few years ago U.S. Treasury Secretary Regan argued that foreign pressure for the United States to reduce its budget deficit was misplaced because budget deficits do not influence interest rates, exchange rates and capital flows. When there are fundamental disagreements about the way the world economy works, there is little reason to believe that coordinated policy will produce improved performance.

It is important to remember that to a very great extent a nation has the ability to achieve its economic goals by itself. Although the levels of demand, inflation, and interest rates in one country do affect the economies elsewhere, a country can manage its own monetary, budget and tax policies to offset many of the potential influences from abroad. Thus changes in domestic monetary policy can counteract the contractionary or inflationary pressures from abroad and structural tax policies designed to encourage investment can offset the effects of a worldwide rise in real interest rates.

There is also a serious risk that economic summits and ministerial meetings will inhibit appropriate changes in national economic policies. Governments may not take the politically painful steps that they should because they believe that foreign actions will make such policies unnecessary or because they want to use their own lack of action as part of a bargaining strategy to induce desired policies on the part of foreign governments. Thus the assertion at the Louvre ministerial and at the Venice summit that the dollar would stop declining may have contributed to a complacency that reduced pressure on the German government to provide adequate domestic stimulus and that may even have contributed to the failure of the American Congress to make greater progress in reducing future budget deficits.

Concluding Remarks

It is unfortunately easy and often politically convenient to exaggerate the potential gains from international economic coordination and to understate the ability of a nation to guide its own economic future. Our politicians and those of other leading countries should not be allowed to escape their responsibilities by blaming poor domestic economic performance on the policies pursued abroad. Similarly, it would be a serious mistake if the pursuit of international coordination in exchange markets and in macroeconomic policy management became an excuse for not pursuing appropriate domestic policies.

Washington's explicit recognition of its responsibility for America's economic future would also reassure a nation that has become unnecessarily frightened by the prospect that international economic coordination will collapse. Unfortunately, ever since the May 1986 summit the U.S. administration and the governments of the other industrial countries have emphatically asserted that international economic cooperation is crucial to a healthy international economy in general and to continued U.S. growth in particular. Since such assertions are not justified by the extent of the actual interdependence of the industrialized nations, Americans have been inappropriately worried about whether policy coordination would continue.

Because foreign governments will inevitably pursue the policies that they believe are in their own best interests, it was inevitable that the process of international coordination would eventually collapse. This began with the actions of the German and Japanese governments in early October and was underscored by the statements of Secretary Baker just before the market crash. But the real problem contributing to the market decline was not the collapse of international macroeconomic coordination per se, but the false impression created by governments that healthy expansion requires such international coordination. Moreover, what appeared as cooperation by the European governments in reducing interest rates since late October was motivated by their desire to offset the contractionary effects of the worldwide stock market declines and the falling dollar, rather than as a gesture of cooperation with the United States.

The United States should now explicitly but amicably abandon the policy of international coordination of macroeconomic policy. We should continue to cooperate with other countries by exchanging information about current and future policy decisions, but we should recognize explicitly that Japan and Germany have the right to pursue the monetary and fiscal policies that they believe are in their own best interests.

It is frightening to the American public and upsetting to our financial markets to believe that the fate of our economy depends on the decisions made in Bonn and Tokyo. Portfolio investors, business managers and the public in general need to be reassured that we are not hostages to foreign economic policies, that the United States is the master of its own economic destiny, and that our government can and will do what is needed to maintain healthy economic growth.

Although international coordination of macroeconomic policy-making sounds like a way to improve international relations more generally, there is a serious risk that it will have the opposite effect. An emphasis on international interdependence instead of sound domestic policies makes foreign governments the natural scapegoats for any poor economic performance. Pressing a foreign government to alter its domestic economic policies is itself a source of friction and the making of unkeepable promises can only lead to resentment. It would in general be far better if the major industrial countries concentrated on the pursuit of sound domestic economic policies and reserved the pursuit of international cooperation for those subjects like international trade and national security in which cooperation is truly essential.

■ *This article is a condensed version of the 1987 Distinguished Lecture on Economics in Government, Joint Session of the American Economic Association and the Society of Government Economists, Chicago, December 28, 1987. A copy of the full lecture is available from the author.*

References

Feldstein, Martin, "Correcting the Trade Deficit," *Foreign Affairs*, Spring 1987a, 795–806.

Feldstein, Martin, *International Economic Cooperation: Summary Report*, National Bureau of Economic Research, 1987b.

Feldstein, Martin, "Rethinking International Economic Cooperation," Oxford Economic Papers, forthcoming.

Feldstein, Martin, *International Economic Cooperation*, Chicago: University of Chicago Press.

Article Thirty-Six

C. FRED BERGSTEN: LOUVRE'S LESSON— THE WORLD NEEDS A NEW MONETARY SYSTEM

A prominent U.S. strategist says the post-Louvre crash shows the system needs more discipline, and argues that 'target zones' would provide it

ONE UNMISTAKABLE LESSON from the global turbulence of the past few years is the need for a new international monetary system.

The near-universal dissatisfaction with unmanaged floating led the Common Market countries to create the European Monetary System a decade ago; more recently, it has prompted the Group of Seven to launch a two-track reform effort—the "indicators" approach to coordination of national macroeconomic policies, and the use of "reference ranges" to limit exchange-rate fluctuations. The failures of both the floating-rate system and its predecessor, the Bretton Woods system of adjustable pegs—combined with the shortcomings of the reform efforts so far—underscore the need for new arrangements.

Unmanaged floating has failed on three crucial counts:

First, it permitted the dollar, the monetary system's key currency, to become overvalued by more than 40% at its peak in early 1985—double the overvaluation that finally destroyed the Bretton Woods system in 1973. The huge trade and financial imbalances triggered by the latest dollar misalignment were the primary cause of the bond market's plunge last spring and the stock market crashes last autumn. They continue to threaten the entire world economy.

Second, floating has failed in its primary job of preserving open markets for world trade. Protectionism has grown steadily throughout the 1980s, mainly in the U.S., but also in Europe and the developing world. There's a double asymmetry here: The overvaluation of currencies breeds import controls, which often remain intact even after the overvaluation is corrected; at the same time, undervaluation breeds protectionism because it generates artificial levels of exports that inevitably spawn demands for protection later after the undervaluation disappears. The endemic overshooting and undershooting under unmanaged floating can thus intensify protectionist pressures at an alarming pace, threatening the open world trading system.

C. FRED BERGSTEN

One paradox of the 1980s is that trade flows have become increasingly circumscribed while capital flows have been increasingly liberalized. There's a direct relationship between the two: In the absence of any systemic counterweights, the vastly greater volume of capital movements can push exchange rates far from their equilibrium levels in terms of trade flows and heighten protectionist pressures. The only way to maintain relative freedom for *both* trade and capital flows is to improve the monetary system so as to avoid large misalignments.

Mr. Bergsten, a former assistant Secretary of the Treasury, is director of the Institute for International Economics in Washington.

Third, floating has had no meaningful impact on the way governments conduct their own economic policies. Countries no longer have any serious international monetary obligations, even on paper. The International Monetary Fund has been rendered irrelevant for the industrial countries. Small, open economies instinctively take into account the international consequences of their actions, but the larger and more self-contained economies needn't do so. As a result, unbridled floating has permitted the the three largest countries—the United States, Japan and West Germany—to pursue diametrically opposite economic policies during the 1980s, leading to huge currency misalignments that have brought about today's massive external imbalances.

Some observers absolve the floating-rate system, instead blaming the misguided economic policies that countries are following. But this misses the point. No system is truly a system unless it has a serious effect on the policies in its member countries, at least to the point of forcing governments to consider the compatibility of their policies with those of their trading partners. The main purpose of any international regime is to push national policies toward sustainable global norms—for the

Bundesbank President Karl Otto Poehl has denounced proposals for the 'robotization' of policymaking with mechanisms and indicators. But Mr. Poehl is attacking a straw-man: No one but gold bugs is proposing that.

longer-run interests of the countries involved if not necessarily for the benefit of incumbent governments that have very short time horizons. No system can prevent governments from adopting inconsistent or irresponsible policies. But it's surely better to try to engineer more stable trade and capital patterns than to leave the process untended.

Countries cherish the "autonomy illusion" of nominal sovereignty over their economic policies. But growing interdependence has made real sovereignty more difficult to maintain. Yet the largest countries, particularly the United States, seem to need constant reminders that unilateral excursions, while successful for a while, always fail in the end—as Presidents Nixon, Carter and now Reagan have all learned. In light of the U.S.'s proclivity to exploit the absence of international rules to pursue disruptive policies, it's a mystery that the other major countries don't leap at offers by American officials—most recently by U.S. Treasury Secretary James Baker—to adopt international mechanisms that might restrain America's own temptations in the future.

The exchange-rate obligations of Bretton Woods and the EMS have worked well in warning countries about the international repercussions of their actions. So have the GATT rules on trade. The systemic flaw of unmanaged floating is that it lacks any such obligations.

In recognition of these problems, the Europeans began to create their own "zone of stability" in the late 1970s. The EMS has worked reasonably well in practice. It demonstrates that international rules can have a meaningful impact under economic conditions of the 1980s, which have changed dramatically from the 1950s and early 1960s, when the similar (but more rigid) Bretton Woods regime enjoyed its biggest success.

Moreover, the EMS has worked in the face of intra-EMS inflation rates and other key economic variables that have differed much more sharply than those of the U.S., Japan and West Germany. So the success of the EMS provides considerable encouragement that such an arrangement could work at the global level as well. To be sure, the EMS won't be subjected to sizable capital flows until the United Kingdom decides to join. But some Europeans, particularly the West Germans, seem to reject the notion of broadening the EMS's concepts to encompass a wider group of countries. Perhaps while Bonn and Frankfurt are confident that they can dominate the EMS, their policymakers fear West Germany couldn't continue to follow the domestic policies it wants as freely if it had to take account of global obligations.

The quest for a better monetary system began when the ideological floaters left the U.S. Treasury in early 1985. At the famous Plaza meeting that September, the Group of Five finance ministers acknowledged that—contrary to the assurances of the ideologues during the previous four years—policy convergence among the major industrial countries had not resulted in international monetary stability, and that direct governmental intervention was required. This reversal opened the door for constructive reform efforts. Beginning with the Tokyo Summit in May 1986, the Group of Seven created a set of economic indicators to provide benchmarks against which to measure the results of their efforts at policy coordination. Their goal was to enhance the prospects that countries' internal and external policy targets would be consistent with each other, and hopefully that the sum of the targets would both be consistent internationally and would promote stable growth for the world as a whole. Within the overall list of indicators, Secretary Baker noted on several occasions that the United States regarded the current account balance and the exchange rate as the most important.

The second reform track—the use of reference ranges for each of the major currencies—was far more important in actual operation, beginning with the Baker-Miyazawa accord on the yen-dollar rate in October 1986 and later the Louvre Accord in February 1987. The idea was to stabilize the currencies within fairly narrow ranges around the rates which existed at that time and then to adopt policy changes needed to support that objective. The U.S. would cut its budget deficit while Japan and West Germany would stimulate their domestic demand. Market pressures forced an upward "rebasing" in April of the yen's range in relation to the dollar, but the enforcement effort continued until even heavier market attacks in the fall rendered the Louvre Accord unsustainable. It was clear by then that the reference ranges alone never would have brought the American current account deficit below $100 billion, if that far, without implementation of the promised policy changes.

For 1988, the issue is not *whether* to reform the international monetary system. The shortcomings of unmanaged floating and the efforts of the recent past provide stark testimony to the need and desire for change. The issue is how to fashion a system that will work.

There's been extensive debate on whether such reform should focus initially on exchange rates themselves or on coordination of national economic policies. But the debate is essentially over tactics; in truth, exchange-rate equilibrium can be preserved only through effective policy coordination, while effective policy coordination will normally produce equilibrium exchange rates. The postwar record both globally and in Europe suggests that success would be more likely if policymakers begin by trying to set appropriate exchange rates. In essence, countries would examine the interaction of national policies through the lens of the exchange rate—viewing the exchange-rate system as a means to the end of more effective coordination of overall national policies.

The most promising strategy for now may be to find a compromise built on the indicators and the reference-range efforts of the past two years. The leading contender today would be a plan to institute target-zones.

That doesn't mean policymakers should rule out an eventual return to fixed rates—possibly along the lines of the EMS, which has a reasonably effective procedure for requiring countries to move quickly to adjust parities by small amounts when imbalances begin to show up. However, such narrow margins could prove harder to maintain between the United States and Japan with their much larger volumes of capital flows. And it isn't clear that the Big Three powers would be as ready as some EMS members to change parities promptly. If they weren't, then the new system, too, could prove too rigid. The present imbalances also make it very hard to choose precise parities any time soon that would offer great hope of remaining in place for very long. But it isn't necessary to return to fixed rates now; the primary objective of the exercise should be to avoid the substantial misalignments that characterized the first half of the 1980s. This could be achieved with a less-sweeping approach.

The most promising strategy for now may be to find a compromise, built on the indicators and reference-range efforts of the past two years, that would avoid the excessive rigidity of the Bretton Woods system and the endemic misalignments of floating. It's interesting to recall that when the Bretton Woods system was breaking down, in the late 1960s and early 1970s, many proponents of monetary reform similarly called for intermediate solutions—then labeled "crawling pegs" and "wider bands." The leading contender today would be target zones, which would permit rates to fluctuate on a day-to-day basis but would limit the extent of such movements and thus prevent misalignments sufficient to damage the international system.

Under target zones, the participating countries would first agree on what the proper current account positions of each of the major countries should be—such as a modest surplus for Japan and deficits for most developing countries—and then decide what exchange rates are needed to bring this about. Then they would establish initial zones that would range from 5% to 10% above and below some optimum exchange rate (adjusted continuously for inflation). The zones would be announced publicly to help stabilize capital flows. They would be revised regularly to make sure that they continued to reflect underlying competitive positions and take account of significant shocks, such as significant changes in worldwide oil prices.

Once the zones were set, rates would be free to fluctuate within them without intervention by the authorities. Most short-term disturbances, such as modest changes in interest rate differentials, would continue to be reconciled through fluctuations in exchange rates. National policies would be no more constrained than under unmanaged floating. But when rates approached the edges of the zones, there would be strong pressure on countries to alter their policies. In some cases, direct intervention in the exchange markets and jawboning might be enough. If that didn't work, countries could then alter their monetary policies—the quickest way to make an impact on the markets. Fiscal policy could then be adjusted to provide an offset, producing a similar macroeconomic outcome but altering the country's external position through a change in the policy mix. To enable this element of the scheme to work properly, several of the major countries (notably the United States and Germany) would have to devise internal reforms to make their budget policies more flexible. Institution of a new international system requiring such changes might help provide the needed spur politically for governments to act at home.

A major operational question would be whether interest rates should be raised in the country whose currency was weakening or reduced in the country whose currency was rising. The answer would depend largely on the outlook for the world economy. If global inflation threatened, the weak-currency country should tighten; if recession loomed instead, the strong-currency country would loosen. If the situation were less clear-cut, both might make adjustments.

In the last issue of *The International Economy*, Bundesbank President Karl Otto Poehl denounced proposals for the "robotization" of policymaking and "those who wish to replace persons and *ad hoc* decisions by regulatory mechanisms and indicators." While correctly noting that "the willingness of each individual country to take into account the implications of its own economic policy for the rest of the world...cannot be decreed from outside," he goes on to say that "no system—no matter how sophisticated it may be—can help when this political willingness is lacking."

But Mr. Poehl is attacking a straw-man: No one, except perhaps the unreconstructed gold standard bugs, is proposing "automatic" or "robotized" rules in a world of sovereign nation-states.

What's more, elsewhere the Bundesbank president has ardently defended the EMS because it has "influenced national decisionmaking processes in economic and monetary policy" and it is "subjecting the participating countries to an exchange-rate discipline...." And it has.

France's mid-1980s decision to reverse the early socialist policies of the Mitterrand administration was largely to avoid violating its obligations to maintain the EMS. And many countries, including the U.S., frequently altered their policies to stay within the confines of the old Bretton Woods regime.

The Bundesbank itself pays considerable attention to its own "target zone" for growth of the money supply, viewing it quite properly as a useful (but not "automatic") guideline which helps fend off critics who favor tighter or more expansionary policies. Why, then, must all international "conflicts of aims only be resolved ad hoc, by the persons involved," as Mr. Poehl has argued?

The target zone approach would in fact effectively meet concerns expressed most frequently by German officials. The nominal exchange rate targets would change automatically if inflation accelerated in some countries, permitting appreciation in the more stable countries (and thus warding off inflationary pressure). The exchange rate could appreciate within the wide zone, further relieving the risk of importing inflationary pressure. Also in light of the wide zone, monetary policy could be targeted to a considerable degree to counter inflationary pressures. And all of the policy adjustments would take global demand conditions fully into account, to avoid giving any push to global inflation (or recession).

Mr. Poehl is correct that individual judgment must be applied in specific cases. The issue is whether to develop and install norms to help guide such decisions, or leave them all to ad hockery. The experience of 1987 with the Louvre Accord should clinch the case for the former: The Louvre Accord sought to stabilize exchange rates at levels that were clearly unsustainable. It defined exchange rates in nominal rather than real terms, setting up a further inherent instability in light of lower inflation in Germany and Japan than in the United States. It apparently sought to maintain existing rates within very narrow margins, providing inadequate scope for short-term fluctuations and thus triggering premature (and ultimately unsuccessful) intervention in both April and October. And the unwillingness of the Big Three countries to carry out major policy changes when exchange rates threatened to pierce the boundaries only encouraged speculators to challenge these targets.

Fortunately, all of these shortcomings of the Louvre Accord can be remedied once the major countries decide that the time has come to improve the international monetary system. Indeed, the structure of reference ranges embodied at the Louvre provides a promising foundation for launching the more far-reaching effort that is needed, as indicated above.

But caution is in order. It would be a mistake to revive

the unrealistic expectations of the Louvre effort by trying to install a target-zone system before the present currency disequilibrium is eliminated. We should wait until a new set of exchange rates and policies produces an acceptable correction of today's massive current account imbalances that is ratified by the markets. The new system would then aim to stabilize the situation, and prevent yet another cycle of costly and disruptive misalignments.

The basic issue isn't whether countries will adjust to the realities of global interdependence. They will, as even the largest learn periodically to their dismay. Nor are countries being asked to conform to international norms or presumptions "to pursue global interests" rather than their own interests. The object is to minimize the costs to a country's *own* economy by providing early warning that it can't escape adverse international consequences from its own actions, and that it should behave accordingly.

The issue is whether countries will adjust constructively and preemptively, or belatedly and reactively. The former course may on occasion mean foregoing some short-term economic benefits. The latter will almost always mean accepting very heavy, lasting costs.

The goal of restructuring the international monetary system is to help push countries toward earlier, less costly changes in their economic policies so that those policies will be more internationally compatible—and thus more sustainable. No system can assure such an outcome on all occasions, or prevent countries from the unhappy results of their own policy failures. But a well-conceived system that is implemented with good faith, based on enlightened definitions of self-interest, could tilt policies in a constructive direction and make a significant difference. Creation of such a system should rank high on the policy agenda for 1988 and beyond. ♦

MENU:
Trade + Project Loans
On-lending
New Money Bonds
Exit Bonds
Debt Equity Swaps
Interest Capitalization

MYER

Article Thirty-Seven

Understanding International Debt Crisis

by James R. Barth, *
Michael D. Bradley **
and Paul C. Panayotacos ***

INTRODUCTION

It is not unusual for borrowing and lending to take place across national
borders. But when Mexico declared a moratorium on foreign debt payments in August 1982 and subsequent debt servicing problems surfaced
in countries such as Argentina, Brazil and Venezuela,[1] it became widely
apparent that international debt is a mixed blessing.[2] Although borrowing funds from abroad enables a country to obtain investment goods
needed for economic growth, the inefficient use of those funds or exogenous shocks[3] causing real interest rates to rise abruptly, oil prices to fluctuate widely, and commodity prices to fall sharply[4] can severely limit a
debtor country's ability or willingness to repay its borrowings.[5] Simi-

* James R. Barth is a Professor of Economics at George Washington University, Washington,
D.C.. Professor Barth has also served as a visiting scholar at the Federal Reserve Bank of Atlanta,
the U.S. Congressional Budget Office, and the Federal Home Loan Bank Board.

** Michael D. Bradley is an Associate Professor of Economics at George Washington University, Washington, D.C..

*** Paul Panayotacos is a doctoral candidate in economics at George Washington University,
Washington, D.C.

1 The only significant Latin American exception to debt- servicing disruption was Colombia.
See Cline, *International Debt and Stability of the World Economy*, 4 INST. FOR INT'L ECON. 30
(Sept. 1983).

2 Actually, the fact that international debt can create problems is not a recent realization. Indeed, a few short years ago it was reported that "The number-one danger confronting the United
States today . . .is the viability of about $25 billion in loans to less developed countries . . ." *See*
Dorfman, *The Bottom Line - The Banks' Biggest Worry*, THE FEDERAL RESERVE SYSTEM 212, (Jan.
1977).

3 *See* P. NUNNENKAMP, THE INTERNATIONAL DEBT CRISIS OF THE THIRD WORLD, (1986).

4 Real interest rates charged to less developed countries (LDC's) jumped from 1% in 1980 to
between 6.73 and 8.50% in 1981-84, oil prices decreased from $35.01 per barrel in 1981 to $28.72
per barrel in 1983 and substantially further since then, and the terms of trade deteriorated mainly
due to falling commodity prices by 9% for non-oil LDC's between 1980 and 1983. Errunza &
Ghalbouni, *Interest Rates and International Debt Crisis*, 157 BANCA NAZIONALE DEL LAVORO Q.
REV., 225-45 (June 1986).

5 Optimal borrowing decisions are part of a country's overall resource allocation problem.
This dynamic resource allocation problem is addressed formally in Cooper & Sachs, *Borrowing
Abroad: The Debtor's Perspective*, in INTERNATIONAL DEBT AND THE DEVELOPING COUNTRIES,
(G. Smith and J. Cuddington eds. 1985).

larly, although lending funds abroad enables a commercial bank to seek higher returns over a wider geographical area, anything that disrupts the fulfillment of the terms of the contract adversely affects the profitability and even the solvency of the creditor. In recent years it has become painfully clear that the nonfulfillment of the contractual terms of international debt as originally agreed upon can spread beyond the immediate debtors and creditors so as to disrupt international trade and the international banking system.[6] It is therefore important to understand the fundamental role of international debt in improving welfare and the ways in which such debt can disrupt economic activity and international relations.

This paper assesses the importance of international debt in the world economy. This is done by first discussing the role of debt in facilitating economic growth as well as the potential problems that may arise due to debt. The magnitude of the current international debt problem will then be described. Lastly, potential solutions to the current problem will be analyzed and the prospects for avoiding future debt problems are assessed.

ECONOMIC RATIONALE FOR INTERNATIONAL DEBT

A basic assumption in economics is that individuals maximize intertemporal utility by choosing a fairly constant consumption path through time that does not exceed their lifetime income.[7] Since income does not follow a perfectly smooth path through time, saving and borrowing serve as shock absorbers enabling individuals to smooth consumption.[8] But the saving and borrowing that occur are based upon the expectation that sufficient income will be earned in the future to maintain consumption as well as to repay any past borrowings.[9] This means that if income is temporarily low in one period, a chosen consumption path can be maintained through borrowing. However, the amount of borrowing that is undertaken in response to the fall in income depends on the extent to which future income is believed to be sufficient to cover the borrowing as well as

---

[6] The widespread nature of the debt problem has been acknowledged by policymakers. For example, Treasury Secretary Baker has stated, "The international debt situation remains a challenge, not only for individual debtor nations but for the international community as a whole." Baker, *Statement Before the Meeting of the OECD Council at Ministerial Level*, TREASURY NEWS, April 17, 1986.

[7] R.E. HALL & J.B. TAYLOR, MACROECONOMICS, 167-201 (1986).

[8] *See e.g.*, S.M. SHEFFRIN, RATIONAL EXPECTATIONS, 146 (1984), "[A]n individual maximizes expected intertemporal utility from consumption or can transfer purchasing power between periods by buying and selling a risky asset."

[9] That is, individuals must choose a consumption path consistent with their lifetime budget constraint. For a discussion of the lifetime budget constraint, see H.R. VARIAN, INTERMEDIATE MICROECONOMICS 180 (1987).

any outstanding borrowings.[10] One role for borrowing, then, is to enable individuals to smooth consumption streams in the face of irregular income streams.[11]

Another role for borrowing is to facilitate investment so as to increase future income.[12] To illustrate this point, consider the situation of a student wanting to attend law school. Upon completion of the requirements for a degree, the student's lifetime income stream will undoubtedly be higher than if the student were not to pursue a professional degree. But at present the student cannot use the future income for current spending. Borrowing against the future income, however, solves the problem for the student with insufficient current resources. A lender will make such a loan, even without physical collateral, so long as the proceeds of the loan are used to increase the future income stream of the borrower. The size of the loan will be bounded by the present discounted expected value of the student's additional lifetime earnings resulting from earning the degree.[13] Since the future is not known with certainty, the willingness of the lender to extend funds depends upon the lender's subjective evaluation of the willingness and ability of the student to repay the loan.[14] One measure of the lender's subjective expectation of repayment is the interest rate charged on the loan. The less likely the repayment, the more risky the loan and, *ceteris paribus*, the higher the interest rate required by the lender to make the loan.[15]

Financial markets thus serve to channel funds from savers (lenders) to dissavers (borrowers) at an interest rate that provides an amount of lending that increases the utility or welfare of all parties involved.[16] Of course, in a world of uncertainty, not all borrowings are repaid in full, if at all, due to an unforseen reduced willingness and ability to repay. To protect against such contingencies, loans are typically made at rates of interest that incorporate any risks of default.[17] Furthermore, without the

---

[10] *Id.* at 182.

[11] *Id.* at 184.

[12] For a discussion of the investment decision, see T. Palm & A. Qayum, Private and Public Investment Analysis (1985).

[13] *Id.* at 64-79.

[14] Complications arising from a potential unwillingness to repay debts are related to "moral hazard problems." See A. Deaton & J. Muellbauer, Economics and Consumer Behavior 389 (1980).

[15] The lender, in this situation, is charging a risk premium. For a discussion of risk-aversion and the associated premium charged for risk, *see* H.R. Varian, *supra* note 9, at 219.

[16] T. Cargill, The Basic Elements of the Financial System and Monetary Policy 27-58 (1968).

[17] Default risk is sometimes reduced through the use of collateral, which then lowers the interest rate. A common example is the collateralized automobile loan. For foreign loans, however, collateral becomes a somewhat nebulous concept due to the general inability to press claims against foreign governments. For an analysis of how loan decisions are made under uncertainty, see Jaffee

expectation of income growth, borrowing is simply impossible. The reason is that if current income is insufficient to finance current consumption, that same level of income, in the future, certainly cannot be sufficient to maintain consumption as well as generate the saving necessary to repay any debt. If income is therefore not expected to grow, it is reasonable to expect any debt to be defaulted upon and thus lenders will not voluntarily extend a loan at any interest rate.[18]

The basic situation just described is no different for international debt.[19] Countries borrow to finance consumption in the presence of current negative income shocks and borrow to finance future income growth. But systematic and repeated borrowing should be associated with the latter type of borrowing, because persistent declines in income are, by definition, not temporary shocks and hence the required lender expectation that income will rapidly return to its "normal" level must be abandoned.[20] In this regard, most recent international borrowing is clearly not temporary and should therefore have been undertaken to finance investment so as to promote future income growth.[21] When external funds are used for this purpose, borrowing is welfare enhancing because the present discounted expected value of the projects financed by loans exceeds the size of the loans which means that the borrowing country anticipates income growth and thus greater consumption growth as well as the ability to repay its loans.[22] In this situation, even a temporary negative shock to income is unlikely to affect the present discounted expected value of investment so that additional short term loans from abroad are appropriate to maintain consumption.[23] A problem arises, however, when the external funds are not used for income enhancing investments. For without additional income growth a country's ability to repay its loans significantly diminishes and thus the likelihood of de-

---

and Russel, *Imperfect Information, Uncertainty, and Credit Rationing*, 90 Q.J. OF ECON. 651-66 (1976).

[18] Difficulties in making this determination due to the moral hazard problem may lead lenders to a system of credit rationing. *Id.* at 657.

[19] LDC's may face some additional problems in valuing the expected real output growth generated by the investment. These difficulties generally come from a lack of developed markets. *See* T. PALM & A. QAYUM, *supra* note 12, at ch. 9.

[20] Systematic and repeated borrowing without income growth would violate the borrower's intertemporal budget constraint. *See* A. DEATON & J. MUELLBAUER, *supra* note 14, at 309-44.

[21] See Tables 1 and 2.

[22] *See* T. CARGILL, *supra* note 16, at 267: "The non-oil developing countries during the 1970s embarked on an ambitious program to build an infrastructure of roads, water projects, communications, and so on to provide a firm base for economic growth. External financing from both private and official sources was extensively relied upon to achieve economic growth objectives. The funds to service and eventually repay the external debt incurred was designed to improve domestic economic growth and improve the ability to compete in world markets. Both would generate the funds required to service and eventually repay the debt over time."

[23] See R.E. HALL & J.B. TAYLOR, *supra* note 7, at 182-184.

fault increases. It is therefore situations in which funds are not used to promote income growth that lead to international debt crises.[24] Of course, even if funds are used to promote growth, an unwillingness to repay all borrowings leads to a similar outcome.

In the next section, we assess the magnitude of current international debt. The economic framework just outlined will be used in analyzing the data presented as well as in subsequent sections discussing proposed remedies to deal with the debt problem.

BURDEN OF INTERNATIONAL DEBT

The current international debt problem can be most easily appreciated with some numbers.[25] As Table 1 shows, the total external debt of less developed countries (LDC's) was nearly $800 billion at the end of 1985.[26] By itself this figure provides relatively little information. When compared to the exports of goods and services or to the gross domestic product of LDC's, however, one finds that both ratios reversed their downward movement form 1978 to 1980. Indeed, these ratios jumped abruptly in 1982—the beginning of the current international debt problem—and have continued to increase, but at a somewhat more moderate rate since then.[27] The alarming aspect of these ratios is that they indicate that corrective action must be taken; external debt cannot forever grow more rapidly than exports and gross domestic product. This is illustrated by observing that the ratio of the debt service payment (interest plus principal repayment) to exports jumped nearly five full percentage points from 1978 to 1982.[28] As a result, almost one-fourth of all exports have been needed simply to service current debt obligations.[29] The crucial role played by exports is more fully appreciated when one realizes that most international debt is denominated in dollars.[30] This means that debt service must be made in dollars, not the debtor country's currency. Debtor countries are thus required to obtain dollars to service their debt,

---

[24] See T. CARGILL, supra note 16, at 268.

[25] For additional data and discussion, see Barth, Bradley and Manage, *The International Debt Crisis: Rhetoric vs. Reality*, 1084 J. SOC. POL. & ECON. STUDIES, 453-82 (1984); Barth and Pelzman, *International Debt: Conflict and Resolution*, CONTEMPORARY INTERNATIONAL ECONOMY: A READER 358-91 (John Adams, ed. 1985).

[26] The International Monetary Fund projection for total external debt is $836.3 billion for 1986. See I.M.F. WORLD ECONOMIC OUTLOOK, 247 (Apr. 1986).

[27] The average annual growth of the ratios of debt to exports and debt to GDP are, respectively, -0.8% and 5.44% (1979-1981), and 2.8% and 4.6% (1983-1985); during 1982, the ratios were 19.2% and 15.9%, respectively. See Table 1.

[28] Debt service payments increased from $19.3 billion to $24.1 billion in the aforementioned years, subsequently dropping to $22.7 by 1985. *Id.*

[29] For recent trends in debt service payments, see OECD, FINANCING AND EXTERNAL DEBT OF DEVELOPING COUNTRIES, 49-52 (1986).

[30] For a discussion of the denomination of debt, see P. NUNNENKAMP, supra note 3, at 4, 49.

TABLE 1. Capital Importing Non-Oil Developing Countries External Debt (1) (billions of U.S. dollars)

	1978	1979	1980	1981	1982	1983	1984	1985
Total Debt	343.4	409.2	490.5	578.5	662.0	703.5	744.2	789.5
Short-term debt	61.6	68.2	94.3	115.5	135.9	117.3	116.4	103.7
Long-term debt	282.3	340.9	396.3	463.0	542.1	586.2	628.0	685.8
Official creditors	118.4	136.9	159.7	181.8	205.0	228.5	250.2	273.1
Financial institutions (2)	82.9	109.9	128.6	153.9	178.9	219.6	242.7	276.6
Other private creditors (3)	80.9	94.1	107.9	127.3	142.2	138.0	135.2	136.1
Debt service payment on short-term and long-term debt (4)	19.3	19.6	17.7	21.2	24.1	21.1	22.0	22.7
Interest payments ratio	7.1	8.0	8.8	11.6	14.0	18.0	18.1	18.2
Amortization ratio (5)	12.2	11.7	8.8	9.6	10.1	8.1	8.9	9.6
Ratio of external debt to exports of goods and services	131.6	122.1	114.7	127.2	151.6	159.6	154.2	164.4
Ratio of external debt to G.D.P.	24.7	24.7	25.2	28.8	33.4	35.7	36.8	38.2

NOTES:

(1) This category includes 120 countries. Figures may not add to totals due to rounding.

(2) Covers only public and publicly guaranteed debt.

(3) Includes all unguaranteed debt on the presumption that this is owed mainly to private creditors.

(4) Payments (interest, amortization, or both) as a percentage of exports of goods and services.

(5) On long-term debt only. Estimates for period up to 1984 reflect actual amortization payments. The estimates for 1985 reflect scheduled payments, modified to take account of actual or pending rescheduling agreements.

SOURCE: *World Economic Outlook*, I.M.F., 1986

and the primary way that dollars are obtained is through exports—the debtor countries sell their goods for dollars. Clearly, external debt cannot be repaid if the size of that debt is growing faster than the pool of dollars earned by the debtor country. But even exports growing faster than the size of the debt is not sufficient to assure that debtor countries will have the capacity over time to repay their debts. The reason is that a country's output is divided among several uses: consumption, investment, government spending and exports. If exports are increasing but aggregate production is not, the other uses of output must be declining. But if investment declines the productive capacity of the economy diminishes and hence the ability of the country to produce goods to be exported in the future also correspondingly diminishes. Consequently, a country's income growth as well as its export growth must exceed debt growth.[31] Otherwise, the dollar earnings from exports can only temporarily satisfy the required debt service payments — with partial or complete default the eventual outcome. Unfortunately, the data in Tables 1 and 2 suggest that even this short-run condition has not been fulfilled. Moreover, in recent years more than half of the debt service payments have been devoted to simply meeting the interest due on the debt,[32] which reflects the abrupt rise in interest rates in the early 1980's and the fact that significant portions of the international debt is short-term and based on variable rather than fixed interest rates. Since 1982, however, this situation has improved as the mix of short and long-term debt has shifted toward long-term.[33] In 1982 short-term debt represented 20% of all debt, whereas by 1985 it had declined to 13%.[34] This has helped ease the frequency of debt negotiations as well as provided the debtor countries with more certainty regarding sources of funds needed for economic growth.[35]

Table 1 also provides useful information about the type and exposure of creditors. As may be seen, financial institutions have steadily increased their exposure to 35% of the total debt in 1985 from 24% in 1978.[36] This relatively large exposure of international banks is what

---

[31] The importance of income and export growth is also stressed by Paul A. Volcker. *See Statement Before the Committee on Foreign Affairs of the House*, 99th Cong., June 18, 1986.

[32] Interest payments as a percentage of total debt service payments increased to an annual rate of 58% in 1982, from 37% in 1982; the ratio jumped to 85% in 1983, and declined to 80% by 1985. *See* Table 1.

[33] On average, short-term debt as a percentage of total debt was 20% during the period 1979-1982; this figure dropped to 15% during the period 1983-1985. *Id.*

[34] *See Id.*

[35] For a discussion on debt negotiations, *see* K. Burke Dillon *et al.*, *Recent Developments in External Debt Restructuring*, in 40 I.M.F. OCCASIONAL PAPER (1986).

[36] In terms of long-term debt, the figures are even more striking: financial institutions almost doubled their exposure to 40% in 1985, from 21% in 1978. *See* Table 1.

leads to concerns over the stability of the international banking system.[37] More specifically, if debt is repudiated or defaulted upon there exists the possibility of large bank failures and even the collapse of the financial system. Moreover, as debtor countries attempt to stimulate their exports and to curtail their imports to generate the needed surpluses in their trade accounts to service their debts, trade is clearly effected for both debtor and creditor countries.[38] These trade effects set in motion calls for protectionism and charges of unfair trade practices as countries intensify their competition with one another under the burden of trying to honor heavy debt obligations.[39]

The figures in Table 1, of course, refer to all LDC's For this reason, it is important to emphasize that not all LDC's are currently experiencing debt problems.[40] The burden of international debt, in other words, is unevenly distributed among the LDC's. Indeed, the vast majority of these countries are not experiencing a "crisis" in meeting their international contractual obligations. The problems instead are concentrated in seventeen countries, most of which are located in Latin America, and certainly it is these debtor countries that most directly concern the United States. Table 2 presents data on the external debt for these seventeen borrowers. As may be seen, the top five heavily indebted Latin American countries accounted for more than two-thirds of the total external debt of all the LDC's in 1985.[41] Despite its seriousness, the debt problem is therefore currently confined to a relatively small number of countries.[42]

Examining the data in Table 2 one notices that the ratio of debt to exports doubled between 1980 and 1984. Specifically, each and every one of the seventeen countries experienced a dramatic increase in this crucial ratio.[43] This means that the burden of fulfilling debt obligations was 200% greater in 1985 than in 1980. This situation also means that the amount of export earnings required for debt service rose significantly, which in turn means that the growth in exports required to simply ser-

---

[37] See OECD, *supra* note 29, at 55-57.

[38] According to I.M.F. estimates, a 1% increase in industrial countries' real GNP would induce a 35% increase in the export earnings of developing countries. *See* I.M.F. Release, July 4, 1986.

[39] Analogous concerns are expressed by de Larosire, *The Debt Problem and Challenges Facing the World Economy*, I.M.F. Release, Nov. 15, 1985, at 6.

[40] For a descriptive synopsis of all indebted countries, *see* THE WORLD BANK, WORLD DEVELOPMENT REPORT, 44 (1985).

[41] Brazil, Mexico, Argentina, Venezuela and Chile accounted for 24.1, 22.2, 11.4, 7.5 and 4.7% of total external debt (for all LDC's), respectively. *See* Table 2.

[42] Debt is also developing into a serious problem in Sub- Saharan Africa. For a discussion, see Krumm, *The External Debt of Sub-Saharan Africa*, in WORLD BANK WORKING PAPER 741, (1985).

[43] The most dramatic increase was exhibited by Nigeria (507.6%) followed by Argentina (222.4%) Chile (198.1%) Uruguay (161.4%) and Colombia (115.4%). *See* Table 2.

TABLE 2. Seventeen Heavily Indebted Developing Countries.

Country	Total Debt Outstanding (1)	Total Debt Service (2)	Ratio of Debt to Exports (%)		Average Annual Growth Rates 1980-84 (%) (3)				
	(billion of U.S. dollars)								
	1985	1985-87	1980	1984	GDP	Exports	Imports	Investment	Per Capita Consumption
Argentina	50.8	20.4	90.0	290.2	−1.6	3.6	−14.7	−16.8	−2.7
Bolivia	4.0	1.6	210.4	382.7	−4.7	−1.7	−15.8	−22.1	−7.8
Brazil	107.3	39.7	171.3	219.8	0.1	10.8	−7.3	−8.6	−1.2
Chile	21.0	9.2	75.5	225.1	−1.4	0.7	−4.2	−11.6	−2.1
Colombia	11.3	6.4	69.7	150.1	1.8	0.8	2.4	2.4	−0.1
Costa Rica	4.2	2.4	139.5	270.8	−0.4	1.1	−9.1	−9.4	−4.8
Ecuador	8.5	3.4	110.9	223.1	1.1	2.6	−13.7	−16.9	−2.3
Ivory Coast	8.0	4.0	119.4	160.5	−2.3	1.3	−8.8	−19.5	−6.6
Jamaica	3.4	1.3	98.2	159.9	1.3	−2.5	−2.1	9.5	−1.4
Mexico	99.0	44.4	136.7	213.5	1.3	10.5	−14.5	−10.1	−1.4
Morocco	14.0	6.0	217.3	337.2	2.5	4.1	−1.0	−2.7	−0.2
Nigeria	19.3	9.1	15.7	95.4	−4.7	−13.3	−12.1	−19.3	−4.3
Peru	13.4	5.2	127.1	247.0	−0.7	−0.6	−10.8	−5.3	−3.7
Philippines	24.8	9.5	81.6	139.1	0.8	3.6	−4.8	−12.4	0.0
Uruguay	3.6	1.4	70.7	184.8	−3.7	2.2	−11.3	−20.2	−4.7
Venezuela	33.6	17.8	48.9	91.4	−1.8	−3.8	−19.3	−15.6	−6.4
Yugoslavia (4)	19.6	13.6	33.3	62.6	0.6	−0.6	−8.1	−2.9	−0.5
Total (5)	445.9	194.9	106.9	203.1	−0.3	1.8	−9.2	−9.7	−1.8

NOTES:
(1) Estimated total external liabilities, including the use of IMF credit.
(2) Debt service is based on known long-term debt and terms at end-1984. It does not take into account new loans contracted or debt reschedulings signed after that date.
(3) Latest year for which data are available. Growth rates are computed from time series in constant prices, using beginning- and end- period values.
(4) Average annual growth rates are for 1980-83, except for GDP which is for 1980-84.
(5) Figures may not add to totals due to rounding.
SOURCE: The World Bank, *World Debt Tables*, 1986.

vice the debt also increased.[44] The emphasis on curtailing imports[45] (and thus conserving the needed dollars) and expanding exports (and thus generating the needed dollars) in these countries is understandable given this situation. Yet, these actions are not only difficult when these countries are experiencing slow growth, depreciating currencies, and falling commodity prices, but also adversely affect the competing domestic suppliers in the creditor countries, which brings calls for protectionist legislation in these countries.[46]

The drive to expand exports at the cost of diverting the debtor countries output from other uses has had negative effects on their economies. While most of the seventeen debtor countries have taken action to increase exports over the last five years, as Table 2 indicates, this export growth has come at the cost of reduced consumption and investment. The reduced investment adversely affects future income growth in these countries because less capital will be available for production.[47] As a consequence, the long-term ability of these countries to repay their debts is actually reduced. The signs of this detrimental effect are already showing—nine of the seventeen countries experienced negative real output growth in the past five years and only one country, Morocco, experienced an annual average output growth rate in excess of 2%.

Reduced consumption can also have negative effects.[48] Falling consumption can generate political and social unrest, thereby increasing pressures to renegotiate the international debt on more favorable terms to the debtor countries, if not actually to repudiate some of the debt.[49] Such drastic actions relating to the willingness of countries to repay their debt would, of course, threaten the solvency of some of the larger international banking institutions, not to mention weaken overall confidence in the banking system. This particular problem will be discussed in the next section.

---

[44] The average annual growth rate of exports between 1980-1984 was positive for all top five Latin American debtor countries, except Venezuela. The highest rate was exhibited by Brazil (10.8%) followed by Mexico (10.5%) and Argentina (3.6%). *See* Table 2.

[45] For example, in response to the 1982 debt crises, Mexico reduced imports by 47.5% in 1983. See Solis and Zedillo, *The Foreign Debt Problem of Mexico*, in International Debt and the Developing Countries, 286 (G.W. Smith & J.T. Cuddington eds. 1986).

[46] For the I.M.F. perspective, see de Larosire, *Interrelationships Between Protectionism and the Debt Crisis*, in I.M.F. Release, (Feb. 6, 1986).

[47] On average, annual investment growth was negative for all 17 countries during the period 1980-1984. The annual average decline for the top five Latin American debtor countries was 13%; in Latin America, Bolivia and Uruguay exhibited the most dramatic declines (22.1% and 20.2% respectively). *See* Table 2.

[48] The average annual decline of per capita consumption for the top five Latin American debtor countries during the 1980-1984 period was 4.92%. *See* Table 2.

[49] The social tensions arising from the debt issue are also acknowledged by J. de Larosire, *supra* note 39 at 5.

A major concern about the current international debt problem is that any defaults or repudiations may set in motion forces leading to a collapse of the international banking system.[50] Table 3 provides data that helps to understand this concern. More specifically, information pertaining to U.S. bank loans to the top three Latin American debtor countries and to all LDC's is presented, broken-down by all reporting banks and the nine largest banks.[51] As may be seen, banks have generally channeled a disproportionately large share of their foreign loans to just three LDC's: Argentina, Brazil and Mexico.[52] As a result, they have been extremely dependent upon events affecting these three countries as regards the possible adverse effect any defaults or loan writedowns would have on their capital. This is especially the case for the nine largest banks, which have put at risk a very large portion of their capital in the event of any nonpayment of their international debt.[53] Indeed, in 1982 and 1983 the loans to the top three Latin American debtor countries exceeded the entire capital of the nine largest banks. Of course, the debt problem for banks appears even more ominous when one includes other debtor countries that are experiencing difficulties servicing their debt.[54]

Table 3 does show that the debt situation for banks - both all reporting banks and the nine largest banks - has improved in recent years. Clearly, international loans by banks have been growing much more slowly since 1982, and have even declined since 1984. As a result, debt-to-capital ratio for banks has significantly declined since 1982.[55]

The data in Tables 2 and 3 raises important issues about the stability of the U.S. banking system. Most importantly, there is the issue as to

---

[50] For an analysis of whether international diversification renders the American banking system more or less prone to failure, see Darby, *The Internationalization of American Banking and Finance: Structure, Risk and World Interest Rates* 1989 in NAT'L BUREAU OF ECON. RES., WORKING PAPERS SERIES (July, 1986).

[51] For a synopsis of the principal sources of data on foreign lending by both U.S.-chartered and foreign banks, see Mills, *Foreign Lending by Banks: A Guide to International and U.S. Statistics*, 10 FED. RES. BULL. 72 (1986).

[52] The average of claims as a percentage of capital for Argentina, Mexico and Brazil (1977-June 1986) was 63.6% for all reporting banks. *See* Table 3.

[53] The average of claims as a percentage of capital for Argentina, Mexico and Brazil (1977-June 1986) was 92.1% for the nine largest banks. *See* Table 3.

[54] The average of claims as a percentage of capital for all non- oil developing countries (1977-June 1986) was 120.8% and 184.2% for all reporting banks and the nine largest banks, respectively. *See* Table 3.

[55] It is instructive to note that claims on Argentina, Brazil and Mexico as a percentage of claims on all non-oil developing nations have actually increased to 59.4% in 1986 (June) from 51.4% in 1982, for all reporting banks, and 58.5% in 1986 from 48.8% in 1982 for the nine largest banks. *See* Table 3.

TABLE 3. Bank Claims on Selected and All Non-Oil Developing Countries.

End of Period	CLAIMS (billions of U.S. dollars)					CLAIMS AS PERCENT OF CAPITAL				
	Argentina	Brazil	Mexico	Total 3 Countries	All Non-Oil Developing Countries	Argentina	Brazil	Mexico	Total 3 Countries	All Non-Oil Developing Countries
ALL REPORTING BANKS (1)										
1977	2.6	12.0	11.2	25.8	46.9	6.4	29.3	27.4	63.1	115.0
1978	2.8	13.4	10.7	26.9	52.2	6.1	29.4	23.5	59.0	116.0
1979	4.8	13.6	11.5	29.9	61.8	9.6	27.3	23.1	60.0	124.0
1980	6.9	14.5	15.7	37.1	75.4	12.1	25.4	27.5	65.1	132.0
1981	8.4	16.8	21.5	46.7	92.8	14.0	28.0	35.9	78.0	148.0
1982	8.2	20.4	24.4	53.0	103.2	11.6	28.9	34.6	75.1	146.0
1983	8.5	20.7	26.3	55.5	106.8	10.7	26.1	33.1	70.0	135.0
1984	8.0	23.9	26.5	58.4	105.8	8.6	25.9	28.8	63.3	115.0
1985	8.4	22.8	24.9	56.1	98.2	8.0	21.6	23.7	53.3	93.0
1986 (June)	8.5	22.3	24.2	54.9	92.5	7.6	20.1	21.8	49.6	83.6
NINE LARGEST BANKS										
1977	1.8	7.7	6.1	15.6	30.0	9.8	41.8	33.2	84.8	163.0
1978	1.8	8.5	6.1	16.4	33.4	9.0	42.5	30.5	82.0	176.0
1979	2.9	8.8	6.5	18.2	39.9	13.2	40.2	29.7	83.1	182.0
1980	4.2	9.4	9.1	22.7	47.9	17.5	39.2	37.9	94.6	199.0
1981	5.2	10.6	11.6	27.4	57.6	19.9	40.6	44.4	105.0	220.0
1982	5.1	13.3	12.9	31.3	64.1	17.6	45.9	44.5	107.9	221.0
1983	5.4	13.3	14.1	32.8	65.8	17.1	42.2	44.8	104.1	209.0
1984	5.1	15.8	14.7	35.6	66.4	13.9	43.1	40.0	97.0	181.0
1985	5.9	15.6	14.1	35.5	62.8	13.9	36.8	33.3	84.0	157.0
1986 (June)	5.9	15.2	13.6	34.7	59.3	13.3	34.5	30.7	78.5	134.2

(1) Data covers 189 U.S. banking institutions for 1986.
SOURCE: *Statistical Release* (Country Exposure Lending Survey), various issues.

whether or not the failure to repay the debt by the debtor countries could set in motion a collapse in the banking system. This could conceivably happen if sufficient debt was not repaid, causing several large banks and numerous other participating smaller banks to become insolvent and thereby reducing depositor confidence enough to set off a run on banks.[56] Such a systemic run on banks could indeed lead to the failure of both solvent and insolvent depository institutions as occurred in the Great Depression. However, two important factors mitigate against any such panic occurring. First, federal deposit insurance now protects nearly all deposits at banks and other depository institutions.[57] And even the uninsured depositors rarely suffer any losses when depository institutions fail.[58] For this reason it is unlikely that depositors will lose confidence in the safety of their deposits and hence would be unlikely to run to withdraw them in the event a relatively few banks were to become insolvent because of their foreign debt. Second, the Federal Reserve System serves as a lender-of-last-resort, which means that it stands ready to lend to any institution that is solvent but finds itself not liquid enough to meet all deposit withdrawals.[59] Any run that therefore spreads to solvent institutions can be readily handled by the Federal Reserve System. Only the insolvent banks will be unable to withstand a run, but such a run only adversely affects the stockholders and any uninsured depositors at those banks. The bulk of the depositors are protected against loss by federal insurance. In short, since the regulatory authorities are obligated to contain systemic runs, but not individual runs on insolvent institutions, the international debt problem should not lead to a collapse of the banking system if the monetary authorities do not default upon their obligation to serve as the lender-of-last-resort.[60]

Of course, the likelihood that any institution is or will become insolvent due to the international debt situation remains unclear. There are a number of reasons for this situation. First, the assets and liabilities (and thus capital which is the difference between the two sides of the balance sheet) of a bank are valued essentially at the time that they were entered

---

[56] Diamond & Dybvig, *Bank Runs, Deposit Insurance, and Liquidity*, 9 J. POL. ECON. 401-09 (1983).

[57] *See* E.J. KANE, THE GATHERING CRISIS IN FEDERAL DEPOSIT INSURANCE, (1985), *and* Barth, Brumbaugh, and Wang, *Insolvency in the Thrift Industry*, CONTEMPORARY POL'Y ISSUES 1-32 (Fall 1985).

[58] *See* Diamond and Dybuig, *supra* note 56.

[59] For a detailed discussion of the role of the lender-of-last- resort in dealing with both domestic and international financial crises, see Barth and Keleher, *Financial Crises and the Role of the Lender of Last Resort*, in ECON. REV., FEDERAL RESERVE BANK OF ATLANTA, 58-67 (Jan. 1984), *and* Humphrey and Keleher, *The Lender of Last Resort: A Historical Perspective*, 4 CATO J. 275-318 (1984)

[60] *See* Edwards, *LDCs' Foreign Borrowing and Default Risk: An Empirical Investigation, 1976-1980*, 74 AM. ECON. REV. 726-34 (1984).

onto the books and thus reflect historic values rather than the current market values. This means that some institutions may already be insolvent (i.e., have negative capital) if the current market value of international debt were substituted for the accounting or book value of the debt.[61]

Under current regulatory rules, it is the financial regulator, not the marketplace, that decides when a depository institution is insolvent and thus should be closed. This means that some currently operating banks may actually be market-value insolvent. Second, even if market-value accounting were used, the value of debt to those countries experiencing difficulties in fulfilling their contractual obligations is not zero. Instead, although it is undoubtedly worth substantially less than its book value, its decline in value since the loans were initially made may be sizeable but not enough to create the solvency problems for even the creditor banks that many fear. Third, the increased use of equity-for-debt swaps may lessen any adverse effects on both banks and debtor countries.[62] Banks benefit from exchanging debt for equity (in the sense of an ownership share in a company's operations in the debtor country) since their initial investment is not simply written-down. Debtor countries benefit from the exchange since their reputations and credibility with respect to honoring obligations suffer less than when defaults occur so that future borrowing is less adversely affected.[63]

In sum, it is not clear that the international debt problem need create any adverse effects insofar as the overall stability of the banking system is concerned.[64] Stockholders of some banks may suffer if the debtor nations fail to fulfill their contractual obligations, but federal deposit insurance and the Federal Reserve System should be able to confine any banking problems to those banks that have become insolvent during the normal course of conducting their business in a risky world.[65]

---

[61] For example, the loan agreement reached in October 1986 between Mexico and foreign lenders ". . . means that the banks can continue carrying Mexico's problem loans on their books at 100 cents on the dollar, but those loans are still being sold or swapped at about 60 cents on the dollar." *See* Witcher and Schmitt, *Growing Market in Third World Debt Raises Questions on the Loans' Value*, Wall St. J., Oct. 7, 1986, at 21, col. 2.

[62] *See generally* Buchheit, *Converting Sovereign Debt Into Equity Investments*, 5 INT'L. FIN. L. REV. 10-14 (1986); Meyier, *Les Contrats d'Echanges de Devises et de Taux d'Interet (Swaps)*, 12 DROIT ET PRATIQUE DU COMMERCE INTERNATIONAL 9-32 (1986) for a discussion of the legal aspects of transferring sovereign loans into equity.

[63] For more information about debt-for equity swaps, see Berg, *U.S. Banks Swap Latin Debt*, N.Y. Times, Sept. 11, 1986, at D1, col. 1.

[64] According to Robert E. Weintraub, ". . . under analysis, the threat of widespread bank failures, of the collapse of our banking system, is found to be imaginary." See Weintraub, *International Debt: Crisis and Challenge*, 4 CATO J. 38 (1984)

[65] In this regard, the Ad Hoc Committee on International Debt and U.S. Financial Policies has argued that "There should be no bailouts, either of debtor nations or of creditor banks." INTERNATIONAL LENDING AND THE INTERNATIONAL MONETARY FUND, 35 (A. Meltzer, ed. 1983).

There are direct linkages between the current international debt problem and international trade. These linkages are reflected in the trade data presented in Table 4. As may be seen, total U.S. imports have, with but one exception, increased significantly year-by-year from 1977 though 1985. Total U.S. exports, on the other hand, increased from 1977 through 1981 but then declined for two years. They rebounded somewhat in 1984 but declined again in 1985. Comparing exports and imports, one observes that what was a surplus in net exports (i.e., exports minus imports) in 1976 became a sizeable deficit in every year thereafter.[66] It is therefore no surprise that there is substantial concern about U.S. trade deficits and increasing calls for protectionist policies in the United States.[67]

Examining the figures in Table 4 one finds that beginning in 1982 a portion of the trade deficit has been accounted for by Latin American.[68] Actually, the top five Latin American debtor countries accounted for the bulk of the Latin American trade imbalance.[69] The reason for this situation is that once the major debtor countries began experiencing difficulties in servicing their debt, they found it necessary to take steps to generate foreign currency (mainly U.S. dollars) and to reduce its use for activities other than fulfilling their contractual obligations to foreign creditors (mainly U.S. banks).[70] This has lead to a contraction in imports that use up foreign currencies and an expansion in exports that generate foreign currencies. However, falling commodity prices, a relatively highly valued U.S. dollar, high real interest rates, and sluggish domestic economic growth have all made these efforts to stimulate exports and to curtail imports particularly burdensome for most debtor countries.[71] After all, not all countries can simultaneously increase their exports while curtailing their imports in an attempt to run trade surpluses. Furthermore, imports are needed by many debtor countries to obtain the investment goods necessary for economic growth.[72]

---

[66] In 1976, the U.S. trade surplus was $13.8 billion. U.S. DEP'T OF COMMERCE BUREAU OF ECONOMIC ANALYSIS.

[67] As stated in a recent International Monetary Fund Publication, ". . . protectionist pressures for trade restrictions continued unabated in 1985." *See Protectionist Pressures Persist, But Capital Controls Ease in '85*, I.M.F. Survey, Sept. 15, 1986, at 273.

[68] It is interesting to note that despite its overall trade deficit following 1976, the U.S. enjoyed a trade surplus with Latin American countries up to 1981 (with the exception of 1977), most of which was accounted from its trade with the top five Latin American debtor countries. *See* Table 4.

[69] The U.S. trade deficit with respect to the top five Latin American debtor countries, as a percentage of its total trade deficit with Latin American countries was, on average (for the period 1982-Sept. 1986), 98.6%. *Id.*

[70] de Larosire, *supra* note 39, at 86-7.

[71] See OECD, *supra* note 29, at 50-1.

[72] For example, imports of machinery, transport equipment and fuels, as a percentage of total

TABLE 4. Trade with Major Latin American Borrowers (billions of U.S. dollars)

	1977	1978	1979	1980	1981	1982	1983	1984	1985	1986 (Sept.)
					U.S. EXPORTS					
Argentina	0.7	0.8	1.9	2.6	2.2	1.3	1.0	0.9	0.7	0.7
Brazil	2.5	3.0	3.4	4.3	3.8	3.4	2.6	2.6	3.1	2.8
Chile	0.5	0.7	0.9	1.4	1.5	0.9	0.7	0.8	0.7	0.6
Mexico	4.8	6.7	9.8	15.1	17.8	11.8	9.1	12.0	13.6	9.4
Venezuela	3.2	3.7	4.6	4.6	5.4	5.2	2.8	3.4	3.3	2.3
Total Top Five	11.7	15.0	20.6	28.0	30.7	22.7	16.1	19.7	21.6	15.8
Total Latin America	16.4	20.2	26.3	36.0	39.0	30.1	22.6	26.3	27.8	19.5
Total World	121.2	136.7	181.8	220.8	233.7	212.3	200.5	217.9	213.1	160.9
					U.S. IMPORTS					
Argentina	0.4	0.6	0.6	0.7	1.1	1.1	0.9	1.0	1.1	0.7
Brazil	2.2	2.8	3.4	3.7	4.5	4.3	4.9	7.6	7.6	5.2
Chile	0.3	0.4	0.4	0.5	0.6	0.7	1.0	0.8	0.8	0.7
Mexico	4.7	6.1	8.8	12.6	13.8	15.6	16.8	18.0	19.1	13.1
Venezuela	4.1	3.5	5.5	5.3	5.6	4.8	4.9	6.5	6.5	4.0'
Total Top Five	11.7	13.4	18.7	22.9	25.5	26.4	28.5	33.9	35.0	23.6
Total Latin America	16.5	18.6	24.8	30.0	32.0	32.5	35.7	42.3	43.4	28.5
Total World	147.7	172.0	206.3	244.9	261.3	244.0	258.0	325.7	345.3	276.0

SOURCE: "Highlights of U.S. Export and Import Trade." U.S. Department of Commerce, Report F1990.

In sum, the international debt problem is definitely linked to international trade. Since most of the Latin American debt owed to U.S. banks was based upon a variable rather than a fixed interest rate and payable in U.S. dollars, the rising value of the dollar and increasing interest rates in the early 1980's made debt servicing extremely burdensome for the Latin American debtor countries. The recent decline in the value of the U.S. dollar and the fall in interest rates has eased the burden for the debtor countries, but the fall in commodity prices for Argentina, Chile and Brazil and the fall in oil prices for Venezuela and Mexico have had the opposite effect.[73] Furthermore, capital flight[74] and the recent world-wide sluggish economic growth's adverse effect on the exports of the debtor countries have both hurt these countries' efforts to acquire foreign currencies.[75]

PROSPECTS FOR RESOLVING INTERNATIONAL DEBT CRISES

The ultimate solution to the current international debt problem is economic growth. Debtor countries can only meet their contractual obligations through economic growth. Such growth, however, requires domestic saving to finance public investment in education, roads, irrigation, telecommunications and other infrastructure and to finance private investment in plant and equipment. Domestic saving can be supplemented, of course, with saving from abroad in the form of aid, grants, loans and equity investments provided by foreign governments, international financial institutions, like the World Bank and the Inter- American Development Bank, and private suppliers of goods and private banks. At present, however, private creditors appear reluctant to increase their overall risk exposure in the heavily indebted LDC's. This obviously reflects the recent and frequent interruptions on the part of these debtor countries in servicing their outstanding external debt. It is clearly in the

---

merchandise imports, constitute 71%, 57%, 48%, and 44% for Brazil, Mexico, Argentina, and Venezuela, respectively. *See* Solis and Zedillo *supra* note 45, at 195.

[73] The average rate of interest paid on total long-term debt declined in 1985 to an estimated 7.6%, down from a peak of 9.3% in 1982; moreover, the dollar value of commodity prices (excluding oil) fell 11.0% in 1985 after the post-recession recovery in 1983 and 1984. That left prices 26% below their 1980 level. See THE WORLD BANK, WORLD DEBT TABLES xiii-xiv (1986).

[74] Capital flight refers to capital outflows motivated by normal portfolio decisions as well as those based on the desire to place assets beyond the control of domestic authorities. Michael P. Dooley finds "that capital flight has been of little consequence in Brazil, while about 40% and 70% respectively, of all external debt in Mexico and Venezuela was matched by capital flight." *See, Capital Flight: A Response to Differences in Financial Risk*, Federal Reserve Board Mimeo, July 18, 1986 at 23.

[75] Industrial countries' demand for developing countries' exports grew by only 2.6% in 1985, following a 10.6% growth in 1985. *Id.*, p.xv. Although capital flight in 1985-86 has decreased to about one-third of its peak 1982 level of $30 million, it is still considered excessive. See OECD, *supra* note 29, at 50.

interest of the creditor banks to have other international financial institutions increase their share of credit to the debtor countries.[76] However, the banks are under pressure to contribute to any additional loans that are made. To the extent that the debtor countries can obtain additional borrowings and thereby avoid defaults it is in their interest to do so, as long as the terms of the loans are viewed by them as being politically and economically achievable. This of course is the source of concern. Although the debtor countries may have sufficient internal resources, including human and natural resources, to achieve sufficient economic growth to repay their debts, the fiscal and monetary policies required may be viewed as unacceptable, at least in the short run.[77] Whether or not external loans are repaid, in other words, depends ultimately upon economic growth,[78] but that in turn depends heavily upon domestic fiscal and monetary policies pursued in the debtor countries.[79] In this regard, it must again be emphasized that economic growth in the debtor countries must be sufficient to service old debt as well as any additional "bridge" loans. When the original loans were made, the lenders expected the borrowing countries to use funds for investment that would enhance productive capacity and thereby enable the country to repay its debt. This did not happen. The debtor countries thus confront the burden of debt repayments with very little additional earning capacity having been generated by investment financed with past debt. New loans must therefore stimulate enough economic growth so that the countries can service *both* the old and new obligations. An analogy might clarify matters. Consider our student mentioned earlier who borrows, purportedly, to go to law school. If the funds were spent instead on a world cruise, the student would not have added to her earning capacity to repay the debt. The student might then argue for additional or new loans, claiming that the money will now be used to finance a law school education to increase her earning capability or productive capacity. However, if a loan is made, the student's future earnings must now rise by enough to cover both the world cruise and the law school debts or a default will eventually occur.

In the sphere of international lending, the situation is even more

---

[76] In October of 1986, Mexico reached agreement on $12.5 billion of new loans. Of this amount, $6 billion will come from banks and will be partially guaranteed by the World Bank. *See, Mexico Reaches Accord With External Creditors*, I.M.F. Survey Oct. 20, 1986 at 305.

[77] Indeed, it was recently reported with respect to the October 1986 debt agreement concerning Mexico that "Many bankers feel the Mexican Government lacks the political support it needs to cut food and transportation subsidies, sell or close inefficient state enterprises, encourage private investment and make the new money bear fruit." See Walsh and Witcher, *Mexico's Bailout Masks Grave Problems that Threaten the Ruling Party's Grip*, Wall St. J., Oct. 2, 1986, at 35, col. 4.

[78] See Cooper and Sachs, *supra* note 5 at 22

[79] A comparison of domestic macroeconomic policies across sound and unsound debtors is given in P. NUNNENKAMP, *supra* note 3.

difficult. At least the student was aware of what policies were appropriate to increase earning power - law school attendance. It is not nearly so clear what macroeconomic policies are appropriate to achieve the "super" economic growth required in the current situation confronting debtor countries.[80] Not only are economists somewhat divided about the choice of appropriate policies to spur growth, but the recent performance of industrialized economies supports the contention that effective policies are always known and readily available.[81]

Finally, even if the proper policies were available, any additional bridge loans are not costless. Given the world-wide pool of saving available at any point in time, diversion of additional funds to heavily indebted countries necessarily implies a reduction of funds available to other countries.[82] Such an allocation of funds means that some other, perhaps more productive, investments will go unfunded. The historical performance of the heavily indebted countries suggests that this is not an unlikely event. If a diversion of funds to the less productive investments occurs, world-wide output growth will necessarily suffer. This reduction in output growth represents a permanent and genuine resource cost of extending additional credit to the heavily indebted countries.[83]

The prospects for resolving the current international debt problem in a manner acceptable to all parties involved are difficult to assess because political as well as economic factors are involved. Banks are reluctant to extend further credit to the debtor countries but are also reluctant to have to adjust their balance sheet and income statements at the present time by writing-down their foreign debt or by attempting to sell it in the recently developed secondary market for such debt.[84] The latter reluctance is strengthened to the extent that international financial institutions become more heavily involved in providing credit to the debtor countries as well as involved in providing some limited guarantees to those banks

---

[80] For an analysis of the difficulties and diversities in macroeconomic policymaking see M.G. RUKSTAD, MACROECONOMIC DESISIONMAKING IN THE WORLD ECONOMY (1986).

[81] Indeed policies may even be implemented that create economic problems. For, as Paul DeGrauwe and Michele Fratianni argue, "The excessive monetary expansion of the seventies is one of the ultimate causes of the present international debt crisis." *See*, DeGrauwe and Fratianni, *The Political Economy of International Lending*, 4 CATO J. 166 (1984).

[82] More generally, an inappropriate allocation of funds reduces the efficiency of the international capital market. For an enumeration of the conditions required to improve the efficiency of the international financial markets see A.K. Swoboda, *Debt and the Efficiency of the International Financial System*, in INTERNATIONAL DEBT AND THE DEVELOPING COUNTRIES, 151-78 (G.S. Smith and J.T. Cuddington, eds. 1986).

[83] *See* Kharas, *The Long-Run Creditworthiness of Developing Countries: Theory and Practice*, 99 Q.J. OF ECON. 425-39 (1984).

[84] The secondary market for LDC debt is currently not very active. A major reason is that under generally accepted accounting rules, if a bank sells a loan at a discount, it has to report a loss from the transaction on its income statement. For more information on the secondary market, see Carns, *Secondary Market for LDC Debt*, BANKING AND ECON. REV. 5-6 (July/Aug. 1986).

that do extend additional credit. The debtor countries, for their part, are reluctant to default, even partially, on their external debt as long as reschedulings and negotiations continue buying them time.

The issue still remains open as to what are appropriate rules governing the extension of credit across national boundaries, particularly when private financial depository institutions are involved.[85] Recent proposals by Treasury Secretary Baker[86] and Senator Bradley[87] presumably are meant to provide just such a set of rules not only to resolve the current debt problem but to avoid future debt problems. Secretary Baker's plan calls on banks to lend more and for debtor countries to adopt certain reforms oriented toward the free market, with the goal of fueling economic growth so that these countries can fulfill their debt obligations.[88] Senator Bradley's plan, on the other hand, includes a reduction in the interest rates charged to debtor countries, forgiveness of three percent of the principal of some countries debts and new loans to stimulate economic growth in these countries.[89]

CONCLUSIONS

The historical existence of borrowing and lending across national borders clearly is evidence that both the debtors and creditors involved viewed such transactions as welfare enhancing. Inevitably, however, countries have now and then experienced severe difficulties servicing their external debts. The most recent debt crisis broke out in 1982 when several heavily indebted LDC's were unable to fulfill their debt obligations. When such crises occur, attention naturally turns to how best to resolve the international debt problem.[90]

This paper has attempted to provide a conceptual framework within which one can can come to understand the causes and effects of international debt crises. This framework operates as follows. To avoid debt problems, external debt must grow less rapidly than exports and domestic output. This is a long-run condition which, if satisfied, means that a country is "solvent." However, exogenous shocks can cause debt to grow more rapidly than exports and output, but this situation must be temporary. In a world of uncertainty, of course, it is not easy to distinguish

---

[85] For a review of the legal issues of international borrowing, see L. KALDEREN & Q.S. SIDDIQI, SOVEREIGN BORROWERS: GUIDELINES ON LEGAL NEGOTIATIONS WITH COMMERCIAL LENDERS, (1984).

[86] See James A. Baker, *Statement Before the Joint Annual Meeting of the I.M.F. and the World Bank*, TREASURY NEWS, Oct. 8, 1985.

[87] See Senator William Bradley, *A Proposal for Third World Debt Management*, United States Senate Memo, June 29, 1986.

[88] See Baker, *supra* note 86, at 4-6.

[89] Bradley, *supra* note 87, at 4.

[90] It is also important to realize that, as Carlos Massad points out, "An early warning system is necessary to provide information far enough in advance to allow corrective policy measures to be adopted before the problems get out of hand." *See Debt: An Overview*, 16 J. DEV. PLANNING 17 (1985).

temporary from longer-run adverse effects on export and income growth. This is especially the case when a debtor country's fiscal and monetary policies importantly influence this growth. And political rather than just economic factors may effect government policies so that whether or not debt obligations are fulfilled involves the willingness of a country to repay its debts as much or even more than a country's ability to repay those debts. It is for this reason that the notion of solvency has limited applicability to an individual debtor country.

Debtor countries do face costs if they default or repudiate their debt, with the major cost being the inability to secure external funds in the future. It is for this reason that countries attempt to establish a reputation for honoring their debts. Debtor countries also attempt to reschedule their debts rather than default or repudiate them entirely. To secure new funds from banks frequently necessary for these reschedulings, the debtor countries agree to conditions set down by the International Monetary Fund[91] so as to signal to banks that credible fiscal and monetary policies are being implemented to generate the required long-term growth in exports and domestic output.[92] In this way, the countries are expressing a willingness to fulfill their debt obligations.

But despite the best of intentions and the most appropriate government policies, some debt may eventually not be fully repaid.[93] It is therefore desirable to obtain information about the market value of such debt so that the position of banks can be continually monitored.[94] Furthermore, debt-for-equity swaps may become more important if the debt situation fails to improve significantly in the near future. Of course, even if some debt is never repaid fully,[95] there is no economic reason to believe that such a situation should lead to a collapse in the international banking system and in international trade.

---

[91] The role of the I.M.F. is therefore, according to J. Richard Zecher, ". . . to enforce contracts, particularly in a troubled time such as the one we are in right now." *See* Zecher *The Interventionist Disease and the I.M.F.'s Agency Cost Role,* 4 CATO J. 342 (1984).

[92] For a discussion of the role of the I.M.F. in the negotiation of new sovereign loans and the rescheduling of outstanding loans, and of the I.M.F.'s relationship with creditor banks, *see* G.P. Nicoletopoulos, *Remarks in a panel of the 78th Annual Meeting of the American Society of International Law on the international debt rescheduling,* 78 AM. SOC'Y OF INT'L LAW PROCEEDINGS 310-12 (1984).

[93] Peter Hakim states that "A significant portion of the debt— perhaps as much as 30%—may have to be written off." *See* Hakim, *The Baker Plan: Unfilled Promises,* CHALLENGE 58 (Sept./Oct. 1986).

[94] According to two scholars, "If a mark-to market policy had been in effect [in the early 1980s], alarm bells would have gone off well before the [current international debt] crisis hit." *See* J.M. GUTTENGAG & R.J. HEARING, THE CURRENT CRISIS IN INTERNATIONAL LENDING 15 (1985).

[95] Rudiger Dornbusch and Stanley Fisher argue that "Equity, good foreign policy, or simple common sense would indicate that certain write-offs are in both debtors' and creditors' interest." *See* Dornbusch and Bisher, *The World Debt Problem: Origins and Prospects,* 16 J. OF DEV. PLANNING 80 (1985). The problem with simply writing down some loans is that it creates a moral hazard problem. See Barth and Pelzman, *supra* note 25, at 385.

Article Thirty-Eight

1988 issue 5
September 9

Table 1

Economic growth and inflation
average annual percent change,
1985-87

	Real GDP	GDP deflator
Belgium	1.8	3.7
Denmark	2.2	5.1
France	2.0	4.3
Germany	2.2	2.5
Ireland	1.9	4.4
Italy	2.8	7.5
Luxembourg	2.9	2.2
Netherlands	2.3	0.5
United Kingdom*	3.4	4.6
Greece*	1.2	17.5
Portugal*	4.1	17.2
Spain*	3.6	8.4
EC 12 average	2.6	5.2

*Nonparticipants in the ERM.

Financial markets in Europe: toward 1992

Europe is abuzz with talk of 1992. After that year, if all goes to plan, 330 million people will be free to reside and do business anywhere in the twelve countries of the European Community (EC). Forward-looking European companies are assessing how green the grass may be on the other side of existing national "fences" — and making plans to protect home turfs from encroachers. The EC political agenda, long topped by farm subsidies, now sports proposals to create a European central bank and wrest concessions from outsiders — Japan, in particular — in return for access to a unified European market.

To some, Europe can withstand competition from U.S. and Japanese companies only with a unified industrial base that reaps economies of scale in research, production, and distribution. Others cheer Project 1992's reliance on market forces and its expansion of individual freedoms to participate in business and the professions Communitywide. An end to regulatory and tax barriers to mobility and trade should cut costs to consumers,

open up job opportunities, and allow faster economic growth. This would revitalize industry and help overcome "Eurosclerosis."

Yet others see Project 1992 as bringing the EC close to the ideals of the 1957 Treaty of Rome: harmonious economic and social development with close political relations among states. These ideals got short shrift so long as attention focused on adding new members, piecemeal regulatory harmonization, and income support for farmers, declining industries, and less developed regions. Today, boosters of the EC are pleased with the policy discipline achieved through the European Monetary System (EMS), which has induced convergence of economic performance in all full participants (see Table 1).

Enthusiasts believe that the EC is ready for a next, major step. Yet the task is Herculean. First, Project 1992 involves wholesale pruning of national regulations catering to parochial customs and vested interests. Second, it would limit the role of the state, contrary to tradition in much of Europe. Third, the

Project requires reform of tax regimes and government spending, which are more distorting of trade, mobility, and allocation decisions than in the United States or Japan.

A year or two ago most observers of the European scene were skeptical of Project 1992. After all, other visionary proposals from the Commission of the European Communities — the EC's executive body — have gone nowhere. This year, however, the idea of a unified, competitive market has fired the imagination of business leaders and gained popularity in many circles. Governments now have adopted a number of key proposals in the face of nationalist and special-interest concerns. No longer is Project 1992 doomed to fade as yet another idea whose time has not come. Instead, enough barriers stand to tumble to make a dramatic difference to the European landscape of the mid- to late-1990s.

Following a brief review of Europe's general approach to integration, this article focuses on a single aspect of Project 1992 — Europe's financial markets. Much remains to be done: Communitywide consensus must be reached on legislation now pending or in draft; countries then must respect timetables and implement the measures in spirit as well as letter; and financial players must adapt to the new rules and the more competitive environment ahead.

Financial integration involves major risks. Obstacles to capital flows and financial service provision could come down before tax and regulatory differences are adequately addressed, driving investment capital toward countries with the lowest tax and regulatory burdens. This, in turn,

could trigger regulatory backlash and new capital controls on the part of countries affected adversely. Another risk is that EMS participants will disagree on policy objectives, notably for economic growth and inflation. Exchange and interest rate instability might ensue, tempting destructive ventures in monetary "independence." The credibility of Project 1992 could be strained and, in the extreme, the unification of Europe's financial markets be postponed indefinitely.

The integration process

Europe's initiative to break down all remaining barriers to economic integration is the most ambitious undertaking since the establishment of the EC in 1957. In June 1985 the heads of EC governments approved a Commission White Paper detailing some 300 measures needed to unify the European market. Six months later the Treaty of Rome was amended to reiterate this objective and facilitate its achievement. By the first half of 1987 the amendment, known as the Single European Act, had been passed by the national parliaments. It calls for the creation, by December 31, 1992, of "an area without frontiers in which the free movement of goods, persons, services and capital is ensured." This objective resembles that of the original Treaty of Rome, which had mandated "the abolition of obstacles to the free movement of persons, services, and capital" by December 31, 1969.*

Nevertheless, on most issues the Act made two significant innovations in EC legislation and practice: qualified majority rule and mutual recognition. Whereas

*In the early 1960s, capital transactions linked to the exercise of basic freedoms established by the treaty (such as commercial credits, direct investments, and personal capital movements) were liberalized. However, treaty signatories had pledged to liberalize financial services and capital flow restrictions only "to the extent necessary for the proper functioning of the common market." They were entitled to reimpose controls, subject to authorization, if capital movements disturbed their own financial markets. During the stormy 1970s and early 1980s, ground was lost because the EC allowed several countries to make extensive use of safeguards, while failing to persuade them to make progress on financial integration. Still, Britain scrapped exchange controls in 1979. More recently, several countries — notably France, Greece, Ireland, and Spain — have unilaterally cut back interest rate controls; and Britain and Portugal have removed other barriers to competition in financial markets. In 1984 the EC membership agreed to tighten recourse to safeguard clauses and all exceptional arrangements subsequently were terminated.

most Commission proposals formerly had to be approved by a unanimous vote of the European Council, the amended treaty allows this gathering of ministers from the twelve countries to pass much legislation by a qualified majority (defined as 54 of 76 weighted votes). Now it takes more than two of the larger countries (with ten votes each), or more than four of the smaller (three-to-five votes each), to block Commission directives — quite a change from before, when any country, however small, could veto proposals of any importance.

Mutual recognition bypasses the tedious approach of trying to conform national regulations and procedures to common, EC-wide standards. The Council now is free to rule that the norms in force in one country are equivalent to those applied in another; no longer need integration stand hostage to endless discussions of how to harmonize, say, product labeling or emission control standards.

The 1985 White Paper also offered a convenient guide to the most blatant obstacles to intra-Community trade in goods and services. These include border controls, discriminatory government procurement practices, subsidies to industries and farmers, technical standards and regulations, unfair business practices, and state-owned or government-sanctioned monopolies and oligopolies.

In principle, an end to these obstacles, by opening up economies of scale and weeding out inefficiency and monopoly profits, would put downward pressure on costs and prices, boost output, and reduce unemployment. How large the benefits would be in practice is much less clear. They surely would depend on rest-of-world developments and the macroeconomic policy stance. Assuming unchanged policies, the European Commission has published rough estimates that full implementation of Project 1992 could lower average EC consumer prices by 6% after six years, raise real GDP by 4.5%, and create almost 2 million jobs — relative to levels otherwise prevailing. With more expansionary fiscal and monetary policies, job creation might reach five million and the GNP gain some 7%. But inflation would run higher too, albeit distinctly less than without Project 1992.

Three years have passed since the White Paper's program was endorsed officially. The tally of approved legislation is up to about one-third of the eventual total. This is more than many had expected. Still, from the 1985 launch date the calendar now is nearly halfway to December 1992. Moreover, many important directives are among the two-thirds not yet approved or submitted.*

---

*Directives already passed would, *inter alia*, simplify border formalities, ease trade in live animals, align laws on auto and truck emissions and dangerous chemicals, facilitate the use of mobile telephones, and grant mutual recognition of prospectuses. In addition, at their June summit, the EC ministers agreed on a schedule to abolish capital controls, eliminate licensing and quota restrictions on trucking, recognize all university diplomas, and fix common rules for food additives and packaging.

Sensitive issues yet to be settled include border controls on individual travelers, largely motivated by differing policies toward terrorism and immigration and by attempts to enforce national gun and drug laws. Initiatives likewise are awaited to curb protectionist government procurement policies; these create major production and trade distortions since the affected outlays run as much as 10% of European GDP. Commission directives approved over a decade ago to open up procurement mostly have been ignored, despite exempting four major sectors (telecommunications, energy, transport, and water supply) in deference to nationalist and strategic considerations.

Among the plethora of topics for decision, tax harmonization promises to be particularly thorny. This comes as no surprise, following an already long history of vain Commission endeavors to bring value added (VAT) and excise taxes into line. Besides, fiscal issues are among the very few that still require resolution by unanimity under the Single European Act, reflecting the profound disagreements extant at the time the Act was drafted. Those disagreements remain: countries that tax alcohol heavily or exempt "necessities" from VAT, for instance, do so out of deeply held beliefs.

Time is short to clear away the outstanding issues of Project 1992. Though Council directives carry the force of law, most grant member countries several years to bring national legislation in line and implement necessary administrative changes. Governments have been known to drag their feet, and the Commission or private parties often have taken them before the European Court to compel action. Council passage of directives therefore cannot be deferred until late 1991 or 1992 if they are to be practically operative by January 1993.

One way to get the 1992 agenda back on track might be to set priorities among the two hundred or so pending legislative items; concentrate on such critical issues as taxes, subsidies, and government procurement; and ignore the rest for now. However expedient, this course would be risky. The Commission has insisted on a "package" approach to the directives, admitting no exceptions. Its intransigence may be working as intended — encouraging members to drop their opposition to particular directives in the knowledge that other countries would be under pressure to cease opposing directives they, in turn, dislike. Abandoning the package approach now could lead the EC down a slippery slope: postponement of the least important directives could be followed by postponement of increasingly more important ones. It is preferable to stick to the present approach, even if not all the work can be completed on time — so long as the direction is unchanged and the message is clear to Europeans and non-Europeans alike.

Financial market integration

Interest in financial liberalization has reawakened because the internationalization of finance and the growth in intra-European trade have rendered controls undesirable and ineffectual. The 1985 White Paper sought complete liberalization of capital movements, including those of a purely monetary nature not linked to commercial transactions. It also aimed to open up the cross-border market for financial services by removing barriers to entry and the free circulation of financial products. The objective was market integration to bring down the costs of auto insurance, mortgage loans, consumer credit, and brokerage services, which in many countries are inflated by feeble national or international competition. To this end, 27 directives were proposed. Ten have been approved; twelve are being discussed; and five are being drafted.

The aspect needing least legislative work is that of *capital controls*. Countries already have made considerable headway or have pledged it under a recently

Table 2

Capital controls
by type of transaction

	Securities		Loans		Other	
	Primary market	Secondary market	Trade related	Other	Deposit accounts	Other*
Belgium**	F/A	F	F	F	F	F
Denmark	F	F	A	A	A	A
France	R/A	F	R	R	F/R	F
Germany	F	F	F	F	F	F
Ireland	A	F/R	F/A	F/A	F/P	F/P
Italy	A/P	F/R	F/A	A	F/P	F/P
Luxembourg**	F/A	F	F	F	F	F
Netherlands	F	F	F	F	F	F
United Kingdom	F	F	F	F	F	F
Greece	A/P	A/P	A	A	R/P	R/P
Portugal	R/A	R/A	A	A	A	A
Spain	A	F/R	A	R/A	F/A	A

The first code refers to capital inflows, the second to outflows.
  F Free of controls.
  A Subject to authorization.
  R Subject to various restrictions as to maturity, size, and use of funds.
  P Prohibited, or subject to authorization that is usually not granted.
 *Money market instruments such as Treasury bills.
**A dual exchange market is maintained.
Source: European Commission.

to impose restrictions on flows with Switzerland.

Efforts to let financial firms operate freely across the EC have focused on three areas: banking, securities, and insurance. With respect to *commercial banking,* the Commission has circulated a directive to allow banks to exercise across EC borders the same banking and securities powers that are permitted them at home. A single-license approach would be adopted: banks' operations throughout the EC would be licensed, regulated, and supervised for the most part by their home country — allowing a Dutch bank, for example, to branch into Italy without having to request permission from host authorities or having to post capital separately at its Italian branch. Given the diversity of national regulatory standards, however, the Commission also has proposed harmonizing accounting norms and essential prudential regulation, such as capital adequacy and limits on equity holdings in nonfinancial firms. Its capital standards recommendation parallels the one recently agreed by twelve central bank governors from the world's leading banking countries — including seven from the EC.

Drafting has begun on a directive covering *investment services.* As in banking, any securities firm reportedly would be able to open branches and market an agreed list of services in other countries. Home-country supervisors would be responsible for the essential regulations such as capital adequacy and the acceptability of major shareholders, while host-country rules would apply to the remainder. The Commission already has submitted a directive banning in-

approved directive. Britain, Germany, and the Netherlands have freed capital flows completely (see Table 2). Five other countries are to follow suit by mid-1990: Belgium and Luxembourg abolishing their two-tier exchange market; Denmark eliminating prior authorization for certain transactions; and France and Italy allowing residents to hold foreign bank accounts and foreigners to tap their domestic credit markets. Four other nations more reliant on capital controls have been given more time to remove them: until 1992 for Spain and Ireland and until the mid-1990s for Greece and Portugal. Capital flows are to be freed not only within the EC but also with countries outside: restricting movements between, say, Italy and a non-EC member, such as Switzerland, is pointless if such flows can be mediated by another EC country, such as Germany or Britain, that is unwilling sider trading and apparently will propose soundness and competence criteria. The EC currently supports the electronic linking of national stock exchanges by subsidizing the exchange of market information in the hope of spawning a screen-based integrated market.

For *insurance services*, the Council recently approved a directive to open up the market for property and casualty insurance for large corporations with home-country control and minimal harmonization; later, in the 1990s, medium-sized contracts will be opened up. Agreement was facilitated by the fact that domestic insurers of major risks long have used techniques such as fronting, coinsurance, and reinsurance to create an international insurance market centered in London. But the Commission has yet to produce directives covering the high-growth potential fields of life and automobile liability insurance. These may not be liberalized before the turn of the century, in part because the European Court is conditioning its approval on adequate harmonization of the consumer protection aspects.

Implications for governments

The legislation on financial services being drafted in Brussels or pending approval by the Council meets resistance from national governments because it limits sovereignty in several respects, notably concerning mutual recognition, reciprocity, and taxation.

To begin with, the principles of mutual recognition and home-country control would increase competition not only among firms across the EC but also among the different national *regulatory systems*. These systems would be under great pressure to converge, since regulations that limit the ability of a country's own banks to offer certain products — say, the French ban on variable-rate mortgages or the German one on money market funds — disadvantage those banks relative to banks from other EC countries that allow these products. Discriminatory rules and incentives, such as limits on the foreign content of pension or insurance funds or obligations on banks to place money in public securities, likewise would not survive because foreign-owned firms could not be required to abide by them. Some governments, having relied on barriers to trade and market segmentation to enforce credit controls or help finance deficits, are therefore reluctant to support the Commission's proposals.

These principles by no means would deprive national regulators of all discretion. Host countries would oversee risk-taking in the securities markets, control bank liquidity, and set monetary policy. Of course, virtually any financial practice could be deemed to affect monetary policy: central banks could argue that authorizing money market funds to compete with bank deposits or banks to pay interest on demand deposits would destabilize the narrow monetary aggregates — as happened in the United States. The Bundesbank further has argued that allowing money market funds (exempt from reserve requirements) would distort competition at the expense of banks. Yet the surge in deregulation suggests that a growing number of European countries understand that trying to keep a lid on financial innovation damages their own financial centers. Still, even if the proposed directives are adopted, the European Court likely will be hearing, for many years to come, cases in which financial firms challenge local interpretation of the principles of mutual recognition and home-country control.

Ending barriers to the provision of financial services by intermediaries from member states implies the necessity for a *common policy* toward firms headquartered outside the EC — much as the elimination of customs duties on intra-EC trade in the early 1960s brought a common tariff against imports from outside the Community. This is a divisive issue. Hitherto, some countries have been very open to non-EC firms and foreign capital, while others have not; the disparity is not sustainable once entry into one country automatically allows entry into others.

Under the proposed directives on banking and securities, existing *subsidiaries* of non-EC firms are to be treated as Community undertakings, subject to a single license and supervision by the member country in which they are incorporated. *Branches* of non-EC banks, however, would remain under the jurisdiction of the authorities in each of the countries in which they operate. This structure could penalize non-EC banks: to enjoy the freedoms of EC banks, they would have to set up subsidiaries within the EC; that could mean significantly higher borrowing costs, since subsidiaries must hold their own capital whereas branches can draw on the full resources of their parents.

The proposed directives also authorize the Commission to deny entry to firms from a non-EC country that fails to grant reciprocal treatment to firms from each of the twelve EC member countries. Moreover, there are indications that such *reciprocity* will be applied to foreign-owned commercial and investment banks already operating in the EC.

Governments are beginning to realize, however, that reciprocity could open a Pandora's box. Some countries interpret reciprocity narrowly as requiring "national," nondiscriminatory treatment for EC firms operating abroad — that they be treated the same way as domestic firms. Other countries interpret it broadly as requiring that EC firms abroad should be extended the same rights as foreign firms operating in the Community. This latter definition could lead, for instance, to a demand that Japan and the United States give powers to banks as wide as those typically granted in the EC. Further, it might force Britain or Luxembourg, say, to exclude existing or new Japanese banks if Portugal or Greece felt that any of its banks did not have reciprocal access to the Japanese market. And U.S. banks might be handicapped within the EC because the United States limits interstate banking and restricts banks' equity holdings in nonfinancial enterprises.

Another concern to governments is that financial market integration will force major changes in *tax systems*. At present, the treatment of interest and dividend income, securities transactions, capital gains, and bank deposits varies a great deal from country to country. For example, Spanish depositors cannot escape taxation on interest income earned at home because of a withholding tax; nor can French depositors because banks in that

Table 3

Withholding taxes
percent of interest and dividend income

	On interest paid to		On dividends paid to	
	Residents	Nonresidents	Residents	Nonresidents
Belgium	25	25	25	25
Denmark	0*	0	30	30
France	**	0-51	0	25
Germany	0***	0***	25	25
Ireland	0-35	0-35	0	0
Italy	12.5-30	12.5-30	10	32
Luxembourg	0	0	15	15
Netherlands	0*	0	25	25
United Kingdom	25	25	0	0
Greece	****	49	42-53	42-53
Portugal	30	30	12	12
Spain	20	20	20	20

Rates indicated are subject to restrictions and exemptions.
*Banks report interest income to the tax authorities.
**Recipients can choose to pay 27% or 47%, depending on the savings instrument, or to lump interest income with other incomes. Banks report interest income to the tax authorities.
***Banks do not report interest income to the tax authorities; a 10% withholding rate will go into effect starting next year.
****Corporations pay 25%; individuals pay 8% plus an amount linked to graduated rates applicable to income taxes.
Source: Arthur Andersen.

country report interest income to the tax authorities (see Table 3). However, they could do so on accounts in, say, Luxembourg or the Netherlands because neither imposes withholding taxes on interest income accrued by residents of other EC countries and further does not report this income to foreign tax authorities. Nonresidents' dividend income poses a similar problem in Ireland and the United Kingdom.

Differences in tax treatment and reporting requirements are offset to some degree by several factors: remaining capital controls, particularly in southern Europe; the fact that most European retail banks do not actively solicit foreign deposits; the local nature of government and corporate bond markets, which deters foreign investors; and the paucity of cross-listings of European companies on the national stock exchanges. However, these offsets will diminish as markets integrate and intermediaries ply their trade throughout the EC. Awareness of the problem blocked agreement earlier this year on the removal of remaining capital controls — until all the countries further agreed that the Commission should develop proposals to reduce tax evasion in time for a vote by the middle of next year.

Basically, the choice is between changing bank secrecy laws or harmonizing withholding tax rates throughout the EC. The key country to persuade is Luxembourg: if it refuses to amend its secrecy laws or impose a common withholding tax, it would tend to become Europe's leading financial center by virtue of its tax haven status alone. This would not, of course, be acceptable to its EC partners. Yet harmonization may not solve the problem, even if Luxembourg and other holdouts succumb to pressure: unless the agreed withholding is quite low (10% or less), there will be an incentive for tax-flight capital to leak outside the EC — to Switzerland, in the first instance, or such havens as Liechtenstein.

There likewise are major intra-EC variances in capital gains taxes and stamp duties on securities transactions. These too will come under pressure. Capital gains taxes on individuals range from zero in Belgium and Greece (and also in many circumstances in Italy and the Netherlands) to a hefty 50% in Denmark. Stamp duties range from zero to 0.5% of the value of stocks and bonds. As individual financial markets become interconnected by pan-European firms, these differences will encourage transactions to be con-

Table 4

Reserve requirements
as of mid-1988

	% of demand deposits in banks
Belgium	0
Denmark	0
France	5.0
Germany	6.6-12.1
Ireland	10.0
Italy*	25.0**
Luxembourg	0
Netherlands	***
United Kingdom	0.5
Greece*	7.5
Portugal	15.0
Spain*	18.5

  *Required reserves are remunerated to some degree.
 **Applied against the increase in deposits since May 1984; the effective level of required reserves is close to 20%.
***A small, variable, and remunerated reserve requirement was introduced in May 1988.

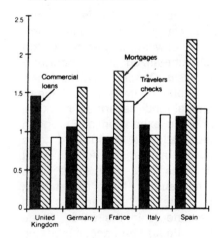

Chart 1

Prices of banking services
average of four lowest-priced countries = 1

Source: Price Waterhouse.

summated via the least burdensome routes.

The taxation of monetary assets also varies greatly, as measured by banks' reserve requirements. Those on demand deposits, for instance, range from zero or close to zero in Belgium, Britain, Denmark, and the Netherlands, to 15% or more in Italy, Portugal, and Spain (see Table 4). As yet there are no plans to harmonize the requirements within the EC because they are viewed as instruments of monetary policy — not as a tax driving a wedge between deposit and loan rates. Nevertheless, as banking systems integrate, deposit and loan transactions will be diverted to banks that can offer better interest rates thanks to less onerous reserve requirements. This will put pressure on central banks — probably even on the Bundesbank — to cut requirements to a minimum and rely on other instruments of monetary policy.

Implications for financial firms

Liberalization and integration are unleashing intense competition and numerous mergers among European financial intermediaries. U.S. experience of banking deregulation in the 1980s has given a preview of what may come to pass. U.S. interstate banking barriers were relaxed about the same time that deposit rate ceilings were phased out, opening new markets to banks just as they were forced to compete more for their customers' funds. Many banks subsequently merged, often across state lines, to pool capital and reach a wider customer base. Others narrowed their focus, specializing to serve selected customers — be they

consumers, middle-market businesses, or large corporations. Virtually all banks sought to cut costs by paring payrolls and branch networks and by adopting explicit pricing for services.

Financial intermediaries in Europe now are shaping strategies for post-1992. Many are looking to expand across borders to compete in markets that are profitable, or can become so once no longer sheltered. A recent study prepared for the EC highlighted the opportunities, finding huge variations in prices for financial services from country to country (see Charts 1-3). These data suggest scope for migration of firms from northern to southern Europe. But there are opportunities for expansion in other directions too. Best placed are firms unburdened by costly labor and managemnet practices, and possessed also of a solid customer base and ample capital. Expansion offers these firms the possibility to widen their product lineup and diversify their assets, liabilities, and revenues.

Cost advantages could be gained by *broad financial product lines* using common distribution networks, funding facilities, managers, and support services. A first wave of product broadening is under way in Europe as different types of credit institutions invade one another's traditional turf. A second wave, involving insurance and securities firms as well as different types of banks, is bound to intensify as integration pressures costs. Insurance and securities firms are particularly interested in distributing their products through bank branches to banks' traditional customers. Some banks, in turn, are attracted by insurance companies' investment management abilities and securi-

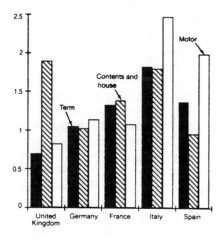

Chart 2

Prices of insurance services

average of four lowest-priced countries = 1

Source: Price Waterhouse.

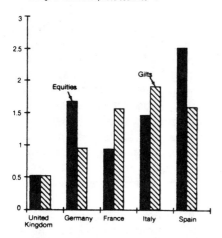

Chart 3

*Prices of institutional
securities services*

average of four lowest-priced countries = 1

Source: Price Waterhouse.

ties firms' research and product innovation skills.

Cross-border expansion also can yield *diversification* benefits. As firms span broader geographic markets, their assets, liabilities, and revenues normally become more diversified. This will be important for banks dependent on such industries as trucking, food, and insurance, which stand to lose the protection afforded by present intra-European barriers. The regional impact of European integration also has implications for financial institutions: over time, for example, cost factors may concentrate European agriculture in the southern regions that enjoy mild weather and cheap labor; in turn, some banks located in these regions could become as farm-dependent and as vulnerable to weather, commodity, and policy cycles as are many banks today in the U.S. Midwest. In principle, diversification through growth can forestall this risk; still, the troubles of some U.S. banks suggest that growth or size alone does not prevent a bank from concentrating its risks unduly.

Cross-border expansion often is thought to promise *economies of scale.* These, however, may elude banks and other financial firms. For them, labor and interest costs do not fall appreciably with volume and typically dwarf the fixed costs associated with offices, computers, and trading floors — the opposite of the variable/fixed cost balance seen in most manufacturing. Adding branches is no sure formula for scale economies in financial services. Concentration in high-volume lines of business may yield savings but, more often than not, they are offset by added costs in other functions; U.S. banks, for example, usually seem

to exhaust size-related economies at a fairly low level of assets ($50 million).

The other presumed advantage of scale — much in vogue in Europe — is the *protection* that size may afford against hostile takeover. Preemptive mergers, however, are not much defense in a world in which size alone poses less and less of a financial obstacle to predators. Today, admittedly, a financial firm reaching the stature of national giant may be able to call its government in aid against takeover; but this may not apply in tomorrow's Europe. Besides, unless a merger embodies a clear vision for improved profitability, the combined firm may wind up more vulnerable than before.

When deciding how to expand abroad, firms may choose among several avenues, ranging from the direct export of financial products without a physical presence, through cooperative agreements with local distributors, to full representation with branches or subsidiaries, whether *de novo* or by merger or acquisition. The appropriate strategy will depend very much upon the nature of the market — wholesale or retail — into which a firm wants to expand.

Europe's *wholesale* financial markets already are quite competitive. Margins tend to be thin and unrealized profit opportunities few. Conceivably, the lifting of capital controls, the linkage of capital and securities markets, and the expansion of European multinationals could lead to a surge in demand for financial services that only large firms could supply. More realistically, no more than a gradual rise in demand is in the cards. Since this could be accommodated handily by the many institutions already active, bank mergers aimed at achieving the critical mass necessary to participate in the wholesale markets will make sense only in a limited number of cases.

By contrast, Europe's *retail* financial markets may be headed for quite a shake-up. In several countries these markets are but little competitive. Of course, breaking into a country's consumer banking or auto or life insurance markets is expensive because a retail network of offices or agents is required.*

A network can be established by opening new branches or purchasing a competitor's. New branches allow full control over product quality but take a major investment of effort and time. Few financial firms are likely to follow this route, given the importance of speed and the already overbanked nature of most European countries.

Purchasing a network has its own drawbacks. In such countries as Italy and, to a lesser extent, France and Germany, many banks are owned by federal or provincial governments or are cooperative associations. These banks are not for sale. The attempt to acquire even privately owned institutions can stir nationalistic feelings, precipitate battles for control, and involve a final purchase price well in excess of the target's book value; this "goodwill" excess must be deducted from core capital (as defined by the new BIS-sponsored capital standards), leaving

*In the absence of such a network, customers might possibly be enticed to bank via automatic teller machines or buy mail-order insurance and money-management products. In practice, however, automatic tellers are costly and need a maintenance force, and field agents are required to handle insurance claims. Besides, for financial services, the European public is attached to the personalized attention that a bank with a local presence can provide.

only banks with ample capital as potential buyers. Besides, firms for sale frequently are financially weak and costly to turn around. It often takes many years to digest an acquisition, tying up management to the detriment of other business goals.

Most financial firms therefore may seek *friendly alliances* ranging from agreements to cross-sell products to joint ventures and, in extreme cases, outright mergers. Because of their limited scope, marketing agreements are easiest to negotiate and also, if desired, easiest to dissolve. For example, a British (home) building society and a French government-owned bank might agree to market the former's mortgage products using the latter's client lists; no integration of the two firms' widely different management structures would be needed — a key advantage in the short term, but possibly not cost effective beyond a time. Joint ventures are best suited to firms having medium-term, well-defined objectives for cooperation. Common ownership is in order when long-term, deeper, and more general forms of cooperation are sought. Large financial concerns, if bent on merger, do best to start with mutual shareholdings, which allow the partners to test the waters while keeping the option of aborting the merger before it is too late.

These considerations suggest that competition in retail financial services will gradually increase throughout the EC as legal impediments are removed. Yet no magic wand can be waved in Brussels to make the process easy, even assuming that EC governments reach early agreement on the many issues still unsettled. In sum, the full benefits from abolition of Europe's barriers to financial services provision will take long to materialize.

Implications for London

Traditionally, wholesale banking and securities trading have tended to gravitate to a single location in any given nation, region, or continent — "the" financial center. Such centers develop because a large scale of operation brings costs down and gives depth to markets by enhancing the liquidity of traded assets. For Europe today, London is the center. Project 1992, however, adds to the possibility that London will lose its edge.

Hitherto, London's favorable tax and regulatory environment has attracted business away from Continental centers, where high taxes and restrictions — such as capital controls, entry limits, product regulations, fixed commissions, and queuing — have raised transactions costs. If the European countries now make steady progress toward economic integration and remove the tax and other measures that distort markets, the coming years could see a return of some financial transactions to the Continent — for example, in syndicated lending, reinsurance, and securities underwriting and trading.

Deregulation in centers such as Paris, Madrid, and Amsterdam, combined with some reregulation in London initiated by the Financial Services Act, is eroding remaining fiscal and regulatory differences. In addition, the cost advantage of trading in a single location is losing significance because the new technologies of screen-based trading, computerized clearing, and cheap telecommunications allow some markets to operate efficiently without all parties present in the same location. Finally, it is generally more efficient and less risky to conduct transactions in a particular currency in its domestic market: the natural supply and demand for investment funds in that currency spring from there, as do the latest bits of information about policy developments that affect prices and flows of assets denominated in that currency. Yet the potential flowering of the Continent's domestic markets need not sound London's death knell. Provided regulators do not impose onerous costs on dealings with investors from outside the EC, London will be a major international financial center for the indefinite future.

The principal threat to London's role lies, rather, in an eventual movement toward a single European currency issued by a European monetary authority. For now, the EC governments are having a hard enough time giving up as much sovereignty as they must in order to comply with the existing Project 1992 agenda. They are not ready to transfer authority over monetary matters to a supranational central bank. Indeed, despite much recent discussion, European integration is nowhere near the stage that can deliver monetary unification.

Some day, at least if Project 1992 is successful, conditions should come together to establish a European central bank in charge of a common currency. Selecting the policy-making location of that putative central bank obviously would be a decision of the highest political magnitude. Establishment of a common currency would set in motion gravitational forces that likely would steer Europe's financial transactions toward a center close to the central bank's operational heart. Yet, as the example of the U.S. Federal Reserve makes plain, there is no necessity that the policy-making and operating centers of the central bank be in one and the same location: the Reserve Board lays down in Washington policy that is executed by the headquarters of the Federal Reserve's second district in New York. For Europe, politics will dictate the policy center. Market depth should properly point to the operating center. Provided its markets stay competitive, London could lay fair claim to become Europe's "second district."

Potential setbacks

Project 1992 promises to compromise the financial policy autonomy of individual EC members. Governments are likely to tolerate this only as long as each is satisfied with the results — particularly in job creation and economic growth. A perception that some countries are coming out ahead at the expense of others, or that it is possible to do better on one's own, could lead to acrimony and backsliding.

Participants in the exchange rate mechanism (ERM) of the EMS have grown accustomed to bending macroeconomic policy to the objective of maintaining a pegged exchange rate between their currencies and the ECU. An end to exchange controls combined with deeper monetary integration will heighten capital mobility and currency substitution: the share of domestic-currency deposits held abroad will grow as will the share of domestic deposits in foreign currencies. French corporations, for example, increasingly will hold mark accounts in Germany or France, and may invest their French francs in Germany. This will render the interpretation of money supply data increasingly difficult. Central banks may try switching to targets for domestic credit but, because of easy access to foreign credit, the predictability of links between this — or any other monetary stock or flow — and ultimate objectives, such as real economic growth or inflation, will worsen steadily.

Countries that are neither active EMS participants nor presently open to capital flows (Greece, Portugal, and Spain) will be able to exercise relatively more control over their monetary aggregates if they are willing to permit their exchange rates to fluctuate freely in response to interest rate differentials and the other factors that affect foreign exchange supply and demand. But, even in these countries, the integration of financial markets will intensify currency substitution and complicate the formulation and implementation of monetary policy.

Some countries may come to regret the loss of monetary autonomy and take steps injurious to the integration process. This could happen through failure to narrow sufficiently the sizable tax and regulatory differences now existing within the EC. Opportunities for financial intermediaries to arbitrage these differences away will grow as remaining exchange controls are lifted, firms from different countries reach out or team up to provide better services, and information and transaction costs are driven down by competition. Without substantial progress to approximate taxes and basic rules, capital could move within

Table 5

Real effective exchange rates
1980-82 = 100

	August 1988
Belgium	80.4
Denmark	110.4
France	102.6
Germany	106.0
Ireland	98.2
Italy	103.2
Luxembourg	n.a.
Netherlands	100.4
United Kingdom	94.7
Greece	78.7
Portugal	81.6
Spain	101.7

Table 6

Germany's trade balance
billions of marks,
FOB/CIF basis

	Total	With EC-member countries	EC members as % of total
1983	42.1	18.7	44.5
1984	54.0	26.4	48.9
1985	73.4	31.6	43.1
1986	112.6	51.4	45.7
1987	117.7	62.3	52.9
1988 1st half*	118.4	78.4	66.2

*Annualized.

the Community in ways not all members will find acceptable.

Some governments may not tolerate the consequences of portfolio and direct investment capital leaving in search of the lowest tax and regulatory burden. To neutralize unwanted pressure on exchange rates, central banks will be tempted to intervene. Intervention resources would appear at first sight to be rather ample. The foreign exchange reserves of the twelve EC countries have nearly doubled in ECU terms since the end of 1982, to around ECU215 billion excluding gold. At last year's meetings at Basle and Nyborg the EMS rules were altered to permit earlier access to common resources for intervention purposes. Nevertheless, central banks likely could not offset through intervention alone the kind of massive portfolio shifts that may occur. Pressure on the monetary authorities to forestall major deflationary adjustments in interest rates then could lead either to a realignment of pegged exchange rates or to the imposition of emergency capital controls. The latter would gravely damage the credibility of the integration process.

Yet another possibility that could derail Project 1992 is dispute over intra-European currency relationships and the desirable pace of domestic demand growth throughout the EC. The unification of markets for goods and services increasingly will pit industries in one country against those of the others. Industry's competitiveness in one country depends, in part, upon the strength or weakness of its currency relative to its EC partners'. As integration proceeds, the appropriateness of parities therefore will become a matter of

ever-growing and legitimate concern.

The situation most likely to give rise to intra-EC tensions is that of Germany. The mark has appreciated little in real effective terms since the early 1980s — very little more than the currencies of France, Italy, and some other EC members (see Table 5). This minimal appreciation has done little to correct Germany's supercompetitive position relative to its EC partners. Its trade surplus with the rest of the EC has risen steadily from under DM20 billion in 1983 to an annualized DM78 billion in the first half of this year (see Table 6). These surpluses, should they keep accumulating, are bound to erode confidence in EMS parities and widen interest rate differentials vis-à-vis Germany. Moreover, they are likely to fuel debate on the willingness of the German authorities to subject industry to the competition unleashed by Project 1992.

The problem is compounded by the low growth of domestic demand in Germany — 2.5% on average during 1985-87 and perhaps 3% this year — even as its EC partners have expanded demand close to 4% per annum. It is widely held, in Europe and elsewhere, that the supply-side adjustments that integration will bring depend on demand-side policies supporting strong domestic growth. Unless the German economy picks up, tensions are bound to worsen.

Growth differentials vis-à-vis Germany acutely concern countries in the ERM. The reasons: the Bundesbank provides the anchor for monetary stability in the ERM; its EMS partners attempt to pursue policies consistent with agreed parities; and diminishing obstacles to trade and capital flows within the EC tend to eliminate whatever few degrees of freedom from German economic policy the other countries have had. If Germany continues to set its monetary policy solely on the basis of domestic considerations, it will force the other countries to throttle down economic growth. That, in turn, could spoil the climate for cooperation so vital to the success of Project 1992.

Statistical appendix

For key to data in tables see 1988 issue 4, August 17.

Chief economist, Rimmer de Vries, Senior Vice President
Publications manager, Sorca E. McFadden, Assistant Vice President
Statistics manager, Elizabeth A. Lue de Grof, Assistant Vice President
Principal authors, Jan G. Loeys, Vice President; Arturo C. Porzecanski, Vice President